INTRODUCING
COMPARATIVE POLITICS

Fourth Edition

Sara Miller McCune founded SAGE Publishing in 1965 to support the dissemination of usable knowledge and educate a global community. SAGE publishes more than 1000 journals and over 800 new books each year, spanning a wide range of subject areas. Our growing selection of library products includes archives, data, case studies and video. SAGE remains majority owned by our founder and after her lifetime will become owned by a charitable trust that secures the company's continued independence.

Los Angeles | London | New Delhi | Singapore | Washington DC | Melbourne

INTRODUCING
COMPARATIVE POLITICS

Concepts and Cases in Context | Fourth Edition

STEPHEN ORVIS

Hamilton College

CAROL ANN DROGUS

Colgate University

FOR INFORMATION:

CQ Press
2455 Teller Road
Thousand Oaks, California 91320
E-mail: order@sagepub.com

SAGE Publications Ltd.
1 Oliver's Yard
55 City Road
London EC1Y 1SP
United Kingdom

SAGE Publications India Pvt. Ltd.
B 1/I 1 Mohan Cooperative Industrial Area
Mathura Road, New Delhi 110 044
India

SAGE Publications Asia-Pacific Pte. Ltd.
3 Church Street
#10-04 Samsung Hub
Singapore 049483

Printed in Canada

Library of Congress Cataloging-in-Publication Data

Names: Orvis, Stephen Walter, 1959- author. | Drogus, Carol Ann, author.

Title: Introducing comparative politics : concepts and cases in context /
Stephen Orvis, Carol Ann Drogus.

Description: Fourth edition | Los Angeles : CQ Press, 2018. | Includes
bibliographical references and index.

Identifiers: LCCN 2016051048 | ISBN 9781506375465 (pbk. : alk. paper)

Subjects: LCSH: Comparative government. | Comparative government—
Case studies.

Classification: LCC JF51 .D76 2018 | DDC 320.3—dc23
LC record available at https://lccn.loc.gov/2016051048

This book is printed on acid-free paper.

Acquisitions Editor: Carrie Brandon
Development Editor: Elise Frasier
Editorial Assistant: Duncan Marchbank
eLearning Editor: John Scappini
Production Editor: Kelly DeRosa
Copy Editor: Talia Greenberg
Typesetter: C&M Digitals (P) Ltd.
Proofreader: Lawrence Baker
Indexer: Joan Shapiro
Cover Designer: Janet Kiesel
Marketing Manager: Amy Whitaker

17 18 19 20 21 10 9 8 7 6 5 4 3 2 1

Brief Contents

Detailed Contents

CHAPTER 3. STATES, CITIZENS, AND REGIMES   98

AP Photo/Sunday Alamba

CHAPTER 4. STATES AND IDENTITY 146

NOEL CELIS/AFP/Getty Images

PART II
POLITICAL SYSTEMS AND HOW THEY WORK

CHAPTER 5. GOVERNING INSTITUTIONS IN DEMOCRACIES 214

Mutai/ Nation Media/Gallo Images/Getty Images

CHAPTER 6. INSTITUTIONS OF PARTICIPATION AND REPRESENTATION IN DEMOCRACIES   282

Photo by Subhendu Ghosh/Hindustan Times via
Getty Images

CHAPTER 7. CONTENTIOUS POLITICS: SOCIAL MOVEMENTS, POLITICAL VIOLENCE, AND REVOLUTION   356

Albin Lohr-Jones/Pacific Press/
LightRocket via Getty Images

CHAPTER 8. AUTHORITARIAN INSTITUTIONS   408

(YOUSSEF KARWASHAN/AFP/Getty Images)

CHAPTER 6. INSTITUTIONS OF PARTICIPATION AND REPRESENTATION IN DEMOCRACIES   282

Photo by Subhendu Ghosh/Hindustan Times via Getty Images

CHAPTER 7. CONTENTIOUS POLITICS: SOCIAL MOVEMENTS, POLITICAL VIOLENCE, AND REVOLUTION   356

Albin Lohr-Jones/Pacific Press/ LightRocket via Getty Images

CHAPTER 8. AUTHORITARIAN INSTITUTIONS   408

(YOUSSEF KARWASHAN/AFP/Getty Images)

REUTERS/Amr Abdallah Dalsh

PART III
POLITICAL ECONOMY AND POLICY

CHAPTER 10. POLITICAL ECONOMY OF WEALTH 522

JOHN THYS/AFP/Getty Images

CHAPTER 11. POLITICAL ECONOMY OF DEVELOPMENT   582

(Photo by Zhao Yuhong/VCG via Getty Images)

CHAPTER 12. PUBLIC POLICIES WHEN MARKETS FAIL: WELFARE, HEALTH, AND THE ENVIRONMENT   634

Lam Yik Fei/Getty Images

Regional and Country Coverage

Preface

The teaching of introductory comparative politics has long been divided, and to some extent confounded, by the question of "country" or "concept": Should the course be taught, as it traditionally has been, as a series of country studies highlighting the key similarities and differences among political institutions around the world, or should it be focused on the important concepts in the discipline? Throughout twenty-five years of teaching introduction to comparative politics, we have been frustrated by this "either/or" proposition, as well as by the textbooks that have been built upon it. The country approach is far too descriptive, and it is not easy to tease major concepts out of country case studies in any sustained way. This makes it difficult for students to get to the intellectual "meat" of our discipline. A purely conceptual approach, on the other hand, leaves students with little concrete knowledge, even when they're given examples here and there. We want our students to know the difference between a president and a prime minister. We've found that it is impossible for them to assess theories in an empirical vacuum. Students need the context that studying actual country cases provides.

We traded syllabi back and forth over the years, trying to combine the two approaches. Our goal was to introduce a set of related concepts and then immediately examine in some detail how they matter in the real world in a comparative context. To do this, we started using two textbooks, one conceptual and the other country-based, in an iterative fashion. But the parts never fit together well, even if written by the same team. In particular, we found that the conceptual books didn't lend themselves well to connecting key theoretical concepts to case study material. We also found that the case studies in most country-based books were either too detailed, leaving the student overwhelmed by unnecessary information, or too simplistic, leaving the student without adequate knowledge with which to understand the utility of the theoretical concepts.

This textbook tries to resolve this country-or-concept dilemma, using what we've come to think of as a "hybrid" approach. The book is organized conceptually, but each chapter introduces concepts and then immediately uses them to examine a series of topical, interesting, and relevant case studies. For instance, chapter 10, on the political economy of wealthy countries, lays out the key concepts in political economy and major economic theories and inserts case studies, where they best fit, of the U.S. laissez-faire model, the German social market economy, and the Japanese developmental state.

We use eleven countries throughout the book as "touchstones" (approximately five cases in each chapter), returning to these countries to illustrate the debates we address. The eleven countries—Brazil, China, Germany, India, Iran, Japan, Mexico, Nigeria, Russia, the United Kingdom, and the United States—span the globe, illustrate a wide array of current and past regimes, and avoid a Eurocentrism still too common in the field of comparative politics. Since we know, however, that not all aspects of comparative politics can best be represented by these eleven countries alone, we reference dozens of others as brief examples (of a paragraph or two) throughout the text.

By the end of the book, students not only will have been introduced to a wide array of important concepts and theoretical debates but also will have learned a lot about each of the eleven countries. We do not and cannot systematically examine all elements of all eleven as a standard country-by-country book would. Instead, after a brief overview of each country in chapter 2 to give students a basic context, we identify the most conceptually interesting elements of each country. For instance, regarding Japan, we cover the developmental state, the role of that state's bureaucracy and level of corruption, its electoral system, and the country's recent efforts to deal with globalization and resuscitate economic growth. Regarding Germany, we cover the rise and structure of the Nazi regime, Germany's cultural nationalism and citizenship debates, its electoral system, and its efforts to reform the social market economy and welfare state in the face of globalization and European Union integration. The case studies are organized and written in a way that allows students to understand the context of the debates and concepts without having to read an entire "country chapter" on each. And we keep the cases concise, which leaves faculty members the option of lecturing to fill in any additional detail that they may feel important or to provide comparisons with cases not covered in a chapter.

Rather than using any one theoretical or methodological approach, in chapter 1 we introduce students to the broad debates in the field to show how comparativists have used various theories and methodologies to understand political phenomena. We do not generally offer definitive conclusions about which approach is best for understanding a particular issue, preferring instead to show students the strengths and weaknesses of each. Occasionally, we make clear that one approach has become the "conventional wisdom" in the field or that we believe it is the most accurate way to analyze a particular phenomenon, but we do this in the context of a broader debate. Our primary focus on eleven countries gives the book an implicit bias toward comparative case studies over large-N quantitative methodology, but we introduce students to the core ideas and benefits of the latter and refer to numerous large-N studies throughout the book as well. We believe our approach will allow faculty to generate debates among students over key approaches and methodologies. By focusing on the key conceptual debates and illustrating them in the real world, the book enables instructors to move their introductory students beyond the memorization of basic information and toward an ability to assess and debate the real issues in our discipline.

The book also moves firmly away from the traditional Cold War division of the world into first-, second-, and third-world countries. While many textbooks claim to do this, we have found that they typically suffer from a "Cold War hangover," with the old division lurking just beneath the surface. We consciously set out to show that many theoretical concepts in the discipline are useful in a wide array of settings, that political phenomena are not fundamentally different in one part of the world than they are in another. For instance, we illustrate the parliamentary system not only with Britain but also with India, we use both the United States and Brazil to analyze the presidential system, and we examine democratization in Russia, Mexico, and Nigeria. Throughout, we try to show how long-standing concepts and debates in the discipline illuminate current "hot topics."

ORGANIZATION OF THE BOOK

This book is divided into three main parts. It first examines the theories and concepts that inform and drive research as a way to frame our investigation, then moves to a survey of political institutions and institutional change, and, finally, to an examination of political economy and policy debates. Part I introduces the major theoretical approaches to the discipline and focuses on the modern state and its relationship to citizens and civil society, regimes, and identity groups. It provides an introduction to the discipline and its key concepts in the modern world, applying them to case studies throughout. Chapter 1 provides a broad overview of key conceptual debates and divides the field into three broad questions to help students organize these debates: What explains political behavior? Who rules? and Where and why? These orient students by grouping the many debates in the field into broad categories tied to clear and compelling questions. "What explains political behavior?" gets at the heart of the discipline's major disputes, which we divide among interests (rational choice and its critics), beliefs (political culture and ideology), and structures (Marxism and institutionalism). "Who rules?" addresses the dispersion of political power, focusing mainly on the debate between pluralist and elite theorists. While that debate is typically subsumed under the study of American politics, we think it helps illuminate important areas of comparative politics as well. "Where and why?" introduces students to the importance of and approaches to comparison.

The rest of Part I focuses on the modern state and its relationship to other key areas of modern politics. Chapter 2 defines and provides an overview of the modern state and the concept of state strength/weakness, and it uses a brief history of the modern state in our eleven case studies to give students an overview of each. Chapter 3 examines modern states in relation to citizens, civil society, and political regimes, arguing that the latter are based first and foremost on political ideologies that define the relationship between state and citizen. Chapter 4 looks at the debate over political identity and the state's relationship to identities based on nationality, ethnicity, religion, race, and gender and sexual orientation. Each of these chapters uses case studies to illustrate and assess the concepts and debates it introduces.

Part II examines political institutions and participation in both democratic and authoritarian regimes as well as regime transitions. It is the "nuts-and-bolts" section of the book, providing what traditionally has been a core feature of the course. Chapters 5 and 6 examine political institutions in democratic regimes. Chapter 5 focuses on governing institutions: executive/legislative systems, the judiciary, the bureaucracy, and federalism. The theme throughout is the question of accountability in democracies. Chapter 6 looks at institutions of participation and representation: electoral systems, parties and party systems, and interest groups. It focuses primarily on how to achieve different kinds of representation and the potential trade-off between active participation and effective governance. Chapter 7 examines contentious politics, taking up social movements as a follow-on to the prior chapter and then moving on to political violence (civil war and terrorism), and revolution (as contentious political episodes). Chapter 8 looks at institutions and participation in authoritarian regimes, drawing on the previous three chapters to show how similar institutions function quite differently in nondemocratic regimes, as well as presenting the active debate over authoritarianism over the past decade. Chapter 9, on regime transition, not only focuses on democratic transitions but also sets them in the longer-term debate over regime change, looking first at military coups and revolutions (as regime change).

Part III examines political economy and some key current policy issues that have been foreshadowed earlier in the book. The conceptual and empirical knowledge that the students have gained in Parts I and II are used to address important current issues. Chapter 10 examines the theoretical and historical relationship between the state and the market economy, including key concepts in political economy, economic theories, and globalization, applying those to wealthy countries, including the debate over convergence versus the varieties of capitalism approach. The chapter includes a discussion of the global financial crisis and its implications. Chapter 11 looks at the political economy of development, using many of the concepts developed in the prior chapter. The theme of chapter 12 is market failure, examining social policy, health policy, and environmental policy in turn. It draws on chapters 10 and 11, as well as material from Part II, to look at different approaches to current hot topics such as universal health care and climate change.

KEY FEATURES

A number of pedagogical features reappear throughout the chapters. Each of them is designed to help students marry the conceptual and country-specific material in the most effective way possible. We think students can manage the concepts without losing sight of the important facts they've learned about the countries if they're given the right tools. Each chapter begins with questions that help students focus on the key issues as they read the chapter, study the cases, and then debate in class. The chapters sometimes provide conclusive answers to some of the key questions, but more often they show students different ways the questions can be answered or approached. Students will find a "case synopsis" at the start of each case study (new in this edition) that briefly gives them the key punchlines, and "case questions" at the end of each case to help them connect the specifics of the case to the larger thematic points we're making, and to compare cases in the same chapter.

"Country and Concept" tables in each chapter showcase empirical material. These provide key data of relevance for our eleven case study countries. The text refers to the tables at various points, but students and faculty can use these for much more, comparing the countries across the variables and asking questions about what might explain the observable variation.

Most chapters also include one or more "In Context" features that present basic data. These allow students to set a case study or idea into a comparative (and sometimes provocative) context. Students can use these to assess how representative some of our case studies are or to see the distribution of an institution, type of event, or set of factors around the world or within a region. For example, the "In Context" in chapter 4 focuses on gender inequality across the Middle East. This is set next to the case study of women in Iran.

In most chapters, we include a "Critical Inquiry" box, in which we ask students to think actively about a particular question. Many of these provide students a limited set of data and ask them, simply by visually examining the data, to develop their own hypotheses about key relationships or evaluate competing hypotheses they've studied in the book. Chapter 6, for instance, includes a "Critical Inquiry" box on the question of what explains women's share of legislative seats around the world. It provides data on the number of women in lower houses broken down by region, electoral system, and length of regime, and it asks students to use these data to informally "test" alternative hypotheses about why women gain better representation. A few "Critical Inquiry" boxes direct students toward more normative questions, using the concepts in the chapter to address them.

In addition to these themed features, readers will find many original tables, figures, and maps throughout the book that illustrate key relationships or variables around the world. Students will find end-of-chapter lists of key concepts with page references to help their study and review, as well as a list of works cited and a list of important print and electronic references for further research. We hope the design of the book strikes a balance as well: colorful and well illustrated to help engage student attention, but without adding significantly to cost.

NEW TO THIS EDITION

We're grateful to the many users who have graciously and enthusiastically provided us with feedback over the course of the last three editions. We've done our best to address their suggestions and comments. This edition includes more substantive changes than any prior revision. Most importantly, we created a new chapter (chapter 7) on contentious politics that is mostly new material. In the aftermath of the Tea Party, Occupy movement, and Arab Spring, we thought this subject deserved much greater attention. This also allowed us to address political violence in a way we hadn't before, including civil war (including violent ethnic conflict), terrorism, and revolution as a form of contentious politics. New case studies include the Occupy and Tea Party movements,

Boko Haram in Nigeria, and Chiapas in Mexico. To make room for this new chapter, we combined the two chapters on identity politics in the previous editions in to one (chapter 4). It addresses both the debates over the political salience of identities and the state's relationship to identity groups (previously in chapter 4) and the debate on how liberal democracies ought to ensure equal citizenship across identity groups (previously in chapter 12).

We also re-designed the material on political economy, creating chapters on the political economy of wealthy countries (chapter 10) and the political economy of development (chapter 11). The conceptual material on the relationship between the state and the market from the prior editions is still present, in chapter 10. This allowed us to create a more coherent final part of the book on political economy and policy that moves from core concepts and political economy of wealthy countries (chapter 10) to the political economy of development (chapter 11) and finally to public policy in key areas in response to market failure (chapter 12) that covers all countries.

Other important content changes also came as a result of user feedback. We've included more systematic presentation of the debate over what explains state strength and weakness in chapter 2; revised our presentation of regime types to include personalist regimes (with a case study of Nigeria) in chapter 3; added a case study of Putin's Russia as an electoral authoritarian regime in chapter 8 (and cut out Nigeria in that chapter, which is well-covered elsewhere in the book); and substantially revised the presentation of the democratization debate in chapter 9.

edge.sagepub.com/orvis4e

Because we know from experience that making the leap into a new textbook is no small chore, CQ Press offers a full suite of high-quality instructor and student ancillary materials (prepared by Rodrigo Praino at the University of Connecticut and Natalie Wenzell Letsa at Cornell University).

SAGE edge offers a robust online environment featuring an impressive array of free tools and resources for review, study, and further exploration.

SAGE edge for Instructors supports teaching by making it easy to integrate quality content and create a rich learning environment for students.

- A comprehensive **test bank** provides multiple-choice, fill-in the blank, and short- and long-essay questions, as well as the opportunity to edit any question and/or insert personalized questions to effectively assess students' progress and understanding.
- **Sample course syllabi** for semester and quarter courses provide suggested models for structuring one's course, especially if switching from a country-by-country or thematic approach to this book's flexible "hybrid" approach.

- Editable, chapter-specific **PowerPoint® slides** offer complete flexibility for creating a multimedia presentation for the course

- An **instructor's manual** features chapter overviews and objectives, lecture starters, ideas for class activities, discussion questions, and country backgrounders that offer basic information on all eleven core countries featured in the book.

- A **TA Guide** provides guidance for graduate students and newer instructors who will benefit from a set of goals, points for review, and discussion questions for each chapter.

- A set of all the **graphics from the text**, including all of the maps, tables, and figures, in PowerPoint, .pdf, and .jpg formats for class presentations.

- **Multimedia content** includes links to video, audio, web, and data links that appeal to students with different learning styles.

- Comprehensive **Video questions** based on the Interactive eBook and Multimedia Videos per chapter to prompt class activities and discussions.

- **Transition Guide** provides a chapter-by-chapter outline of key changes to the third edition.

SAGE edge for Students provides a personalized approach to help students accomplish their coursework goals in an easy-to-use learning environment.

- Mobile-friendly **eFlashcards** strengthen understanding of key terms and concepts.

- Mobile-friendly practice **quizzes** allow for independent assessment by students of their mastery of course material.

- A customized online **action plan** includes tips and feedback on progress through the course and materials, which allows students to individualize their learning experience.

- **Chapter summaries** with **learning objectives** reinforce the most important material.

- **Multimedia content** includes links to video, audio, web, and data that appeal to students with different learning styles.

- EXCLUSIVE! Access to certain full-text **SAGE journal articles** have been carefully selected for each chapter. Each article supports and expands on the concepts presented in the chapter. This feature also provides questions to focus and guide your interpretation.

ACKNOWLEDGMENTS

We have developed numerous debts in the process of writing this book. Perhaps the longest standing is to our students over twenty-five years of teaching introduction to comparative politics at Hamilton College. Figuring out how to teach the course in a way that is interesting, relevant, and clear to them led us to develop the approach taken in this book. We kept them in mind as we wrote the book: Will it be clear to them? Will it interest them? Will it help them see the important concepts and how they matter in the real world?

We owe a substantial thank you to the office of the Dean of Faculty at Hamilton College as well. It has provided support for research assistants for this project over ten years and four editions, primarily from the Steven Sands Fund for Faculty Innovation. The office also provided sabbatical support for Steve Orvis on Hamilton's program at Pembroke College, Oxford University, where the first elements of this project were written. Additional thanks go to the fellows and staff at Pembroke College for providing a hospitable venue for a sabbatical leave for research and writing on the first edition. Deep thanks go as well to ten especially talented Hamilton College undergraduates who worked for us as research assistants on the four editions, pulling together vital data and information for many of the book's case studies. They are Charlie Allegar, Henry Anreder, Emily Drinkwater, Luke Forster, Laura Gault, Derek King, Katie McGuire, Joshua Meah, Maya Montgomery, and Natalie Tarallo. This new edition also benefited from tremendous research assistance from Carolyn Morgan, Ph.D. candidate at Ohio State University. All were invaluable help for two faculty members taking on a project of this magnitude. Thanks go also to Andrew Rogan and Dawn Woodward for assistance in preparing the bibliographies in the book. We are very grateful to Carolyn Morgan for ably updating and crafting the ancillary materials for this book. Thanks also to Nathan Gonzalez for drafting the initial case studies on Mexico added to the second edition.

The staff at CQ Press have been pleasant, professional, and efficient throughout this process. Our association began with a chance meeting between one of us and a sales representative from CQ Press, in which "complaints were made" about the quality of textbooks in the field and the sales rep asked the inevitable: "So, how would you write one?" A quick response was met with the sales rep's enthusiastic statement: "We're looking for a book just like that! Can my acquisitions editor call you to talk about it?" We said sure, but, to be honest, didn't expect to hear from anyone. A week later the phone rang—Charisse Kiino, now Executive Director of College Editorial for SAGE Publishing, was on the line to talk through the ideas further. This led to a long process through which Charisse expertly led us, starting with developing a proposal and draft chapter and responding to the first round of reviews. Charisse patiently walked us through the process with constant good cheer and support. Our development editor for the first, third, and fourth editions, Elise Frasier, was invaluable, putting forth tremendous ideas for pedagogical elements of the book that we would have never thought of on our own, doing much of the research to develop these elements, and being herself an insightful reader and critic of the text. Of all the people we mention in this preface, she has provided the most valuable input and content for this book.

Finally, our production editor Kelly DeRosa and copy editor Talia Greenberg have been fabulous in the final stages of this fourth edition, improving the prose in innumerable places, pointing out inconsistencies, and working with us in an open, honest, and professional way that has made a tedious process as easy as it could be. We deeply appreciate the work of all at CQ Press who have made the process of writing this book as painless as we could imagine it being.

We wish also to thank the numerous reviewers who read chapters of the book at various stages. Their comments led us to revise a number of elements, drop others, and further develop still others. They have collectively made it a much better book that we hope will serve students well. They are:

William Avilés, *University of Nebraska–Kearney*

Dinorah Azpuru, *Wichita State University*

Jody Baumgartner, *East Carolina University*

Dilchoda Berdieva, *Miami University*

Michael Bernhard, *University of Florida*

Gitika Commuri, *California State University–Bakersfield*

Jeffrey Conroy-Krutz, *Michigan State University*

Carolyn Craig, *University of Oregon*

Brian Cramer, *Rutgers University*

William Crowther, *University of North Carolina–Greensboro*

Andrea Duwel, *Santa Clara University*

Clement M. Henry, *University of Texas–Austin*

Eric H. Hines, *University of Montana*

Jennifer Horan, *University of North Carolina–Wilmington*

John Hulsey, *James Madison University*

Christian B. Jensen, *University of Iowa*

Neal G. Jesse, *Bowling Green State University*

Alana Jeydel, *American River College*

Amie Kreppel, *University of Florida*

Eric Langenbacher, *Georgetown University*

Ricardo René Larémont, *Binghamton University, SUNY*

Carol S. Leff, *University of Illinois at Urbana-Champaign*

Paul Lenze, *Northern Arizona University*

M. Casey Kane Love, *Tulane University*

Mona Lyne, *University of Missouri–Kansas City*

Rahsaan Maxwell, *University of Massachusetts*

Mary McCarthy, *Drake University*

Scott Morgenstern, *University of Pittsburgh*

Stephen Mumme, *Colorado State University*
Armando Razo, *Indiana University Bloomington*
Nils Ringe, *University of Wisconsin–Madison*
Sharon Rivera, *Hamilton College*
David Sacko, *U.S. Air Force Academy*
Edward Schwerin, *Florida Atlantic University*
Brian Shoup, *Mississippi State University*
Tony Spanakos, *Montclair State University*
Boyka Stefanova, *University of Texas–San Antonio*
Sarah Tenney, *The Citadel*
Markus Thiel, *Florida International University*
Erica Townsend-Bell, *University of Iowa*
Kellee Tsai, *Johns Hopkins University*
Dwayne Woods, *Purdue University*
Eleanor E. Zeff, *Drake University*
Darren Zook, *University of California, Berkeley*

Last, but far from least, we have to extend thanks to our children, Nick and Will. They didn't contribute ideas or critique the book, but they showed real enthusiasm for understanding things like who the prime minister of Britain is and why there is a Monster Raving Loony Party, and they endured and even participated in occasional dinner table debates on things like the relative merits of parliamentary systems and different concepts of citizenship. Most of all, they gave of themselves in the form of great patience. This project became more of an obsession, at least at key points, than our work usually is. The first two editions took us away from them more than we like and made our family life rather hectic. They bore it well, going on with their lives in their typically independent way. Now they're older and mostly off on their own, so they don't bear the brunt of it, and have become active citizens of whom we are very proud. We preserve our dedication of the book to them and their generation, who give us great hope.

About the Authors

Stephen Orvis is Professor of Government at Hamilton College. He is a specialist on sub-Saharan Africa (Kenya in particular), identity politics, democratic transitions, and the political economy of development. He has been teaching introduction to comparative politics for more than twenty-five years, as well as courses on African politics, nationalism, and the politics of identity, political economy of development, and weak states. He has written a book and articles on agricultural development in Kenya, as well as several articles on civil society in Africa and Kenya, and is currently doing research on political institutions in Africa.

Carol Ann Drogus is Senior Associate Director of Off-Campus Study at Colgate University. She is a specialist on Brazil, religion, and women's political participation. She taught introduction to comparative politics for more than fifteen years, as well as courses on Latin American politics, gender and politics, and women in Latin America. She has written two books and numerous articles on the political participation of women in religious movements in Brazil.

1 INTRODUCTION

KEY QUESTIONS

- How much power do different people or groups have in different political systems?
- Do self-interest, beliefs, or underlying structural forces best explain how people act in the political realm?
- What kinds of evidence can help us determine why political actors do what they do?
- What can be learned from comparing political behavior and outcomes across countries?

Understanding political developments and disputes around the world has never seemed more important than it does today. Civil war in Syria has produced the largest flow of refugees in decades, as over a million people fled the war for the relative safety of Europe. Their arrival has raised questions about Europeans' identity and the continuation of the famous "open borders" within the European Union (EU). And the EU was already reeling from the effects of the financial crisis of 2008–2009. That crisis began in the United States but ultimately hit Europe harder. Greece, the first stop for those million-plus migrants, was essentially bankrupted by the financial crisis and nearly forced out of the EU before the migrants arrived. A housing bubble that burst in the United States and a civil war in the Middle East threaten the well-being and even identity of Europe, and in turn leaves the United States trying to assist its most important allies and contain a war halfway around the world.

Many people now see the world as more complicated and less comprehensible than it was during either the Cold War (1944–1989), when clear and predictable divisions seemed to dominate the globe, or the post–Cold War era (1989–2001), when the international realm seemed peaceful and stable and foreign politics was of little importance. The end of communist rule in the Soviet Union and Eastern Europe seemed to

In an increasingly globalized world, civil war in one country can have impacts around the world. Here, migrants arrive on the island of Lesbos in Greece. In 2015 the Syrian civil war produced a massive refugee crisis that flooded Europe with requests for asylum. The political and economic effects of this movement of people were huge, burdening the weak Greek economy, leading to greater support for anti-immigrant parties in many European countries, and influencing the successful British vote to leave the European Union.

Sipa via AP Images

foreshadow a period in which understanding political differences among countries would be both easier and less important. Instead, we have witnessed dramatic political change: several countries split into two or more new countries, ethnic and religious civil wars increased significantly, and two full-scale genocides have occurred. On the other hand, the number of countries that could claim to have democratic governments has also increased substantially, and East Asia, led by China, has achieved unprecedented economic growth that lifted more people out of poverty more quickly than ever before in history.

Diversity of political, economic, and social life among nations exists in every period of history. Comparative politics attempts to understand this diversity, assessing current events in the light of fundamental and long-standing questions: Why do governments form? Why does a group of people come to see itself as a nation? Why do nations sometimes fall apart? How can a government convince people that it has the right to rule? Do some forms of government last longer than others? Do some forms of government serve their people's interests better than others? How do democracies form, and how do they fall apart? Can democracy work anywhere, or only in particular countries and at particular times? Are certain political institutions more democratic than others? Can government policy reduce poverty and improve economic well-being? This book introduces you to the many and often conflicting answers to these questions by examining them comparatively. It will also help you start to assess which are the most convincing and why.

THE BIG ISSUES

Current "hot-button" political issues around the world are just the latest manifestations of a set of enduring issues that students of comparative politics have been studying for the last half-century. We could list many such issues, but for the moment, let's focus on just five to illustrate the major areas of interest in comparative politics: political development, regime type and change, participation and representation, policy-making processes, and political economy. The logical starting point is the question of **political development.**

political development
The processes through which modern nations and states arise and how political institutions and regimes evolve

Political Development You may be accustomed to seeing development applied to the field of economics, where it relates to the growth of modern industrial economies, but the word has important political dimensions as well. Historically, the biggest political development questions are about how and why modern nations and states arose. Why did the entity now known as France, and a group of people who think of themselves as French, come into existence? Is this process similar for all countries? If not, how and why does it vary?

Political scientists initially thought about these issues in a European context, but since World War II most questions about political development have emerged out of the experiences of former colonies in Latin America, Africa, and Asia. As these colonies gained independence, the relationship between economic and political development came into focus. Most observers assumed that former colonies would go through a process of economic development dubbed **modernization**—the transformation of poor agrarian societies into wealthy industrial societies. Political scientists initially assumed that as this transformation occurred, political systems that were more or less democratic also would emerge.

modernization
The transformation of poor agrarian societies into wealthy industrial societies, usually seen as the process by which postcolonial societies become more like societies in the West

In fact, neither economic nor political development has occurred as planned. Some countries, such as South Korea, have achieved rapid economic transformation and have established electoral democracies. Many others, however, have not. Democracy has emerged in some very poor countries (Ghana), while nondemocratic governments have presided over great economic change in others (Vietnam). In many countries, a sense of being a nation has never fully emerged, and some have even collapsed into civil war (Democratic Republic of the Congo). Middle-income countries such as Iraq and Syria have also seen civil war, while what once seemed like a rapidly modernizing Iran became a theocracy. Many saw the EU as a new stage of political development, as "modern" states willingly gave up sovereignty, moving beyond national interests; financial crisis and immigration, however, have brought that development into question. Even though the assumptions of modernization have not adequately answered the key questions, scholars continue to examine political development because finding an answer remains crucial, as the cases of Syria, Afghanistan, and Iraq demonstrate so vividly today.

Regime Type and Change Closely related to the issue of political development is the question of regime type and regime change. Americans often use regime to refer to some sort of "bad" government: we (democracies) have governments, whereas they (nondemocracies) have regimes. Political scientists, however, think of regimes in more neutral terms, as sets of political institutions that define a type of government. France has existed as a state and a nation for centuries, but it has had numerous regimes. The long-standing monarchy was overthrown by the world's first modern social revolution in 1789 that created a very brief republic, which itself was ultimately overthrown by Napoleon Bonaparte, who created a dictatorship. His regime collapsed and the monarchy was restored in 1815, followed by two other regimes, until a long-lived democracy finally emerged under the third republic, lasting from 1870 until it was overthrown by Nazi Germany in 1940. Since World War II, France has been democratic again, but under two quite different regimes, with distinct constitutions. Despite being a state and nation for centuries, France has had (depending on how you count) at least nine regimes.

Political scientists classify regimes into a limited number of categories, or regime types. Two broad categories are democratic and authoritarian regimes. Many definitions of a democracy exist, but for purposes of systematic comparison, most political scientists adhere to what is often called the "minimal definition" of a **democracy** as a regime in which citizens have basic rights of open association and expression and the ability to change the government through some sort of electoral process. This is not to say that democratic regimes are all the same. Besides being "more" or "less" democratic, they are also organized in different ways, for example, as presidential or parliamentary systems (see chapter 5).

Conversely, an **authoritarian regime** is simply a regime lacking democratic characteristics. As is the case with democratic regimes, numerous kinds of authoritarian regimes exist. The most important of these in the twentieth century were fascist regimes such as Nazi Germany, communist regimes such as the Soviet Union, modernizing authoritarian regimes such as the military government in Brazil from 1964 to 1985, personalist dictatorships such as Idi Amin's in Uganda (1971–1979), and theocratic regimes such as the Islamic Republic of Iran since 1979.

In recent years, a third broad regime category has become more widespread. The electoral authoritarian regime includes some elements of democracy such as elections, but the ruling party has sufficient control over seemingly democratic processes to ensure that it remains in power. Most of these regimes have emerged out of attempts to create new democracies during the last two decades. The largest example in the world today is Russia.

Once the various regime categories are identified, we can ask questions about how they differ and how they are similar. On the surface, the answer seems obvious: democracies have elections, and authoritarian regimes have dictators. In fact, the differences and similarities are much more complex. Some formally democratic regimes have significant informal limits on citizen input and participation, whereas some

democracy
A regime in which citizens have basic rights of open association and expression and the ability to change the government through some sort of electoral process

authoritarian regime
A regime lacking democratic characteristics, ruled by a single leader or small group of leaders

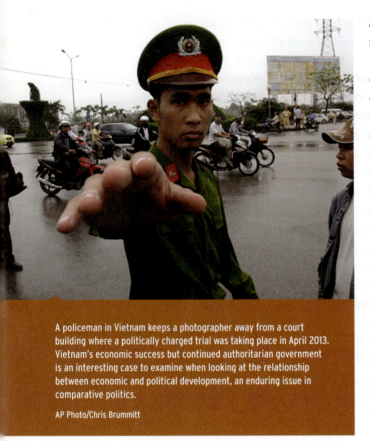

A policeman in Vietnam keeps a photographer away from a court building where a politically charged trial was taking place in April 2013. Vietnam's economic success but continued authoritarian government is an interesting case to examine when looking at the relationship between economic and political development, an enduring issue in comparative politics.

AP Photo/Chris Brummitt

authoritarian regimes allow dissent and even power sharing within certain bounds.

As the French example suggests, we also need to ask questions about regime change, the process through which one regime is transformed into another. This process can take numerous forms. Revolutions, such as the overthrow of Russia's autocratic regime in 1917 and the triumph of Chinese communists in 1949, are violent upheavals of entire societies that result in the creation of new regimes. Military coups d'état also often involve violence, but usually focus only on the old government that the military has chosen to overthrow, such as in many Latin American countries in the 1950s and 1960s and in Mali in West Africa much more recently (2012). A more recent form of regime change has been the spread of democracy since the late 1970s, commonly referred to as democratic transition. Democratic transitions seemed to be the sole remaining form of regime change around the millennium, but in the last decade the establishment or reestablishment of electoral authoritarian regimes has become increasingly common, in some cases after what appeared to be a democratic transition, as in Egypt since 2011.

Participation and Representation Closely related to the issues of regime type and democratization are popular participation and representation. Political scientists have long sought to understand why and how people participate in the political process, as well as how that participation differs across cultures and regimes. In some countries citizens participate as part of self-conscious identity groups, such as ethnic, religious, or racial groups (see chapter 4). In other countries identity groups have little relevance to politics. When and why do these differences emerge? What are the effects of strong "identity politics" on the stability of democracy? Citizens participate individually by voting or asking their government for assistance, but they may also band together in what is called civil society to pursue common interests via the political process. **Civil society** is defined as the sphere of organized, nongovernmental, nonviolent activity by groups larger than individual families or firms. The most familiar elements of civil society in the United States are interest groups such as the Sierra Club or the U.S. Chamber of Commerce. Political scientist Robert Putnam (2000) worried about a decline in American participation in civil society, creating a large debate about changing forms and extent of participation in democracies around the world.

civil society
The sphere of organized, nongovernmental, nonviolent activity by groups larger than individual families or firms

Political participation also occurs through the medium of political parties, of course. Different regimes have quite distinct kinds of parties and electoral systems that encourage different kinds of citizen participation. It is no surprise, then, that political scientists want to know which party and electoral systems most accurately represent the interests of citizens in the political process. How can citizens ensure that their representatives actually represent them? Can representation exist in authoritarian regimes? How do different societies conceptualize political representation in different cultural contexts?

Policymaking Another major issue in comparative politics is policymaking. All governments, whatever the regime, ultimately make policies that govern society. How do different regimes decide which policies to pursue? What role do different political institutions have in the policy-making process? Who is most influential in the process and why? Do the policies that finally gain approval reflect the will of the people? Which decisions should be made at the level of the national government, and which should be delegated to more local governments such as states or provinces? Different regimes provide different answers to these questions.

Political Economy Political economy is the study of the interaction of political and economic phenomena. In the modern world, virtually all governments are concerned with and (at least in theory) held responsible for the economic well-being of their people. Political economists try to understand why certain kinds of economic institutions and policies arise in certain countries but not others, relating political economy to political development. They also ask if some types of regimes produce better economic outcomes than others. Many observers have argued, for instance, that modernizing authoritarian regimes can achieve more rapid economic growth in poor countries than democratic regimes can, but in recent years political scientists have found substantial evidence that the relationship is far less black and white. Some authoritarian regimes, such as China's, have been quite capable of achieving growth, whereas others, including Zimbabwe's, have not. Similarly, some kinds of democratic regimes seem capable of achieving beneficial economic outcomes while others do not.

These big issues do not encompass all of comparative politics, but they do raise the most prominent questions that comparativists—political scientists who study comparative politics—have been grappling with for the past half-century. Today, these questions are alive and well in the countries making headlines, from Russia and Ukraine to Libya and Syria. Comparativists try to look beyond the momentary hot topics to examine these enduring questions systematically, seeking ever clearer understanding of how politics works in the world and how it might be made better. Doing this requires some thought about how to study a very complex subject.

political economy
The study of the interaction between political and economic phenomena

COMPARATIVE POLITICS: WHAT IS IT? WHY STUDY IT? HOW TO STUDY IT?

politics
The process by which human communities make collective decisions

comparative politics
One of the major subfields of political science, in which the primary focus is on comparing power and decision making across countries

political science
The systematic study of politics and power

first dimension of power
The ability of one person or group to get another person or group to do something it otherwise would not do

second dimension of power
The ability not only to make people do something but to keep them from doing something

third dimension of power
The ability to shape or determine individual or group political demands by causing people to think about political issues in ways that are contrary to their own interests

Politics can be defined as the process by which human communities make collective decisions. These communities can be of any size, from small villages or neighborhoods to nations and international organizations. **Comparative politics** is one of the major subfields of **political science,** the systematic study of politics. Politics always involves elements of power, the first concept we need to examine closely.

Individuals or groups can have power over others in a variety of ways. If someone holds a gun to your head, he has a great power over you at that moment. If your boss tells you to do something, you do it because she is paying you and could fire you. But if someone has control over a resource you need—say, admission into a college—she also may have power over you. Political theorist Steven Lukes (1974) usefully categorized power into three dimensions. The **first dimension of power** is the ability of one person or group to get another person or group to do something it otherwise would not do: when someone points a gun and asks for your wallet, you hand it to him. The focus here is on behavior and active decisions: making someone do something. A **second dimension of power,** first articulated by Peter Bachrach and Morton Baratz (1962), sees power as the ability not only to make people do something but to keep them from doing something. Bachrach and Baratz argued that a key element of political power is the ability to keep certain groups and issues out of the political arena by controlling the political agenda and institutions to allow certain groups to participate and voice their concerns, while preventing or at least discouraging others from doing so: if it takes large amounts of money to run for office, poor people are likely not to try. A **third dimension of power,** which Lukes contributed, is the ability to shape or determine individual or group political demands by causing people to think about political issues in ways that may be contrary to their own interests. The ability to influence how people think produces the power to prevent certain political demands from ever being articulated: if workers making the minimum wage believe that raising it will result in fewer jobs, they won't demand a higher wage in the first place. We will examine the role of all three of these dimensions of power in this chapter and in the rest of the book.

What Is Comparative Politics?
In comparative politics, the primary focus is on power and decision making within national boundaries. This includes the politics of entire countries as well as more local-level politics. Politics among national governments and beyond national boundaries is generally the purview of the field of international relations, and while comparativists certainly take into account the domestic effects of international events, we do not try to explain the international events themselves. Perhaps it is self-evident, but comparativists also compare; we systematically examine political phenomena in more than one place and during more than one

period, and we try to develop a generalized understanding of and an explanation for political activity that seem to apply to many different situations.

Why Study Comparative Politics? Studying comparative politics has multiple benefits. First, comparativists are interested in understanding political events and developments in various countries. Why did the peaceful regime change happen in Tunisia in 2011 but not in Bahrain and Yemen? Why did the Socialist Party win back the presidency in France in 2012 after seventeen years of conservative presidents? Also, as the Middle East example shows, understanding political events in other countries can be very important to foreign policy. If the U.S. government had better understood the internal dynamics of Syrian politics, it might have been able to respond more effectively to the outbreak of civil war there.

Second, systematic comparison of different political systems and events around the world can generate important lessons from one place that can apply in another. Americans often see their system of government, with a directly elected president, as a very successful and stable model of democracy. Much evidence suggests, though, that in a situation of intense political conflict, such as an ethnically divided country after a civil war, a system with a single and powerful elected president might not be the best option. Only one candidate from one side can win this coveted post, and the sides that lose the election might choose to restart the war rather than live with the results. A democratic system that gives all major groups some share of political power at the national level might work better in this situation. That conclusion is not obvious when examining the United States alone. A systematic comparison of a number of different countries, however, reveals this possibility.

Third, examining politics comparatively helps us develop broad theories about how politics works. A **theory** is an abstract argument that provides a systematic explanation of some phenomenon. The theory of evolution, for instance, explains how species change in response to their environments. The social sciences, including political science, use two different kinds of theories. An **empirical theory** is an argument that explains what actually occurs. Empirical theorists first *describe* a pattern and then attempt to *explain* what causes it. The theory of evolution is an empirical theory in that evolutionary biologists do not argue whether evolution is inherently good or bad; they simply describe evolutionary patterns and explain their causes. A good empirical theory should also allow theorists to *predict* what will happen as well. For example, a comparison of democratic systems in post–civil war situations would lead us to predict that presidential systems are more likely to lead to renewed conflict.

On the other hand, a **normative theory** is an argument that explains what *ought to occur.* For instance, socialists support a normative theory that the government and economy *ought* to be structured in a way that produces a relatively equal distribution of wealth. While comparativists certainly hold various normative theories, most of the discipline of comparative politics focuses on empirical theory. We attempt to explain

theory
An abstract argument that provides a systematic explanation of some phenomenon

empirical theory
An argument explaining what actually occurs; empirical theorists first notice and describe a pattern and then attempt to explain what causes it

normative theory
An argument explaining what ought to occur rather than what does occur; contrast with empirical theory

the political world around us, and we do this by looking across multiple cases to come up with generalizations about politics.

How Do Comparativists Study Politics?　Clearly, political scientists do not have perfect scientific conditions in which to do research. We do not have a controlled laboratory, because we certainly cannot control the real world of politics. Physicists can use a laboratory to control all elements of an experiment, and they can repeat that same experiment to achieve identical results because molecules do not notice what the scientists are doing, think about the situation, and change their behavior. In political science, however, political actors think about the changes going on around them and modify their behavior accordingly.

Despite these limitations, comparativists use the scientific method (as explained in the "Scientific Method in Comparative Politics" box) to try to gain as systematic evidence as possible. We use several research methods to try to overcome at least some of the difficulties our complex field of study presents. Research methods are systematic processes used to ensure that the study of some phenomena is as objective and unbiased as possible.

One common research method we use is the single case study, which examines a particular political phenomenon in just one country or community. A case study can generate ideas for new theories, or it can test existing theories developed from different cases. A single case can never be definitive proof of anything beyond that case itself, but it can be suggestive of further research and can be of interest to people researching that particular country. Deviant case studies that do not fit a widely held pattern can be particularly helpful in highlighting the limits of even widely supported theories. Case studies also deepen our knowledge about particular countries, useful in and of itself. Scholars engaging in case study research search for common patterns within the case or use a method known as process tracing, which involves careful examination of the historical linkages between potential causes and effects, to demonstrate what caused what in the particular case. Case studies serve as important sources of information and ideas for comparativists using more comparative methods.

Scholars use the comparative method to examine the same phenomenon in several cases, and they try to mimic laboratory conditions by selecting cases carefully. Two approaches are common. The most similar systems design selects cases that are alike in a number of ways but differ on the key question under examination. For instance, Michael Bratton and Nicholas van de Walle (1997) looked at transitions to democracy in Africa, arguing that all African countries share certain similarities in patterns of political behavior that are distinct from patterns in Latin America, where the main theories of democratization were developed. On the other hand, the most different systems design looks at countries that differ in many ways but are similar in terms of the particular political process or outcome in which the research is

research methods
Systematic processes used to ensure that the study of some phenomena is as objective and unbiased as possible

single case study
Research method that examines a particular political phenomenon in just one country or community and can generate ideas for theories or test theories developed from different cases

comparative method
The means by which scholars try to mimic laboratory conditions by careful selection of cases

interested. For instance, scholars of revolution look at the major cases of revolution around the world—a list of seemingly very different countries like France, Russia, China, Vietnam, Cuba, Nicaragua, and Iran—and ask what common elements can be found that explain why these countries had revolutions. Both comparative methods have their strengths and weaknesses, but their common goal is to use careful case selection and systematic examination of key variables to mimic laboratory methods as closely as possible.

With about two hundred countries in the world, however, no one can systematically examine every single case in depth. For large-scale studies, political scientists rely on a third method: **quantitative statistical techniques.** When evidence can be reduced to sets of numbers, statistical methods can be used to systematically compare a huge number of cases. Recent research on the causes of civil war, for instance, looked

quantitative statistical techniques
Research method used for large-scale studies that reduces evidence to sets of numbers so that statistical analysis can systematically compare a huge number of cases

Scientific Method in Comparative Politics

Political science can never be a pure science because of imperfect laboratory conditions: in the real world, we have very little control over social and political phenomena. Political scientists, like other social scientists, nonetheless think in scientific terms. Most use key scientific concepts, including the following:

- Theory: An abstract argument explaining a phenomenon
- Hypothesis: A claim that certain things cause other things to happen or change
- Variable: A measurable phenomenon that changes across time or space
- Dependent variable: The phenomenon a scientist is trying to explain
- Independent variable: The thing that explains the dependent variable
- Control: Holding variables constant so that the effects of one independent variable at a time can be examined

In using the scientific method in political science, the first challenge we face is to define clearly the variables we need to include and measure them accurately. For instance, one recent study of civil wars by Paul Collier and Anke Hoeffler (2001) included, among other variables, measurements of when a civil war was taking place, poverty, ethnic fragmentation, and dependence on natural resources. They had to ask themselves, What constitutes a "civil war"? How much violence must occur and for how long before a particular country is considered to be having a civil war? In 2007 critics of the U.S. presence in Iraq argued

that Iraq was experiencing a civil war, while defenders of the United States denied this, so should the internal conflict in Iraq in 2007 be counted as a civil war or not?

A second challenge we face is figuring out how to control for all the potentially relevant variables in our research. In a laboratory, scientists control many of the variables they work with, holding them constant so that they can examine the effects of one independent variable at a time. Political scientists can rarely do this directly, as we cannot hold variables constant. A common alternative is to measure the simultaneous effects of all the independent variables through quantitative studies, such as Collier and Hoeffler's study of civil wars. Single-case studies and the comparative method attempt to control variables via careful selection of cases. For instance, a comparative case study examining the same questions Collier and Hoeffler studied might select as cases only poor countries, hypothesizing that the presence of natural resources only causes civil wars in poor countries. The question becomes, In the context of poverty, is ethnic fragmentation or the presence of natural resources more important in causing civil war? If, on the other hand, we think poverty itself affects the likelihood of civil war, we might select several cases from poor countries and several others from rich countries to see if the presence of natural resources has a different effect in the different contexts. None of this provides the perfect control that a laboratory can achieve; rather, it attempts to mimic those conditions as closely as possible to arrive at scientifically defensible conclusions.

Young men look for diamonds in Sierra Leone. Recent statistical research has supported the theory that conflicts such as the civil war in Sierra Leone in the 1990s are not caused primarily by ethnic differences, as is often assumed, but by competition over control of mineral resources.

AP Photo/Adam Butler

at all identifiable civil wars over several decades, literally hundreds of cases. The results indicated that ethnic divisions, which often seem to be the cause of civil war, are not as important as had been assumed. Although they may play a role, civil war is much more likely when groups are fighting over control of a valuable resource such as diamonds. Where no such resource exists, ethnic divisions are far less likely to result in war (Collier and Hoeffler 2001).

Each of these methods has its advantages and disadvantages. A single case study allows a political scientist to look at a phenomenon in great depth and come to a more thorough understanding of a particular case (usually a country). The comparative method retains some, but not all, of this depth and gains the advantage of systematic comparison from which more generalizable conclusions can be drawn. Quantitative techniques can show broad patterns, but only for questions involving evidence that can be presented numerically, and they provide little depth on any particular case. Case studies are best at generating new ideas and insights that can lead to new theories. Quantitative techniques are best at showing the tendency of two or more phenomena to vary together, such as civil war and the presence of valuable resources. Understanding how phenomena are connected, and what causes what, often requires case studies that can provide greater depth to see the direct connections involved. Much of the best scholarship in recent years combines methods, using quantitative techniques to uncover broad patterns and comparative case studies to examine causal connections more closely.

No matter how much political scientists attempt to mimic laboratory sciences, the subject matter will not allow the kinds of scientific conclusions that exist in chemistry or biology. As the world changes, ideas and theories have to adapt. That does not mean that old theories are not useful; they often are. It does mean, however, that no theory will ever become a universal and unchanging law, like the law of gravity. The political world simply isn't that certain.

Comparative politics will also never become a true science because political scientists have their own human passions and positions regarding the various debates they study. A biologist might become determined to gain fame or fortune by proving a particular theory, even if laboratory tests don't support it (for instance, scientist Woo Suk Hwang of South Korea went so far as to fabricate stem cell research results). Biologists, however, neither become normatively committed to finding particular research results nor ask particular questions because of their normative beliefs. Political scientists, however, do act on their normative concerns, and that is entirely justifiable. Normative theories affect political science because our field is the study of people. Our normative positions often influence the very questions we ask. Those who ask questions about the level of "cheating" in the welfare system, for instance, are typically critics of the system who tend to think the government is wasting money on welfare. Those who ask questions about the effects of budget cuts on the poor, on the other hand, probably believe the government should be involved in alleviating poverty. These normative positions do not mean that the evidence can or should be ignored. For example, empirical research suggested that the 1996 welfare reform in the United States neither reduced the income of the poor as much as critics initially feared nor helped the poor get jobs and rise out of poverty as much as its proponents predicted (Jacobson 2001). Good political scientists can approach a subject like this with a set of moral concerns but recognize the results of careful empirical research nonetheless, and change their arguments and conclusions in light of the new evidence.

Normative questions can be important and legitimate purposes for research projects. This book includes extensive discussions of different kinds of democratic political institutions. One of the potential trade-offs, we argue, is between greater levels of representation and participation on the one hand and efficient policymaking on the other. But this analysis is only interesting if we care about this trade-off. We have to hold a normative position on which of the two—representation and participation or efficient policymaking—is more important and why. Only then can we use the lessons learned from our empirical examination to make recommendations about which institutions a country ought to adopt.

Where does this leave the field of comparative politics? The best comparativists are aware of their own biases but still use various methods to generate the most systematic evidence possible to come to logical conclusions. We approach the subject with our normative concerns, our own ideas about what a "good society" should be, and what role government should have in it. We try to do research on interesting questions as scientifically and systematically as possible to develop the best evidence we can to provide a solid basis for government policy. Because we care passionately about the issues, we ought to study them as rigorously as possible, and we should be ready to change our normative positions and empirical conclusions based on the evidence we find.

THREE KEY QUESTIONS IN COMPARATIVE POLITICS

Comparative politics is a huge field. The questions we can ask are virtually limitless. Spanning this huge range, however, are three major questions. The first two are

CRITICAL inquiry

An Orientation to Comparative Politics

Although you are only starting your study of comparative politics, it is never too early to start developing the ability to understand and ultimately conduct systematic research in the field. Throughout this book, you'll see boxes labeled "Critical Inquiry." Most of these will present you with some key evidence, such as data on several variables for a select number of countries. We will ask you to use these data to test or challenge other findings, or to develop hypotheses of your own that attempt to answer some of the key questions we address in that particular chapter. We may invite you to use online and other resources for additional research as well, so you can start to formulate conclusions about whether the hypotheses are true or not. In some chapters, we also present normative questions for consideration, as these are also essential to the study of comparative politics. While you won't be able to come to definitive conclusions, these exercises will give you a taste of how comparative politics is done. They will also allow you to think about the limits of the research you've done or encountered, the role of normative questions in the field, and what could be done to answer the questions more definitively.

fundamental to the field of political science, of which comparative politics is a part. The third is comparativists' particular contribution to the broader field of political science.

Probably the most common question political scientists ask is, What explains political behavior? The heart of political science is trying to understand why people do what they do in the world of politics. We can ask, Why do voters vote the way they do? Why do interest groups champion particular causes so passionately? Why does the U.S. Supreme Court make the decisions it does? Why has Ghana been able to create an apparently stable democracy, while neighboring Mali had its own democracy overthrown by the military? By asking these questions, we seek to discover why individuals, groups, institutions, or countries take particular political actions. Political scientists have developed many theories to explain various kinds of political actions. Below, we discuss them in terms of three broad approaches that focus on interests, beliefs, and structures.

The second large question animating political science is, Who rules? Who has power in a particular country, political institution, or political situation and why? Formal power is often clear in modern states; particular officials have prescribed functions and rules that give them certain powers. For example, the U.S. Congress passes legislation, which the president has the power to sign or veto and which the U.S. Supreme Court can rule as constitutional or not. But does the legislation Congress passes reflect the will of the citizens? Are citizens really ruling through their elected representatives (as the U.S. Constitution implies), or are powerful lobbyists calling the shots, or can members of Congress do whatever they want once in office? The Constitution and laws can't fully answer these broader questions of who really has a voice, is able to participate, and therefore has power.

Virtually all questions in political science derive from these two fundamental questions, and virtually all empirical theories are involved in the debate these two questions raise. Comparativists add a third particular focus by asking, Where and why do particular types of political behavior occur? If we can explain why Americans on the left side of the political spectrum vote for Democrats, can we use the same explanation for the voting patterns of left-leaning Germans and Brazilians? If special interests have the real power over economic policy in the U.S. presidential system, is this the case in Britain's parliamentary democracy as well? Why have military coups d'état happened rather frequently in Latin America and Africa but very rarely in Europe and North America? Comparativists start with the same basic theories used by other political scientists to try to explain political behavior and understand who really has power; we then add a comparative dimension to develop explanations that work in different times and places. In addition to helping develop more scientific theories, comparing different cases and contexts can help us determine which lessons from one situation are applicable to another.

What Explains Political Behavior?

The core activity in all political science is explaining political behavior: Why do people, groups, and governments act as they do in the political arena? It's easy enough to observe and describe behavior, but what explains it? In daily discussions we tend to attribute the best of motives to those with whom we agree—they are "acting in the best interests" of the community or nation. We tend to see those with whom we disagree, on the other hand, as acting selfishly or even with evil intent. You can see this tendency in the way Americans use the phrase "special interest." We perceive groups whose causes or ideological leanings we agree with as benevolent and general; those we disagree with are "special interests." Logically, however, any **political actor**, meaning any person or group engaged in political behavior, can be motivated by a variety of factors. Political scientists have developed three broad answers to the question of what explains political behavior: interests, beliefs, and structures. Each answer includes within it several theoretical approaches.

Interests We commonly assume that most people involved in politics are in it for their own good. Even when political actors claim to be working for the greater good or for some specific principle, many people suspect they are just hiding their own self-interested motives. The assumption of self-interest (broadly defined) is also a major element in political science theories about political behavior.

Rational choice theory assumes that individuals are rational and that they bring a set of self-defined preferences into the political arena. This does not mean that all people are greedy or selfish, but rather that they rationally pursue their preferences, whatever those may be. The theory borrows heavily from the field of economics, which makes the same assumptions in analyzing behavior in the market. Political

political actor
Any person or group engaged in political behavior

rational choice theory
An explanation for political behavior that assumes that individuals are rational beings who bring to the political arena a set of self-defined preferences and adequate knowledge and ability to pursue those preferences

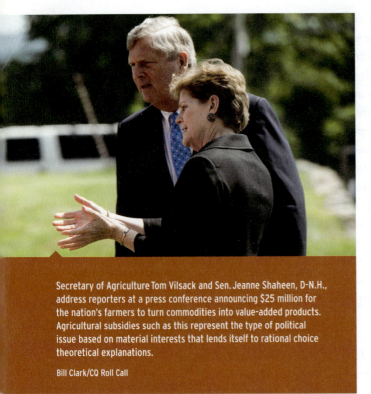

Secretary of Agriculture Tom Vilsack and Sen. Jeanne Shaheen, D-N.H., address reporters at a press conference announcing $25 million for the nation's farmers to turn commodities into value-added products. Agricultural subsidies such as this represent the type of political issue based on material interests that lends itself to rational choice theoretical explanations.

Bill Clark/CQ Roll Call

scientists use this theory to explain political behavior and its results by making assumptions about political actors' preferences, modeling the political context in which they pursue those preferences, and demonstrating how political outcomes can be explained as the result of the interactions of those actors in that context. For instance, the allocation of money for building new roads is the result of an agreement among members of a congressional committee. All of the members of the committee have certain interests or preferences, based mainly on the stated desires of the voters in the districts they represent as well as the members' own desire for reelection. The committee members pursue those interests rationally, and the final bill is a negotiated settlement reflecting the relative power of the various committee members, as well as their interests within the context of the committee and Congress more broadly.

Rational choice theorists start their analyses at the level of the individual, but they often seek to explain group behavior. They model group behavior from their assumptions about the preferences of individual members of groups. Group behavior is considered a result of the collective actions of rational individual actors in the group in a particular context. Racial or ethnic minority groups, women's groups, or environmental and religious groups can all be analyzed in this way. Rational choice theorists would argue, for instance, that environmentalists are just as rational and self-interested as oil companies but simply have different preferences. Environmentalists gain benefits from breathing clean air and walking through unpolluted forests; they pursue those preferences in the same way that the oil industry pursues its opposition to environmental regulations. While self-defined preferences may be easier to see when analyzing battles over material goods and money, they exist throughout the political arena. Rational choice theorists thus are not interested in the second or third dimensions of power we mentioned earlier; they examine behavior, not institutions that prevent behavior, and they do not ask how and why people have certain preferences. They instead accept people's preferences and actions as given and then ask how they can be explained via rationality.

This raises one of the major criticisms of rational choice theories. Critics contend that rational choice theorists have difficulty explaining outcomes because they often cannot know in advance exactly which individuals or groups might be involved in a particular political dispute and exactly how they will define their preferences. When a new political issue arises, individuals or groups have to figure out if they are interested in it, and if so, what preferences they will pursue. In economics, this usually isn't a problem. It's a pretty safe assumption that people engage in economic activity to make money: businesses seek to maximize profits, and workers look for the highest wage. Knowing preferences in advance is much more difficult in political science. For instance, how can a rational choice theorist explain the electoral choice of a voter who is both a devout Catholic and a union member if the two available candidates are (a) a Democrat who favors raising the minimum wage and other workers' benefits but also favors legalized abortion, and (b) a Republican with the opposite views? Will that person vote as a Catholic or as a union member? How can we use rational choice theory to figure out his preferences in this situation?

Many comparativists also ask whether rational choice theories can explain the different political behaviors seen around the world. For most of the twentieth century, for example, the most important French labor unions were closely affiliated with the Communist Party and pursued many objectives tied to party beliefs, beyond the basic "shop floor" issues of wages and working conditions. In the United States, by contrast, no major unions were tied to communist or socialist parties, and unions focused much more on improving wages and working conditions, with less concern for broader social changes. In Britain, labor unions were not communists, but they created their own party, the Labour Party, to represent their interests in government. Rational choice theorists might be able to explain political outcomes involving these unions after correctly understanding the preferences of each, but they have a hard time explaining why unions in different countries developed strikingly different sets of preferences. Did something about the working conditions of these three countries produce different definitions of "self-interest," or do different workers define their interests differently based on factors other than rational calculation?

Psychological theories also focus on individual interests but question the assumption of rational action and are particularly interested in how political preferences are formed. They explain political behavior on the basis of individuals' psychological experiences or dispositions. Psychological theories look for nonrational explanations for political behavior. Comparativists who study individual leaders have long used this approach, trying to explain leaders' choices and actions by understanding personal backgrounds and psychological states. More recently, political scientists have examined the role of emotions in explaining political behavior. Roger Petersen (2002) and Andrew Ross (2013) look at emotions such as fear to explain violent ethnic and religious conflict, while Bethany Albertson and Shana Gadarian (2015) argue that anxiety is important to understanding Americans' response to threatening issues such as terrorism and climate change. In sharp contrast to rational choice theory, psychological theories are often interested in the third dimension of power: influences on the formation of individual political demands. Critics of the psychological approach argue that the inherent focus on the individual that is fundamental to psychological theories makes them irrelevant to explaining group behavior. If so, their utility in political science is limited. Explanations beyond the level of individual motivation, however, might help explain these situations.

psychological theories
Explanations for political behavior based on psychological analysis of political actors' motives

Beliefs Beliefs are probably second only to self-interest in popular ideas about political behavior. If people think a political actor is not simply self-interested, they usually assume she is motivated by a value or belief. Environmentalists care about the environment; regardless of their own personal interests, they think everyone ought to have clean air to breathe and forests to explore. People who are against abortion believe that life begins at conception and therefore abortion is murder; self-interest has nothing to do with it. Political scientists have developed various formal theories that relate to this commonsense notion that values and beliefs matter. The main approaches focus on either political culture or political ideology.

A **political culture** is a set of widely held attitudes, values, beliefs, and symbols about politics. It provides people with ways to understand the political arena, justifications for a particular set of political institutions and practices, and definitions of appropriate political behaviors. Political cultures emerge from various historical processes and can change over time, although they usually change rather slowly as they are often deeply embedded in a society. They tend to endure, in part, because of **political socialization**, the process through which people, especially young people, learn about politics and are taught a society's common political values and beliefs. Theories of political culture argue that the attitudes, values, beliefs, and symbols that constitute a given country's political culture are crucial explanations for political behavior in that country. Widely accepted cultural values, they argue, can influence all three dimensions of power: getting people to do something, excluding them from the political arena, and influencing their political demands.

Two broad schools of thought within political culture theory exist: modernist and postmodernist. **Modernists** believe that clear attitudes, values, and beliefs can be identified within any particular political culture. The best-known example of this approach was presented by Gabriel Almond and Sidney Verba in their 1963 book, *The Civic Culture*. Based on a broad survey of citizens of five countries in North America and Europe, the authors developed a typology, or list of different types, of political cultures. They saw each country as dominated primarily by one particular type of political culture and argued that more stable and democratic countries, such as the United States and Great Britain, had a **civic culture.** This meant that their citizens held democratic values and beliefs that supported their democracies; these attitudes led citizens to participate actively in politics but also to defer enough to the leadership to let it govern effectively. On the other hand, the authors described Mexico as an authoritarian culture in which citizens viewed themselves primarily as subjects with no right to control their government, suggesting that these attitudes helped to produce the electoral authoritarian regime that ruled the country until 2000.

Critics of the modernist approach question the assumption that any country has a clearly defined political culture that is relatively fixed and unchanging, and they contest the argument that cultural values cause political outcomes rather than the

---

political culture
A set of widely held attitudes, values, beliefs, and symbols about politics

political socialization
The process through which people, especially young people, learn about politics and are taught a society's common political values and beliefs

modernists
Theorists of political culture who believe that clear sets of attitudes, values, and beliefs can be identified in each country that change very rarely and explain much about politics there

civic culture
A political culture in which citizens hold values and beliefs that support democracy, including active participation in politics but also enough deference to the leadership to let it govern effectively

Police confront protesters in Mexico City in 1968. Political culture theory argues that countries like Mexico were not democratic because they did not have a democratic political culture. Critics contend that culture can change quickly, so it isn't a very good explanation of regime type. Mexico transitioned to an electoral democracy in 2000.

other way around. They note that **subcultures** (distinct political cultures of particular groups) exist in all societies. Racial or religious minorities, for instance, may not fully share the political attitudes and values of the majority. The assumption that we can identify a single, unified political culture that is key to understanding a particular country can mask some of the most important political conflicts within the country. Furthermore, political attitudes themselves may be symptoms rather than causes of political activity or a governmental system. For example, Mexican citizens in the 1960s may not have viewed themselves as active participants in government for a very rational reason: they had lived for forty years under one party that had effectively suppressed all meaningful opposition and participation. They really did not have any effective voice in government or any chance for effective participation. According to this view, the political institutions in Mexico created the political attitudes of Mexicans, rather than vice versa.

Some political scientists also accuse modernists of ethnocentrism, in that many modernist approaches argue that Anglo-American values are superior to others for establishing stable democracies. Still other critics suggest that political culture is more malleable than *The Civic Culture* assumed. The attitudes that surveys identified in the 1960s were just that—attitudes of the 1960s. Over time, as societies change and new political ideas arise, attitudes and values change accordingly, sometimes with breathtaking speed (Almond and Verba 1989). Many cultural theorists, for instance, have argued that both Arab and Islamic cultures tend to have nondemocratic values that

subcultures
Groups that hold partially different beliefs and values from the main political culture of a country

support authoritarian regimes in the Middle East. The revolts of the "Arab Spring" in 2011 suggest that those theorists either misunderstood the cultures or the cultures changed rapidly, and the differential outcomes of those revolts—democracy in Tunisia but a return to electoral authoritarian rule in Egypt—suggest that "Islamic" or "Arab" culture is far from monolithic.

Some modernist approaches examine change in political culture. Ronald Inglehart (1971) coined the term **postmaterialist** in the 1970s to describe what he saw as a new predominant element in political culture in wealthy democracies. He argued that as a result of the post–World War II economic expansion, by the 1960s and 1970s most citizens in wealthy societies were less concerned about economic (materialist) issues and more concerned about "quality of life" issues. They had become "postmaterialist." Economic growth had allowed most citizens to attain a level of material comfort that led to a change in attitudes and values. Individuals had become more concerned with ideas like human rights, civil rights, women's rights, environmentalism, and moral values.

This postmaterialist shift in political culture led to a sea change in the issues that politicians came to care about and the outcomes of elections. It explained, for instance, why many self-identified Catholic voters in the United States shifted from voting Democratic in the middle of the twentieth century to voting Republican by the end of the century. In the 1950s they voted their mostly working-class economic interests, supporting the party that created what they saw as "pro-worker" policies. Later, as they achieved greater economic security as part of an expanding middle class, they came to care more about postmaterialist moral values, such as their religious opposition to abortion, and they shifted their party allegiance accordingly. As the bulk of American voters went through this shift in political culture, political battles focused less on economic issues and more on debates over moral and cultural values. More recently, Russell Dalton, Christian Welzel, and their colleagues have argued that postmaterialist and more participatory values have come to characterize not only Western societies but many societies around the world, and that those more participatory values result in stronger democracy and ability to govern, in contrast to *The Civic Culture*'s thesis that too much participation threatens democracy (Dalton and Welzel 2014).

The postmaterialist thesis shows how political culture can change over time as a result of other changes in society. Nonetheless, these theorists continued to argue that it was useful to think about societies as having identifiable political cultures that explain much political behavior. The **postmodernist** approach, on the other hand, pushes the criticism of modernism further, questioning the assumption that one clear set of values can be identified that has a clear meaning to all members of a society. Postmodernists, influenced primarily by postmodern French philosophers such as Michel Foucault, see cultures not as sets of fixed and clearly defined values but rather as sets of symbols subject to interpretation. When examining political culture, postmodernists focus primarily on **political discourse**, meaning the ways in which a

postmaterialist
A set of values in a society in which most citizens are economically secure enough to move beyond immediate economic (materialist) concerns to "quality of life" issues like human rights, civil rights, women's rights, environmentalism, and moral values

postmodernist
An approach that sees cultures not as sets of fixed and clearly defined values but rather as sets of symbols subject to interpretation

political discourse
The ways in which people speak and write about politics; postmodern theorists argue that political discourse influences political attitudes, identity, and actions

society speaks and writes about politics. They argue that a culture has a set of symbols that, through a particular historical process, has come to be highly valued but is always subject to varying interpretations. These symbols do not have fixed values upon which all members of a society agree; instead, political actors interpret them through political discourse. Influencing discourse can be a means to gain power in its third dimension: influencing how people think about politics.

One example of a symbol that American political actors use in political discourse is "family values." No American politician would dare oppose family values. In the 1980s Republicans under President Ronald Reagan used this concept in their campaign discourse very effectively to paint themselves as supporters of the core concerns of middle-class families. As a result, Democrats and their policies came to be seen at times as threatening to the ideal of the nuclear family. In the 1990s under President Bill Clinton, Democrats were able to gain back some political advantage by reinterpreting family values to mean what they argued was support for "real" American families: single mothers trying to raise kids on their own, or two-income families in which the parents worried about the quality of after-school programs and the cost of a college education. Democrats created a new discourse about family values that allowed them to connect that powerful symbol to the kinds of government programs they supported. Family values, the postmodernists would argue, are not a fixed set of values on which all agree, but rather a symbol through which political leaders build support by developing a particular discourse at a particular time. Such symbols are always subject to reinterpretation.

Critics of the postmodern approach argue that it really cannot explain anything. If everything is subject to interpretation, then how can one explain or predict anything other than "things will change as new interpretations arise"? Postmodernists respond that the discourses themselves matter by setting symbolic boundaries within which political actors must engage to mobilize political support. The ability of political leaders to interpret these symbols to develop support for themselves and their policies is a central element to understanding political activity in any country.

Advocates of political culture, whether modernist or postmodernist, argue that explaining political behavior requires understanding the effects of political culture at the broadest level. A related but distinct way to examine the effect of beliefs is the study of **political ideology,** a systematic set of beliefs about how a political system ought to be structured. Political ideologies typically are quite powerful, overarching worldviews that incorporate both normative and empirical theories that explicitly state an understanding of how the political world does operate and how it ought to operate. Political ideology is distinct from political culture in that it is much more consciously elaborated. In chapter 3 we examine the predominant political ideologies of the last century: liberalism, communism, fascism, modernizing authoritarianism, and theocracy.

Advocates of a particular political ideology attempt to mobilize support for their position by proclaiming their vision of a just and good society. The most articulate

political ideology
A systematic set of beliefs about how a political system ought to be structured

proponents of an ideology can expound on its points, define its key terms, and argue for why it is right. Communists, for instance, envision a communist society in which all people are equal and virtually all serious conflicts disappear, meaning government itself can disappear. They appeal to people's sense of injustice by pointing out the inequality that is inherent in a capitalist society, and they encourage people to work with them through various means to achieve a better society in the future.

A political ideology may be related to a particular political culture, but political ideologies are conscious and well-developed sets of beliefs rather than vague sets of values or attitudes. Some scholars take political ideology at face value, at least implicitly accepting the idea that political leaders, and perhaps their followers as well, should be taken at their word. These scholars believe that political actors have thought about politics and adopted a particular set of beliefs that they use as a basis for their own political actions and for judging the actions of others. Comparativists Evelyne Huber and John Stephens (2001), for instance, argue that the strength of social democratic ideology in several northern European governments partly explains why those states have exceptionally generous welfare policies.

Critics of this approach point to what they see as the underlying motives of ideology as the real explanation for political behavior. The Italian Marxist Antonio Gramsci (1971) argued that the key element we need to understand is **ideological hegemony**, or the ruling class's ability to propagate a set of ideas that justifies and perpetuates its political dominance. For Gramsci, ideology is a means by which the ruling class convinces the population that its rule is natural, justified, or both (see the "Who Rules?" section in this chapter on page 25 for a discussion of the ruling class). Clearly, this ties directly to the "third dimension" of power. Advocates of rational choice models might argue that a particular leader or group adopts a particular ideology because it is in its own self-interest; for example, business owners support an ideology of "free markets" because it maximizes opportunities to make profits. Similarly, advocates of a political culture approach see cultural values as lying behind ideology. In the United States, for instance, vague but deep-seated American values of individualism and individual freedom may explain why Americans are far less willing to support socialist ideologies than are Europeans.

Structures   The third broad approach to explaining political behavior is **structuralism.** Structuralists argue that broader structures in a society at the very least influence and limit, and perhaps even determine, political behavior. These structures can be socioeconomic or political. An early and particularly influential structuralist argument was **Marxism**, which argues that economic structures largely determine political behavior. Karl Marx contended that the production process of any society creates discrete social classes—groups of people with distinct relationships to the means of production. He argued that in modern capitalist society the key classes are the **bourgeoisie**, which owns and controls capital, and the **proletariat**, which owns no capital and must sell its labor to survive. According to Marx, this economic structure

ideological hegemony
The ruling class's ability to spread a set of ideas justifying and perpetuating its political dominance

structuralism
Approach to explaining politics that argues that political behavior is at least influenced and limited, and perhaps even determined, by broader structures in a society such as class divisions or enduring institutions

Marxism
Structuralist argument that says that economic structures largely determine political behavior; the philosophical underpinning of communism

bourgeoisie
The class that owns capital; according to Marxism, the ruling elite in all capitalist societies

proletariat
A term in Marxist theory for the class of free-wage laborers who own no capital and must sell their labor to survive; communist parties claim to work on the proletariat's behalf

explains political behavior: the bourgeoisie uses its economic advantage to control the state in its interest, while the proletariat will eventually recognize and act on its own, opposing interests. These groups are acting on their interests, but those interests are determined by the underlying economic structure.

A more recent structuralist theory is **institutionalism**. Institutionalists argue that political institutions are crucial to understanding political behavior. A **political institution** is most commonly defined as a set of rules, norms, or standard operating procedures that is widely recognized and accepted and that structures and constrains individuals' political actions. Major political institutions often serve as the basis for key political organizations such as legislatures or political parties. In short, institutions are the "rules of the game" within which political actors must operate. These rules are often quite formal and widely recognized, such as in the U.S. Constitution.

Other institutions can be informal or even outside government but nonetheless be very important in influencing political behavior. In the United States, George Washington established a long-standing informal institution, the two-term limit on the presidency. After he stepped down at the end of his second term, no other president, no matter how popular, attempted to run for a third term until Franklin Roosevelt in 1940. Voters supported his decision and reelected him, but after his death the country quickly passed a constitutional amendment that created a formal rule limiting a president to two consecutive terms. Informal institutions can be enduring, as the two-term presidency tradition shows. It held for more than 150 years simply because the vast majority of political leaders and citizens believed it should; in that context, no president dared go against it.

Broadly speaking, two schools of thought exist among institutionalists. **Rational choice institutionalists** follow the assumptions of rational choice theory outlined above. They argue that institutions are the products of the interaction and bargaining of rational actors and, once created, constitute the rules of the game within which rational actors operate, at least until their interests diverge too far from those rules. Barry Weingast (1997), for instance, claimed that for democracies to succeed, major political forces must come to a rational compromise on key political institutions that give all important political players incentives to support the system. Institutions that create such incentives will be self-enforcing, thereby creating a stable democratic political system. Weingast applied this argument to several countries, including the United States. He argued that political stability in early U.S. history was due to the Constitution's provision of federalism, a particular separation of powers, and the equal representation of each of the states in the Senate. This gave both North and South effective veto power over major legislation, which enforced compromise and, therefore, stability. The Civil War broke out, in part, because by the 1850s the creation of nonslave states threatened the South's veto power. This changed context meant that Southern leaders no longer saw the Constitution as serving their interests, so they were willing to secede. Rational choice institutionalists argue that political actors will abide by a particular institution only as long as it continues to serve their interests. Therefore, a changed context

institutionalism
An approach to explaining politics that argues that political institutions are crucial to understanding political behavior

political institution
A set of rules, norms, or standard operating procedures that is widely recognized and accepted by the society, structures and constrains political actions, and often serves as the basis for key political organizations

rational choice institutionalists
Institutionalist theorists who follow the assumptions of rational choice theory and argue that institutions are the products of the interaction and bargaining of rational actors

requires institutions to change accordingly or face dissolution. By looking at institutions and their effects, however, they often include the second dimension of power in their analyses, in contrast to the rational choice theorists mentioned earlier who focus solely on the first dimension of power.

historical institutionalists
Theorists who believe that institutions explain political behavior and shape individuals' political preferences and their perceptions of their self-interests, and that institutions evolve historically in particular countries and change relatively slowly

Historical institutionalists believe that institutions play an even bigger role in explaining political behavior. They argue that institutions not only limit self-interested political behavior but also influence who is involved in politics and shape individuals' political preferences, thus working in all three dimensions of power. By limiting who is allowed to participate, institutions can determine what a government is capable of accomplishing. Stephan Haggard and Robert Kaufman (1995), for example, argued that two key institutions—a strong executive and a coherent party system—shaped political participation in ways that allowed certain countries in Latin America and East Asia to respond positively to economic crises in the 1980s and 1990s, improving their economies and creating stable democracies. Beyond limiting who can participate and what can be accomplished, institutions can create political preferences. Because societies value long-standing political institutions, their preservation is part of political socialization: citizens come to accept and value existing institutions and define their own interests partly in terms of preserving those institutions. Historical institutionalists thus argue that institutions profoundly shape political outcomes independent of people's self-interests, and can even help create political values and beliefs, operating on all three dimensions of power.

Critics of institutionalism argue that institutions are rarely the actual explanation for political behavior. Skeptics who follow rational choice theory argue that institutions are simply based on rational actions and compromises among elites who will continue to be "constrained" by these only as long as doing so serves their interests. Scholars who focus on beliefs suggest that institutions are derived from a society's underlying values and beliefs or a more self-conscious ideology, which both shape institutions and explain political behavior.

Political scientists look to three sources as explanations for political behavior: interests, beliefs, and structures. Scholars can use each of these approaches to analyze the same political event. For instance, Chile made one of the most successful transitions to democracy in the 1990s. A rational choice institutionalist might argue that this resulted from the strategic interaction of the major political actors, regardless of what they personally believed about democracy. They came to a compromise with the former military regime and with one another around a set of constitutional rules that, given the political context, they thought was better for them than the available nondemocratic alternatives. Therefore, they agreed to act within the democratic "game." A political culture theorist would point to values in Chilean society that favored democracy, values that perhaps derived in part from the European origins of much of the population, as well as the country's past history with democracy. A historical institutionalist, on the other hand, would argue that Chile's prior stable democratic institutions were easy to resurrect because of their past success and that these institutions represented a legacy that many other Latin American countries did not have. So the question becomes, Which of these theories is most convincing and why, and what evidence can we find to support one or another explanation? This is the primary work of much of political science and the kind of question to which we will return frequently in this book. The theories we use are summarized in Table 1.1.

Who Rules?

The second great question in comparative politics is, Who rules? Which individual, group, or groups control power, and how much do they control? At first glance, the answer may seem obvious. In a democracy, legislators are elected for a set term to make the laws. They rule, after the voters choose them, until the next election. Because of elections, it is the voters who really rule. In a dictatorship, on the other hand, one individual, one ruling party, or one small group (such as a military junta) rules. This ruler(s) has all the power and keeps it as long as he pleases, or at least as long as he is able.

President of Chile Michelle Bachelet attends a military parade in 2015 in the capital. Feminist theorists often argue that women are kept out of political power because of the association of political leadership with military experience and prowess. Women heads of state throughout the world, though still small in number, have begun to challenge that norm.

Fernando Lavoz/LatinContent/Getty Images

Comparativists, however, question this superficial view. Even in democracies, many argue that the voters don't really hold the power and that a small group at the top controls things. Conversely, many argue that dictatorships may not be the monoliths they appear to be in that those officially in charge may unofficially have to share power with others in society in one way or another. Political scientists, in trying to dig beneath the surface of the question, have developed many theories that can be grouped into two broad categories: pluralist theories and elite theories.

Pluralist Theories: Each Group Has Its Voice Pluralist theories contend that society is divided into various political groups and that power is dispersed among them so that no group has complete or permanent power. This is most obvious in democracies in which different parties capture power via elections. When pluralists look at political groups, however, they look at far more than just parties. They argue that politically organized groups exist in all societies, sometimes formally and legally but at other times informally or illegally. These groups compete for access to and influence over power. Policy is almost always the result of a compromise among groups, and no single group is able to dominate continuously. Furthermore, over time and on different issues, the power and influence of groups vary. A group that is particularly successful at gaining power or influencing government on one particular issue will not be as successful on another. No group will ever win all battles. Pluralists clearly tend to think about power in its first dimension; they do not believe that any one group has

pluralist theories
Explanations of who has power that argue that society is divided into various political groups and that power is dispersed among these groups so that no group has complete or permanent power; contrast to elite theory

TABLE 1.1	**What Explains Political Behavior?**			
TYPE	**INTERESTS** Understanding what internal factors explain political actions		**BELIEFS** Understanding the effect of values or beliefs	
Theory or framework	**Rational choice**	**Psychological theory**	**Political culture**	**Political ideology**
Assumptions	Political actors bring a set of self-defined preferences, adequate knowledge, and ability to pursue those interests and rationality to the political arena.	Nonrational influences explain political behavior.	A set of widely held attitudes, values, beliefs, and symbols about politics shapes what actors do.	Systematic set of beliefs about how the political system ought to be structured motivates political action.
Unit of analysis	Individual actors	Group and individual identity and behavior	Individual actors and groups, political institutions, discourses, and practices	Individual actors and groups
Methods	Observe outcome of political process; identify actors involved, relative power, and preferences; demonstrate how outcome was result of actors' self-interested interactions.	Explain actors' choices and actions by understanding their personal backgrounds and psychological states.	Modernist approach identifies clear attitudes, values, and beliefs within any particular political culture—for example, civic culture or postmaterialist culture. Postmodernist approach holds that cultures do not have fixed and clearly defined values but rather a set of symbols subject to interpretation; focuses primarily on political discourse.	Analyze written and verbal statements of political actors and correlate them with observed behavior.
Critiques	Some difficulty predicting future behavior; hard to explain variation across cases.	Difficult to verify connections between internal state and actions, particularly for groups.	Political culture is not a monolithic, unchanging entity within a given country. Cultural values are not necessarily the cause of political outcomes; the causal relationship may be the other way around. If everything is subject to interpretation, then how can anything be explained or predicted?	Focus on ideology obscures what may be underlying motives, or the real explanation, for political behavior.

STRUCTURES Understanding how broad structures or forces shape or determine behavior	
Marxism	**Institutionalism**
Economic structures determine political behavior. Production process creates distinct social classes—groups of people with the same relationship to the means of production.	Political institutions are widely recognized and accepted rules, norms, or standard operating procedures that structure and constrain individuals' political actions—the "rules of the game."
Groups and social classes in particular	Interaction of both formal and informal institutions with groups and individuals
Conduct historical analysis of economic systems.	Rational choice institutionalists follow rational choice theory; institutions are products of the interactions and bargaining of rational actors. Historical institutionalists examine the historical evolution of institutions to demonstrate how these institutions limit self-interested political behavior and shape individuals' political preferences.
Ignores noneconomic motives and ignores groups other than social classes.	Difficult to determine if institutions, rather than self-interest or culture, limit behavior.

the ability to exclude other groups from the political arena or to influence how another group thinks to the extent necessary to gain permanent power over them.

This pluralist process is less obvious in countries that do not have electoral democracies, but many pluralists argue that their ideas are valid in these cases as well. Even in the Soviet Union under Communist rule, some analysts saw elements of pluralism. They believed that for most of the Soviet period, at least after the death of Joseph Stalin in 1953, the ruling Communist Party had numerous internal factions that were essentially informal political groups. These were based on positions in the party and government bureaucracy or on economic position, regional loyalty, or personal loyalty to a key leader. For instance, people in the KGB (the secret police) and the military were each a political group, quietly lobbying to expand the influence and power of their organizations. Leaders of particular industries, such as the oil industry, were a group seeking the ruling party's support for greater resources and prestige for their area of the economy. Pluralist politics were hidden behind a facade of ironclad party rule in which the Communist Party elite made all decisions and all others simply obeyed.

Dictatorships in postcolonial countries can also be analyzed via pluralism. On the surface, a military government in Africa looks like one individual or small group holding all power for as long as it is able or desires. Pluralists argue, however, that many of these governments have very limited central control. They rule through patron–client relationships in which the top leaders, the patrons, mobilize political support by providing resources to their followers, the clients. The internal politics of this type of rule revolves around the competition among group leaders for access to resources they can pass on to their clients. The top clients are themselves patrons of clients further down the chain. Midlevel clients might decide to shift their loyalty from one patron to another if they don't receive adequate resources, meaning those at the top must continuously work to maintain the support of their clients. In many cases, patrons use resources to mobilize support from others in their own ethnic group, so the main informal groups competing for power are ethnically defined (see chapter 4). Various factions compete for power and access to resources, again behind a facade of unitary and centralized power.

Elite Theories   While pluralists see competing groups, even in countries that appear to be ruled by dictators, proponents of **elite theories** argue that all societies are ruled by an elite that has effective control over virtually all power. Elite theories usually focus on the second and third dimensions of power to argue that certain elites have perpetual power over ordinary citizens. The longest tradition within elite theory is Marxism, mentioned above. Marx argued that in any society, political power reflects control of the economy. In feudal Europe, for instance, the feudal lord, by virtue of his ownership of land, had power over the peasants, who were dependent on the lord for access to land and thus their survival. Similarly, Marx contended that in modern capitalist society, the bourgeoisie, by virtue of their ownership of capital, are the **ruling class,** as the feudal lords were centuries ago. The general population, or proletariat, is forced to sell its labor by working in the bourgeoisie's businesses in order to survive and must generally serve the desires of the bourgeoisie. Thus, in *The Communist Manifesto* Marx famously called the modern state "the executive committee of the whole bourgeoisie."

In postcolonial societies, Marxist analysts often argue that at least part of the ruling class is outside the country it rules. With the end of colonialism, a new situation of **neocolonialism** arose. The leaders of the newly independent countries in Africa and Asia benefited politically and economically by helping Western businesses maintain access to their countries' wealth. The new governments came to serve the interests of Western corporations as much as or more than they served their own people.

The Marxist tradition is only one type of elite theory. C. Wright Mills, in *The Power Elite* (1956), argued that the United States was ruled by a set of interlocking elites sitting at the top of economic, political, and military hierarchies. Mills shared with the Marxist tradition an emphasis on a small group controlling all real power, but he did not see the economy as the sole source of this power. He believed that the economic, political, and military spheres, while interlocking, are distinct and that all serve as key elements in the ruling elite. A more recent example of this view was put forward

---

elite theories
Theories that all argue societies are ruled by a small group that has effective control over virtually all power; contrast to pluralist theory

ruling class
An elite who possess adequate resources to control a regime; in Marxist theory, the class that controls key sources of wealth in a given epoch

neocolonialism
A relationship between postcolonial societies and their former colonizers in which leaders benefit politically and economically by helping outside businesses and states maintain access to the former colonies' wealth and come to serve the interests of the former colonizers and corporations more than they serve their own people

by Charles Lindblom (1977), who referred to the "privileged position of business" in a capitalist society. In his view, government is dependent on business for taxes and the bulk of the population is dependent on business for employment, so business is in a unique position to influence those in power. Modern democracies, including the United States, are not fully governed by "the people" in any real sense of the word, according to elite theorists, but rather by interlocking elites.

More recently, feminist scholars have also developed elite theories of rule based on the concept of **patriarchy,** or rule by men. They argue that throughout history men have controlled virtually all power. Even though women have gained the right to vote in most countries, men remain the key rulers virtually everywhere. Today, social mores and political discourse are often the chief sources of patriarchy rather than actual law, but men remain in power nonetheless, and the political realm, especially its military aspects, continues to be linked to masculinity. A leader needs to be able to command a military, "take charge," and "act boldly and aggressively"—all activities most societies associate with masculinity. The second and third dimensions of power help preserve male control despite women now having the same formal political rights as men. Men also continue to enjoy greater income and wealth than women and can translate economic status into political power. According to feminist theorists, men thus constitute an elite that continues to enjoy a near monopoly on political power in many societies.

Similarly, some analysts argue that a racial elite exists in some societies in which one race has been able to maintain a hold on power. Historically, this was done via laws that prevented other races from participating in the political process, such as under apartheid in South Africa or the Jim Crow laws of the southern United States. But, as with feminists, analysts of race often argue that one race can maintain dominance through a disproportionate share of wealth or through the preservation of a particular political discourse that often implicitly places different races in different positions in a hierarchy. Michelle Alexander (2010) argued that laws and discourse around crime, drugs, and "colorblindness" constitute a "new Jim Crow" in the United States; they systemically disempower and disenfranchise black men, in particular, by disproportionately putting a large number of them in the criminal justice system. More generally, race theorists contend that in the United States, cultural attributes associated with being white, such as personal mannerisms and accent and dialect of English, are assumed to be not only "normal" but implicitly superior and are thus expected of those in leadership positions. This gives an inherent advantage to white aspirants for political positions, even when no overt discrimination against others exists.

Determining whether pluralist or elite theories best answer the question of who rules requires answering these questions: Who is in formal positions of power? Who has influence on government decision making? Who benefits from the decisions made? If the answer to all of these questions seems to be one or a select few small groups, then the evidence points to elite theory as more accurate. If various groups

patriarchy
Rule by men

Protesters meet on Wall Street in New York City in January 2015, demanding the end of the "New Jim Crow" and support for the Black Lives Matter movement. Michelle Alexander (2010) called the systematic exclusion of a large percentage of black men from full citizenship via imprisonment for minor crimes the "new Jim Crow." The Black Lives Matter movement that exploded in 2014 was aimed at ending police brutality and excessively harsh sentencing of drug crimes, to undo the "new Jim Crow."

Keith Getter / Contributor

seem to have access to power or influence over decision making, or both, then pluralism would seem more accurate. Table 1.2 summarizes these theories, which we investigate throughout this book.

Where and Why?

"What explains political behavior?" and "Who rules?" are central questions to all political scientists. The particular focus of comparative politics is to ask these questions across countries in an attempt to develop a common understanding of political phenomena in all places and times. The third major question that orients this book is "Where and why?" Where do particular political phenomena occur, and why do they occur where they do and how they do?

For instance, Sweden is famous for its extensive and expensive welfare state, while the U.S. government spends much less money and attention on providing for people's needs directly via "welfare." Why are these two wealthy democracies so different? Can their differences be explained on the basis of competing rational choices? Did business interests overpower the interests of workers and poor people in the United States, while a large and well-organized labor movement in Sweden overcame a small, weaker business class to produce a more extensive welfare state? Or has the Swedish Socialist Party, which has been dominant over most of the last century, simply been successful at convincing the bulk of the population that its social democratic ideology produces a better society, while Americans' cultural belief in "making it on your own" leads them to reject any form of socialism? Or are the differences because a strong nongovernmental institution, the Landsorganisationen I Sverige (LO), arose in Sweden, uniting virtually all labor unions and becoming a central part of the policy-making process, whereas in the United States the country's more decentralized labor unions were weaker institutions and therefore not as capable of gaining the government's ear on welfare policy? Comparative politics attempts to resolve this kind of puzzle by examining the various theories of political behavior in light of the evidence found.

We engage in similar comparative efforts when seeking to understand who rules. A case study of the United States, for instance, might argue (as many have) that a corporate elite holds great power in American democracy, perhaps so great that it

TABLE 1.2	Who Rules?

	Pluralist theory	Elite theory
Key arguments	Society is divided into political groups.	All societies are ruled by an elite with control over virtually all power.
	Power is dispersed among groups.	Marxism: Political power reflects control of the economy; it is based on the economic power of the bourgeoisie, who owns and controls capital and is the ruling elite in capitalist societies.
	No group has complete or permanent power.	The power elite: Elite consists of military and political elite as well as economic elite.
	Even authoritarian regimes have important pluralist elements.	Patriarchy: The ruling elite is male; social mores and political discourse keep men in power. The political realm, especially the military, is linked to masculinity.
		Critical race theorists: The ruling elite is white; assumed superiority of white cultural characteristics keeps whites in power.

raises questions of how democratic the system actually is. A Marxist might argue that this is due to the unusually centralized and unequal control of wealth in the United States. A political culture theorist would point instead to American culture's belief in individualism, which leads few to question the leaders of major businesses, who are often depicted as "self-made" individuals whom many citizens admire. An institutionalist, on the other hand, would argue that American political institutions allow corporations to have great influence by funding expensive political campaigns and that members of Congress have little incentive to vote in support of their parties and so are more open to pressure from individual lobbyists. A comparativist might compare the United States and several European countries, examining the relative level of corporate influence, the level of wealth concentration, cultural values, and the ability of lobbyists to influence legislators in each country. This study might reveal comparative patterns that suggest, for instance, that corporate influence is highest in countries where wealth is most concentrated, regardless of the type of political system or cultural values. We examine this kind of question throughout the book.

PLAN OF THE BOOK

This book takes a thematic approach to exploring comparative politics. Each chapter examines a set of issues by presenting the major theoretical ideas and debates in that area of comparative politics and then examining how those ideas and issues play out in the real world in a set of countries. The rest of Part I looks at a set of key

COUNTRY AND CONCEPT
Case Study Benchmarks

Country	Population	Age structure	Monetary unit	Major natural resources
Brazil	204,259,812	0-14 years: 23.3%; 15-64 years: 68.9%; 65 years and over: 7.8%	Real	Bauxite, gold, hydropower, iron ore, manganese, nickel, petroleum, phosphates, platinum, timber, tin, uranium
China	1,367,485,388	0-14 years: 17.1%; 15-64 years: 72.9%; 65 years and over: 10%	Renminbi	Aluminum, antimony, coal, iron ore, lead, magnetite, manganese, mercury, molybdenum, natural gas, petroleum, tin, tungsten, uranium, vanadium, zinc, hydropower potential
Germany	80,854,408	0-14 years: 12.9% 15-64 years: 65.7%; 65 years and over: 21.5%	Euro	Arable land, coal, construction materials, copper, iron ore, lignite, natural gas, nickel, potash, salt, timber, uranium
India	1,251,695,584	0-14 years: 28.1%; 15-64 years: 66%; 65 years and over: 6%	Rupee	Arable land, bauxite, coal (world's fourth-largest reserves), chromite, diamonds, iron ore, limestone, manganese, mica, natural gas, petroleum, titanium ore
Iran	81,824,270	0-14 years: 23.7%; 15-64 years: 71%; 65 years and over: 5.3%	Rial	Coal, chromium, copper, iron ore, lead, manganese, natural gas, petroleum, sulfur, zinc
Japan	126,919,659	0-14 years: 13.1%; 15-64 years: 60.3%; 65 years and over: 26.6%	Yen	Negligible mineral resources, fish
Mexico	121,736,809	0-14 years: 27.6%; 15-64 years: 65.6%; 65 years and over: 6.8%	Peso	Petroleum, silver, copper, gold, lead, zinc, natural gas, timber
Nigeria	181,562,056	0-14 years: 43%; 15-64 years: 53.9%; 65 years and over: 3.1%	Naira	Arable land, coal, iron ore, lead, limestone, natural gas, niobium, petroleum, tin, zinc
Russia	142,423,773	0-14 years: 16.7%; 15-64 years: 69.7%; 65 years and over: 13.6%	Ruble	Broad natural resource base, including major deposits of coal, natural gas, oil, timber, and many strategic minerals
United Kingdom	64,088,222	0-14 years: 17.4%; 15-64 years: 64.9%; 65 years and over: 17.7%	Pound sterling	Arable land, chalk, clay, coal, gold, gypsum, iron ore, lead, limestone, natural gas, petroleum, potash, salt, sand, silica, slate, tin, zinc
United States	321,368,864	0-14 years: 19%; 15-64 years: 66.1%; 65 years and over: 14.9%	Dollar	Bauxite, coal, copper, gold, iron, lead, mercury, molybdenum, natural gas, nickel, petroleum, phosphates, potash, silver, timber, tungsten, uranium, zinc

Source: CIA, *The World Factbook* (https://www.cia.gov/library/publications/the-world-factbook/index.html).

relationships crucial to understanding modern politics. These relationships all involve the modern state (defined fully in chapter 2). To understand the modern political world, we must first understand what the modern state is, how it functions, and how it arose. We then look at the relationship of states to citizens (chapter 3) and group identity (chapter 4). Part II examines the basic institutions of modern politics in both democratic and authoritarian regimes and explores the process of transition from one regime to another. Part III turns to an examination of political economy and public policy.

Throughout the book, we draw on a set of eleven countries to illustrate the ideas, debates, institutions, and issues we are examining. Each chapter focuses on a comparison of several of these countries, chosen to illustrate the key ideas and debates in the chapter. The eleven countries include a majority of the most populous countries in the world and provide a representative sample of different kinds of modern political history. They include four wealthy democracies (the United States, Britain, Germany, and Japan), two postcommunist countries (Russia and China), the largest and one of the most enduring democracies in the world (India), the world's only theocracy (Iran), and three examples of countries that have worked to establish democratic systems after lengthy authoritarian regimes (Brazil, Mexico, and Nigeria). Our task is to see what we can learn from a comparative examination of politics in this diverse array of settings.

KEY CONCEPTS

authoritarian regime (p. 5)

bourgeoisie (p. 22)

civic culture (p. 18)

civil society (p. 6)

comparative method (p. 10)

comparative politics (p. 8)

democracy (p. 5)

elite theories (p. 28)

empirical theory (p. 9)

first dimension of power (p. 8)

historical institutionalists (p. 24)

ideological hegemony (p. 22)

institutionalism (p. 23)

Marxism (p. 22)

modernists (p. 18)

modernization (p. 4)

neocolonialism (p. 28)

normative theory (p. 9)

patriarchy (p. 29)

pluralist theories (p. 25)

political actor (p. 15)

political culture (p. 18)

political development (p. 4)

political discourse (p. 20)

political economy (p. 7)

political ideology (p. 21)

political institution (p. 23)

political science (p. 8)

political socialization (p. 18)

politics (p. 8)

postmaterialist (p. 20)

postmodernist (p. 20)

proletariat (p. 22)

psychological theories (p. 17)

quantitative statistical techniques (p. 11)

rational choice institutionalists (p. 23)

rational choice theory (p. 15)

research methods (p. 10)

ruling class (p. 28)

second dimension of power (p. 8)

single case study (p. 10)

structuralism (p. 22)

subcultures (p. 19)

theory (p. 9)

third dimension of power (p. 8)

 Sharpen your skills with SAGE edge at **edge.sagepub.com/orvis4e.** **SAGE edge for students** provides a personalized approach to help you accomplish your coursework goals in an easy-to-use learning environment.

WORKS CITED

Albertson, Bethany, and Shana Kushner Gadarian. 2015. *Anxious Politics: Democratic Citizenship in a Threatening World.* Cambridge, UK: Cambridge University Press.

Alexander, Michelle. 2010. *The New Jim Crow: Mass Incarceration in the Age of Colorblindness.* New York: The New Press.

Almond, Gabriel A., and Sidney Verba. 1963. *The Civic Culture: Political Attitudes and Democracy in Five Nations.* Princeton, NJ: Princeton University Press.

———. 1989. *The Civic Culture Revisited.* Newbury Park, CA: Sage.

Bachrach, Peter, and Morton S. Baratz. 1962. "Two Faces of Power." *American Political Science Review* 56 (4): 947–952.

Bratton, Michael, and Nicholas van de Walle. 1997. *Democratic Experiments in Africa: Regime Transitions in Comparative Perspective.* Cambridge, UK: Cambridge University Press.

Collier, Paul, and Anke Hoeffler. 2001. *Greed and Grievance in Civil War.* Washington, DC: World Bank.

Dalton, Russell, and Christian Welzel, eds. 2014. *The Civic Culture Transformed: From Allegiant to Assertive Citizens.* Cambridge, UK: Cambridge University Press.

Gramsci, Antonio. 1971. *Selections from the Prison Notebooks of Antonio Gramsci.* Edited and translated by Quintin Hoare and Geoffrey Nowell Smith. New York: International.

Haggard, Stephan, and Robert R. Kaufman. 1995. *The Political Economy of Democratic Transitions.* Princeton, NJ: Princeton University Press.

Huber, Evelyne, and John D. Stephens. 2001. *Development and Crisis of the Welfare State: Parties and Policies in Global Markets.* Chicago: University of Chicago Press.

Inglehart, Ronald. 1971. "The Silent Revolution in Europe: Intergenerational Change in Post-Industrial Societies." *American Political Science Review* 65 (4): 991–1017. doi:10.2307/1953494

Jacobson, Linda. 2001. "Experts Debate Welfare Reform's Impact on Children." *Education Week* 21 (September 19): 1–8.

Lindblom, Charles E. 1977. *Politics and Markets: The World's Political Economic Systems.* New York: Basic Books.

Lukes, Steven. 1974. *Power: A Radical View.* London: Macmillan.

Mills, C. Wright. 1956. *The Power Elite.* New York: Oxford University Press.

Petersen, Roger. 2002. *Understanding Ethnic Violence: Fear, Hatred, and Resentment in Twentieth-Century Eastern Europe.* New York: Cambridge University Press.

Putnam, Robert. D. 2000. *Bowling Alone.* New York: Simon and Schuster.

Ross, Andrew A. G. 2013. *Mixed Emotions: Beyond Fear and Hatred in International Conflict.* Chicago: University of Chicago Press.

Weingast, Barry R. 1997. "The Political Foundations of Democracy and the Rule of Law." *American Political Science Review* 91 (2): 245–263. doi:10.2307/2952354

RESOURCES FOR FURTHER STUDY

Blank, Rebecca. 2001. "Declining Caseloads/Increased Work: What Can We Conclude about the Effects of Welfare Reform?" *Economic Policy Review* 7 (2): 25–36.

Dahl, Robert Alan. 1961. *Who Governs? Democracy and Power in an American City.* Yale Studies in Political Science No. 4. New Haven, CT: Yale University Press.

Gaventa, John. 1980. *Power and Powerlessness: Quiescence and Rebellion in an Appalachian Valley.* Urbana: University of Illinois Press.

Katznelson, Ira, and Helen V. Milner, eds. 2002. *Political Science: State of the Discipline.* New York: Norton.

King, Gary, Robert O. Keohane, and Sidney Verba. 1994. *Designing Social Inquiry: Scientific Inference in Qualitative Research.* Princeton, NJ: Princeton University Press.

Landman, Todd. 2003. *Issues and Methods in Comparative Politics: An Introduction.* 2nd ed. New York: Routledge.

Marx, Karl, and Friedrich Engels. 1978. *The Marx-Engels Reader.* Edited by Robert C. Tucker. 2nd ed. New York: Norton.

WEB RESOURCES

CIA, World Factbook
 (https://www.cia.gov/library/publications/the-world-factbook)

Organisation for Economic Co-operation and Development (OECD), Data Lab
 (http://www.oecd.org/statistics)

Pew Research Center, Global Attitudes & Trends
 (www.pewglobal.org)

The World Bank, Data
 (http://data.worldbank.org)

2 THE MODERN STATE

KEY QUESTIONS

- What are the common characteristics of all modern states, and how do these characteristics give their rulers power?

- Do the characteristics of modern states limit power in any way?

- Why are some states stronger than others? Why do some states fail completely?

state
An ongoing administrative apparatus that develops and administers laws and generates and implements public policies in a specific territory

Political development—the origin and development of the modern state—is the starting point for the study of comparative politics. What do we mean by "the modern state"? In everyday language, *state* is often used interchangeably with both *country* and *nation*, but political scientists use the term in a more specific way. *Country*, the most common term in daily discourse, is not used in political science because its meaning is too vague. *Nation*, which we discuss in depth in chapter 4, refers to a group of people who perceive themselves as sharing a sense of belonging, and who often have a common language, culture, and set of traditions. *State*, on the other hand, does not refer directly to a group of people or their sense of who they are, though most states are closely related to particular nations. One way to think about the state is to ask how and when we "see" or contact the state. Capitols, courts of law, police headquarters, and social service agencies are all part of the state. If you have attended a public school, gotten a driver's license, received a traffic ticket, or paid taxes, you've come into contact with the state, which provides public goods, enforces laws, and raises revenue via taxes. These observations lead to a useful, basic definition of the **state** as an ongoing administrative apparatus that develops and administers laws and generates and implements public policies in a specific territory.

South Sudanese parade their new flag shortly before the referendum in January 2011 that granted them independence from neighboring Sudan at the conclusion of a long civil war. The world's newest state fell into civil war in December 2013 when the president accused the vice president, his chief political rival, of trying to overthrow the government. A cease-fire was declared and the vice president returned to the government in April 2016, though tensions remained high. New states are almost always quite fragile, as South Sudan demonstrates.

REUTERS/Benedicte Desrus

The *ongoing* nature of the state sets it apart from both a *regime* and a *government*. Regimes are types of government such as liberal democracy or fascism (see chapter 3). Americans use *government* and *state* interchangeably, but "governments" are transient. They occupy and utilize the ongoing apparatus of the state temporarily, from one election to the next in a democracy. Americans often refer to governments as *administrations* (e.g., the Obama administration), but the rest of the world uses the word *government* in this context (e.g., the May government of Great Britain).

Modern states have come to be an exceptionally powerful and ubiquitous means of ruling over people. Any number of groups or individuals, such as dictators, elites, or democratically elected politicians, can rule through the state's institutions. Identifying and understanding the key features of the state help us analyze how governments rule and how much power they have. Looking at how much institutional apparatus a particular country has developed and how effectively that apparatus can be deployed (Are people really paying taxes? Are neighborhoods run by drug lords or the police?) can help identify the effective limits of official rule. States with stronger institutions are stronger states and give their rulers greater power.

In addition to understanding what the state is and how it operates, comparativists study its origins and evolution: Why did modern states become so universal? Where did they first emerge, and why did strong states develop sooner in some places and later or not at all in others? A glance at the Country and Concept table on page 57 shows clearly that even within our group of eleven case study countries, the age and strength of the state varies greatly. These states range from over three hundred to just fifty years old, and they include some of the weakest and strongest, as well as some of the most and least corrupt, in the world. Though they vary widely, all modern states share some basic characteristics that set them apart from earlier forms of political organization.

CHARACTERISTICS OF THE MODERN STATE

Territory   The first characteristic of the modern state is so obvious that you might overlook it. A state must have **territory,** an area with clearly defined borders to which it lays claim. In fact, borders are one of the places where the state is "seen" most clearly via the signs that welcome visitors and the immigration officers who enforce border regulations.

territory
An area with clearly defined borders to which a state lays claim

The size of modern states varies enormously, from Russia, the geographically largest at 6,520,800 square miles, to the seventeen states with territories of less than 200 square miles each. The differences between vast Russia and tiny Tuvalu are significant, but territories and borders help both claim the status of state.

A glance at any map of the world shows no territories not enclosed by state borders (except Antarctica). Many states have inhabited their present borders for so long that we may think of them as being relatively fixed. In truth, the numbers of states and their borders continue to change frequently. The most recent examples are Kosovo's independence from Serbia in 2008 and South Sudan's independence from Sudan in 2011. Border changes and the creation of new states, as both these examples attest, are often attempts to make states coincide more closely with nations, groups with a shared identity that often seek to share a distinct territory and government (that is, a state).

External and Internal Sovereignty   To have real, effective **external sovereignty**, that is, sovereignty relative to outside powers, a state must be able to defend its territory and not be overly dependent on another power. Governments that lack sovereignty are not truly modern states. Examples include the Japanese-backed and controlled state Manchukuo (Manchuria) from 1932 to 1945, the collaborationist Vichy government in France during World War II, and all colonial states; although they had a local government and clearly defined territory, they were not sovereign states because their most crucial decisions were subject to external authority.

external sovereignty
Sovereignty relative to outside powers that is legally recognized in international law

Modern states also strive for **internal sovereignty**—that is, to be the sole authority within a territory capable of making and enforcing laws and policies. They must defend their internal sovereignty against domestic groups that challenge it, just as they must

internal sovereignty
The sole authority within a territory capable of making and enforcing laws and policies

New States and the United Nations

Since 1959, the vast majority of new member states in the United Nations (UN) have been admitted after declaring independence. In the 1960s and 1970s, most newly admitted states were former colonies. In the 1990s, most newly admitted states were the result of the breakup of the Soviet Union and other Eastern-bloc countries. New UN members continue to be added in the twenty-first century:

- **1945–1959:** Eighty-one member states admitted.
- **1960–1969:** Forty-two member states admitted.
- **1970–1979:** Twenty-five member states admitted.
- **1980–1989:** Six member states admitted.
- **1990–1999:** Thirty-one member states admitted.
- **2000–2009:** Five member states admitted.
- **2010– :** One member state admitted.

The example of Kosovo reminds us of another important aspect of territoriality: states exist within an international system of other states (see Table 2.1 on level of state recognition). It is not enough for a state to claim a defined territory; other states must also recognize that claim, even if they dispute a particular border. Political scientists call internationally recognized states sovereign. Essentially, a sovereign state is legally recognized by the family of states as the sole legitimate governing authority within its territory and as the legal equal of other states. This legal recognition is the minimal standard for external sovereignty. Legal external sovereignty, which entails being given the same vote in world affairs as all other states, is vital for sovereignty.

defend it externally. Internal challenges typically take the form of a declaration of independence from some part of the state's territory and perhaps even civil war. States rarely are willing to accept such an act of defiance. From the American Civil War in the 1860s to the former Soviet republic of Georgia in the 1990s, when the region of South Ossetia tried to break away, most states use all the means in their power to preserve their **sovereignty** over their recognized territories.

States try to enforce their sovereignty by claiming, in the words of German sociologist Max Weber, a "monopoly on the legitimate use of physical force" (1970). Put simply, the state claims to be the only entity within its territory that has the right to hold a gun to your head and tell you what to do. Some governments claim a virtually unlimited right to use force when and as they choose. At least in theory, liberal democracies observe strict guidelines under which the use of force is permissible. For example, law enforcement can be called in when a citizen runs a red light or fails to pay taxes, but not when she criticizes government policy. All states, though, insist on the right to use force to ensure their internal as well as external sovereignty. As one political philosopher reportedly said in response to students who complained about the university calling in police during a demonstration, "The difference between fascism and democracy is not whether the police are called, but when."

sovereignty
Quality of a state in which it is legally recognized by the family of states as the sole legitimate governing authority within its territory and as the legal equal of other states

TABLE 2.1 — The Shifting Borders of Modern States: Not Recognized, Limited Recognition, and Majority Recognition States

NOT RECOGNIZED

State	Disputed since	Status
Nagorno-Karabakh	1991	Claimed by Azerbaijan.
Somaliland	1991	Claimed by Somalia.
Transnistria	1990	Claimed by Moldova.

LIMITED RECOGNITION

State	Disputed since	Status
Abkhazia	2008	Recognized by only by 4 countries: Russian Federation, Nicaragua, Nauru, Venezuela.
Kosovo	2008	Recognized by 108 countries.
South Ossetia	2008	Recognized by only by 4 countries: Russian Federation, Nicaragua, Nauru, Venezuela.
Palestine	1988	Recognized as a proposed state by 136 UN member states.
Turkish Republic of Northern Cyprus (TRNC)	1983	Recognized only by Turkey.
Sahrawi Arab Democratic Republic (SADR)	1976	Recognized by 46 countries as legitimate government of Western Sahara.
Republic of China (Taiwan) (ROC)	1949	Recognized by 21 countries.

MAJORITY RECOGNITION

State	Disputed since	Status
Cyprus	1974	Recognized by all countries except Turkey.
People's Republic of China (PRC)	1949	Not recognized by the Republic of China (Taiwan); the PRC does not accept diplomatic relations with the 22 other UN member states that recognize the ROC.
Israel	1948	Not recognized by Iran or the Sahrawi Arab Democratic Republic (SADR); no diplomatic relations with 34 countries.
North Korea	1948	Not recognized by South Korea and Japan.
South Korea	1948	Not recognized by North Korea.

Sovereignty does not mean, however, that a state is all-powerful. Real internal and external sovereignty vary greatly and depend on many factors. Because the United States is wealthy and controls much territory, its sovereignty results in much greater power than does the sovereignty of Vanuatu, even though both are recognized as legitimate sovereigns over a clear territory. Wealthier states can defend their territories from attack better than poorer and weaker ones, and they can also more effectively ensure that their citizens comply with their laws. Even the United States, though, cannot completely control its borders, as the undocumented immigrants and illegal narcotics crossing its long border with Mexico attest.

Legitimacy The ability to enforce sovereignty more fully comes not only from wealth but also from legitimacy. Weber argued that a state claims a "monopoly on the *legitimate* use of physical force" [emphasis added]. **Legitimacy** is the recognized right to rule. This right has at least two sides: the claims that states and others make about why they have a right to rule, and the empirical fact of whether their populations accept or at least tolerate this claimed right. Virtually all modern states argue at length for particular normative bases for their legitimacy, and these claims are the basis for the various kinds of regimes in the world today (a subject explored in chapter 3).

Weber described three types of legitimate authority: traditional, charismatic, and rational-legal. **Traditional legitimacy** is the right to rule based on a society's long-standing patterns and practices. The European "divine right of kings" and the blessing of ancestors over the king in many precolonial African societies are examples of this. **Charismatic legitimacy** is the right to rule based on personal virtue, heroism, sanctity, or other extraordinary characteristics. Wildly popular leaders of revolutions, such as Mao Zedong in his early years in power, have charismatic legitimacy; people recognize their authority to rule because they trust and believe these individuals to be exceptional. **Rational-legal legitimacy** is the right to rule of leaders who are selected according to an accepted set of laws. Leaders who come to power via electoral processes and rule according to a set of laws, such as a constitution, are the chief examples of this. Weber argued that rational-legal legitimacy distinguishes modern rule from its predecessors, but he recognized that in practice most legitimate authority is a combination of the three types. For example, modern democratically elected leaders may achieve office and rule on the basis of rational-legal processes, but a traditional status or personal charisma may help them win elections and may enhance their legitimacy in office.

Legitimacy enhances a state's sovereignty. Modern states often control an overwhelming amount of coercive power, but its use is expensive and difficult. States cannot maintain effective internal sovereignty in a large, modern society solely through the constant use of force. Legitimacy, whatever its basis, enhances sovereignty at a much lower cost. If most citizens obey the government because they believe it has a right to rule, then little force will be necessary to maintain order. This

legitimacy
The recognized right to rule

traditional legitimacy
The right to rule based on a society's long-standing patterns and practices

charismatic legitimacy
The right to rule based on personal virtue, heroism, sanctity, or other extraordinary characteristics

rational-legal legitimacy
The right of leaders to rule based on their selection according to an accepted set of laws, standards, or procedures

is an example of the third dimension of power we discussed in chapter 1. For this reason, regimes proclaim their legitimacy and spend a great deal of effort trying to convince their citizens of it, especially when their legitimacy is brought into serious question.

Where modern states overlap with nations, national identity can be a powerful source of legitimacy. This is not always the case, however, and most modern states must find additional ways to cultivate the allegiance of their inhabitants. They usually attempt to gain legitimacy based on some claim of representation or service to their citizens. The relationship between states and citizens is central to modern politics, and chapter 3 addresses it at length. We explore the contentious relationship among states, nations, and other identity groups more fully in chapter 4.

bureaucracy
A large set of appointed officials whose function is to implement the laws of the state, as directed by the executive

Bureaucracy Modern **bureaucracy**, meaning a large set of appointed officials whose function is to implement laws, is the final important characteristic of the state. In contemporary societies, the state plays many complicated roles. It must collect revenue and use it to maintain a military, pave roads, build schools, and provide retirement pensions, all of which require a bureaucracy. Weber saw bureaucracy as a central part of modern, rational-legal legitimacy, since in theory individuals obtain official positions in a modern bureaucracy via a rational-legal process of appointment and are restricted to certain tasks by a set of laws. Like legitimacy, effective bureaucracy strengthens sovereignty. A bureaucracy that efficiently carries out laws, collects taxes, and expends revenues as directed by the central authorities enhances the state's power. As we discuss further below, weak legitimacy and weak bureaucracy are two key causes of state weakness in the contemporary world.

In summary, the modern state is an ongoing administrative apparatus that develops and administers laws and generates and implements public policies in a specific territory. It has effective external and internal sovereignty, a basis of legitimacy, and a capable bureaucracy. As we argue below, no state has all of these characteristics perfectly; the extent to which particular states have these characteristics determines how strong or weak they are.

HISTORICAL ORIGINS OF MODERN STATES

Now that we have clarified what a state is, we need to understand the diverse historical origins of modern states, which greatly influence how strong they are as well as their relationships to their citizens and nations. A world of modern states controlling virtually every square inch of territory and every person on the globe may seem natural today, but it is a fairly recent development. The modern state arose first in Europe between the fifteenth and eighteenth centuries. The concept spread via conquest, colonialism, and then decolonization, becoming truly universal only with the independence of most African states in the 1960s.

FIGURE 2.1   **The Anatomy of a State**

States

A state is an administrative entity that endures over time, develops laws, creates public policies for its citizens, and implements those policies and laws.

A state must have a legitimate and recognized claim to a defined territory that forms its borders and legitimate and recognized authority to govern within its territory.

It also must have the institutions needed to administer the state's laws and policies.

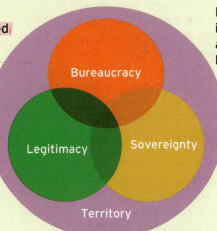

Nations

Sometimes the people of a nation may identify as belonging to a particular state and thereby enhance the legitimacy of the state. Some nations strongly overlap with states.

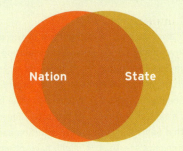

But states may contain one or more nation, or a national movement or a group within a state might contest the state's legitimacy. Some nations exist across a number of state borders or may take up only part of a state.

For instance, the Kurdish people live across the borders of at least five states: Armenia, Iran, Iraq, Turkey, and Syria.

Somaliland: Internal versus External Sovereignty

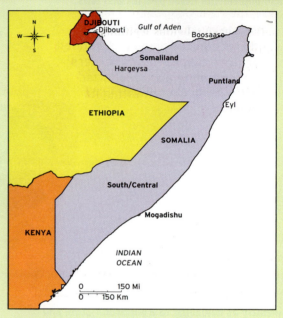

MAP 2.1

Source: William Clark, Matt Golder, and Sona Nadenichek Golder, Map 4.1, *Principles of Comparative Politics*, 2e. p. 92.

Somaliland is an interesting recent case of disputed sovereignty. It is a state that has achieved almost unquestioned internal sovereignty, a stable (albeit uncertain) constitutional democracy, and a growing economy. No other state recognizes it, however, so it has no international, legal external sovereignty. This unusual outcome is a result of the collapse of the larger state of Somalia and the international efforts to resolve that country's civil war. Somaliland, the northernmost region of Somalia, originally was a separate colony from the rest of what is now Somalia; it fell under British control while the rest of the country was an Italian colony. In 1960 the former British colony gained independence for a few days but then quickly agreed to become part of the larger state of Somalia, which had also just gained independence.

When Somali dictator Siad Barre was deposed in 1991, the rebel movement in Somaliland declared the region independent within a few months, restoring its colonial borders. A conference of the elders of all the major clans of Somaliland in 1993 produced a new government with a parliament modelled after traditional Somali institutions, with representation based on clan membership. In 2001 a referendum approved a new constitution that was fully democratic, with a bicameral legislature: one house is filled by directly elected representatives and the other by clan elders. The country held successful democratic elections for president, parliament, and local governments in 2005 and 2010. Since then, elections have been repeatedly postponed; the announcement that elections scheduled for mid-2015 would be delayed to 2017 was met by riots in the capital.

Despite growing concerns about its democracy, Somaliland's economy has grown substantially, based mainly on exports of livestock to the Middle East and money sent home by Somalis living and working around the world. The government has established much better social services and greater security than exist in the rest of war-wracked Somalia. Yet because it has no official recognition from other governments, Somaliland receives very limited foreign aid, has only one embassy in its capital (that of neighboring Ethiopia), and sends no ambassadors abroad. Most of the world fears that officially recognizing Somaliland's external sovereignty will encourage other regions of Somalia to attempt to break away as well, so recognition of the de facto state, expected eventually by many, awaits resolution of the larger civil war in Somalia. Ironically, it looks far more like a modern state than the official government of the larger Somalia, which is internationally recognized as a sovereign state but only partially controls a modest portion of its territory. Indeed, some observers argue that Somaliland's lack of recognition has forced it to create a stronger state than it might have otherwise in order to survive militarily and financially, and the search for international recognition has become a strong basis for a growing sense of nationalism (Richards and Smith 2015).

feudal states
Premodern states in Europe in which power in a territory was divided among multiple and overlapping lords claiming sovereignty

Modern States in Europe Prior to approximately 1500, Europe consisted of **feudal states,** which were distinct from modern states in several ways. Most important, they neither claimed nor had undisputed sovereignty. Feudal rule involved multiple and overlapping sovereignties. At the heart of it was the relationship between lord and vassal in which the lord gave a vassal the right to rule a piece of land known as a fief and tax the people living on it, in exchange for political and military loyalty. The system often involved several layers of these relationships, from the highest and most powerful king in a region to the local lord. The loyalty of the peasants—the bulk of the population who had virtually no rights—followed that of their lord. At any given time, all individuals were subject to the sovereignty of not only their immediate lord but also at least one higher lord and often others, and that loyalty could and did change. In addition, the Catholic Church claimed a separate and universal religious sovereignty over all and gave religious legitimacy to the kings and lords who recognized church authority.

By the fifteenth century, feudalism was giving way to **absolutism**, rule by a single monarch who claimed complete, exclusive sovereignty over a territory and its people. Absolutist rulers won battles for power among feudal lords by using superior economic and military resources to vanquish their rivals. Scholars debate the extent to which the absolutist state was a truly modern state, but it certainly introduced a number of the modern state's key elements. Perry Anderson (1974) argued that the absolutist state included at least rudimentary forms of a standing army and diplomatic service, both of which are crucial for external sovereignty; centralized bureaucracy; systematic taxation; and policies to encourage economic development. It took centuries for these to develop into fully modern forms, however. Legitimacy remained based largely on tradition and heredity, and most people remained subjects with few legal rights. Perhaps of greatest importance, the state was not conceived of as a set of ongoing institutions separate from the monarch. Rather, as Louis XIV of France famously declared, "*L'état, c'est moi*" (The state, that's me).

> **absolutism**
> Rule by a single monarch who claims complete, exclusive power and sovereignty over a territory and its people

The competition among absolutist states to preserve external sovereignty reduced their number from about five hundred sovereign entities in Europe in 1500 to around fifty modern states today. The states that survived were those that had developed more effective systems of taxation, more efficient bureaucracies, and stronger militaries. Along the way, political leaders realized that their subjects' loyalty (legitimacy) was of great benefit, so they began the process of expanding public education and shifting from the use of Latin or French in official circles to the local vernacular so that rulers and ruled could communicate directly, thus adding a new dimension to the rulers' legitimacy. This long process ultimately helped create modern nations, most of which had emerged by the mid-nineteenth century.

The truly modern state emerged as the state came to be seen as separate from an individual ruler. The state retained its claim to absolute sovereignty, but the powers of individual officials, ultimately including the supreme ruler, were increasingly limited. A political philosophy that came to be known as liberalism, which we discuss in greater depth in chapter 3, provided the theoretical justification and argument for limiting the power of officials to ensure the rights of individuals. The common people were ultimately transformed from subjects into citizens of the state. Bellwether events in this history included the Glorious Revolution in Great Britain in 1688, the French Revolution of 1789, and a series of revolutions that established new democratic republics in 1848.

Premodern States Outside Europe Outside Europe, a wide variety of premodern states existed, but none took a fully modern form. The Chinese Empire ruled a vast territory for centuries and was perhaps the closest thing to a modern state anywhere in the premodern world (including in Europe). African precolonial kingdoms sometimes ruled large areas as well, but their rule was typically conceived of as extending over people rather than a precisely defined territory, having greater sovereignty closer to the capital and less sovereignty farther away. Virtually all premodern empires included multiple or overlapping layers of sovereignty and did not include a modern sense of citizenship.

The Export of the Modern State Europe exported the modern state to the rest of the world through colonial conquest, beginning with the Americas in the sixteenth century. The earliest colonies in the Americas were ruled by European absolutist states that were not fully modern themselves. Over time, European settlers in the colonies began to identify their interests as distinct from the monarch's and to question the legitimacy of rule by distant sovereigns. The first rebellion against colonial rule produced the United States. The second major rebellion came at the hands of black slaves in Haiti in 1793, which led to the first abolition of slavery in the world and to Haitian independence in 1804. By the 1820s and 1830s, most of the settler populations of Central and South America had rebelled as well. As in the United States, the leaders of these rebellions were mostly wealthy, landholding elites. This landed elite often relied on state force to keep peasant and slave labor working on its behalf, so while some early efforts at democracy emerged after independence, most Central and South American states ultimately went through many decades of strongman rule over relatively weak states. Independence nonetheless began the process of developing modern states.

The colonial origins of early modern states in the Americas created distinct challenges from those faced by early European states. European states went through several centuries of developing a sense of national identity. In the Americas, the racial divisions produced by colonization, European settlement, and slavery meant that none of the newly independent states had a widely shared sense of national identity. Where slavery continued to exist, as in the United States, citizenship was restricted to the "free" and therefore primarily white (and exclusively male) population. Where significant Native American populations had survived, as in Peru and Guatemala, they continued to be politically excluded and economically marginalized by the primarily white, landholding elite. This historical context would make the ability of the new states to establish strong national identities difficult and would produce ongoing racial and ethnic problems, explored further in chapter 4.

After most of the American colonies achieved independence, growing economic and military rivalry among Britain, France, and Germany spurred a new round of colonization, first in Asia and then in Africa. This time, far fewer European settlers were involved. The vast majority of the populations of these new colonies remained indigenous; they were ruled over by a thin layer of European officials. Colonizers effectively destroyed the political power of precolonial indigenous states but did not exterminate the population en masse. Challenges to this new wave of colonialism were quick and numerous. The independence of the first-wave colonies and the end of slavery raised questions about European subjugation of African and Asian peoples. Colonization in this context had to be justified as bringing "advanced" European civilization and Christianity to "backward" peoples. Education was seen as a key part of this "civilizing" mission. It had a more practical aspect as well: with limited European settlement, colonial rulers needed indigenous subjects to serve in the bureaucracies of

A British colonial official arrives with his camel carriage and entourage at an office in the Punjab, India in 1865. European colonial states in Africa and Asia consisted of a small number of European officials, with military force behind them, ruling over the local population. To rule, they had to rely on local leaders and staff, who collaborated with colonial rule.

Photo by SSPL/Getty Images

MAP 2.2   Spread of Modern Independent States

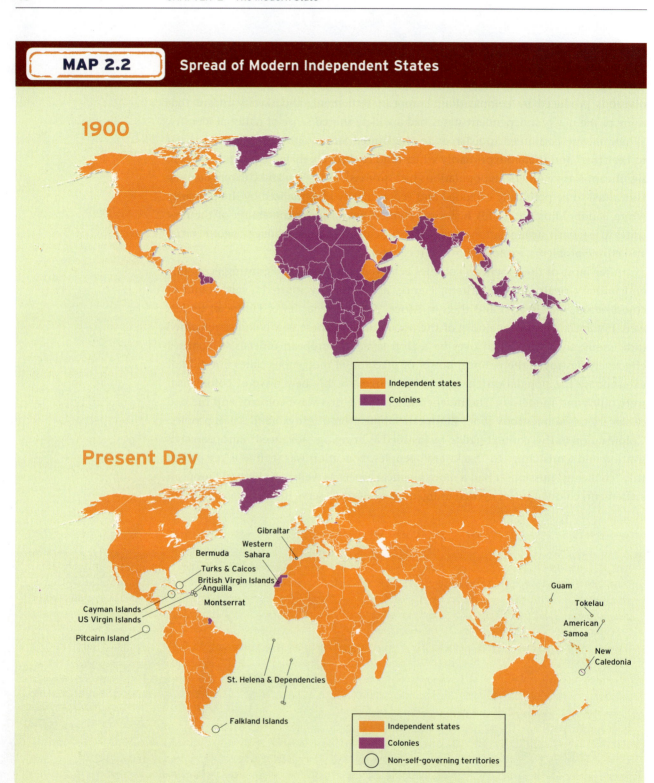

1900

Independent states
Colonies

Present Day

Gibraltar
Western
Sahara
Bermuda
Turks & Caicos
British Virgin Islands
Anguilla
Montserrat
Cayman Islands
US Virgin Islands
Pitcairn Island
Guam
Tokelau
American
Samoa
New
Caledonia
St. Helena & Dependencies
Falkland Islands

Independent states
Colonies
Non-self-governing territories

Is ISIS a State?

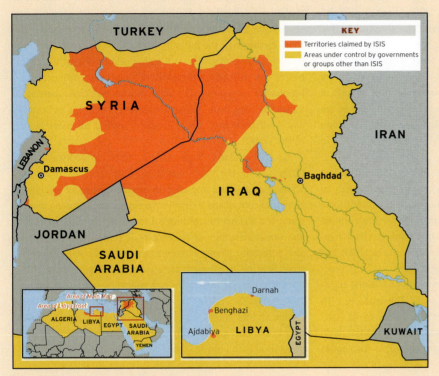

state or state in formation. So, as of 2016, how did it fare in terms of our core components of statehood: territory, sovereignty, legitimacy, and bureaucracy?

The proclamation of the caliphate came after ISIS had gained control over significant amounts of territory in Syria and Iraq. At its height in 2015, it had effective control over as many as six million people in a territory the size of Belgium, though it lost about a quarter of that by September 2016. Much of ISIS's territory, however, was only nominally under its control. It actually administered policies in only a handful of significant cities along key roadways, while having loose control and free range of movement over the mostly uninhabited spaces in between. It also had eight affiliates around the world, but only the affiliate in Libya controlled significant territory of its own, which it lost in December 2016.

On June 29, 2014, Abu Bakr al-Baghdadi, the head of the Islamic State in Iraq and al-Sham (ISIS), declared the creation of a new caliphate, an Islamic state carved by force out of parts of Syria and Iraq. To most outsiders, ISIS is simply the latest and most brutal Islamist terrorist organization, famous for videotapes of beheadings. ISIS, however, has proclaimed itself to be something else: a state, albeit one based on its interpretation of a set of religious principles that harken back to medieval Islam. ISIS is clearly a terrorist organization, but is it also a state, or can it become one?

Charles Tilly, one of the foremost scholars of the rise of modern states in Europe, famously declared that "war made the state, and the state made war" (1975, 42). War or the threat of war forced leaders of early modern, European states to develop taxation and conscription, which in turn required functioning bureaucracies and some sense of legitimacy. More recently, Rosa Brooks (2015) noted that "[s]tate formation . . . has always been a bloody business." ISIS's brutality does not distinguish it from earlier states that have become respected members of the international state system. Brutality alone cannot rule it out as a

Within its territory, or at least in the key cities, ISIS does exercise internal sovereignty. It is divided into twenty provinces (twelve in Syria and Iraq plus the eight affiliates elsewhere), each with its recognized leadership. In its heartland it gains revenue via taxing the local population in various ways, looting cash from banks it captures, and exporting (illegally) resources like oil and antiquities. It uses this revenue to pay its fighters, many of whom have come from elsewhere to join what they see as a religious cause, and to fund government administration and some social services.

External sovereignty is much less clear. Of course, it is actively waging war in both Iraq and Syria and being attacked on multiple fronts. It is not recognized by any UN member and, in fact, is uninterested in such recognition. Indeed, its ideology rejects the modern state system, proclaiming that all Muslims should be united in one caliphate under ISIS leadership, a re-creation of the medieval, Islamic caliphate. Like some regimes before it (Nazi Germany comes to mind), it is inherently expansionist. ISIS's failure to recognize the international state system suggests the system's members will never recognize it.

(Continued)

(Continued)

It has established an extensive bureaucracy that is not only military. It has taken over or established schools, health clinics, and *sharia* courts in the major cities it controls, and attempted to regulate currency values and issue identity documents. Given the limited reports of what is going on in its territory, the extent and effectiveness of its public services are uncertain. Of course, in some of the areas it controls, years of war and rule by weak states have meant limited services are the norm; it's probable that ISIS is doing as well or better than the internationally recognized states did before it, at least in some areas.

ISIS bases its legitimacy on its religious claims. The last Islamic caliphate was the Ottoman Empire, dismantled by Western powers at the end of World War I. Al Qaeda under Osama bin Laden saw itself as laying the groundwork for the eventual restoration of the caliphate but did not think it could happen any time soon; ISIS believes it is obliged to establish and expand the caliphate now, by any means necessary. ISIS's proclamation of the caliphate inspired thousands of Islamist fighters from around the world to join its ranks. The brutality with which it treats both its external enemies and any of its "citizens" who dare question it or try to flee is justified in the name of establishing the caliphate. Its leader and other ideologues

cite Muslim scripture frequently, claiming they are re-creating the original, medieval Muslim government and spurning any connection to modernity. While it has attracted Muslims who share its ideology, the brutality with which it treats many of the Muslims it governs raises significant questions about whether it has or can maintain any significant legitimacy. While most of its population shares ISIS's Sunni Muslim tradition, there is no indication they share its specific ideology or accept its brutality any more than they would brutality visited on them by any other "state."

So is the Islamic State really a "state" in political science terms? Clearly, the answer has to be "only partially." It has consciously established and tried to expand aspects of statehood: territorial control and internal sovereignty, a functioning bureaucracy, and a claim to legitimacy. Indeed, its claim to the caliphate—an Islamic form of statehood—is central to its legitimacy and popularity among radical Islamists. While it has provided some political goods such as services, security—individual and territorial—is the most universal political good any state must provide, and ISIS is failing that. Its rejection of the international system and its brutality mean it remains in a state of constant war, losing and gaining territory regularly and threatening its population with horrific violence on a daily basis.

the colonial states. These chosen few were educated in colonial languages and customs and became local elites, although European officials remained at the top of the colonial hierarchy and exercised nearly unlimited power. In time, the indigenous elites began to see themselves as equal to the ruling Europeans and chafed at colonial limits on their political position and economic advancement. They became the key leaders of the movements for independence, which finally succeeded after World War II. By the 1960s, modern states covered virtually every square inch of the globe, as Map 2.2 demonstrates.

Postcolonial countries faced huge obstacles to consolidating modern states. Although they enjoyed legal external sovereignty and had inherited at least minimal infrastructure from colonial bureaucracies, legitimacy and internal sovereignty remained problematic for most. The colonial powers had typically established borders with little regard for precolonial political boundaries, and political institutions that had no relationship to precolonial norms or institutions. Numerous political entities and many distinct religious and linguistic groups were brought together under one colonial state. The movements for independence created genuine enthusiasm for the new nations, but the colonizers had previously tried to inhibit a strong sense of national unity. Political loyalty was often divided among numerous groups, including the remnants of precolonial states. Finally, huge disparities in wealth, education, and access to power between the elite and the majority of the population reduced popular support for the state. All of this meant the new states were mostly very weak versions of the modern state. The differences between strong and weak states, and the causes of state weakness and collapse, are the last subjects we need to address to complete our conceptual overview of the modern state.

STRONG, WEAK, AND FAILED STATES

The modern state as we have defined it is what Weber called an **ideal type,** a model of what the purest version of something might be. Nothing in reality perfectly matches an ideal type; no state indisputably enjoys complete external or internal sovereignty, absolute legitimacy, a monopoly on the use of force, and a completely effective and efficient bureaucracy. Some states, however, are clearly much closer to this ideal than others. States typically use their sovereignty, territory, legitimacy, and bureaucracy to provide what political scientist Robert Rotberg (2004) called "political goods" to their population. Political goods include security; the rule of law; a functioning legal system; and infrastructure such as roads, public education, and health care. Modern states are also expected to pursue economic policies that will enhance their citizens' well-being, though exactly what those policies ought to be is quite controversial. While some political goods, such as basic security, are universally recognized, others, such as specific economic policies, are the core of many contemporary political debates around the world, which we will investigate in subsequent chapters.

A **strong state** is generally capable of providing political goods to its citizens, while a **weak state** can only do so partially. State strength, however, exists on a continuum, with no state being perfectly strong in all conceivable categories, and changes in state strength can go in both directions. Francis Fukuyama (2014), for instance, argues that the U.S. state has weakened in the last several decades due mainly to what he calls "gift exchange" between legislators, lobbyists, and campaign donors that weakens the state's ability to make independent decisions based on some sense of the public interest. As the Country and Concept table (page 57) shows for our case studies, stronger states tend to be wealthier and consume a larger share of economic resources; they are simply economically bigger than weak states. They also are less corrupt, indicating the presence of stronger bureaucracies, and tend to be more legitimate. Weak states, on the other hand, are often characterized by what Thomas Risse (2015) termed "limited statehood": they provide some political goods widely but others only in certain areas of the country. Other actors—local strongmen, religious institutions, or nongovernmental organizations (NGOs)—may substitute for a weak state in some regions, providing political goods the state cannot or will not.

A state that is so weak that it loses sovereignty over part or all of its territory is a **failed state.** Failed states make headlines—for example, Syria, the Democratic Republic of the Congo, South Sudan, and Afghanistan. In extreme cases, the state

ideal type
A model of what the purest version of something might be

strong state
A state that is generally capable of providing political goods to its citizens

weak state
A state that only partially provides political goods to its citizens

failed state
A state that is so weak that it loses effective sovereignty over part or all of its territory

A group of soldiers stand guard in a town in Syria liberated from ISIS control in February 2015. Failed states make headlines around the world and have implications far beyond their borders. The Syrian civil war gave ISIS the opportunity to create a proto-state within its and Iraq's territory, and it produced a massive refugee crisis that has had profound effects in the European Union.

Massoud Mohammed / Barcroft Medi via Getty Images

collapses totally, as Somalia did in 1991, resulting in two decades of near-total anarchy. It became known to many Americans due to the infamous "Black Hawk Down" episode in 1993, in which sixteen U.S. soldiers were killed and dragged through the streets of the capital. State failure can have effects far beyond the state's borders.

Virtually all elements of state strength are interconnected. If a state lacks the resources to provide basic infrastructure and security, its legitimacy most likely will decline. Lack of resources also may mean civil servants are paid very little, which may lead to corruption and an even further decline in the quality of state services. Corruption in some bureaucracies, such as the military and border patrol, can cause a loss of security and territorial integrity. If the state cannot provide basic services, such as education, citizens will likely find alternative routes to success that may well involve illegal activity (e.g., smuggling), undermining sovereignty that much further. If the state does not apply the rule of law impartially, citizens will turn to private means to settle their disputes (mafias are a prime example of this phenomenon), threatening the state's monopoly on the legitimate use of force. Continuing patterns of lawless behavior create and reinforce the public perception that the state is weak, so weak states can become caught in a vicious cycle that is difficult to break.

Why some states are strong while others are weak has long been a major question in the study of political development. Economists Douglass North and John Wallis and political scientist Barry Weingast used a rational choice institutionalist argument to address this question (2009). They argued that the earliest states were based on elite coalitions created to limit violence among themselves. Power remained very personal, as the earliest states were really just temporary agreements among competing elites, each of whom had control over the means of violence. Elites abided by these agreements in order to gain economic advantages from the absence of warfare and the ability to extract resources. Eventually, some elites negotiated agreements that recognized impersonal organizations and institutions that were separate from the individual leaders. As these developed and functioned credibly, greater specialization was possible, and distinct elites who controlled military, political, economic, and religious power emerged. This required the rule of law among elites. Together with ongoing, impersonal organizations, the rule of law allowed the possibility of a true monopoly over the use of force as individual elites gave up their control of military power. Once established among elites, such impersonal institutions and organizations could expand eventually to the rest of society.

Fukuyama (2014) argued that the continuation of this story—the development of modern states in nineteenth-century Europe—took several different paths. Some, like Prussia (which became Germany), first developed a strong bureaucracy and military in the face of external military threat and only later developed the rule of law and democratic control over the state. Others, such as the United States, saw the rule of law and relatively widespread democratic accountability develop first, resulting in political parties that became corrupt "machine politics"; a modern bureaucracy arose only after industrialization produced a middle class and business interests that demanded reforms to create a more effective government. Following Samuel Huntington (1968), Fukuyama argued that states such as Italy and Greece, which did not develop as strong states early enough, faced the problem of a politically mobilized populace without adequate economic opportunity. This led to corruption as political leaders used the state's resources to provide for their political followers rather than creating a bureaucracy based on merit and equity.

Comparativists have developed several other arguments to explain why states are weak. A common one for non-European countries is the effects of colonialism. In most of Africa and Asia, postcolonial states were created not by negotiations among local elites but between them and the departing colonial power, and political institutions were hastily copied from the departing colonizers; the kind of elite accommodation to which North, Wallis, and Weingast (2009) pointed did not occur. Not having participated seriously in the creation of the new institutions, elites often did not see themselves as benefitting from them and therefore changed or ignored them. In Africa, postcolonial rulers, lacking functioning impersonal institutions, maintained power by distributing the state's revenue to their supporters, and therefore created authoritarian regimes to narrow the number of claimants on those resources. Economic decline beginning in the late 1970s and pressure for democratization a decade later meant those leaders had to try to extract more and more resources from their citizens, leading to a period of widespread state failure and civil war in the 1990s (Bates 2008).

Some scholars point to variation in colonial and early postcolonial rule to explain differences in state strength. Lange (2009) looked at different kinds of colonial rule among British colonies, arguing that more directly ruled colonies in which the colonizer had built strong bureaucracies early on (e.g., Mauritius) developed stronger states after independence than did colonies where the colonizer had relied on local institutions to rule on its behalf (e.g., Nigeria). Andrew Kelly and James Mahoney (2015) argued that in the Americas, the weakest states developed where the earliest Spanish conquest occurred, around the capitals of precolonial kingdoms such as in Mexico and Peru. Stronger states emerged at locations of less population density and therefore greater European settlement, and later colonization, whether Spanish (Argentina) or British (the United States and Canada). Hillel David Soifer (2015), on the other hand, suggested that in nineteenth-century Latin American countries where modernizing elites were united in a single, major capital, state-strengthening reforms were possible; where they were divided into regional economies and centers of political power, such as in Colombia, reform was impossible. He notes that the Latin American states that were relatively strong or weak by 1900 remain so today.

Others have looked to the nature of the economy or the modern international system to explain state weakness. Wealth certainly plays a role: states need resources to provide political goods. The type of economic activity within a state, however, may make a significant difference. Countries with tremendous mineral wealth, such as oil or diamonds, face a situation known as the **resource curse.** A government that can gain enough revenue from mineral extraction alone does not need to worry about the strength of the rest of the economy or the well-being of the rest of the population. If the asset exists in one particular area, such as the site of a key mine, the government simply has to control that area and export the resources to gain revenue in order to survive. Rebel groups likewise recognize that if they can overpower the government, they can seize the country's mineral wealth, a clear incentive to start a war rather than strive for a compromise with those in power. Once again, in this situation, elite compromise to create stronger institutions seems unlikely. Ryan Saylor (2014), though, argued that how strong this logic is depends on who holds political power. Commodity booms focused on a single resource can strengthen the state if those controlling the export of the commodity also lead the political coalition ruling the country; in that case, they have an incentive to provide greater public goods and institutions that benefit their own economic interests but also strengthen the state. In countries that already have relatively strong states, like Norway when it discovered oil in the North Sea, abundant resources may simply provide greater wealth and strengthen the state further, but in weak states, greater wealth may do little to strengthen the state and even weaken it, given the incentives it provides to various political actors.

The neighboring states of Sierra Leone and Liberia in West Africa are a classic case of the worst effects of the resource curse. Ironically, both countries began as beacons of hope. Britain founded Sierra Leone to provide a refuge for liberated slaves captured from slaving vessels, and the United States founded Liberia as a home for former American slaves. Descendants of these slaves became the ruling elite in both countries. Both countries, however, also became heavily dependent on key natural resources. The bulk of government revenue came from diamond mining in Sierra Leone and from iron-mining and rubber plantations owned by the Firestone Tire Company in Liberia. The ruling elites kept firm control of these resources until rebellion began with a military coup in Liberia in 1980. The new regime was just as brutal and corrupt as its predecessor, leading to a guerrilla war led by the man who became West Africa's most notorious warlord: Charles Taylor. After taking control of a good portion of Liberia, Taylor helped finance a guerrilla uprising in neighboring Sierra

resource curse
Occurs when a state relies on a key resource for almost all of its revenue, allowing it to ignore its citizens and resulting in a weak state

Measuring State Strength

In response to growing international concern about state failure, the Fund for Peace developed a Fragile States Index to highlight countries of imminent concern. In 2016 the twelfth annual index ranked 178 countries on twelve factors in three categories considered essential to state strength:

- Social indicators
  - demographic pressures,
  - refugees or internally displaced persons,
  - vengeance-seeking group grievance, and
  - sustained human flight;

- Economic indicators
  - uneven economic growth and
  - poverty/severe economic decline;

- Political indicators
  - legitimacy,
  - deterioration of public services,
  - rule of law/human rights abuses,
  - security apparatus,
  - factionalized elites, and
  - intervention of external political actors.

Map 2.3 shows the least and most stable countries.

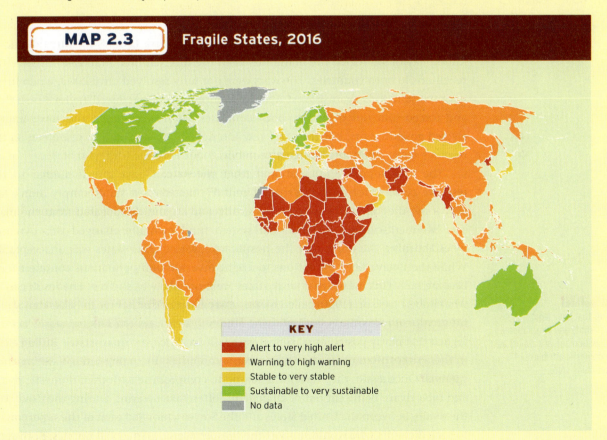

MAP 2.3 **Fragile States, 2016**

KEY

- Alert to very high alert
- Warning to high warning
- Stable to very stable
- Sustainable to very sustainable
- No data

Source: Fund for Peace, 2016, "Fragile States Index 2016" (http://fsi.fundforpeace.org/rankings-2016).

(Continued)

(Continued)

We can use the Fragile States Index to ask a couple of interesting questions. First, what kind of argument can we make about why states are weak or stable based on the index? Look at which countries are most threatened, most sustainable, and in between on the index. Based on what you know about the countries (and it never hurts to do a little research to learn more!), what hypotheses can you generate about why states are weak or strong? Do some of these relate to the arguments we outlined above about why states are weak or strong? Can you come up with other arguments that we haven't discussed in this chapter? If so, on what kinds of theories (from chapter 1) are your hypotheses based?

A second interesting question is, How can we really measure state strength? Take a look at the indicators page of the index: http://fsi.fundforpeace.org/indicators. The index measures those twelve indicators and then adds them up, weighting them all equally, to arrive at an overall score for each country. Do the indicators each measure an important element of state strength? Is it feasible to think we can measure the indicators and arrive at a number to represent each of them in each country? Does it make sense to weight all the indicators equally, or are some more important than others? If you think some are more important, which ones and why? Does your answer connect to any of the theories of state strength and weakness we discussed earlier?

Comparativists don't all agree on the answers to these questions, but we look at evidence and try to generate testable hypotheses for state strength, weakness, and failure in an effort to help states develop stronger institutions. We do this because the human consequences of state weakness—civil conflict, refugees, and human rights violations—and the consequences for the international system are severe.

Leone. Once the guerrilla forces gained control of Sierra Leone's lucrative diamond mines, Taylor smuggled the diamonds onto the international market to finance the rebellions in both countries. The wars were not fully resolved until 2003, when international sanctions against West African diamonds finally reduced Taylor's cash flow and forced him out of power. Both countries are now at peace and have fragile, elected governments, but they still rely too heavily on key natural resources, so the resource curse could cause further problems.

The contemporary international legal system can have effects similar to the resource curse. Prior to the twentieth century, the weakest states simply didn't last very long; they faced invasions from stronger rivals and disappeared from the map. The twentieth-century international system fundamentally changed this dynamic by establishing the norm that the hostile takeover of other states was unacceptable. While there have been exceptions, outright invasion and permanent conquest have become rare. This means that weak states are more likely to survive. The result can be what Robert Jackson (1990) called **quasi-states**: states that have legal sovereignty and international recognition but lack most domestic attributes of a modern state. Jackson argued that many postcolonial states, especially in Africa, are quasi-states. Ruling elites in these states often come to rely on external resources, including foreign aid, for their survival. Once again, they have little reason to compromise with their domestic rivals, and their rivals, being cut out of all benefits, often take up arms. During the Cold War, the rivalry between the United States and the Soviet Union led each of the superpowers to back dictators who would support their respective sides in global politics. Both sides provided generous aid to dictators who ruled with little interest in providing political goods to their people. Many of these states failed a few years after the end of the Cold War because the elimination of the U.S.–Soviet global rivalry meant that neither side was interested in continuing to support the dictators.

quasi-states
States that have legal sovereignty and international recognition but lack almost all the domestic attributes of a functioning state

COUNTRY AND CONCEPT
The Modern State

Fragile States Index, 2016

Country	Approximate year modern state established	Rank among 177 countries	Score (12 = lowest risk of state failure, 144 = highest risk of state failure)	GDP per capita (ppp)	Government expenditure as % of GDP	Corruption Perception Index, 2015 (0 = highly corrupt, 10 = highly clean)	Legitimacy (0 = least legitimate, 10 = most legitimate)
Brazil	1889	117	65.3	$16,200	38.6%	3.8	4.68
China	1949	86	74.9	$13,200	29.3%	3.7	5.36
Germany	1871	165	28.6	$46,200	44.3%	8.1	5.84
India	1947	70	79.6	$5,800	27.0%	3.8	5.21
Iran	1925	47	86.9	$17,400	15.0%	2.7	2.04
Japan	1867	157	35.1	$37,500	42.3%	7.5	6.13
Mexico	1924	107	70.4	$18,000	28.1%	3.5	3.50
Nigeria	1960	13	103.5	$6,100	13.4%	2.6	data unavailable
Russia	1917	65	81.0	$24,400	38.2%	2.9	3.18
United Kingdom	1707	162	32.4	$39,800	45.1%	8.1	6.21
United States	1787	159	34.0	$54,400	38.9%	7.6	5.83

Sources: Fragile state data are from the Fund for Peace, 2016. Data on GDP per capita are from the *CIA World Factbook* (https://www.cia.gov/library/publications/resources/the-world-factbook/index.html). Data on government expenditure as percentage of GDP are from the Heritage Foundation's 2016 Index of Economic Freedom (http://www.heritage.org/index/ranking). Data on corruption are from Transparency International, 2015. Data on state legitimacy are from Bruce Gilley, "State Legitimacy: An Updated Dataset for 52 Countries," *European Journal of Political Research* 51 (2012): 693–699 (doi:10.1111/j.1475-6765.2012.02059.x).

In the post–Cold War era, the international system and major powers have come to see weak and failed states as a significant problem. Weak states produce corruption and illegal activity. They have porous borders through which illegal arms, contagious diseases, terrorists, and illegal drugs might pass. They undermine economic growth and political stability, and democracy is difficult or impossible to foster when a state is unable to provide at least the basic political goods citizens expect. Somalia and Afghanistan are only the best-known examples of this worst-case scenario. For all these reasons, "state-building" (or "nation-building"—the terms are often used interchangeably, even though comparativists draw a sharp distinction between a state and a nation) has become a common element of the international political system. Wealthy countries and international organizations, including the UN, implement programs to try to rebuild states after conflicts, as in Sierra Leone and Liberia. They try to build or rebuild political institutions, train bureaucrats in proper procedures, hold democratic elections, and restore basic services. Much of the comparative research outlined above suggests that state-building is a very long and complicated process, while official "state-building" programs often focus on a five- to ten-year program and only certain elements of the state. Should international efforts focus first on building a coherent national army, a bureaucracy, or democratic political institutions? Or should they instead focus on economic development, assuming political change will follow? Not surprisingly, whatever approach is used, success has been rare. Indeed, no extremely weak or failed states have become strong in the past quarter-century, though some formerly failed states have stabilized but remain quite weak.

CASE STUDIES OF STATE FORMATION

We have chosen eleven countries to illustrate the trends, theories, and debates in comparative politics. We introduce all eleven below by describing the historical development of each state and its relative strength or weakness, and we present them from strongest to weakest as measured by the Fragile States Index. The Country and Concept table above presents some basic information about all of them. The various measures of state strength in the table produce some surprises. Despite Iran's important international role and its moves toward acquiring nuclear weapons, by most measures it is a fairly weak state. Similarly, the external power of the United States does not translate into its being the strongest state in the world, though it is certainly one of the stronger ones. A measure of legitimacy that includes not just human rights but citizens' perceptions of the effectiveness of their government suggests that China's government may be more legitimate than many Western observers believe.

The Strongest States

The strongest states among our case studies were all established as modern states in the eighteenth and nineteenth centuries, industrialized relatively early, and are among the world's wealthiest countries. In other ways, however, their origins lay in quite different circumstances, from the consolidation of independent monarchies in the United Kingdom and Germany to a negotiated agreement in the United States and a defensive strengthening against Western encroachment in Japan. Only one, the United States, began as a colony. In fact, all four were at least briefly colonial powers themselves. They all have firm control of their territory and strong militaries, though in the case of Germany territorial consolidation (or reconsolidation) was not complete until 1990. All also have high levels of legitimacy based on liberal democracy, though questions persist about the ability of their political systems to continue to provide political goods adequately. They have relatively strong senses of national unity, though three of the four face significant questions about immigration and racial differences. That, along with the related issues of uneven economic development and potentially violent groups internally (terrorists, among others), are their most common weaknesses. None is the very strongest according to the Fragile States Index (see Map 2.3, page 55), but all are in the top thirty. Despite this, each still has elements of relative weakness: no state is perfectly strong.

CASE Study

GERMANY: THE FIRST MODERN WELFARE STATE

CASE SYNOPSIS

The modern German state emerged relatively late in Europe after uniting many of the widely dispersed German-speaking people. Its initial strengths rested in a relatively modern bureaucracy and military. Its sovereignty was briefly eliminated under occupation after World War II, and its territory was divided by the Cold War. Nonetheless, the German state, under several different regimes, consciously and effectively created an industrial powerhouse in the heart of Europe that was also the first modern welfare state. Language-based nationalism was the initial basis of legitimacy, and eventually became associated with Nazism. Democracy as a basis of legitimacy emerged twice, disastrously after World War I and successfully after World War II, but was only secure and universal throughout Germany after 1990. Today, the German state is widely considered to be one of the world's strongest, most legitimate, wealthiest, and most stable. This combination makes it the strongest state of our eleven cases as measured by the Fragile States Index.

- FRAGILE STATES INDEX 28.6 (165 of 177); weakest on "group grievance" and "refugees and IDPs"

- TERRITORY Widespread sense of national identity among German-speaking people, but consisted of many states until 1871; boundaries changed with wars until 1990; brief colonial empire prior to World War I

- SOVEREIGNTY Established over much of German-speaking people by 1871; divided by the Cold War, 1945–1990

- **LEGITIMACY** Based on nationalism first; failed liberal democracy after World War I led to Nazi rule; divided state with liberal democratic and communist regimes until united under democratic constitution in 1990

- **BUREAUCRACY** Foundation of early modern state; first modern welfare state; extensive since World War II

A unified Germany first emerged under Otto von Bismarck, the chancellor (equivalent of a prime minister) of Prussia, the largest of many German principalities. Bismarck came to power in 1862 and set about conquering lands populated by German speakers. The Prussian bureaucracy and military, modernized in a reform that began in 1807 in response to Napoleon's invasion, were key sources of Bismarck's ability to build one German-speaking state. The bureaucracy and military were recruited on the basis of merit and average citizens were increasingly treated as equals before the law, creating a stronger state than neighboring ones. In 1871 a united Germany was proclaimed, with the Prussian king named as the German kaiser and Bismarck as the chancellor. This new Germany had a legislature and elections, but virtually all power was in the hands of Kaiser Wilhelm I and Bismarck; the bureaucracy and military remained central to the state and Bismarck's power.

The new German state became actively involved in the economy, using its formidable bureaucracy to pursue rapid industrialization in an attempt to catch up with the economic might of Britain, then Europe's most powerful state. The primary opposition to Bismarck came out of this industrialization in the form of the Social Democratic Party (SDP), founded in 1875, which demanded greater workers' rights and democracy. Bismarck successfully resisted the party's efforts, both by brutal repression when necessary and by creating Europe's first social welfare programs. The latter included health insurance and old-age pensions. The military and bureaucracy remained central to the state's strength, and the regime's ability to forestall democracy.

By 1900 Germany had become an industrial powerhouse with aspirations to

East Berliners stand atop the Berlin Wall in 1989, shortly before it was brought down to reunite the divided German state. Reunification in 1990 meant the elimination of the separate and largely illegitimate East German state, whose territory was absorbed by the much stronger and more legitimate West German state. This was only the most recent change in the boundaries of the German state.

AP Photo/Michel Lipchitz

become an empire. It colonized several territories in Africa before World War I, but its defeat in "the Great War" destroyed the country's first regime and its colonial empire. As Allied forces moved on Berlin in 1918, the kaiser fled, and the leaders of the SDP proclaimed a democratic republic, trying to shift the basis for legitimacy from nationalism to democracy. The new democracy, known as the Weimar Republic, survived only fourteen years. Defeat in the war and subsequent reparations to the victorious Allies left the nation devastated and led to support for political extremists, including the growing Nazi Party. Adolf Hitler became chancellor in 1932 and effectively eliminated democracy a year later (see chapter 3). Hitler vastly expanded the state's strength, particularly its military element, in his drive for domination, but his defeat at the end of World War II led to Germany's territorial division. While the United States, Britain, and France united the areas of the country they controlled under one government, the Soviet Union refused to allow its sector to rejoin the rest. It became the German Democratic Republic (GDR), better known as East Germany, a communist state so closely controlled by the Soviet Union that its own sovereignty was quite limited. The rest became the Federal Republic of Germany (FRG), governed by the Basic Law (the equivalent of a constitution) that took effect in 1949. West Germany, as it came to be known, reemerged as a democratic and industrial powerhouse in Central Europe. It joined France in creating what would become the European Union.

Germany and the city of Berlin were to remain divided for nearly forty years. They were reunited only at the end of the Cold War in 1989, dramatically signaled by the destruction of the Berlin Wall. By 1990 Germany had been reunified under the constitution of the former West Germany. Reunification was economically and politically difficult, requiring the integration of the much poorer East German population into the larger and wealthier West German state. Once the worst of its reunification pains were behind it, Germany led the transformation of the European Community into the European Union, giving up significant economic sovereignty to the larger body. This culminated in the creation of the euro currency and the European Central Bank in 1999. Despite the recent difficulties over the role of the euro, the EU nonetheless represents a new phase in the development of states, one in which states for the first time voluntarily ceded elements of sovereignty to a larger body. While the financial crisis in 2008–2009 and the refugee crisis of 2015–2016 took a significant toll, Germany clearly remained the dominant power in the EU, working hard to maintain the Union in the face of threats of dissolution.

While Germany was founded on the basis of a sense of nationalism based on speaking German (see chapter 4), it has seen significant immigration, initially from Turkey and more recently in the form of refugees from the Syrian civil war. This has posed a continuous challenge and significant debate over national identity and the integration of non-German and Muslim immigrants. This continuing conflict is reflected in its two weakest indicators on the Fragile States Index: "group grievance" and "uneven economic development."

CASE Questions

1. Germany has had multiple types of governments and was even divided into two states for forty years, yet today it is one of the world's strongest states. What explains this unusual outcome of a tumultuous history?
2. Which single element of state strength that we identified earlier in the chapter is most influential in explaining the German case and why?

CASE Study

UNITED KINGDOM: THE LONG EVOLUTION OF A STRONG STATE

CASE SYNOPSIS

The modern British state developed over centuries of evolution and internal war but was finally united in 1707. Legitimacy shifted slowly from a monarchy to a liberal democracy. Industrialization made it the most powerful state in the world by the nineteenth century. While it lost its empire and yielded some sovereignty to the EU in the twentieth century, Britain nonetheless remains a strong, modern state with an effective bureaucracy and fairly extensive welfare state. Questions of sovereignty have arisen recently, as the Scottish almost voted to secede from the country in 2014, and the country voted to leave the EU in 2016. As in both Germany and the United States, questions surrounding immigration and identity provide some of the most significant remaining areas of state weakness.

- FRAGILE STATES INDEX 32.4 (162 of 177); weakest on "poverty and economic decline," "uneven economic development," and "group grievance"

- TERRITORY Consolidated from three nations (England, Wales, and Scotland) by 1707; colonial empire from mid-nineteenth to mid-twentieth century; question of Scottish secession

- SOVEREIGNTY Aided by island status; fully developed by 1707; partially yielded to European Union; exit from European Union in 2016

- LEGITIMACY Traditional legitimacy of monarchy with some limits since thirteenth century; slow transition to liberal democratic legitimacy since 1688

- BUREAUCRACY Industrialization in nineteenth and twentieth centuries expanded and modernized; welfare state since World War II

The full union of England and Scotland under the Act of Union of 1707 officially established the Kingdom of Great Britain (later changed to the United Kingdom officially, though "Great Britain" or simply "Britain" are also commonly used) and marked the start of the modern state. England and Wales (the western section of the island) were previously united in 1542. When King James VI of Scotland also became King James I of England the entire island was finally brought under a single state, eventually creating a single British parliament and eliminating the separate Scottish and Welsh parliaments. Both Scotland and Wales came to be primarily English speaking, linguistically uniting the kingdom, though some cultural distinctions remain to this day, including a distinct Welsh language spoken by a minority.

The greatest threat to the early English monarchs' sovereignty came from religious wars between Protestants and Catholics. After King Henry VIII broke with the Catholic Church and established the Church of England (known as the Anglican Church in the United Kingdom and the Episcopal Church in the United States) in 1534, religious conflicts dominated politics for well over a century. This culminated in a civil war in the 1640s that brought to power a nonroyal, Protestant dictatorship under Oliver Cromwell. The monarchy was restored after about twenty years, only to be removed again, this time peacefully, by Parliament in the Glorious Revolution of 1688. After this, the doctrine of liberalism gained greater prominence, and slowly the two faiths learned to live under the same government. The Glorious Revolution began a long transition in the basis for legitimacy from the traditional monarchy to liberal democracy that began shortly before the union with Scotland.

Starting in the mid-eighteenth century, Britain was one of the first countries to begin industrializing. By the nineteenth century, rapid economic transformation helped it become the most powerful state in the world that controlled a global empire. The empire declined rapidly after World War II, however. The war helped inspire a growing nationalist movement across Asia and Africa that resulted in nearly all British (and other) colonies gaining their independence by the 1960s.

The front page of the *London Evening Standard* newspaper broadcasts the resignation of British prime minister David Cameron following the result of the UK's vote to leave the EU in the June 23, 2016, "Brexit" referendum. One of the most stable states in the world, the UK nonetheless faces major changes in its sovereignty with the Brexit vote and the continued possibility of Scotland voting to secede.

DANIEL SORABJI/AFP/Getty Images

Industrialization expanded the domestic strength of the state as well, and helped create its modern bureaucracy. The growing middle class and military weakness in the Crimean War produced reforms of the civil service starting in the 1850s that required certain kinds of education for civil service appointments, signaling a shift away from government appointments based on patronage. A century later, the sacrifices made to win World War II produced a consensus in favor of a more egalitarian society, leading to the creation of the British welfare state, greatly expanding the bureaucracy and enhancing legitimacy. Starting in the 1960s, the British state slowly yielded some sovereignty to what became the European Union (EU). Its embrace of the EU, however, has always been partial: it did not adopt the common currency, the euro, and in 2016 a popular referendum in support of leaving the EU, known as "Brexit," passed, sending economic shockwaves throughout the world and forcing the government's leader to resign. The British people, concerned about growing immigration and EU rules imposed on them, voted to regain full national sovereignty, despite warnings that they could face severe economic hardship.

Britain successfully molded a national identity out of English, Welsh, and Scottish national identities, though the latter two reemerged and helped create "devolution"—the passing of some powers (such as over education)—to newly created Welsh and Scottish parliaments in 1998. A growing Scottish nationalist movement successfully demanded a referendum on Scottish independence in 2014, which lost 55 percent to 45 percent. The Scottish Nationalist Party remains the dominant political force in Scotland, and after the Brexit vote, it vowed to hold a new referendum on independence because Scotland heavily favored staying in the EU. In Northern Ireland, the relatively poor, Catholic majority long fought to join the Republic of Ireland but the wealthier Protestant minority, supported by the British, have kept it part of the United Kingdom. More recent questions of national identity have arisen, as in Germany, around the question of immigration, both regarding Muslims and Eastern Europeans allowed to enter Britain because they are part of the EU. Since World War II, the previously homogenous Britain has seen large-scale immigration from its former colonies in the Caribbean, Africa, and South Asia, in particular, creating new categories of people such as "black Britons." A growing debate over the place and role of Muslim immigrants (in Britain, mostly from South Asia) has raised questions about national identity that inevitably affect legitimacy and were a major force behind the Brexit vote. Like Germany, this is reflected in relatively weak scores on relevant indicators on the Fragile States Index.

CASE Questions

1. In contrast with the United States, the modern British state arose from a long, historical evolution. What impact has this history had on the modern state, and what differences might this create compared with the U.S. case?
2. What are the weakest elements of the British state, and what effects do these weaknesses have?

THE UNITED STATES: A CONSCIOUSLY CRAFTED STATE

CASE SYNOPSIS

The United States established its sovereignty and legitimacy in an unusually clear and explicit way, first via a Declaration of Independence and then a consciously crafted constitution. The new state's sovereignty was tested in the War of 1812 against its former colonizer and again in the Civil War, but it held. The state simultaneously expanded its territory dramatically via invasion of Native American lands, land purchases from European colonial powers, and war with Mexico. Its modern bureaucracy developed more slowly than most in Europe, but industrialization and a major reform movement ended its famously corrupt "machine politics," slowly expanding a bureaucracy based on merit from the late nineteenth century through World War II. Today, it is the world's leading superpower externally; internally the strength of its state is high but not the highest in the world (at least according to the Fragile States Index). This is due in large part to continuing inequality among the population stemming from the legacy of slavery and immigration.

- FRAGILE STATES INDEX 34.0 (159 of 177); weakest on "uneven economic development" and "group grievance"

- TERRITORY Consolidated from separate colonies; expanded via purchase, invasion, and war

- SOVEREIGNTY Established via negotiation to create central government; challenged by Civil War over issue of slavery

- LEGITIMACY Constitution established liberal state under which democratic rights slowly extended over two hundred years to mass of citizenry

- BUREAUCRACY Small and corrupt until early twentieth century; progressive reforms created modern form, and modest welfare state added since World War II

At first glance, the origin of the United States in a conference that brought together thirteen separate colonies appears most unusual. Few states were created so completely by design rather than by slow historical evolution. Yet while the origin of the U.S. state was unusual, its early trials and tribulations, and questions about its very existence, were similar to those of many other postcolonial states.

North America's colonial history was not unlike that of South America, despite primarily British rather than Spanish and Portuguese conquest. From early on, the economy of the southern colonies was based on large-scale plantation agriculture, which used extensive labor. Because British conquest decimated the Native American population through disease and displacement, African slaves with no rights and no possibility of gaining freedom became the chief source of plantation labor. While most northern colonies allowed slavery, their economies did not depend on it. Slavery created a racial division that has plagued the nation ever since.

Acting as representatives of poor and rich alike, the white, wealthy authors of the Declaration of Independence adopted the enlightened views then prevalent among European intellectuals. They envisioned a nation in which "all men are created equal and endowed by their Creator with certain inalienable rights." The first effort at creating a state, however—the Articles of Confederation—fell into disarray within a few years, in part because of a lack of effective sovereignty. The Articles severely curtailed the national government's power, preserving for the separate thirteen states the right to approve all taxes and trade policies. This weakness led to the adoption of the U.S. Constitution, the document on which the state's legitimacy has depended ever since. The Constitution created a stronger, more sovereign central government with powers to establish a coherent national economy and foreign policy. The individual states did retain significant areas of sovereignty, however, such as responsibility over policing, infrastructure, and education; this created one of the first examples of federalism, in which a state's power is divided among multiple levels of government.

The Constitution also made clear that the political elite at the time had a very limited concept of "all men are created equal." They certainly meant "men," since women had no political rights, but they did not mean "all." To secure the support of the southern states, slavery was preserved. By counting each slave as two-thirds of a person (but not giving slaves any rights), slaveholding states received more representation in Congress than their number of voters justified.

Under the aegis of white settlers, the United States dramatically expanded its territory at the expense of native populations and Mexico; industrialization produced a stronger economy; and the population of the new state continued to grow. Immigration and industrialization increased the size and power of the northern states relative to the southern

The signing of the Declaration of Independence in 1776 was a unique event at the time: a state was being created by conscious design rather than emerging from political battles among rival monarchs. It would take much more work to draft a working form of government and a civil war to create a real sense of national unity. Many colonies would follow the example of the United States in later centuries, demanding independence and writing their own constitutions.

The Granger Collection, NYC

ones, while a growing abolitionist movement questioned the continuing legitimacy of slavery, a position on which the new Republican Party took the strongest stand. Southern leaders ultimately tried to secede, leading to the Civil War, a four-year, failed effort to preserve a slaveholding society.

After the war, the Constitution was amended to end slavery and guarantee equal rights to all regardless of race, but African Americans did not truly achieve full citizenship, including the right to vote, for another hundred years with the passage of the Civil Rights and Voting Rights Acts in 1964 and 1965, respectively. (A prior milestone in the expansion of democratic legitimacy was granting voting rights to [initially white] women in 1920.) The Fragile States Index suggests that this racial legacy continues to weaken the state, lying behind its weakest indicators: "uneven economic development" and "group grievance."

The United States became a global power with the second industrial revolution of the late nineteenth century. Cities grew dramatically as immigrants poured into urban areas to provide labor for rapidly expanding factories, and a growing middle class emerged. This brought demands for changes in the state. Since the expansion of the franchise under Andrew Jackson in the 1820s, partisan competition in the United States was characterized by "machine politics," in which victorious parties appointed their supporters to virtually all bureaucratic posts. The country was famous for corruption. Starting in the 1880s with the Pendleton Act, reformers established a civil service under which most jobs would be permanent and based on some concept of merit, rather than on the whims of the next elected politician. The same reform movement ultimately produced the national income tax, which became the state's primary source of revenue. These reforms created the state's modern bureaucracy, a process that wasn't fully developed until World War II.

Further expansion occurred with the New Deal in the 1930s, under which an expanded government helped provide jobs and old-age pensions to people in need as part of the effort to pull the country out of the Great Depression. The New Deal, followed by the Great Society programs of the 1960s, increased the size and reach of the U.S. state. Nonetheless, it remained quite a bit smaller than most of its European counterparts, which you can see clearly by comparing the United Kingdom and United States in the "Government Revenue" column in the Country and Concept table on page 57.

These new roles also strengthened the central government vis-à-vis the states. While the formal rules in the Constitution did not change, the central government's ability to fund popular programs gave it much greater power than it had possessed a century earlier. Federalism continues to divide sovereignty in the United States among the national (or federal) government and the fifty states, making the United States a more decentralized (and, critics contend, fragmented) state than most wealthy countries. Nonetheless, the state is far more centralized and involved in American lives than it was a century ago.

While the United States generally has firm external sovereignty via control of its territory and by far the most powerful military in the world, territorial boundaries still raise questions. Significant illegal immigration from neighboring Mexico shows the limits of sovereignty for even the most powerful state. As is the case with Germany, the country also continues to struggle with how immigrants are incorporated into the national identity (see chapter 4). Furthermore, Fukuyama (2014) argues that in recent decades the influence of lobbyists and campaign donors, and the growing role of the judiciary in making policy decisions (see chapter 5 for more on this), have significantly weakened the state, as decision making has become increasingly difficult and bureaucratic agencies less autonomous from political pressures.

CASE Questions

1. The United States is unusual in that it is a state created by self-conscious design rather than historical evolution. What impact does that origin have on the strength of its state and the differences between it and other states?
2. What are the weakest elements of the state in the United States, and what effects do these weaknesses have?
3. Do you agree with Fukuyama (2014) that the American state has become weaker in recent decades? What evidence do you see in favor of or against this argument?

CASE Study

JAPAN: DETERMINED SOVEREIGNTY

CASE SYNOPSIS

Japan is one of the few places in the world that successfully avoided European colonization and then established a modern state strong enough to allow interaction with the West while resisting domination. The military ultimately took control of this state, created an empire, expanded industrialization, established a modern bureaucracy that became a core element of the state, and then lost power at the end of World War II. After five years of occupation, in which Japan's sovereignty was forfeited for the first time in four hundred years, Japan reemerged as a sovereign state fully in control of its traditional territory and with a new source of legitimacy: liberal democracy. Its earlier bureaucracy, though, survived the war and became an exceptionally powerful force. Today, despite significant economic problems, it remains one of the strongest states in the world.

- FRAGILE STATES INDEX 35.1 (157 of 177); weakest on "demographic pressures" (aging population) and "poverty and economic decline"
- TERRITORY Fully consolidated by 1603; colonial empire in Asia in late nineteenth and early twentieth centuries
- SOVEREIGNTY Feudal system with unusually strong center since 1603; nearly complete isolation until modern state established in 1867
- LEGITIMACY Traditional but unusually weak monarchy since 1100s; monarch only symbolic since 1867 and rule by modernizing elite; liberal democracy since 1950
- BUREAUCRACY Developed with industrialization prior to World War II; exceptionally powerful influence on state since World War II

Japan reduced its monarchy to a largely symbolic role much earlier than European countries did. Following nearly a century wherein warring states competed for control, Tokugawa Ieyasu claimed the title of shogun in 1603 and fully established sovereignty over the entire territory. The new state came to be called the Tokugawa Bakufu, or shogunate, and was roughly similar to European feudal states, though more centralized than most. Like neighboring China, Japan already had a history of a quasi-modern centralized bureaucracy that established uniform law across the country.

The Tokugawa Shogunate isolated itself from outside influence until U.S. warships forced their way into the harbor at Edo (present-day Tokyo) in 1853. A series of unfavorable treaties with the United States, France, and Britain produced immediate protests, led by a modernizing elite humiliated by concessions to Western powers. After a series of battles, the shogunate ceded power in October 1867, establishing what came to be known as the Meiji Restoration, so called because the new government claimed to be restoring the Emperor Meiji to his full powers. In truth, the new government was controlled by modernizing elites in the bureaucracy and, increasingly, the military.

Japan was the first non-Western state to create a fully modern economy. By first isolating itself from Western control and then borrowing Western technology, Japan's unusually strong state helped create what is now the world's third-largest economy, as evidenced by the neon lights and bustle of its famed Ginza Street in downtown Tokyo.

REUTERS/Kimimasa Mayama

The Meiji government created the first truly modern state in Japan. The threat of dominance by Western powers gave the new government the incentive to launch a series of rapid modernizations, borrowing openly and heavily from the West. The new state ultimately included a modern army and navy, the beginnings of compulsory education, and the establishment of a single school to train all government civil servants. Significantly, the bureaucracy and new military had nearly complete autonomy. The military helped Japan gain colonial control over Taiwan in the 1890s and Korea in 1905, briefly creating a Japanese empire. The Meiji government introduced the first written constitution in 1889, formally codifying state institutions, including the first, though extremely weak, parliament. After a brief period of greater parliamentary power after World War I, the military reasserted power at the expense of civilian leaders and ushered in a period of growing Japanese imperialism. This ultimately led to Japan's alliance with fascist Germany and Italy in World War II, and its attack on Pearl Harbor.

World War II ended with the United States dropping atomic bombs on Hiroshima and Nagasaki in August 1945. The Japanese surrender led to the country's full occupation by the United States. The United States completely demilitarized Japanese society and wrote a new democratic constitution for the country that prohibited Japan from creating a military or engaging in war, although Japan ultimately did create a "self-defense" force that has since become the second-richest military in the world. In spite of the fact that one party has won all but two national elections since 1950, liberal democracy has fully replaced monarchy as the basis for the state's legitimacy, though the monarch remains as a symbol of the nation, as in the United Kingdom.

The long-standing bureaucracy was the only major political institution to survive into the postwar era more or less intact. It became very powerful, working much more closely with Japanese businesses and the ruling party than did bureaucrats in most Western countries. Since 1990, however, Japan's bureaucracy has been rocked by a seeming inability to restart economic growth and a series of corruption scandals. Economic stagnation over the past two decades has combined with a rapidly aging population to present seemingly intractable economic problems, reflected in "demographic pressures" being by far its weakest indicator in the Fragile States Index. Nonetheless, more than seventy years after its defeat in World War II, the country remains the third-largest economy in the world.

CASE Questions

1. Japan is virtually unique in emerging early on as the world's strongest non-Western state. What best explains this unusual history?
2. How do the strengths and weaknesses of the Japanese state compare with the case studies of relatively strong Western states such as Germany, the United Kingdom, and the United States?

Moderately Strong States

The following six countries can be considered moderately strong (or weak) states. They have many of the functions of modern states in place and provide citizens many political goods. In various important ways, however, they are notably weaker than the strongest states. This weakness often manifests itself in particular areas, including much higher levels of corruption, weaker rule of law, and more difficult intergroup conflicts. They are all middle-income countries, not nearly as wealthy as the strongest states but much wealthier than the poorest. The modern state emerged in most of them in the early to mid-twentieth century and was challenged by regional, cultural, or linguistic groups in several cases. Like Germany and Japan, most have seen multiple bases for legitimacy over the last century, though India, the largest and one of the most enduring democracies in the world, is an exception. Questions of legitimacy, then, are very much alive in some of these countries. With relatively minor exceptions, they face no serious threats to their territory, despite sometimes seething discontent in particular regions. With only moderately strong bureaucracies, however, internal sovereignty is notably weaker than in the strongest states; the state simply does not have the capacity to deliver political goods nearly as uniformly. In some ways, some of the cases—particularly India, Brazil, and China—seem to be getting much stronger, but in other ways they and others are getting weaker. It is unclear whether stronger states will emerge in these cases or not, though that is certainly possible.

CASE Study

BRAZIL: A MODERATELY STRONG, AND NOW LEGITIMATE, MODERN STATE

CASE SYNOPSIS

While maintaining a large sovereign territory since independence, Brazil has faced repeated questions about the state's legitimacy. Various Brazilian leaders have responded by claiming legitimacy on the basis of charismatic appeals, clientelism, modernization, and democracy. Brazil's democracy now seems to be fully established. While the state presided over rapid economic growth and reduced poverty for a number of years, "uneven economic development" remains one of its biggest weaknesses. It also continues to be plagued by corruption, which undermines the rule of law and

CASE SYNOPSIS

bureaucratic effectiveness, as well as a security apparatus that sometimes seems beyond civilian control. It is nonetheless a moderately strong modern state, exercising effective control over its territory and people, enjoying democratic legitimacy, and having the largest economy in the Southern Hemisphere.

- FRAGILE STATES INDEX 65.3 (117 of 177); weakest on "demographic pressures" and "uneven economic development"

- TERRITORY Colonial creation; Portuguese half of South America

- SOVEREIGNTY Inherited peacefully at independence; legacy of weak central government vis-à-vis states and local elites

- LEGITIMACY Monarchy until 1889; limited democracy thereafter; legacy of military intervention claiming legitimacy based on modernization; now consolidated democracy

- BUREAUCRACY Expanded greatly since 1964 under state-guided development; high levels of corruption

ike most countries, Brazil's modern state was the product of European colonial rule. The Portuguese effectively subjugated the small indigenous population, and colonial Brazil became a major producer of sugarcane and other agricultural products, farmed largely with African slave labor. Indeed, Brazil had more slaves than any other colony in the Americas. A Portuguese, landowning elite emerged as the socially and economically dominant force in the colonial society.

In contrast with the Spanish colonies in South America, Brazil gained independence from Portugal as a single country, creating by far the largest territory in South America under one sovereign government. In most of South America, the landowning elite rebelled against Spanish rule. In contrast, the Portuguese royal family actually fled to Brazil in 1808 to evade Napoleon's conquest of Portugal. In 1821 King João VI

Brazilians protest in Sao Paulo in 2016 against former president Lula da Silva and his successor, Dilma Rouseff. Rouseff was impeached in the midst of a massive corruption scandal that forced numerous national leaders to resign and/or face trial. It was the biggest crisis for Brazil's democracy since the end of military rule.

Photo by Victor Moriyama/Getty Images

returned to Portugal, leaving his son in Brazil to rule on his behalf. A year later, his son declared Brazil independent and himself emperor, with no real opposition from Portugal.

The new state's economy remained agricultural and used slave labor until the late nineteenth century, making it the last slaveholding society in the world. Liberal elites, facing growing international pressure, finally convinced the government to abolish slavery in 1888 and convinced military leaders to overthrow the emperor in a bloodless coup and establish a republic a year later.

The leaders of the new republic created Brazil's modern state, drafting a democratic constitution, but one that gave voting rights only to literate men, restricting the voting population to 3.5 percent of the citizenry. This disenfranchised virtually all the former slaves, who were illiterate. The new system was federal from the start; a compromise among regional elites, who held most political power, gave significant power to local governments and thereby kept the country united.

Economic influence was shifting to urban areas, but political control remained vested in the rural landowning elite. Known as *coronéis,* or "colonels," these rural elites used their socioeconomic dominance to control votes in a type of machine politics. Meanwhile, in the growing urban areas, **clientelism,** the exchange of material resources for political support, developed as the key means of mobilizing political support. As more urban dwellers became literate and gained the right to vote, elite politicians sought their support by providing direct benefits to them, such as jobs or government services to their neighborhoods. Corruption and clientelist use of bureaucratic jobs as perks for supporters simultaneously bloated and undermined Brazil's young bureaucracy, weakening the state.

clientelism
The exchange of material resources for political support

Getúlio Vargas used clientelism and military support to gain complete power and eliminate democracy in the 1930s. He created a new regime, the quasi-fascist *Estado Novo* (New State), that he ruled from 1937 to 1945. He significantly expanded the state's economic role and power, creating state-owned steel and oil industries, and expanded health and welfare systems to gain popular support (which also strengthened the state's bureaucracy). When the end of World War II discredited fascism, Vargas was forced to allow a return to democratic rule.

The New (democratic) Republic was plagued by economic problems and political instability. By the early 1960s, the elite and military saw growing working-class militancy as perhaps the first stage of a communist revolution. In a preemptive strike, the military overthrew the elected government in 1964 with U.S. and considerable upper- and middle-class support. The military ruled until 1985, leading what we will term a "modernizing authoritarian" regime (see chapter 3), which produced very rapid economic growth and industrialization, further expanding the state's size and capabilities. By the late 1970s, growing inequality and a slowdown in economic growth led newly formed labor unions and followers of liberation theology in the Catholic Church to demand democracy, forcing the military to cede power. Democratic governments have ruled since, firmly establishing liberal democracy as the basis for legitimacy.

In the first decade of the new millennium, Brazil's democratic governments oversaw a new period of rapid economic growth that substantially reduced poverty and strengthened the state. Declining oil prices and a massive corruption scandal in the national oil company slowed growth beginning in 2014, tarnishing the state's image domestically and internationally. In 2016 the president was impeached and other top political leaders forced to resign and/or face court cases, as Brazil's democracy faced its greatest crisis since military rule.

CASE Questions

1. Brazil is the strongest of our "moderately strong states." What are the main elements that make it significantly weaker than the "strong states" above?
2. What has been the role of democracy in strengthening or weakening the Brazilian state over the last century?

CASE Study

MEXICO: CHALLENGES TO INTERNAL SOVEREIGNTY

CASE SYNOPSIS

Mexico's first postcolonial state was extremely weak, rocked by regional and ideological divisions that initially produced great instability and later a weak, personalist dictatorship. Revolution in the 1910s through the 1920s finally resulted in the start of a modern state, ruled over by a single, dominant party for three-quarters of a century. It consciously used an interventionist economic development strategy, funded mainly by oil production, to initiate industrialization and greatly expand the state's bureaucratic capabilities. Economic success amid continuing poverty and declining legitimacy ultimately created a movement for democracy, which succeeded in peacefully ousting the long-ruling party from power in 2000, changing the basis of the state's legitimacy. Today, Mexico has a stable democracy but faces challenges to its internal sovereignty in the south from indigenous groups and, more threateningly, in the north from drug cartels who seem more powerful than the state's security forces. This important middle-income country has seen significant economic success in the last generation but is plagued by growing questions of internal sovereignty.

- FRAGILE STATES INDEX 70.4 (107 of 177); weakest on "group grievance" and "security apparatus" (drug cartels and corrupt police forces)

- TERRITORY Spanish colonial creation; half its original size following the Mexican-American War (1846–1848)

- SOVEREIGNTY Achieved in War of Independence (1810–1821); recent challenges by southern guerrilla movement and northern drug cartels

- LEGITIMACY Nineteenth-century divisions (liberal versus conservative *caudillos*); revolution followed by twentieth-century electoral authoritarian regime; twenty-first-century democracy

- BUREAUCRACY Developed with single-party domination over the twentieth century; part of ruling party's clientelist networks until 2000

Under colonial rule starting in 1519, Spain exploited Mexico for its gold and silver, but most important was the country's large, disciplined population that provided valuable labor for the colonial regime. Because of this, Mexico did not become an important market for the African slave trade, retaining instead a large indigenous population. Mexico became a sovereign state with the War of Independence (1810–1821), but in the immediate aftermath found itself bitterly divided along regional (north–south) and ideological (liberal–conservative) lines. These divisions manifested themselves in successive military coups, with strongmen (*caudillos*) constantly changing allegiances in support of one side or another. The conflicts resulted in a weak state and a limited capacity to develop a functioning bureaucracy. The internal rifts also had a negative impact on Mexico's ability to defend its sovereignty, as evidenced by the Mexican-American War (1846–1848), which forced it to sell much of what is now the American Southwest to the United States, shrinking Mexican territory to under one-half of its original size. The instability of the nineteenth century did eventually end, but at the cost of political freedoms. Porfirio Díaz, a *caudillo* who had mastered the art of consolidating power through bribery and intimidation, founded an authoritarian regime and ruled from 1876 until 1910. His rule based its legitimacy on an ability to deliver political order and unprecedented economic growth. The Díaz regime's primary supporters were the upper class and business elite. Its enemies were the peasant class (*campesinos*), who lost land to foreign speculators only to find the state unresponsive to their grievances. When Díaz reneged on a promise to retire in 1910, anti-Díaz forces, supported by the rural poor, instigated the Mexican Revolution (1910–1920). Despite Díaz's resignation in 1911, the revolution became a civil war, with various factions turning against the newly installed government, notably the guerrillas led by General Francisco "Pancho" Villa in the north and the peasant armies of Emiliano Zapata in the south.

Ultimately, Villa and Zapata were defeated and President Plutarco Elías Calles (1924–1928) established the modern Mexican state, as well as the longest-ruling political party in Mexican history, eventually named the Partido Revolucionario

The two best-known leaders of the Mexican Revolution, Pancho Villa (center) and Emiliano Zapata (holding *sombrero*), pose with other revolutionary leaders. The Mexican Revolution (1910–1920) created the modern Mexican state but ultimately produced seventy-five years of rule by one party, the Institutional Revolutionary Party (PRI). In 2000 Mexico finally made a transition to a democratic form of government via free and fair elections. The long PRI rule created a moderately strong, if repressive, state that has made Mexico a growing player on the world stage.

Institucional (Institutional Revolutionary Party, or PRI). While the PRI embraced the revolution-era democratic constitution of 1917, in practice it formed an electoral authoritarian system that governed Mexico from 1929 to 2000. The party was able to maintain power through systemic corruption, bribery, and intimidation, as well as clientelism and effective voter mobilization tactics (see chapter 3).

The PRI's legitimacy rested mainly on its association with the values of the Mexican Revolution, especially land reform and the empowerment of the *campesinos*. It created a functioning bureaucracy that, while corrupt, made important strides in furthering literacy, access to health care, and overall economic development. It used oil wealth and trade with the United States to achieve significant industrialization, transforming Mexico into a middle-income country, though with sharp income and regional inequality. All of this expanded the size, scope, and capability of Mexico's state.

Starting in the early 1980s, the party moved away from its traditional policies that protected the rural poor, adopting policies more favorable to a free-market economy with less government intervention. This led to a fissure within the party and the creation of a new party that garnered an unprecedented 30 percent of the vote in the 1988 presidential election, amid widespread claims of electoral fraud. The PRI's unending string of questionable electoral victories finally seemed to be taking a toll on its fragile legitimacy. The 1988 election was the start of growing demands for real democracy, finally established in 2000 with the bellwether election of Vicente Fox of the National Action Party as president, the first non-PRI president in over seventy years. This move from electoral authoritarianism to democratic competition reflects changing notions of legitimacy, from clientelism and modernization to liberal democracy.

Despite its democratization, Mexico remains plagued by severe economic and regional disparities along with questions over the strength of the state. First, Mexico has experienced large-scale flight of labor to the United States, symptomatic of the desperate economic situation faced by millions of Mexicans. In the south, indigenous farmers became the backbone of the Zapatista Army of National Liberation (EZLN). Based in the southern state of Chiapas, the EZLN waged a guerrilla campaign in 1994 in the tradition of Zapata's fighters during the Mexican Revolution, though it has since reverted to more peaceful methods of demonstration against the state.

By far the most critical challenge to Mexican sovereignty today, however, comes in the north, where a war among rival drug cartels has killed an estimated 75,000–100,000 people in the last decade. While U.S. consumers have been supporting the border states' manufacturing, or *maquiladora,* economy, America has also been the prime market for the Mexican drug trade. Endemic police corruption, lack of alternative economic opportunities, a supply of small arms from north of the border, and a large appetite for drugs there have all led to the degradation of government authority in the northern region. This has called into question the state's ability to keep a monopoly on the legitimate use of force for the first time since the end of the Mexican Revolution. A surge in economic growth starting in 2011 and drop in drug-related deaths in 2015, however, raised hopes that the Mexican state would grow stronger and overcome its most serious difficulties.

CASE Questions

1. Since the revolution a century ago, Mexico has been marked by exceptional political stability—the same regime ruled for nearly eighty years—yet it is only a moderately strong state. Why?
2. Which elements of state strength best explain the increasing strength of the Mexican state over the last twenty to thirty years?

CHINA: ECONOMIC LEGITIMACY OVER POLITICAL REFORM

China established its territory, sovereignty, and a relatively modern bureaucracy centuries before anything similar developed in Europe. The Chinese state, though, was severely weakened from the late nineteenth to mid-twentieth centuries. Out of that chaotic period emerged the world's second major communist regime, which created a

CASE SYNOPSIS

modern, if brutal, state. The Communists regained full sovereignty, expanded the state's territory to include the still-disputed region of Tibet, and reestablished a strong bureaucracy that controlled the entire economy. The regime's legitimacy was based on communist doctrine, augmented by Mao's initial charisma, but clearly declined over the years. Since Mao's death, the regime has still officially proclaimed communism as its ideology, but in reality it bases its legitimacy on economic success. The ruling party has presided over an increasingly strong, modern state that has achieved perhaps the most remarkable economic advance in human history. China has become the second-largest economy in the world and an economic and political superpower, though an economic slowdown in 2015–2016 raised questions about its continued strength. It also is still plagued by corruption, weak rule of law, and questions about its legitimacy in the absence of any significant political reform.

- FRAGILE STATES INDEX 74.9 (86 of 177); weakest on "human rights and rule of law" and "state legitimacy"

- TERRITORY Established in ancient empire, though with changing boundaries; Communist rulers annexed disputed territory of Tibet

- SOVEREIGNTY Longest continuous sovereign entity in world history under empire; civil war in early twentieth century; sovereignty restored by Communist revolution in 1949 and start of modern state

- LEGITIMACY Traditional empire; nationalist government came out of civil war; communist ideology until 1978; modernizing authoritarian state since then

- BUREAUCRACY Ancient Confucian system of merit; great expansion under Communist rule; growing problem of corruption

The Chinese empire, first united in 221 BCE, "built a centralized, merit-based bureaucracy that was able to register its population, levy uniform taxes, control the military, and regulate society some eighteen hundred years before a similar state was to emerge in Europe" (Fukuyama 2014, 354). While it was not a fully modern state, it developed one central element of a modern state very early.

The empire's demise began in the mid-nineteenth century. While trade with the outside world had long existed, the United States and European powers began demanding greater access to Chinese markets, leading to the Opium Wars from 1840 to 1864 that gave Western powers effective sovereignty over key areas of the country. What had been one of the strongest states in the world was dramatically weakened. Foreign domination and economic stagnation produced growing discontent. Sun Yat-sen, an American-educated doctor, started a nationalist movement that proclaimed its opposition to the empire and to foreign imperialism. By 1911 military uprisings signaled the empire's imminent collapse, and on January 1, 1912, the empress resigned and the Republic of China was established.

The new nationalist government quickly became a dictatorship and ushered in more than a decade of chaos and war. Warlords gained control of various parts of the country as the Chinese state's sovereignty and territorial control crumbled. In the 1920s, the nationalists slowly regained control with the help of an alliance with a new political force, the Chinese Communist Party (CCP). Once fully back in power, the nationalists turned against the Communists. The state's sovereignty, however, was seriously compromised by reliance on warlords, the continuous threat of civil war with the CCP, and Japanese invasion. The nationalists ruled a very weak state.

The CCP under Mao Zedong moved to the countryside after the nationalists broke the alliance. Starting in the southeast, Mao put together a revolutionary movement that began an intermittent civil war with the government. In 1934–1935, Mao led the famous Long March, a six-thousand-mile trek by party supporters. The CCP took effective sovereignty over the northwestern section of the country and began creating the prototype of its future Communist regime. The Japanese invasion of 1937 left the country's territory and sovereignty divided among the CCP, the nationalist government, and Japan. After the Japanese withdrawal at the end of World War II, the Communist revolution triumphed in 1949, despite U.S. military support for the nationalists, who fled to the island of Taiwan and formed a government there.

Communist rule created the first modern Chinese state, but at a horrific cost. The new government instituted massive land reform programs and campaigns against corruption, opium use, and other socially harmful practices. It also took control of the economy, creating a Soviet-style command economy with a massive bureaucracy, which attempted to industrialize the world's largest agrarian society. The result was a famine that killed at least twenty million people, and political purges that sent many others to "re-education camps," prison, or execution. During the Cultural Revolution from 1966 to 1976, Mao mobilized his followers against what he saw as entrenched

A protester carries a portrait of Chinese dissident Li Wangyang, who died under mysterious circumstances after taking part in the famous Tiananmen Square protest in 1989. The Chinese state has presided over the most successful period of economic growth in human history, but it has preserved its authoritarian regime. Can an increasingly wealthy and powerful state remain nondemocratic for the long term, in contrast with the pattern of European history?

REUTERS/Tyrone Siu

bureaucrats in his own party and state, causing widespread political uncertainty, repression, and economic and social dislocation.

The Cultural Revolution ended with Mao's death in 1976. Deng Xiaoping, one of Mao's earliest comrades who had been removed from power during the Cultural Revolution, established his supremacy over the party and state in 1979. Deng initiated a series of slow but ultimately sweeping reforms that reduced the state's direct control of the economy. He also began to reestablish organized, party control over the state and more uniform laws to govern the country. These reforms continue today, a near four-decade process of introducing a market economy and stronger state that is still not complete. The result has been the fastest economic growth in the world that has moved millions of Chinese out of poverty, spurred a huge exodus from rural areas to cities, and allowed much greater inequality than existed under Mao.

While rebuilding a modern bureaucracy, Deng and his successors have resisted most efforts to achieve greater freedom and democracy. While the state's legitimacy is still officially based on communism, its pursuit of capitalist development has meant its real legitimacy is implicitly based on its ability to modernize the economy and provide wealth. Thus, China now has what we will call a modernizing authoritarian regime (see chapter 3). Many observers see a fundamental contradiction between allowing economic freedoms but denying political ones and argue that ultimately the CCP will have to allow much greater political freedom if its economic success is to continue. Under its latest president, Xi Jinping, the regime has actually restricted freedoms further and intervened in the economy more in response to declining growth and insta- bility in the stock market. This, along with the social and environmental effects of extremely rapid economic growth, widespread corruption, and growing inequality, are the major weaknesses facing the Chinese state today.

CASE Questions

1. What impact does the legacy of Mao's communist system have on the strength of the modern Chinese state today?
2. China boasts the oldest and most enduring premodern state in world history. What impact does this have on the strength of its modern state?

CASE Study

INDIA: ENDURING DEMOCRACY IN A MODERATELY WEAK STATE

CASE SYNOPSIS

Indian territory and sovereignty emerged out of colonial rule and the nationalist movement for independence. Most unusual for postcolonial states, its democracy has survived and remains the basis of legitimacy. Its state remains relatively weak, however, manifested in continuing corruption, religious tensions, and poverty. India was famed for its strong bureaucracy after independence, but reforms to reduce the bureaucracy's role in economic policy and growing corruption have weakened it. In recent years, the state has presided over a growing economy, and many observers see elements of a potential economic superpower, hobbled most significantly by its weak state.

- FRAGILE STATES INDEX 79.6 (70 of 177); weakest on "group grievance" (Muslim–Hindu conflicts primarily) and "demographic pressures"

- TERRITORY Created by British colonial rule, though divided into India and Pakistan at independence

- SOVEREIGNTY Established with independence in 1947; dispute with Pakistan over control of Kashmir region

- LEGITIMACY Continuous liberal democracy; secular government questioned by Hindu nationalists and other religious movements

- BUREAUCRACY Created by British colonialism; central to economic policy; weakening due to external pressure for reform and growing corruption

The territory that is now India, Pakistan, and Bangladesh was once divided among many kingdoms and languages, most of which practiced Hinduism. Muslim invaders created the Moghul Empire in 1526, which dominated most of northern and central India and ruled over a mostly Hindu population. Like other premodern rulers, both the Hindu kings and Muslim emperors had only loose sovereignty over daily life. At the local level, members of the elite caste, the Brahmin, governed.

The British government took direct control of its largest colony in 1857. The colonial state required educated local people to fill its administrative offices. The resulting all-Indian civil service and military and the start of a modern bureaucracy helped create greater unity among the subcontinent's disparate regions, and newly educated

Indians filled the offices of these new institutions. Unfortunately for the British, the first stirrings of nationalism would arise from this educated elite.

India's independence movement, led by the charismatic Mahatma Gandhi, was the first successful anticolonial effort of the twentieth century and inspired similar movements around the world. The leadership of the main nationalist movement, the Indian National Congress that has ruled India for most of its independent history, was primarily Hindu, but the Congress operated on democratic and secular principles and claimed to represent all Indians. Nonetheless, as the nationalist movement developed, India's Muslim leaders increasingly felt unrepresented in the organization, and by the end of the 1930s, some began to demand a separate Muslim state.

The push for independence succeeded after World War II. Muslim leaders, however, demanded and received from the British a separate Muslim state, Pakistan. In 1947 the simultaneous creation of the two states (against Gandhi's fierce opposition) resulted in the mass migration of millions of citizens, as Hindus moved from what was to be Pakistan into what would become India, and Muslims went in the other direction. At least a million people perished in violence associated with the massive migration, probably the largest in world history.

India thus gained independence under the rule of the Congress Party in a democratic and federal system. Its bureaucracy inherited from colonial rule, the Indian Civil Service, was a backbone of state strength and a key institution in the country's development. For the first several decades it was considered one of the strongest bureaucracies in the postcolonial world, but growing corruption has weakened it substantially in recent decades.

Besides economic development, the government's other great challenge was the demand for greater recognition by India's diverse ethnic and religious groups. Throughout the 1950s, leaders of local language groups demanded, and some received,

An election official shows workers on a tea plantation how to use a new electronic voting system. While India's state is weakened by corruption, suffers from widespread religious and ethnic tensions, and remains extremely poor despite recent economic gains, it has endured as the world's largest democracy for almost seven decades.

REUTERS/Rupak De Chowdhuri

states of their own within the federal system. The legitimacy of the democratic system as a whole was questioned by only a few groups, however, most of which were communist inspired.

When Indira Gandhi (no relation to Mahatma) gained leadership of the Congress Party and the country as prime minister in 1971, she increasingly centralized power in her own hands. In 1975 she declared a "state of emergency" that gave her the power to disband local governments and replace them with those loyal to her. This was the only period that threatened the survival of India's democracy. Her actions were met with increasing opposition, however, and she was forced to allow new democratic elections two years later, in which the Congress Party lost power for the first time in its history.

Starting with a large but unsuccessful Sikh movement for an independent Sikh state in the 1970s and 1980s, religious movements came to replace language-based ones as the most threatening to India's secular democracy. Since then, political battles have increased between Muslims and Hindu nationalists, in particular, many of whom reject the official secularism of the national government. A renewed Hindu nationalist party won a national election and formed the government from 1998 to 2004 and again since 2014. They have, however, preserved India's official principles of secular democracy as the core source of legitimacy.

Since the mid-1990s, governments of both major parties have reduced the role of the state in the economy and India has achieved much higher growth rates, carving out a major niche in the global economy in areas related to computer services in particular. It remains, however, a country with growing inequality, widespread malnutrition, and the largest number of poor people in the world. While growth has strengthened the state's resources, a weakened bureaucracy, widespread corruption, and continuing religious tensions have weakened it.

CASE Questions

1. What have been the effects of colonialism on the relative strength of the Indian state?
2. What are the weakest elements of the Indian state, and how do these differ from the strong states discussed earlier? What explains these differences?

CASE Study

RUSSIA: STRONG EXTERNAL SOVEREIGNTY WITH WEAK RULE OF LAW

CASE SYNOPSIS

Russia has had three dramatically different regimes over the centuries, with a fourth emerging in the new millennium. For most of the twentieth century, the communist state controlled virtually all economic and political activity far more tightly than any state does today. It also controlled a vast, multinational empire along its borders, one that was lost with the dissolution of the Soviet Union. The smaller but still vast Russian state continues to be plagued by ethnic and national differences, some of which have resulted in violent conflict. The various regimes' claims to legitimacy have been drastically different and have always been challenged. After a period of weakness in the 1990s, the state has become stronger in most areas in the new millennium as it has shifted from a democracy to an electoral authoritarian regime. While it has strengthened its external sovereignty, it remains much weaker internally, with questions about its legitimacy, high levels of corruption, and a weak rule of law.

- FRAGILE STATES INDEX 81.0 (65 of 177); weakest on "group grievance," "security apparatus," and "human rights and rule of law"

- TERRITORY Multinational empire consolidated under tsar; communist state of USSR broken into fifteen countries in 1991, reducing Russia to pre-imperial borders; military annexation of the Crimea in 2014

- SOVEREIGNTY Feudal state with unusually strong monarchy under tsar; modern state established by communist rule; postcommunist state weak but getting stronger; continuing challenges to central control from regions

- LEGITIMACY Traditional monarchy overthrown by communist revolution; democracy in 1990s; electoral authoritarian regime with strong nationalist appeal since

- BUREAUCRACY Extremely powerful under Communist Party rule, controlling economy; postcommunist weakening with growing corruption; perhaps strengthening since 2000

Ivan IV Vasilyevich (Ivan the Terrible) took the title Russian "tsar" (emperor) in 1547 and greatly increased the monarch's power and the state's territory. By 1660 Russia was geographically the largest country in the world. The country became a vast, multinational empire in which more than one hundred languages were spoken, governed by a monarchy that would last until 1917. The tsar was an absolutist ruler with even greater power than most monarchs in Europe. The Russian state was an early modern absolutist state in terms of effective sovereignty and control over territory.

As industrialization began and Russian cities grew in the nineteenth century, both liberal democratic and Marxist movements arose. Tsar Alexander III was finally forced to agree to the creation of an elected legislature, the *Duma*, in 1905. He dissolved the body after only three months, however; Russia's first, very brief experiment with democracy was over.

Not long afterward, Russia was drawn into World War I, which proved economically disastrous. Because it was still primarily a poor and agricultural society, soldiers were sent to the front ill equipped and hungry, and as conditions worsened, mass desertions occurred. A crisis of legitimacy undermined the state's ability to maintain its territorial integrity and military force. The makings of another electoral democracy emerged in February 1917, only to be overtaken by a communist revolution that October. The communists assassinated the tsar and his family, after which many of the non-Russian areas of the empire declared themselves independent. It took the communist movement three years to reconstruct what had been the tsarist empire, more or less preserving prior Russian territory. A new government called the Union of Soviet Socialist Republics (USSR), or the Soviet Union (see chapter 3 for more details), was formed, a brutal but nonetheless modern state. The Communist Party created a dictatorial regime that it tightly controlled. A new basis for legitimacy was established in Communist ideology, but most analysts believe the regime's real legitimacy was fairly short-lived.

The Communists modernized Russia, but at tremendous human cost (estimates range as high as twenty million dead). Joseph Stalin (1929–1953) rapidly industrialized the country, taking resources and laborers from the countryside as needed and completely controlling all economic activity. The secret police dealt with anyone who opposed the state's methods, creating one of the most oppressive police states in history. Yet Stalin also created a superpower, which became the only serious rival to the United States after World War II. After his death, Soviet leaders reduced the degree of

Russian president Vladimir Putin talks to military officers in September 2015. The new Russian state emerged from the collapse of the Soviet Union in 1991. After a decade as a very weak state, it became significantly stronger under Putin, who has emphasized military strength and expansion, including occupying Crimea and sending troops to defend the Assad regime in the Syrian civil war.

Sasha Mordovets/Getty Images

terror but maintained centralized control over an increasingly bureaucratic form of communism. The Communist model, while successful at early industrialization, could not keep pace with the West's economic growth. Recognizing the need for change, a new leadership under Mikhail Gorbachev began reforms in 1985 that soon resulted in the collapse of the Soviet state.

When elements of the Soviet military who were opposed to Gorbachev's reform attempted a coup in August 1991, Boris Yeltsin, the leader of the Russian part of the Soviet federation and himself a Communist reformer, stood up to the tanks and proclaimed the end of Soviet rule. The military, faced with masses of people in the streets and with the eyes of the world on it, was forced to back down. By December, Gorbachev had agreed to the dissolution of the Soviet state. The old tsarist empire split into fifteen separate states, with Russia the largest by far.

Today, Russia remains a multiethnic state, with a federal system of government that gives some power, at least in theory, to the various regions, which are defined loosely along ethnic lines. After the dissolution of the Soviet regime, Russia gained a new claim to legitimacy as an electoral democracy. It was very fragile, however; the state became demonstrably weaker, as powerful mafias and super-rich "oligarchs" controlled most political power and economic wealth. Yeltsin's handpicked successor, Vladimir Putin (1999–2008, 2012–), consciously set out to strengthen the state by centralizing power in the executive, strengthening the central government vis-à-vis regional governments, reducing crime, and restoring order. In the process, however, he effectively eliminated democracy; although the trappings of elections and offices with clear mandates continue to exist, Russia in fact is now an electoral authoritarian regime under Putin's tight control. He has increasingly championed nationalism as a basis for legitimacy, most famously in his successful annexation in 2014 of the Crimean peninsula, a primarily Russian-speaking area of Ukraine. Despite Putin's successful strengthening of Russia's external sovereignty, he has undermined the rule of law and weakened the state in other ways; Russia scores very poorly on the Fragile States Index on "group grievances," "human rights," and the quality of the "security apparatus."

CASE Questions

1. Russia has seen exceptionally dramatic swings in the claims to legitimacy of its different regimes. What impact might that have on the strength of its state?
2. What explains the unusual combination of great external sovereignty versus weaker internal strength in the Russian case?

The Weakest States

The weakest states in the world appear to be quite fragile. The Fragile States Index characterizes them with words such as *warning* and *alert*. In many cases, their territorial integrity is at least threatened, if not outright violated. Even where they maintain official control, that control is often rather weak: their borders are porous, with huge black markets in people and goods. Corruption is rife and many institutions therefore function only sporadically, leaving much of the population dependent on personal networks and clientelist ties to survive. They are by and large quite poor, with many dependent on the export of key primary commodities, making the resource curse a common problem. These states provide very limited political goods for their citizens, undermining legitimacy, whatever its basis. The weakest can accurately be characterized as "quasi-states," maintaining legal sovereignty and the access to the international system that entails, but only minimally achieving internal sovereignty. Our case studies are not among the very weakest, but nonetheless they illustrate the contours of extreme state weakness.

IRAN: CLAIMING LEGITIMACY VIA THEOCRACY

CASE SYNOPSIS

The Pahlavi dynasty established the first modern Iranian state nearly a century ago, ruled by a modernizing authoritarian regime under the shah that expanded sovereignty internally and externally, and attempted to reduce the influence of Islam. Growing inequality and secularization, however, produced a backlash that became the 1979 Islamist revolution. The revolutionary leader, Ayatollah Khomeini, and his successors created an Islamic regime, but within the confines of a modern (though corrupt) bureaucratic state whose territory and sovereignty are secure. The Islamic regime has expanded the social services the state provides and, therefore, the size and reach of the bureaucracy. It has also asserted international influence via threatened nuclearization, though questions over its legitimacy continue to weaken it.

- FRAGILE STATES INDEX 86.9 (47 of 177); weakest on "state legitimacy," "human rights and rule of law," and "factionalized elites"

- TERRITORY Solidified in nineteenth century; smaller than ancient kingdoms

- SOVEREIGNTY Never formally colonized, though heavily influenced by British and Russian imperialism

- **LEGITIMACY** Traditional monarchy until first modern state; modernizing authoritarian state under shah in twentieth century; Islamic theocracy since 1979
- **BUREAUCRACY** Expanded by shah's modernization policies; expanded social services under Islamic republic; continuing problem of corruption

ran is the modern descendant of the great ancient empire of Persia and has been ruled by two major empires since. These premodern states united the territory but relied on local elites to rule, especially in peripheral areas; neither created a fully modern state. In the nineteenth century the empire's real power was drastically reduced by Russian and British imperialism. Like China, Iran was never formally colonized, but the government became extremely dependent upon and compliant with the Russians and British, granting them very favorable terms for key resources such as oil and depending on them for military support. This era also saw the modern, much reduced, borders of Iran clearly demarcated. European imperialism severely compromised Iran's sovereignty and reduced its territory, in spite of never officially colonizing the country. By the start of the twentieth century, popular discontent with this foreign influence led to street demonstrations from citizens demanding a new constitution. In 1906 the shah (the supreme ruler) allowed the creation of a democratic legislature, but the state remained weak, divided, and heavily influenced by Russia and Britain.

In the midst of this, Colonel Reza Khan led a coup d'état that overthrew the weakened empire and established what came to be known as the Pahlavi dynasty, ruled first by Reza Shah and then by his son, Mohammed Reza Pahlavi. The Pahlavis created the first truly modern state in Iran. During their rule from 1925 to 1979, they increased the size of the central army tenfold, dramatically expanded the bureaucracy, and gained

Worshippers pray at a mosque in Tehran. The increasingly authoritarian regime in Iran bases its legitimacy on a version of Islamic theology that claims all state authority should be derived from religious law. Mosques are a major source of regime communication to followers and legitimacy for the clerics, who are the most powerful figures in the government.

REUTERS/Raheb Homavandi

full control over the provinces. The Pahlavis established a modernizing authoritarian regime, expanding both the state and the economy, increasing agricultural and industrial production, and building tremendous infrastructure, with the government itself directly involved in most of these efforts. They continued to welcome extensive foreign investment, especially in the growing oil sector. They also centralized power in their hands; the elected legislature continued to exist with an elected prime minister, but its power was greatly reduced, and eliminated completely in 1953.

In the 1950s, the shah launched a series of social and economic reforms to modernize, as he saw it, Iranian society, which further expanded the role and reach of the state and its bureaucracy. He staked his claim to legitimacy on these modernizations, which included land reform and secularization; the latter reduced the role of Islamic law. An economic crisis in the late 1970s created growing opposition to his policies, which favored wealthier and urban over poorer and rural sectors of society. The opposition coalesced behind the leadership of an exiled Islamic spiritual leader, Ayatollah Ruhollah Khomeini. Protests spread through the streets and mosques, and local Islamic militias took over entire neighborhoods. Facing growing opposition, the shah went into what was supposed to be temporary exile in January 1979 but never returned, his legitimacy completely gone. A month later, Khomeini came back from exile to complete the Iranian revolution and establish the Islamic Republic of Iran, the first theocratic government in the modern era.

The Islamic Republic has gone through phases of greater openness to political debate and greater repression (see chapter 8), but it has endured and remains regionally powerful. While basing its claim to legitimacy firmly in theocracy, it includes limited elements of democratic rule that have had more influence at some times than others. Patronage from oil revenue and corruption are probably more important than elections in maintaining the government's authority. Questions remain, however, about its legitimacy, as seen in the massive street protests against the presidential election outcome in 2009. While politically quiescent since then, the country continues to seethe with opposition to the government, which responds with increasing repression. Its bid to become a nuclear power, or at least to acquire much greater nuclear capabilities, has recently made Iran the center of major global debate and treaty. While it is an important regional player and focus of global attention, over time the Islamic Republic has become a weaker and weaker state.

CASE Questions

1. Iran and China share one aspect of their history: strong but informal Western influence in the nineteenth century. What impact did this have on the development of the modern states in the two countries? In what ways were those impacts similar and different?
2. What are the weakest elements of the Iranian state, and what affects do they have?

CASE Study

NIGERIA: AN EXTREMELY WEAK STATE

CASE SYNOPSIS

With the exception of the 1967–1970 civil war, the Nigerian state has maintained its sovereignty and territory, mostly under military rule. It is extremely weak, however. The long-ruling military claimed legitimacy via promises to end corruption, restore economic growth, and return the country to democracy, but those promises were rarely fulfilled. The democratic regime that has been in place since 1999 is a great improvement over previous regimes, but it has had only limited success in solving the deeply entrenched problems the country faces. While the state's territory is intact, its sovereignty is threatened by ethnic militia and the radical Islamist group Boko Haram (an affiliate of ISIS); it suffers from widespread corruption that undermines bureaucratic efficiency; and its legitimacy is now based on a rather fragile democracy. The state's weakness originated in colonial rule but has been exacerbated by the country's oil wealth, which has been a huge incentive for corruption.

- FRAGILE STATES INDEX 103.5 (13 of 177); weakest on "security apparatus" and "factionalized elites"
- TERRITORY Created by colonial rule out of numerous precolonial political entities; divided by civil war, 1967–1970
- SOVEREIGNTY Gained with independence in 1960 but threatened by recent demands for secession; weak internally
- LEGITIMACY Nationalist movement divided along ethnic and regional lines; limited legitimacy of postcolonial democratic government; six military coups; weak democracy since 1999
- BUREAUCRACY Colonial creation; suffers from extreme levels of corruption fueled by oil wealth

Nigeria, like most African states, is a product of colonialism. It is by far the largest African country in terms of population (approximately one-seventh of all Africans are Nigerians) and a major oil producer. Prior to colonial conquest, the territory that is now Nigeria was home to numerous and varied societies. The northern half was primarily Muslim and ruled by Islamic emirs (religious rulers) based in twelve separate city-states. The southern half consisted of many societies, the two biggest of which were the Yoruba and Igbo. The Yoruba lived in a series of kingdoms, sometimes politically united and sometimes not, though they shared a common language and religion. The Igbo in the southwest also shared a common language and culture but were governed only at the most local level by councils of elders; they had no kings or chiefs.

The British conquest began around 1870, part of what came to be known as the "scramble for Africa." The British eventually established "indirect rule," under which colonial authorities, in theory, left precolonial kingdoms intact to be ruled by local leaders. In northern Nigeria, this meant ruling through the emirs, who in general accepted British oversight as long as they were left to run their internal affairs mostly as they pleased. In the south, kings and chiefs fulfilled this role where they existed, but where there were no chiefs the British simply invented them. British colonialism gave local rulers more power than they had before, in exchange for rulers' acquiescence in implementing unpopular policies such as forced labor and the collection of colonial taxes. This undermined the legitimacy of those who had been precolonial rulers and prevented newly invented rulers from gaining legitimacy.

As in India, the colonial state required educated natives to help staff its bureaucracy. In the south, Christianity and Western education expanded rapidly; southerners filled most of the positions in the colonial state. The northern emirs, on the other hand, convinced colonial authorities to keep Christian education out in order to preserve Islam, on which their legitimacy was based. This meant that northerners received far less Western education. As the colonial state and bureaucracy expanded, especially after World War II, more and more southerners moved north to take up positions as clerks for the government. Their presence would prove explosive after independence.

The educated elite became the leadership of the nationalist movement after World War II. These elite were primarily employed in the government. For this reason, they had little interest in spurring economic growth by supporting Nigerians engaged in the key agricultural export sectors at the time; government policy before and after independence extracted resources from the productive economy to funnel benefits to

An activist holds a poster demanding the release of Nnamdi Kanu, a leader of the movement to create a separate country of Biafra in southeastern Nigeria. The first Biafran effort resulted in a three-year civil war and at least a million deaths in 1967-1970. After decades of what seemed to be resolution of the problem, a new Biafran movement arose in the new millennium, fueled by feelings that the region, in spite of its oil wealth, is politically and economically marginalized.

PIUS UTOMI EKPEI/AFP/Getty Images

political leaders themselves and their key supporters, a pattern that continued after the discovery of oil. Given the history of divisions in the country, it is no surprise that the nationalist movement was split from the start. The British ultimately negotiated a new government for an independent Nigeria that would be federal, with three regions corresponding to the three major ethnic groups, and political parties formed mainly along regional and ethnic lines.

As in virtually all African countries, the new government was quite fragile. In contrast with their approach in India, the British began introducing the institutions of British-style democracy just a few years before independence in their African colonies. Nigerians had no prior experience with electoral democracy and little reason to believe it would be a superior system for them. In response to fraudulent elections and anti-Igbo violence, the army, led primarily by Igbo, overthrew the elected government in January 1966 in the first of six military coups. A countercoup six months later brought a new, northern-dominated government to power, but the Igbo military leadership refused to accept it. In January 1967, they declared their region the independent state of Biafra. Not coincidentally, large-scale oil production had just begun, and the oil wells were in the area claimed as Biafra. A three-year civil war ensued that cost the lives of a million people. The central government defeated the separatists in Biafra and reestablished a single state in 1970. Interrupted by only four years of elected rule, the military governed Nigeria until 1999. While all military leaders pledged to reduce corruption and improve development, in reality, oil revenue overwhelmed all other economic activity and fueled both corruption and the desire of those in power to stay there. A weak state grew ever weaker and more corrupt.

In 1999 the military finally bowed to popular and international pressure and carried out the country's first free and fair election in twenty years. While many observers have questioned the integrity of all four elections since, Nigeria's democracy nonetheless remains intact, with little threat of further military intervention. Democracy has become the basis of legitimacy, but that democracy in practice remains very imperfect. With corruption still quite significant, the provision of political goods is limited. The democratic government has also faced growing religious tension in the northern states, many of which have adopted Islamic law. A violent Islamist group, Boko Haram, initiated an armed insurgency that has killed thousands, mostly in the northwestern part of the country, since 2010, though the president elected in 2015 initiated a military campaign that severely weakened the group. In the oil-rich areas of the former Biafra, ethnic militias have demanded greater benefits for their people, and pro-Biafra demonstrations erupted in 2015. Despite the area's natural resources, its residents are among the poorest in the country. While the country has seen significant economic growth in the new century, and for the first time in decades much of it is coming from non-oil sectors of the economy, oil and the resource curse remain a key problem.

CASE Questions

1. Nigeria and India are our only two case studies of states that were put together during colonialism from multiple premodern political entities (a common history in Africa and Asia). What impacts does this history have on the strength of the two states? In what ways were those impacts similar and different?

2. What are the weakest elements of the Nigerian state, and what effects do they have?

CONCLUSION

The modern state is a political form that has been singularly successful. Its characteristics—territory, sovereignty, legitimacy, and bureaucracy—combine to produce an exceptionally powerful ruling apparatus. Arising nearly five hundred years ago, it has spread to every corner of the globe. In fact, the modern world demands that we all live in states. Although state strength can be used to oppress the citizenry, many political scientists argue that long-term strength must come from legitimacy and the effective provision of political goods. In strong states, rulers command military force to prevent foreign attack and domestic rebellion, and they control a set of state organizations that can effectively influence society in myriad ways. When this all works well, it can give ruling elites legitimacy and therefore greater power. Weak states, on the other hand, lack the capacity, and often the will, to provide political goods. This threatens their legitimacy and often leaves them dependent on international support or key resources for their survival. While they may appear strong

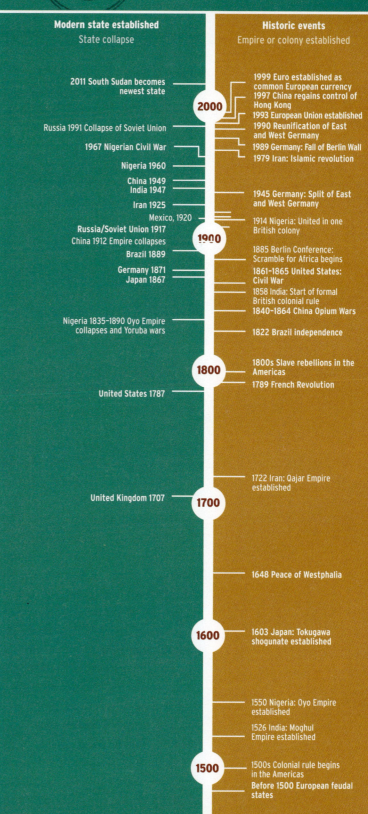

Modern state established
State collapse

Historic events
Empire or colony established

2011 South Sudan becomes newest state

2000

1999 Euro established as common European currency
1997 China regains control of Hong Kong
1993 European Union established
1990 Reunification of East and West Germany

Russia 1991 Collapse of Soviet Union

1989 Germany: Fall of Berlin Wall
1979 Iran: Islamic revolution

1967 Nigerian Civil War

Nigeria 1960

China 1949
India 1947

1945 Germany: Split of East and West Germany

Iran 1925

Mexico, 1920

1914 Nigeria: United in one British colony

Russia/Soviet Union 1917
China 1912 Empire collapses

1900

Brazil 1889

1885 Berlin Conference: Scramble for Africa begins

Germany 1871
Japan 1867

1861-1865 United States: Civil War
1858 India: Start of formal British colonial rule
1840-1864 China Opium Wars

Nigeria 1835-1890 Oyo Empire collapses and Yoruba wars

1822 Brazil independence

1800

1800s Slave rebellions in the Americas
1789 French Revolution

United States 1787

1722 Iran: Qajar Empire established

United Kingdom 1707

1700

1648 Peace of Westphalia

1600

1603 Japan: Tokugawa shogunate established

1550 Nigeria: Oyo Empire established

1526 India: Moghul Empire established

1500

1500s Colonial rule begins in the Americas
Before 1500 European feudal states

because they use a great deal of force against their own people, this is in fact often a sign of weakness: they have no other means of maintaining their rule. The weakest states are prone to collapse; they become failed states, as violent opponents can challenge the state's monopoly on the use of force with relative ease.

This raises a long-standing question: How can weak states become stronger? The answer usually involves the creation of impersonal institutions and the rule of law. This can lead citizens to trust the state, giving it greater legitimacy and strength that it can use to provide political goods. The strongest modern states are virtually all democracies, which are based on such notions as treating all citizens equally and limiting what the state can do, though electoral democracy certainly is no guarantee of state strength.

The strongest states in Europe and elsewhere resulted from centuries of evolution in most cases, as ruling elites ultimately compromised to create more impersonal and powerful institutions that would allow greater economic growth and protect them from attack. These states often began their modern era with strength in one or two particular areas, such as the bureaucracy and military, and developed strength in other areas decades or even centuries later. Postcolonial states had very different historical origins, based on colonial conquest rather than agreements among domestic elites. With independence, these states took the modern form but not necessarily all of the modern content. They often lacked a strong sense of national unity based on a shared history. The international system, however, demands that they act like states, at least internationally. Their rulers therefore act accordingly, often gaining significant power in the process, even in relatively weak states. Lack of wealth, or wealth in the form of a resource curse, also produces very weak states, often in combination with a problematic colonial legacy.

Political scientists have used various theoretical approaches to understand the modern state. Both Marxist and political culture theorists have long made arguments about how and why states develop. Marxists see them as reflecting the power of the ruling class of a particular epoch. Under capitalism, that ruling class is the bourgeoisie, and the liberal state in particular represents the bourgeoisie's interests. In postcolonial countries, weaker states reflect the weak, dependent nature of the ruling elite there. Cultural theorists argue that underlying values, in particular a strong sense of nationalism, are crucial to maintaining a strong state, which must be based on some shared sense of legitimacy. Without this, effective sovereignty will always be limited.

In recent years, rational choice and institutionalist theories have become more prominent. The modern state, these theorists argue, emerged in response to the rational incentives of the emerging international state system, rewarding rulers who developed effective sovereignty, military force, and taxation. Once established, strong state institutions tend to reinforce themselves as long as they continue to function for the benefit of the elites whom they were created to serve, and provide adequate political goods to the citizenry. Weaker states develop where colonial rule did not provide the same set of incentives, and variation in colonial rule often led to variation in postcolonial state strength. As modern states demand more from citizens, they develop a rational interest in establishing some type of popular legitimacy, a subject we look at in much greater depth in the next chapter.

KEY CONCEPTS

absolutism (p. 45)

bureaucracy (p. 42)

charismatic legitimacy (p. 41)

clientelism (p. 73)

external sovereignty (p. 38)

failed state (p. 51)

feudal states (p. 44)

ideal type (p. 51)

internal sovereignty (p. 38)

legitimacy (p. 41)

quasi-states (p. 56)

rational-legal legitimacy (p. 41)

resource curse (p. 54)

sovereignty (p. 39)

state (p. 36)

strong state (p. 51)

territory (p. 38)

traditional legitimacy (p. 41)

weak state (p. 51)

Sharpen your skills with SAGE edge at **edge.sagepub.com/orvis4e.** **SAGE edge for students** provides a personalized approach to help you accomplish your coursework goals in an easy-to-use learning environment.

WORKS CITED

Anderson, Perry. 1974. *Lineages of the Absolutist State.* London: New Left Books.

Bates, Robert H. 2008. *When Things Fell Apart: State Failure in Late-Century Africa.* Cambridge, UK: Cambridge University Press.

Brooks, Rosa. 2015. "Making a State by Iron and Blood." *Foreign Policy,* August 19 (https://foreignpolicy.com/2015/08/19/making-a-state-by-iron-and-blood-isis-iraq-syria/).

Fukuyama, Francis. 2014. *Political Order and Political Decay: From the Industrial Revolution to the Globalization of Democracy.* New York: Farrar, Straus, and Giroux.

Fund for Peace. 2016. "Fragile States Index 2016" (http://www.fsi.fundforpeace.org).

Huntington, Samuel. 1968. *Political Order in Changing Societies.* New Haven, CT: Yale University Press.

Jackson, Robert H. 1990. *Quasi-States: Sovereignty, International Relations, and the Third World.* Cambridge Studies in International Relations, No. 12. New York: Cambridge University Press.

Kelly, Andrew S., and James Mahoney. 2015. "The Emergence of the New World States." In *The Oxford Handbook of Transformations of the State,* edited by Stephan Leibfried, Evelyne Huber, Matthew Lange, Jonah D. Levy, Frank Nullmeier, and John D. Stephens, 99–115. Oxford, UK: Oxford University Press.

Lange, Matthew. 2009. *Lineages of Despotism and Development: British Colonialism and State Power.* Chicago: University of Chicago Press.

North, Douglass Cecil, John Joseph Wallis, and Barry R. Weingast. 2009. *Violence and Social Orders: A Conceptual Framework for Interpreting Recorded Human History.* Cambridge, UK: Cambridge University Press.

Richards, Rebecca, and Robert Smith. 2015. "Playing in the Sandbox: State Building in the Space of Non-Recognition." *Third*

World Quarterly, 36 (9): 1717–1735. doi:1 0.1080/01436597.2015.1058149

Risse, Thomas. 2015. "Limited Statehood: A Critical Perspective." In *The Oxford Handbook of Transformations of the State*, edited by Stephan Leibfried, Evelyne Huber, Matthew Lange, Jonah D. Levy, Frank Nullmeier, and John D. Stephens, 152–168. Oxford, UK: Oxford University Press.

Rotberg, Robert I., ed. 2004. *When States Fail: Causes and Consequences*. Princeton, NJ: Princeton University Press.

Saylor, Ryan. 2014. *State Building in Boom Times: Commodities and Coalitions in Latin America and Africa*. Oxford, UK: Oxford University Press.

Soifer, Hillel David. 2015. *State Building in Latin America*. Cambridge, UK: Cambridge University Press.

Tilly, Charles, ed. 1975. *The Formation of National States in Western Europe*. Studies in Political Development No. 8. Princeton, NJ: Princeton University Press.

Weber, Max. 1970. "Politics as Vocation." In *From Max Weber: Essays in Sociology*, edited by H. H. Gaert and C. Wright Mills. London: Routledge and Kegan Paul.

RESOURCES FOR FURTHER STUDY

Boix, Carles. 2015. *Political Order and Inequality: Their Foundations and Their Consequences for Human Welfare*. Cambridge, UK: Cambridge University Press.

Jessop, Bob. 1990. *State Theory: Putting Capitalist States in Their Place*. Cambridge, UK: Polity Press.

Levi, Margaret. 2002. "The State of the Study of the State." In *Political Science: State of the Discipline*, edited by Ira Katznelson and Helen V. Milner, 33–55. New York: Norton.

Mann, Michael. 2012. *The Sources of Social Power*. New ed., vols. 1–4. Cambridge, UK: Cambridge University Press.

Pierson, Christopher. 1996. *The Modern State*. New York: Routledge.

Poggi, Gianfranco. 1990. *The State: Its Nature, Development, and Prospects*. Cambridge, UK: Polity Press.

WEB RESOURCES

Brookings Institution Index of State Weakness in the Developing World
  (https: www.brookings.edu/research/index-of-state-weakness-in-the-developing-world/)
Comparative Constitutions Project
  (http://comparativeconstitutionsproject.org)
The Fund for Peace, Fragile States Index 2016
  (fsi.fundforpeace.org)
The Heritage Foundation, Index of Economic Freedom
  (http://www.heritage.org/index/ranking)
International Crisis Group
  (http://www.crisisgroup.org)
Organisation for Economic Co-operation and Development (OECD), Better Life Index
  (http://www.oecdbetterlifeindex.org)

Organisation for Economic Co-operation and Development (OECD), Country Statistical Profiles
(http://www.oecd-ilibrary.org/economics/country-statistical-profiles-key-tables-from-oecd_20752288)

Transformation Index BTI
(http://www.bti-project.org/home)

Transparency International, Corruption Perception Index
(http://www.transparency.org/policy_research/surveys_indices/cpi)

United Nations
(http://www.un.org/en)

The World Bank, Worldwide Governance Indicators
(http://info.worldbank.org/governance/wgi/index.aspx#home)

3

STATES, CITIZENS, AND REGIMES

KEY QUESTIONS

- How do different ideologies balance the rights of citizens with the state's ability to compel obedience?

- On what grounds do different regimes give citizens an opportunity to participate in politics? Who rules where citizens do not seem to have such an opportunity? Can this be justified?

- To what extent does ideology explain how different regimes are organized and justify themselves? What else helps explain how different kinds of regimes actually function?

- Do our case studies reveal patterns that suggest where different regime types emerge and why?

The proper relationship between a state and its people, individually and collectively, is one of the most interesting and debated questions in political science. All successful modern states are able to compel their citizens to obey and to regulate many areas of their lives. No modern state can do this, however, without answering questions about the legitimate boundaries of such compulsion and regulation. States vary on how far and under what circumstances they can compel individuals and groups to obey those in authority, how extensively they can intervene in people's lives, and how and whether some areas of individual and collective life should not be subject to the state's power. These differences are embodied in what political scientists call regimes. The Country and Concept table on page 100 demonstrates the wide variety of regimes and the levels of freedom that they allow their citizens among just our eleven case studies.

This chapter examines variations in the relationships between states and citizens embedded in different regimes. A **regime** is a set of formal and informal political institutions that defines a type of government. Regimes are more enduring than governments but less enduring than states. Democratic regimes, for example, may persist through many individual governments. The United States elected its forty-fifth presidential government in 2016, yet its democratic regime has remained intact for

The broom (to sweep away corruption) is the symbol of the new All Progressives Congress party in Nigeria. The new party was created by three opposition parties to challenge the ruling People's Democratic Party, which controlled Nigeria from 1999 to 2015. The new party gained power in a historic election in 2015, the first change in government via election in the nation's history.

AP Photo/Sunday Alamba

over two centuries. Similarly, a modern state may persist though many regime changes from democratic to authoritarian or the other way around. The state—the existence of a bureaucracy, territory, and so on—is continuous, but its key political institutions can change. The Country and Concept table shows the great variation around the world in regime stability over the last century, from the single, continuous regimes of the United States and the United Kingdom to the eight regimes Nigeria has seen.

Political scientists categorize regimes in many different ways. We think it is most useful to define regimes primarily based on their distinct political ideologies, which are usually explicitly stated and elaborately developed. Among other things, political ideologies make normative claims about the appropriate relationship between the state and its people: who should be allowed to participate in politics, how they should participate, and how much power they should have. We will focus on the major political ideologies that have been used to underpin regimes over the last century. We will also examine the ways in which regimes diverge from their ideological justifications because no regime operates exactly as its ideology claims.

regime
A set of formal and informal political institutions that defines a type of government

COUNTRY AND CONCEPT
Modern Regimes

Country	Current regime	Year established	Number of regimes in 20th and 21st centuries	Freedom House score
Brazil	Liberal democracy	1989	5	Free
China	"Communist" modernizing authoritarian	1949: People's Republic established	3	Not free
Germany	Liberal democracy	1945: Federal Republic of Germany established 1991: Reunited with German Democratic Republic	4	Free
India	Liberal democracy	1947: Independence	2	Free
Iran	Theocracy	1979: Islamic Republic proclaimed	4	Not free
Japan	Liberal democracy	1947	2	Free
Mexico	Liberal democracy	2000: First free and fair election	3	Partly free
Nigeria	Democracy (though with neopatrimonial elements)	1999	8	Partly free
Russia	Electoral authoritarian	2000: Putin's election	3	Not free
United Kingdom	Liberal democracy	1688: Glorious Revolution	1	Free
United States	Liberal democracy	1789: Constitution adopted	1	Free

Source: Data for the Freedom House score are from Freedom House, "Freedom in the World, 2016" (https://www.freedomhouse.org/report/freedom-world/freedom-world-2016).

CITIZENS AND CIVIL SOCIETY

Before we begin discussing any of this, however, it is helpful to understand the historical development of the "people" over whom modern states claim sovereignty. Ideas about how the people stand in relation to the state have evolved in tandem with the modern state described in chapter 2. At the most basic level, a **citizen** is a member of a political community or state. Notice that a citizen is more than an inhabitant within a state's borders. An inhabitant may be a member of physical and cultural communities, but a citizen inhabits a political community that places her in a relationship with the

citizen
A member of a political community or state with certain rights and duties

state. In the modern world, everyone needs to be "from" somewhere. It is almost inconceivable (although it does happen) to be a "man without a country." By this minimal definition, everyone is considered a citizen of some state.

The word *citizen,* however, is much more complex than this simple definition suggests. Up until about two or three hundred years ago, most Europeans thought of themselves as "subjects" of their monarchs, not citizens of states. Most people had little say in their relationship with the state; their side of that relationship consisted of duty and obedience. The very nature of the absolutist state meant that few mechanisms existed to protect subjects and enable them to claim any "rights." If the king wanted your land or decided to throw you in jail as a possible conspirator, no court could or would overrule him.

This began to change with the transition to the modern state. As the state was separated from the person of the monarch and its apparatus was modernized, states gained both the ability and the need to make their people more than just subjects. The concept of sovereignty, like the state itself, was divorced from the person of the sovereign, and many European philosophers and political leaders began to toy with the idea that sovereignty could lie with the people as a whole (or some portion, such as male landowners) rather than with a sovereign monarch. This was an important step in the development of the concept of modern citizenship: citizens, unlike subjects, were inhabitants of states that claimed that sovereignty resided with the people. Thus, after the French Revolution overthrew the absolutist *ancien régime,* people addressed one another as "citizen."

Over time, as the modern state developed, people began to associate a complex set of rights with the concept of citizenship. In the mid-twentieth century, the philosopher T. H. Marshall (1963) usefully categorized the rights of citizenship into three areas: civil, political, and social. **Civil rights** guarantee individual freedom and equal, just, and fair treatment by the state. Examples include the right to equal treatment under the law, habeas corpus, and freedom of expression and worship. **Political rights** are those associated with political participation: the right to vote, form political associations, run for office, or otherwise participate in political activity. **Social rights** are those related to basic well-being and socioeconomic equality, such as public education, pensions, or national health care. Marshall believed that modern citizenship included basic legal (civil) status in society and protection from the state as well as the right to actively participate in the political process. He argued that full citizenship also requires enough socioeconomic equality to make the civil and political equality of citizenship meaningful. Modern conceptions of citizenship go beyond just the focus on rights, however; others stress the participatory role of citizens in

Marianne is a key symbol of France, created during the French Revolution to represent liberty and reason. Here, she is depicted at the storming of the Bastille prison on July 14, 1789, a key event in the revolution, which helped usher in liberalism and the modern conception of citizenship in Europe.

Rue des Archives/The Granger Collection, NYC

civil rights
Those rights that guarantee individual freedom as well as equal, just, and fair treatment by the state

political rights
Those rights associated with active political participation—for example, to free association, voting, and running for office

social rights
Those rights related to basic well-being and socioeconomic equality

the political community, the obligations of citizenship, or citizenship as an identity. A citizen, then, is a member of a political community with certain rights, perhaps some obligations to the larger community as well, and ideally (for most theorists) an active participant in that community.

Participation, of course, typically happens in organized groups of one sort or another, what we call "civil society." We defined civil society in chapter 1 as the sphere of organized, nongovernmental, nonviolent activity by groups larger than individual families or firms. Like citizenship, civil society in Europe developed in conjunction with the modern state. Absolutist states would not have conceived of such a realm of society separate from the state itself, for what would this have meant? If a monarch could dispose of lands and goods, grant monopolies on tax collection, and determine which religion the realm would follow, what could "society" mean apart from that? The rise of religious pluralism and of modern, capitalist economies alongside the modern state meant that there were now areas of social life outside the immediate control of the state.

This history should not be romanticized or thought of as a linear movement toward modern, democratic citizenship. Change was neither inevitable nor always positive. The same changes that gave us the modern state, however, also gave us the modern concept of the citizen and the modern concept of an independent civil society in which citizens could organize collectively for all sorts of purposes, from religious worship to charitable activity to political action.

Today, ideas of citizenship and civil society are connected to regime claims to legitimacy via the concept of "popular sovereignty." Recall that a claim to legitimacy is a key characteristic of modern states: all modern regimes make some claim to legitimacy, and most do so based on representing and speaking on behalf of "the people." Although it is a distinctly European and liberal democratic notion, the idea of popular sovereignty has deeply influenced all subsequent political ideologies. Even dictators claim to be working on behalf of the citizenry. They may claim that they must deny

Immigrants and supporters demonstrate in front of the Greek parliament, demanding citizenship for children of immigrants who were born in Greece. Citizenship gives full rights to immigrants. Laws on who can be a citizen and how that happens vary from state to state and help define national identity.

George Panagakis/Pacific Press/ LightRocket via Getty Images certain rights in the short term to benefit society as a whole in the long term (or, in the case of theocracy, that God has willed certain exceptions to citizens' rights), but they still lay some claim to working toward the well-being of the citizens.

Some argue that a "postnational" citizenship is now emerging as the latest chapter in this history, especially in the European Union (EU) (Lister and Pia 2008). We can see this in several major institutions around the world: the rights of citizenship are embedded in key United Nations documents, the International Criminal Court in the Hague exists to enforce those rights on behalf of the world community, the EU has a "social charter" that sets standards for treatment of citizens in all EU countries, and most EU members have a common immigration policy that allows people to travel freely within the Union as if they were travelling in only one country. The EU's difficulties, however, in responding to both the 2008–2009 financial crisis and the 2015–2016 refugee crisis raised serious doubts about the viability of this expanded concept of citizenship. In terms of participation, as international organizations such as the World Trade Organization become more important, citizens are forming international groups to try to influence those policies. Keck and Sikkink (1998) called this phenomenon "transnational civil society." These new trends are undoubtedly important and may still grow, but for now almost all citizenship in terms of core rights still resides within the nation-state. Even in the EU, one gains "European" citizenship only via citizenship in a member state.

In practice, regimes vary enormously in their relationships to both citizens' rights and civil society. Virtually no country fully provides all three types of rights described by Marshall. Similarly, the manifestation of civil society ranges from flourishing, lively groups of independently organized citizens, like the many interest groups and political movements in the United States or Europe, to highly controlled or actively repressed groups, such as the government-controlled labor union in China. In short, modern citizens and civil society are much like the modern state: the ideas represent an ideal type but are not universally implemented in contemporary societies. By looking at regimes' political ideologies, we can learn how they attempt to justify and legitimize their various relationships with their citizens.

REGIMES, IDEOLOGIES, AND CITIZENS

Not all political ideologies have been embodied in regimes, but virtually every regime has some sort of ideology that attempts to justify its existence in the eyes of its citizens and the world. Regimes are much more than just the legal and institutional embodiments of their ideologies, however. Although all regimes have formal rules and institutions that reflect, at least to some extent, their ideological claims to legitimacy, they also have informal rules and institutions, and these may conflict with their ideological claims. Informal institutions may be more important than formal ones; rulers may not actually believe the ideology they proclaim; or the realities of being in power, of trying to govern a complex society, may necessitate ideological modifications. As we noted in chapter 2, weak states in particular are characterized by relatively weak formal institutions. In these states, knowing the informal rules and

Major Political Ideologies and Regime Types

LIBERAL DEMOCRACY

ORIGINS   Social contract theory. Legitimate governments form when free and independent individuals join in a contract to permit representatives to govern over them.

KEY IDEA   Individuals are free and autonomous, with natural rights.

Government must preserve the core liberties—life, liberty, and property—possessed by all free individuals.

CHARACTERISTICS   Representative democracy. Citizens have direct control, and leaders can be removed.

Separation of powers, federalism, and social citizenship supplement, but are not essential to, legitimate government.

WHO HAS POWER   Legislature.

COMMUNISM

ORIGINS   Marxism. Ruling class oppresses other classes, based on mode of production. Historical materialism means that material (economic) forces are the prime movers of history and politics.

KEY IDEA   Proletariat will lead socialist revolution. Socialist society after revolution will be ruled as a dictatorship of the proletariat over other classes; will eventually create classless, communist society in which class oppression ends.

CHARACTERISTICS   Lenin believed that the vanguard party can lead socialist revolution in interests of present and future proletariat. Vanguard party rules socialist society using democratic centralism and is justified in oppressing classes that oppose it.

WHO HAS POWER   Vanguard party now; proletariat later.

FASCISM

ORIGINS   Organic conception of society. Society is akin to a living organism rather than a set of disparate groups and individuals.

KEY IDEA   Rejects materialism and rationality; relies instead on "spiritual attitude."

The state creates the nation, a "higher personality"; intensely nationalistic.

Corporatism. The state recognizes only one entity to lead each group in society (for example, an official trade union).

CHARACTERISTICS   The state is at the head of the corporate body. It is all-embracing, and outside of it no human or spiritual values can exist. "Accepts the individual only in so far as his interests coincide with those of the State" (Benito Mussolini, 1933).

WHO HAS POWER   A supreme leader.

MODERNIZING AUTHORITARIANISM

ORIGINS   End of colonialism and desire to develop; technocratic legitimacy.

KEY IDEA   *Modernization theory.* Postcolonial societies must go through the same process to develop as the West did. Development requires national unity; democracy would interfere with unity.

CHARACTERISTICS   Four institutional forms: one-party regimes, military regimes, bureaucratic-authoritarian regimes, and personalist regimes. Neopatrimonial authority is common.

| WHO HAS POWER | A modern elite—a relatively few, highly educated people—who are capable of modernizing or "developing" the country; the claim to rule based on special knowledge is technocratic legitimacy. |

PERSONALIST REGIME

ORIGINS	One-party regime or military coup
KEY IDEA	Claims to modernizing authoritarianism but really based on neopatrimonial authority
CHARACTERISTICS	Extremely weak institutions, instability and unpredictability
WHO HAS POWER	Individual ruler

ELECTORAL AUTHORITARIANISM

ORIGINS	Primarily failed transitions to democracy.
KEY IDEA	Legitimacy is based on a combination of liberal democratic and modernizing authoritarian ideologies.
CHARACTERISTICS	Allows limited freedoms of expression and association. Allows limited political opposition to hold some elected offices but ensures ruling party/leader holds most power. Informal institutions are often more important than formal institutions. Contradictions exist between democratic and authoritarian elements.
WHO HAS POWER	Ruling party.

THEOCRACY

ORIGINS	Ancient religious beliefs.
KEY IDEA	Rule is by divine inspiration or divine right.
CHARACTERISTICS	Islamist version: • *Islamism*. Islamic law, as revealed by God to the Prophet Mohammed, can and should provide the basis for government in Muslim communities. • *Ijtihad*. The belief that Muslims should read and interpret the original Islamic texts for themselves, not simply follow traditional religious leaders and beliefs. • *Sharia*. Muslim law should be the law of society for all Muslims.
WHO HAS POWER	God is sovereign, not the people.

institutions at work may be more important to understanding how their regimes actually function than knowing the formal institutions embodied in their constitutions.

Even where informal institutions predominate, though, ideologies are important. The major political ideologies have defined the terms of the most important political debates of the past century: liberal democracy versus communism versus fascism versus theocracy. (For a description of the major ideologies, see the "Major Political Ideologies and Regimes" box on page 104.) Most regimes have come to power in the name of one or another of the ideologies outlined below, and many have made serious efforts to rule along the lines prescribed by them. We begin with liberal democracy.

While it is certainly not universally accepted, it has become powerful enough that all regimes, implicitly or explicitly, must respond to its claims. In fact, approximately 90 percent of the world's constitutions, including those of many authoritarian regimes, mention "democracy" somewhere (Elkins, et al. 2014, 141).

Liberal Democracy

Democracy means different things to different people: many people find it hard to define, yet they think they know it when they see it. The word literally means rule by the *demos*, or the people, but that doesn't tell us very much. In this book, we will follow the main convention in comparative politics and use a "minimal definition" of the term, typically referred to as *liberal democracy*. The two words of the phrase are stated together so frequently that in many people's minds they have become one. The distinction between the two, however, is important to understanding both the development of liberal democracy and current debates over its expansion around the world, which we discuss in subsequent chapters.

Liberalism, the predecessor of liberal democracy, arose in the sixteenth and seventeenth centuries amidst the religious wars in England and the later revolution in France. The key liberal thinkers of the period created a model of political philosophy known as **social contract theory.** Although there are many variations, all social contract theories begin from the premise that legitimate governments are formed when free and autonomous individuals join in a contract to permit representatives to govern over them in their common interests. The originators of this idea, Thomas Hobbes and John Locke in England and the Baron de Montesquieu and Jean-Jacques Rousseau in France, started from an assertion that had not been part of Europe's political landscape since ancient Athens: all citizens should be considered free and equal. They theorized an original "state of nature" in which all men (and they meant men—women weren't included until much later) lived freely and equally with no one ruling over them. They argued that the only government that could be justified was one that men living in such a state of nature would freely choose.

Beginning with Locke, all social contract theorists ultimately came to the same basic conclusion about what such a freely chosen government would look like. Locke argued that in the state of nature, government would only arise if it helped preserve the core liberties of all free men: life, liberty, and property (a phrase Thomas Jefferson later modified as "life, liberty and the pursuit of happiness" in the Declaration of Independence). This became the central doctrine of liberalism: a regime is only justified if it preserves and protects the core liberties of autonomous, free, and equal individuals. A state can only infringe on these liberties in very particular circumstances, such as when an action is essential for the well-being of all or when a particular citizen has denied others their rights. Preservation of rights is essential and severely limits what governments can do.

social contract theory
Philosophical approach underlying liberalism that begins from the premise that legitimate governments are formed when free and independent individuals join in a contract to permit representatives to govern over them in their common interests

Key Characteristics of Liberal Democracy The classical liberal doctrine on the preservation of rights justifies limited government to enhance individual freedoms, but it says nothing about how a government will come to power or make decisions. Liberals argued that men in a state of nature would desire a government over which they had some direct control, with leaders they could remove from office if necessary, as protection against a state trying to destroy basic liberties. Representative democracy thus became the universal form of liberal governance. By voting, citizens would choose the government that would rule over them. Those chosen would be in office for a limited period, with some mechanism for removal if necessary.

With elected representatives, some type of legislature would be essential and central to government. This would be a body in which elected officials would debate and decide the important issues of the day. While kings and courts had long existed in Europe as the executive and judicial branches, liberals argued that the most important branch ought to be the legislative, the body of elected representatives of free and equal citizens. Montesquieu added the idea of giving each branch of government independent powers as a way to divide and thereby further limit the state overall. (This doctrine, adopted in the United States but not in the United Kingdom, is not essential to liberal democracy but is rather an extension of the liberal ideal of limited government.)

For all of their forward thinking about equality and limited government, most liberals still conceived of the citizens to which these concepts applied as male property owners only. They argued that while everyone had some basic civil rights, only men who owned property were adequately mature, rational, and independent of the whims of others to be given the right to vote and participate in governing. Restricting full citizenship to this group meant that all citizens could be considered equal: different men held different amounts of property and had different abilities, but compared with the rest of society they were roughly similar. It was not long before groups not initially granted full citizenship, such as men without property, women, and racial minorities, began asking why they weren't considered as free and autonomous as anybody else. This question produced the largest political struggles of the nineteenth and twentieth centuries in Europe and the United States, struggles to fully democratize liberalism. As citizenship slowly expanded to include more and more groups, real inequality among citizens increasingly began to conflict with the proposition that "all men [and later, all people] are created equal."

Modern liberal democratic regimes arose from this history. Leaders in these regimes justify their actions by claiming to preserve and protect core civil and political liberties: freedom from government intervention in private lives (except under clearly defined and limited circumstances), freedom of religious practice, freedom of expression, freedom of association, and the rights to vote and hold office. Citizens in a liberal democracy use these freedoms to create civil society, though civil society's strength,

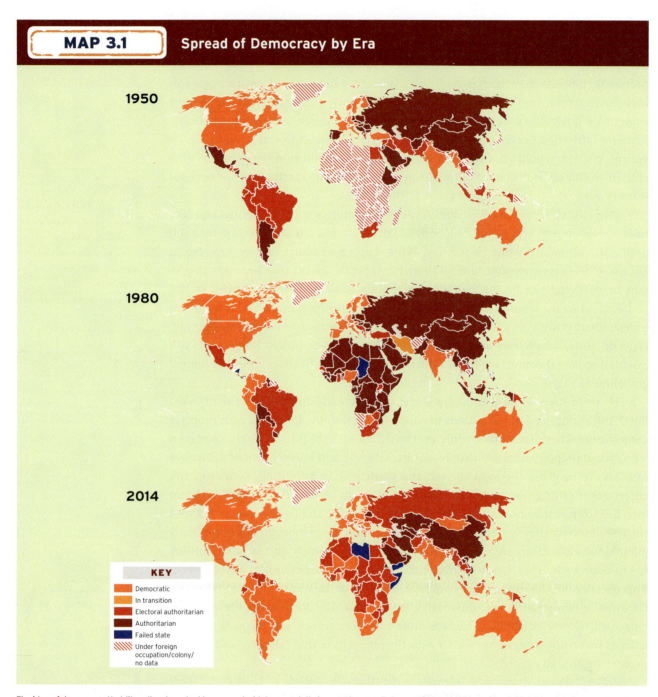

MAP 3.1   Spread of Democracy by Era

1950

1980

2014

KEY
- Democratic
- In transition
- Electoral authoritarian
- Authoritarian
- Failed state
- Under foreign occupation/colony/ no data

The idea of democracy that liberalism launched has spread widely, especially in recent years. Between 1950 and 1980, most colonial rule came to an end, but democracy did not spread very far. By 2014, however, many more countries had become democratic, and many authoritarian regimes had become somewhat more open electoral authoritarian regimes that allowed some limited political competition, as we discuss later in this chapter. Only a relative handful of purely authoritarian regimes remain.

Source: Data from Polity IV Project: Political Regime Characteristics and Transitions, 1800–2014 (http://www.systemicpeace.org/polityproject.html). The "Polity" variable employed, with the following coding by the authors: democracy (6–10); electoral authoritarian, (–5–5); authoritarian, (–10–6). Countries labeled "in transition" or "failed state" are Polity IV classifications.

organization, and daily relationship with the state vary from country to country. All liberal democracies are characterized by some system of elections by which voters, now defined almost universally as all adult citizens (certain categories of citizens, however, are still excluded: one of the largest is ex-felons, prevented from voting in many U.S. states), choose key members of the government, who serve limited terms and may be removed. Some liberal democracies include other safeguards, such as separation of powers. Many include the provision of extensive government services to attempt to achieve something closer to equal social citizenship.

The debate continues, of course, over how much power liberal freedoms actually give to the average citizen vis-à-vis the elite. Marxists, among other elite theorists, argue that liberal rights to vote and join organizations do not give any real power to the average citizen. They contend that elites such as major business leaders gain disproportionate influence in any "democracy" and influence government policy in their favor, often against the interests of average citizens, who have no real recourse in spite of the rights liberalism provides. Other ideologies, such as fascism or theocracy, which we discuss below, argue that liberal democracy places undue emphasis on individual rights over the needs of building a good state and society based on other criteria like achieving modernization or obeying divine law.

Political scientist Robert Dahl captured the essentials of the liberal democratic system of government by noting the eight key guarantees it provides: freedom of association, freedom of expression, the right to vote, broad citizen eligibility for public office, the right of political leaders to compete for support, alternative sources of information, free and fair elections, and institutions that make government policies depend on votes and other forms of citizen preferences. We include these in our working definition of **liberal democracy.**

Varieties of Democracy Liberal democracy is certainly not the only form of democracy that democratic theorists have imagined or advocated. Perhaps the best known alternative is **social democracy**, which combines liberal democracy with a much greater provision of social rights of citizenship and typically greater public control of the economy as well. Advocates of social democracy argue that citizens should not only control the political sphere but also key elements of the economic sphere. They favor public ownership or at least extensive regulation of key sectors of the economy to enhance equal citizenship and the well-being of all. They believe in

What Makes a Democracy a Democracy?

The alternative definitions of democracy raise a set of important normative questions worthy of debate: What are the essential elements of democracy? Are Dahl's eight attributes of liberal democracy enough to give citizens true political equality? If not, what more is required? Are social democrats correct that a minimum level of social equality is necessary for true "rule of the people"? Is electing representatives to rule on behalf of citizens enough, or do citizens need to participate more actively in actual decision making? Should areas of life beyond what we normally think of as "political" be subject to democratic control as well?

liberal democracy
A system of government that provides eight key guarantees, including freedoms to enable citizen participation in the political process and institutions that make government policies depend on votes and other forms of citizen preferences

social democracy
Combines liberal democracy with much greater provision of social rights of citizenship and typically greater public control of the economy

maintaining a market economy, but one that is regulated in the interests of the greater good of the citizens as a whole. They also believe that Marshall's third category, social rights, is very important to achieving full democracy, so they favor generous social programs.

Social democratic parties emerged in the late nineteenth century to demand that citizens gain social citizenship: decent living standards so that they could be respected in their communities and fully participate in citizenship as moral equals. Social democratic ideology did not create a separate regime type, but it became an important variant in the internal debates of liberal democracy. Its proponents argue that without social citizenship and full participation, democracy is not yet achieved, in spite of the presence of basic civil and political rights.

Proponents of **participatory democracy** argue that real democracy must include far more than the minimal list of institutional guarantees. Real democracy requires direct citizen participation in the decisions that affect their lives. Therefore, advocates of participatory democracy support the decentralization of decision making to local communities to the greatest extent possible, with the goal of direct citizen involvement. Many also support the democratization of the workplace, advocating for worker participation in the key decisions of the companies for which they work.

participatory democracy
A form of democracy that encourages citizens to participate actively, in many ways beyond voting; usually focused at the local level

CASE Study

UNITED KINGDOM: "CRADLE OF DEMOCRACY"

CASE SYNOPSIS

Britain's unusual liberal democracy has evolved slowly, and often contentiously, over centuries. Citizenship rights have expanded to include all adult citizens despite the absence of a single, written constitution. Parliamentary sovereignty gives Britain an unusually centralized form of democracy (which we explore in detail in chapter 5) but one that has preserved and expanded basic liberal rights for a very long time. Like all liberal democracies, Britain continues to debate how much the power of the central government ought to be limited and how universal social rights should be.

- REGIME First liberal democratic regime

- CITIZEN AND STATE Gradual but contentious expansion of citizens' rights in nineteenth and early twentieth centuries

- CLAIM TO LEGITIMACY Parliamentary sovereignty

- RECENT TRENDS Constitutional reforms in the new millennium, devolution, and Supreme Court

Many of the most important developments in the history of liberal democracy occurred in the United Kingdom (UK), or England before it became the UK. The core ideas of limiting a sovereign's power and creating what was called a parliament (from the French word *parler*, meaning to talk) arose long before they were codified in the philosophy of Locke and others. The earliest important milestone was the Magna Carta, signed by King John in 1215 under pressure from feudal lords. It included the first right to trial by peers, guaranteed the freedom of the (Catholic) church from monarchical intervention, created an assembly of twenty-five barons (chosen by all the barons of England) that became the first parliament, and guaranteed nobles the right to be called together to discuss any significant new taxes. All of these rights and guarantees were strictly designed to preserve the dominance of the nobility, but they were a significant first step in limiting the monarch's individual power.

Four centuries later, religious divisions between Catholics and Protestants led to the English civil war; Locke developed his ideas largely in reaction to the deep religious divisions and violence of that war. The Glorious Revolution of 1688 saw Parliament's bloodless removal of King James II from the throne and the installation of a new king and queen, a dramatic expansion of parliamentary power over the monarch. The following year, Parliament passed a Bill of Rights that substantially expanded the rights of citizenship. From that point forward, Parliament gained increasing power vis-à-vis the monarchy, and the power of the prime minister—an individual appointed by the king but who worked closely with Parliament—grew significantly.

The growing power of the elected Parliament was significant, but political citizenship was still restricted primarily to men with substantial property holdings, who constituted less than 5 percent of the population. The nineteenth century saw significant challenges to this system: the franchise was extended first to the growing middle class in 1832 (though the electorate remained all male and grew only to about 7 percent of the population) and then to most adult males via reforms in 1867 and 1884. A movement for women's suffrage emerged by the mid-nineteenth century, but women were not given the right to vote until 1918. None of this expansion of political citizenship occurred easily. Large-scale pressure from civil society was necessary to achieve each reform. Liberal rights expanded, but only when those without them demanded (vociferously, and sometimes violently) that they be included in full citizenship.

The modernistic Scottish Parliament building in Edinburgh (left) is a sharp contrast to the stately British Parliament building in London (right). Britain devolved certain powers to the newly created Scottish and Welsh parliaments in 1997, a major change to Britain's liberal democratic regime. Scotland held a referendum in September 2014 on the question of declaring full independence from Great Britain, but it was defeated. After the "Brexit" vote to leave the EU, the Scottish National Party promised to hold another referendum on independence.

Photograph © 2005 Scottish Parliamentary Corporate Body

parliamentary sovereignty
Parliament is supreme in all matters; key example is the United Kingdom

The British model of liberal democracy is unusual, in part because of its history. No equivalent of the American or French Revolution occurred to cause a single, definitive break from monarchy. The development of the liberal democratic regime in Britain was much more gradual. No unified, written British constitution exists, though many of the elements of a constitution—the fundamental rules of how the regime works—are written down in various laws passed by Parliament. In the absence of a single constitution, British democracy is based on the concept of **parliamentary sovereignty,** which holds that Parliament is supreme in all matters. Members can write any law they choose via majority vote. Rights are preserved only by a collective consensus that Parliament should not reverse them. This is a great example of a powerful but *informal* political institution, a set of implicit rules and norms that are not violated even though in theory they could be. Political culture theorists would explain this institution by pointing to British cultural values. Institutionalists might suggest that the institution, established originally in the Bill of Rights of 1689, has served citizens' interests well and therefore is preserved. In any case, the system has continued to operate with only limited change for more than three centuries.

The two most important recent changes to Britain's democratic regime have addressed decentralization of power from Parliament to both regional governments and the judiciary. In 1997 the British Parliament allowed devolution of some powers (such as over education and social services) to newly created Scottish and Welsh parliaments, which had ceased to exist when the two kingdoms were integrated into the United Kingdom centuries earlier. While devolution was welcomed in both areas, in Scotland a nationalist party that gained power in the Scottish parliament pushed for full independence. It held a referendum in 2014 on the question of Scotland becoming a completely independent country, breaking apart the United Kingdom created three centuries earlier. After a vociferous campaign in which English political leaders across the political spectrum campaigned to preserve the United Kingdom, the referendum failed by a vote of 55 to 45 percent, though the Scottish nationalist movement promised a new referendum after Britain as a whole voted to leave the European Union in 2016, a move very unpopular in Scotland. In 2005 the government also created a freestanding Supreme Court as a final court of appeals, a job that had previously been done by the unelected House of Lords in Parliament. Though it lacks the power to reverse acts of Parliament that the U.S. Supreme Court has vis-à-vis Congress, its existence is another step in reducing the power of Britain's Parliament.

In the twentieth century, Britain's democracy also wrestled with the notion of social rights. After World War II, based on a sense that all citizens had shared the sacrifices necessary to win the war and therefore should share in the rewards, the British government expanded its welfare state extensively. This included the National Health Service, which essentially made access to health care a universal right, plus other universal benefits such as an annual "child allowance" from the government for all parents raising children. New rules instituted in 2013 ended the universality of the child allowance, restricting it primarily to parents with incomes of less than 50,000 British pounds (about $75,000). The debate over what should and should not be a social right in Britain's liberal democracy continues.

CASE Questions

1. What does the UK case teach us about the process of establishing and expanding liberal rights?
2. The UK's regime is unusual among liberal democracies in that it doesn't have a written constitution. Look back at the core tenets of liberal democracy: Does the UK regime seem to qualify fully as a liberal democracy? Why or why not?

Communism

The first and most influential ideological alternative to liberal democracy was communism, which became the basis for regimes in Russia, China, and a number of other countries. Karl Marx, the originator of communism, grounded his philosophy on what he called **historical materialism**, the assertion that material (economic) forces are the prime movers of history and politics. He believed that to understand politics, one must first understand the economic structure of a society and the economic interests that arise from it. As the material forces in the society—technology, raw materials, and the way they are combined to make goods—change, so too will the political, social, and ideological systems. Feudalism produced all-powerful lords and monarchs, with religious sanction from the church as the chief ideological justification, to keep the peasants in their place, producing a surplus for the lords. The shift to capitalism produced liberalism, in which political power was no longer vested in the landed aristocracy but was instead given to all men of property. This allowed the rising bourgeoisie, the owners of capital, to gain political power. Capitalism requires labor that is paid a wage and can move from place to place, so the feudal system that required peasants to stay on the land where they were born was abolished, and many peasants were forced off their land to work for a daily wage in cities.

historical materialism
The assumption that material forces are the prime movers of history and politics; a key philosophical tenet of Marxism

Liberal democracy, according to Marx, is the political and ideological shell that allows capitalism to work and that serves the interests of the bourgeoisie, capitalism's ruling class. When Marx was developing his ideas, only men of property had full political rights in most countries. Even where those rights had expanded to others, as in the United States by the 1830s, Marx argued that this was only a charade. He called liberal rights "equal rights for unequal people," arguing that where workers did have the vote, it was virtually meaningless because those with wealth were the only ones with any real power. Civil society, he argued, was a realm dominated by capitalists as well, a sphere created to give capitalists independence from the state and a means by which they could control the state.

mode of production
In Marxist theory, the economic system in any given historical era; feudalism and capitalism in the last millennium in Europe

Marx saw the transition from one **mode of production** to another, such as from feudalism to capitalism, as a process of social revolution. He argued that all modes of production ultimately create contradictions they cannot overcome, leading to revolution. Capitalism, he believed, would be characterized by an ever greater division between the bourgeoisie and the proletariat, workers who must sell their labor for a wage to survive. Marx believed that as more and more wealth and power accrued in the hands of capitalists, the proletariat would become so poor that they would not be able to consume all of capitalism's products, creating an economic crisis that would usher in a new era of social revolution. Just as the liberal revolutions had been led by the bourgeoisie and had established liberal democracy, the next revolutions would be communist revolutions led by the proletariat—what Marx called the "specter haunting Europe" in *The Communist Manifesto* (1848/1888). Marx believed this revolution was inevitable and that it was the job of the communist movement to recognize when and where social revolutions were emerging and bring them to fruition to create a new and better society and political system.

The communist society that Marx believed would emerge from these revolutions would abolish class distinctions and collectively own the means of production. All people (or at least men—Marx was no more feminist than most other nineteenth-century philosophers) would be paid the same amount for the same work, and everyone would have to work. This he saw as the first stage of communism, which he also called socialism. He was quite explicit about who would rule during this stage: the

dictatorship of the proletariat
In the first stage of communism in Marxist thought, characterized by absolute rule by workers as a class over all other classes

dictatorship of the proletariat, an absolute rule by workers as a class over all other classes. This dictatorship was not of one man but of the entire class, which would control and ultimately eliminate all other classes. Civil society distinct from this workers' state would no longer be needed. This was justified in Marx's view because all governments, including all liberal democracies, have been class dictatorships; liberal democracies are simply dictatorships of the bourgeoisie. As this socialist society developed, everyone eventually would become equal in the sense of all being part of the proletariat. At that point, the second, higher stage of communism would develop in which no state would be necessary because no class divisions would exist, and all dictatorships would end.

Marx believed that communism was both inevitable and the final stage of human historical evolution. Just as political systems and ideologies are the product of economic forces, Marx believed human nature was as well. With class division and exploitation eliminated, he believed that human nature itself would change from being self-interested and greedy under capitalism to being what he viewed as more fully human under communism. This would facilitate the creation of his ultimate and, he believed, inevitable goal of a communist utopia. Critics dispute this utopian goal and therefore the means to achieve it. Liberals reject the notion that any end, whether feasible or not, justifies violating the fundamental rights of any individual or group, as would occur under the dictatorship of the proletariat. They fear instead that a communist state would simply become a dictatorship of an individual or small group over all of society.

Postmodern theorists have argued that Marxism, or any theory claiming certainty about the "laws" of human history, inevitably will result in a **totalitarian state** that attempts to control every aspect of society in the name of achieving an unreachable utopia. Various political ideologies could be used to justify the creation of a totalitarian state. Both Marxism and its twentieth-century arch-rival, fascism—which we discuss below—were the primary examples, however. The history of communism in Russia illustrates the potential and pitfalls of the communist dream.

totalitarian state
A state that controls virtually all aspects of society and eliminates all vestiges of civil society; Germany under Hitler and the Soviet Union under Stalin are key examples

CASE Study

RUSSIA: THE FIRST SELF-PROCLAIMED COMMUNIST REGIME

CASE SYNOPSIS

For seventy years, Russia's communist regime, based on the principles of Marx as modified by Vladimir Lenin, claimed to be working on behalf of the proletariat. Regime leaders argued, however, that only highly trained and educated communists could use Marxist analysis to serve the proletariat's interests effectively. This claim to legitimacy justified repression of all public dissent. The regime thus restricted citizenship to those who accepted the party's wisdom and rule; those who opposed the party were traitors to the class that rightfully should rule. Civil society under Communist Party rule was completely eliminated, and the state, led by the party, controlled virtually all aspects of individuals' lives, including where they worked, the clubs and organizations to which they could belong, and the prices they paid at the cash register.

- REGIME Communist; totalitarian under Stalin; finally, bureaucratic socialism with battles for resources behind the scenes
- CITIZEN AND STATE Citizenship only for those who accepted the party's rule
- CLAIM TO LEGITIMACY Vanguard party ruling on behalf of proletariat
- KEY INSTITUTIONS Decision making in soviets, with final authority in politburo
- CONTEXT Revolution in the "wrong country"

Marx was an active revolutionary for most of his life, but he did not live to see a communist revolution succeed. Based on his analysis of capitalism, he believed the revolution would start in the wealthiest and most advanced capitalist societies, such as the United Kingdom, Germany, and France. Russia at the turn of the twentieth century, however, was still primarily rural, with growing multinational investment controlled by foreigners and an unstable and oppressive political system. The liberal, bourgeois revolution, let alone the socialist one, had yet to happen there. In fact, late in his life Marx wrote to Russian revolutionaries, telling them to wait for the revolutions in the wealthier parts of Europe before pursuing their own socialist dreams.

As Russians writhed in the throes of World War I, a disastrous and unpopular war for them, Vladimir Lenin, inspired by Marx's writing, led his forces to victory in the October Revolution of 1917 and created the first Communist regime, the Soviet Union. Lenin knew that according to Marx, Russia was not ripe for revolution, so to legitimize his regime, Lenin modified Marx's political theories. He argued that where capitalism had not developed sufficiently to produce the economic crisis and socialist revolution, a committed band of revolutionaries, a **vanguard party,** could still lead a revolution. This party would take power and rule on behalf of the proletariat until the country

vanguard party
Vladimir Lenin's concept of a small party that claims legitimacy to rule based on its understanding of Marxist theory and its ability to represent the interests of the proletariat before they are a majority of the populace

Vladimir Lenin, leader of the Russian revolution, modified Marxist doctrine to adapt it to Russian circumstances, arguing that a vanguard party of committed revolutionaries could lead a precapitalist, agrarian nation into communism.

Fine Art Images/Heritage Images/Getty Images

was fully industrialized and therefore fully proletarian. Socialism, the first stage of communism, would last longer than Marx had envisioned, but the revolution could occur sooner. Lenin also believed that once the revolution succeeded in Russia, the proletariat of the wealthier European countries would see the possibility of a proletarian regime and rise up to create their own. He fully expected the communist revolution to spread quickly across Europe and create a set of socialist regimes that would build communism together.

Once in power, and seeing that the revolution was not going to spread rapidly across Europe, Lenin had to figure out how the Soviet Union would survive as the lone socialist state. The dictatorship of the proletariat would, for the time being, be the dictatorship of the single vanguard party, which was justified in ruthlessly suppressing all opposition that represented other class interests. The party thus became the sole representative of the people.

The regime consisted of a set of soviets, or legislative bodies, which made decisions at all levels. Officially, the soviet was the decision-making body at each level of the regime, but in reality each was tightly controlled by the Communist Party, which was the only legal party to which any politically active person had to belong. At the top of the entire system was the **politburo,** the party's chief decision-making organ. This small, mostly male group collectively and secretly selected each new general secretary of the party. The general secretaries were the country's most powerful rulers, and most served in that position until death.

Lenin recognized by 1921 that while central state control of the government had merit, similar control of the economy was hurting production, especially in agriculture, the largest sector of the economy. Once again, ideological modification seemed essential. In response, he created the New Economic Policy, under which state control of the economy was partially loosened. Lenin died from a stroke at a relatively young age only three years later.

After a five-year succession struggle, Joseph Stalin came to power and radically reversed Lenin's economic policies. Stalin launched a plan to institute state control of the economy, taking ownership of virtually all land and extracting huge surpluses from agriculture to build industry. The result was rapid industrialization that transformed the Soviet Union from a poor agricultural country into an industrial powerhouse and superpower by World War II. Those who opposed Stalin's policies were ruthlessly suppressed; estimates of deaths under his reign range from two to twenty million. He created a totalitarian state that he tightly controlled, eliminating all vestiges of civil society.

Stalin's successors reduced aspects of his reign of terror and created what became an oppressive but predictable communist system. Political scientists of the time debated extensively how centralized or pluralist this regime was. While it certainly was not pluralist in the democratic sense of the term, many observers argued that factions jockeyed for power and influence behind the scenes. Understanding how the regime actually functioned required far more than just understanding the Leninist beliefs on which it was founded. A new subfield of comparative politics emerged called

politburo
The chief decision-making organ in a communist party; China's politburo is a key example

"Kremlinology," in which experts looked for informal signs of who had real power. For instance, which officials were standing or sitting closest to the top leaders indicated who had the most influence at a particular moment. Pluralists and institutionalists argued that behind the façade of a totalitarian state and the complete absence of public debate, numerous factions battled to gain resources and power.

Stalin's policies had industrialized the economy, but the inefficiencies of central state control grew over time, and the wealth and productivity of the Soviet Union had declined compared with that of Western countries. By the mid-1980s, a new generation of leaders headed up by General Secretary Mikhail Gorbachev realized the Soviet Union had to try to increase economic productivity and allow a modicum of open political debate to survive. Gorbachev launched modest economic and political reforms that moved in that direction. Those reforms initiated a cycle of events over which Gorbachev eventually lost control. In August 1991, after the military's failed attempt at a coup d'état that was intended to restore some of the old order, the Soviet Union began to crumble. In December 1991, it officially ceased to exist, and fifteen separate states, including Russia, emerged once the dust had settled. This began the difficult process of regime change in Russia that we explore further in chapter 9.

The Russian Communist Party set the basic model of communist rule that was copied, with some modifications, in China and elsewhere after World War II. Only China, Cuba, Vietnam, and North Korea still maintain a claim to communism, and only North Korea fully maintains the centralized economic system that was at the heart of the effort. Cuba has experimented with limited liberalization of the economy, and China and Vietnam have essentially allowed capitalism to emerge. While still claiming to be communist, the latter two are in fact modernizing authoritarian regimes.

CASE Questions

1. No regime perfectly matches the ideology on which it is based. What are the most important ways in which the Soviet regime differed from Marxist ideology, and what explains those differences?
2. Can the problems that arose in the Soviet regime best be explained as the result of inherent flaws in Marxist ideology, flaws in Lenin's ideas, or flawed implementation of those ideas in this particular case?

Fascism

Fascism was the other major European alternative to liberal democracy in the early to mid-twentieth century. It was self-consciously both antiliberal and anticommunist. Fascist ideology conceives of society as being akin to a living organism rather than a set of disparate groups and individuals. The state is central to and dominant within this organic society; it regulates and ensures the smooth functioning of the organism, much as the brain does for the body. Italian fascist leader Benito Mussolini, in *Fascism: Doctrine and Institutions* (1933/1968), argued that "the State is all-embracing; outside of it no human or spiritual values can exist. . . . The Fascist State . . . interprets, develops, and potentiates the whole life of a people." He goes on to say that the state creates the nation (that is, the collective identity of the people), which is itself a "higher personal-ity." Fascists are thus intensely nationalistic, but they conceive of the nation as created by and loyal to the state first and foremost. Unlike liberals, who emphasize individual freedom, fascists argue that the individual is and should be subsumed within the state. Mussolini, for example, said the fascist "accepts the individual only in so far as his interests coincide with those of the State, which stands for the conscience and the universal will of man as a historic entity." Thus, the interests of the state are justifiably dominant over both individual citizens and civil society. This state, in turn, is led by one man who becomes the supreme leader and head of the state, which itself is both the head and the spirit of the nation. He rules on behalf of the entire "body" of society so that it can function properly.

Fascist belief in society as an organic whole leads to the argument that society should not have competing organizations that could potentially work against one another. Fascists reject the liberal notion of civil society as a sphere of voluntary orga-nizations independent of the state. Instead, just one organization, controlled by the state, should represent the interests of each component of society. This idea is known as **corporatism.** In fascist (and some other authoritarian) societies, the state creates one trade union to "represent" all workers—one business association, one farmers' association, one women's association, etc.—all tightly controlled by the state.

Fascists also reject Marxists' emphasis on materialism and economic life. Instead, Mussolini calls fascism "a spiritual attitude," describing a fascist life as "serious, austere, religious." Fascists reject much of the rationality that is the basis for most of Western philosophy, appealing instead to spiritual principles and traditions of a nation as a living organism. Fascist doctrine sees life as a struggle and proclaims a life of action. It views each nation as a unique and historical force that must work to maximize its power and position in the world, and it accepts war as a part of this struggle for the glorification of the state, the nation, and the leader.

Fascists share the modern conception of citizenship in the sense of a direct rela-tionship between citizens and a state. Like communists, however, they define citi-zens not as everyone legally in the state's territory but much more narrowly. Only those loyal to the state can be citizens, and even these citizens do not have rights in the liberal sense. Because individuals have no existence outside of the state, the concept of preexisting individual rights is nonsensical. Citizens are left only with duties, which they fulfill as part of achieving a more complete life. Fascists, like communists, thus justify the complete elimination of civil society, but in contrast to communists, Mussolini openly admitted that the fascist state was and should be totalitarian. Liberals, of course, reject fascism because they start from the premise that the individual exists independently of society and the state. Marxists would accept the

corporatism
System of representation in which one organization represents each important sector of society; two subtypes are societal and state corporatism

elimination of civil society and other restrictions of rights, but not in the name of the organic nation, which they view as detrimental to the real interest of the proletariat on whose behalf they claim to rule.

GERMANY: RISE OF THE NAZI PARTY AND A TOTALITARIAN STATE

CASE SYNOPSIS

Fascists came to power in the same era in Germany, Italy, Spain, and Portugal. Adolf Hitler created Nazi puppet regimes as well in the countries he conquered. Nazi rule followed the precepts of fascism, denying all individual rights in the name of the strength of the state and the glorification of the nation, defining citizenship in terms of who supported that effort, repressing opponents as necessary, and replacing an autonomous civil society with corporatist control. The Nazis, in contrast to most fascists, added explicit racism, especially vis-à-vis Jews, to their ideological justification. The horror of their rule delegitimized fascism the world over. While some regimes adopt certain fascist practices, and some political leaders are accused of having "neo-fascist" tendencies, virtually no major political leader openly espouses fascist ideology today.

- REGIME Nazism merged fascism and racism; totalitarian, but with internal factions
- CITIZEN AND STATE Citizenship based on race/nationality and support for Nazi regime
- CLAIM TO LEGITIMACY National/racial grandeur and state as head of organic society
- RECENT TRENDS Nazism delegitimizes fascism, but "neofascists" still exist

Fascists generally glorify the nation, but they do not explicitly proclaim one nation as inherently superior to all others. They also do not define the nation as being of one racial or cultural group. Under the leadership of Adolf Hitler, Germany's National Socialists (Nazis) married fascism and racism to claim that the German nation, defined in racial terms as "Aryan," was superior to all others and deserved to rule over them.

Germany's economy was in dire straits in the 1920s, due in part to its defeat in World War I and the subsequent war reparations. The Great Depression that started in 1929 made things even worse. Blaming the mainstream parties in power for their increasingly difficult lives, German voters began shifting their allegiance to the "radical" parties: the Communists and Nazis. By the 1932 election, the Nazis won 37 percent of the vote, the largest percentage of any party. Thus, Adolf Hitler did not grab power via a violent revolution or military coup; he was elected. Following the norms of Weimar's parliamentary democracy, Hitler became chancellor (the German equivalent of a prime minister), Germany's key leader of government. Because his party did not have a majority of seats in the Reichstag (the German parliament), he had to invite members of other parties to join his government to form a coalition. Members of the Nationalist Party, the chief mainstream conservative party, sympathized with enough of Hitler's goals to agree to be his partners in government. They believed that, despite Hitler's antidemocratic rhetoric and writings, they could use their influence in the government to keep him in check. They were wrong.

Shortly after Hitler became chancellor, the Reichstag burned to the ground. Hitler arrested a Communist activist and launched an anti-Communist campaign, claiming that a communist revolution threatened the nation. In reality, it is almost certain that the Nazis themselves burned the Reichstag to initiate their grab for total power. Hitler used the "emergency" to ban personal liberties, allowing him to arrest Communist members of the Reichstag as well as other opponents. After seeing what happened to the Communist legislators, members of the Reichstag, with Nazi Party militia surrounding the building, agreed to pass the Enabling Act that effectively eliminated the Reichstag's legislative powers, and a dictatorship was born. Hitler and his party immediately used this new law to ban all opposition parties and replace all trade unions with the party-controlled German Labor Front, beginning the process of creating the totalitarian state that fascist doctrine calls for.

Adolf Hitler among supporters in Bavaria. Fascists believe in a strong leader ruling the state, which would be the head of the corporate body of society. All German citizens were expected to obey and glorify the leader as symbol of the state and nation.

Photo12/UIG via Getty Images

Pluralists, however, argue that even this totalitarian state had factions within it. Some members of the National Socialist Party took the socialist part seriously, favoring government control of the economy to build a stronger nation. Hitler, however, sided with business in the interest of rapid economic growth. Early in June 1934, he had "radical elements" in the party, who wanted to institute actual socialism, murdered during the "Night of the Long Knives" (*Nacht der Langen Messer*). From then on, large industries worked relatively closely with the Nazis. They initially favored Hitler's elimination of trade unions and later benefited from heavy government investment in infrastructure and military production in the buildup to World War II. Just as was true behind the scenes in the Soviet Union, factions continued to exist within the Nazi regime, with fierce internal battles for power in various ministries. While the regime was as close as any has ever been to being fully totalitarian, factionalism nonetheless continued to exist.

Nazism combined fascism with racism, aimed primarily at Jews. The regime slowly and systematically implemented anti-Semitic policies, first encouraging boycotts of Jewish businesses and firing Jewish civil servants in 1933, then officially classifying people as Jewish and registering Germany's entire population by race in 1935. Jewish businesses were looted and burned during *Kristallnacht* ("Night of Broken Glass") in November 1937, and shortly thereafter, Jewish citizenship was eliminated and Jews were encouraged to emigrate from Germany to "purify" the state. The Holocaust did not begin in earnest until the start of World War II, when Jews could no longer flee in large numbers. By the end of the war approximately six million Jews had died at the hands of the Nazis and their allies across Europe. In addition to Jews and political opponents, the systematic killing included the sick and disabled who, according to the Nazis, could not contribute to the national good; homosexuals because they were considered "morally depraved"; members of various faiths other than the official, Nazified, German Evangelical Church because they were seen as denying the supremacy of fascism; and "gypsies" (Romanis) because they were seen as impure and flawed.

The horror of Nazi rule, and fascist rule in general, delegitimized fascist ideology the world over. No regime proclaims itself as fascist today. While small fascist political movements and parties exist, none that claims the name has any significant political influence. Many observers, however, argue that fascist tendencies exist in many countries. Parties that espouse a virulent nationalism, often defined on a cultural, racial, or religious basis and opposed to immigrants they see as threats to the "soul of the nation," are frequently termed **neofascist.** These groups usually deny the label, however. The best-known example of neofascism is France's National Front, led originally by Jean-Marie Le Pen. Le Pen argued that the greatest danger facing France is the immigration of Muslims, mainly from North Africa. He claimed that Muslim immigration is destroying the French nation, and he called for policies that would reward white French women for having more babies and would severely restrict or even eliminate immigration. Shockwaves rippled through France and much of Europe in 2002, when Le Pen came in second in the presidential election. Marine Le Pen succeeded her father as head of the National Front and toned down some of his rhetoric to try to broaden

neofascist
Description given to parties or political movements that espouse a virulent nationalism, often defined on a cultural, racial, or religious basis and opposed to immigrants as threats to national identity

the party's support. By 2014, the party came in first, with nearly a quarter of the vote, in elections for France's seats in the EU parliament, and achieved a similar result in elections for France's regional governments a year later. In the wake of the 2008–2009 global financial crisis, extreme right-wing, anti-immigrant parties that many see as neofascist made significant electoral gains in the Netherlands, Finland, Austria, Hungary, and Greece as well. In the United States in 2016, a number of commentators saw Republican President-elect Donald Trump as espousing neofascist ideas as well, including opposition to virtually all immigration, banning or registering groups based on their identity, and claiming that national strength was the greatest of virtues. While fascism is dead, many believe neofascism is not.

CASE Questions

1. Based on the German case, what seems to explain the rise of fascist regimes? Can you tie your answers to this question to some of the theories of political behavior discussed in chapter 1?
2. How could we best determine if contemporary extreme right parties such as the National Front are "neofascist"? What core principles would we look for to determine this? If we did believe a particular party fits this label, what should we do about it in a liberal democracy?

Modernizing Authoritarianism

While no regime currently uses fascism as an acceptable claim to legitimacy, the argument that the needs of the state and nation must take precedence over liberalism's individual rights remains common. Many regimes that arose after the end of colonial rule based their legitimacy on **modernizing authoritarianism**: their common claim to legitimacy was that they would modernize or "develop" their countries, and doing so required restricting or eliminating individual rights and elections. Modernizing authoritarianism is not as consciously elaborated as the other ideologies we have discussed, but it nonetheless appeals to a common set of precepts. Many postcolonial states are relatively weak, so the formal institutions based on modernizing authoritarianism may reveal less about how they actually rule than their informal institutions. All modernizing authoritarian regimes, however, share a set of core assumptions that underpin their official claim to legitimacy.

The first of these assumptions is that development requires the leadership of a "modern elite." In societies with relatively few highly educated people, the assumption is that power should be in the hands of those who understand the modern world and how to advance within it. They should be the ones who rule, at least until their societies are "ready" for democracy.

This assumption is an appeal to **technocratic legitimacy**, a claim to rule based on knowledge that was part of **modernization theory**. This theory of development

modernizing authoritarianism
A claim to legitimacy based the need to "develop" the country via the rule of a modernizing elite

technocratic legitimacy
A claim to rule based on knowledge or expertise

modernization theory
Theory of development that argues that postcolonial societies need to go through the same process that the West underwent in order to develop

argued that in order to develop, postcolonial societies needed to go through the same process of modernization that the West had undergone. Modernization theorists argued that the modern elite—a "new type of enterprising men" in the words of Walt Rostow (1960), one of the pioneers of the theory and a founder of the American foreign aid program—would lead the development process. Modernization theorists assumed, as we noted in chapter 1, that democracy would arise along with economic development. The leaders of the modernizing authoritarian regimes, however, recognized the contradiction between democracy and the idea that development requires the leadership of an educated elite. They believed that in a country in which a large percentage of the population was illiterate, democracy would not necessarily put the "right" people in power. In their eyes, this legitimized truncating democracy and limiting citizens' rights in favor of some form of authoritarian rule led by elites who claimed to have special leadership abilities based on their education.

The second common assumption of modernizing authoritarian regimes is that they can produce the benefits of "development." The word *development* means many things to many people (see chapter 11), but in political discourse throughout the postcolonial world since the 1950s, for most people it means creating a wealthy society like those in the West. For the poorest countries, this meant transforming poor, overwhelmingly agricultural societies into urbanized, industrialized societies with dramatically higher productivity and wealth. For middle-income countries, such as Brazil, development meant continuing the industrialization that had already started, "deepening" it from relatively low-technology to higher-technology and higher-productivity industries. All of this required the application of modern science and technology, which the educated and technocratic elite claimed to understand and be able to employ on behalf of the entire country. The goal, and the main justification for authoritarian rule, was development.

Development also required national unity, the third assumption underpinning these regimes. Postcolonial elites argued that achieving the Herculean task of "catching up" to the West necessitated unusual measures. Their countries did not have time for lengthy debates about what policies to pursue. Instead, the modern elite should take control to move the country forward. Debate and democracy had to wait until the "big push" for development was completed, or at least well underway.

All of these assumptions have faced severe criticism. Liberals reject the notion that individual rights must be subsumed in an effort to achieve greater collective ends. They also question the assumption that democracy is necessarily so divisive that effective policymaking cannot occur. Marxists, as noted in chapter 1, argue that modernizing authoritarian regimes really represent neocolonialism. The local ruling class is working in its own interests, not those of the country as a whole and, furthermore, works on behalf of global capitalist forces, which influence policy behind the scenes and against the interests of the poor majority. Fascists, on the other hand, would likely be more sympathetic to many of the arguments of modernizing authoritarianism, in that the two doctrines share the notion that national greatness requires restricting individual rights.

Tanzania's One-Party Regime

From the 1960s until the 1980s, the African state of Tanzania was an interesting example of a modernizing authoritarian one-party regime. Julius Nyerere, the president from 1962 to 1985, has been called Africa's "philosopher-king," in part because he was unusually self-conscious and explicit in justifying his regime. He argued that political parties in Western democracies are based primarily on social class divisions and that since Africa had few and minor class divisions, there was no need for opposing parties. He suggested that in Africa, "when a village of a hundred people have sat and talked together until they agreed where a well should be dug they have practised democracy" (1966). He thereby justified a one-party regime. His party, the Tanzanian African National Union (TANU), overwhelmingly won the country's first election on the eve of independence, and it didn't take much effort to change the constitution to legally eliminate the opposition.

In addition to his idea of "African democracy," Nyerere envisioned creating an "African socialism," dubbed *ujamaa* in Swahili. He argued that this would return the country to its precolonial origins, but with distinctly modern additions. The centerpiece of the effort was the creation of *ujamaa* villages in which Tanzanians would live and work communally. This arrangement would also facilitate the provision of more modern social services such as schools, health clinics, and clean water. While Nyerere justified *ujamaa* as a return to precolonial "traditions," it was in fact an example of a modernizing authoritarian regime in action. It distorted precolonial practices and postcolonial realities against the will of the people in the interests of "development." Nyerere's vision of precolonial Africa was historically inaccurate, and the rural majority had no interest in farming communally or moving into villages. Nyerere ultimately turned to force to create his vision; the state moved millions into new villages and tried to force communal labor. The results were disastrous for agricultural production and the country's economy, though the government was able to improve health care and education, achieving the amazing feat of nearly universal literacy in one of the world's poorest countries.

Nyerere's commitment to village democracy ultimately proved limited as well; public debate became more and more circumscribed over time. His twin goals of African democracy and African socialism were contradictory. The bulk of the population didn't support Nyerere's vision of African socialism; had they

Tanganyika African National Union (TANU) youth league members carry hoes in a parade in 1968. The youth league was an important element of the ruling party in Tanzania's modernizing authoritarian regime. The hoes symbolize agriculture, the backbone of the economy and key to the regime's claims to legitimacy based on "development."

ASSOCIATED PRESS

been able to exercise full democratic rights, they would have voted against it. Throughout TANU's rule, however, the party did hold parliamentary elections once every five years, allowing two party-approved candidates to compete for each seat. Though the candidates could not question the ruling party's overall policies, they could and did compete over the question of who would best represent the area, so the elections were fair, if not free.

By 1985, Nyerere realized that his vision had produced a bankrupt country and that the key economic policies would have to change. He resigned the presidency voluntarily, only the third African president ever to do so, rather than implement a reversal of his vision. In the 1990s and following the trend across the continent (see chapter 9), Nyerere argued in favor of opening the country to multiparty democracy, saying the time for one-party rule was over. The country did allow full legal opposition, starting with the election of 1995, but TANU (renamed CCM, Chama Cha Mapinduzi, or Party of the Revolution) continues to rule against only token opposition.

one-party regime
A system of government in which a single party gains power, usually after independence in postcolonial states, and systematically eliminates all opposition

military regime
System of government in which military officers control power

Modernizing authoritarianism has taken different institutional forms. The most common civilian form is the **one-party regime,** once common in Africa and Asia. In many of these countries, a single party gained power after independence and systematically eliminated all opposition in the name of development and national unity. These regimes eliminated all effective opposition. Some, such as Kenya and Côte d'Ivoire, achieved notable economic progress, while many others did not. **Military regimes** frequently took power in postcolonial states via coups d'état; they often justified elimination of the previous government in terms of modernizing authoritarianism. Often citing prolonged economic stagnation or growing social unrest as their impetus, military leaders argued that they would "clean up the mess" of the prior government and get the country at least started down the road to development before returning it to civilian and democratic rule. Brazil under military rule from 1964 to 1985 was a classic case of this type of regime.

CASE Study

BRAZIL: A MODERNIZING AUTHORITARIAN REGIME IN MILITARY FORM, 1964–1985

CASE SYNOPSIS

Brazil's modernizing authoritarian regime was one of the more conscious and committed, and emerged in one of the stronger postcolonial states. It elaborated a clear ideological justification for what it did, combining the need to further economic development with the need to fight communism during the Cold War. The military leaders saw themselves as a technocratic elite, and they hired civilian technocrats to augment their policy expertise. The elite believed democracy had to be suppressed because it would, at best, slow development and, at worst, lead to a communist takeover. The regime produced a period of rapid economic growth, but as that growth slowed in the late 1970s, regime legitimacy plummeted and the military was ultimately forced to allow a return to democracy.

- REGIME Modernizing authoritarian and military

- CITIZEN AND STATE Repressive, but not as severe as many in Latin America at the time

- CLAIM TO LEGITIMACY Modernization and anticommunism

- KEY INSTITUTIONS Military presidency; limited civilian opposition in legislature

- CONTEXT State-led industrialization produces "Brazilian Miracle"

Brazil emerged from World War II as a semi-industrialized economy and returned to being a democracy, albeit a very unstable one, with deep ideological and class tensions. When João Goulart became president in 1960, workers and the poor saw him as sympathetic to their cause, which emboldened them to organize street protests to claim a greater share of the fruits of development. This led to rising concern from business owners, landowners, and other conservatives, who organized their own counterdemonstrations. It was not long before the Brazilian military, with quiet support from the United States, decided that the instability threatened the country's development. Military officials overthrew Goulart and Brazil's democracy in a coup d'état in 1964.

The Brazilian military came to power at the height of the Cold War, just five years after Fidel Castro had led a communist revolution in Cuba. During the 1950s, it developed the National Security Doctrine, which argued that national security included encouraging economic development and protecting the country from domestic insurrection. It was a classic statement of modernizing authoritarian beliefs, but it added anticommunism to the common justifications for authoritarian rule and justified military involvement in particular by pulling those elements together under the rubric of "national security." The military regime suppressed independent unions and returned the country to the corporatist model that had been in place during the quasi-fascist regime of the 1930s. It then expanded industrialization via significant government investments in new industries, particularly in heavy industry such as auto manufacturing and airplanes. The regime explicitly claimed legitimacy on the basis of technocratic expertise and anticommunism, and brought many talented economists into the government to develop the new economic plan. The result came to be known as the "Brazilian Miracle," a period of particularly rapid economic growth that was at its zenith from 1967 to 1973. Despite this growth, however, much of the population remained mired in poverty, as inequality increased substantially.

The Brazilian military government certainly repressed its opponents as necessary to implement its economic model, though it was less repressive than were many

Brazil's military regime was less violent than its infamous neighbors in Chile and Argentina of the same period, but violence was certainly used to repress dissent, and student and worker protests were often targets. Here, police carrying pistols force rioting students to the ground in the 1960s.

Bettmann / Contributor

Latin American military governments. It allowed elections for a national congress but restricted competition to only two legal parties: the opposition party was limited in what it was allowed to say, the congress itself had little real power, and the military resorted to electoral tampering to maintain government party control. Ultimate decision making remained firmly in the hands of top military leaders.

By the late 1970s, increased oil prices had contributed to an economic slowdown across the country. Independent unions once again formed, in open violation of the law. Strikes became more common and had greater impact than before, given the rapid industrialization of the past two decades; there were now more industrial workers, and their industries were more important to the economy. Trade unions and political activists in the Catholic Church became more active in civil society, playing a key role in starting a movement for democracy that eventually brought Brazil's modernizing authoritarian regime to an end in 1985, when the first civilian president since 1964 took office. Modernizing authoritarianism stakes its claim to legitimacy on economic development; once that collapsed in Brazil, the regime was severely weakened.

CASE Questions

1. What similarities and differences are there between the military regime in Brazil and fascist regimes in Europe earlier in the century?
2. Compare the Brazilian case with the box above on the one-party regime in Tanzania during the same era. What common elements and what differences do you see? Does it make sense to think of both of them as "modernizing authoritarian"?

Personalist Regimes

personalist regime
System of government in which a central leader comes to dominate a state, typically not only eliminating all opposition but also weakening the state's institutions to centralize power in his own hands

Modernizing authoritarian regimes arose primarily in postcolonial states, many of which are relatively weak states with weak formal institutions. Informal institutions are therefore often quite important to understanding how these regimes function. In the very weakest states, **personalist regimes** often arose. In these regimes, few if any institutions constrained individual power. Power can thus be quite personalized, and the rule of law is inconsistent at best. Personalist regimes can arise via either one-party rule or military coup, but either way a central leader comes to dominate. Even the military or party that helped bring him to power will lose power vis-à-vis the individual leader. These leaders not only eliminate all opposition but also weaken the state's institutions even more in order to centralize power in their own hands. Mobutu Sese Seko of Zaire (now the Democratic Republic of the Congo) and Ferdinand Marcos of the Philippines were classic examples of personalist regimes. They often justify their rule by using the arguments of modernizing authoritarianism, but they rarely put those ideas into practice. Instead, the arguments are simply a fig-leaf to justify centralizing power in the hands of one leader and his closest confidants. They rarely achieve any real development. Actual practice and informal rule typically trump ideology and formal institutions.

Comparativists studying Africa have suggested that many personalist regimes are imbued with **neopatrimonial authority.** German sociologist Max Weber (1925/1978) defined "patrimonial" societies as those in which rule is based on reciprocal personal ties and favors, not bureaucratic institutions or formal laws. Many African regimes combine the trappings of modern, bureaucratic states with underlying informal patterns of patrimonial authority that work behind the scenes to determine real power; hence, the term *neopatrimonial.* Constitutions, laws, courts, and bureaucracies all exist, but power really derives mainly from personal loyalty, personal favors, and patronage. Patron-client relations are central in these regimes. Personalist rulers maintain their power by distributing patronage to their followers, who are personally loyal to the rulers. Politics becomes a competition among key patrons for access to the state's resources that they then distribute to their supporters. Neopatrimonial authority can exist to some degree in a variety of regimes but is the hallmark of personalist ones. Nigeria has had a series of military regimes but its last one, led by General Sani Abacha, was the only one to become a true personalist regime.

neopatrimonial authority
Power based on a combination of the trappings of modern, bureaucratic states with underlying informal institutions of clientelism that work behind the scenes; most common in Africa

CASE Study

NIGERIA: A PERSONALIST REGIME IN UNIFORM, 1993–1998

CASE SYNOPSIS

Nigeria had a weak state at independence, but its long period of military rule weakened it further. Over time, military rule, using massive oil wealth, fueled corruption and undermined institutions. The final military dictator, General Sani Abacha, created a truly personalist regime. He eliminated the remaining institutional constraints and ruled via whim, repressing his opponents far more brutally than earlier Nigerian military leaders had and engaging in massive corruption, a classic example of neopatrimonial authority. Though he claimed that he would put the country on a path to democracy, he successfully resisted all efforts in that direction until his untimely death, at which point other military leaders recognized the danger of such a personalist regime and helped establish the democratic regime that continues in power today.

- **REGIME** Personalist and military
- **CITIZEN AND STATE** Repression, and use of neopatrimonial authority via massive corruption
- **CLAIM TO LEGITIMACY** Restoring democracy
- **KEY INSTITUTIONS** Elimination of virtually all institutional constraints on personal power
- **CONTEXT** Prevented return to democracy until personalist ruler's sudden death

The last of Nigeria's six military coups d'état took place in November 1993. The country had been in turmoil since June, when the last military leader had annulled the results of what most observers saw as a free and fair election because his favored candidate lost. Northerners had led almost all of Nigeria's regimes, both civilian and military, in the country's regionally based political competition. A westerner had won the election, which the incumbent military leader found unacceptable. Instead of accepting the results, he appointed a hand-picked interim government headed by a civilian but with one of the top military leaders, General Sani Abacha, in the position of secretary of defense. Massive protests involving millions of Nigerians ensued over the next months, as the country demanded that the fairest elections in the country's history be respected. By November, Abacha overthrew the interim government in a bloodless coup, promising to restore democracy via yet another election in the next few years.

The military ruled Nigeria continuously from 1983 to 1999 (except for the four-month interim government in 1993), but under three leaders. Each one ruled in part via repression and neopatrimonial authority, using Nigeria's vast oil wealth to buy the support of other military leaders and many prominent civilians as well. Throughout

Nigerian soldiers keep pro-democracy demonstrators at bay in 1998. General Sani Abacha ruled Nigeria via a corrupt, personalist regime from 1993 to 1998. Via repression and corruption, he resisted a growing movement for democracy throughout his rule. Only after his death did the country establish a democratic regime, in place since 1999.

AP Photo

this era, the institutions of government declined as corruption rose. Abacha's rule was the final and most extreme stage of this long saga; institutional constraints disappeared almost completely as he created a truly personalist regime. By the time of his sudden death in 1998, even many military leaders were glad to see the end of the regime, and the military leadership that took power immediately promised and carried out democratic elections, ushering in the democratic regime still in power today.

While all of the country's military regimes had used repression as needed, they did not undermine all institutional constraints or eliminate all political expression. Abacha quickly proved himself much more ruthless, and the already atrophied institutions crumbled after he used corruption to co-opt both military and civilian leaders. Over his first two years in office, he eliminated much of the judiciary's autonomy and habeas corpus, assassinated or imprisoned numerous political opponents including the winner of the 1993 election, and banned many organizations. This culminated in the conviction by military tribunal and hanging of the famed poet and leader of the Ogoni ethnic movement, Ken Saro-Wiwa. Saro-Wiwa's death led to nearly universal international condemnation of the regime, which nonetheless ruled for another three years, until Abacha died of a heart attack.

Corruption was the other hallmark of Abacha's personalist regime. He and his closest associates looted the Nigerian treasury of an estimate $3 billion during his six years in power, some of which the subsequent democratic government was able to recover from British and Swiss banks. Neopatrimonial authority, of course, requires more than just stealing money for yourself; you have to use the state's resources to secure the loyalty of key political figures. In spite of the hotly contested 1993 election and protests, a number of prominent civilian politicians quickly agreed to serve in Abacha's government in exchange for opportunities for corruption themselves. As repression increased, both civilian and military political leaders faced the choice of being co-opted and thereby being able to gain great wealth, fleeing the country (which thousands did), or becoming victims of the repression. This choice is not unusual in the context of a fully personalist regime in which virtually no institutional constraints operate to protect people. Once the personalist dictator died unexpectedly, the complete lack of legitimacy for his regime resulted in a rapid transition to the democratic regime that remains in power today.

CASE Questions

1. How and why was Nigeria's military government different from Brazil's?
2. What elements of neopatrimonial authority do you see in Abacha's regime? How do you think a country can best begin to move away from this type of rule? Will creating a democracy, as Nigeria ultimately did, eliminate neopatrimonial authority?

Electoral Authoritarianism

Since the end of the Cold War and the wave of democratizations that followed, modernizing authoritarian regimes have become far less common. A related but distinct regime type, however, has become more common: **electoral authoritarian regimes.** These regimes "allow little real competition for power . . . [but] leave enough political space for political parties and organizations of civil society to form, for an independent press to function to some extent, and for some political debate to take place" (Ottaway 2003, 3). In electoral authoritarian regimes, opposition parties are allowed to exist and win some elected offices, but the ruling party manipulates electoral rules and processes enough to ensure that it maintains virtually all effective power. Such regimes typically allow some limited freedom of expression as well, but they ensure that this also does not threaten the ruling party's grip on power.

Some scholars have referred to electoral authoritarian regimes as "hybrid regimes" because they seem to combine some democratic and some authoritarian elements. This is clear ideologically: they attempt to legitimize themselves using a combination of democratic and modernizing authoritarian ideas. Unlike modernizing authoritarian regimes, they proclaim themselves democratic and point to democratic elements to justify this claim, in particular the presence of regularly scheduled elections (however flawed they are in practice). At the same time, electoral authoritarian regimes invoke ideas from modernizing authoritarianism as well, justifying limits on democracy as essential for national unity and development. This combination means that, as in modernizing authoritarian and personalist regimes, informal political institutions are often more important than formal institutions.

Electoral authoritarian regimes have become far more common in the last twenty years. This is undoubtedly due in part to the growing international acceptance of liberal democratic norms: in the post–Cold War and postcommunist world, it is no longer legitimate to proclaim a regime as purely authoritarian (of whatever ideology). Electoral authoritarian institutions—such as minimally competitive elections and a national legislature in which opposition parties are allowed to hold a few seats and, within limits, criticize the ruling party—provide a veneer of democratic legitimacy to regimes that in an earlier era might have been modernizing authoritarian. This is especially true in states that at least began a transition to democracy, typically in the 1990s. Full reversion to modernizing authoritarianism is unacceptable to the citizenry and the international community, and even the beginning of a transition to democracy usually unleashes popular pressure that the regime can better manage by allowing some limited opposition to exist, rather than repressing it entirely. Our case study of Russia is an example of this path to electoral authoritarian rule (see chapter 8). Mexico, however, shows that some electoral authoritarian regimes have been around much longer.

electoral authoritarian regime
Type of hybrid regime in which formal opposition and some open political debate exist and elections are held; these processes are so flawed, however, that the regime cannot be considered truly democratic

MEXICO

MEXICO: ELECTORAL AUTHORITARIANISM UNDER THE PRI

CASE SYNOPSIS

Though it existed long before the term was coined, Mexico's Institutional Revolution Party, or PRI (Partido Revolucionario Institucional), created a classic electoral authoritarian regime. The party's dominance was unquestioned for sixty years. Throughout, however, it held elections for the presidency and the lower house of the legislature that allowed internal elite competition and rotation of power across factions within the party. Opposition parties won a handful of seats but never enough to threaten the regime. This system provided a veneer of democratic legitimacy, and the PRI pursued policies that kept many workers and peasants loyal to it for decades. Like modernizing authoritarian regimes, the PRI based its legitimacy partly on the claim it was modernizing the country, and it achieved significant economic development (see chapter 11). This combination of claims to democratic and modernizing legitimacy under what was really authoritarian rule is the hallmark of electoral authoritarian regimes.

- REGIME Electoral authoritarian

- CITIZEN AND STATE Corporatism, clientelism, electoral fraud, and repression if necessary

- CLAIM TO LEGITIMACY Revolutionary nationalism and modernization

- KEY INSTITUTIONS Presidential power nearly unlimited for six years; regular elections and orderly succession

- RECENT TRENDS Transition to democracy, 1988–2000

deologically, the PRI claimed legitimacy partly on the basis of the legacy of the Mexican Revolution (1910–1920). While the revolution included many different leaders and groups with varying purposes, the bulk of its support came from its promises to end the extreme inequality of nineteenth- and early-twentieth-century Mexico. The PRI claimed it represented peasants, workers, and the downtrodden generally, and for a long time it maintained their loyalty and support. It mobilized that support, though, via clientelism and corporatism, and while it allowed official opposition, the PRI made sure that it won virtually every election in the name of the revolution.

The PRI traces its origins to President Plutarco Elías Calles (1924–1928), who used the party to remain influential without running for office again, given the state's commitment to the revolutionary slogan of "No Reelection," meaning that officeholders could not be reelected to subsequent terms. This insured that no individual would become permanently dominant, helping rotate power among elites within the party. The PRI's main electoral constituency has been referred to as a three-legged stool comprising laborers, peasants, and bureaucrats, though over time the party became more like a big tent that includes liberals, radicals, and even conservatives. This broad base increased the PRI's competitive edge and allowed it to poach potential rivals from opposition parties. Pitched battles did take place internally; power and the presidency shifted from radical to more conservative factions via elections every six years, but the party's control was never in doubt.

Throughout, the president remained the central and most powerful figure within both the state and the party apparatus. The president appointed the official leaders of the party as well as all governors and senators. Some early presidents such as Calles and Lázaro Cárdenas (1934–1940) remained influential even after leaving office, but the PRI eventually developed a system in which a president would govern unencumbered for one term and then retire from public life altogether. At the end of every six-year presidential term (called the *sexenio*), a new leader, chosen by his predecessor but reflecting the balance of power among factions within the party, would step in and take over the reins of the country.

While this system of orderly succession forestalled the emergence of a personalist regime, it came at great cost: Mexican presidents were known to take advantage of their limited time in office and guaranteed safe retirement to engage in widespread graft, and they encouraged their close associates to do the same. In addition, outgoing presidents often escalated government spending at the end of their term to facilitate the election of their successor, which resulted in predictable cycles of inflation at the start of each *sexenio*.

Despite its many problems, the electoral authoritarian regime remained in place thanks in part to robust control of and support from the Mexican Labor Confederation,

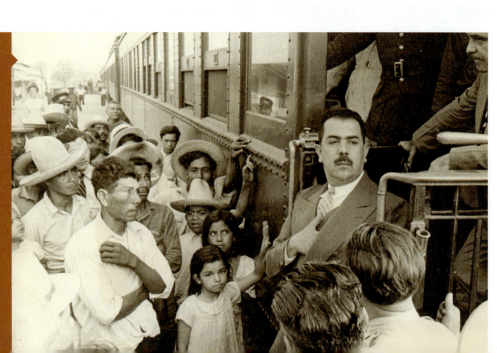

Lázaro Cárdenas (1934-1940) was the most important and famous Mexican president during the era of the PRI's electoral authoritarian state. He set the "populist" policy course for the party, helping it to create a sense of legitimacy based on its provision of patronage to core constituencies, especially unionized workers and peasants. His political and economic framework stayed in place, with minor changes, until the 1980s debt crisis forced the PRI to shift to a more open-market economy. This was the beginning of the end of the PRI's political dominance.

Bettmann / Contributor

or CTM (Confederación de Trabajadores de Mexico). Under a corporatist arrangement, the CTM became the overwhelmingly powerful labor union in Mexico and went so far as to organize militias capable of checking the military's power. The CTM, and a similar peasant union, mobilized support for the party in exchange for better working conditions and patronage.

The regime used clientelism, which at its most basic level took the form of vote buying, to maintain rural support. Between the end of the revolution and the start of World War II, the state engaged in large-scale land reform. By the 1970s, clientelism was exercised through massive government spending on agricultural development projects. This helped guarantee a loyal rural constituency that to this day remains the electoral backbone of the PRI.

When corporatism and clientelism were not enough to ensure the outcome of a vote—especially in the face of the mobilization capabilities of opposition forces among conservative Catholic activists and leftist students in the universities—the ruling party resorted to electoral fraud. Favorite tactics included stuffing ballot boxes, moving polling locations at the last minute, having supporters vote multiple times, and, if necessary, altering the numbers once the votes had been tallied.

Always concerned about maintaining the veneer of democratic legitimacy, electoral authoritarian regimes such as Mexico's prefer to maintain control via clientelism and behind-the-scenes electoral fraud rather than outright violence. If necessary, though, the PRI was not above using force to guarantee its rule. The most infamous example of this came when the military opened fire on antigovernment student protesters on October 2, 1968, in what came to be known as the Tlatelolco Massacre—days before the start of the Mexico City Olympics.

These strategies allowed the PRI to win 98 percent of all mayoral and congressional elections between 1946 and 1973. By the late 1980s, though, opposition parties began to make inroads that could no longer be ignored. Part of this shift was due to urbanization and free-market reforms, which made traditional clientelism more difficult to maintain. In 1988 Cuauhtémoc Cárdenas (son of former PRI president Lázaro Cárdenas) was part of a left-wing faction that defected from the PRI to form a new party in response to the government's increasingly market-oriented economic policies. Cárdenas ran for president and garnered 30 percent of the vote to the PRI's 52 percent (compare this with the 1976 election, in which the PRI trounced the opposition with 98.7 percent of the vote). To this day, many believe that Cárdenas, who claimed victory but was denied the presidency, was the actual winner at the polls. A year later, the conservative Partido Acción Nacional (PAN), or National Action Party, became the first opposition party to elect a governor.

Given the tense political climate that emerged following the closely contested and controversial 1988 election, the ruling party was forced to introduce concrete steps toward providing electoral fairness and broader representation in government. The first free election took place in 1994, though voters opted for continuity and bureaucratic experience, and gave the election to Ernesto Zedillo of the PRI. Although the PRI kept the presidency, the days of one-party rule were numbered. A new, democratic, three-party system emerged, and the PRI would have to compete alongside the others. In 2000 the election of the PAN's Vicente Fox finally broke the PRI's seventy-one-year monopoly on the presidency, ushering in a new era in Mexican politics. Unhappiness with the state of the economy, though, led Mexican voters in 2012 to put the PRI back in power under the leadership of new president Enrique Peña Nieto, but this time the party is in power freely and fairly in a democratic regime. Critics contend, however, that continuing violence under Peña Nieto has restricted the press and other freedoms, reflected in Freedom House shifting Mexico's status from "free" to "partly free."

CASE Questions

1. Electoral authoritarian regimes typically base their legitimacy on a combination of nondemocratic and democratic claims. What were the most important bases of legitimacy for the PRI-led regime, and how democratic were these claims?
2. Understanding most regimes requires understanding both formal and informal institutions. How important were the two types of institutions in understanding the key elements of Mexico's regime? Do formal or informal institutions seem more important, and why?

Theocracy

theocracy
Rule by religious authorities

Theocracy is rule by religious authorities. They rule on behalf of God and following His dictates. It's very unlikely that you would have found theocracy included in a textbook on comparative politics forty years ago. If it were mentioned at all, it would have been in connection with the "divine right of kings" of medieval and early modern Europe under which the monarchy was thought to represent God on Earth, sanctioned as such by the universal Catholic Church. Today, the prime example of theocracy is not Christian but Muslim. Like other kinds of regimes, the Muslim theocracy in Iran is based on a well-elaborated political ideology. Iran currently is the world's only true theocracy, but political movements aimed at achieving similar regimes exist throughout the Muslim world. Some other countries, such as Saudi Arabia, have monarchies that are closely tied to and in part legitimized by Islamic religious authority, but their primary basis for legitimacy is the monarchy itself. We focus on Islamic theocracy as an ideology and regime type not because it is the only conceivable kind of theocracy but because it is the only contemporary example of a theocratic regime and because theocratic political ideology is an important challenger to liberal democracy today.

The political ideology that has inspired such fear in much of the West and such admiration in some of the Muslim world is typically known as "Islamic fundamentalism," a name that implies a set of ideas that is often quite different from what its adherents actually believe. The word *fundamentalist* implies "traditional" to many people, but nothing could be further from the truth in this case. "Traditional" Islamic beliefs, as developed over the centuries, hold that religious law ought to be the basis for government, but in practice local cultural traditions and rulers compromised these precepts significantly. In many countries in the twentieth century, traditional Muslim religious authorities compromised with modernity and the increasing secularization of the state by withdrawing from politics nearly completely and quietly accepting secular, modernizing authoritarian regimes. Indeed, many Islamists argue that the rise of a new, politicized Islamic movement over the past century is in large part a reaction to Western imperialism; it is not at all "traditional," but rather a reaction to twentieth-century events (Abu-Rabi 2010). Bassam Tibi (2012) says it involves "the invention of tradition" rather than the re-creation of an actual tradition.

Given this reality, most scholars prefer the term **Islamism** instead of *Islamic fundamentalism*. While it has many variations, Islamism is generally defined as a belief that Islamic law, as revealed by Allah to the Prophet Mohammed, can and should provide the basis for government in Muslim communities, with little equivocation or compromise with other beliefs or laws. Islamism arose in the nineteenth and twentieth centuries with the goal of "purifying" Muslim society of the creeping influences of the West and secularism that traditional Muslim religious leaders had often been willing to accept. In line with this, most Islamists explicitly reject the Muslim concept of *taqlid,* the acceptance of all past legal and moral edicts of the traditional clergy, and instead embrace *ijtihad,* the belief that Muslims should read and interpret the original Islamic texts for themselves. They base their ideology on their interpretation of the Quran and Sunnah, the two holiest books of Islam, and take as their primary model the seventh-century Muslim society and state created by Mohammed and his immediate followers. Islamists vary in the degree to which they are willing to compromise with aspects of the contemporary world. Not all, for instance, support stoning as punishment for adultery, but most adhere to a fairly strict belief in Muslim law, **sharia**. Past compromises by traditional clergy are therefore unacceptable.

Islamists believe that sovereignty rests with Allah, so they ultimately reject democracy and its idea of popular sovereignty. Some, however, such as the early Palestinian leader Taqi al-Din al-Nabhani (1905–1978), reserve a place for *shura*, which means "consultation with the people." He believed the Muslim state should be led by a caliph, a supreme religious and political leader, but that the caliph should be acceptable to the population as a whole and be advised by an elected council. Some religious authorities have since used this concept to argue in favor of allowing an ideologically limited civil society, one that stays within the bounds of Islamic practices,

Islamism
The belief that Islamic law, as revealed by God to the Prophet Mohammed, can and should provide the basis for government in Muslim communities, with little equivocation or compromise

sharia
Muslim law

ideas, and law. Much debate has arisen over how compatible Islamism is with democracy (Tibi 2012), but those who argue that the two can be combined base that argument on the concept of *shura*. Some Islamists, such as the Muslim Brotherhood in Egypt, have been willing to go a step further and participate in democracy as a means of gaining power. After the "Arab Spring" overthrew the regime of Hosni Mubarak, the Brotherhood created a political party and won the first presidential election, though it was overthrown in a military coup in 2013. Other Islamists reject the notion of democracy altogether, maintaining that any compromise with democracy violates Allah's sovereignty. Our case study of Iran shows the tension between the sovereignty of Allah and the idea of *shura*.

jihad
Derived from an Arabic word for "struggle" and an important concept in Islam; the Quran identifies three kinds of *jihad*

As the electoral participation of some groups demonstrates, while all Islamists place great significance on *jihad*, not all advocate violence. *Jihad* means "struggle," and, although it is not one of the "five pillars" of the faith, it is an important concept in Islam. The Quran identifies three kinds of *jihad*. The first and most important is the individual's internal struggle to renounce evil and live faithfully. The second is the struggle of the individual to right evils and injustice within the *umma,* the Muslim community. The third and least important is protection, armed and violent if necessary, of the *umma*. The most radical Islamists argue that the *umma* is under attack externally from the West and internally via secularization and Westernization. For groups like Al Qaeda and the Islamic State, this justifies violence outside and within the *umma*. Furthermore, following *ijtihad,* these individuals reject the traditional teaching that violent *jihad* should only be carried out on the orders of high religious authorities. They argue instead that individuals, and religiously untrained leaders like Osama bin Laden, can discern for themselves when and where violent *jihad* is not only a justifiable option but a moral necessity.

Although Iran's Muslim regime is a recent development and the sole contemporary version of theocracy today is Islamic, theocracy is one of the oldest forms of government still in existence. Islamists believe in giving sovereignty not to "we the people" but rather to Allah. They vary widely, however, in the methods they use to achieve Islamist regimes and in the details of what those regimes would look like. Liberal critics reject this notion of sovereignty from God, and Marxists famously reject the concept of God altogether. Fascists might have some sympathy with the idea of a strong central ruler governing on behalf of all, but the goal for fascists would not be to follow God's will but to strengthen the nation. Islamist philosophers and ideologues have created many variants of Islamist regimes in the abstract, but only one has gained power and ruled for a sustained period: Iran's revolutionary Islamic government.

THE ISLAMIC REPUBLIC OF IRAN: THEOCRATIC STATE, 1979–

CASE SYNOPSIS

Iran's Ayatollah Khomeini helped create the first true theocracy in the modern world. It follows Shiite Islamist principles and includes some democratic elements justified via the concept of *shura*. The power of those democratic elements, however, has varied over time. Khomeini's death allowed stronger reformist movements and politicians to emerge in the 1990s. Conservative clergy have since used the religious institutions that the revolution created to frustrate reforms and preserve what they see as the pure path of the Islamist regime. Since the election of reformist president Hassan Rouhani in 2013, conservative and reformist forces have contended in an uneven seesaw for influence over the regime.

- REGIME Theocracy, but tension between theocratic and democratic elements
- CITIZEN AND STATE Islamist faithful only; democratic space and participation vary over time
- CLAIM TO LEGITIMACY Sovereignty of Allah under Shiite Islam
- KEY INSTITUTIONS Supreme leader; secular president and limited parliament
- RECENT TRENDS Growing repression, but reformist electoral victories in 2013 and 2016

slam in Iran is unusual in that the vast majority of the country's population and major religious authorities are Shiites, not Sunnis. In the seventh century, Islam split over the succession to the Prophet Mohammed. Those who became Shiite believe the Prophet's son-in-law, Imam Ali, was the rightful heir to the leadership of the *umma* and that descendants of Imam Ali remain the only rightful religious authorities. Major Shiite religious authorities are chosen from among those who can claim to be his heirs. Sunnis, who constitute approximately 85 percent of the world's Muslims, believe that any religiously educated person of appropriate stature and training can become a major leader of the *umma*, and they reject the claim that a particular bloodline should rule. Iran and Iraq are two of only four Muslim countries with Shiite majorities; Iran is nearly all Shiite. The Islamic Republic in Iran nonetheless exemplifies the ideology and contradictions of Islamist theocracy more broadly.

Prior to 1979, Iran had a modernizing authoritarian regime under the leadership of the Pahlavi dynasty; father and then son ruled the country from 1925 to 1979. The dynasty, however, kept whatever benefits came out of this modernization for itself and its close supporters, and domestic opposition mounted. One of the country's major religious leaders, Ayatollah Ruhollah Khomeini, emerged as a major spokesperson and leader of this opposition. Jailed and later forced into exile in neighboring Iraq and then France, Khomeini was the symbol and most popular leader of the revolution that swept the shah from power in 1978–1979 (see chapter 7). His Islamist ideals became the basis for the new government.

Khomeini's most original contribution to Islamist doctrine was the concept of the supreme leader. He argued that one leader with enough religious authority and popular support should be the ultimate guide of the Islamic state, with the power to veto any law. Khomeini also believed, however, in consultation, or *shura*, and so was quite willing to allow the existence of an elected parliament, the Majlis, as long as its laws were subject to the approval of the supreme leader or other clergy he might deputize to fulfill that function. Because of this, tensions between theocratic legitimacy, resting in clerical authority, and quasi-democratic elements such as elections have characterized the regime since its beginning. A new constitution in December 1979 established Iran as an Islamic Republic that specifically followed Shiite doctrine and declared Allah as sovereign. Khomeini became the supreme leader and a Guardian Council of twelve clergy was formed as his main watchdogs over the government. The council must approve or veto every law the parliament passes, as well as approve all candidates for office. A directly elected president administers the government on a daily basis. While the constitution preserved the pre-Islamic court system, *sharia* became the sole source of law and clergy head all major courts. Clergy also monitor all of the president's cabinet ministers, who are in charge of the various departments of the government.

Women vote in Iranian parliamentary elections in April 2016. The elections saw a significant increase in reformist candidates getting elected, the latest shift in Iran's long battle between conservatives based primarily in the clergy and security apparatus, and reformers in office via elections.

ATTA KENARE/AFP/Getty Images

The regime is clearly theocratic, since supreme religious authorities can ultimately make or unmake any governmental decision. Some democratic elements have been allowed, however. Regular elections for president and parliament have been held on schedule since the regime's beginning (see chapter 8). Nonetheless, the Guardian Council can disapprove any candidate for office who is deemed not adequately committed to the goals of the Islamic revolution, which has meant the degree of openness of the elections has varied greatly. In the first parliamentary election in 1980, a large number of parties competed and entered parliament, and a "moderate" won the presidency. He claimed commitment to the revolution but also took a practical stance toward modifying Islam to meet the necessities of running a modern state. By 1983 Khomeini forced him and other moderates out of office and in 1986 banned all parties, arguing that they were divisive. Informally, he allowed factions to continue to exist, but the elimination of all parties kept opposition forces repressed.

As real political options narrowed and the power of the Majlis vis-à-vis the Guardian Council declined, elections excited less interest and voter turnout dropped. A decade later, in the late 1990s, elections again became exciting and popular after the clergy allowed another moderate reformer, Mohammad Khatami, to run for president. Following his election, however, the clergy proceeded to frustrate virtually every reform effort he undertook and made sure that a candidate more loyal to them, Mahmoud Ahmadinejad, won the election of 2005. Ahmadinejad was reelected in what most observers believe to have been a fraudulent election in 2009, which was followed by massive street protests, several deaths, and thousands of arrests of regime opponents. In 2013 a somewhat more moderate candidate, Hassan Rouhani, was elected president, though he was far more deferential to the ruling clergy than Khatami had been a decade earlier. In 2016 a significant number of reformist candidates were elected to the Assembly of Experts, which will choose the next supreme leader, when the current one dies, and the parliament, raising hopes that greater reforms might be possible.

Despite some periods of greater openness, citizen ability to voice opinions and engage in political activity has been quite limited. When allowed, a very active press has emerged, but whenever this press begins to question the goals of the revolution beyond certain limits, religious authorities close it down, and a period of repression sets in. Nonetheless, the country has seen growing pressure for change and a more active civil society than is present in many Middle Eastern countries.

CASE Questions

1. How important are democratic elements in Iran's theocratic regime? Compare these to the democratic elements in Mexico's electoral authoritarian regime: Which of the two seems to give greater power to democratic institutions such as elections?
2. Does it make sense to categorize the Iranian regime as theocratic, or should it be considered electoral authoritarian instead? Why do you answer as you do?

CONCLUSION

All political ideologies involve the question of the proper relationship between individual citizens and the state. Most citizens of established democracies probably consider liberal democracy's insistence on limited state power and citizens' rights, especially the right to participate in politics through voting, as the presumptive norm. Liberal democracy, however, is an outlier in this regard. Communism, fascism, modernizing authoritarianism, electoral authoritarianism, and theocracy all tilt the balance in varying degrees in favor of the state. Each finds some grounds for arguing that government should not rest in the hands of citizens or elected representatives alone. Most ideologies offer some sort of rationale for giving a select group, whether it's the working class, the fascist state itself, or a technocratic or religious elite, more say and limiting the participation of others. In these ideologies, real citizenship is thus restricted to members of the key party, those loyal to the nation, those capable of helping the country achieve development, or those who are part of the faithful. This was true for much of liberalism's history as well, of course, as male property owners were the sole citizens. Despite this history, all long-standing liberal regimes have been democratized over the last century as the formal rights of citizenship have expanded to include virtually all adults.

The question of who actually has power, though, may be less clear than formal ideological differences suggest. Pluralist theorists have argued that in almost all regimes, even some of the most totalitarian, factions exist. Elites clearly rule, but they do not rule in a fully united manner. They are divided into factions that vie for power, resources, and influence, often behind the façade of a united and repressive regime. And critics argue that elites often control real power in liberal democracies as well, despite widespread formal rights. Liberal equality of citizenship may exist legally, but it never exists in reality, even where fairly extensive social rights are practiced. The sharp distinctions between liberalism and its ideological alternatives may be less in practice than they are in theory.

Ideology offers what regimes hope is a compelling justification for their actions and often serves as a blueprint on which their formal institutions are based, but regimes rarely abide strictly by their ideologies. Democracies vary in their institutional structures, for instance, and even the most established ones have only relatively recently granted full citizenship rights to all adult citizens regardless of gender or race. Similarly, communist regimes modified Marx's ideal of rule by the proletariat in favor of Lenin's concept of rule by the vanguard party. In weaker, postcolonial states, some modernizing authoritarian regimes have failed to meet their own goals of technocratic government, or personalist regimes have ruled in the interests of the key leadership with only a façade of ideological legitimacy. In these regimes, informal institutions often explain more about how a regime actually works than the official ideology does. In other instances, practical circumstances make leaders choose paths that diverge from their own stated ideology, as when Lenin espoused the New Economic Policy.

Because ideology alone does not explain how regimes arise and function, comparativists have used a wide array of theories to examine regimes. Political culture theorists, for instance, have argued that the first communist dictatorship emerged in Russia in part because of the long-standing authoritarian elements in Russian political culture, bred under centuries of tsarist rule. Marxists, of course, use their structural theory to explain the rise of particular regimes, arguing that ideology is simply a mask to justify class dictatorships of various sorts: liberal democracy emerged to serve the interests of the bourgeoisie and foster capitalism; modernizing authoritarian regimes further neocolonialism and the interests of both the budding capitalist elites in postcolonial societies and global corporations. Institutionalists, on the other hand, argue that what matter most are not just regimes' ideological blueprints but how well developed their formal institutions are—and, therefore, how important informal institutions and practices are. Ideology is important to understanding regimes' claims to legitimacy, but understanding why certain regimes arose in certain places and how they actually govern requires far more, which we discuss at length later in the book. First, though, we turn to another crucial issue for modern states: their relationship to identity groups.

KEY CONCEPTS

citizen (p. 100)

civil rights (p. 101)

corporatism (p. 119)

dictatorship of the proletariat (p. 114)

electoral authoritarian regime (p. 132)

historical materialism (p. 113)

Islamism (p. 137)

jihad (p. 138)

liberal democracy (p. 109)

military regime (p. 126)

mode of production (p. 114)

modernization theory (p. 123)

modernizing authoritarianism (p. 123)

neofascist (p. 122)

neopatrimonial authority (p. 129)

one-party regime (p. 126)

parliamentary sovereignty (p. 112)

participatory democracy (p. 110)

personalist regime (p. 128)

politburo (p. 117)

political rights (p. 101)

regime (p. 99)

sharia (p. 137)

social contract theory (p. 106)

social democracy (p. 109)

social rights (p. 101)

technocratic legitimacy (p. 123)

theocracy (p. 136)

totalitarian state (p. 115)

vanguard party (p. 116)

Sharpen your skills with SAGE edge at **edge.sagepub.com/orvis4e.**
SAGE edge for students provides a personalized approach to help you accomplish your coursework goals in an easy-to-use learning environment.

WORKS CITED

Abu-Rabi, Ibrahim M. 2010. "Editor's Introduction." In *The Contemporary Arab Reader on Political Islam*, edited by Ibrahim M. Abu-Rabi, vii–xxv. New York: Pluto Press.

Acemoglu, Daron, and James A. Robinson. 2006. *Economic Origins of Dictatorship and Democracy*. Cambridge, UK: Cambridge University Press.

Elkins, Zachart, Tom Ginsburg, and James Melton. 2014. "The Content of Authoritarian Constitutions." In *Constitutions in Authoritarian Regimes*, edited by Tom Ginsburg and Alberto Simpser, 141–164. Cambridge, UK: Cambridge University Press.

Keck, Margaret E., and Kathryn Sikkink. 1998. *Activists beyond Borders: Advocacy Networks in International Politics*. Ithaca, NY: Cornell University Press.

Lister, Michael, and Emily Pia. 2008. *Citizenship in Contemporary Europe*. Edinburgh, UK: Edinburgh University Press.

Marshall, T. H. 1963. *Class, Citizenship, and Social Development: Essays*. Chicago: University of Chicago Press.

Marx, Karl, and Friedrich Engels. 1888. *The Communist Manifesto*. Translated by Samuel Moore with Friedrich Engels. London: William Reeves Bookseller. (Originally published as *Manifest der Kommunistischen Partei* in London in 1848.)

Moore, Barrington, Jr. 1966. *Social Origins of Dictatorship and Democracy: Lord and Peasant in the Making of the Modern World*. Boston: Beacon Press.

Mussolini, Benito. 1968. *Fascism: Doctrine and Institutions*. New York: Howard Fertig. (Originally delivered as address to National Cooperative Council, Italy, in 1933.)

Nyerere, Julius K. 1966. *Freedom and Unity: Uhuru Na Umoja; A Selection from Writings and Speeches, 1952–65*. London: Oxford University Press.

O'Donnell, Guillermo A. 1979. *Modernization and Bureaucratic-Authoritarianism: Studies in South American Politics*. Text ed. Berkeley: Institute of International Studies, University of California.

Ottaway, Marina. 2003. *Democracy Challenged: The Rise of Electoral Authoritarianism*. Washington, DC: Carnegie Endowment for International Peace.

Polity IV Project. 2010. "Political Regime Characteristics and Transitions, 1800–2009" (http://www.systemicpeace.org/polity/polity4.htm).

Rostow, W. W. 1960. *The Stages of Economic Growth: A Non-Communist Manifesto*. Cambridge, UK: Cambridge University Press.

———. 2009. "The Contingent Power of Authoritarian Elections." In *Democratization by Elections: A New Mode of Transition*, edited by Staffan I. Lindberg, 291–313. Baltimore, MD: Johns Hopkins University Press.

Tarrow, Sidney G. 1998. *Power in Movement: Social Movements and Contentious Politics*. New York: Cambridge University Press.

Tibi, Bassam. 2012. *Islamism and Islam*. New Haven, CT: Yale University Press.

Weber, Max. 1978. *Economy and Society*. Edited by Guenther Ross and Claus Wittich. Berkeley: University of California Press. (Originally published as *Wirtschaft und Gesellschaft* in Germany in 1925.)

RESOURCES FOR FURTHER STUDY

Brownlee, Jason. 2007. *Authoritarianism in an Age of Democratization*. Cambridge, UK: Cambridge University Press.

Dahl, Robert A. 1971. *Polyarchy: Participation and Opposition*. New Haven, CT: Yale University Press.

Esposito, John L. 1997. *Political Islam: Revolution, Radicalism, or Reform?* Boulder, CO: Lynne Rienner.

Held, David. 1996. *Models of Democracy.* 2nd ed. Stanford, CA: Stanford University Press.

Husain, Mir Zohair. 2003. *Global Islamic Politics.* 2nd ed. New York: Longman.

Marx, Karl, and Friedrich Engels. 1978. *The Marx-Engels Reader.* Edited by Robert C. Tucker. 2nd ed. New York: Norton.

McCann, James A., and Jorge I. Domínguez. 1998. "Mexicans React to Electoral Fraud and Political Corruption: An Assessment of Public Opinion and Voting Behavior." *Electoral Studies* 17 (4): 483–503. doi:10.1016/S0261-3794(98)00026-2

Mill, John Stuart. 1870. *The Subjection of Women.* New York: D. Appleton.

Pitcher, Anne, Mary H. Moran, and Michael Johnston. 2009. "Rethinking Patrimonialism and Neopatrimonialism in Africa."

African Studies Review 52 (1): 125–156. doi:10.1353/arw.0.0163

Roy, Olivier. 2004. *Globalized Islam: The Search for a New Ummah.* CERI Series in Comparative Politics and International Studies. New York: Columbia University Press.

Sargent, Lyman Tower. 1987. *Contemporary Political Ideologies: A Comparative Analysis.* 7th ed. Chicago: Dorsey Press.

Schedler, Andreas, ed. 2006. *Electoral Authoritarianism: The Dynamics of Unfree Competition.* Boulder, CO: Lynne Rienner.

Sherman, John W. 2000. "The Mexican 'Miracle' and Its Collapse." In *The Oxford History of Mexico,* edited by Michael C. Meyer and William H. Beezley, 537–568. Oxford, UK: Oxford University Press.

Suchlicki, Jaime. 2008. *Mexico: From Montezuma to the Rise of the PAN.* 3rd ed. Washington, DC: Potomac Books.

WEB RESOURCES

CIRI Human Rights Data Project
(http://www.humanrightsdata.com)
United States Citizenship, Involvement, Democracy (CID) Survey
(http://www.icpsr.umich.edu/icpsrweb/civicleads/studies/4607)
DataGov, Governance Indicators Database
(http://infor.worldbank.org/governance/wgi/index.aspx#home)
Freedom House, Freedom in the World Survey
(https://freedomhouse.org/report/freedom-world-2016/table-scores)

4 STATES AND IDENTITY

KEY QUESTIONS

- How and why do identity groups form and become politically salient?
- How does the social construction of identity groups influence who has power?
- What are the implications of identity groups' demands on the ideal of equal citizenship in the modern state?
- What are the different political issues faced by different types of identity groups?

The great political battle of the second half of the twentieth century was between liberalism and communism, but nationalism won. Nationalist, ethnic, and religious movements seemed to be the main beneficiaries of the fall of communism, and they emerged as the greatest challenges to democracy. Since the end of the Cold War, an internationalist Islamist movement has gained strength in many countries, a number of countries in the former Soviet sphere have been wracked by ethnically based political battles, and full-scale genocide has occurred in Bosnia and Rwanda. From the battles to create new governments in Iraq and Afghanistan to secessionist struggles in Chechnya and Ukraine to debates over same-sex marriage in many countries, "identity politics" has come to the fore.

Comparativists studied political conflicts based on identity long before the post–Cold War era. As we noted in chapter 2, states and nations are intimately connected. Internationally, the state is seen as the representative and voice of the nation. Domestically, political leaders can gain legitimacy and power by proclaiming their nationalism and castigating their opponents as "traitors" to the nation. As modern states developed, many actively championed the creation of nations over which to rule. This process usually involved attempts to homogenize a disparate populace, which often led to the exclusion of certain groups from the "nation"

University students in the Philippines march under a pride flag in support of gay rights. Gay rights movements are spreading rapidly in postcolonial countries around the world.

NOEL CELIS/AFP/Getty Images

or the rise of movements that claimed an identity distinct from the "nation" that the state was proclaiming.

We noted in chapter 3 that groups based on some sense of common identity are only one of many kinds of political groups, but they often have a particularly intense hold on people's loyalties. Few people would risk their lives defending the Sierra Club or Chamber of Commerce, but everyone is expected to do so for their nation, and many would do so for

their ethnic or religious group as well. The potential for this ultimate political commitment means that states must and do care deeply about identity politics. All states seek to develop and gain legitimacy from some sense of identity, but the "wrong" identity can be the gravest threat a state can face.

Even when identity groups, such as women's or gay rights movements, do not threaten the existence of a state, they still raise fundamental questions about equal citizenship, particularly about individual versus group rights. States throughout the world have created new policies to try to address these concerns, and globalization has meant that even states with very little open political space or only weak demands for change have nonetheless felt pressure to address at least some of these issues.

COUNTRY AND CONCEPT
Ethnicity, Race, Religion, Gender, and Sexuality

Country	Largest ethnic/ racial group, % of population	Index of ethnic fractionalization*	Major modern, identity-based, violent conflicts	Gender Inequality Index (2014)	% of respondents who say, "I am a religious person" †	% of respondents who say that "homosexuality is never justifiable" ‡‡
Brazil	White, 47.7%; Mulatto (mixed white and black), 43.1%	0.5408	None	0.997	79.70%	34.30%
China	Han Chinese, 91.6%	0.1538	Uyghur dispute, 1949– Tibetan dispute, 1959–	0.943	12.50%	49.40%
Germany	German, 91.5%	0.1682	Nazi repression of Jews/ Holocaust, 1933-1945	0.963	49.50%	17.80%
India	Hindi, 41%	0.4182	• India/Pakistan partition, 1947-1948 • Kashmir dispute, 1947– • Hindu-Muslim conflicts/ riots, 1950–(intermittent) • Sikh independence movement, 1960s-1984	0.795	88.80%	73.10%
Iran	Persian, 61%	0.6684	Islamic Revolution, 1978-1979	0.858	80.80%	81.30%
Japan	Japanese, 98.5%	0.0119	None	0.961	20.90%	17.60%
Mexico	Mestizo, 62%	0.5418	Chiapas Rebellion, 1994–	0.943	74.20%	39.10%
Nigeria	Hausa and Fulani, 29%	0.8505	• Biafran civil war, 1967-1970 • Ogoni and related movements, 1993– • Muslim-Christian battles over sharia, 1999–(intermittent); Boko Haram Islamist group	0.841	95.90%	63.90%

Russia	Russian, 77.7%	0.2452	• War of Transniestira, 1990–1992 • Chechen Wars, 1994–1996, 1999–	1.019	53.10%	54.10%
United Kingdom	White British, 87.2%	0.1211	Northern Ireland nationalist movement, 1921–1998	0.965	47.20%	18.10%
United States	White alone, 79.96%	0.4901	• Civil War with slavery as key issue, 1861–1865 • Urban race riots, 1965–1968	0.995	67.00%	24.00%

Source: Data are from the most recent country census results, the *CIA World Factbook*, the United Nations (http://hdr.undp.org/sites/default/files/2015_human_development_report.pdf), and the World Values Survey. Ethnic fragmentation data are from Alberto Alesina et al., "Fractionalization," *Journal of Economic Growth* 8, no. 2 (2003): 155–194. http://www.nsd.uib.no/macrodataguide/set.html?id=16&sub=1, Updated November 11, 2011.

*0 = perfectly homogeneous and 1 = highly fragmented.

† = World Values Survey question: "Independently of whether you attend religious services or not, would you say you are:" Percentages listed are indicative of those who agreed that they are "a religious person." Selected samples: Brazil 2014, China 2012, Germany 2013, India 2012, Japan 2010, Mexico 2012, Nigeria 2011, Russia 2011, United States 2011, Iran 2005, United Kingdom 2006.

†† = World Values Survey question: "Please tell me for each of the following actions whether you think it can always be justified, never be justified, or something in between:" a range of 0–10. The percentages listed here are indicative of respondents who agreed that homosexuality is never justifiable. Selected samples: Brazil 2014, China 2012, Germany 2013, India 2012, Japan 2010, Mexico 2012, Nigeria 2011, Russia 2011, United States 2011, Iran 2005, United Kingdom 2006.

These groups and debates raise a number of important questions in comparative politics. First, why do these identities emerge and become politically important in the first place? Second, what can the policy outcomes of debates over the place of identity groups tell us about who rules? Why do particular groups make the demands they do, and why do governments respond as they do to those demands? Equal citizenship is central to at least the ideal of the modern state, but do these groups' demands indicate a failure to achieve that ideal? We examine all these questions below, looking at identity groups based on nationalism, ethnicity, religion, gender, and sexual orientation.

The Country and Concept table above portrays the ethnic, racial, and religious diversity; status of women; attitudes toward gay rights; and the major conflicts that have arisen from that diversity in our case study countries. Our case studies run the gamut from one of the most ethnically homogeneous societies in the world, Japan, to two of the most diverse, India and Nigeria. Levels of religiosity, gender equality, and acceptance of homosexuality vary widely as well. Some have seen frequent identity-based violent conflicts, while others have had none. We explore and try to explain these differences throughout this chapter.

UNDERSTANDING IDENTITY

Many people view their national, ethnic, religious, or gender identity as natural, or even divinely ordained, but the intensity and political impact of those identities vary widely across countries and over time. While group membership of some sort may be "natural" to human beings, a particularly intense political loyalty to the nation, ethnic group, religion, gender, or sexual orientation is not, given how greatly it varies. The **political saliency**—the political impact and importance—of identity groups is created, not innate. Explaining this process is our first major task. Given the enduring importance of identity to politics, it's not surprising that social scientists have developed several different approaches to understanding how identities are formed and why they become politically salient.

The oldest approach is now commonly called **primordialism.** It provides the central assumptions of many people's understanding of group origins and differences, and it is implicit in the arguments of most nationalist, ethnic, and racial leaders. The purest primordialists believe exactly what we mentioned above: that identity groups are in some sense "natural" or God given; that they have existed since "time immemorial;" and that they can be defined unambiguously by such clear criteria as kinship, language, culture, sex, or phenotype (physical characteristics, including skin color, facial features, and hair). Based on these assumptions, many primordialists see conflict among groups as understandable, and perhaps even inevitable, given their innate differences. Resolving these conflicts, therefore, seems unlikely to primordialists; the best option is probably separate states for the "naturally" distinct and conflicting ethnic or national groups, for instance, and acceptance of "inherent" gender differences. Few social scientists are pure primordialists today; virtually all have been convinced that group identities change enough that the argument that they are somehow "natural" is insupportable. However, the approach still holds important popular and political influence.

A more nuanced primordial argument is based on political culture or psychology. Because cultural values and beliefs are deeply ingrained, they can be the basis of immutable group identities. Religious tenets understood in this way served as the basis of an influential work by Samuel Huntington titled *The Clash of Civilizations* (1996/1997). Huntington argued the world can be divided into seven or eight major "civilizations" based largely on religious identity, and that major wars of the future will occur along the boundaries of these civilizations.

The currently dominant alternative to primordialism is **constructivism.** Like primordialism, it is based partly on political culture, but instead of accepting cultural identities as unchanging, constructivism uses the postmodern ideas of political culture outlined in chapter 1, emphasizing the shifting interpretation of symbols and stories. Constructivists argue that a complex process, usually referred to as **social construction,** creates identities. Societies collectively "construct" identities as a wide array of actors continually discuss the question of who "we" are.

political saliency
The degree to which something is of political importance

primordialism
A theory of identity that sees identity groups as being in some sense "natural" or God given, as having existed since "time immemorial," and as defined unambiguously by such clear criteria as kinship, language, culture, or phenotype

constructivism
A theory of identity group formation that argues that identities are created through a complex process usually referred to as social construction

social construction
Part of constructivist approach to identity, the process through which societies collectively "construct" identities as a wide array of actors continually discuss the question of who "we" are

According to constructivism, this discourse is crucial to defining identities or "imagined communities" (Anderson 1991). Identity communities are "imagined" in the sense that they exist because people believe they do: people come to see themselves as parts of particular communities based on particular traits. These communities are flexible, though they typically change relatively slowly. Furthermore, individuals are members of a number of different groups at the same time. Elites can attempt to mobilize people using the discourse and symbols of any one of several identities in a particular time and place.

This creation of social and cultural boundaries, even where no legal ones exist, is central to the social construction of identity. As a group defines who "we" are, it also creates boundaries that define who "they" are. To take the most obvious example, the concepts and identities of "man" and "woman" could not exist without each other. If human beings were a species of only one sex, neither word would exist. On the other hand, the growing transgender movement has questioned the binary nature of the traditional gender division of "man" and "woman." Most theorists today see gender existing on a continuum; gender boundaries, like ethnic or racial ones, are set by society, not by nature. Constructivists argue that identities and boundaries are created in part by the interpretation and reinterpretation of symbols and stories. Through families, the media, and the public education system in all countries, individuals develop a sense of identity as they learn the importance and meaning of key symbols and stories. The state always plays an important role in this process. As a government develops and implements educational curricula, it requires that children be taught the "national history," which can include only certain events interpreted in certain ways if the "facts" are to support a specific national identity. The end result of this only partly planned and always amorphous process is adherence to certain beliefs, values, symbols, and stories that come to constitute an identity: for example, a flag, a monarch, the struggle for independence, the fight for racial equality, and monuments to fallen heroes.

Pakistani transgender women henna their hands as they prepare to celebrate Eid al-Fitr, one of the most important Muslim holidays. Gender identity movements threaten all other identity categories and today most often conflict with claims based on religion.

A MAJEED/AFP/Getty Images

Gender identity plays a distinct role from most other identities in this process. On the one hand, few gender-based movements have demanded a separate state or autonomy for a particular territory the way other groups might. On the other hand, social constructions of gender—and, in particular, symbols of what a "proper" woman is within a national, ethnic, religious, or racial group—are frequently key ways in which other group boundaries are demarcated (Yuval-Davis and Anthias 1989). By having babies, women literally reproduce the community. As the primary childcare providers in almost all societies, they also pass on key cultural elements to the next generation. Finally, women serve as symbolic markers of community identity and boundaries. Anne McClintock (1991), for instance, showed how the idea of a "pure" Afrikaner woman in South Africa under apartheid helped solidify Afrikaner nationalism, distinguishing Afrikaners from other white South Africans and creating a feminine ideal around which Afrikaner men could rally vis-à-vis the black majority. A more recent example is the wearing of the Islamic veil, which has become an issue of debate both in Europe and in several Middle Eastern countries. What women do, how they behave, what they wear, and where and how they are seen are often central to the social construction of not only gender but also other identities.

Constructivists believe identity conflicts can be resolved, given that they are not inherent, but often look beyond formal political solutions, focusing on trying to shift identity-based discourses over the longer term to create more inclusive identities and respect for all identities. For instance, they may suggest rethinking how students learn about gender and sexuality to give people of all genders and sexual orientations a greater sense of recognition and belonging. This can reduce stigmatization of those groups and thereby reduce possible future tension and conflicts. In the United States in the 1990s, historians influenced by constructivism suggested significant and controversial changes to the teaching of U.S. history in public schools to include more material on racial minorities' roles. Critics suggested this would undermine national unity by emphasizing differences, while supporters saw it as teaching a more inclusive national story that could help reduce long-standing racial tensions and misunderstandings.

Like most contemporary social scientists, in this text we adopt a primarily constructivist approach to understanding identity.

THE POLICY DEBATE

Once we have a framework for understanding how identity groups are constructed and evolve, we can examine why and how states respond to these groups, whose political demands can raise fundamental questions about equal citizenship or even threaten the existence of a state. States, whether to avoid greater conflict or to live up to their ideals, sometimes must recognize and grant groups some of what they demand. Making these concessions, however, can cause clashes with other groups with equally strong, or even opposing, demands and values. Political autonomy for one ethnic group can lead others to demand the same. Equal treatment of all citizens regardless of gender or sexual orientation often conflicts with deeply held religious beliefs or long-standing cultural practices. Recent controversies over transgender rights are just the latest in a long history of clashes of deeply held values. Even when the principle of equal citizenship is not questioned, major controversies arise over what "equal treatment" means.

Much of the debate over how states should accommodate identity group demands has taken place in the context of democratic theory: normative theories about how democracy ought to work. A number of the institutionalized solutions proposed, however, can apply in any modern state, since they all grapple with the demands of mobilized groups asking for greater inclusion. At the heart of the debate is the question of individual versus group rights and recognition. Liberal democracy in its classic formulation is based on individual rights and the equal treatment of all citizens regardless of their personal, cultural, or social differences. Contemporary identity groups ask, Is that enough?

The Demands of Identity Groups

Before turning to the policy debate, we have to understand what identity groups demand. The universal demand revolves around what Charles Taylor (1994) called the "politics of recognition." They want the state and society to recognize them as distinct groups with distinct and legitimate concerns. They usually seek legal rights at least equal to those of other citizens. While the last vestige of legalized racial discrimination was eliminated with the end of apartheid in South Africa in 1994, legal discrimination against women, especially in areas of property ownership and family law, remains fairly common, and legal discrimination against homosexuals remains the norm in most of the world.

Members of ethnic or religious groups sometimes seek **autonomy** to control their own affairs, either in a particular region where they are in the majority or over areas of their lives influenced by cultural traditions or religious beliefs, such as family law and property rights. When a demand for autonomy becomes nationalist, becoming a demand for complete secession, states will virtually always resist, which often leads to civil war. To mitigate this possibility, states may grant autonomy or group rights.

autonomy
The ability and right of a group to partially govern itself within a larger state

A third demand that many groups make is for representation and full participation in the political process. As long as they accept the basic integrity of the state and thereby view themselves as part of the political community, they will want representation and participation. This may appear to be a simple legal matter of ensuring basic political rights, but it often becomes more complicated and controversial as groups question whether they are truly allowed to participate on an equal footing with other citizens and whether institutional changes are necessary for them to achieve that equality.

A final demand is for better social status. Virtually all identity groups that mobilize to demand changes begin in a socially marginalized position: they are typically poorer and less educated than the average citizen and may be socially segregated as well. Harkening back to T. H. Marshall's (1963) ideas of the social rights of citizenship (see chapter 3), they argue that they need better education and economic positions and greater respect from and acceptance in society as a whole. How to achieve those improvements has proven quite controversial.

Arguments for Group Rights and Recognition

Some theorists argue that individual rights, no matter how fully respected, will never allow full inclusion of culturally distinct or socially marginalized groups. Social or cultural differences, as well as histories of exclusion and repression, mean that legal equality alone is not enough. More must be done, usually in the form of rights for or preferential policies that target the distinct needs and weak social positions of particular groups. Theorists making these arguments support policies of several types: (1) recognizing and actively supporting the preservation of distinct cultures; (2) granting some degree of governing autonomy to particular groups; (3) reforming representative institutions such as electoral systems and political parties to enhance or guarantee participation and representation for members of particular groups; and (4) actively intervening to improve the socioeconomic status of distinct groups, usually via government intervention in the market.

Two of the most prominent advocates of group rights and preferences are political theorists Will Kymlicka (1995) and Iris Marion Young (2000). Kymlicka contended that collective rights for minority cultures are justified "to limit the economic or political power exercised by the larger society over the group, to ensure that the resources and institutions on which the minority depends are not vulnerable to majority decisions" (1995, 7). He argued that most people find it very difficult to cross cultural barriers fully; without recognition and protection of their distinct cultures, they will not be able to participate completely in the larger society and make the choices on which democratic citizenship depends. Kymlicka and Norman (2000) encouraged a policy based on **multicultural integration** rather than **assimilation.** The latter, as practiced in the United States and elsewhere, has the goal of eventually integrating immigrants' cultures into the larger culture of the whole society. Conversely, multicultural integration

> does not have the intent or expectation of eliminating other cultural differences between subgroups in the state. Rather, it accepts that ethnocultural identities matter to citizens, will endure over time, and must be recognized and accommodated within [political] institutions. The hope is that citizens from different backgrounds can all recognize themselves, and feel at home, within such institutions. (14)

Critics have asked whether respecting cultural differences might undermine individual rights, especially freedom of expression and gender equality. Kymlicka and Norman, though, were clear that only cultural practices not violating fundamental liberal rights should be allowed and encouraged via multicultural integration.

multicultural integration Accepts that ethnocultural identities matter to citizens, will endure over time, and must be recognized and accommodated within political institutions; in contrast to assimilation

assimilation A belief that immigrants or other members of minority cultural communities ought to adopt the culture of the majority population

Predating Kymlicka's arguments, an institutional expression of this general idea is **consociationalism** (Lijphart 1977). Consociationalism accepts ethnically or religiously divided groups and political parties, granting each some share of power in the central government. Switzerland, Northern Ireland, and Belgium are examples of this system. Power sharing can be done formally, as in Lebanon, where power is divided along religious lines: by agreement of all parties, the president is always a Christian, the prime minister a Sunni Muslim, and the Speaker of the parliament a Shiite Muslim. It can also be done more informally. The electoral system can be designed to encourage the formation of parties based on key identities. The parties, once elected, can then work out power-sharing arrangements in some type of government of national unity. Typically, each major ethnic or religious party will have, in effect, a veto over major legislation, so all must agree before laws are passed. Consociationalists also suggest using federalism by creating ethnically or religiously homogeneous states or provinces so that central governments can try to shift the focus of identity politics from the center to the regional governments. This type of federalism has been the most common response to identity-based conflicts in the post–Cold War era.

The best-known recent effort at consociationalism was the Belfast Agreement of 1998 that ended the religiously based conflict in Northern Ireland, one of the oldest communal conflicts in the world. The origins of the conflict date back to British colonial rule, when English and Scottish Protestant plantation owners oversaw a Gaelic, Catholic population. In the nineteenth century, an Irish nationalist movement arose, and most of Ireland gained independence in 1920. The six northern counties, however, remained part of Great Britain, gaining only limited local government under Protestant control. The nationalist movement, demanding that the northern counties join the Irish Republic, continued its efforts throughout the twentieth century, and the conflict became particularly violent starting in the late 1960s. By the early 1990s, it became clear to both sides that they could not achieve their core aims unilaterally. The nationalists recognized they could not militarily defeat the British, and the unionists (Protestants favoring continued union with Great Britain) acknowledged they could not continue to rule unilaterally without paying a steep price in terms of lives, political stability, and economic well-being.

This set the stage for the historic Good Friday agreement creating a consociational solution that, while far from perfect, is holding to date. Under the agreement, Northern Ireland would remain part of Great Britain, and Ireland renounced its longstanding claim to the territory. Government would devolve, however, from direct rule from London to local rule in Northern Ireland. A National Assembly would be elected based on a proportional electoral system that ensured that nationalists and unionists would have seats in parliament equal to their share of the national vote (see chapter 6 for details on proportional electoral systems). The first minister and deputy first minister, who are elected by the National Assembly, share executive power. They must each win a majority vote of both the nationalist and unionist members of the National Assembly (every member, once elected, must declare herself to be officially

consociationalism
A democratic system designed to ease ethnic tensions via recognizing the existence of specific groups and granting some share of power in the central government to each, usually codified in specific legal or constitutional guarantees to each group

unionist, nationalist, or other). Cabinet positions are then shared among all parties in the assembly based on their share of the total seats. In this way, both sides of the sectarian divide must support the government. Despite a promising start, compromise between the main parties remained elusive, and a government wasn't formed until 2007. Numerous efforts to forge cross-community relationships in civil society and integrate institutions such as schools have begun, but they have been far from successful so far. Indeed, in late 2012, forty days of Protestant rioting broke out in Belfast after the Catholic-controlled city council voted to limit the number of days the British flag would be flown over City Hall. The riots were stoked by fears that higher Catholic birthrates would soon make Protestants a minority, shifting the balance of power in the consociational government. The Storemone House Agreement of 2014 created a Commission on Flags, Identity, Culture, and Tradition to recommend policies in these areas to prevent further conflict. Despite these problems, the consociational system has succeeded in ending almost all of the violent conflict and establishing a government in which the former antagonists are sharing power peacefully, at least for now.

Political philosopher Iris Marion Young (2000) offered a different approach to justifying group rights, one focused more on forms of participation and deliberation than specifically delineated and institutionalized rights or power-sharing schemes. She focused not on identity and culture but rather on what she termed "structural social groups," or groups of people who share a structural position and therefore similar experience in social and political institutions. A structural position can be based on economic position, physical attributes, or a variety of other factors. Structural groups can therefore overlap with cultural groups, but they are not the same thing. She argued that collective rights or preferences for such groups are justified in the interests of justice and greater democracy. Democracy, she suggested, should have as one of its primary goals the seeking of justice. Both democracy and justice are enhanced when all important social perspectives are included in the discussion. She further argued that groups in structurally marginalized positions are typically not included unless governments intervene to ensure that they are. Her goal was inclusive democracy:

Inclusion ought not to mean simply the formal and abstract equality of all members of the polity of citizens. It means explicitly acknowledging social differentiations and divisions and encouraging differently situated groups to give voice to their needs, interests, and perspectives. (2000, 119)

Young's position leads her to favor adjusting political discussion and debate to recognize and value the forms of communication that marginalized groups, such as women or speakers of different languages, are often more comfortable using. She also suggested that if a history of discrimination or current practices prevents members of marginalized social groups from being elected or appointed to political positions, some reform is warranted. This could take the form of rules for how parties select candidates, reserved legislative seats for particular groups, reserved positions on appointed boards for particular groups, or the drawing of electoral districts to increase the likelihood that members of particular groups will be elected.

Arguments against Group Rights

Critics of group rights argue that "special" group rights or preferences undermine the norm of equal citizenship, serve to perpetuate a group's distinct and therefore unequal position, and threaten the common identity and bonds on which citizenship and national identity are based.

The classic liberal position is that only individuals can have rights and all individuals should have them equally. This implies support for government policies of nondiscrimination, but it does not justify giving distinct rights or preferences to members of particular groups or treating them differently in any other way. Once legal equality is achieved, individuals are and should be free to pursue political participation as they desire and are able. The state should not intervene in any way in response to either cultural or social differences, which, even if acknowledged to exist, are beyond the state's rightful purview.

Indeed, proponents of this approach fear that group rights will undermine political stability and democracy, both of which, they argue, require a common identity and a shared set of values. Nationalism underlies the development of the modern state and of democracy, and each state is given international legitimacy as a representative of "a people." A sense of commonality, then, is essential to domestic and international legitimacy for all states. From this perspective, group rights and preferences will preserve group differences rather than encourage commonality, undermining political stability.

An institutionalist approach that attempts to get beyond group identities is known as the **centripetal approach,** championed most strongly by political scientist Donald Horowitz (1985). He argued that ethnic or religious conflict can best be resolved by giving political leaders incentives to moderate their demands and broaden their appeal beyond their particular groups. Certain electoral systems can encourage this by requiring winning candidates to gain votes over a broad geographic area

centripetal approach
A means used by democracies to resolve ethnic conflict by giving political leaders and parties incentives to moderate their demands

containing multiple religious or ethnic groups, for instance. Also, rules for recognition of parties can require them to have representation and leadership across ethnic or other identity lines. Creating ethnically or religiously mixed states or provinces in a federal system can also encourage compromise within each one, moderating tensions. Our case study of Nigeria is a classic example of this approach.

Finally, all liberal theorists ask, To what extent can and should group rights be supported if those groups pursue goals contrary to a state's liberal ideals? Should a religious group that explicitly opposes equal rights for men and women not only be allowed to participate in the political process but also be given specific preferences? Our case study of Nigeria, once again, provides an example of this issue, as some states in their democracy have instituted a form of Muslim *sharia* law that opponents see as violating core democratic values.

We now turn to look at the debates in the context of each of the major identity categories of importance today: nation, ethnicity, race, religion, and gender and sexual orientation.

NATIONS AND NATIONALISM

The nation remains a fundamental building block of the global political system and the starting place for any discussion of identity. Each state claims to be the sole legitimate representative of a nation, and each nation claims a right to its own state. Despite this, clearly defining the word *nation* is no easy task. Writing over a century ago, French theorist Ernest Renan (1882) concluded that no single cultural feature was crucial. Instead,

> a nation is a soul, a spiritual principle. Two things, which are really only one, go to make up this soul or spiritual principle. One of these things lies in the past, the other in the present. The one is the possession in common of a rich heritage of memories; and the other is actual agreement, the desire to live together, and the will to continue to make the most of the joint inheritance.

The resemblance of Renan's deduction to contemporary notions of social construction is striking. A nation is an "imagined community," imagined through shared memories. All of those memories beyond the immediate experience of the individuals themselves are shared only because a group has learned to share them, in part through state-sponsored education.

The distinction between a nation and an ethnic group, in particular, is often not clear. The Irish are members of a nation, but when they immigrate to the United States, they become, sooner or later, part of an "ethnic group." The Zulu in South Africa are an ethnic group, but the Palestinians, who are less culturally distinct from their Arab neighbors than are the Zulu from neighboring South African groups, are generally regarded as a nation. As Renan concluded long ago, no particular set of cultural markers fully distinguishes a nation from an ethnic group. The only clear definition ties back to the state. A **nation** is a group that proclaims itself a nation and has or seeks control of a state. This desire to be a nation and thus to control a national state is **nationalism.** Ethnic groups, on the other hand, do not think of themselves as nations and do not desire to control their own state as much as they want autonomy within a larger state. Clearly, and to the potential detriment of states' territorial integrity, an unsatisfied ethnic group can develop into a nation demanding its own state. David Siroky and John Cuffe (2014) used a large statistical analysis of secessionist cases since 1960 and found that this is most likely to happen when an ethnic group that has had a degree of political autonomy within a state loses it.

Not surprisingly, most nationalist leaders are primordialists: each claims his nation has existed since the beginning of time as a mighty and proud people. As we saw in chapter 2, however, most scholars see nationalism as a fundamentally modern concept tied to the rise of the modern state and economy. The first European nations, such as France and England, were largely the products of preexisting states. Once nationalism emerged as an idea, though, political and intellectual elites started propagating a sense of national identity long before they controlled their own states, as the development of Germany demonstrates. In former colonies, nationalism emerged as a movement for independence from colonial oppressors. And once the creation of the state is accomplished, the process of developing a national identity continues. As Italian nationalist Massimo d'Azeglio declared shortly after the unification of Italy in the 1860s: "We have made Italy. Now we must make Italians." While there are a few scholars who argue that nations are inherently based on older ethnic groups (Gat 2014; Smith 1998), most scholars support the idea that nations are modern entities tied in some way to the development of the modern state and economy.

Nationalism has a complicated relationship with liberal democracy as well. At least until the mid-twentieth century, many nationalists saw themselves as carving

nation
A group that proclaims itself a nation and has or seeks control of a state

nationalism
The desire to be a nation and thus to control a national state

A supporter of Republican presidential nominee Donald Trump displays his support for the nominee outside the party's 2016 national convention in Cleveland. Trump's promise to build a wall along the U.S. border with Mexico, deport millions of illegal immigrants, and ban Muslim immigration led critics to claim he was basing his campaign on a form of cultural nationalism—specifically, white nationalism—not seen in a major party's presidential candidate for decades.

Spencer Platt/Getty Images

cultural nationalism
National unity based on a common cultural characteristic wherein only those people who share that characteristic can be included in the nation

jus sanguinis
Citizenship based on "blood" ties; for example, in Germany

civic nationalism
A sense of national unity and purpose based on a set of commonly held political beliefs

jus soli
Citizenship dependent on "soil," or residence within the national territory; for example, in France

democratic nations out of the remnants of feudal or colonial empires. Before "we the people" can declare ourselves sovereign, "we" must have a sense of "us" as a "people": who is and is not included in "us" defines who has the rights of democratic citizenship. In this context, two distinct forms of nationalism have crucial implications. **Cultural nationalism** is national unity based on a common cultural characteristic, and those people who don't share that particular characteristic cannot be included in the nation. Cultural nationalists advocate a legal definition of citizenship based on **jus sanguinis,** citizenship based on blood rather than residence. For instance, prior to 2000, anyone whose parents were ethnically German could gain automatic German citizenship, while citizenship for all others was extremely difficult to procure. Cultural nationalism poses obvious challenges for democracy, for how can those lacking the "national" characteristics be full citizens with democratic rights? For this reason, most observers see **civic nationalism** as more supportive of democracy. In civic nationalism, the sense of national unity and purpose is based on a set of commonly held political beliefs. Those who share the beliefs are part of the nation. Civic nationalists support legal citizenship based on **jus soli,** or residence on the state's "soil," thus automatically conferring citizenship on second-generation immigrants, whatever their cultural characteristics.

Immigration is often the context in which debates about national identity are played out. In 2015 Europe faced a collective crisis over a massive flow of immigrants from the Middle East, mainly Syria. Who should be allowed in, what political rights should they be given, and why? British voters chose to leave the European Union in 2016, desiring to assert their national identity vis-à-vis the EU and reduce the flow of immigrants into the country. Simultaneously, Donald Trump mounted a surprisingly successful campaign for president of the United States, in part by declaring his desire to build a wall the length of the U.S. border with Mexico and to ban all Muslim immigrants. Officially, the United States proclaims a civic nationalism based on the principles in the Declaration of Independence and Constitution. A recent survey, though, showed that over 90 percent of Americans think that for a person to be a "true American" he must speak English; among Americans with the strongest sense of national identity, two-thirds believed that a "true American" has to be Christian and one-third believed a "true American" has to be white (Theiss-Morse 2009). Clearly, cultural (in this case linguistic, religious, and racial) nationalism exists alongside official civic nationalism. Our case study of Germany is another example of the continuing tension between civic and cultural nationalism.

DEUTSCHLAND BUNDESREPUBLIK

NATIONALISM IN GERMANY

CASE SYNOPSIS

Germany demonstrates the underlying complexity of what may seem to be a very stable national identity. It long maintained a strictly cultural nationalism that left millions of immigrants and their children without political rights. A 2000 reform changed this, though citizenship is far from automatic. Neither civic nor cultural nationalism has become the unquestioned and universal conception of "we." The massive Syrian refugee crisis simply added fuel to this long-running debate. These political battles between contending visions of the national identity are fought in the realm of citizenship laws, meaning they have a direct bearing on who gains democratic rights and who does not.

- BACKGROUND Nationalism precedes the modern state
- CONTEXT Cultural nationalism and *jus sanguinis* until recent reform
- ISSUES Turkish immigrants, Syrian refugees, and continuing debate over who is "German"

German nationalism long predates the modern German state. For centuries, German speakers lived side by side with Slavs and other ethnic groups while retaining their German language and culture. While a common language and culture existed, it took Napoleon's invasion in the early nineteenth century and the influence of the Romantic movement to foment modern German nationalism. Advocates of Romanticism envisioned the nation as an organic whole with a "distinct personality" (note the similarity to fascist ideas outlined in chapter 3). Intellectual elites shaped German nationalism by defining "Germany" in linguistic and cultural terms that juxtaposed German identity with the identities of the neighboring Slavs in the east and French in the west.

As outlined in chapter 2, Otto von Bismarck united much of what is now Germany in 1871. He tried to use education to create greater cultural homogeneity in the new state; his new *Reich* (the German nation and its territory) included large populations of linguistic minorities and excluded huge numbers of German speakers in Austria and eastern Europe. By 1913, German citizenship was legally based on *jus sanguinis*, legally codifying the long-standing cultural understanding of what it meant to be "German."

Nazi ideology developed out of this cultural nationalism, marrying it to explicit racism. The Nazis considered the master "Aryan" race as superior to all others, and

Adolf Hitler's regime stripped "non-Aryans" of citizenship rights, expelling or extermi-nating many, especially Jews. With the end of World War II, the Soviet Union expelled millions of ethnic Germans from eastern Europe, and others left voluntarily as Soviet control tightened. Citizenship in the new West Germany continued to reflect the con-cept of the cultural nation: all ethnic Germans were welcomed into West Germany and automatically granted citizenship. This open-arms policy was in stark contrast to the treatment of the growing number of non-German immigrants, who rarely gained citizenship no matter how many generations their ancestors had resided in Germany. Access to political power required being part of the German cultural nation.

The debate over who is and should be "German" continues today, especially in the context of growing immigration. The large numbers of Turks who immigrated to Germany in recent decades were initially welcomed to fulfill essential jobs. Following German national self-conception, these immigrants were known as *gastarbeitern*, or "guest workers"; they were to stay as long as they were employed and then return home. Today, nearly three million ethnic Turks live in Germany, and many have raised children there. Until recently, however, very few could gain German citizenship because of Germany's *jus sanguinis* law. Starting in the 1980s, a movement demand-ing a shift to a multicultural understanding of citizenship arose, supported by labor unions and the new Green Party. In 2000 the government (then controlled by the Social Democrats and Greens) finally allowed German-born children of immigrants who had been in the country at least eight years to apply for citizenship, provided they could pass a German language test and renounced their prior citizenship. In 2004 and 2007 the government added rules that required immigrants to attend an extensive "integration course" on German culture and society and pass a test at the end of it, in addition to the language requirement. Citizenship did not shift to a fully multicultural model, in that non-Germans have to assimilate to German culture at

A Turkish woman walks past a Turkish grocery store in an immigrant neighborhood in Berlin. Until 2000, Germany's *jus sanguinis* definition of citizenship meant that millions of Turkish residents and their German-born children were not citizens. Since then, more have gained citizenship, though a restrictive process means only a minority of longtime Turkish residents have become citizens so far.

Sean Gallup/Getty Images

least enough to pass the key tests, but it moved to an assimilationist model of cultural nationalism, from *jus sanguinis* to *jus soli*. As a result, approximately 1.5 million former Turkish citizens now have German citizenship, though after an initial spurt of applications the rate dropped significantly, probably due to the testing demands and the fact that until 2014 Germany did not allow Turks to have dual citizenship. Over 40 percent of Turkish residents remain noncitizens, despite the fact that many have lived in Germany for decades.

The revised citizenship law did not end the debate over the place of Turks in the German nation. Some argue it helped create a backlash against Muslim immigrants in general. In 2010 a member of the board of the national bank, Thilo Sarrazin, wrote a book titled *Germany Does Away With Itself (Deutschland Schafft Sich Ab)* that argued that Germany was becoming literally stupider and culturally weaker due to the presence of too many Muslim immigrants. This touched off a raging debate, and he was forced to resign, but a poll showed that as many as a third of Germans agreed with his sentiments and the book became a best seller. The European refugee crisis of 2015–2016 ignited more debate over immigration and German identity. Chancellor Angela Merkel pursued a policy of welcoming as many as 1.1 million refugees from Syria. While press reports of Germans welcoming refugees into their communities were common, an opinion poll showed that one-third of the country feared that the massive immigration would threaten their values and culture. The ability to speak German remains crucial to Germans' sense of national identity: a 2016 survey found that 79 percent of Germans believed immigrants speaking the language was "very important" and another 19 percent thought it was "somewhat important"; only 2 percent thought it was not important. In sharp contrast, only 29 percent said immigrants following German customs and traditions was very important (Pew Research Center 2016b).

The refugee crisis provoked a clear political backlash as well. An anti-immigrant group, PEGIDA (Patriotic Europeans Against the Islamization of the Occident), formed in December 2014 and mobilized tens of thousands of supporters in multiple anti-immigrant demonstrations in 2015. A new, far-right party called Alternative for Germany includes cultural nationalism explicitly in its platform and states that "Islam does not belong to Germany." In 2016 the party had the approval of 10–15 percent of German voters (Sauerbrey 2016).

CASE Questions

1. Most theorists of nationalism argue that it is a modern phenomenon rather than a relic of ancient history. In what ways is that true or not true in the German case?
2. What does the German case suggest about the debate over whether civic or cultural nationalism is more beneficial in a democracy?

ETHNICITY

Now that we have defined and illustrated what a nation is, defining an ethnic group becomes an easier task. An **ethnic group** is a group of people who see themselves as united by one or more cultural attributes or a sense of common history but do not see themselves as a nation seeking its own state. Like a nation and all other identity categories, ethnic identity is imagined: people's perceptions are what matter, not actual attributes or some "objective" interpretation of history. Ethnic groups may be based on real cultural attributes, such as a common language, but even these are subject to perception and change. In the former Yugoslavia, Serbs, Croats, and Bosniaks all spoke closely related versions of what was known as Serbo-Croatian. As ethnic conflict and then war emerged in the early 1990s, each group began claiming it spoke a distinct language—"Serbian," "Croatian," or "Bosnian"—and nationalists in all three groups began to emphasize the minor linguistic differences among them. People think of African "tribes" as modern remnants of ancient, unchanging groups, but the Nigerian case below shows how even there, ethnicity is socially constructed and quite modern. (See the "What's in a Name?" box on page 165 for a fuller discussion of "tribes" in Africa.)

If ethnic groups do not desire to have their own state, what do they want? All identity groups wish to be recognized. For ethnic groups, recognition may take the form of official state support of cultural events, school instruction in their language, official recognition of their language as one of the "national" languages, or inclusion of the ethnic group's history in the national history curriculum. In short, many ethnic group leaders demand the kind of policies Kymlicka and Norman (2000) envisioned with their notion of "multicultural integration." If an ethnic group resides primarily in one area, it also may demand some type of regional autonomy, such as a federal system of government in which its leaders can control their own state or province. The issue of federalism became so contentious in India in the 1960s that the national government created a commission to examine it. The commission recommended the creation of a number of new states based on linguistic boundaries. Even when an ethnic group is not regionally concentrated, it will typically demand greater representation and participation in government, perhaps especially when a federal option is not possible.

In contrast to national identity, ethnicity is not always political. In the United States today, white ethnic identities— such as Italian American or Irish American—have very little political content. Irish Americans may be proud of their heritage and identify culturally with Ireland, but few feel any common political interests based on that identification. This can change, of course: a century ago many Irish Americans felt their identity was tied very strongly to their political interests. A crucial question, then, is when and why ethnicity becomes politically salient. Leadership can be a key catalyst. Because of the potential intensity of ethnic attachments, they are a tempting resource for ambitious politicians. A leader who can tie ethnic identity to political demands can gain tremendous support.

What's in a Name? Tribe, Ethnicity, and Nation

When Westerners think of Africans and Native Americans, they think of "tribes," but no one refers to the Basques in Spain or Scots in Britain as a tribe. Instead, they are ethnic groups, linguistic groups, or "nations." We defined a nation as a group of people who have or want their own state. By that definition, Basques and Scots only partially qualify: some of them want their own state, but many simply want greater autonomy within Spain or Britain. In this sense, they are very similar to a good portion of the Zulu in South Africa. So why are the Zulu a tribe while the Scots and Basques are not?

People tend to understand the word *tribe* in primordialist and negative terms; that is, they are "traditional" groups that have survived into the modern world and therefore cause political problems. As our case study of Nigeria shows, nothing could be further from the truth. Modern African ethnic groups arose in their current form during the colonial era and only sometimes originated in precolonial identities or states. The Kalenjin of Kenya consist of eight separate groups speaking closely related languages that assumed a common ethnic identity only in the 1950s, primarily via a popular radio program. To call the Kalenjin a "tribe," evoking the word's connotation of a small and primitive group, masks this history.

The real reason *tribe* is associated with Africans and Native Americans is rooted in eighteenth- and nineteenth-century racism. At least since Julius Caesar, *tribe* has implicitly meant a backward and inferior group of people. Caesar used *tribus* to refer to the "barbarian," blue-eyed blonds he conquered in northern Europe. Later, European slavers and colonists used it to classify people they saw as backward and inferior. Contemporary scholars of Africa prefer the term *ethnic group* for people in Africa, Europe, or anywhere else who have an identity derived from some cultural characteristic but who are not a nation in the way scholars define that term. Many Native Americans, on the other hand, prefer the term *nation*, even though most of them do not seek complete sovereignty from the larger states in which they reside.

Constructivists point out, however, that leaders cannot do this at will. The context is important. If a group believes those in power have discriminated against it economically, socially, or politically, members may see their political interests and ethnic identity as one and the same. Their history, which they may pass from parent to child, is one of discrimination at the hands of the powerful "other." On the other hand, relative wealth can also lead to ethnic mobilization. If an ethnic group is based in a particular region that has a valuable resource such as oil, group members may feel that they should receive more benefits from what they see as "their" resource. This is a central issue in the ethnic and religious divisions in Iraq because the country's oil reserves are located in both Kurd and Shiite areas but not in Sunni areas. Sunni leaders, not surprisingly, want oil revenue fully controlled by the central government in Baghdad, not by regional governments; they fear being dominated by the larger groups within whose territory the oil is located. Fear, then, is also a common source of ethnic mobilization. With the fall of communism in eastern Europe and the former Soviet Union, many people felt great fear about the future. The old institutions had collapsed, and the new ones were untested. In this situation, it is relatively easy for a political leader to mobilize support with an ethnic or nationalist appeal that suggests that other groups will take advantage of the uncertain situation and try to dominate. Our case study of Nigeria illustrates all of these elements of ethnic politics.

CASE Study

THE EVOLVING ROLE OF ETHNICITY IN NIGERIA

CASE SYNOPSIS

Nigeria demonstrates that although they are socially constructed and usually quite modern, once ethnic divisions are politicized, they become difficult to contain. Both military and civilian governments struggled with these forces, and at times their efforts at control exacerbated rather than ameliorated the problems. Nigeria's centripetal policies have had limited success in the context of economic inequality, fear, political insecurity, and conflict over oil. Ethnic conflict was a primary force frustrating the two prior attempts at democracy, and religious and ethnic tensions threaten to undermine the current democracy.

- BACKGROUND Colonial origins of ethnic identity
- CONTEXT Centripetalism and federalism, resource battles, and civil war
- ISSUES Oil and ethnic conflict

As outlined briefly in chapter 2, Nigeria is the quintessential colonial creation. People of many languages and cultures were brought together within its boundaries, where approximately four hundred languages are now spoken. Three groups emerged as numerically predominant: the Hausa in the north, the Yoruba in the west, and the Igbo in the east. We say "emerged" because that is exactly what happened. While many Nigerians perceive their ethnic identity in primordial terms, those identities were socially constructed primarily in the twentieth century. The Hausa are a Muslim people sharing a common language who were governed in twelve separate city-states by Muslim emirs in the eighteenth and nineteenth centuries. The Yoruba shared a common language and a common indigenous religion, but for most of their precolonial history were divided among several kingdoms, which sometimes lived in peace but suffered prolonged warfare in the late precolonial period. Under colonial rule, most Yoruba converted to Christianity, though today a large minority is Muslim. The Igbo, on the other hand, had no conception of themselves as a people prior to colonial rule. They lived in small, mostly independent villages ruled by councils of elders. The word *Igbo* first appears in documents in the 1930s. Under colonial rule, members of this group converted to Christianity more quickly and completely than did the Yoruba or Hausa.

Despite their different origins, all three identities had emerged as ethnic groups by the end of colonial rule. Each came to perceive its collective interests as "tribal," defined by region and language. Indirect rule (described in chapter 2) played a part in this, as colonial chiefs became leaders over what the British, and the Nigerians, increasingly came to see as "tribes." Missionaries and anthropologists were crucial in the recognition of the Igbo and other stateless societies as distinct groups. As they wrote down "tribal histories" that told primordialist stories of ancient and noble traditions and political unity, and transcribed a common "Igbo" language, they codified that language and Igbo culture.

For all three groups, internal political disagreements faded in the face of their common interests vis-à-vis the colonizer and, increasingly, one another. As members of these groups moved to the growing colonial cities to work, they began to compete for jobs, with members of each group supporting their own, so separate patron–client networks developed within each group, establishing the importance of ethnicity to people's material well-being. Those who became Christian were the first to be educated in colonial schools and in the English language, which gave them an advantage in the job market. The Igbo in particular benefited from this; the Hausa, being Muslim and therefore receiving little Christian education, lost out. Military employment, however, required less education than did most sectors of the economy, and the Hausa and other northerners found greater success in this arena. Southerners, and especially the Igbo, dominated in education, civil service, and private business.

The approach of independence in 1960 provided a context for solidifying ethnic and regional identity, and separate nationalist movements emerged in each of the three major regions, each led by one of the three major ethnic groups. Budding national leaders mobilized followings on ethnic and regional bases. Leaders of the three groups and the British negotiated a federal system of government for the new state that gave some autonomy to each of the three regions. This meant that a coalition of two of the three would be required to form a national government. The newly

Members of the Movement for the Actualization of the Sovereign State of Biafra (MASSOB) with a Biafran flag drive past a police station in southeastern Nigeria. The demand for an independent country of Biafra led to civil war from 1967 to 1970. Despite what most observers saw as a successful reintegration of the country after the civil war, a new movement for independence emerged in the impoverished, oil-rich region in the new millennium.

PIUS UTOMI EKPEI/AFP/Getty Images

independent government was fragile from the start. The three major parties, one representing each ethnic group, consolidated their power over the minorities in their own regions. The minorities, members of Nigeria's over three hundred much smaller ethnic groups, resented the political power of the larger groups and began demanding their own regions. By the 1990s, this pressure would result in the creation of thirty-six states out of the original three regions. Growing tensions between the central government and the regions, as well as friction among the three major parties, led to a chaotic and violent second election in 1964. The military stepped in with the nation's first coup d'état in 1966, led mainly by Igbo officers. Whatever the military's actual reason for taking power, the Yoruba and Hausa saw the coup as an Igbo effort to grab total power. In response, widespread rioting broke out in northern cities. Hausa attacked Igbo working as civil servants and in business, and tens of thousands were killed. Many survivors left the north, returning to their ethnic "homeland" in the southeast. This violence merged with a battle over a new resource, oil, located in the eastern region dominated by the Igbo. By 1967, an Igbo military leader declared the eastern region the independent country of Biafra. The result was a three-year civil war (1967–1970), ultimately unsuccessful, in which more than a million people perished. Nigeria was preserved, but at great human cost.

Each democratic constitution has tried to contain ethnoregional conflict through federalism and centripetal rules that govern how political parties could form. The 1979 constitution required all political parties to have representatives in all areas of the country; to win the presidency, a candidate had to win not just the most votes but also at least 25 percent of the vote in two-thirds of the nineteen states. Northerners' numerical strength and predominance in the military gave them control of most Nigerian governments. In part because of this, when the current democracy began in 1999, leading northern politicians decided to support a Yoruba for president. His handpicked successor eight years later was a northerner, creating an informal agreement that the presidency would alternate between a northerner and southerner. The untimely death of the second president in 2010, however, meant his vice president, a southerner, took power, causing northerners to feel cheated out of their full presidential term. This ultimately produced a split in the ruling party and the election in 2015 of a northerner as the new president.

In the southeastern part of the country, local ethnic movements emerged anew in the mid-1990s around the issue of benefits from oil. Members of these movements, which contained both peaceful and violent elements, argued that all the oil revenue went to the central government and they were left with environmental devastation and poverty, in spite of living in the oil-rich region. The best known of these movements originated among the Ogoni, who were led by internationally known poet Ken Saro-Wiwa until his execution at the hands of the military government in 1995. He and his movement successfully linked Ogoni ethnic demands with environmental and oil revenue concerns in a locally powerful movement. With Saro-Wiwa's execution, the peaceful Ogoni movement declined and violent clashes became more common, mostly involving young men from the Ijaw ethnic group. A 2009 cease-fire temporarily halted the violence, but the government's failure to follow through on reforms meant it did not last long. In 2010 the largest violent group, the Movement for the Emancipation of the Niger Delta (MEND), detonated bombs in the capital at Nigeria's celebration of its fiftieth anniversary of independence; this was the first time the ethnic violence had spread beyond the oil-producing region itself. Several violent groups have since declared their existence in the region, and in 2016 the violence was great enough to cause oil production to drop to its lowest level in twenty years. Amid this, the Movement for the Actualization of the Sovereign State of Biafra (MASSOB) has gained support for its call to recreate an independent state. While none of these movements is explicitly ethnic in name or stated purpose, all are led and supported by particular ethnic groups.

CASE Questions

1. What are the effects of Nigeria's colonial origins on its ethnic conflicts?
2. Why have the Nigerian government's efforts to control ethnic conflict via centripetal policies had only limited success?

RACE

While the distinction between ethnic group and nation is relatively clear, the difference between ethnic group and race is much more ambiguous. In a particular context, it may seem obvious, but a consistent distinction is difficult to apply systematically. Following Stephen Cornell and Douglas Hartman (2007, 25), we define a **race** as "a group of human beings socially defined on the basis of physical characteristics." Most ethnic identities focus on cultural rather than physical characteristics, though many do see specific physical characteristics as markers of particular groups as well. Most racial groups are distinguished by physical characteristics, though they and others may also perceive cultural distinctions. The distinction between race and ethnicity, then, is not perfect, but this is probably the best we can do.

race
A group of people socially defined primarily on the basis of one or more perceived common physical characteristics

Perhaps more important than the actual definitions of race and ethnicity is the difference in these identities' origins and social construction. Ethnic identity usually originates at least partially in a group's self-assertion of its identity. Most ethnic groups represent people who are themselves claiming an identity and the political demands that often go with that claim. Race, in contrast, originates in the imposition of a classification by others. Race in its modern sense began with Europeans' expansion around the globe and their encounter with markedly different peoples. Primarily to justify European domination and slavery, European explorers and colonists classified the native populations of the lands they conquered as distinct and inferior races. Embedded within the very classification was an assertion of power (the third dimension of power outlined in chapter 1). This legacy continues today: almost every racial classification system marks current or quite recent differences in power along racial lines. Ethnicity can also represent starkly different positions in a power structure (as many have argued has been the case in Nigeria), but in many cases it does not (as in the case of German Americans or Italian Americans today). Ethnicity and race, then, usually differ in how they are marked (culture versus physical characteristics), their origins (self-assertion versus external imposition), and the degree of power differences embedded in their contemporary social construction.

For the concept of race, just as for that of nation and ethnicity, we emphasize perception. Genetically, members of racial groups, such as white and black Americans, have as much in common with one another as they do with members of their own groups: genetic variation is no greater across the two groups than it is within each. Races are constructed by focusing on particular differences, such as skin color, and ignoring the far more numerous similarities.

Like all socially constructed categories, racial identity varies across time and place, as the cases of the United States and Brazil demonstrate. In the United States, race was historically defined by descent—the infamous "one-drop" rule that defined everyone with any African ancestry as black in order to ensure that children of black slaves and white masters were legally slaves. More recently, racial categorization is self-identified—legally, you are what you tell the Census Bureau you are. In contrast, Brazilians define race purely based on visual cues. The black–white dichotomy that characterizes U.S. racial history makes little sense to most Brazilians, where what Americans would call "interracial" marriage is quite common. Brazil's white population, facing a country in which at least half of the population was of slave descent, actively encouraged the creation of intermediate racial categories as buffers between them and poor, uneducated blacks. The result is more than a dozen unofficial racial categories between "white" and "black." Even the census was employed to encourage people to identify with some intermediate category instead of "black." The policy worked: the 1890 census recorded 44 percent of the population as "white"; the 1950 census put the figure at 62 percent. More recently, growing racial awareness has meant a shift in self-definition. For the first time in decades, the 2010 census found that a minority—48 percent—of Brazilians identified as "white." Still, most of the rest identified as mixed-race, not "black." In the last decade, an affirmative action program based on race for university admissions has become quite controversial. One of the main issues is the question of who is "black" and therefore deserves the admission preference.

Given the power dynamic inherent in racial classification, a political element nearly always exists. Like ethnicity, whether this leads to political mobilization of a racial group depends on the ability of particular leaders to articulate a common agenda by using the symbols of racial identity and discrimination in a compelling way. A dominant or majority group, such as white Americans, typically will not see itself as pursuing a common political agenda, though members of other races may think otherwise. Groups in a minority or subordinate position are more likely to view their political interests as tied to their racial identity, in part because they face discrimination on that basis.

Politicized racial groups usually desire recognition, representation, and improved social status. Autonomy is a less common goal because racial groups usually do not share a distinct geographical home. Recognition usually means official governmental recognition of the race as a socially important group through such means as inclusion on a census form, the teaching of the group's historical role in the larger national history, and the celebration of its leaders and contribution to the nation's culture. In addition, racial groups desire representation in the sense of full formal and informal participation in their government and society, which in turn, they argue, requires improved social status. Thus, racial demands typically do not involve such mechanisms as federalism but instead focus on inclusion in public and private employment, political offices, and the educational system. Frequently, as in the United States, members of minority races may argue that past discrimination justifies some type of preferential system that works relatively rapidly to achieve representation equal to their share of the population and greater socioeconomic equality. Mechanisms to do this might include numerical targets or goals for hiring, increased funding for training and education, or adjustments to the electoral system that make the election of racial minorities more likely or guaranteed. As the case of the United States shows, racial politics can be at least as intense as ethnic or national politics, so state leaders often see it as in their interests to respond, or at least appear to respond, to racial demands.

CASE Study

RACIAL POLITICS IN THE UNITED STATES

CASE SYNOPSIS

The election of Barack Obama as president in 2008 was clearly an event of great import, the biggest milestone in the fight for racial equality in the United States since the Voting Rights Act of 1965. The debate over whether the United States will overcome the inequalities and prejudices built into the country's socially constructed racial system will continue, however. High levels of racial disparity exist across a wide spectrum of American society and politics. As segregation and discrimination have become more informal and (some argue) ambiguous, racial identities have as well, now being legally based on self-identification rather than governmental imposition. A crucial question is

CASE SYNOPSIS

whether recent immigrant groups, like their European predecessors a century ago, will assimilate into the white majority or remain distinct; the answer will play a major role in how Americans think about race and its political impact over the next century.

- **BACKGROUND** Slavery, legal segregation, and the making of "white" America
- **CONTEXT** Demands for representation, equal treatment under the law, and improved social status; immigration and social construction of new racial categories
- **ISSUES** The meaning of Obama's election; continued inequality; racial disparity in the criminal justice system

On the night Democrat Barack Obama was elected the first African American president in U.S. history, he stood before a massive crowd in Chicago and said, "If there is anyone out there who still doubts that America is a place where all things are possible; who still wonders if the dream of our founders is alive in our time; who still questions the power of our democracy, tonight is your answer. . . . It's the answer spoken by young and old, rich and poor, Democrat and Republican, black, white, Latino, Asian, Native American, gay, straight, disabled, and not disabled. . . ." He claimed a new era had begun. By 2010, the anti-Obama and overwhelmingly white Tea Party had become a major new force in party politics, giving the Republican Party a massive electoral victory. Four years later, a series of highly publicized police killings of black men led to the creation of the Black Lives Matter movement and hundreds of demonstrations across the country, the largest African American protest movement since the 1960s. Had Obama's election changed the direction of racial politics in the United States for the better, or had it created a white backlash that made things worse?

Obama's election is but one event in America's long racial history. While most Americans today see racial categories as self-evident and more or less fixed, nothing could be further from the truth. Initially, the black–white racial division had to be defined legally to distinguish clearly between black slave and white citizen. The "one-drop" rule classified anyone with virtually any black heritage as black and therefore as a slave, ensuring that the offspring of slave women and white masters remained slaves and thus property. In the immediate aftermath of slavery, legal racial definitions remained important in underpinning the segregationist laws of the Jim Crow era. By the late twentieth century, race was legally categorized based on individual preferences: Americans belong to the racial category they say they do. Names of the racial groups themselves have marked different eras and identities, imposed or chosen. Descendants of slaves who had once been known as "colored" demanded that they be called "Negro" (1950s), "black" (1960s–1970s), and then "African American" (1980s on). As unprecedented numbers of Caribbean and African immigrants have arrived recently, the question of what term, if any, captures all Americans of African descent is still very much alive. Many Caribbean immigrants do not identify as "African American," while newly arrived Africans, and their American-born children, may be giving a whole new meaning to the term.

The clear categorization of all European immigrants as white that is so accepted today was by no means automatic either. The predominantly Anglo population of the United States in the nineteenth century did not view immigrants from southern and eastern Europe as racial equals. This changed only with the slow assimilation of Irish, Italians, Poles, Jews, and others into the white majority. A study of this era is aptly titled *How the Irish Became White* (Ignatiev 1995). Their ultimate success in becoming "white" had significant effects. First, no discernible socioeconomic differences exist today between these groups and the larger white population. Second, assimilation helped preserve a clear white majority in the country. Given the huge number of immigrants, had they ultimately been classified into something other than white, the country would likely have no clear racial majority. Third, white "ethnics," as they are sometimes called, may view their ethnic origin as a source of pride and cultural distinction, but it has virtually no impact on their political allegiance or behavior.

Other current American racial identities were socially constructed even more recently than African American and white identities. Immigrants from China, Japan, and other Asian countries, as well as residents of Mexican descent, identified themselves primarily by nationality until the mid-twentieth century. Chinese immigrants, for instance, thought of themselves as Chinese, and later Chinese American, but not as Asian American. Chinese and Japanese immigrants and their descendants were legally barred from citizenship for decades. Starting in the 1940s, American immigration policy and thinking about these groups began to change, as labor needs and America's global role changed. By the 1950s, Japanese and Chinese Americans had become known as the "model minority" who, once legally allowed, rapidly advanced up the educational and income ladders of the society. By dubbing them thus and claiming their success was based on a laudable culture and values, many analysts at least implicitly contrasted them with African Americans, whose culture and values allegedly held them back from succeeding. Part of the explanation for Asian education and therefore professional success, however, is disproportionately highly educated

A protestor videotapes a demonstration after the police shot and killed Alton Sterling in Baton Rouge, Louisiana, in July 2016. The Black Lives Matter movement that developed in response to a series of high-profile police shootings of African American men became the largest racial protest movement since the civil rights effort of the 1960s. Alongside Donald Trump's candidacy for the presidency, the new racial debate suggested Barack Obama's election as president had not ushered in a new era of improved race relations.

Mark Wallheiser/Getty Images

Asian immigrants arriving in the first place (Wu 2014). Intellectual and political activists in Asian communities, influenced by the black power movement in the 1960s, began to resist the "model minority" designation and conceive of themselves and their political demands in new ways, focusing their identity on their common experiences of discrimination in the United States rather than their nations of origin. They coined the term *Asian American* to unite them under one identity. This movement began with a student strike in San Francisco in 1968, as Japanese, Chinese, and Filipino students came together from separate ethnically defined organizations to form a new Asian American Political Alliance.

Similarly, leaders of Mexican and other South and Central American groups in the 1960s began to use the more overarching term *Hispanic* to assert a common identity tied to their common language and experience of discrimination. Hispanics became the largest "minority" group in the country in 2000 and grew by an additional 43 percent by 2010. While most Americans probably think of Hispanic as a racial category, it is legally a linguistic category: Hispanics are defined as Spanish speakers or descendants of Spanish speakers. Officially, these individuals can be of any race. The U.S. Census, however, still has not come to reflect accurately the self-perception of Hispanic Americans. In the 2010 census, 53 percent of Hispanics identified themselves racially as white, but another 37 percent identified themselves as "some other race," indicating an unwillingness to accept any of the official U.S. racial categories. A 2005–2006 survey of Hispanics found that fully 51 percent said that "Hispanic/Latino" is a racial category (Latino National Survey). While the construction of the category "Hispanic/ Latino"—socially, politically, and legally—is still very fluid, a Hispanic/Latino racial identification may well emerge, becoming the newest addition to the construction of racial categories in the United States.

Throughout this evolution of racial categories, African Americans have been the most politically mobilized racial group. Two major branches of thinking about black identity have competed for support throughout. From Frederick Douglass to Martin Luther King Jr. and Jesse Jackson, a liberal integrationist strand has focused primarily on proclaiming and demanding racial equality within the existing U.S. political and social system. King's core demands were the rights enshrined in the Declaration of Independence and the U.S. Constitution: a system that actually operates on the precept that "all men are created equal." The legal elements of this effort were achieved with the Civil Rights Act of 1964 and the Voting Rights Act of 1965, finally granting African Americans the complete rights of citizenship.

Running parallel to this way of defining black identity and demands is black nationalism. Melanye Price (2009) identified four key elements of this ideology: (1) black self-determination in the sense of control over their own community institutions; (2) obtaining and maintaining their own financial, political, and intellectual resources for a self-sustaining community; (3) severing ties with whites that foster ideas of racial inferiority; and (4) a global view of black oppression and liberation. Groups like the Black Panthers worked to improve the lives of poor blacks in urban areas, provided self-defense training and protection (from the police as well as from criminals), and educated blacks about the glories of their African past, all with little support from white society. Advocates of this approach argued that not until black power was achieved in this way could blacks ultimately force racist whites to move toward racial equality. Survey data from the 1990s showed that only about 15 percent of African Americans could be characterized as adherents of black nationalism (Price 2009).

The removal of legal and political restrictions in the 1960s did not fully eliminate either the effects of past discrimination or all current discrimination. In recent years, the African American political movement has focused on: (1) "affirmative action"—that is, programs in education, employment, and business that include specific hiring and admission policies directed toward minorities; (2) equal treatment by the police and judicial system; (3) greater funding for programs to improve conditions for the poor, who are disproportionately black and Hispanic; (4) changes in the electoral system to enhance the possibility that African Americans will be elected into public office; and (5) encouragement of African American voting and other forms of participation in the electoral process.

Propelled by the shooting deaths of a number of young, black men at the hands of the police, several of which were captured on videotape and widely circulated via social media, the most recent African American political effort has come to be known as the Black Lives Matter movement, named after the hashtag widely used on social media. The latter was coined after the 2013 acquittal in Florida of the man accused of shooting Trayvon Martin, but the movement exploded with the police killing of Michael Brown in Ferguson, Missouri, in August 2014. It is a decentralized effort of multiple groups using the hashtag and name, demanding reforms in how police treat African Americans and prosecution of police officers who kill African Americans. In the fall of 2014, hundreds of demonstrations took place in cities and university campuses across the country in support of the Black Lives Matter effort. A continuing string of high-profile police shootings, two in the same week in Louisiana and Minnesota in July 2016, gave impetus to additional protests. While no police officers were convicted of any crime in the thirteen high-profile killings of blacks in 2014 to 2016, the movement had put the issue on the national political agenda. Legislation was introduced (but not passed) in Congress, and some presidential candidates called for police reforms and reductions in the harsh sentencing laws that disproportionately affect African Americans (Alexander 2010). While many saw the movement as a resuscitation of the civil rights movements of the 1960s, others criticized its decentralization as a fundamental flaw in efforts to make change happen.

Overall, then, has the Obama candidacy and presidency had a major impact? Initially, many African Americans, in particular, claimed it did, saying they can honestly tell their children (or at least their sons) that they can "become whatever they want to be." On the other hand, the widely publicized criticisms of police officers' treatment of African Americans, the racialized effects of 1990s-era antidrug laws that put far more African Americans and Hispanics behind bars than whites (Alexander

2010), and continuing racial disparity in political representation and socioeconomic outcomes suggest otherwise. Figures 4.1 and 4.2 show recent data for education and income for the largest racial groups. Asian Americans have surpassed whites' income and level of education, though the higher income per household is a product of Asian households having more workers per household; individual Asian American wages continue to be below white wages for workers with similar educational backgrounds.

African Americans and Hispanics continue to suffer much lower levels of both income and education. The ratio of white incomes to black and Hispanic incomes remained constant (white incomes are about twice black and Hispanic averages) between 1989 and 2010, while the disparity of wealth levels hit their highest level in 2010 (white wealth was over six times the average for blacks and Hispanics). The Great Recession increased this disparity by 50 percent (Lowrey 2013). School segregation actually increased from 1991 to 2004 across all racial categories, and residential segregation remains extensive. While residential segregation has declined since 1970 for African Americans, it has remained high, the highest for any racial group, and has actually increased for Latinos. Asian American residential segregation has declined and is only moderate—still significant, but well below the rates for African Americans and Latinos (Schmidt et al. 2010, 109–120).

Obama's rapid ascent raises new questions about political representation of racial minorities: Has their underrepresentation finally started to end, a half-century after the Voting Rights Act? It has certainly improved since then, but unevenly; no group is fully represented except whites, who are overrepresented, as the data in Figures 4.4 and 4.5 demonstrate. The House of Representatives in 2016 was notably closer to being representative than the Senate, but even in the House, Hispanics remain significantly underrepresented. African Americans have come close to parity in the House but have little representation in the Senate, to which only eight African Americans have ever been elected.

Much evidence suggests that African Americans and Hispanics also continue to face discrimination in how they are treated by police and the judicial system, the target of the Black Lives Matter movement. Data on police treatment of civilians with whom they interact are rare; no good national database exists on the subject. Economist Roland Fryer (2016) combed the records of ten police departments and concluded that police are significantly more likely to use some type of physical force on blacks than on whites, even when controlling for the arrest rate and type of crime alleged, though he also found no racial bias in the likelihood of police shooting blacks versus whites beyond what would be expected as a rational response to different criminal behavior. Fryer examined police behavior only after a person was stopped by police but not the racial disparity in how frequently people were stopped. An earlier study looked at county-level data and found unarmed blacks' risk of being shot by police was 3.5 times greater than whites' risk (Ross 2015). Much stronger evidence exists on racial disparity in treatment by the larger criminal justice system. Blacks are 5.0 times and Hispanics 1.4 times more likely to be in state prisons (the vast majority of American prisons) than whites. The highest disparities are mostly in northeastern and midwestern states, with southern states having much lower levels of racial disparity in incarceration rates (Nellis 2016). Approximately one-third of African American men spend some part of their lives in the criminal justice system. Crime surveys show far less racial disparity in criminal behavior, suggesting a significant element of racial bias in the system. Given that a felony record typically denies a person access to public housing, many jobs, and the right to vote, the long-term implications of this are large (Alexander 2010).

Citizen attitudes and voting patterns also present stark disparities. A 2016 study found that 43 percent of blacks but only 11 percent of whites believed that the country will *not* make progress on equal rights; blacks were twice as likely to believe that racial discrimination is a major obstacle to their individual success; and blacks were almost four times more likely to support the Black Lives Matter movement. This disparity had significant partisan implications as well: nearly 60 percent of white Republicans but only 20 percent of white Democrats believed that too much attention was paid to race (Pew Research Center 2016a). Many celebrated Obama's winning 2 percent more white votes than did the Democratic candidate in 2004, but his opponent still won 55 percent of white votes. Obama won via gaining 95 percent of the African American vote and 67 percent of the Hispanic vote. Obama voters overall were about 60 percent white, compared with 90 percent white for his opponent. Obama's share of the white vote dropped to 39 percent in 2012, below the share Michael Dukakis received in 1988 when he lost in a landslide. Fifty-six percent of Obama's voters were white in 2012 (down 4 percent from 2008), compared with 89 percent for his opponent, Mitt Romney.

Michael Tesler and David Sears (2010) used extensive survey research to show that racial resentment—sentiments measured by survey data showing feelings of antipathy toward another race—among whites played a bigger role in the 2008 election than it had in any other election since the measurements began. Since Obama's election, evidence suggests the effects of racial resentment have become much stronger. Pasek et al. (2012) used three extensive surveys to conclude that white racial resentment increased slightly from 2008 to 2012; antiblack attitudes lowered Obama's job approval ratings by 2 to 3 points and cost him 4 percentage points in the 2012 election. Tesler (2016) used extensive survey and experimental data to show that by the end of Obama's first term as president, racial resentment made a much bigger difference to whites' political attitudes than it had prior to 2008 on a wide array of subjects, including their likelihood to vote for Republicans for Congress, their approval rating of Hillary Clinton, their support for government involvement in health care, their support for raising taxes on the wealthiest Americans, and even their party identification. Tesler argued that a "spillover of racialization" explains these findings: whites' negative feelings toward Obama based on racial resentment affected their attitudes to everything related to him, including their opinion of his dog. Simultaneously, not only African Americans but also Hispanics and Asian Americans became much more likely to identify as Democrats between 2008 and 2012, and the worse their impression of

FIGURE 4.1-4.5   Racial Disparity in the United States

Figure 4.1 Percent Population with College Degree

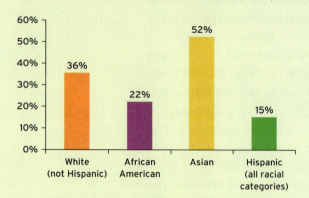

Figure 4.2 Median Household Income 2014 ($US)

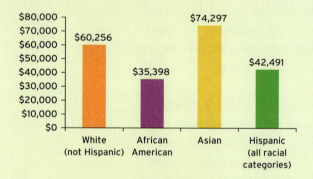

Figure 4.3 Racial Groups as Percentage of U.S. Population

As percentage of US population

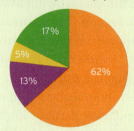

Figure 4.4 Racial Disparity in House of Representatives

As percentage of House

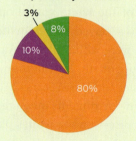

Figure 4.5 Racial Disparity in Senate

As percentage of Senate

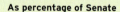
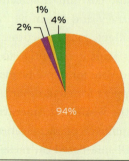

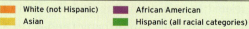

Sources: Income data are from "Income and Poverty in the United States: 2014," United States Census Bureau (http://www.census.gov/content/dam/Census/library/publications/2015/demo/p60-252.pdf); education data are from "Educational Attainment," U.S. Census Bureau (http://www.census.gov/hhes/socdemo/education/data/cps/historical/index.html); population data are from QuickFacts–United States Census Bureau (http://www.census.gov/quickfacts/table/RHI425214/00); and political representation data are from "Membership of the 114th Congress: A Profile," Congressional Research Service (https://www.fas.org/sgp/crs/misc/R43869.pdf).

Note: There are 435 total seats in the U.S. House of Representatives and 100 seats in the Senate.

whites was, the more likely that was true; Tesler concluded they had come to see the Republican Party as a party of and for white people.

Tesler found, also, that racial resentment affected less-educated whites' political attitudes far more than it affected more-educated whites' attitudes, which could help explain the less-educated whites' strong support for Donald Trump's candidacy in 2016; Philip Klinkner (2016) found high levels of racial resentment among supporters of Donald Trump's 2016 presidential campaign. While the debate continues over the effects of Obama's presidency on racial attitudes, a large body of survey research suggests that his presidency has been the "most racial" rather than "post-racial" (Tesler 2016).

CASE Questions

1. How has the social construction of race in U.S. history influenced the political position of different racial groups in American democracy?
2. What are the possible long-term political impacts of rising Asian and Hispanic immigration to the United States, and why?
3. What impact has the Obama presidency had on American racial attitudes and racial politics?

RELIGION: RECOGNITION, AUTONOMY, AND THE SECULAR STATE

Religion is both the oldest and, in a sense, newest basis for questions of inclusion and clashing values. As we noted in chapter 3, religious divisions within Christianity in early modern Europe led to civil wars and the emergence of liberalism. Eventually, secular states became universal in Western societies, which, at least in theory, relocated religion into the private sphere. The secular state reached its zenith after World War II and the onset of independence of numerous secular states across Africa and Asia. In the past generation, however, and with renewed emphasis since the terrorist attacks of September 11, 2001, religion has again become a major issue in almost all societies.

Religion as Group Identity

We can apply most of what we have learned about ethnic groups to religious groups as well. One might assume that religious group membership can be more inclusive and flexible than ethnicity, more like civic than cultural nationalism. Virtually all religions allow conversion to the faith, so while you may not be able to become Chechen, except perhaps through marriage, you can convert to Islam. In practice this may be more difficult than in theory, however, especially where religious identity has become a divisive cultural marker and a basis for political mobilization. It is unlikely that members of other groups will want to convert at this point, or be accepted if they did. Conversion is much more likely when the political salience of religious identity is relatively low.

While religious conflict is often based on a deep sense of religiosity, that is not always the case. The three major groups in the former Yugoslavia were defined primarily by religion: Serbs are Orthodox Christian, Croats are Catholic, and Bosniaks are Muslim. Ironically, because Communists had ruled the country since World War II, religious belief and practice were very low among all three groups prior to the conflict; religious affiliation was a marker of identity based on birth, not a matter of personal faith. As the conflict spread, religious observance increased within all three groups. Once people start shooting at you because of your religion, it starts to loom larger in your consciousness.

The demands of religiously mobilized groups are comparable to those of ethnic groups: they want some version of multicultural integration, involving recognition and often some autonomy. For religious groups, recognition certainly involves the right to practice one's faith openly, but it might also include demands that the state officially recognize the religion in the form of state-sponsored religious holidays or recognize and perhaps fund religious schools. A desire for autonomy could be expressed as a demand for federalism if the religious group lives in a particular region. Within its own province, the group could then practice its religion and use the provincial government to support it. Demands for autonomy can also take the form of asking that religious leaders and organizations be granted legal control over marriage, death, and other personal matters.

State Response to Religion: Differing Forms of Secularism

The vast majority of the world's states officially respond to religion by maintaining some version of secularism, with most of the exceptions being in the Middle East. In liberal democracies, few question the right of citizens to practice any religion they choose in the private sphere (with the possible exception of religious practices that break other kinds of laws, such as those against drug use or polygamy). In most societies, religious groups may organize, build houses of worship, and do charitable work as they desire. Controversies arise over what role, if any, the state should play in this process and what role, if any, the religious groups should play in secular politics and policy.

Current approaches to secularism reflect the broader debate over multiculturalism and group rights. The version of secularism most familiar to Americans we might call the **neutral state model**: the state should be neutral about, but not opposed to, religion. Religious perspectives in politics are treated the same as any other perspectives, with the state (at least in theory) being a neutral arbiter that does not choose sides in the debate. The United States is a chief example of this form of secularism. Recent controversies have therefore involved actions that seem to question the state's neutrality, such as posting the Ten Commandments in courtrooms or public school classrooms, or

neutral state model
A model of secularism wherein the state is neutral about, but not opposed to, religion

requiring children to pray in school or learn about creationism instead of the theory of evolution. Other controversies implicate the state in actively supporting religion, such as government funding for religious groups' charitable work or abstinence programs in schools in lieu of sex education courses.

A more absolute version of secularism the French call *laïcité.* It developed in societies whose political origins lay in a battle to separate the state from a single, dominant religion. France, Turkey, and our case study of Mexico are all examples of this. The French and Mexican revolutions and the establishment of the modern state in Turkey after the demise of the Ottoman Empire each involved the creation of a secular republic independent of the politically powerful Catholic Church in France and Mexico and the Islamic caliphate in Turkey. The result was a secularism advocating that religion should play no part in the public realm. The state is not neutral toward religions but rather is actively opposed to religion having any role in the public sphere. Private religious practice remains acceptable, as long as it is kept private. Religious references in political discourse, while not illegal in most cases, are nonetheless considered inappropriate. This type of secularism in our case study of Mexico dates back to the nineteenth century. The PRI government after the revolution (1920–2000) increased the state's anticlericalism even more. After democratization in 2000, some leaders of the main conservative party, the Partido de Acción Nacional (National Action Party), began to express their religious believes in public, albeit in a limited way. When church leaders urged voters to elect people who opposed abortion rights, though, many Mexicans believed it had crossed a line that it should not have. Controversies arise in this type of secularism when a religious group seeks an independent public role for its religious beliefs; the case of Islamic girls wearing veils in France and Turkey provides another example of this.

A third variant of secularism Alfred Stepan (2011) termed **positive accommodation,** arguably the closest to the tenets of multicultural integration. It sees the state as neutral among but willing to support religions that it recognizes as important elements in civil society. Our case study of Germany is the classic model of this type. Since the end of World War II, it has officially recognized various Judeo-Christian faiths, the leaders of which register with the government to gain recognition. The state even collects a tax on their behalf to help fund them, and they help administer some of Germany's extensive welfare programs. Controversies in this type of secular state involve deciding which religious groups gain recognition and how they have to be organized to do so. Most Sunni Islamic sects, for instance, are nonhierarchical, which means that each mosque is independent. This has raised questions in Germany about if and how the state should recognize Muslim groups the way it has Judeo-Christian ones. Some individual German states have recognized some Muslim groups, but no national policy on the question existed as of 2016.

A model related to "positive accommodation" is the established religion model of Scandinavia and our case study of Britain. In relatively religiously homogeneous societies such as these, the state has long recognized an official church. In

laïcité
A model of secularism advocating that religion should play no part in the public realm

positive accommodation
A model of secularism wherein the state is neutral among but willing to support religions that it recognizes as important elements in civil society

Islamic Headscarves in France and Turkey

France is at least nominally largely Catholic, but it is home to the largest Muslim population in Europe, most of whom are immigrants from North Africa. The population of Turkey is nearly all Muslim. Both countries have faced considerable controversy over young women wearing Islamic headscarves to school. The issue aroused such passion in part because each state's sense of national identity includes its particular conception of secularism; any questioning of it threatens national identity itself.

In October 1989, the principal of a junior high school in a Paris suburb expelled three Muslim girls for wearing the *hijab*, the Muslim headscarf, in school. This immediately became a major national controversy that pitted defenders of *laïcité* and feminists, who viewed the headscarf as a form of oppression, against defenders of religious freedom and multicultural understanding. The government ultimately determined that religious symbols could be worn in schools unless "by their nature . . . or by their ostentatious or protesting character . . . [they] disturb the order or normal functioning of public services" (Fetzer and Soper 2005, 79). Given the vagueness of this language, dozens of Muslim girls were expelled from school, so the controversy continued. After heated debate, the French parliament banned the wearing of all "conspicuous religious symbols" in schools in 2004, and since then, more Muslim girls have been expelled from school for wearing the *hijab*. Critics contend that the law is an anti-Muslim attack on religious freedom, since students have long worn small crosses and yarmulkes to school without incident. Supporters argue that the law is essential to the preservation of a secular republic under the threat of encroaching Islamist ideology and to the preservation of French gender equality.

More recently, the *burqa*, the full-body and full-face covering worn by some Muslim women, has also become controversial. In 2010 parliament banned wearing the *burqa* in public places because it saw it as contradicting the French ideals of *laïcité*, equality between the sexes, and *fraternité* (brotherhood), allowing an exception only for places of worship. Most Muslims argued against the ban, saying it would further marginalize them from mainstream French life. Critics also noted that fewer than two thousand women in the entire country regularly wear the *burqa*; they suggested that the campaign was more about political leaders appealing to nationalist sentiments to gain political support, and "Islamophobia," than it was about an actual policy problem. In 2016 a new controversy arose over Muslim women wearing the "burkini," a full-body swimsuit, on French beaches, with arguments for and against paralleling the earlier debates.

Kemal Atatürk founded the modern Turkish state after World War I based on an explicit campaign to modernize and Westernize the country, in part by eliminating the role of Islam

in the former seat of the Muslim caliphate. Whenever Muslim parties that called for Turkey to recognize its place in the Muslim Middle East gained too much power, they were banned or the military carried out a coup. The Muslim headscarf on women, though, was not banned in universities and government offices until 1981, and the ban wasn't regularly enforced until after the military forced an Islamist government out of power in 1998.

A new Islamist party, the Justice and Development Party (JDP), arose in 2001, led by the popular, charismatic mayor of Istanbul, Recep Tayyip Erdoğan. The JDP modified past Islamist parties' demands, preserving its embrace of Islamic principles on social issues but also supporting globalization, economic modernization tied to the West, and Turkey's application to join the European Union. It won the 2002 national election and the military did not carry out a coup, as it had in the past when a party it didn't like won an election; Erdoğan and the JDP have been the ruling party ever since, surviving a failed coup attempt by some elements in the military in 2016.

The JDP came to power promising to allow women to wear headscarves more widely, including in universities, but it did not pass legislation to that effect until February 2008. The secular elite reacted swiftly. Millions of secularists held pro-ban demonstrations, and the Constitutional Court ruled in June 2008 that the new law was unconstitutional. After winning a referendum in 2010 to amend the constitution, the JDP government felt it had the political strength to stop enforcing the ban on headscarves in universities. While it has not changed the constitution further, women are now allowed to wear headscarves at universities. Furthermore, the prime minister stated in 2013 that the state would allow female public officials and civil servants to wear headscarves, though the constitutionality of that is a point of contention and could result in a court ruling in the future. In 2013 women MPs were allowed to wear headscarves in parliament for the first time, and in 2015 girls were allowed to wear them in high schools and judges were allowed to wear them in court.

French and Turkish secularism have long envisioned a strictly secular public sphere, a vision that rising Islamic sentiment is challenging. Both states have reacted by restricting women's ability to wear clothing that symbolizes their Islamic faith, though by 2013 Turkey was moving toward fewer restrictions while France was moving toward more. A similar debate emerged after the 2011 "Jasmine revolution" in Tunisia. The long-banned Islamist party quickly emerged as a powerful political force, and women increasingly donned headscarves in what had been the most secular Arab state, raising concerns among secularists that the revolution would result in a religious "takeover" of government.

modern, secular democracies, however, this recognition has become largely symbolic, in that other religions do not experience active discrimination. As under positive accommodation, the state might fund religious schools, for instance, but not exclusively those of the established church. The questions under this model are similar to those under positive accommodation: Under what circumstances are religions recognized and accommodated? The established religion model, of course, also has nondemocratic versions, such as in Saudi Arabia, where the regime's legitimacy is tied closely to its support of a particular version of Islam, and key clerics play important roles in establishing laws on personal behavior that follow their interpretation of *sharia*.

These models of secularism have influenced how various European states have responded to the growing Muslim presence and demands in their societies. Germany's formal recognition of several religious groups has led Muslims there to ask for the same, to become part of the system, and to organize themselves in a manner that allows the German state to recognize them. Germany's long-standing church–state relationships have shaped not only the government's response to the Muslims but also what Muslim groups have requested. Similarly, the presence of the official Church of England and the tradition of teaching religion in both religious and secular schools have meant that Britain has been willing to include the study of Islam in its secular school curriculum and has been more willing to fund Muslim schools than has France (Fetzer and Soper 2005). These potential processes of integration, furthermore, raise the question Kymlicka (1995) addressed regarding if and how liberal democratic states should accommodate religious and cultural practices such as polygamy and requiring women to wear Islamic veils that potentially violate democratic norms. Since most European states have a model of secularism similar to Germany's or Britain's, these issues are crucial to both the accommodation of growing Muslim populations and the future of secular states across the continent.

Most postcolonial states are also officially secular, while making various accommodations for religions. On the whole, perhaps the biggest difference between African and Asian states, in particular, and European states is that the former are much more religious, as the Country and Concept table (pages 148–149) indicates for most of our case study countries. Stepan (2011) argued that in our case study of India, among others, a new model of secularism has arisen, what he termed the "respect all, positive accommodation, principled distance" model. The state in multireligious societies under this model attempts to respect and give autonomy to all major religions but also includes an element of "positive accommodation" in terms of state funding of religions. Philosophically, it closely resembles Kymlicka's multicultural integration in the sense that particular groups may be given particular rights in the interests of both social harmony and their inclusion in the broader society. As our case study of India demonstrates, that can be a difficult process in practice.

CASE Study

INDIA: SECULARISM IN A RELIGIOUS AND RELIGIOUSLY PLURAL SOCIETY

CASE SYNOPSIS

India's battle over secularism and the role of religion raises the classic questions about equal citizenship and clashing values that have arisen in the West, but in very different circumstances. Faced with a multireligious and relatively devout population, the founders of India's democracy agreed to a secular state but defined that state via the "respect all, positive accommodation, principled distance" form of secularism. Recognizing religious groups' autonomy to follow their own laws, however, has pitted communal rights against individual rights of equal citizenship. The state has come to treat Hindus and Muslims differently in this arena, granting much greater autonomy to the Muslim minority. Much of this debate has involved, as is so often the case, questions about women's rights within the religious community. Despite the goals of the country's first leaders, the state's official secular stance does not seem to be reducing the role of religion. Indeed, religious movements seem stronger now than at any time since independence and have raised serious challenges to Indian secularism.

- BACKGROUND Religiously devout and pluralistic society

- CONTEXT Secularism based on "respect all, positive accommodation, principled distance"

- ISSUES Growing Hindu–Muslim disputes; religious autonomy versus uniform laws; Ayodhya mosque/temple controversy

On February 27, 2002, a train full of Hindus returning from a pilgrimage to a disputed temple site unexpectedly stopped in a small town in Gujarat, a western state in India and the birthplace of Mahatma Gandhi. A Muslim mob set the train on fire, killing fifty-eight passengers. In response, Hindu nationalists called for a massive protest, which the state government supported. The protest quickly became a rampage against Muslims and their businesses; as many as 2,000 Muslims were killed and 150,000 displaced, and for three days the police did nothing to stop the violence.

This was only the largest recent example of major religious violence in India. Religious divisions led to the partition of India and Pakistan at independence, which left India with a population that is more than 80 percent Hindu but that has numerous religious minorities, including a Muslim minority that comprises about 13 percent of the population. After partition, religion was not a major division in India's secular democracy for two decades, but since the 1970s it has become increasingly important. India has seen major debates over what exactly secularism should mean, especially in the area of personal law governing marriage, divorce, and inheritance.

India's "respect all, positive accommodation, principled distance" model has arisen from three ideas of secularism that have competed throughout India's history: the state as modernizer working to reduce the influence of all religions, the state as neutral arbiter among religions, and the state as protector of religious minorities against the Hindu majority. Much of the top leadership of the nationalist movement saw religion as backward and standing in the way of modernization. For them, secularism meant that the state should work to reduce the influence of religion in public life. Most recognized, however, that the country was very religiously observant and diverse. Ultimately, the constitutional statutes regarding the place of religion were based on the idea of equal respect for all religions. For the most part, religious organizations were left the authority to mind their own affairs, though within limits. Article 26 of the country's constitution "provides freedom to manage religious affairs, subject to public order, morality and health," and Article 25

> provides for freedom of conscience and free profession, practice and propagation of religion subject to public order, morality, and health. It confers on the state the right to regulate or restrict any economic, financial, political, or other secular activity, which may be associated with religious practice. (Rao 2006, 53–54)

These clauses seem to grant religious groups autonomy to practice their faiths but also grant the state the ability to limit these practices when it deems necessary, an ambiguous stance that has led to decades of dispute.

Not surprisingly, these principles have been put into practice in varying ways over the years. The state does not allow religious education in publicly financed schools, but it does allow and even aids religious schools that have religious curricula. Given the decentralized nature of both Hinduism and Islam, the government has also intervened at times to facilitate interactions among

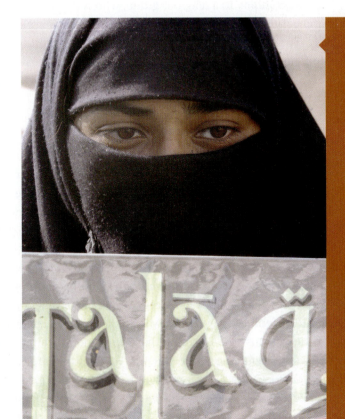

An Indian Muslim girl in 2005 holds a sign protesting the "triple Talaq," under which Muslim men can divorce their wives simply by stating three times they choose to do so. In 2016 a major case, in which a Muslim woman argued that Muslim marriage should be governed by the uniform civil code rather than Muslim religious law, was presented before the Indian Supreme Court.

INDRANIL MUKHERJEE/AFP/Getty Images

religious organizations of the same faith or has informally recognized certain groups as representing these religions. The southern state of Tamil Nadu, for instance, helps administer Hindu temples and their large endowments, with prominent members of the government on the boards of directors of the temples. These temples own half a million acres of prime agricultural land and manage great wealth, making the happiness of their membership politically important.

Personal law came to be the most controversial religious question in India, especially involving Muslims. Uncertainty over Islamic law led to the creation of the All India Muslim Personal Law Board (AIMPLB) in 1973 to oversee the implementation of *sharia* in personal law. By the 1980s, it had established itself as the unofficial voice of the Muslim community on personal law, but its position soon came into dispute. In 2000 it issued what it hoped would be a definitive treatise giving a detailed version of proper *sharia* personal law, but that failed to quell growing questions about the board's position. Critics within the Muslim community argued that the board had become beholden to a particular version of Islam and therefore did not represent the larger community (Jones 2010). By 2005 the board had split, and two additional boards had been created, the All India Shia (Shiite) Personal Law Board and the All India Muslim Women's Personal Law Board, the latter an Islamic feminist effort to interpret *sharia* in ways that expand rights for women. As in other cases where the state recognizes and gives autonomy to a religious group, who is the official arbiter of the group's traditions and beliefs is an important and often contested question.

The constitution's ambiguous position of granting autonomy to religious groups to follow their own personal law while simultaneously promising to work toward an eventual "uniform civil code" is at the heart of growing legal disputes. At independence, a debate was already underway over a Hindu Code Bill that would reform Hindu law to outlaw polygamy for Hindus and grant women greater rights to divorce and inheritance. Legislation in 1955 gave limited rights to Hindu women, including banning polygamy for Hindus, but it still prevented women from inheriting agricultural land, the most important form of wealth in the country. While only a partial victory for women's rights, the act nonetheless established the principle that Hindu law was subject to secular legal principles. The latter did not govern Muslim law, leaving a disjointed legal framework that remains to this day (Harel-Shalev 2013).

The biggest battle over personal law and religion occurred in 1986. Shah Bano, a seventy-three-year-old Muslim woman divorced from her husband of more than fifty years, went to court to seek financial support from him because a law in the criminal code, which applies to all citizens regardless of religion, requires husbands to provide for their former wives. Under Muslim law, however, a husband is not usually obligated to support his wife for more than three months after divorce. The case went all the way to the Supreme Court, which ruled that the state's criminal code overrides Muslim personal law and, therefore, Shah Bano's husband had to support her. This seemingly innocuous personal case led to large-scale protest and intense political drama. The

AIMPLB launched a campaign against the ruling that included a demonstration of half a million people in Bombay, numerous conferences attended by tens of thousands of people, and even a thirty-five-thousand-strong women's protest. In response, secular liberals, reformist Muslims, and women's movements launched counterdemonstrations and demanded further reforms directed toward fulfilling the constitution's promise of a uniform civil code.

The case pitted individual equal rights of citizenship directly against communal rights of religious law and practice. After some hesitation, the Congress Party government introduced the Muslim Women's (Protection of Rights on Divorce) Bill in parliament in February 1986. The vociferous parliamentary debate, framed mainly in terms of the rights of a religious minority versus universal equal rights, was closely watched across the country. The bill ultimately passed; the communal rights of the religious minority had won out. Ironically, in the new millennium, courts have interpreted its provisions in ways that favor Muslim women, giving them greater benefits after divorce (Basu 2008). In a related case, in 2016 a Muslim woman petitioned the Supreme Court, asking it to annul both Muslim men's right to divorce a woman simply by declaring three times they wished to do so and polygamy, arguing that a uniform civil code ought to govern both. Despite protests from the AIMPLB, the Court agreed to hear the case and will consider a prior government report on the status of women in India that recommended banning both practices.

These cases occurred in the context of rising religiously inspired participation in electoral politics. Although a small minority, Muslims in India participate actively in party politics. Where they constitute a sizable group, they often support a Muslim-identified party, which can win elections as long as Muslims make up around a third of the electorate. Where they are a smaller minority, they choose a secular party they hope will support their interests, though Hindu politicians usually lead such parties. While it was dominant, the ruling Congress Party received the most Muslim votes. Since the Congress's decline in the late 1980s, Muslims also have supported state-level and ethnic parties. This participation, though, has not resulted in equal representation or socioeconomic status in Indian society. A 2006 government commission on the status of Muslims found that they remain underrepresented in most levels of government and have poverty and education rates similar to *dalit*s, the so-called "untouchables" (Harel-Shalev 2013). After the 2014 election, Muslims occupied just 4.5 percent of parliamentary seats, down from 6 percent after the 2009 election.

Growing Muslim movements are in part a reaction to the growth of Hindu nationalism and its party, the Bharatiya Janata Party (BJP) (see chapter 6), which was the ruling party from 1999 to 2004 and again since 2014. The BJP's ideology, *Hindutva,* is based on a claim that Hinduism lies at the core of Indian national history and identity. Most Hindu nationalists do not claim that Muslims have no rights in India, but they do argue that Muslims and others must recognize the cultural influence and centrality of Hinduism to true Indian nationalism. The party actively opposes what it sees as "appeasement" of Muslims and other religious minorities and instead calls for a uniform civil code and the end of quotas reserving educational and civil service positions for Muslims or other minorities (an Indian form of affirmative action). Hindu nationalists reject official secularism, arguing it is a Western import of little relevance to deeply religious India: "According to the BJP, India will emerge as a strong nation only when it becomes a cohesive *Hindu Rashtra,* a Hindu nation-state" (Rao 2006, 76). At the state level, BJP governments have actively worked to rewrite Indian textbooks to remove what they see as bias in favor of the Muslim role in the country's history. While in power at the national level, however, the party has moderated its views substantially and has not pursued the uniform civil code. Despite this partial moderation, the Hindu nationalists have caused significant fear and opposition among Muslims.

Since the start of the U.S.-led war in Afghanistan, fears of Islamic militancy have risen in India. The disputed northern region of Kashmir has long been a flashpoint. The Kashmiri movement was originally a regionally based drive for autonomy or independence from both India and Pakistan, rejecting both Hindu and Muslim domination. India's continued refusal to allow a referendum on Kashmir's independence, however, has led the movement in an increasingly religious direction, with the active support of neighboring Pakistan. Terrorist bombs that destroyed a Mumbai hotel and killed hundreds in 2008 raised tensions further, though in response, Muslims led a major demonstration against terrorism. Howard Spodek (2010) argued that while violent Muslim militancy certainly exists in India, it is unlikely to achieve a widespread following; India's democracy continues to allow Muslim participation, and its economic success is reducing the young, unemployed population that is typically subject to militant recruitment. A potentially violent conflict was avoided when an appeals court ruling in 2010 divided ownership of the disputed temple site in Ayodhya (from which the Hindu pilgrims were returning when attacked in 2002) between Hindus and Muslims, and no major reaction occurred. In early 2011, the country's Supreme Court stayed the appeals court ruling, however, pending its own decision. By 2016, the Court was still considering the case.

CASE Questions

1. Why has personal law involving things like marriage and divorce become such a contentious subject in Indian politics? What does this teach us about how religion becomes politicized?
2. Indian policy on religion is ambiguous: on the one hand, it attempts to grant religious groups autonomy, while on the other hand it strives to create uniform laws for all. Why has India not been able to resolve this ambiguity, and how might it best do so in the future?

GENDER AND SEXUAL ORIENTATION: THE CONTINUING STRUGGLE FOR RECOGNITION, SOCIAL STATUS, AND REPRESENTATION

The women's movement and changes in women's position, activity, and status have been the most dramatic social and political revolution of the last generation, especially in wealthy countries. The number of women in the workforce in wealthy countries, in professional positions, and in higher education has skyrocketed since the 1960s. Jeane Kirkpatrick wrote in the early 1970s in her classic study of the United States, *Political Woman*:

> Half a century after the ratification of the nineteenth amendment, no woman has been nominated to be president or vice president, no woman has served on the Supreme Court. Today, there is no woman in the cabinet, no woman in the Senate, no woman serving as governor of a major state, no woman mayor of a major city, no woman in the top leadership of either major party. (1974, 3)

Today, every item on the list has been checked off. While women still make up a small percentage of each of the offices Kirkpatrick mentions, they are present in noticeable numbers, and many other countries outstrip the United States in percentage of women in high offices. Hillary Rodham Clinton, the Democratic nominee for president in 2016, won the most votes but lost the election in the Electoral College. While this final, political "glass ceiling" remains to be shattered, women's participation in American politics has been transformed since Kirkpatrick's statement.

While many might argue that what is commonly known as the "gay rights movement" has not achieved as much progress as the women's movement, it has nonetheless had a dramatic, and rapidly growing, impact. Particularly in Western countries, gays and lesbians are often comfortable living in the open, and in many countries they have successfully fought for the right to marry, serve in the armed forces, and, like women, not face employment discrimination. Both of these interrelated movements, though, continue to face opposition to their demands, greater in some countries than others.

Both movements emerged from the tumultuous 1960s in the West. Women active in other movements such as the anti–Vietnam War effort began to demand equal treatment and recognition, both within the other movements and in society more broadly. While the women's movement arose gradually, the gay rights movement burst forth suddenly and dramatically. While various countries had small "homophile" organizations earlier, the modern gay rights movement was born in New York City in 1969 at the famous Stonewall riots. New York police raided a popular gay bar, the Stonewall Inn, on June 28, setting off five days of sometimes violent defense of the bar and attacks on the police. In the context of the racial and feminist movements of the late 1960s, the effect of Stonewall was dramatic: "Literally overnight, the Stonewall riots transformed the homophile movement of several dozen homosexuals into a *gay liberation movement* populated by thousands of lesbians, gay men, and bisexuals who formed hundreds of organizations demanding radical changes" (Eskridge 1999, 99).

The women's and gay rights' movements have fundamentally challenged social and political norms. Norms of gender and sexuality, of course, are closely intertwined. What it means to be a "man" in every society is tightly woven with what it means to be a "heterosexual man." And because particular notions of gender help define what it means to be a member of a nation, ethnic group, race, or religion, challenging gender and sexual orientation norms challenges the validity of other identity groups. Women, gays, and lesbians who demand recognition of gender and sexual orientation as distinct categories of concern have thus come into conflict not only with nationalists in the West but also with postcolonial nationalists who demanded national unity to throw off colonial rule, leaders of racial or ethnic groups who demanded unity to overcome oppression, and religious groups who demanded recognition and autonomy.

Most recently, the transgender movement has questioned not only gender norms but the definition of gender itself. The success of the feminist and gay rights movements has empowered transgender people to demand recognition and equal social status. The "coming out" of Caitlyn Jenner as a transgender woman in 2015 was simply the most public event in a longer history. In 2016 the U.S. government issued guidance for schools suggesting that giving transgender students equal access to all facilities, bathrooms in particular, based on their self-declared gender identity was necessary to fulfill laws on gender equality (Title IX of the Educational Amendments of 1972, in particular), and the military began to allow transgender soldiers to serve openly.

Transgender rights, though, also posed some problems for elements of the women's movement, as it raised the question of who is a "woman." Women's colleges, for instance, struggled with whether they should accept transgender women (who were assigned the male gender at birth) as students, including whether they should accept transgender women who had or had not had surgery to change their anatomy (not all transgender people desire, or are able, to have surgery to reconcile their anatomy with their gender identity). Some feminists also questioned whether transgender women who had spent most of their lives living as men could understand the discrimination women face and therefore be included as legitimate members of women's movements.

The question of exactly who should be included in the group has long been a question for the gay rights movement as well. Originally referred to as "homosexual," by the late 1960s the group had adopted the term "gay and lesbian" in some countries, in part because "homosexual" had been a term used by psychiatrists to classify the practice as a mental disorder. By the 1980s, though, it was becoming clear that not all people who were not heterosexual identified themselves as gay or lesbian. Sex research has long shown that sexual preferences do not fit into absolute categories but rather extend along a continuum, from sole preference for the opposite sex on one end and for the same sex on the other and a range of variation in between. Eventually, the categories "bisexual" and "transgender" were added to produce "lesbian, gay, bisexual, and transgender" (LGBT), the most common current designation in the United States. Even though transgender refers to gender identity rather than sexual orientation (transgender people can be of any sexual orientation), their movement arose within the "gay rights" movement, and they share the common issue of demanding to live their true identity in the public sphere rather than being forced to hide "in the closet." Recently, some activists and theorists have adopted the word *queer*, formerly considered derogatory, as an affirmative term to include the entire LGBT group or sometimes as an addition to the label, as in LGBTQ.

Debating Goals

As they challenged other groups, feminists and LGBT rights advocates also debated among themselves what their full agenda ought to be. This debate mirrors the broader debate on multiculturalism and group rights. Liberal feminists, like proponents of liberal equality more generally, focus on gaining equal rights with men as their main goal, and they tend not to challenge social or political norms beyond that, accepting existing political and economic systems but demanding equal treatment within them. Similarly, LGBT activists who favor what is known as an assimilationist approach seek equal civil and political rights but generally are willing to adopt the cultural norms of mainstream, heterosexual society: for instance, they favor same-sex marriage, the expansion of a heterosexual institution to include them.

Many feminist and LGBT theorists and activists, though, demand more than just equal treatment in legal, political, and economic contexts. Like other proponents of group rights, many feminists have come to believe that major social and political institutions need to change if women are to make full use of legal equality. Carole Pateman (1988), for instance, questioned the terms of equal citizenship itself, contending that citizenship as typically conceived is inherently male and patriarchal, with its greatest expression being military service. Echoing the ideas of Iris Young (2000) on including all voices in democracy, Pateman argued for a new conception of citizenship that values women's lived experience—one that places motherhood, for instance, on the same moral level as military service. Similarly, the **liberationist** approach to LGBT rights seeks to transform sexual and gender norms, not simply to gain equal rights with heterosexuals but also to liberate everyone to express whatever sexual orientation and gender identity they wish; the goal is to gain social acceptance and respect for all, regardless of their conformity to preexisting norms or institutions. Those favoring a liberationist approach question the importance of same-sex marriage because they question the entire idea of marriage as a patriarchal, heterosexual institution from which everyone should be liberated. They certainly favor equal rights, but they seek much greater change than that, calling for a new "sexual citizenship" (Bell and Binnie 2000).

liberationist
Member of the LGBT movement who seeks to transform sexual and gender norms so that all may gain social acceptance and respect regardless of their conformity to preexisting norms or institutions

Objectives and Outcomes

Recognition   Both women and the LBGT community initially demand recognition of themselves as a group and their concerns as legitimate. Recognition is especially central to the LGBT community because they have been forced to hide throughout most of human history. In this context, being publicly recognized and "coming out" as gay or transgender is the first crucial political act and demand. In gaining recognition, these groups have raised a fundamental question about how the state should regulate the "private" sphere. Liberal political debate is generally restricted to what is deemed "public," with private matters left to the individual, family, and religious institutions. Each society defines for itself, however, what is public and what is private. In most societies, including those in the West, men's treatment of their wives was long a private concern: verbal, physical, and sexual abuse, as long as it did not go as far as murder (and sometimes even when it did), was typically ignored and considered a private, family matter. On the other hand, the act of engaging in sex with someone of the same sex was considered morally offensive and therefore subject to public sanction. In reality, all liberal democracies regulate the "private" sphere in one way or another; the question is how they will do so. The women's and LGBT movements have demanded, and in many cases achieved, changes to this regulation.

Social, Legal, and Economic Status   While women have made many gains, their social and legal status is still not uniformly equal to men's. Women's groups worldwide have sought greater access for women to education and participation in the labor force at all levels, and while women have not achieved full parity, they have made tremendous gains. Many people have an image of Western women as having achieved nearly equal status with men while women in postcolonial countries continue to be mired in oppression. In fact, in many postcolonial countries, this image no longer applies. The gender gap in educational access and attainment has narrowed substantially in most Latin American and African countries and in some Asian ones as well over the last two decades, although, as is true everywhere, professional status and labor force participation rates lag behind education. Aili Mari Tripp (2013) asked not what kind of country but what kind of regime produces the best outcomes for women, finding that even when controlling for the wealth of the country, democracies provider better outcomes for women overall, including in countries that recently went through democratic transitions. The Country and Concept table (pages 148–149) shows that some postcolonial societies are not that much more unequal in gender terms than are wealthier countries, while Map 4.1 displays gender inequality rankings around the world.

Concerns about achieving greater social and economic status have led women to demand reproductive rights and state support for childbearing and child rearing. Women's movements have successfully championed the spread of access to contraception in much of the world, and birth rates have fallen significantly in most countries over the last generation. Legalized abortion remains a controversial subject, with women successfully leading efforts in many societies to support it even as moral and religious objections keep it illegal in quite a few others. Women in approximately

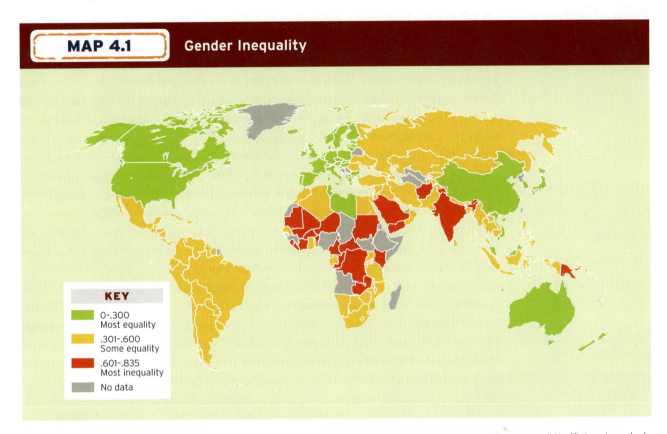

MAP 4.1   **Gender Inequality**

KEY

- 0–.300 Most equality
- .301–.600 Some equality
- .601–.835 Most inequality
- No data

Source: Gender Inequality Index 2016, International Human Development Indicators, United Nations Development Programme (http://hdr.undp.org/en/composite/GII).

sixty countries currently have access to legal abortion. Women, especially in wealthier countries, have also demanded greater state support for childbearing and child rearing to facilitate their participation in the labor force. Support has included paid and unpaid maternity leave, paid and unpaid paternity leave (for fathers to help with child rearing), and access to affordable and high-quality childcare.

A key target of women's groups worldwide has been the achievement of legal status equal to that of men in areas of family law, including rights concerning custody of children, land ownership, and inheritance of family property. These gains have been achieved in virtually all wealthy countries but not in all postcolonial countries. In many of the latter, women still face various legal inequities vis-à-vis men that prevent them from independently owning land or inheriting property; in some cases, women are even restricted from having independent access to banking and travel. While virtually all countries have active women's movements working toward these goals, women in most developing societies remain poorer and less educated, on average, than in wealthier countries, so their movements lack the resources that have helped wealthier women achieve many gains.

Members of the LGBT community cannot proclaim their identity publicly in most countries because of laws criminalizing their behavior, so repealing those laws is always one of the first priorities. Beyond decriminalization of their behavior, they have worked for passage of antidiscrimination laws that prevent government, employers, educators, and adoption agencies from discriminating based on sexual orientation.

States around the world have responded to the LGBT movement in various ways, as Map 4.2 demonstrates. Some have not only decriminalized homosexual activity but have legalized same-sex marriage; others have severe penalties for any homosexual activity. The biggest issue of recent years has been same-sex marriage. A handful of states have granted complete rights to marry, starting with the Netherlands in 2001 and by 2016 including fifteen countries, as shown on Map 4.2. Proponents of same-sex marriage argue it is a matter of equal civil rights for all. Opponents disagree based on religious beliefs or on the argument that heterosexual marriage is a key building block of social order and should be preserved as such. In contrast to many of the debates over inclusion, in this case those arguing for the status quo do so on the basis of preserving particular group rights (religious justifications for heterosexual marriages), while those seeking change argue for treating all individuals equally.

While the LGBT movement began in the United States, its success there was comparatively slow. Sodomy laws against homosexual activity were not eliminated by the Supreme Court until 2003, gay men and lesbians were not allowed to serve openly in the military until 2010, and same-sex marriage was not legalized nationwide until 2015, long after a number of other countries had made similar changes. It remains legal to discriminate on the basis of sexual orientation in the workplace in most of the country: twenty-one states have laws protecting against employment discrimination on the basis of sexual orientation (eighteen of which include gender identity as well), but no federal antidiscrimination legislation exists. The Employment Non-Discrimination Act (ENDA) to do so has been introduced in Congress every year since 1974 but has never passed. Its current version includes protection on the basis of gender identity.

Fewer postcolonial societies have active LGBT movements. Higher levels of religiosity and cultural traditions in many of these societies mean greater social opposition to public proclamation of homosexuality, as Map 4.2 and the Country and Concept table (pages 148–149) demonstrate. In a growing number of postcolonial countries, however, active gay rights movements have arisen. Indeed, South Africa became the first country in the world to include sexual orientation in its constitution as a category protected from discrimination. In 2005 a South African court interpreted this to apply to marriage, making it also one of the first countries to legalize gay marriage. Fledgling LGBT movements elsewhere in Africa, such as in Zimbabwe, Kenya, and Uganda, face much greater popular and legal resistance. In many African and Middle Eastern countries, homosexual activity remains explicitly illegal. Our case study of Brazil is an example of a postcolonial society with an active LGBT movement that has had some notable policy successes, including legalizing gay marriage in 2013.

Political Representation   After a long struggle, women have gained recognition as a group with legitimate concerns and basic political rights in many societies (though not all). In terms of rights, members of the LGBT group are unusual in the

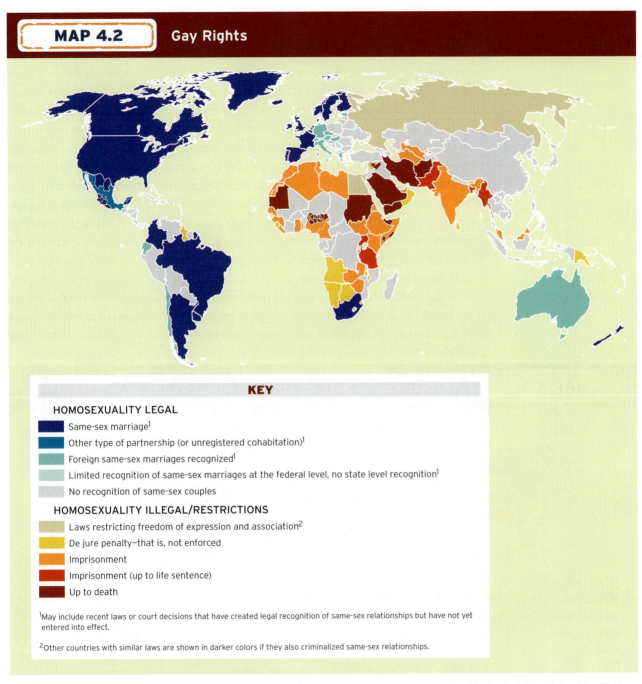

MAP 4.2   Gay Rights

KEY

HOMOSEXUALITY LEGAL

- Same-sex marriage[1]
- Other type of partnership (or unregistered cohabitation)[1]
- Foreign same-sex marriages recognized[1]
- Limited recognition of same-sex marriages at the federal level, no state level recognition[1]
- No recognition of same-sex couples

HOMOSEXUALITY ILLEGAL/RESTRICTIONS

- Laws restricting freedom of expression and association[2]
- De jure penalty—that is, not enforced
- Imprisonment
- Imprisonment (up to life sentence)
- Up to death

[1]May include recent laws or court decisions that have created legal recognition of same-sex relationships but have not yet entered into effect.

[2]Other countries with similar laws are shown in darker colors if they also criminalized same-sex relationships.

Sources: Wikipedia, Homosexuality Laws (http://en.wikipedia.org/wiki/File:World_homosexuality_laws.svg); *Washington Post*, "The State of Gay Rights Around the World" (https://www.washingtonpost.com/graphics/world/gay-rights/).

sense that they secured basic political rights as individuals long before civil rights; that is, as individuals they could vote or run for office like any other citizen, as long as they kept their sexual orientation or transgender identity private. As a group, though, they were unwelcome until quite recently in all societies. Once they gain social and legal acceptance, the barriers to political participation are greatly reduced.

Women's movements, however, have focused great effort on improving their representation in the political process. Jane Mansbridge (2000) argued that "descriptive representation"—representation by people who look like you and have similar life experiences—is particularly important when social inequality results in groups of citizens not trusting their elected representatives who hail from a different group, communication among members of different groups might be difficult, or unforeseen issues arise between elections. Most feminists believe that greater descriptive representation will produce greater substantive representation: the effective representation of women's issues and concerns. Tiffany Barnes and Stephanie Burchard (2013) used a statistical analysis of survey data to demonstrate that descriptive representation in the form of more women in legislatures produces greater female political engagement in the citizenry. Barnes (2016) also used evidence from Argentina to show that women legislators collaborate more than their male counterparts because women are in a more marginalized position in the legislative process than men and therefore benefit more from collaboration.

While women have definitely gained ground in parliaments around the world, they remain just 22.7 percent of the total members of parliament worldwide (see Map 4.3), and only fourteen women were heads of government in 2016. Parliamentary

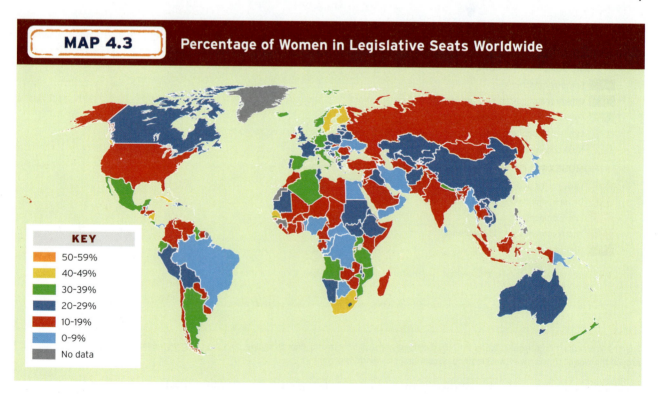

MAP 4.3 **Percentage of Women in Legislative Seats Worldwide**

KEY
- 50–59%
- 40–49%
- 30–39%
- 20–29%
- 10–19%
- 0–9%
- No data

Source: Inter-Parliamentary Union, "Women in National Parliaments" (http://www.ipu.org/wmn-e/classif.htm).

Note: Andorra and Rwanda are the only two countries with women occupying 50 percent or more legislative seats. Percentages are for lower and single houses only. Data for upper houses, where available, can be found at the source website above. South Africa's estimate does not include the thirty-six special rotating delegates appointed on an ad hoc basis; all percentages given are therefore calculated on the basis of the fifty-four permanent seats.

CRITICAL INquiry

The World Values Survey: Attitudes toward Women, Religion, and Homosexuality

This chapter treats claims for inclusion by religious groups, women, and gays and lesbians separately, though we note that they share many similarities and can be understood using the same philosophical debate. The Critical Inquiry table provides data from the World Values Survey of attitudes toward all three groups and a few other key variables for a selection of countries. What patterns can you see in the data? Do attitudes for all three areas go together? Why or why not? What hypotheses can you generate to explain the patterns you find? Can you tie these hypotheses to some of the theories that explain political behavior that we've examined throughout the book?

	Importance of religion (% responding "very" and "rather important")	Membership in church (% active members)	Trust people of another religion (% responding "trust completely" and "trust somewhat")*	Importance of democracy (%)**	When jobs are scarce, men should have more right to a job than women (%)	Men make better political leaders (% responding "agree" and "strongly agree")	Homosexuality justified (% responding always justified) †***	Don't want homosexuals as neighbors (%)†
Argentina	56.1	17.0	53.1	71.6	15.0	26.9	28.4	11.0
Brazil	89.4	49.5	57.5	65.9	16.8	28.4	23.4	11.1
Colombia	85.4	49.1	28.6	70.3	22.4	27.4	11.6	34.6
Chile	50.3	23.1	40.8	72.8	17.6	27.0	29.1	25.7
Burkina Faso	94.8	23.8	52.3	58.8	50.5	57.6	3.9	80.5
Ghana	98.5	69.2	44.4	72.8	49.3	81.3	1.6	79.7
Rwanda	72.3	29.2	39.0	55.0	42.3	45.7	0.3	88.4
South Africa	83.9	56.2	53.8	55.2	30.0	51.6	17.2	37.9
Germany	38.0	14.1	50.0	84.6	15.5	19.8	36.6	22.4
France	40.8	4.3	75.0	77.2	18.1	20.7	47.8	28.8
United Kingdom	40.1	19.0	65.4	76.0	15.8	27.8	32.0	16.8
United States	68.4	34.5	69.0	72.7	5.7	19.4	31.9	20.4
Egypt	99.8	0.4	40.0	86.6	83.4	86.4	–	–
Iran	94.3	19.9	–	64.0	69.0	78.0	2.5	92.4
Iraq	97.5	7.0	32.8	66	65.2	79.3	1.2	80.3
Morocco	98.7	1.5	22.4	64.8	60.6	57.4	0.7	85.5
India	91.3	14.0	50.0	59.3	52.4	52.0	1.9	65.0
Indonesia	98.0	37.6	37.8	70.5	54.2	59.0	1.6	65.9
Japan	19.0	3.7	10.1	64.4	30.0	27.6	22.7	–

Source: World Values Survey (http://www.wvsevsdb.com/wvs/WVSAnalizeQuestion.jsp); selected samples: Argentina 2013, Brazil 2014, Colombia 2012, Chile 2011, Egypt 2012, Germany 2013, Ghana 2011, India 2012, Iraq 2013, Japan 2010, Morocco 2011, Rwanda 2012, South Africa 2013, United States 2011; Burkina Faso 2007, France 2006, Indonesia 2006, Iran 2005, United Kingdom 2005.

*Percentage combines answers "trust completely" and "trust a little" in the survey.

**Percentage combines answers 8–10 from the survey, where the survey used a scale of 1–10, with 1 being "not at all important" and 10 being "absolutely important."

***Percentage combines answers 8–10 from the survey, where the survey used a scale of 1–10, with 1 being "not at all justified" and 10 being "absolutely justified."

†World Values Survey notes that questions having to do with homosexuality were not asked in some countries for "cultural reasons."

representation varies widely but not systematically by region. A number of postcolonial states have higher percentages of female representatives than do the United States or some European countries; Rwanda and Bolivia were the only countries above 50 percent in 2016. Women's movements in many countries have championed the creation of quotas for women's legislative participation, in the form of either rules that require a certain percentage of each party's candidates to be women or a certain percentage of women in the legislature itself. Quotas are typically set at anywhere from 25 to 50 percent of the total seats or candidates. While only ten states had any type of quota before 1980, over one hundred had them by 2010. The majority of these, however, have been voluntarily adopted within parties. Aili Mari Tripp and Alice Kang (2008) concluded from a large statistical analysis that quotas have a greater effect on the number of women in legislatures than do economic development, religion, or other commonly used explanations for why women gain representation. Quotas also are associated with greater substantive representation of women's issues (Krook and Schwindt-Bayer 2013, 565).

Quotas for women in legislatures, especially those mandated by law (more typical in Asia and Africa than in Europe), raise the key questions in the debate over multiculturalism and inclusion in democracies. Supporters of simple liberal equality argue that women are free to vote and run for office, and if they are elected they are free to serve. Any type of quota violates the principle of equal citizenship for all. Supporters of quotas, on the other hand, argue for the group right of descriptive representation, following Iris Young's argument that democracies need to ensure that the voices of marginalized groups are included in policy discussions.

IRAN: WOMEN'S SOCIAL GAINS, POLITICAL AND CULTURAL RESTRICTIONS, AND ISLAMIC FEMINISM

CASE SYNOPSIS

Economic needs and the women's movement have combined to achieve significant social, educational, and economic gains for Iranian women, but far fewer legal, political, and cultural successes. These changes have had a profound effect on Iranian families in terms of frequency and age of marriage, number of children, and frequency of divorce. An active women's movement continues and includes both secular and Islamic women. Its success has been much greater when reformists have controlled the government, and its gains are at least partially reversed when conservatives are elected.

CASE SYNOPSIS

- **BACKGROUND** "Modernization" under the shah; greater restriction under the Islamic Republic
- **CONTEXT** Women's movement mixes secular and Islamic women; active participation in 2009 antiregime protests
- **ISSUES** Contradiction between social and economic gains and restrictive laws
- **GENDER INEQUALITY INDEX** 0.515—114 of 155 in 2014

In 2003 Iranian human rights lawyer and feminist activist Shirin Ebadi won the Nobel Peace Prize amid great adulation from much of the world but condemnation from the Iranian government. Four years later, the government responded to a new wave of women's activity against discrimination with a crackdown on public morality, especially women's public appearance. "Chastity police" arrested hundreds and harassed thousands of Iranians, mostly women, for not abiding by a particular interpretation of Islamic teachings about what women can do and how they can appear in public. These events were part of a long-standing dispute over women's rights in Iran. While the Iranian government certainly does not treat women equally in cultural and political areas, it has nonetheless allowed and often even encouraged significant social and economic gains. This has created a contradiction, as educated and employed women demand greater equality and the government continues to deny it.

Under the shah's modernization program of the 1960s and 1970s, women were encouraged to reject their traditional roles and appearance in order to "modernize" along Western lines. The effort had a much more significant effect in urban than rural areas. Like the rest of the shah's policies, though, it increasingly came to be seen as imposed by a dictator doing the West's bidding, and women were active participants in

Iranian women wait in line to vote in the 2013 presidential election. Women under the Islamic Republic have made massive gains in education and control over reproduction (lower fertility and more access to contraception) but continue to lag in employment and access to political power. While large numbers of women's NGOs operate within the country, very few women are in major leadership positions in government.

ATTA KENARE/AFP/Getty Images

the 1978–1979 revolution that created the Islamic Republic. The revolutionary process itself brought women into the political arena in unprecedented numbers.

As the Islamist clerics under the Ayatollah Khomeini consolidated their power in 1979–1980, however, one of their first acts was to reverse the shah's Family Protection Law, which had Westernized much of the country's family law. The new regime eliminated women's right to divorce while giving men nearly an unlimited right to leave their wives; required women to wear the *hijab,* the Islamic veil, in public; forced women out of the legal profession and restricted them from several other professions; banned contraception; and segregated the education system. Many women who had been active in the revolution felt betrayed and protested these changes, including hundreds of thousands who took to the streets in March 1979 to protest mandatory veiling.

During the 1980s most of the social gains women had made since the 1960s were at least partially reversed: women's employment levels dropped, their political participation was minimal (only 4 women out of 270 MPs were elected to the first parliament after the revolution), and without access to contraception they bore more children. The absence of men during the Iran–Iraq War (1980–1988), however, gave women an opportunity to enter school at all levels to an unprecedented degree, which the government encouraged as part of a literacy campaign. Indeed, the regime's gender segregation of schools increased girls' enrollment, as conservative parents were more willing to send their daughters to all-female schools. Any critical political activity was still severely repressed, but women found new paths to enter the public arena via the education system.

In the early 1990s, the various restrictions put on women's economic roles came into direct conflict with the government's economic liberalization program. Spurred by a renewed women's movement and facing economic necessity, the government partially reversed various laws restricting the advancement of women. Over the course of the decade, most restrictions on what women could study and where they could work were eliminated, and the government reintroduced and actively supported contraception and mandated maternity leave. Women were also allowed to reenter the legal profession in any position except that of courtroom judge. Fertility rates dropped, women advanced through the educational system, female literacy increased dramatically, more women chose not to marry, and the age of first marriage increased (Bahramitash and Kazemipour 2006). The reformist government under President Mohammad Khatami (1997–2005) accelerated these trends with an explicit policy of furthering women's position in society. From the revolution to 2002, women's life expectancy increased from fifty-eight to seventy-two years, their literacy rate increased from 31 to 69 percent, the share of women still single in their early twenties increased from 21 to 54 percent, their fertility rate dropped from an average of 6.5 live births to 2.7, the gap between men and women in age of marriage and level of education dropped dramatically, and women's share of seats in public universities rose to 60 percent (Bahramitash and Kazemipour 2006). The rapid gains, in fact, led to a conservative backlash in the new millennium that put quotas on the number of women allowed in certain fields of study and at universities away from their homes (Aryan 2012).

Women's improved status did not translate into large gains in employment, however. Women continue to be employed at much lower rates than men and tend to work in lower-paid sectors, especially the government and universities. They constitute only 2 percent of all top political, decision-making, and managerial positions (Nejadbahram 2012, 82–84). Many women and men argue that women pursue education in such high numbers in part because few economic alternatives are open to them (Rezai-Rashti and Moghadam 2011). Universities appealed to young women also because they were places where they could get away from restrictions imposed on them at home and in the larger society. Nonetheless, women's dramatic educational advances created huge social changes and ultimately were supported by most families (Aryan 2012).

Among other outcomes of these social changes, Iran's divorce rate tripled from 2000 to 2010, despite laws making divorce extremely difficult for women. One in seven marriages now ends in divorce. Women frequently waive their right to financial support under Islamic law in order to gain their husband's agreement to divorce. Anthropologist Pardis Mahdavi (2009) studied sexual relationships in contemporary Iran and reported she never met a woman who was "happily married" but did find very high levels of extramarital affairs, instigated by both wives and husbands.

As these dramatic social and economic changes were taking place, an active women's movement reemerged that involved both secular and Islamic feminists. The latter asserted their right to interpret the holy texts (*ijtihad*) and argued that Islam actually emphasizes gender equality. They used the Prophet Mohammad's wives and daughters as examples of women actively involved in the public sphere. They argued that

> true Islam . . . combined equality of opportunity for men and women to develop their talents and capacities and to participate in all aspects of social life, because it acknowledged women's maternal instinct and their essential role within the family. (Paidar 1995, 241)

These feminists rejected what they saw as Western society's sexual objectification of women and the individualistic assumptions of much Western feminism, but they nonetheless argued for a place of equality within Iran's Islamic society.

As the broader reform movement grew in the 1990s (see chapter 8), the women's movement became more active. This was clear in the growing role of women's NGOs. Their number increased from none in 1995 to 480 by 2004, and they were very active in providing services and education for women, especially in urban areas (Koolaee 2012, 140). Inspired in part by Shirin Ebadi's Nobel Prize, the women's movement proclaimed itself publicly at its first major demonstration at Tehran University

Women in Iran and the Middle East

Improvements in the status of women in Iran since the late 1980s have made it roughly equal with the average of other Middle Eastern states on a variety of measures of women's well-being and equality, below average on political representation, but well ahead of the regional average in reduced fertility rate and women's education.

	Gender Inequality Index (2014)	Fertility rate (births per woman, 2015)	Ratio of female to male labor force participation (2013)	Percentage female adult literacy rate (2015)	Percentage female population with at least secondary education (2014)	Percentage female seats in parliament (2016)
Iran	0.515	1.9	17:74	82.5	62.2	6
Middle East	0.537	3.2	13:38	79.9	34.7	14

Sources: United Nations Educational, Scientific and Cultural Organization (http://www.uis.unesco.org/DataCentre/Pages/global-ranking.aspx), (http://data.uis.unesco.org/Index.aspx?queryid=166). All other data in the table are from Human Development Report 2015 (http://hdr.undp.org/sites/default/files/2015_human_development_report_1.pdf).

in 2005, demanding constitutional changes to end gender discrimination. Despite police harassment, some five thousand women managed to attend. Subsequently, the movement began the Campaign for One Million Signatures to change the constitution (Hoodfar and Sadeghi 2009). Under the increased repression of the government of President Mahmoud Ahmadinejad (2005–2013), the movement was divided over how overtly political it should be, but nonetheless the campaign was perhaps the largest civil society activity at the time.

Despite severe cultural and legal restrictions on women, the Islamic constitution gave them full rights to participate in politics, except for being barred from holding the office of the president. Prior to 1991, only women who were clearly identified as Islamists had been elected to the parliament. In that year's election, secular women activists were added to their ranks. When the Guardian Council prevented reformist candidates from running for parliament in 2000, however, the number of women MPs dropped and only recovered in the 2016 election (after reformist Hassan Rouhani was elected president), when a record seventeen women were elected. From the start of the Islamic Republic, most of the small number of women MPs worked actively to achieve greater equality for women. In the area of family law, women were granted slightly more rights to divorce and greater rights over guardianship of children, which came with child allowances from the government. Such legal victories, though, have remained relatively rare and minor.

At the height of the reformist movement under President Mohammad Khatami, the government reduced the severity of the cultural restrictions on women's public actions. It did not enforce the rules about veiling and public segregation of the sexes with the zeal of earlier or subsequent governments. The election of President Ahmadinejad ended the Khatami-led reform effort. Ahmadinejad's renewed efforts to restrict women and segregate them in public included not only the cultural crackdown starting in 2007 but also banning numerous women's (and other dissident) publications and websites and expanding the gender segregation of public amenities. More than one city built women-only parks behind high walls within which women could enjoy being outdoors and exercise without being veiled. This crackdown, however, did not eliminate the women's movement. A women's coalition formed during the 2009 campaign and women were active participants in the massive protests that followed the rigged elections.

Newly elected president Hassan Rouhani said during his 2013 campaign that he believed men and women should be treated equally and promised to create a Ministry of Women's Affairs. He initially disappointed women activists, though, when he appointed only one woman to his cabinet. By 2016, he had appointed four women vice presidents and three governors but had never established the Ministry of Women's Affairs. While he has said he wants to reduce the enforcement of veiling, he had little effective control over the "morality police" who enforce the rule, so little had changed.

CASE Questions

1. What does the contradiction in Iran between significant socioeconomic and educational advance, on the one hand, and severe political and cultural restrictions, on the other, teach us about which areas are most important for the advancement of gender equality? Does it suggest one area should be the primary target for change first?
2. What would the various theories on multiculturalism argue about the Iranian case? Would any of them justify some of the policies toward women in the name of respecting religious belief and cultural differences? Why or why not?

CASE Study

BRAZIL: LGBT RIGHTS IN A NEW DEMOCRACY

CASE SYNOPSIS

The LBGT community in Brazil has had significant success, including the legalization of same-sex marriage in 2013. The transition to democracy—which emphasized expanded rights for all, even though "sexual orientation" was explicitly rejected for inclusion in the new constitution—established a political context in which Brazilian policy has shifted significantly. In terms of recognition, the first and most important goal of the LGBT movement, Brazil has achieved a great deal. The community is widely known and celebrated. On the other hand, opposition from both traditionalist Catholic and evangelical Protestant movements continues, and the world's highest rate of violence against LGBT citizens remains a major concern.

- BACKGROUND Decriminalization of homosexual behavior in nineteenth century
- TYPE OF MOVEMENT Primarily assimilationist, though with liberationist elements
- SUCCESSES Antidiscrimination laws in some places; same-sex marriage
- CONTINUING CHALLENGES Harassment and violence against gays

São Paulo, Brazil's largest city, annually hosts what is reputed to be the biggest gay pride parade and gathering on the planet. Although Brazil is the world's largest predominantly Catholic country, it has a long history and reputation of being relatively open about sexuality in general. It has a well-established LGBT community, but it only developed an open political movement with the transition to democracy in the late 1970s. The first explicitly gay rights group formed in São Paulo in 1979. By the early 1980s, about twenty mostly male gay rights groups existed, but many of these did not survive more than a few years and were plagued by divisions over the inclusion of lesbians and transvestites. Both of the latter formed separate organizations at various points. Until 1992, the major annual meeting of the movement was called the Brazilian Meeting of Homosexuals; in 1993 this became the Brazilian Meeting of Lesbians and Homosexuals; in 1998 the Brazilian Meeting of Lesbians, Gays, and Transgenders. Finally, in 2005 the Brazilian Association of Lesbians, Gays, Transvestites, and Transsexuals was founded, bringing all the major groups under one umbrella.

The movement's growth, despite its divisions, has been impressive. The leadership of the union-based Workers' Party (PT) (see chapter 6) rhetorically embraced gay rights activists and their cause at the first party convention in 1981. The AIDS crisis first hurt and then strengthened the movement in the 1980s. Initially, AIDS hit the gay male population the hardest. As awareness grew, however, infection rates among gay men dropped significantly. Simultaneously, and partly as a result of active pressure from the movement, Brazil developed an AIDS prevention and treatment policy that became a global model of success. Several hundred gay rights groups now constitute the overall movement. In 2006 Juan Marsiaj noted that "the size and diversity of the Brazilian GLT movement make it the largest and one of the strongest of its kind in Latin America" (172).

In 1823 Brazil became one of the first countries in the world to eliminate anti-sodomy laws. While homosexual activity is legal, the law only partially enforces antidiscrimination. The gay rights movement worked hard to get "sexual orientation" included in the 1988 constitution's antidiscrimination clause but was unsuccessful. A national antidiscrimination law focusing on discrimination by commercial enterprises and government offices finally passed the Congress in 2000. A law to outlaw all forms of discrimination on the basis of sexual orientation and gender identity passed one house of Congress in 2006 but never passed both houses of Congress to become law, in part due to strong opposition from legislators affiliated with evangelical Christian movements.

In contrast to the United States, the federal government controls marriage law in Brazil. The PT introduced a bill in the National Congress in 1995 to legalize civil unions nationwide, but it never passed. Court cases have expanded the rights of same-sex couples, however. The constitution's antidiscrimination clause does not list "sexual orientation" specifically but does mention "and other forms of discrimination." Using this clause, the courts legalized civil unions in 2011 and same-sex marriage in 2013.

Activists march in the Walk of Lesbian and Bisexual Women in São Paulo, Brazil, in 2016. The sign in the center front reads, "Being a lesbian is a political act." Brazil has one of the largest and most active gay rights movements in the world, and it legalized same-sex marriage in 2013.

Cris Faga/NurPhoto via Getty Images

In spite of these developments, harassment of and violence against LGBT citizens remains a major concern and common occurrence, and Congress still has not passed a law fully criminalizing such behavior. Brazil leads the world in its murder rate for transgender people (partly because it has one of the highest murder rates in the world in general). A Brazilian activist group has estimated that an antigay/transgender murder takes place virtually every day somewhere in the country. After a particularly gruesome video of brutal treatment of a transgender woman in a Brazilian prison, the state of Rio de Janeiro passed reforms of its prison system that allowed transgender inmates to serve their terms in a prison for their gender of choice and to continue hormone treatments while incarcerated.

Opposition to further LBGT rights, though, continues. In 2013 a member of Congress who is an evangelical minister was elected chair of a key congressional committee and introduced a bill that would allow psychologists to treat homosexuality as a pathology, but the bill failed to pass and a poll showed that 84 percent of Brazilians believed he should step down from his position. More recently, another member of Congress, Jair Bolsonaro, has become a major opponent of LGBT rights, including wanting to reverse the legalization of same-sex marriage. In 2016 he was a leading contender in opinion polls for the next presidential election.

CASE Questions

1. What differences do you see in how gay rights have advanced in the United States and Brazil? What explains these differences: differences in the political systems, the cultures, or the gay rights movements themselves?
2. How do the gay rights movements in these two cases compare with the women's movements in Russia and Iran? What similarities do you see in how and why groups organize and achieve success, or not?

CONCLUSION

Identity politics is so common and explosive in part because the very construction of the groups often creates and reflects differences in political power. As identity categories are created, a sense of superior and inferior status is often embedded within them. How a group is defined influences what it may claim in order to gain or enhance its power: anything from specific legal protections like antidiscrimination laws or the right to school their children in a local language to regional autonomy, power-sharing arrangements, or national statehood. Similarly, actions taken in pursuit of redress of grievances may range from lobbying, voting, and constitutional reform to armed violence and secession. In countries with significant immigration, like the United States and Germany, new immigrants continually raise new issues: their racial or ethnic categorization must be clarified, and the ongoing construction of their categories will influence their place and political power in the broader "nation" they are attempting to join.

Each person belongs to various identity groups, but whether people act politically based on these group memberships depends on a variety of factors. First, the group in question must have a preexisting sense of itself: it must be an "imagined community" with both perceived historic ties and a forward-looking agenda. Second, it must have some felt grievance. Finally, groups seem to need political leadership, elites who can build on and strengthen the identity and link it to particular grievances and appropriate action.

Identity groups always pose challenges to the modern state. Under some circumstances, nationality, ethnicity, race, or religion can challenge the very existence of a state. Even when this is not the case, though, all identity groups raise questions of inclusiveness and equal citizenship. In liberal democracies, such challenges cut to the heart of one of the defining characteristics of the regime. Demands for inclusive citizenship can also raise challenges when they clash with the demands of other identity groups. States must then resolve the question of which groups' demands to meet. This can be particularly difficult when, for instance, women or LGBT groups demand individual civil rights in the name of equality, while a religious, ethnic, or other minority group claims a conflicting right to respect for its cultural practices.

The outcomes of protracted and intense political battles always reveal something about who rules in a particular political system. Policy outcomes reflect the relative power of different political forces. In the political disputes we examined in this chapter, a dominant group protecting the status quo exists in almost all cases. Lack of identity-based conflict may indeed reflect nearly complete domination by that group, as the "second face of power" (see chapter 1) would suggest. Where questions about the inclusion of minority or marginalized identity groups have become politically salient, those groups have at least gained enough power to raise their demands. Their success demonstrates growing power; continuing limitations on their demands equally demonstrate limits on their power.

The trend toward greater mobilization around issues of identity is strong right now, but as always in comparative politics, we cannot assume that what is true today will be true tomorrow. We do believe that identity will continue to be a key challenge to the politics of nation-states, and particularly liberal democracies, and these challenges are likely to arise in other places if more countries expand their openness to global ideas and increase the scope of their civil societies. In the future, however, new conflicts and new political trends will arise, and students of comparative politics will be challenged to document and explain the patterns, sources, and outcomes of future political conflicts. Much will depend on how political institutions in various countries function, the subject we turn to next.

KEY CONCEPTS

assimilation (p. 154)
autonomy (p. 153)
centripetal approach (p. 157)
civic nationalism (p. 160)
consociationalism (p. 155)
constructivism (p. 150)
cultural nationalism (p. 160)
ethnic group (p. 164)
jus sanguinis (p. 160)
jus soli (p. 160)
laïcité (p. 181)

liberationist (p. 191)
multicultural integration (p. 154)
nation (p. 159)
nationalism (p. 159)
neutral state model (p. 180)
political saliency (p. 150)
positive accommodation (p. 181)
primordialism (p. 150)
race (p. 169)
social construction (p. 150)

 Sharpen your skills with SAGE edge at **edge.sagepub.com/orvis4e.**
SAGE edge for students provides a personalized approach to help you accomplish your coursework goals in an easy-to-use learning environment.

WORKS CITED

Alesina, Alberto, Arnaud Devleeschauwer, William Easterly, Sergio Kurlat, and Romain Wacziarg. 2003. "Fractionalization." *Journal of Economic Growth* 8 (2): 155–194.

Alexander, Michelle. 2010. *The New Jim Crow: Mass Incarceration in the Age of Colorblindness.* New York: The New Press.

Anderson, Benedict. 1991. *Imagined Communities: Reflections on the Origin and Spread of Nationalism.* New York: Verso.

Aryan, Khadijeh. 2012. "The Boom in Women's Education." In *Women, Power, and Politics in 21st Century Iran*, edited by Tara Povey and Elaheh Rostami-Povey, 35–52. Burlington, VT: Ashgate.

Bahramitash, Roksana, and Shahla Kazemi-pour. 2006. "Myths and Realities of the Impact of Islam on Women: Changing Marital Status in Iran." *Critique: Critical Middle Eastern Studies* 15 (2): 111–128.

Barnes, Tiffany. 2016. *Gendering Legislative Behavior: Institutional Constraints and Collaboration.* Cambridge, UK: Cambridge University Press.

Barnes, Tiffany, and Stephanie Burchard. 2013. "'Engendering' Politics: The Impact of Descriptive Representation on Women's Political Engagement in Sub-Saharan Africa." *Comparative Political Studies* 46 (7): 767–790. doi:10.1177/0010414012463884

Basu, Srimati. 2008. "Separate and Unequal: Muslim Women and Un-uniform Family Law in India." *International Feminist Journal of Politics* 10 (4): 495–517. doi:10.1080/14616740802393890

Bell, David, and Jon Binnie. 2000. *The Sexual Citizen: Queer Politics and Beyond.* Cambridge, UK, and Malden, MA: Polity Press and Blackwell.

Cornell, Stephen, and Douglas Hartmann. 2007. *Ethnicity and Race: Making Identities in a Changing World.* 2nd ed. Thousand Oaks, CA: Pine Forge Press.

Eskridge, William N., Jr. 1999. *Gaylaw: Challenging the Apartheid of the Closet.* Cambridge, MA: Harvard University Press.

Fetzer, Joel S., and J. Christopher Soper. 2005. *Muslims and the State in Britain, France, and Germany.* Cambridge, UK: Cambridge University Press.

Fryer, Roland G. 2016. *An Empirical Analysis of Racial Differences in Police Use of Force.* National Bureau of Economic Research, Working Paper 22399. July 2016 (http://www.nber.org/papers/w22399.pdf).

Gat, Azar, with Alexander Yakobson. 2014. *Nations: The Long History and Deep Roots of Political Ethnicity and Nationalism.* Cambridge, UK: Cambridge University Press.

Gurr, Ted Robert. 1970. *Why Men Rebel.* Princeton, NJ: Princeton University Press.

Harel-Shalev, Ayelet. 2013. "Policy Analysis beyond Personal Law: Muslim Women's Rights in India." *Politics & Policy* 41: 384–419. doi:10.1111/polp.12016

Hoodfar, Homa, and Fatemeh Sadeghi. 2009. "Against All Odds: The Women's Movement in the Islamic Republic of Iran." *Development* 52 (2): 215–223. doi:10.1057/dev.2009.19

Horowitz, Donald L. 1985. *Ethnic Groups in Conflict.* Berkeley: University of California Press.

Huntington, Samuel P. 1997. *The Clash of Civilizations and the Remaking of World Order.* New York: Touchstone. (Originally published in 1996 by Simon and Schuster.)

Ignatiev, Noel. 1995. *How the Irish Became White.* New York: Routledge.

Jones, Justin. 2010. "'Signs of Churning': Muslim Personal Law and Public Contestation in Twenty-first Century India." *Modern Asian Studies* 44 (1): 175–200. doi:10.1017/S0026749X09990114

Kirkpatrick, Jeane J. 1974. *Political Woman.* New York: Basic Books.

Klinkner, Philip. 2016. *The Easiest Way to Guess if Someone Supports Trump? Ask if Obama Is a Muslim* (http://www.vox.com/2016/6/2/11833548/donald-trump-support-race-religion-economy).

Koolaee, Elaheh. 2012. "Women in the Parliament." In *Women, Power, and Politics in 21st Century Iran,* edited by Tara Povey and Elaheh Rostami-Povey, 137–151. Burlington, VT: Ashgate.

Krook, Mona Lena, and Leslie Schwindt-Bayer. 2013. "Electoral Institutions." In *The Oxford Handbook of Gender and Politics,* edited by Georgina Waylen, Karen Celis, Johanna Kantola, and S. Laurel Weldon, 554–578. Oxford, UK: Oxford University Press.

Kymlicka, Will. 1995. *Multicultural Citizenship: A Liberal Theory of Minority Rights.* Oxford, UK: Clarendon Press.

Kymlicka, Will, and Wayne Norman, eds. 2000. *Citizenship in Diverse Societies.* Oxford, UK: Oxford University Press.

Latino National Survey. University of Washington Institute for the Study of Ethnicity, Race and Sexuality (http://depts.washing ton.edu/uwiser/LNS.shtml).

Lewis-Beck, Michael S., Charles Tien, and Richard Nadeau. 2010. "Obama's Missed Landslide: A Racial Cost?" *PS: Political Science & Politics* (January): 69–76. doi:10.1017/S1049096509990618

Lijphart, Arend. 1977. *Democracy in Plural Societies: A Comparative Exploration.* New Haven, CT: Yale University Press.

Lowrey, Annie. 2013. "Wealth Gap among Races Has Widened since Recession." *New York Times*, April 28 (http://www.nytimes.com/2013/04/29/business/racial-wealth-gap-widened-during-reces sion.html?emc=eta1).

Mahdavi, Pardis. 2009. *Passionate Uprisings: Iran's Sexual Revolution.* Stanford, CA: Stanford University Press.

Mansbridge, Jane. 2000. "What Does a Representative Do? Descriptive Representation in Communicative Settings of Distrust, Uncrystallized Interests, and

Historically Denigrated Status." In *Citizenship in Diverse Societies,* edited by Will Kymlicka and Wayne Norman, 99–123. Oxford, UK: Oxford University Press.

Marshall, T. H. 1963. *Class, Citizenship, and Social Development: Essays.* Chicago: University of Chicago Press.

Marsiaj, Juan P. 2006. "Social Movements and Political Parties: Gays, Lesbians, and Travestis and the Struggle for Inclusion in Brazil." *Canadian Journal of Latin American and Caribbean Studies* 31 (62): 167–198.

McClintock, Anne. 1991. "'No Longer in a Future Heaven': Women and Nationalism in South Africa." *Transition* 51: 104–123.

Nairn, Tom. 1977. *The Break-Up of Britain: Crisis and Neo-Nationalism.* London: New Left Books.

Nejadbahram, Zahra. 2012. "Women and Employment." In *Women, Power, and Politics in 21st Century Iran,* edited by Tara Povey and Elaheh Rostami-Povey, 73–89. Burlington, VT: Ashgate.

Nellis, Ashley. 2016. *The Color of Justice: Racial and Ethnic Disparity in State Prisons.* June 14, 2016 (http://www.sentencingproject.org/publications/color-of-justice-racial-and-ethnic-disparity-in-state-prisons/#II).

Paidar, Parvin. 1995. *Women and the Political Process in Twentieth-Century Iran.* Cambridge, UK: Cambridge University Press.

Pasek, Josh, Jon A. Krosnick, and Trevor Tompson. 2012. *The Impact of Anti-Black Racism on Approval of Barack Obama's Job Performance and on Voting in the 2012 Presidential Election* (http://www.stanford.edu/dept/communication/faculty/krosnick/docs/2012/2012%20Voting%20and%20Racism.pdf).

Pateman, Carole. 1988. *The Sexual Contract.* Stanford, CA: Stanford University Press.

Pew Research Center. 2016a. *On Views of Race and Inequality, Blacks and Whites Are Worlds Apart.* June 27 (http://www.pewsocialtrends.org/2016/06/27/on-views-of-race-and-inequality-blacks-and-whites-are-worlds-apart/).

Pew Research Center. 2016b. *Europeans Fear Wave of Refugees Will Mean More Terrorism, Fewer Jobs: Sharp Ideological Divides across EU on Views about Minorities, Diversity and National identity.* July 11 (http://www.pewglobal.org/2016/07/11/europeans-fear-wave-of-refugees-will-mean-more-terrorism-fewer-jobs/).

Price, Melanye T. 2009. *Dreaming Blackness: Black Nationalism and African American Public Opinion.* New York: New York University Press.

Rao, Badrinath. 2006. "The Variant Meanings of Secularism in India: Notes toward Conceptual Clarifications." *Journal of Church and State* 48 (1): 47–81. doi:10.1093/jcs/48.1.47

Renan, Ernest. 1882. *What Is a Nation?* (http://www.nationalismproject.org/what/renan.htm).

Rezai-Rashti, Goli, and Valentine Moghadam. 2011. "Women and Higher Education in Iran: What Are the Implications for Employment and the 'Marriage Market'?" *International Review of Education* 57 (3/4): 419–441.

Ross, Cody T. 2015. "A Multi-Level Bayesian Analysis of Racial Bias in Police Shootings at the County-Level in the United States, 2011–2014." *PLoS ONE* 10 (11): e0141854. doi:10.1371/journal.pone.0141854

Sauerbrey, Ann. 2016. "What Is German?" *New York Times.* May 26 (http://www.nytimes.com/2016/05/27/opinion/what-is-german.html?smprod=nytcore-ipad&smid=nytcore-ipad-share&_r=0).

Schmidt, Ronald, Sr., Yvette M. Alex-Assensoh, Andrew L. Aoki, and Rodney E. Hero. 2010. *Newcomers, Outsiders, and Insiders: Immigrants and American Racial Politics in the Early Twenty-first Century.* Ann Arbor: University of Michigan Press.

Siroky, David, and John Cuffe. 2014. "Lost Autonomy, Nationalism and Separatism."

Comparative Political Studies 48 (1): 3–34. doi:10.1177/0010414013516927

Smith, Anthony D. 1998. *Nationalism and Modernism.* New York: Routledge.

Spodek, Howard. 2010. "In the Hindutva Laboratory: Pogroms and Politics in Gujarat, 2002." *Modern Asian Studies* XVIV (2): 349–399. March.

Stepan, Alfred. 2011. "The Multiple Secularisms of Modern Democratic and Non-Democratic Regimes." In *Rethinking Secularism*, edited by Craig Calhoun, Mark Juergensmeyer, and Jonathan van Antwerpen, 114–144. Oxford, UK: Oxford University Press.

Taylor, Charles. 1994. "The Politics of Recognition." In *Multiculturalism: Examining the Politics of Recognition,* edited by Amy Gutmann, 25–74. Princeton, NJ: Princeton University Press.

Tesler, Michael. 2016. *Post-Racial or Most-Racial? Race and Politics in the Obama Era.* Chicago: University of Chicago Press.

Tesler, Michael, and David O. Sears. 2010. *Obama's Race: The 2008 Election and the Dream of a Post-Racial America.* Chicago: University of Chicago Press.

Theiss-Morse, Elizabeth. 2009. *Who Counts as an American? The Boundaries of National Identity.* Cambridge, UK: Cambridge University Press.

Tripp, Aili Mari. 2013. "Political Systems and Gender." In *The Oxford Handbook of Gender and Politics*, edited by Georgina Waylen, Karen Celis, Johanna Kantola, and S. Laurel Weldon, 514–535. Oxford, UK: Oxford University Press.

Tripp, Aili Mari, and Alice Kang. 2008. "The Global Impact of Quotas: On the Fast Track to Increased Female Legislative Representation." *Comparative Political Studies* 41 (3): 338–361. doi:10.1177/0010414006297342

Wu, Ellen D. 2014. *The Color of Success: Asian Americans and the Origins of the Model Minority.* Princeton, NJ: Princeton University Press.

Young, Iris Marion. 2000. *Inclusion and Democracy.* Oxford, UK: Oxford University Press.

Yuval-Davis, Nira, and Flora Anthias, eds. 1989. *Woman-Nation-State.* Consultant ed., Jo Campling. Basingstoke, UK: Macmillan.

RESOURCES FOR FURTHER STUDY

Baksh, Rawwida, and Wendy Harcourt, eds. 2015. *The Oxford Handbook of Transnational Feminist Movements.* Oxford, UK: Oxford University Press.

Brass, Paul R. 1991. *Ethnicity and Nationalism: Theory and Comparison.* Newbury Park, CA: Sage.

Brubaker, Rogers. 1992. *Citizenship and Nationhood in France and Germany.* Cambridge, MA: Harvard University Press.

Chandra, Kanchan, ed. 2012. *Constructivist Theories of Ethnic Politics.* Oxford, UK: Oxford University Press.

Cordell, Karl, and Stefan Wolff, eds. 2011. *Routledge Handbook of Ethnic Conflict.* New York: Routledge.

Gellner, Ernest. 1983. *Nations and Nationalism.* Oxford, UK: Blackwell.

Ghai, Yash P., ed. 2000. *Autonomy and Ethnicity: Negotiating Competing Claims in Multi-Ethnic States.* Cambridge, UK: Cambridge University Press.

Hobsbawm, Eric J. 1990. *Nations and Nationalism since 1780: Programme, Myth, Reality.* Cambridge, UK: Cambridge University Press.

Hunter, Shireen T., ed. 2002. *Islam, Europe's Second Religion: The New Social, Cultural, and Political Landscape.* Westport, CT: Praeger.

Hutchinson, John, and Anthony D. Smith, eds. 2000. *Nationalism: Critical Concepts in Political Science,* Vol. IV. New York: Routledge.

Joppke, Christian, and John Torpey. 2013. *Legal Integration of Islam: A Transatlantic Comparison.* Cambridge, MA: Harvard University Press.

Juergensmeyer, Mark. 1993. *The New Cold War? Religious Nationalism Confronts the Secular State.* Berkeley: University of California Press.

Kaufman, Stuart J. 2001. *Modern Hatreds: The Symbolic Politics of Ethnic War.* Ithaca, NY: Cornell University Press.

Lovenduski, Joni, ed. 2005. *State Feminism and Political Representation.* Cambridge, UK: Cambridge University Press.

Lowe, Chris. 1997. "Talking about 'Tribe': Moving from Stereotypes to Analysis." With Tunde Brimah, Pearl-Alice Marsh, William Minter, and Monde Muyangwa (http://www.africaaction.org/talking-about-tribe.html).

Mazur, Amy G. 2002. *Theorizing Feminist Policy.* Oxford, UK: Oxford University Press.

Parekh, Bhikhu C. 2000. *Rethinking Multiculturalism: Cultural Diversity and Political Theory.* Cambridge, MA: Harvard University Press.

Sinno, Abdulkader H., ed. 2009. *Muslims in Western Politics.* Bloomington: Indiana University Press.

Taras, Raymond, and Rajat Ganguly. 2002. *Understanding Ethnic Conflict: The International Dimension.* 2nd ed. New York: Longman.

Van Deburg, William L., ed. 1997. *Modern Black Nationalism: From Marcus Garvey to Louis Farrakhan.* New York: New York University Press.

Wimmer, Andreas. 2013. *Waves of War: Nationalism, State Formation, and Ethnic Exclusion in the Modern World.* Cambridge, UK: Cambridge University Press.

WEB RESOURCES

Center for American Women and Politics
(http://www.cawp.rutgers.edu)
Conflict Analysis Resources, Royal Holloway, University of London
(http://www.rhul.ac.uk/economics/home.aspx)
Correlates of War
(http://www.correlatesofwar.org)
Fractionalization Data, The MacroData Guide
(http://www.nsd.uib.no/macrodataguide/set.html?id=16&sub=1)
International Lesbian, Gay, Bisexual, Trans and Intersex Association
(http://ilga.org)
Quota Project
(http://www.quotaproject.org)
The Religion and State Project, Bar Ilan University, Israel
(http://www.religionandstate.org)
Research Network on Gender Politics and the State
(https://pppa.wsu/research-network-on-gender-politics-and-the-state/)
OutServe-Servicemembers Legal Defense Network
(http://www.outserve-sldn.org)
UNDP Human Development Reports, Gender Inequality Index
(http://hdr.undp.org/en/statistics/gii)
World Values Survey
(http://www.worldvaluessurvey.org)

5 GOVERNING INSTITUTIONS IN DEMOCRACIES

KEY QUESTIONS

- A democracy must limit the power of its executives to provide accountability. Which institutional choices best ensure accountability, and how?

- How much power should a minority have in a democracy? How do different democracies seek to guarantee that minorities are protected from possible majority tyranny? Do some institutional choices seem to guarantee this better than others?

- Do greater participation and representation of many voices in government result in less effective policymaking?

- How can we explain why an institution that works well in one setting might not work as well in another?

- What explains why particular democratic institutions arise in particular countries but not in others?

Americans are taught from a young age the importance of the three branches of government—executive, legislative, and judicial—and how essential their separate but equal status is for democracy. Understanding politics, however, requires far more than simply understanding the formal institutions of government. The social, cultural, and historical contexts in which those formal institutions exist can have significant bearing on how institutions function in practice. On paper, a president in one country may have similar powers as a president in another country, but what each can achieve might vary greatly in the two distinct contexts. The actual power of particular institutions often changes over time as well, as changing socioeconomic and cultural factors give greater resources to one or another institution, or a particular leader helps strengthen or weaken an institution. The first question we must ask, then, has to do with **institutionalization:** To what degree are a state's government processes and procedures established, predictable, and routinized? Comparativists look at how institutionalized the political institutions of a particular state are. This varies within and across all regimes. It is important to examine in democracies and even more important in authoritarian regimes, where it tends to vary more, as we'll see in chapter 8.

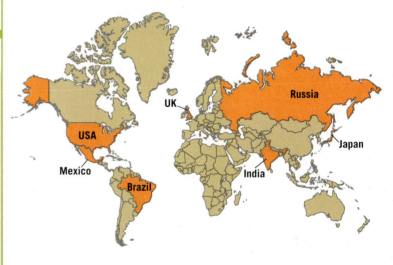

The study of institutions in democracies, which is the focus of this and the next chapter, raises other important questions for democratic theory and comparative politics. The first question involves who rules: Do certain institutional arrangements achieve greater **political accountability,** meaning the ability of the citizenry to directly or indirectly control political leaders and institutions?

Argentine political scientist Guillermo O'Donnell (1999) used the terms *vertical* and *horizontal accountability* to analyze the extent to which the power of key state institutions is under democratic control. **Vertical accountability** refers to the ability of individuals and groups in a society to hold state institutions accountable, whereas **horizontal accountability** refers to the ability of the state's institutions to hold one another accountable. The latter represents indirect control on the part of the citizenry, in that particular institutions implicitly act on behalf of the citizenry to limit the power of and thereby control other institutions or leaders. For instance, a legislature presumably should have enough power vis-à-vis the executive branch to limit what the executive can do, to ask him to justify his actions, and ultimately to punish him

institutionalization
The degree to which government processes and procedures are established, predictable, and routinized

political accountability
The ability of the citizenry, directly or indirectly, to control political leaders and institutions

vertical accountability
The ability of individuals and groups in a society to hold state institutions accountable

horizontal accountability
The ability of state institutions to hold one another accountable

executive
The branch of government that must exist in all modern states; the chief political power in a state and implements all laws

legislature
Branch of government that makes the law in a democracy

judiciary
Branch of government that interprets the law and applies it to individual cases

if he acts in ways unacceptable to the state's constitution or majority opinion in the country. Similarly, the court system may have the power to rule legislative or executive actions unconstitutional, thus preserving the basic system of government against politicians' attempts to abrogate it.

This chapter focuses on horizontal accountability, as we examine the relative power of governing institutions in relation to one another. We examine vertical accountability in greater detail in the next chapter, looking at institutions of participation and representation.

Note that only one of the branches of government, the executive, is essential to a modern state as we defined it in chapter 2. Modern states are sovereign entities that administer territories and people; therefore, an executive power and accompanying bureaucracy are essential to their existence. The **executive** is the chief political power in a state. The position is filled through elections in a democracy and typically is embodied in the single most powerful office in the government, referred to as a president or prime minister in most countries. The modern state, however, also includes a bureaucracy, a large set of lesser officials whose function is to implement the laws of the state, as directed by the executive. We explore both executive powers and modern bureaucracies in this chapter.

The executive is essential, but as the idea of horizontal accountability suggests, a legislature with autonomy from the executive is an important institution of democratization, even if it is not crucial to the modern state itself. Similarly, a judiciary is essential for the state to punish crime and enforce property and contract rights, but it need not have a political role independent of the executive, although in a democracy this can be an important element of horizontal accountability. The process of democratization is in part a matter of creating mechanisms through which the power of the executive is limited. In democratic theory, the **legislature** makes the law, and the **judiciary** interprets it. The power and autonomy of each, however, vary significantly in practice.

Many political scientists believe that forces in the modern world are strengthening the executive branch. The contemporary state has more technically sophisticated functions to carry out than in earlier eras. Legislators often delegate the more technical decisions implied in particular laws to bureaucrats because the legislators lack the technical competence to make those decisions. This has meant the size and power of bureaucracies have expanded, which makes controlling the executive paramount. Some political scientists also worry about limiting the role of the judiciary, seeing a "judicialization" of politics in which courts and judges replace elected officials as key decision makers.

A second crucial question in democracies is, How much power should be given to the majority that, at least in theory, rules? Democracy implies majority rule, but how much power the majority has over dissident minorities is a fundamental question. Some formal institutions give the representatives of the majority far greater power

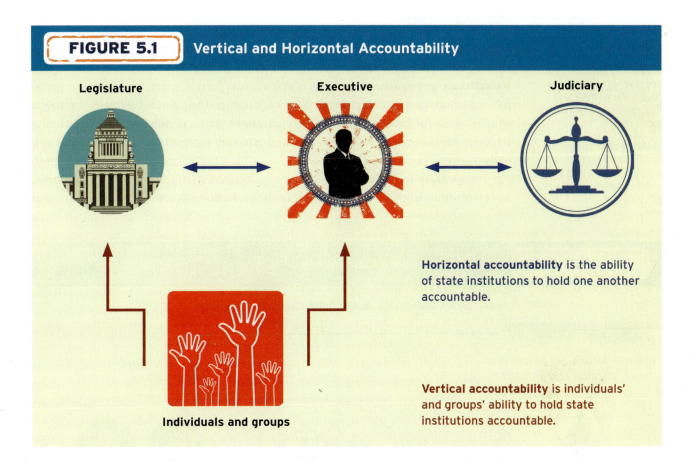

FIGURE 5.1   Vertical and Horizontal Accountability

Legislature   **Executive**   **Judiciary**

Horizontal accountability is the ability of state institutions to hold one another accountable.

Individuals and groups

Vertical accountability is individuals' and groups' ability to hold state institutions accountable.

than do others. The United Kingdom and United States stand in sharp relief on this issue and illustrate the range of available options. As we discuss below, the British Parliament has the legal right to pass any legislation it pleases, which gives the majority party tremendous powers. In contrast, the U.S. Constitution divides and thereby limits power significantly. Even when the same party controls both houses of Congress and the presidency, that party's power is limited by the ability of the Supreme Court to declare laws unconstitutional and by the various powers reserved specifically for state governments. Both countries are democracies, but they address the question of how formal institutions should protect minorities quite differently.

A final key question is, What is the potential trade-off between popular participation in the government and representation of many viewpoints, on the one hand, and effective governance, on the other? If the institutions of a particular regime strongly limit one another and many different groups are represented in the decision-making process, do these factors limit the ability of the government to make effective policy? Comparativist Arend Lijphart (1999) examined this potential trade-off. He suggested that we think of democracies on a continuum from what he termed "majoritarian" to "consensus." **Majoritarian democracies** concentrate power in

majoritarian democracy
A type of democratic system that concentrates power more tightly in a single-party executive with executive dominance over the legislature, a single legislative branch, and constitutions that can be easily amended

consensus democracy
A democratic system with multiparty executives in a coalition government, executive-legislative balance, bicameral legislatures, and rigid constitutions that are not easily amended

coalition government
Government in a parliamentary system in which at least two parties negotiate an agreement to rule together

a single place and office; they have a single-party executive, executive dominance over the legislature, a single legislative branch, and constitutions that can be easily amended. **Consensus democracies,** in contrast, have multiparty executives called a **coalition government** (in which at least two parties negotiate an agreement to rule together), executive-legislative balance, bicameral legislatures (with two roughly equally powerful houses), and rigid constitutions that are not easily amended. If a trade-off exists between representation and effective policymaking, majoritarian systems ought to be more effective because they have much more concentrated power. They seem likely to produce less horizontal accountability, however, since they have few institutions to check the executive. G. Bingham Powell (2000) noted, though, that

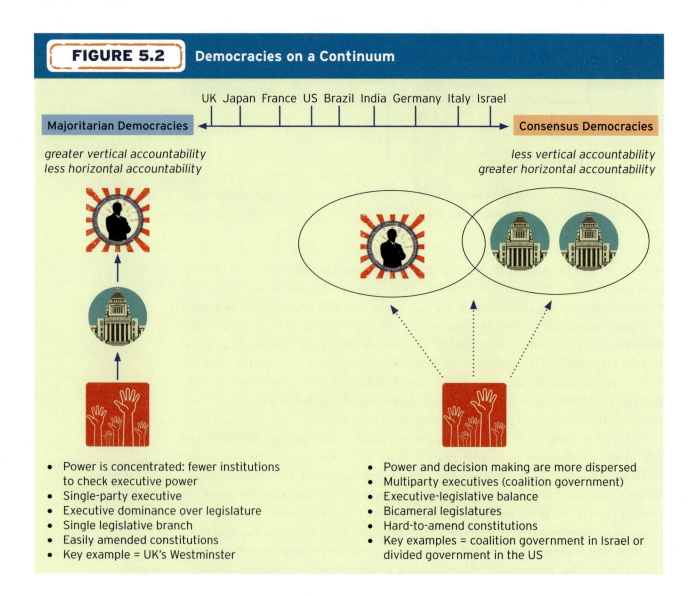

FIGURE 5.2   **Democracies on a Continuum**

UK Japan France US Brazil India Germany Italy Israel

Majoritarian Democracies   ←――――――――――――――→   **Consensus Democracies**

greater vertical accountability
less horizontal accountability

less vertical accountability
greater horizontal accountability

- Power is concentrated: fewer institutions to check executive power
- Single-party executive
- Executive dominance over legislature
- Single legislative branch
- Easily amended constitutions
- Key example = UK's Westminster

- Power and decision making are more dispersed
- Multiparty executives (coalition government)
- Executive-legislative balance
- Bicameral legislatures
- Hard-to-amend constitutions
- Key examples = coalition government in Israel or divided government in the US

COUNTRY AND CONCEPT
Snapshot of Governing Institutions

| Country | Executive-legislative system | Judicial system | | | Bureaucracy: corruption (scale of 0–100, 100 = least corrupt)[1] |
		Type of legal system	Right of judicial review	Federal system	
Brazil	Presidential	Code law	Yes	Symmetric federalism	38
China	NA	Code law	No	Unitary	37
Germany	Parliamentary	Code law	Yes	Symmetric federalism	81
India	Parliamentary	Common law	Yes	Asymmetric federalism	38
Iran	Semipresidential (authoritarian)	Islamic *sharia*	No	Unitary	27
Japan	Parliamentary	Code law	Yes	Unitary	75
Mexico	Presidential	Code law	Yes	Symmetric federalism	35
Nigeria	Presidential	Common law and *sharia*	Yes	Symmetric federalism	26
Russia	Semipresidential	Code law	Yes (but weak)	Asymmetric federalism	29
United Kingdom	Parliamentary	Common law	No	Unitary	81
United States	Presidential	Common law	Yes	Symmetric federalism	76

[1] Transparency International, Corruption Perceptions Index, 2016 (http://www.transparency.org/cpi2015#results-table).

vertical accountability is likely to be greater in majoritarian systems because voters know exactly who is responsible for government policy. In consensus systems with coalition government and multiple participants in the policy-making process, on the other hand, responsibility is less clear.

Comparativist George Tsebelis (2002) studied limits on effective policymaking as well. He argued that a key distinction among political systems and institutions is the number of veto players they have. A **veto player** is an individual or collective actor whose agreement is essential to effect policy change. Veto players may exist on the basis of institutional positions defined by a constitution or via partisan battles and political support. Tsebelis further argued that the greater the number

veto player
An individual or collective actor whose agreement is essential for any policy change

of veto players and the greater the ideological distance among them, the less likely policy change will be. We will see how both the arrangement of governing institutions (examined in this chapter) and institutions of participation and representation (examined in chapter 6) create veto players. We will examine the trade-offs among horizontal and vertical accountability, representation, and effective policymaking in both chapters.

The Country and Concept table shows the great variation in our case studies' governing institutions, even among those that are democracies. We begin with the relationship between the executive and legislative branches, which, more than anything else, distinguishes different kinds of democracies. We then examine the roles of the judiciary and the modern bureaucracy and their relationships to the executive and legislative branches. We also look at the question of federalism and the extent to which the overall power of the state is either centralized in national institutions or dispersed among subnational units of government; federalism can be another means of achieving accountability.

EXECUTIVES AND LEGISLATURES

head of state
The official, symbolic representative of a country, authorized to speak on its behalf and represent it, particularly in world affairs; usually a president or monarch

The executive is indispensable to any state or regime and fulfills two very important roles. First, as **head of state,** the executive is the official, symbolic representative of a country, authorized to speak on its behalf and represent it, particularly in world affairs. Historically, heads of state were monarchs, who still exist as symbolic heads of state in a number of countries, including the United Kingdom and Japan. Second, as **head of government,** the executive's task is to implement the nation's laws and policies. The two parts of the executive function may be filled by one individual or two, but both are essential to any regime. Legislatures are less ubiquitous because authoritarian regimes can dispense with them. They are, however, crucial to democratic regimes because a legislature's very democratic function is to debate public policy and pass laws. We discuss the executive and legislature together because the relationship between them distinguishes three classic models of democratic government: parliamentarism, presidentialism, and semipresidentialism.

head of government
The key executive power in a state; usually a president or prime minister

Parliamentarism: The Westminster Model

parliamentarism
A term denoting a parliamentary system of democracy in which the executive and legislative branches are fused via parliament's election of the chief executive

If you ask Americans to define democracy, many will start with the "separation of powers." The oldest model of modern democracy, however, does not separate the executive and legislature. Commonly known as the Westminster, or parliamentary, model, it originated in Britain. Lijphart called **parliamentarism** the purest form of his "majoritarian" model in which power is concentrated in one place, creating very few institutional veto players. The fusion of the executive and legislative branches provides for an exceptionally powerful executive. This fusion exists in the office of

the **prime minister (PM)** (in Germany, the chancellor), whose relationship to the legislature is the key distinguishing feature of the model. The PM is not only the executive but also a member of the legislature. She is the leader of the majority party or leading coalition party in the legislature. The PM, then, is not elected directly to executive office but rather is named after the legislative election determines the dominant party in parliament. Citizens cast one vote for a party or individual, depending on the electoral system, to represent them in parliament; the majority in parliament then names the prime minister. In practice, when citizens vote for parliament, they know who the PM candidate for each party is, so their vote for their preferred **member of parliament (MP)** or party is indirectly a vote for that party's leader to serve as PM.

Formally, the PM serves at the pleasure of parliament. Should a parliamentary majority lose confidence in the PM, members can cast a **vote of no confidence** that forces the PM to resign. At that point, the leading party in parliament can choose a new leader who will become PM, or the resigning PM will ask the head of state to call new parliamentary elections. Parliamentary systems often do not have fixed terms of office, and while the parliament can oust a prime minister if she no longer has the loyalty of the majority of MPs, a PM can similarly dissolve parliament and call for new elections. In practice, votes of no confidence are usually called by the opposition in parliament and are only successful in removing the government about 5 percent of the time, but they provide the opposition a means to highlight the government's weaknesses and usually result in opposition gains in the next election (Williams 2011).

Parliamentary systems separate the two functions of the executive. They have a "nonexecutive head of state," who embodies and represents the country ceremonially. Countries lacking a hereditary monarchy typically replace the monarch in this function with an elected head of state who, somewhat confusingly to Americans, is often called the "president." In most cases, this president's role, like the queen's in Britain, is small and ceremonial. Countries tend to elect esteemed elder statesmen (or, less often, women) who gracefully perform the ceremonial role while leaving all important executive functions to the head of the government, the PM. When a PM is the leader of the party that holds a majority of the seats in parliament and that party votes regularly as a bloc (as is almost always the case in parliamentary systems), the PM is an extremely powerful executive. Whatever legislation she puts forth is almost automatically passed into law by the legislature. A prime minister is in a somewhat different position if her party does not have a clear majority in parliament. In this situation, the PM will head a coalition government, in which at least two parties negotiate an agreement to rule together. A vote of no confidence is far more likely in a coalition government because if one party in the coalition is unhappy with a PM's policies, it can leave the coalition, causing the coalition to lose its majority. Smaller parties in the coalition often become partisan veto players; the PM must ensure that

prime minister (PM)
The head of government in parliamentary and semipresidential systems

member of parliament (MP)
An elected member of the legislature in a parliamentary system

vote of no confidence
In parliamentary systems, a vote by parliament to remove a government (the prime minister and cabinet) from power

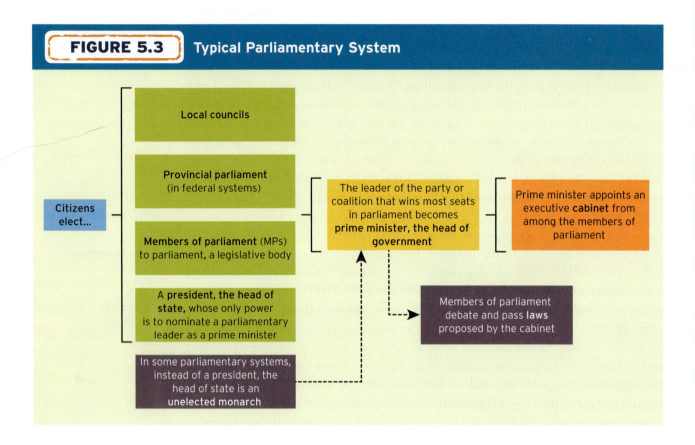

FIGURE 5.3   Typical Parliamentary System

Citizens elect...

Local councils

Provincial parliament (in federal systems)

Members of parliament (MPs) to parliament, a legislative body

A president, the head of state, whose only power is to nominate a parliamentary leader as a prime minister

In some parliamentary systems, instead of a president, the head of state is an **unelected monarch**

The leader of the party or coalition that wins most seats in parliament becomes **prime minister, the head of government**

Prime minister appoints an executive **cabinet** from among the members of parliament

Members of parliament debate and pass **laws** proposed by the cabinet

she has their support before she can get her legislation through parliament, a process that can involve extensive negotiations.

The prime minister also appoints the other ministers (what Americans call "secretaries") to the cabinet, but given the close executive relationship with parliament, these individuals cannot be whomever the prime minister pleases. The cabinet, especially in a coalition, serves as a check on the PM. Cabinet ministers must also be MPs, and in a coalition government the prime minister must consult with the other parties in the coalition about the distribution of "portfolios" (cabinet seats). Normally, all parties in the coalition, and certainly the biggest ones, get some representation in the cabinet. The cabinet, then, is often the site of the most important negotiations over policy. Whether all cabinet members are from the same party or from different parties in a coalition, once they have agreed to put forth a piece of legislation, it should pass through the legislature quite easily, as the classic case of Britain demonstrates. When no single party has a majority in parliament and therefore a coalition government is required, the process becomes more complex, as our case study of India illustrates.

PARLIAMENTARY RULE IN BRITAIN AND INDIA

CASE SYNOPSIS

Britain and India illustrate how similar governing institutions function differently in distinct social and political contexts. As a British colony, India adopted Britain's Westminster model almost completely. Differences in the party systems and the socioeconomic and cultural contexts of the two countries, however, influence how the model functions in practice. In Britain, the parliamentary system is the classic case of Lijphart's majoritarian democracy, with few veto players. Britain has only two strong parties, so one has ruled unimpeded almost all of the time. Vertical accountability clearly exists, but horizontal accountability is limited. The Indian system under Congress Party dominance was equally majoritarian. Since 1989, however, coalition government in India has substantially increased the potential veto players, adding a degree of consensual democracy.

- EXECUTIVE POWER Depends on number and strength of parties; greater in Britain

- LEGISLATIVE POWER Greater than formal powers might suggest; parliament as "watchdog," even though government legislation almost always passes

- ACCOUNTABILITY Stronger vertical accountability but coalition governments likely to weaken it

- VETO PLAYERS Weak in Britain, with stronger and fewer parties

- POLICYMAKING Strong; coalition government weakens in India

- RECENT TRENDS PMs becoming more "presidential," but efforts to strengthen parliament via more committees and resources

Britain's prime minister is often called the most powerful democratic executive in the world. The power of the office derives not just from its formal functions but also from the nature of Britain's parties and the strength of British institutions. Like the United States, Britain has two major parties (Labour and Conservative) that almost always alternate in power: one or the other wins a majority of legislative seats in virtually every election. This means that coalition governments are very rare (the coalition government from 2010 to 2015 was the first since World War II). Unlike parties in the United States, British parties are highly disciplined in the legislature, meaning that MPs almost always vote in support of their party's position on legislation. This is partly an effect of the parliamentary system itself. Ambitious MPs want to become cabinet ministers, and the head of the party controls these positions; thus, MPs demonstrate loyalty to the party leadership. As head of the majority party, the PM can usually get legislation passed with ease. The system has very few veto players.

The British PM appoints approximately twenty cabinet ministers who run the individual departments of government and whom the PM is supposed to consult before making major decisions. By tradition, the PM's power is checked by the cabinet and the practice of collective responsibility, which means that all cabinet members must publicly support all government decisions. A cabinet member who cannot do so is expected to resign. Since cabinet members are themselves senior leaders of the majority party and MPs, collective responsibility constitutes an informal legislative agreement to policies prior to their formal introduction in Parliament.

Many argue that the cabinet's role has declined over the last generation and that PMs have begun to look more presidential. The two most important PMs of the last generation, Conservative Margaret Thatcher (1979–1990) and Labourite Tony Blair (1997–2007), centralized decision making in an inner circle of advisers and paid less attention to input from the cabinet as a whole. More than most PMs, they became charismatic figures in their own right, and their campaigns looked more like U.S. presidential campaigns, with a great deal more attention paid to the individual attributes of the party leader than is traditional in Britain. Their popularity waned, however; both faced increasing resistance, showing that democratic control still exists in the British system. Many observers saw the 2010 election as furthering the "presidentialization" of the British PM, though. For the first time, the campaign featured American-style televised debates among the three main contenders.

In Britain, a vote of no confidence is extremely rare. A more common means of removing unpopular PMs is for the majority party to replace them. This has happened three times since 1990, most recently when Prime Minister David Cameron lost the referendum vote he called on whether Britain would remain within the European Union.

Theresa May leaves her official residence, 10 Downing Street, shortly after her selection as British prime minister in July 2016. She replaced David Cameron, who failed to defeat a referendum on Britain leaving the European Union and therefore resigned. The shift from Cameron to May, both in the Conservative Party that controlled a majority of Parliament at the time, was one of several changes of the head of the executive in Britain's parliamentary system that came without an election. Instead, the ruling party simply chose a new leader, who became prime minister.

Chris J Ratcliffe/Getty Images

He opposed the so-called "Brexit" and said he would resign if the referendum passed. It did, and he announced his resignation immediately afterward. Within days, Theresa May had emerged as the cabinet minister with strongest support among Conservative MPs (the majority party) and was duly approved by the queen as the new prime minister. Once again, control of the executive branch had changed hands (though remained within the same party) without an election. In all three cases, this happened when the PM had become exceptionally unpopular, so the change reflected popular will at least to some extent.

In parliamentary systems, the government can also change if the PM calls an election. In Britain until 2011, the maximum term allowed between elections was five years, but a PM could call earlier elections to take advantage of an electoral opportunity for her party. Margaret Thatcher did this in 1987 after winning the Falklands War, taking advantage of the popularity of the military victory to secure another term in office. The coalition government that ruled from 2010–2015 changed this, putting in place fixed terms for Parliament for the first time in the country's history. The Liberal Democratic Party (LDP) insisted on this as part of its agreement to form a coalition government; the LDP wanted to ensure that Conservative prime minister David Cameron, whom they had agreed to support, could not simply call a new election as soon as he thought he could win an outright majority. The new law mandates elections every five years in May. Early elections can only occur if two-thirds of Parliament vote for them or a vote of no confidence removes a prime minister and Parliament cannot form a new government in two weeks, neither of which is very likely. Arguably, this reform reduced the purely majoritarian characteristics of Britain's parliamentary system: removing the prime minister's power to dissolve Parliament and call an early election seems likely to increase Parliament's power vis-à-vis the executive and make coalition government more likely (since the PM cannot call an election when it is likely his party will win a majority) (Schleiter and Belu 2016).

Given the power of the PM, what powers does Parliament have? In Britain's **bicameral legislature,** the lower house, the House of Commons, has virtually all legislative power. The older upper house, the House of Lords, consists of members known as "peers"; these are appointees of the PM and traditionally were aristocrats who inherited their positions. In 1999 the Blair government ended the institution of "hereditary peers," allowing only a small minority to remain in office until further reforms. The only significant power held by the House of Lords for many years was to act as a final court of appeal for individual cases, and the Constitutional Reform Act of 2005 removed even that, creating a new Supreme Court as the final court of appeal. The Commons, though, retains considerable power. As noted above, even the most powerful PMs must take account of the views of their party's MPs in the Commons, especially if the PM's popularity is waning.

bicameral legislature
A legislature that has two houses

Parliament also serves an important watchdog function. The PM must attend Parliament weekly for Question Time, a very lively, televised debate among the major politicians of the day. During Question Time, the PM is expected to respond to queries from MPs and defend the government's policies. In addition, MPs have the right to question cabinet ministers about the activities of their departments, who must respond personally in Parliament, giving a public airing of issues of concern, large and small. The House of Commons recently created more committees that hold hearings on proposed legislation. In the British system, the fate of legislation introduced by the government (the cabinet) is rarely in doubt, but the committees allow MPs to investigate the implications of proposed laws, and at times the ruling party will allow legislation to be amended if committees identify problems.

Traditionally, MPs rarely voted against their party, but that has been changing. Since the 1970s, the number of times at least one MP voted against her party has slowly climbed, reaching 39 percent of all votes under the coalition government of 2010–2015 (Russell and Cowley 2016). Prior to the 1970s, prime ministers never saw Parliament defeat their legislation entirely, but since then every prime minister has suffered a defeat at least once. Even with these recent changes, though, the British Parliament does not modify legislation nearly as much as the U.S. Congress does. Nonetheless, the executive branch must pay attention to the opinions of the majority-party MPs. A recent examination of the influence of the British Parliament since World War II found that Parliament is more influential than most observers think, but that the influence mostly comes as legislation is being prepared; the PM and cabinet consult with their party's MPs and modify legislation in advance to avoid formal defeats in parliamentary votes (Russell and Cowley 2016). Parliamentary debate also provides a means for dissident MPs to voice their opinions, with an eye primarily to communicating with their constituents—something more common in Britain than in many other parliamentary systems (Proksch and Slapin 2015). The prime minister's formal powers may seem to allow him to ignore Parliament as long as he has control over his party, but his political survival actually requires that he attend to it closely.

Despite few formal differences, the role and power of the Indian prime minister and parliament are significantly different from the British model on which it was based. The divergence between the systems is due mainly to differences in the number of parties in the two countries. Like Britain and most parliamentary systems, India's MPs almost always vote with their party. Unlike Britain, India has multiple parties rather than just two. One party dominated the government for the first forty years after the nation's independence, but coalition governments have been the norm since.

For four decades, one-party dominance meant that PMs were far less constrained than their British counterparts. The Indian National Congress (commonly called the Congress) ruled nearly continuously from 1947 to 1989. The country's first prime minister, Jawaharlal Nehru (1947–1964), was a hero of the nationalist movement for independence and a deeply popular and respected figure. His cabinet consisted of leaders of the major factions within the ruling party and served as the actual governing body, debating policy as a cabinet is expected to in a parliamentary system. Shortly after his death, his daughter, Indira Gandhi (1966–1977, 1980–1984), was selected to lead the Congress and therefore became PM, centralizing power even more than her father had.

Her son, in turn, was PM from 1984 to 1989. The Congress Party lost its dominant position after 1989, and every government from then until 2014 was a coalition of one large party and a number of smaller ones. This profoundly changed the role of the PM, who remains the central executive and by far most important leader in the country, but now must compromise with other parties in order to form a government. This has produced the predictable drop in stability, as seen in the number of PMs India has had: in its first thirty years of independence (1947–1977), the country had only three PMs; in its second thirty years (1977–2007), it had twelve, only three of whom served full terms.

The 2014 election saw one party, the Bharatiya Janata Party (BJP), win an outright majority in the lower and more powerful house of parliament for the first time since 1989, meaning the new prime minister, Narendra Modi, should in theory be free to write policies as he wishes. In fact, policy changes were slower than expected, as opposition to him in the upper house, which the BJP did not control, blocked some of his proposals. The government did pass major legislation overhauling the country's tax system in 2016, an idea that both major parties had supported for years but could not get through parliament. Prime Minister Modi put together a coalition in the upper house of parliament by amending the bill, reaching out to state-level chief ministers (the equivalent of U.S. governors), and giving key political figures governmental appointments, not unlike a president would put together a coalition in a presidential system without a majority party.

The rise of coalition government made small parties that negotiate membership in these coalitions quite important, a trend that did not change significantly after the 2014 election gave one party a majority in the lower house of parliament. Not surprisingly, coalition government has meant that parliament has become less effective (Pelizzo 2010); parliament passes fewer laws now than it did under the dominance of the Congress, and MPs spend far less time there. Parties are more important for their votes in putting together a coalition government than they are for their legislative activity, and most of the 544 MPs are focused more on their states than on the national government. Many of the small parties have little support outside a particular state, so the political fortunes of many MPs are tied to their role in state-level politics more than they are to the national parliament. These small parties, in fact, often decide to join coalition governments based on the parties' interests at the state level rather than any ideological affinity with the national government.

For all of these reasons, many Indians have bemoaned the "decline of parliament" as an institution, but B. L. Shankar and Valerian Rodrigues (2011) argued that the shifts in parliament and greater party fragmentation reflect the changing nature of Indian society: more groups are now represented, MPs themselves are more diverse and therefore don't always agree, and MPs are increasingly focused on their local constituents—not necessarily bad things in a democracy. Coalition governments have also allowed the opposition in parliament to be more assertive, something that clearly continued even after the BJP won a parliamentary majority in 2014. Under the single-party dominance of the Congress, opposition parties were reduced to protests such as walkouts of parliament. Now, parliamentary committees in India have become stronger. Opposition MPs have also started regularly introducing their own legislation, something relatively rare in parliamentary systems because without some government support, legislation has little chance of being passed. Virtually unheard of in the era of Congress dominance, opposition bills are now quite regular, and some manage to pass with a coalition of small parties supporting them. Similarly, parliamentary debate now more regularly features opposition MPs.

CASE Questions

1. Based on the United Kingdom and India, what factors are most important in explaining why parliamentary systems operate differently in different countries?
2. Lijphart saw the "Westminster model" as the most majoritarian of all systems. Why do some parliamentary systems support his claim but others do not?

Presidential Systems: The Separation of Powers

presidentialism
A term denoting a presidential system of democracy in which the executive and legislature are elected independently and have separate and independent powers

separation of powers
Constitutionally explicit division of power among the major branches of government

Presidentialism needs little introduction for American students because the best known and most enduring example is the United States. In a presidential system, the roles of head of state and head of government are filled by the same person, who is given the title "president." The crucial, defining aspect of a presidential system, however, is not this fusion of executive roles. Rather, it is the concept of **separation of powers.** The American founders, following the ideas of the French liberal political theorist, the Baron de Montesquieu, argued that the functions of the executive and legislative branches should be separate, and everything about any presidential system reflects this choice, no matter how the particulars of any specific constitution may differ. This means that the executive and legislative branches are elected separately in their own (though possibly concurrent) elections, and the president must be independently and directly (or nearly directly) elected. Regardless of the electoral or party system in place, this institutional feature gives presidential systems an element of consensual democracy: institutional veto players are built into the founding documents of the system.

Some countries elect a president by plurality; others use a two-round system to achieve an absolute majority. No matter how the elections are administered, the important thing is that the president's legitimacy as head of state and government derives from a national election. Similarly, the legislature's legitimacy arises from the direct election of the representatives, who should therefore reflect the popular will. The president and legislature are both legitimized independently by the electoral process, and creating laws requires the agreement, in some way, of both the president and a majority in the legislature.

In contrast to parliamentary systems, presidents and their legislatures generally cannot interfere with one another's time in office. Presidents serve a fixed term, and

Parliaments and Presidents

Map 5.1 shows how many parliamentary, presidential, and semi-presidential systems exist today and where they are located.

What patterns do you see in terms of where different systems have been adopted? What might explain those patterns? Which theoretical arguments from chapter 1 can help you explain the patterns? Choose a country that you think might not fit the patterns you've noticed, and do some background research to figure out why it's different. What does that tell you about why countries choose particular institutions and not others?

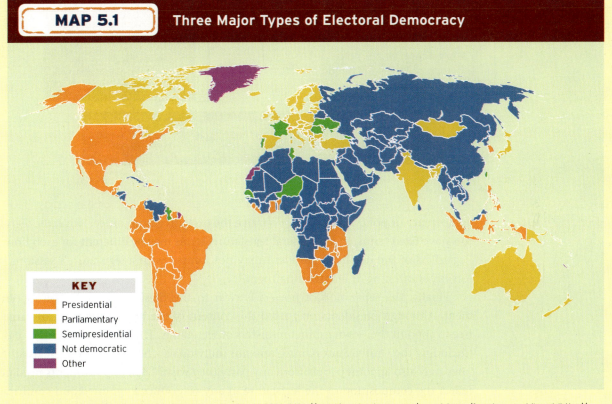

MAP 5.1 Three Major Types of Electoral Democracy

KEY
- Presidential
- Parliamentary
- Semipresidential
- Not democratic
- Other

Source: Data are from Freedom House, Freedom in the World 2016 (http://www.freedomhouse.org/report-types/freedom-world) and (http://en.wikipedia.org/wiki/File:Forms_of_government.svg). Modified by the authors.

it is very difficult for a legislature to remove the president from office. Most countries make provision for some kind of impeachment process, but impeachment requires extraordinary measures and can only be justified in extreme circumstances. Barring this, no matter how much legislators disagree with the president or question his

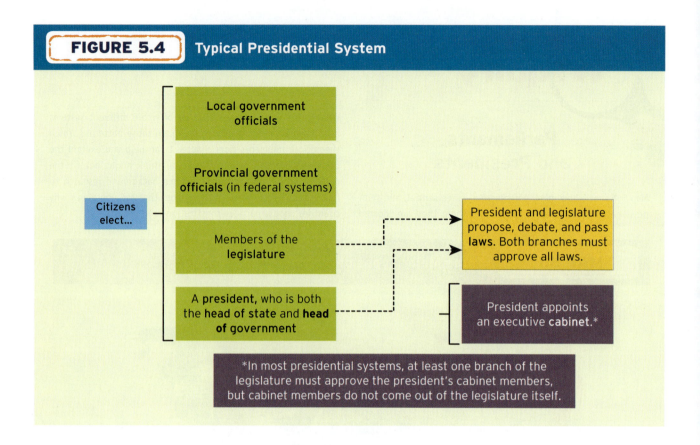

FIGURE 5.4   **Typical Presidential System**

Local government officials

Provincial government officials (in federal systems)

Members of the legislature

A **president,** who is both the **head of state** and **head of** government

Citizens elect...

President and legislature propose, debate, and pass **laws**. Both branches must approve all laws.

President appoints an executive **cabinet**.*

*In most presidential systems, at least one branch of the legislature must approve the president's cabinet members, but cabinet members do not come out of the legislature itself.

competence or policy, they cannot remove the executive from office. Similarly, legislators have fixed terms. In a bicameral legislature, terms may be different for each house. Regardless of the details, a president may not tamper with a legislature's sessions by forcibly shortening or lengthening them.

Finally, the separation of powers is clear in the president's powers of appointment. Although presidents may need the consent of the legislature, they are largely free to appoint their own cabinet ministers or secretaries. They may, and in many cases (including the United States) must, appoint individuals who are not in the legislature. They may also appoint people from any party they wish. Their appointments need not reflect the composition of the legislature in any way. Once appointed and confirmed by the legislature, the officers serve at the president's pleasure, and the legislature can interfere only minimally with their activities. In practice, of course, most presidents try to appoint to their cabinet a group of people more or less representative of the major political factions in their party. The separation from the legislature, though, means they only do this to the extent they think is politically expedient, rather than being required to in order to form a government, as in a parliamentary system. Thus, the cabinet is typically a far less important decision-making body than in a parliamentary system. Also, because members of the legislature are not vying directly for cabinet appointments, the president has less control over them than a PM does, so the legislature becomes a more important and independent decision-making body. Ironically, this means that legislatures in presidential systems are typically more powerful than legislatures in parliamentary systems. How easily a president can get her preferred policies approved by the legislature depends on whether she has majority support (via her own party or a coalition of parties) in the legislature as well as her ability to bargain with legislators, which is influenced by the specific powers the president has, as the cases of the United States and Brazil demonstrate.

PRESIDENTIALISM IN THE UNITED STATES AND BRAZIL

CASE SYNOPSIS

Most countries in the Western Hemisphere have presidential systems, although the socioeconomic and political contexts of these systems vary widely, as the cases of the United States and Brazil show. The Brazilian president enjoys significant powers that the American one does not, but Brazil's many parties make passing legislation at least as difficult for the president. Both countries have inherent institutionalized veto players, a characteristic they share with all presidential systems. The bargaining necessary among branches of government, especially when they are controlled by differing parties, creates a degree of consensual democracy. How much this serves as a form of horizontal accountability depends very much on context. As in parliamentary systems, the number and strength of political parties matter; Brazil's fragmented legislature with many, weak parties may limit accountability. In the United States, the president is more powerful, but is certainly checked by a Congress controlled by the opposing party.

- EXECUTIVE POWER Weak but growing over time; stronger with fewer parties, as in the United States

- LEGISLATIVE POWER Strong

- ACCOUNTABILITY Horizontal accountability stronger than vertical accountability

- VETO PLAYERS Built into system in legislature and executive

- POLICYMAKING Problems of gridlock in the United States and many weak parties in Brazil

- RECENT TRENDS Greater gridlock in the United States; coalition instability and impeachment in Brazil

n the United States, the office of the president was one of the more controversial parts of the Constitution when it was written. Many leaders, most notably Thomas Jefferson, feared that a single executive would inevitably become authoritarian. In part for this reason, the president's formal powers in the Constitution are modest by modern standards: (1) approving or vetoing legislation passed by Congress (Congress can override a veto with a two-thirds majority vote); (2) appointing cabinet secretaries and Supreme Court justices, other federal judges, and political appointees in the bureaucracy, subject to the Senate's approval; (3) serving as head of state and commander in chief of the armed forces; and (4) entering into treaties and declaring war, again subject to Senate approval.

While these formal powers are largely unchanged, informal presidential power expanded over time, ironically beginning with Thomas Jefferson, who successfully proclaimed the right of the president to expand the country via the Louisiana Purchase. Andrew Jackson became the de facto head of his party, giving the president greater influence over Congress, and Franklin Roosevelt created vast new social programs that increased the size and reach of the federal bureaucracy that the president controls. The U.S. president ultimately has become the symbolic leader of the nation, the undisputed leader of his party, and both the chief initiator and implementer of legislation. While legislation formally starts in Congress, in practice Congress looks to the president for major legislative initiatives. Members of Congress initiate considerable legislation, but the most important legislation usually starts as a presidential initiative.

While the presidency has certainly become more powerful over time, the U.S. Congress has substantial powers as well. Because legislators are independently elected, Congress jealously guards its autonomy from the executive branch. The U.S. House of Representatives and Senate have perhaps the most extensive and expensive staffs of any legislature in the world. Committees and subcommittees are crucial in investigating, amending, and passing legislation. Individual members have great freedom

Dilma Rousseff became Brazil's first woman president in 2010, replacing her mentor, the wildly popular Luis Inácio "Lula" da Silva. Brazil's democracy faced its greatest crisis since military rule when Rousseff was impeached in 2016 in the midst of a massive corruption scandal. Despite greater formal powers, Brazilian presidents have had difficulty keeping coalitions together in the legislature and passing legislation because of Brazil's many political parties. The collapse of Rousseff's legislative coalition led to her impeachment, which her supporters called a "soft coup."

William Volcov/BrazilPhotoPress/LatinContent/Getty Images

to introduce legislation compared with members of most national legislatures, and it's entirely possible that individual legislation will become law if it gains the support of the chairs of key committees or subcommittees. Most observers argue that the U.S. Congress is the most powerful legislature in the world, not only because it legislates on behalf of the most powerful country but because of its autonomy from the executive branch.

One possible result of the separation of powers is "gridlock," or the inability to pass major legislation, which has become an issue of great concern in recent years. The United States has only two major parties, but these have long been relatively weak; individual legislators are not beholden to party leaders, and they vote as they choose on each piece of legislation. This alone can occasionally produce gridlock, but stalemates are more likely when one party controls the presidency and the other controls Congress, which has become the norm in the U.S. presidential system (see Figure 5.5). Frank Baumgartner and colleagues (2014) compared legislative productivity in the United States during periods of divided versus united government (when the same party controls both the executive and legislative branches) and found that while Congress passes just as many laws under divided government, it is less likely to pass important legislation that alters major policies. One of the president's main jobs has become trying to get his legislation passed, either by cajoling members of his own party to support him or by negotiating and compromising with the opposing party in Congress, especially when it is in the majority.

Compromises, though, have become increasingly difficult to achieve in recent years. Several trends seem to account for this. While still weak relative to many other democracies, American parties appear to be gaining greater unity; their legislators vote more and more frequently in lockstep. The parties are also becoming more ideologically polarized (McCarty 2014) and national elections are becoming more competitive, in the sense of parties splitting the national vote evenly (Lee 2014). In the House of Representatives, fewer districts, though, are individually competitive; more and more have clear majorities for one party or the other, meaning individual legislators only need to worry about appealing to their party's supporters. These phenomena reinforce one another: as national competition increases, parties need to distinguish themselves from one another ideologically, leading to polarization. Individual congressional candidates use these ideological positions to gain the support of their party stalwarts in their relatively homogenous districts. Legislators therefore oppose the other party's proposals, not only because they disagree but also in order to gain an electoral advantage with their constituents. This would not produce gridlock in a parliamentary system; the majority party would simply have control of both the executive and legislature and be able to govern unimpeded, for better or worse. In a presidential system, though, it makes governing extremely difficult. Very little major legislation has been passed in recent years, and an annual battle over the national budget and debt ceiling repeatedly threatened to close the government and undermine the country's credit rating.

When not trying to negotiate the maze of the legislative process, the U.S. president oversees a vast bureaucracy. Most are permanent civil servants, but several thousand

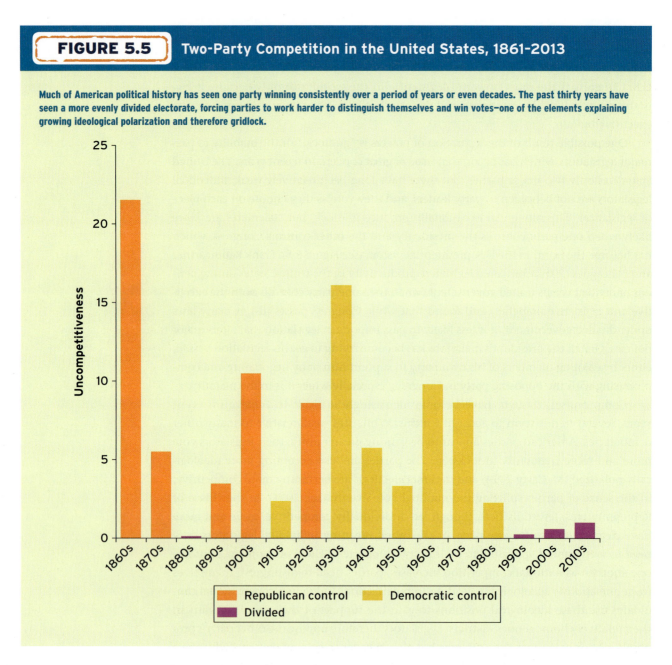

FIGURE 5.5   Two-Party Competition in the United States, 1861-2013

Much of American political history has seen one party winning consistently over a period of years or even decades. The past thirty years have seen a more evenly divided electorate, forcing parties to work harder to distinguish themselves and win votes—one of the elements explaining growing ideological polarization and therefore gridlock.

Source: Frances Lee, "American Politics Is More Competitive Than Ever. That's Making Partisanship Worse," *Washington Post*, January 9, 2014 (https://www.washingtonpost.com/news/monkey-cage/wp/2014/01/09/american-politics-is-more-competitive-than-ever-thats-making-partisanship-worse/).

at the top of the bureaucratic hierarchy serve at the president's pleasure. This gives the president great influence over the implementation of laws passed by Congress. For most of the nation's history, this power has been relatively uncontroversial; under President George W. Bush, however, this executive power became a subject of contention. Especially controversial were presidential "signing statements" that President

Bush attached to more than one thousand provisions of legislation he signed into law. The precedent for such signing statements is quite old, but issuing signing statements only became frequent under Presidents Ronald Reagan and Bill Clinton in the 1980s and 1990s. The strongest of them, "constitutional signing statements," assert the president's authority not to implement certain aspects of legislation because in his opinion they violate his constitutional powers. President Bush controversially asserted these rights via signing statements on legislation involving torture and treatment of prisoners of war. He contended that the legislation unduly restricted his ability to conduct war as commander in chief; his critics argued that Bush's signing statements unconstitutionally and unilaterally revoked parts of legislation with which he didn't agree, violating Congress's power to legislate. Despite criticizing Bush's action, President Barack Obama had himself issued thirty-seven signing statements by October 2016, in some cases reversing earlier Bush statements. Obama, on the other hand, has been criticized for expanding presidential power by issuing rules and regulations, especially during his second term. His frustration with Congress's inability to pass legislation led him to adopt the slogan "We Can't Wait" to justify issuing executive orders on a wide array of policies. These included policies regarding global warming, access to guns, net neutrality, airline passenger rights, and deportation of undocumented immigrants. Obama issued 50 percent more regulations that the Congressional Budget Office defined as having "significant economic or social impacts" than Bush did (Applebaum and Shear 2016). These controversial assertions of powers by presidents of both parties are only the latest salvos in a two-hundred-year battle over the power of the U.S. presidency.

The fears of Thomas Jefferson were partly justified: the presidency of the United States is a very powerful office. On the one hand, the separation of powers in the presidential system, particularly in the context of relatively weak parties in the United States, limits what presidents can do. On the other hand, presidents' leadership of their party and control over foreign policy and thousands of key appointments give them far greater powers than many of the authors of the Constitution envisioned. This divided power in the context of a very old democracy with well-established institutions and only two main parties produces a system that is often seen as slow to make policy, particularly in recent years, as gridlock has come to be seen as the norm.

Presidentialism, however, can look very different when transplanted to different geographic, social, and institutional settings, as the example of Brazil shows. As in most of Latin America, Brazil's democratic regimes have always been presidential. The current system dates to a constitution approved in 1988. Brazil's president has more extensive formal powers than her U.S. counterpart, but a legislature with many weak political parties and the most decentralized federal system in the world make these powers substantially less effective than they appear on paper. It seemed that Brazilian presidents were slowly strengthening the powers of the presidency via the incentives they could provide supporters in Congress and growing discipline within the major parties. The impeachment of President Dilma Rousseff in 2016, however—arguably the biggest crisis for Brazil's democracy since the end of military rule—showed that the president continues to be at the mercy of her ability to maintain a coalition of support in Congress.

Brazil's president is directly chosen in a two-round election: if no candidate wins an absolute majority on the first vote, a second vote takes place two weeks later between the top two candidates. The president can serve up to two four-year terms, as in the United States, and has the typical powers of the office: head of state and government, commander in chief of the armed forces, and appointment powers. In Brazil she also has several unusual powers: (1) the authority to issue "provisional decrees" (PDs), which become law for thirty days unless the National Congress approves them permanently; (2) a line-item veto, which allows her to eliminate individual measures in a bill sent from the National Congress without vetoing the entire law; (3) a monopoly over initiation of all legislation involving the budget; and (4) the ability to declare legislation "urgent," moving it to the top of the National Congress's agenda.

The Brazilian president must operate in a system with many fragmented parties. Brazil's electoral system gives politicians little incentive to form broad, inclusive parties or to follow party leaders once they are in the National Congress. Both houses of Brazil's bicameral legislature, the Chamber of Deputies (the lower house) and the Senate (the upper house), include numerous parties. After the 2014 election, the Chamber of Deputies included twenty-six parties, the biggest of which—the president's party—had only 13 percent of the seats (68 out of 513) and in the Senate, only 15 percent of the seats (12 out of 81). The only way for presidents to get their legislation passed is to build coalitions among several parties. Indeed, in the last few elections, several parties have supported the two major presidential candidates, a result of preelection negotiations regarding sharing power after the election. After the election, the president appoints members of parties supporting her to the cabinet and other major offices, like a prime minister would in a parliamentary system. Such presidential coalitions have been quite large and ideologically diverse, averaging nine parties each. Much of the debate over legislation, then, happens within the informal governing coalition rather than between them and the opposition.

Presidents can also use the line-item veto to negotiate with individual legislators to gain their support for particular bills. As in the United States, Brazilian legislators engage in "pork-barrel" politics; that is, they seek to include specific spending projects for their home areas in the national budget. This is the contemporary continuation of a long Brazilian tradition of patronage politics in which elected officials bring home government resources as a primary means of gaining support. The president's line-item veto allows the executive to decide which of these individual items to keep and which to eliminate, so she can exchange approval of a legislator's pet project for support on a crucial piece of legislation.

The first president directly elected under the 1988 constitution, whose party had only 3 percent of the seats in the Chamber of Deputies, ruled largely through PDs, issuing 150 of them in his first year in office. Often, when one expired, he would simply reissue it the next day, essentially making it last as long as he pleased. Subsequent presidents recognized the need to include the National Congress and used the various negotiation strategies to pass legislation. In 2001 the Brazilian Congress passed a reform to limit the president's ability to reissue PDs and to discourage their use altogether. While Brazilian presidents continue to use them, they cannot be used continually to, in effect, allow a president to rule by decree.

Overall, however, the powers of Brazil's president remain limited. Major presidential proposals fail to pass the National Congress more often than in any other major Latin American country, and of those that do, virtually all are modified (Hiroi and Renno 2016). Each piece of legislation requires extensive horse trading, not only with party leaders but also with individual legislators looking for favors. Early in President Lula's (2003–2010) first term, his administration combined not only cabinet seats and provision of "pork" to gain legislative victories but also illegal payments to some legislators to gain their support, which erupted into a major corruption scandal that cost some of his closest aides and several members of Congress their jobs. Pereira et al. (2011) argued that, while reprehensible, it was a logical extension of the situation in which the Brazilian president found himself: he had an ambitious legislative agenda and was not able to manipulate the legal means of bargaining adequately to get his proposals passed into law.

Dilma Rousseff, elected to succeed Lula in 2010 and Brazil's first woman president, is from Lula's Workers' Party (PT), which is the most united and ideologically driven party in the country. A declining economy and massive corruption scandal, though, led to her coalition unraveling entirely. She and the PT joined forces with a centrist party to win the 2015 election, appointing one of the other party's leaders as vice president. A leader of the second-largest party in her coalition who nonetheless opposed her won the seat of speaker of the assembly and used that to undermine her authority whenever possible. The massive corruption scandal that erupted in 2014 involved the national oil company, which Rousseff headed before becoming president. While she was not directly implicated in that scandal, her popularity plummeted and Congress, led by the speaker of the assembly, ultimately impeached her in 2016 on charges that she illegally hid the extent of the country's budget deficit prior to her 2015 reelection. The much more conservative vice president took over as president after her impeachment, but his own government was immediately hit with corruption scandals as well, forcing two of his cabinet members to resign within months of taking office. Rousseff and her supporters charged their conservative opponents with using impeachment to carry out a "soft coup" to gain power and avoid ending up in jail themselves. Sixty percent of Congress, in fact, was under indictment on one charge or another in 2016, many of them involving the national oil company scandal.

It seemed prior to the massive corruption scandal that the Brazilian presidency and parties were becoming stronger institutions. In many ways, they are, but the spectacular dissolution of Rousseff's presidential coalition and her impeachment, whatever its motives, make it unclear what the future strength of the presidency will be.

CASE Questions

1. Many comparativists argue that presidential systems are ineffective at making policy. Based on Brazil and the United States, what are the most important factors influencing how true that statement is?

2. The writers of the U.S. Constitution worried that executive power would become too great and erode democracy. Based on our two case studies, to what extent was that a valid concern?

Semipresidentialism: The Hybrid Compromise

The third major executive-legislative system is the most recently created. **Semipresidentialism** splits executive power between an elected president and a prime minister. The president is elected directly by the citizens as in a presidential system and serves as the head of state, but she also has significant powers in running the government. The official head of government is the PM, who is the leader of the majority party or coalition in parliament, as in a parliamentary system. The president appoints the PM, who must also obtain majority support in the parliament. Legislation requires the signature of the president, as well as support of the PM as head of the ruling party or coalition in parliament. The parliament can force the PM and cabinet to resign through a vote of no confidence. For semipresidentialism to be successful, the powers and duties of the president and PM as dual executives must be spelled out clearly in the constitution. For example, the president may be given power over military decisions (as in Sri Lanka) or foreign policy (as in Finland), whereas the prime minister typically concentrates on domestic policies. The specific division of powers varies greatly, however, and is not always clearly delineated.

The semipresidential system originated in France in the 1958 constitution establishing the Fifth Republic. Charles de Gaulle, a World War II hero and undisputed political leader of France at the time, envisioned the presidency as a stabilizing and powerful position, legitimated via national election. He assumed that the same party would win the presidency and a legislative majority. So long as it did, semipresidentialism gave the president, as head of the majority party who also appoints the PM, unparalleled power to govern.

This worked as intended until the 1980s, when for the first time the president was elected from one party and the majority of the legislature from another, a situation the French humorously call **cohabitation.** Under cohabitation, the president must compromise with the legislature by appointing a PM from the majority party in the legislature rather than from his own party. A compromise had to be worked out regarding the specific powers of the president and the PM, since the French constitution did not draw clear boundaries. In practice, the compromise has been that the president runs foreign policy while the PM and the legislature control

semipresidentialism
A term denoting a semipresidential system of democracy in which executive power is divided between a directly elected president and a prime minister elected by a parliament

cohabitation
Sharing of power between a president and prime minister from different parties in a semipresidential system

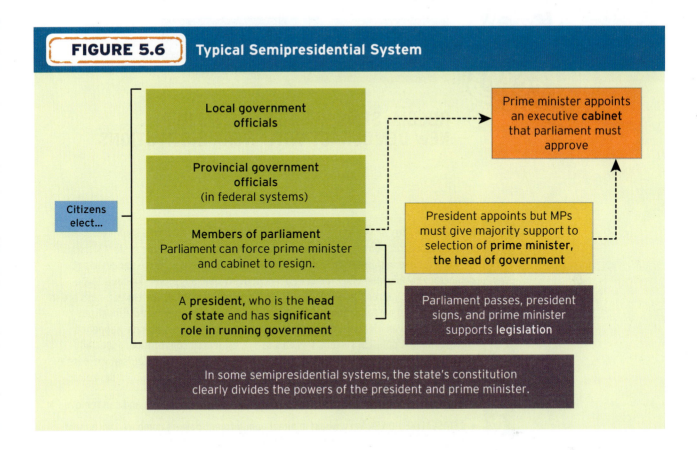

FIGURE 5.6 **Typical Semipresidential System**

Citizens elect...

- Local government officials
- Provincial government officials (in federal systems)
- Members of parliament
  Parliament can force prime minister and cabinet to resign.
- A **president,** who is the **head of state** and has **significant role in running government**

President appoints but MPs must give majority support to selection of **prime minister, the head of government**

Prime minister appoints an executive **cabinet** that parliament must approve

Parliament passes, president signs, and prime minister supports **legislation**

In some semipresidential systems, the state's constitution clearly divides the powers of the president and prime minister.

domestic policy. Critics of semipresidentialism fear that it gives the president too much power, but cohabitation clearly limits those powers significantly. If a majority in the legislature is elected in opposition to the president, he is forced to accept the results and live with cohabitation and the limits it imposes. However, cohabitation can also produce gridlock and inability to legislate effectively, as in a purely presidential system.

In addition to cohabitation, a second crucial institutional question in semipresidential systems is whether the president has the power to remove the PM. Robert Elgie (2011) argued that if he does, the semipresidential system is much less stable because neither the president nor the majority in parliament will have an incentive to compromise. If the president cannot remove the PM, the legislature has greater power, making the president more likely to compromise with it, which produces greater power sharing among contending factions. The semipresidential system, then, can produce stronger or weaker institutional veto players depending on the context: under cohabitation and with more limited presidential powers, veto players are stronger and compromise more likely. Our case study of Russia, however, shows the dangers of having fewer or no veto players; it demonstrates Elgie's argument that if the president can dismiss the PM at will, compromise is unlikely and the stability of democracy is in danger.

РОССИЯ

CASE Study

RUSSIA: SEMIPRESIDENTIALISM IN A NEW DEMOCRACY WITH WEAK INSTITUTIONS

CASE SYNOPSIS

Russia is the largest and one of the most important countries with a semipresidential system. Its current government demonstrates the worst fears of the system's critics: that in a regime with weak institutions, a powerful presidency can be dangerous to democracy by allowing one official to achieve overwhelming power. Vladimir Putin used the already strong presidency in Russia's semipresidential system to amass great presidential and personal power, transforming a young and weak institutionalized democracy into an electoral authoritarian regime. While this might have happened with a different political system, Russia's semipresidential constitution, especially as amended by Putin, gives the president great powers; even if the legislature were controlled by an opposition party, its ability to act as a veto player would be limited.

- EXECUTIVE POWER Initially strong, now nearly unlimited; appoints and can remove PM

- LEGISLATIVE POWER Very weak; minimal appointment powers compared with most semipresidential systems; cabinet ministers do not need to be members of legislature

- ACCOUNTABILITY Minimal

- VETO PLAYERS None

- POLICYMAKING Strong, but centered almost entirely in executive

- RECENT TRENDS Under Putin, even further expansion of presidential powers

The Russian constitution adopted in 1993 created a semipresidential system with an exceptionally strong presidency. The president is directly elected to a six-year term (it was a four-year term until a 2012 constitutional amendment), with a maximum of two terms possible. He must be elected by an absolute majority: if no candidate wins a majority in the first election, a second is held between the top two candidates. The president appoints the prime minister with the approval of the parliament, the Duma, but if the Duma votes against the president's candidate for PM three times, it is automatically dissolved and new elections are called. This means that unless the president's opponents in the Duma think they will gain from an election, they will be very hesitant to oppose his nominee. The president also appoints all cabinet members, who do not need approval by the Duma. Neither the PM nor the rest of the cabinet need to be members of the Duma, and the vast majority have not been.

The Russian system, then, does not link the president and parliament via the PM and cabinet as fully as the original French model. This structure frees the president to appoint anyone he pleases to the cabinet, regardless of which party controls parliament. Furthermore, the president has direct control over several key ministries (Foreign Affairs, Defense, and Interior) and the Federal Security Service, the successor to the KGB; in these areas, his authority bypasses the PM and the cabinet altogether. Perhaps most important, the president can issue decrees that have the force of law and cannot be vetoed by the Duma or challenged in court, which gives him the power to rule without legislative support. A constitutional amendment in 2000 also gave the president the power to appoint and dismiss all governors of Russia's eighty-nine regions (see the section on federalism below), who in turn appoint half of the members of the upper house of parliament. Election of governors was restored in 2012, but the law was then amended in 2013 to allow appointment in certain circumstances, returning significant power to the president. The Duma can vote no confidence in the prime minister but must do so twice to remove him from office. It can also impeach the president by a two-thirds vote, but it has only attempted to do so once, in 1999, and failed.

Russia's two major post-Communist presidents, Boris Yeltsin (1991–2000) and Vladimir Putin (2000–2008, 2012–), used the powers of the presidency quite differently. Yeltsin was the hero of the post-Communist revolution. He led the opposition to an attempted Soviet military coup in August 1991, which ultimately resulted in the demise of the Soviet Union. He also was the architect of the 1993 constitution. His rule, however, was chaotic. Because he was not a member of any political party, he was unable to marshal strong support for his reforms. For most of his presidency, his chief opposition was the former Communist Party, which had a plurality (but not a majority) of seats in the Duma. Yeltsin fought many battles with a hostile parliament and often enacted laws by decree. His war with parliament came to a head in 1999, when the Communists attempted to impeach him on charges of illegally prosecuting a war

Are two chief executives better than one? Dmitry Medvedev (right) was Vladimir Putin's prime minister and succeeded him as president in 2008. Putin then became Medvedev's prime minister, leading some observers to wonder who really was in charge. In 2012 Putin returned as president and Medvedev once again became a much weakened prime minister, as it became clear that Putin had retained the greatest power throughout.

VLADIMIR RODIONOV/AFP/Getty Images

Semipresidential Systems

Semipresidentialism spread rapidly in the 1990s with the wave of democratization in Africa and eastern Europe. Between 1990 and 1992, the number of semipresidential systems worldwide increased from ten to thirty-nine, and by 2010 there were fifty-three (Elgie 2016). Fifteen are former colonies of two semipresidential European countries, France and Portugal. Freedom House rated twenty-two semipresidentialist countries as "free" in 2010, seventeen as partly free, and thirteen as not free.

Region	Number of semipresidential regimes	Free	Partly free	Not free
Sub-Saharan Africa	17	4	6	7
Americas	2	1	1	0
Asia	5	2	3	0
Eurasia	7	0	4	3
Europe	17	15	2	0
Middle East and North Africa	5	1	1	3
Total	53	23	17	13

Sources: Data are from Robert Elgie, "The Semi-Presidential One" (http://www.semipresidentialism.com/?p=1053); Freedom House, *Freedom in the World 2016* (http://www.freedomhouse.org/report-types/freedom-world).

against the breakaway region of Chechnya and engaging in corruption. He appointed seven prime ministers over his tenure and more than two hundred cabinet ministers. His final prime minister was Putin, whom he anointed as his successor as president.

Putin, a former KGB agent and leader, would prove to be a much stronger president than Yeltsin, winning 53 percent of the vote in the first-round election in 2000. In the 2003 Duma election, his followers organized a new party, United Russia, which won control of parliament and proceeded to pass every major bill he submitted. By 2012, only four parties remained in the Duma, all of which supported Putin. He used his powers of decree and control over the prosecution of corruption to eliminate many of the "oligarchs" who had arisen under Yeltsin and come to control major sectors of the economy, replacing them with his supporters or taking direct state control of some companies. He also severely restricted nongovernment sources of media. After winning the 2004 election with more than 70 percent of the vote, he reformed the constitution to gain effective control over the country's regional governments and, therefore, the upper house of the legislature. Facing a constitutional limit of two terms as president, Putin anointed Dmitry Medvedev as his successor, who was duly elected in May 2008. Putin himself became head of his ruling party in the Duma and PM, and he unofficially remained the chief leader of the country. After a term as prime minister, Putin was legally eligible to begin another two terms as president in 2012.

He and Medvedev "agreed" to switch roles, with Putin running for and winning the presidency and Medvedev becoming prime minister again.

The 2012 election, though, was not the overwhelming victory that the 2004 and 2008 elections had been; Putin won only 65 percent of the vote even though he had legally eliminated most serious opposition contenders, and his party's parliamentary majority was reduced from 70 to 53 percent of the seats in the Duma. The election took place amidst large-scale opposition demonstrations over what seemed to be obvious electoral fraud and dismay that he was extending his time in office. Passing laws that massively increased penalties for unauthorized gatherings, Putin cracked down on opposition demonstrations against him, which were growing in Moscow in spring 2012. He also changed the electoral system (see chapter 8) to favor United Russia in the 2016 legislative elections. As his and the ruling party's popularity dropped, restrictions on association and the media, and changes to the electoral rules, were a successful effort to ensure that his party won the 2016 parliamentary election while avoiding the large-scale protests that outright electoral fraud produced in 2012.

CASE Questions

1. Some comparativists argue that the detailed logic of formal institutions is frequently not the most important element to understand in a political system. Instead, we ought to focus on how strong institutions are, regardless of how they are organized. What does our case study of Russia suggest about this argument?
2. In Russia, the semipresidential system clearly has not been very effective at enhancing accountability. Is this outcome inherent in semipresidential systems, or is it the result of specific factors in Russia?

COMPARING EXECUTIVE-LEGISLATIVE INSTITUTIONS

In comparing parliamentary, presidential, and semipresidential systems, comparativists ask three major questions: Which system is most democratic in the sense of providing greatest accountability? Which system is most effective at making public policy? Which system provides the greatest political stability for a democratic regime? All three systems provide vertical accountability in that major leaders are subject to electoral sanction by voters. The question is, How frequent and effective is this vertical accountability? Also, how much horizontal accountability exists? Lijphart (1999) argued that the more majoritarian systems provide less representation and accountability because power is so concentrated; on the other hand, concentration of power could well make policymaking easier. More consensual systems tend to be just the opposite: the distribution of power among major parties and institutions makes more robust horizontal accountability, often based on the presence of veto players, but may threaten effective policymaking.

Accountability

In all three types of executive-legislative systems, a trade-off often exists between vertical and horizontal accountability. In theory, the Westminster system, the most purely majoritarian system, is extremely democratic because it makes the legislature, the elected body of the people, supreme. In practice, the question of accountability is far more complex. First, much depends on the electoral system and number of parties. In multiparty systems such as contemporary India, parliamentarism may be more consensual, promoting negotiation, coalition building, and representation of a wide range of views in the cabinet. In a primarily two-party system like Britain's, however, in which one party almost always has a majority of parliamentary seats, the PM may be an unusually powerful executive because she is guaranteed legislative support. Some critics also argue that the modern world, particularly given the rise of television and other media, has strengthened the hand of the PM. Prime ministers are becoming similar to presidents—presidents who always have a legislative majority—and therefore vest too much power in the hands of a single individual. On the other hand, Powell (2000) argued this can provide greater vertical accountability: at election time citizens know whom to hold responsible for government policy.

Presidentialism seems to have greater horizontal accountability because of the separation of powers. The independent legislature can limit the president's prerogatives on a regular basis, and the members of the legislature are likely to have more influence on policymaking than under a parliamentary system. Again, how true this is depends in part on the nature of parties. A presidential system with strong parties that vote in lockstep and in which the president's party has a majority in the legislature will function much like a parliamentary system with a strong majority party. On the other hand, a presidential system with weaker parties (as in the United States) or with a divided government (with the presidency and legislature controlled by different parties) provides for much greater horizontal accountability, though perhaps at the expense of effective policymaking. Many analysts claim the United States has faced this problem regularly in recent years.

Similarly, accountability in semipresidential systems depends on the strength and number of parties and the president's powers. If the president heads a strong party that controls a majority of the legislature, little horizontal accountability exists, though vertical accountability may be clearer. On the other hand, if a party opposed to the president controls the legislature, as under cohabitation in France in the 1980s, the president will have to compromise regularly with the prime minister. In this situation, horizontal accountability increases via more veto players.

Policymaking

Making public policy effectively in a democracy always requires compromise. A parliamentary system in which the PM's party controls a majority of the legislature is generally thought to be most effective at making policy precisely for the same reason critics say it is less democratic: there are no institutional constraints on the ruling party's actions. This allows it to decide what policies it wishes to pursue and make them law relatively quickly, compromising very little with opponents. Of course, the ruling party's members will ultimately face voters' judgment, but in the short term they face no formal constraints. Many observers contend this explains why PM Margaret Thatcher in the United Kingdom changed economic policies so much more successfully than did U.S. president Ronald Reagan, elected at about the same time and with a very similar ideology. Thatcher had a majority in Parliament who passed her proposals more or less without question, while Republican Reagan spent much of his term with a Democratic majority in Congress with whom he had to compromise.

In a parliamentary system with a coalition government, however, policymaking requires more compromises. For years, small parties representing ultra-Orthodox Jews were essential members of the cabinet in Israel's coalition governments. They used this power to bargain for passage of legislation exempting their sons from mandatory military service if they are studying the Torah. After the 2013 election, however, the prime minister managed to put together a coalition without them, and changes to the unpopular law were quickly passed.

In a review of the political science literature on this question, David Samuels (2007) concluded that overall, presidential systems are less likely to change the status quo via legislation, and when they do, change will take longer and be more expensive than in parliamentary systems. In semipresidential systems, much depends on whether the president, PM, and parliamentary majority are from the same party. If so, little compromise will likely be necessary. If one or more are from different parties, compromise is more essential and successful policymaking less likely. This, of course, makes short-term horizontal accountability stronger.

Stability

The biggest debate in recent years among comparativists examining these institutions has been over whether one system is more stable than another. Looking mainly at new democracies, political scientist Juan Linz (1990) initiated the debate, arguing that presidentialism has many potential disadvantages. He saw the separation of powers as leading to what he called "dual legitimacy." Since both the legislature and the executive are independently and directly elected, each has legitimacy. Linz thought that since neither had a higher claim to legitimacy, there could be no democratic resolution of conflicts between them. He also argued that the direct election of the president could lead to chief executives with a "winner-take-all" mentality who would overemphasize their national mandate and be less willing to compromise; in this sense, he saw them as tending to be more majoritarian than consensual. Finally, Linz claimed that presidentialism is too inflexible: fixed terms mean that any serious problem for which a president might need to be removed—or even a president's death in office—could provoke a political crisis, as happened in Nigeria in 2010.

Following Linz, most scholarship has found that presidentialism is likely to be more crisis-prone and threatening to the survival of a new democracy than is parliamentarism (Samuels 2007). This is much more likely to be true, however, in a multiparty system, especially if the president does not have a working majority in the legislature. The smaller the size of the president's party and the greater the overall fragmentation of the legislature, the greater the likelihood of regime collapse in presidential systems (Samuels 2007). Paul Chaisty and colleagues (2015), however, examined nine cases of this type of fragmentation (including our case study of Brazil), what they termed "coalitional presidentialism," and found it to be more stable than often assumed. As in Brazil, presidents used their powers over cabinet and other appointments, and the national budget, to form coalitions that are able to govern. MPs in the nine countries believed this system helped maintain stability, but at the cost of horizontal accountability; too many legislators took the opportunity to gain presidential favors by supporting the ruling coalition, harming parliament's ability to hold the president accountable. Linz's critics argue that presidential institutions themselves are not the problem. After extensive quantitative analysis, political scientist José Antonio Cheibub concluded that the society, not the institution, is the problem. Presidential systems "tend to exist in societies where democracies of any type are likely to be unstable" (2007, 3). All of these concerns are relatively muted in a more established democracy in which regime collapse does not seem to be a real possibility. In those cases, the fixed terms of the presidential system, some argue, provide greater continuity and stability, especially compared with some of the more fragmented parliamentary systems with many parties, like Italy or Israel.

Semipresidentialism, with its combination of a parliament and president, seems more difficult to analyze. On the one hand, Linz argued semipresidentialism poses the dangers of the strong presidency—dual legitimacy and unwillingness to compromise. On the other hand, the PM's dependence on parliament means that her cabinet will, if necessary, reflect a coalition of parties in a fractionalized system and allow a degree of flexibility not found in pure presidential systems. Empirical research has found

Antiabortion activists demonstrate in front of the U.S. Supreme Court before the Court ruled against a Texas law restricting abortion clinics. The Court ruled that Texas had excessively restricted women's constitutional right to an abortion. The long saga over abortion, dating back to the famous *Roe v. Wade* case in 1973, raises the crucial questions about the judiciary in a democracy: When and why should nonelected officials make important policy decisions, and is the judicialization of politics excessively increasing the judiciary's political role?

MANDEL NGAN/AFP/Getty Images

that while the specific powers of the president in semipresidential systems are important (presidents should not be allowed to override the legislature or dismiss the PM), these systems are no less stable than parliamentary systems, even under cohabitation (Schleiter and Morgan-Jones 2009). Furthermore, voters in semipresidential systems are quite capable of assigning responsibility for policies to particular officials, in spite of the dual executive, making accountability clear, and semipresidential systems seem just as capable of making policy decisions as other systems.

Executive-legislative institutions are at the heart of the biggest debates over how well democracies represent and govern their citizens. The effects of different institutional arrangements often appear reasonably clear in the abstract, but in practice the social, cultural, and political contexts make analysis much more complex. This complexity means that debates over democracies' varying effectiveness will continue to be a major subject of research in comparative politics for some time to come.

JUDICIARY

The judiciary is the least studied branch of government in comparative politics, which is unfortunate since it is becoming more important in many countries. On a daily basis, the job of the judiciary is to enforce a state's laws. Its more important political role, however, is to interpret those laws, especially the constitution. Most democracies have some version of **judicial review,** the authority of the judiciary to decide whether a specific law contradicts a country's constitution. Vested in unelected judges, this makes the court a veto player in the political system. It is clearly a potential means to limit majority rule and achieve horizontal accountability, but it also raises a fundamental question: Why should unelected officials have such power? How much power they actually have, though, depends not only on formal rules but also on the strength of the judiciary as an institution. New democracies have often had to build new judicial institutions, and the weakness of these has become a major concern in comparative politics. In this section, we discuss judicial review and its relationship to democracy, the judicialization of politics, and the question of judicial independence and institutional strength.

judicial review
The authority of the judiciary to decide whether a specific law contradicts a country's constitution

Judicial Review and the "Judicialization" of Politics

Two legal systems, common law and code law, emerged in modern Europe and spread to most of the world via colonialism (see Map 5.2). **Common law** developed in the United Kingdom and was adopted in most former British colonies, including the United States (it is sometimes referred to as Anglo-American law). Under common law, judges base decisions not only on their understanding of the written law but also on their understanding of past court cases. When a judge finds a law ambiguous, he can write a ruling that tries to clarify it, and subsequent judges are obliged to use this ruling as precedent in deciding similar cases.

common law
Legal system originating in Britain in which judges base decisions not only on their understanding of the written law but also on their understanding of past court cases; in contrast to code law

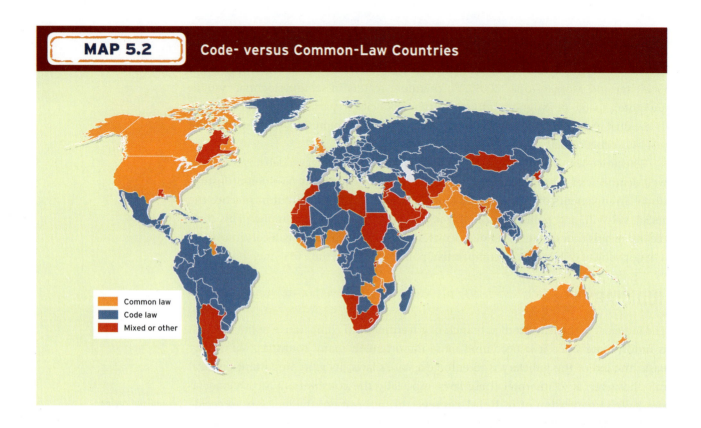

MAP 5.2   **Code- versus Common-Law Countries**

Common law
Code law
Mixed or other

code law
Legal system originating in ancient Roman law and modified by Napoleon Bonaparte in France, in which judges may only follow the law as written and must ignore past decisions; in contrast to common law

Code law is most closely associated with the French emperor Napoleon Bonaparte, who codified it in what became known as the Napoleonic Code. (It is also known as civil law.) Under code law, which has its origins in ancient Roman law and was spread in modern Europe via Napoleon's conquests, judges may only follow the law as written, interpreting it as little as necessary to fit the case. Past decisions are irrelevant, as each judge must look only to the existing law. Like common law, code law spread globally via colonialism, especially to former French, Spanish, and Portuguese colonies.

The two systems logically led to different kinds of judicial review. Common-law countries, such as the United States, usually have decentralized judicial review: the same courts that handle everyday criminal cases can also rule on constitutional issues and can do so at any level. If a constitutional question begins in a lower court, it can be appealed upward, ultimately to the highest court. Code-law countries usually have centralized judicial review: a special court handles constitutional questions. Another important distinction is the question of who can initiate cases. Most common-law systems, including that of the United States, have concrete judicial review: only someone who has actually been negatively affected by the law in question can initiate a case. Most code-law systems have abstract judicial review; certain public officials or major political groups can call on the courts to make a constitutional ruling even before the law is fully in effect. The length of appointments to whatever court handles judicial review is also important. Some countries have lifetime appointments; others limit judges' terms.

The fundamental question about judicial review in a democracy is why judges, who are typically not elected and therefore not subject to vertical accountability, should be allowed to make decisions with major political consequences. Proponents argue that the difference in democratic legitimacy between judges and elected officials is far less sharply defined than is often assumed. First, legislatures and executives are never perfectly representative or accountable, so the difference between them and the judiciary may be less than it appears. Second, the judiciary's horizontal accountability to executives and legislatures can be seen as an indirect source of democratic accountability. Judges are typically appointed by elected officials, so their stands on issues reflect the ideas of those officials and their constituents. Robert Dahl, one of the foremost scholars of democracy, argued in a widely read 1957 article that U.S. Supreme Court justices are part of political coalitions just as elected officials are, and that they reflect the same political divisions that divide elected officials. Advocates of judicial review also argue that even if the judiciary is an imperfect democratic institution, it plays several crucial roles. It provides a check on executive and legislative power, serving as a mechanism of horizontal accountability. In the United States, many argue as well that judicial review exists to protect minority rights that might be trampled by a legislature or executive acting on majority opinion. In practice, however, most studies have shown that courts are more likely to rule in favor of those in power than on behalf of marginalized or oppressed minorities.

However one answers the questions raised by judicial review, it is certainly becoming more widespread, a process that Tate and Vallinder called the "judicialization" of politics. They argued that judicialization is "one of the most significant trends in late-twentieth and early-twenty-first-century government" (1995, 5). Taylor (2008) argued that this is happening not only because the judiciary has chosen to act as a veto player but also because other political actors increasingly use the judicial system to conduct their policy battles, making the judicial venue a "veto point."

Judicial Independence and Institutional Strength

Under any legal system, new or old, the judiciary must constitute a strong institution if it is to carry out its function properly in a system of horizontal accountability. Judicial review only matters in practice to the extent the key courts are willing and able to act independently of the other branches of government. This requires **judicial independence,** the belief and ability of judges to decide cases as they think appropriate, regardless of what other politically powerful officials or institutions desire. Judicial systems that lack independence are weak institutions in which corruption is common; judges may accept bribes to decide cases in a particular way or refuse to rule against powerful individuals. This can affect everyday criminal and civil cases as well as constitutional questions. No particular formal procedure or power guarantees judicial independence, though Ferejohn and Pasquino (2003) found that the distinct constitutional courts common in code-law countries are particularly independent and effective. This

judicial independence
The belief and ability of judges to decide cases as they think appropriate, regardless of what other people, and especially politically powerful officials or institutions, desire

type of court has been very common in new democracies over the last several decades. Legal scholar Samuel Issacharoff (2015) argued that their creation facilitated the process of democratic transition by allowing political actors crafting new constitutions to leave some controversial problems for courts to decide later, and the courts in turn have played a crucial role in helping young democracies resist efforts to undermine democratic rules.

What undoubtedly matters most to judicial independence, though, is informal factors that help make formal independence real in practice. Any number of factors can influence how much courts can actually practice the official powers granted them. Ferejohn, Rosenbluth, and Shipan (2007) argued that political structure is key: countries with more fragmented political systems provide more political space for the judiciary to act independently. For instance, a presidential system's division of the executive and legislature raises the possibility of a divided government in which the judiciary may feel it can act more independently because the other branches disagree with one another. A parliamentary system with many parties that requires a coalition government can create a similar context for judicial independence. Similarly, weaker parties in which leaders have limited control over legislators encourage judicial independence. In new democracies, these same factors make political leaders fear that their opponents will gain power and exclude them via extraconstitutional means, so they support creating judicial review as a safety measure (Yadav and Mukherjee 2014). Judicial independence is less likely when courts do not feel they have the power to counter a strong majority consensus among elected officials. Matthew Ingram (2016), on the other hand, argued that judges' beliefs were a crucial ingredient. Examining local courts' strength and independence in our case studies of Brazil and Mexico, he found that the presence of judges who were ideologically committed to reforms explained where reforms happened better than did the structure of political competition.

A study of post-Communist countries found that even where judicial review is well established in the constitution, high courts use it rarely and warily, in part because they lack legitimacy and therefore do not believe themselves to be strong enough to withstand pressure from more powerful officials. Given that the judiciary lacks both military and financial resources, legitimacy is crucial to its institutional strength; without widespread support and acceptance on the part of other officials and the general populace, the judiciary has little power. Gibson, Caldeira, and Baird (1998) found that judiciaries typically gain legitimacy only over time as the populace comes to understand their role more fully and is satisfied with key court decisions. Leading judges are often acutely aware of this and decide cases so as to enhance the institutional strength of the judiciary; judges' actions, no less than those of other political leaders, can at times be understood via rational choice theory (Hirschl 2009). Diana Kapiszewski (2012) made a historical institutionalist argument that greater judicial ability to stand up to the executive successfully comes from informal institutions within the judiciary that gain it greater legitimacy and professionalization. These institutions arise in particular political contexts that give political leaders incentives to allow their initial development, and once created, they tend to endure. As we will see in the case study of Brazil and in chapter 9, the institutional strength of the judiciary in new democracies, and therefore judicial independence, is important and not automatic.

CASE Study

THE JUDICIARY: BRAZIL

CASE SYNOPSIS

Brazil's relatively young democracy does not have one of the world's strongest judicial systems, but the judiciary has nonetheless achieved what many courts have not: a degree of judicial independence that has partially curbed executive and legislative power, and helped battle widespread corruption. But code law and abstract judicial review have put tremendous strain on the court system, particularly at the top. This has encouraged the judicialization of politics and made the highest court a key veto point in Brazil's fragmented democracy, raising the classic question of whether too much horizontal accountability excessively limits the ability to govern. Also, while judicial independence has been an important achievement, it has not helped eliminate corruption within the judiciary itself.

- CODE LAW Special constitutional courts and abstract judicial review
- JUDICIALIZATION The constitutional court as veto point
- INSTITUTIONALIZATION Moderate independence, but not complete legitimacy; huge inefficiency

Brazil's 1988 constitution created a complex judicial system with constitutional protection for its autonomy in most personnel, budgetary, administrative, and disciplinary areas. The system is headed by the Supreme Federal Tribunal (STF), which hears constitutional cases. Under the STF is the Supreme Justice Tribunal, the court of final appeal for nonconstitutional cases. Judges to these highest courts are appointed by the president with approval of the Senate (the upper house of the legislature).

Judges in the two levels of federal courts below these are appointed by the judiciary itself based on criteria of merit. Most serve life terms up to seventy years of age. As is typical in code-law countries, in addition to these constitutional and criminal courts, separate codes and courts exist for labor disputes, military issues, and elections. This system is replicated in large part within each state of Brazil's federal system, resulting in a total of approximately 16,900 judges in hundreds of separate courts.

Initially, Brazil's top judges seemed hesitant to use their independence vis-à-vis the president. By 1992, though, the STF had gained confidence, and its rulings helped lead to the president's impeachment on corruption charges, a watershed event in the four-year-old democracy. The top court has since ruled against a number of major political leaders on both constitutional questions and corruption charges, though in favor of the executive in other situations. The court's most prominent role began in 2014, as the giant scandal involving the national oil company exploded. The federal judge overseeing it, Sergio Moro, became something of a national hero as major political figures were indicted. As the breadth and depth of the scandal emerged, Brazilians increasingly saw the judiciary as a source of relative probity and therefore legitimacy: "For a public sick of corruption, [the judiciary] represented hopes that the old culture of impunity was finally over, that democratic institutions were growing stronger, that the division of powers was functioning and justice was being done" (Watts 2016). The impeachment of President Dilma Rousseff, though, raised potential problems. The impeachment, of course, came from Congress, not the judiciary, but the political controversy over whether it was justified had the potential to threaten the perceived impartiality of the judiciary's role in the broader scandal.

Oliveira (2005) found that STF justices decided cases most frequently based on values of professionalism and expansion of the court's role vis-à-vis the other branches of the government; they were rarely submissive to political demands from elected leaders. Kapiszewski (2012) argued that this professionalism was based on a history of professionalizing the courts that dates back to the 1930s in Brazil. Also, the exceptionally fragmented National Congress would not approve judicial appointees they perceived as heavily partisan, so appointments of widely respected legal professionals became the

Brazil's Supreme Federal Tribunal meets in December 2015 to consider a motion from President Dilma Rousseff to end the Senate's attempt to impeach her. The court modified the impeachment process but allowed it to continue, and the president was impeached in May 2016. The Brazilian court had gained significant autonomy since the return to democracy, but the highly politicized nature of the president's impeachment threatened to undermine its legitimacy if it was seen as too biased in favor of or opposed to the impeachment of Rousseff.

EVARISTO SA/AFP/Getty Images

norm. This independence enhanced horizontal accountability vis-à-vis the executive, but it also left few restraints on the judiciary.

Carlos Santiso (2003) pointed out, however, that while Brazil's judiciary serves an important function in horizontal accountability, its own lack of vertical accountability has become a major problem. Virtually all observers view the judiciary as slow, inefficient, and corrupt. Scandals involving judges have sometimes gone unpunished, many courts have a backlog of cases stretching out for years, and Brazilian judges are some of the most highly paid in the world.

Part of the problem with the huge number of cases is the system of code law and judicial review established in the constitution. Brazil allows an unusually wide array of political leaders to bring constitutional cases to the STF. This resulted from a transition to democracy in which no party had full control, so each wanted to ensure access to the judiciary if its opponents tried to usurp too much power (Yadav and Mukherjee 2014, 142–143). Constitutional cases can come to the STF either on appeal from lower courts or directly from key political actors, including most government agencies, national business or labor organizations, state governments, and political parties. The STF typically processes 70,000 cases per year, probably the highest number in the world. It even has a drive-up window for lawyers to file cases! To handle the workload, individual judges are allowed to decide most cases; indeed, 90 percent are decided by a single judge. Political leaders and groups have taken advantage of the code-law system that allows them to file constitutional cases directly to judicialize Brazilian politics. If they cannot win in a state legislature or at the federal level, they take a case to court, making a constitutional argument if possible. Just initiating a case can often bring significant publicity to a group's pet cause. Taylor (2008) found this tactic to be particularly common in policy areas in which there are concentrated costs to particular groups; they are very likely to make a constitutional challenge to try to protect themselves, even after losing the legislative battle. Brazil's independent judiciary has become a powerful veto point in Brazil's already fragmented political system.

Judicial independence has also made it difficult to clean up corruption or reform the parts of the system that almost everyone agrees aren't working. Brazil has long been one of the most unequal societies in the world, and stories abound of wealthy people bribing judges to ensure that court decisions go their way. The poor are more likely to be brought to court, more likely to be convicted, and more likely to be sentenced to long terms in Brazil's overcrowded and often violent prisons. So while Brazil's top court has become an important player in the national policy-making process, and a venue for other actors to pursue their policy goals, the judiciary as a whole remains only moderately institutionalized, and its continuing problems limit its legitimacy.

Judicial leaders have successfully fought against reforms of this system. In December 2004, to reduce the number of cases in the courts, the legislature passed some minimal reforms and created a National Judicial Council composed of both top judges and nominees outside the judiciary to oversee the budget and administration of the courts. The initial results of this reform were positive, cutting the number of cases almost in half. Still, much work remains to be done.

CASE Questions

1. What does Brazil teach us about the question of whether the power of an unelected judiciary is justified in a democracy?
2. What does Brazil teach us about the trade-off between the benefits of the judiciary checking the other branches of government, on the one hand, and the role of the judiciary as a veto player or veto point, on the other?

BUREAUCRACY

Chapter 2 identified a bureaucracy as one of the key characteristics of a modern state. All states have an executive branch that includes a bureaucracy of some sort. The ideal modern bureaucracy consists of officials appointed on the basis of merit and expertise who implement policies lawfully, treat all citizens equally according to the relevant laws, and are held accountable by the elected head of the executive branch. This ideal is an important component in the full development of an effective modern state; as we noted in chapter 2, a state (whatever type of regime it has) will have greater capacity to rule its territory and people if it has an effective bureaucracy. A bureaucracy in this modern sense is also a key component of liberal democracy, as it recruits officials according to merit, administers policies according to law, treats citizens equally, and insulates bureaucratic officials from the personal and political desires of top leaders. On the other hand, bureaucracy can be a threat to democracy, so bureaucrats themselves must be held accountable. Who will prevent them from abusing their independence and autonomy? Because they are not elected, vertical accountability does not exist, meaning that horizontal accountability is very important.

Bureaucracy can limit the executive in a number of ways, even as it enhances a state's capacity. Prior to modern reforms, bureaucratic positions in most societies were based on political patronage: leaders appointed all officials to suit the leaders' interests. (China was a major exception—Confucian ideas of merit in that country go back millennia.) Professionalization involved recruitment based on merit and a reduction of political patronage. It also came to mean that bureaucratic officials held technical expertise, on which political leaders often have to rely to make decisions in an increasingly complex world. Knowledge and expertise are key sources of bureaucrats' independent power. Modern bureaucracies developed into formal, hierarchical organizations in which career advancement, at least ideally, was based on performance and personal capability rather than on political connections.

Bureaucratic professionalization keeps the bureaucracy at least partially insulated from the whims of political leaders, but it raises the question of how the political leadership will hold the bureaucracy accountable. This can be understood as a **principal-agent problem.** The principal (the elected or appointed political leadership in the executive or legislative branches) assigns an agent (the bureaucrat) a task to carry out as the principal instructs; the problem is how the principal makes sure the agent carries

principal-agent problem
A problem in which a principal hires an agent to perform a task but the agent's self-interest does not necessarily align with the principal's, so the agent may not carry out the task as assigned

out the task as assigned. Bureaucratic agents might well have strong incentives to deviate from their assigned tasks. Rational choice theorists argue that bureaucrats, however professional, are as self-interested and rational as any other actors. Bureaucrats' preferences are usually to expand their sphere of influence and the size of their organization to enhance their own prestige and salary. This can expand the size of the bureaucracy, create inefficiencies, and distort the principals' purposes. Self-interest can also lead to corruption, if bureaucrats exchange favorable treatment of political leaders or ordinary citizens for bribes or other advantages.

Numerous solutions to this problem have emerged over the years. In every state the political leadership of the executive branch selects a certain number of **political appointees** to head the bureaucracy. These appointees, starting at the top with cabinet ministers, serve at the pleasure of the president or prime minister and, among other things, are assigned the task of overseeing their respective segments of the bureaucracy. Different countries allow different numbers of political appointees: the United States typically allows six or eight for each significant department in the federal government, whereas two are more typical for each ministry in the United Kingdom. (The United States uses the term *department* to designate the major agencies of the government, whereas most of the world uses *ministry* to mean the same thing, harkening back to the religious influence on the early modern state.)

Political appointees' power over professional bureaucrats is limited by the legal means through which the latter are hired, paid, and earn career advancement; bureaucrats, however, must answer to political appointees within those legal limits. In democracies, legislators can write laws that are as specific as possible to limit bureaucrats' discretion. Whether they choose to do so, though, depends on a number of factors. If legislators trust bureaucrats or see them as sharing similar preferences, if they are not capable of writing detailed legislation, and if they can turn to the courts to control bureaucrats if necessary, then they are less likely to try to control bureaucratic behavior via detailed legislation (Huber and Shipan 2002). **Legislative oversight** is another

political appointees
Officials who serve at the pleasure of the president or prime minister and are assigned the task of overseeing their respective segments of the bureaucracy

legislative oversight
Occurs when members of the legislature, usually in committees, oversee the bureaucracy

David Wildstein, a political appointee of New Jersey governor Chris Christie, looks toward his attorney at a hearing at the state assembly in 2014. A scandal over the closing of traffic lanes on the George Washington Bridge into New York City erupted that year, with many blaming Christie's political appointees for using the bureaucracy for partisan purposes, undermining bureaucratic autonomy. Hearings are a key element of legislative oversight of the bureaucracy.

Emile Wamsteker/Bloomberg via Getty Images

key means of horizontal accountability; members of the legislature, usually in committees, oversee the bureaucracy by interviewing key leaders, examining budgets, and assessing how successfully a particular agency has carried out its mandate. Often, citizens use the judicial system to try to achieve accountability by taking individual officials or entire agencies to court, arguing that they have either failed to carry out their duties or have done so unlawfully.

None of these efforts to influence the bureaucracy works perfectly, in large part because principals never know exactly what their agents within a bureaucracy are doing, especially as technocratic knowledge becomes more important. For most of the twentieth century, governments relied heavily on professional socialization to maintain standards. They recruited people who had been trained to abide by key professional norms of neutrality and legality, and they believed they could count on most of these recruits to behave in the general "public" interest in alignment with their training. Some states, such as France and Japan, went so far as to recruit almost exclusively from one high-profile educational institution so that government bureaucrats garnered great prestige and professional status.

New Public Management (NPM)
Theory of reform of bureaucracies that argues for the privatizing of many government services, creating competition among agencies to simulate a market, focusing on customer satisfaction, and flattening administrative hierarchies

Rational choice theorists, however, argued that training could not overcome the incentives and self-interest inherent in the bureaucracy, which tend to produce inefficiency and corruption. Following this line of argument, the **New Public Management (NPM)** movement arose. The movement first emerged in the United States and United Kingdom in the 1980s and was associated with President Ronald Reagan and Prime Minister Margaret Thatcher. NPM advocates contended that inherent inefficiencies meant that the bureaucracy required radical reforms to make it operate more like a market-based organization. Reforms included privatizing many government services so that they would be provided by the market, creating competition among agencies and subagencies within the bureaucracy to simulate a market, focusing on customer satisfaction (via client surveys, among other things), and flattening administrative hierarchies to encourage more team-based activity and creativity. The ideas of NPM became widely popular and were implemented in many wealthy democracies to varying degrees. Some countries, such as the United Kingdom and New Zealand, cut the size of their bureaucracies extensively via NPM, while others, including Germany and Japan, implemented it slowly and partially. While NPM reduced the size of government significantly in some countries, one of the few detailed studies of its effects, across thirty years in our case study of the United Kingdom, concluded that even though the size of the civil service was cut by one third, overall costs went up slightly and the quality and fairness of services (measured by the number of citizen complaints) declined slightly (Hood and Dixon 2015).

Bureaucracy and Corruption

One of NPM's main targets was bureaucratic corruption. Where the state and its institutions are generally weak, reform requires not only making the bureaucracy more efficient but also strengthening it as an institution. When bureaucratic rules and norms are extremely weak, corruption and massive inefficiency are likely (O'Dwyer 2006). Political elites may be able to use a weak bureaucracy to pursue personal or financial interests of their own, citizens may be able to gain favors from the state via bribery, and bureaucrats themselves may steal from the state. Bribery and rent seeking are two primary types of corruption in bureaucracies. In the least institutionalized bureaucracies, citizens often have to bribe officials to get them to carry out the functions they are mandated to do. The political leadership may not be interested in encouraging the bureaucracy to function effectively because they benefit from their own ability to purchase favors from bureaucrats. Alternatively, they may simply have lost all ability to control their agents in the bureaucracy, often because of very low bureaucratic salaries. **Rent seeking** is the gaining of an advantage in a market without engaging in equally productive activity; it usually involves using government regulations to one's own benefit. In weakly institutionalized bureaucracies, for example, businesses may be able to bribe officials to grant them exclusive rights to import certain items, thereby reaping huge profits for little effort.

rent seeking
Gaining an advantage in a market without engaging in equally productive activity; usually involves using government regulations for one's own benefit

The rent-seeking model of corruption is based on a rational choice theory of why corruption is greater in some countries than in others (see Map 5.3). Rational choice theories, as always, focus on individual incentives, arguing that economic conditions are particularly important in explaining corruption: countries with more highly regulated economies and greater inequality are likely to be more corrupt. The former provides opportunities for corruption, as bureaucrats can demand bribes frequently; the latter means that average citizens have fewer resources to get what they want and therefore are more willing to pay bribes. Numerous other theories, however, have also sought to explain the puzzle of corruption.

One of the oldest theories is based on political culture: corruption is greater where societies lack shared values about the importance of the public sphere, instead placing personal, family, or ethnic interests above those of the society as a whole. Others have noted that greater corruption is found in postcolonial societies; they contend that the lack of legitimacy of a postcolonial state that has no firm roots in the society leads citizens to believe one should gain whatever one can from the public sphere. Nigerian sociologist Peter Ekeh (1975) argued that in Africa, two "publics" exist: a "primordial public," which includes ethnic, religious, and community identities in which people feel reciprocal moral responsibility toward one another, and an amoral "civic public" involving the state, toward which people feel no obligation and therefore take from freely.

Much recent scholarship is institutionalist, focusing on the effects of political institutions in particular. The general consensus has been that in democracies with stronger parties and greater political competition, corruption is lower. Competition among institutions, such as in presidential and federal systems, is also seen as likely to reduce corruption by increasing horizontal accountability. Vineeta Yadav (2011) recently argued, however, that strong parties actually increase corruption. Based on

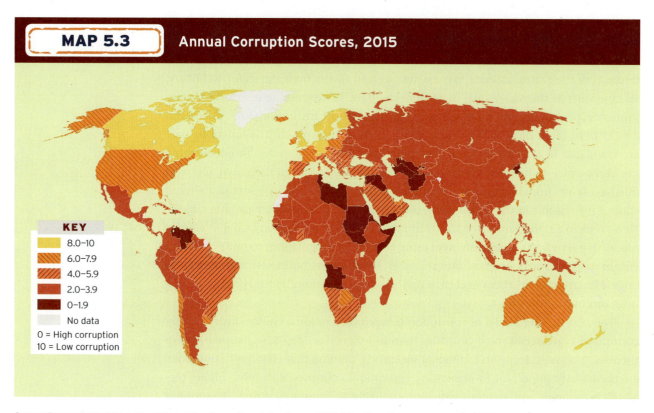

MAP 5.3   Annual Corruption Scores, 2015

KEY
8.0–10
6.0–7.9
4.0–5.9
2.0–3.9
0–1.9
No data
0 = High corruption
10 = Low corruption

Source: Transparency International Corruption Perceptions Index Scores, 2015 (http://www.transparency.org/cpi2015).

case studies of Brazil and India, as well as a much wider statistical analysis, she argued that stronger parties that control the legislative process actually encourage greater corruption because they need higher levels of cash for campaigns.

Michael Johnston (2005), one of the foremost scholars of corruption, combined theories based on economic factors and political institutions to argue that, rather than trying to predict the total amount of corruption, we need to understand its variation in different kinds of societies. He elaborated four models of different types of corruption, based on wealth level and the nature of the political system. Corruption in wealthy, established democracies is primarily based on "influence markets," in which corporations use access to politicians, usually via generous contributions to campaigns and parties, to gain preferential treatment from key bureaucracies, as in the case of Japan and the United States. In middle-income countries with newer and less well-institutionalized democracies, "elite cartels" emerge in which key political and business leaders form networks to gain control of the government and systematically use it to their joint political and financial benefit, as in Brazil. In middle-income countries that just recently became democracies, institutions are even weaker and political competition more intense, uncertain, and personal; in these countries, "oligarchs and clans" scramble for spoils in the system, as in Russia. In the least institutionalized (and

Wealth, Corruption, and Democracy

The table below shows the levels of wealth, corruption, and democracy for a selection of countries around the world, including our eleven case studies. Michael Johnston argued that corruption isn't necessarily higher or lower in countries that are wealthier and more democratic, but different. Based on the table, what trends do you see? Are wealthier countries clearly less corrupt? Are democratic countries clearly less corrupt? Which of the two (wealth or democracy) seems most influential in determining the level of corruption? What do your answers suggest for Johnston's argument?

Corruption Perceptions Index			
Country	GDP per capita (current US $)	CPI	Polity IV score
Norway	$97,299.6	91	10
United States	$54,629.5	5	10
Japan	$36,194.4	75	10
United Arab Emirates	$43,962.7	70	-8
Germany	$47,773.9	81	10
United Kingdom	$46,297.0	81	10
Czech Republic	$19,502.4	56	9
Chile	$14,528.3	70	10
Russia	$12,735.9	29	4
Brazil	$11,726.8	38	8
Mexico	$10,325.6	35	8

Country	GDP per capita (current US $)	CPI	Polity IV score
Botswana	$7,123.3	63	8
Colombia	$7,903.9	37	7
China	$7,590.0	37	-7
Thailand	$5,977.4	38	-3
Iran, Islamic Republic of	$5,442.9	27	-7
Indonesia	$3,491.9	36	9
Georgia	$4,435.2	52	7
Philippines	$2,872.5	35	8
India	$1,581.5	38	9
Nigeria	$3,203.3	26	7
Vietnam	$2,052.3	31	-7
Pakistan	$1,316.6	30	7
Kenya	$1,358.3	25	9
Rwanda	$695.7	54	-3
Mozambique	$585.6	31	5
Uganda	$714.6	25	-1
Niger	$427.4	34	6
Congo, Democratic Republic of the	$442.3	22	-4

Polity IV is a measure of how well institutionalized democracy is within a given country, with 10 being fully institutionalized democracy and -10 being fully institutionalized authoritarian regime.

Sources: GDP data are from the World Bank, GDP per Capita (current US $). (http://data.worldbank.org/indicator/NY.GDP.PCAP.CD/countries); CPI scores are from Transparency International, Corruption Perceptions Index, 2015 (http://www.transparency.org/cpi2015/results/#myAnchor1); Polity IV scores are from Polity IV, Case Format (http://www.systemicpeace.org/inscrdata.html).

often poorest) states with personalized or neopatrimonial rule, corruption often takes the form of the "Official Mogul," a strongman who uses the resources of the state as he pleases to favor his political allies and punish his enemies, as in much of Africa.

The extent of the problem and the possible remedies for corruption vary, Johnston argued, across these four types of countries, though corruption is an important issue in all of them. Johnston (2014) and other scholars (Börzel and van Hüllen 2015; Mungiu-Pippidi 2015) have argued that bringing corruption under control requires far more than simply reforming the bureaucracy via programs like NPM; instead, it requires a mobilized citizenry with adequate information to demand greater account-ability. Where these do not exist, they must be established before specific policy reforms aimed at reducing corruption will work. Leslie Schwindt-Bayer and Margit Tavits (2016) found that majoritarian democracies in which clarity of responsibility for corruption is strongest facilitated voters' ability to hold corrupt politicians responsible; consensual democracies, they suggested, allow officials to blame each other for corruption, limiting voters' ability to know whom to hold responsible. Japan demonstrates both the power and limits of bureaucracy, and the complex issues that arise when bureaucracy weakens.

BUREAUCRATIC CONTROL AND CORRUPTION: JAPAN

CASE SYNOPSIS

As technocratic expertise becomes ever more important, major economic and social forces have pushed most countries in the direction of enhanced bureaucratic autonomy and power. This process can give rise to corruption, especially in countries with a historical legacy of strong bureaucracy such as Japan. Reform efforts to create greater horizontal accountability have been difficult to put into effect, even though models like NPM have long been available on which to draw. Entrenched bureaucratic power, especially when supported by elected officials who benefit from it, can be very difficult to overcome, as the Japanese case demonstrates.

- BUREAUCRATIC STRENGTH Strong from 1950s to 1980s, later reduced by globalization
- CORRUPTION "Iron triangles" and bureaucrats' political influence
- REFORM Limited effects of NPM; frustration of recent reform efforts

The sweeping victory of the Democratic Party of Japan (DPJ) in 2009 (see chapter 6 for details) over the long-ruling Liberal Democratic Party (LDP) was the most important electoral outcome in Japan since World War II. One of the DPJ's major campaign promises was to reform the entrenched bureaucracy, seen by many Japanese as a source of unaccountable power that was preventing necessary reforms. The Japanese economy boomed for four decades after the war, thanks in part to Japan's long-standing tradition of a highly professionalized, elite bureaucracy. Fears that the bureaucracy was becoming too powerful and corrupt, though, were realized in the revelations of the "recruit scandal" in 1988. Numerous scandals involving both bureaucrats and politicians have occurred since, but the power of the bureaucracy has been trimmed only partially.

The fact that the Japanese bureaucracy was the only major political institution to survive the post–World War II U.S. occupation largely intact gave it a tremendous advantage vis-à-vis other institutions in the new democracy. As in France, Japan's top bureaucrats are recruited primarily from one source: the law faculty at the University of Tokyo. From the 1950s through the 1970s, the unwritten rule was that the top graduates of that school would enter the elite corps of the bureaucracy to begin their ascent to the top. Bureaucrats' great prestige and potentially high income came from the common practice of *amakudari*, or the "descent from heaven," and rigid **iron triangles** among business leaders, politicians, and key bureaucrats. Under *amakudari,* retiring civil servants gained lucrative positions in the businesses they previously regulated. Among other things, this gave bureaucrats an incentive to maintain favorable conditions for and relations with key corporations in their regulatory area. The term *iron triangle* was coined in reference to the United States, but the phenomenon is even stronger in Japan. Key bureaucrats, business leaders, and politicians cooperate to set policy to their mutual interest. In a classic example of the type of corruption Michael Johnston (2005) termed the "influence market," businesses give generous contributions to top politicians; in exchange, the politicians secure favorable treatment from key bureaucrats, and bureaucrats grant the favors because they will eventually be working in the businesses themselves.

The power of Japan's bureaucracy was unusual for a democracy: it controlled

iron triangle
Three-sided cooperative interaction among bureaucrats, legislators, and business leaders in a particular sector that serves the interests of all involved but keeps others out of the policy-making process

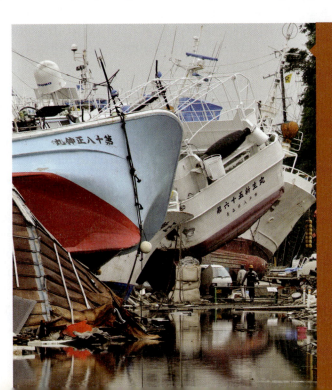

The tsunami that devastated parts of coastal Japan in 2011 piled large vessels in heaps like these. The government was criticized, and the ruling party lost the subsequent election, for its failure to respond adequately to the crisis. Part of the problem was lack of coordination among various bureaucratic agencies, caused by reforms the government had put in place to try to reduce the bureaucracy's influence over policymaking.

KAZUHIRO NOGI/AFP/Getty Images

the key information and expertise needed to guide the growing economy and was a source of highly prestigious employment. Until a 2014 reform, the prime minister only made around two hundred political appointments, as compared with the several thousand that a U.S. president makes, giving him little executive oversight. Combined with little legislative oversight due to the iron triangles, the bureaucracy was left with great power vis-à-vis the other branches in Japan's democracy. At the height of its power, most major legislative initiatives began not with the prime minister or the legislature but rather in the relevant bureaucracy. Interestingly, this power did not result in the further growth of the bureaucracy. Though it retained great regulatory powers in the economy, the number of officials as a percentage of all employment was and remains the lowest among wealthy democracies, undoubtedly in part because of *amakudari*.

While most Japanese knew that corruption was fairly common, they thought it did not affect the top echelons until major scandals broke out in the 1980s and 1990s. Combined with the economic stagnation of the 1990s, the scandals diminished the prestige of the bureaucracy in general. At the height of the bureaucracy's power in the 1960s, forty-three top university graduates competed for each top bureaucratic position; by the 1990s only eleven did (Pempel 2000, 160). Business stagnation made *amakudari* more difficult, and the prestige of the bureaucracy plummeted. While corruption is relatively low now (Japan ranked number 18 on Transparency International's Corruption Perception Index in 2015), the iron triangles continue to mean that a great deal of public expenditure on things like infrastructure is based on political and personal interests of politicians and bureaucrats rather than clear need. A series of scandals in 2016, for example, rocked the early preparations for the 2020 Tokyo Olympics, forcing the resignation of one key official involved in the process.

Changes to Japan's bureaucratic system have long been proposed but have seldom succeeded. Electoral reforms in 1993, a direct response to the worst scandals, seem to have had limited effect on the role of money in the election process (see chapter 6). The ideas of NPM filtered in from the United States and United Kingdom but also had relatively little impact. Neither Japanese bureaucrats nor politicians had significant interest in reforming a system from which they all benefited, and given the small size of Japan's bureaucracy, some of NPM's analysis clearly did not fit.

Longtime Japan analyst Karel van Wolferen (2010) argued that the DPJ government that came to power in 2009 tried to implement the most serious reform effort to date. Its key leaders wanted to fundamentally reduce the power of the bureaucracy vis-à-vis the PM and cabinet by building up the strength of elected offices. To that end, the first DPJ prime minister centralized key decision making in the cabinet and eliminated several important roles for senior bureaucrats, including what had been a crucial meeting of senior bureaucrats to coordinate policy across ministries, arguing that elected officials should make decisions and bureaucrats should implement them. He also instituted regular and important meetings of the elected cabinet, following the British model, which had not been the case before. This stark break with past practices and strong barrier between the elected officials and senior bureaucrats ultimately left key decision makers inadequately informed on important issues and bureaucrats feeling marginalized (Shinoda 2012).

In mid-2010 a new DPJ prime minister moved back to a policy of greater cooperation between elected officials and bureaucrats. The government, however, proved inept in responding to the unprecedented crisis of the 2011 earthquake and tsumani, which killed twenty thousand people, displaced hundreds of thousands, and threatened nuclear catastrophe. Part of the problem was the various ministries' inability to coordinate policy, a result of the government having eliminated regular meetings among senior bureaucrats from different ministries (Shinoda 2012). The third DPJ PM reversed almost all of the prior practices, reinstating bureaucrats' role in coordinating and setting policy in several areas. In spite of this, the Japanese public saw the government as incompetent, and the LDP swept back into power in the election of December 2012. The new prime minister, Shinzo Abe, created the Cabinet Bureau of Personnel Affairs in 2014 and appointed a close aide to run it. It was given power to appoint over six hundred key bureaucrats, tripling the number of appointments the prime minister controlled in the past, in a clear effort to use the elected executive's power of appointment to control and curtail the independent bureaucrats.

The relative power of the bureaucracy today remains in dispute. It is certainly more powerful than in most wealthy democracies, but globalization and deregulation have reduced its control of the economy (see chapter 10). In addition, it has become more internally divided, allowing more voices within and without to have an effect on key questions in Japanese politics. Even though recent reforms appear not to have had a major impact, the longer trend seems to point in the direction of at least somewhat greater accountability.

CASE Questions

1. Political scientists debate whether increasing bureaucratic power is inherent in our highly technological and complex era or is simply the result of inadequate political will and institutions with which to keep the bureaucracy in line. What does the Japanese case teach us about the answer to this debate?
2. Does Japan suggest that the design of political institutions or the nature of economic policies is more important in explaining the relative strength of the bureaucracy in a modern state?

FEDERALISM

So far, we have only considered governmental institutions at the national level. In every country, of course, they exist at lower levels as well, though their role and autonomy vis-à-vis the national government vary widely. The most important distinction is between unitary and federal systems. In **unitary systems** the central government has sole constitutional sovereignty and power, whereas in **federal systems** the central

unitary systems
Political systems in which the central government has sole constitutional sovereignty and power; in contrast to a federal system

federal systems
Political systems in which a state's power is legally and constitutionally divided among more than one level of government; in contrast to a unitary system

government shares constitutional sovereignty and power with subunits, such as states, provinces, or regions. Local governments exist in unitary systems, but they derive their powers from the central government, which can alter them as it pleases. In federal systems, some subnational governments have constitutionally derived powers that can only be changed via constitutional amendment.

The first modern federal system was the Dutch Republic of the United Provinces in what is now the Netherlands, but the best-known early example is the United States. Both states originally were contiguous units within larger empires that declared independence and banded together. In the case of the United States, separate and sovereign states—the original thirteen British colonies—came together to form a federation only after a looser union, a confederation, failed to produce a viable central state. Political scientist William Riker (1964) provided a now-classic rational choice explanation for how American federalism emerged, arguing that it resulted from a bargain among self-interested leaders of separate states who were motivated primarily by military concerns—protecting themselves from external threat.

Australia and Switzerland are other examples of federalism that arose from separate states that came together to form a new state. Most modern federations, however, came about in exactly the opposite way: through states trying to remain together, often after colonial rule, as our case study of India below demonstrates. In some cases, such as India, federations arose via democracy and implicit bargaining between regional elites and the central government. In other cases, such as Russia, authoritarian rulers imposed federalism to help them rule a vast, heterogeneous territory.

Why Countries Adopt Federalism

While federal systems are a minority of the world's governments, they include most of its geographically largest countries. As the Country and Concepts table for this chapter (page 219) shows, among our case studies, all of the larger countries except China are federal systems. This is not accidental. Larger countries tend to adopt federal systems in part to provide some level of government closer to the populace than the national government.

A second purpose of federalism is to limit the power of the majority by decentralizing and dividing governmental power. Federal systems usually have bicameral legislatures, with the second (usually referred to as the upper) house representing the interests of the states or provinces. They also have some sort of judicial review to settle disputes between the levels of government. Both institutions limit the power of the executive and the majority controlling the lower (and usually more powerful) house of the legislature. Federal systems, then, typically institutionalize several veto players that do not exist in unitary systems.

Finally, as we mentioned in chapter 4, federalism is often a means to protect the interests of religious or ethnic minorities. When regional minority communities feel threatened by other groups' control of the national government, a federal system that creates separate states or provinces with clear ethnic or religious majorities can ease tensions. This explains why some relatively small states have chosen federal systems. Belgium, for instance, was created in 1830 as a buffer against potential French expansion. Federalism there is combined with consociationalism: the national cabinet and many other appointments must be split 50–50 between the two major language groups, the Flemish and Walloons; separate elections and parties exist for each group; and governments are virtually always a coalition of the two largest parties from each side. Despite its prolonged existence as a nation-state, regionalism in Belgium has always remained strong and seems to be increasing. In 2010 a Flemish nationalist party that calls for Flemish independence won an unprecedented 30 percent of the Flemish vote to become the largest party in the Belgian parliament. It took a world-record 541 days for the ethnically divided political parties in parliament to form a coalition government after the election.

Federalism and Accountability

A key determinant of the extent to which federalism limits majority power and provides accountability is the relative power and autonomy of the national and subnational governments. These factors, in turn, depend on the specific powers set out for each level of government in the constitution, the resources each level of government controls, and the composition and relative strength of the upper house in the legislature. The constitutions of all federal systems lay out the powers of both the central government and the states or provinces. Military, foreign, and monetary policies are always placed under the authority of the national level, as they are essential to the sovereignty of the modern state and a modern economy. States or provinces typically have power over education, transportation, and sometimes social services (at least partially). In more decentralized systems, like the United States and Brazil, states also have separate judicial systems that handle most criminal law.

The real power of each level of government, however, depends not only on formal powers ordained by the constitution but also on resources and bargaining among the units. Two key questions, and areas of political combat between the levels of government in any federal system, are how much each level of government can collect in taxes and how much each can spend. The power of taxation is particularly important, as it gives subnational units greater autonomy than they would have if they were wholly dependent on the central government for their revenue. In the most centralized unitary states, such as the United Kingdom and Ireland, the central government collects more than three-quarters of total government revenue; in the least centralized federal systems, such as Germany and Switzerland, the central government collects less than a third. Similarly, the central government in some unitary systems is responsible for around 60 percent of all expenditures, whereas in decentralized federal systems it is responsible for as little as 30 percent. During the twentieth century, revenue collection in federations became more centralized, reflecting the growing power of national governments over state or provincial ones.

The upper and weaker house of the legislature in a federal system is usually designed to represent the state or provincial governments, while the lower and more powerful house represents individual voters. The upper house's power and composition help determine the extent to which federalism limits majority rule. Its powers can be quite sweeping, as in the case of the U.S. Senate, which must approve all legislation, or much more limited, as in Germany's Bundesrat, which can only delay bills unless they directly relate to the *Bundesländer* (state governments). Because states or provinces are typically of different sizes, smaller ones are often overrepresented in the upper house. In the U.S. Senate, every state has two seats: in 2010 the twenty least populous states had just under 10 percent of the U.S. population but elected 40 percent of the senators. Given that Senate legislation requires the approval of 60 percent of the body on important issues, the representatives of just over 10 percent of the population can stop legislation, an unusually severe restriction on majority rule. Population shifts to cities are causing the population gap between large and small states to increase and leaving small states increasingly rural and conservative and larger states increasingly urban and liberal, meaning the representation gap has partisan implications favoring conservatives. The ratio of representation of the smallest states to the largest in the U.S. Senate is about 66 to 1. The same ratio in the German Bundesrat is only 13 to 1; this ratio, combined with the weaker powers of the Bundesrat, shows clearly that German federalism does not restrict majority rule nearly as much as American federalism does.

The degree of institutionalization in federal systems is also important to accountability, especially at the local level. Examining Latin America, Edward Gibson (2013) argued that especially in poorer and more rural states or provinces, a federal system can preserve nondemocratic rule within a national democracy. As the large, federal Latin American countries such as Mexico, Argentina, and Brazil became democratic, some politically powerful "bosses" in particular states were able to use clientelism to maintain their rule largely unchallenged. In these cases, the new democratic institutions were not followed, so federalism allowed semi-authoritarian rule to continue at the state level, even though a democratic regime existed at the national level. Our case study of Russia is even more extreme: as democracy at the national level withered, federalism weakened with it.

Federalism and Minority Rights

Most federal systems today exist in heterogeneous societies; part of their purpose is to give some local autonomy to ethnic or religious minorities. While all of the issues outlined above apply to these federal systems, other factors also come into play in preserving ethnic minority autonomy. The United States is an example of a **symmetrical federal system**: all states have the same relationship with and rights in relation to the national government. In contrast, many federal systems in ethnically divided societies are **asymmetrical**: some states or provinces have special rights or powers that others do not. These special relationships are often negotiated individually between the leaders of a particular group and the central government, sometimes at the end of a civil war or under

symmetrical federal system
A federal system in which all subnational governments (states or provinces) have the same relationship with and rights in relation to the national government

asymmetrical federal system
A federal system in which different subnational governments (states or provinces) have distinct relationships with and rights in relation to the national government

the threat of civil war or secession. A recent comparative study concluded that federal systems on the whole help to accommodate ethnic and religious divisions, resulting in less conflict than occurs in unitary systems with heterogeneous populations. However, the study also found that federal systems work best where there has not been a history of severe repression of one group over another; in such cases, even the best designed federal institutions may not be able to overcome the tensions and lack of trust between a regionally based group and the central government (Amoretti and Bermeo 2004).

Trends in Federalism

Ever since Riker's (1964) classic study, rational choice theorists have argued that federalism is inherently unstable. They view federalism as based on a negotiated agreement among political coalitions, and as those coalitions change over time, they will demand changes in the federal agreement. Federalism, then, always involves negotiation of the federal arrangement in some way, whether via constitutional amendment, as has happened in Germany, or via evolving judicial interpretations of the constitution, as in the United States. In most cases, though, rational choice theorists argue that either a dominant majority is likely to centralize power, reducing the extent of or even eliminating federalism, or regional minorities will come to feel like they are not getting what they should from the system and demand greater autonomy, perhaps even secession. In Riker's classic analysis, this dynamic led to the American Civil War. More recently, a similar dynamic meant that the post-Communist federations of the Soviet Union, Czechoslovakia, and Yugoslavia all collapsed as the Cold War ended, producing twenty-three separate nation-states. One of those, Russia, is itself a federation that faced similar problems and, as our case study below shows, resolved them via extreme centralization and the effective end of both federalism and democracy (Filippov and Shvetsova 2013). Political parties that have a truly national reach can serve as integrative forces helping to limit the fragmenting tendencies of federalism (our case study of Russia in the 1990s famously lacked these, as we explore in chapter 9), while parties that have only regional interests can exacerbate the problems (Thorlakson 2013).

Recent trends elsewhere also demonstrate the continuing negotiations involving federalism, and the potential for greater centralization or secession. The most decentralized federal systems have become more centralized as the federal governments have gained a greater share of total revenue and used it to override state prerogatives in areas such as civil rights, education, and even the drinking age. (Since the 1980s, the U.S. federal government has enforced the mandatory minimum drinking age of twenty-one by denying transportation funding to states that refuse to abide by it; therefore, all states comply.) In some unitary systems, such as in the United Kingdom, decentralization has taken place. This is often termed **devolution** because it devolves power from the center to the regions or subnational units. A British parliamentary report commented that devolution differs from federalism because parliamentary sovereignty means that devolution of power is reversible. The "devolved" institutions in Scotland, Wales, and Northern Ireland remain subordinate to the British Parliament. Interestingly, Britain is

devolution
Partial decentralization of power from central government to subunits such as states or provinces, with subunits' power being dependent on central government and reversible

an example of "asymmetrical devolution," since each region has its own set of devolved responsibilities (Leeke, Sear, and Gay 2003). Devolution, though, hasn't fully satisfied the members of the Scottish National Party, in particular, who used their new devolved powers to demand a referendum on independence. Though it failed in 2014, after Britain's vote to leave the EU in 2016, the party was promising to hold another referendum, which most observers believed would succeed in creating a separate Scotland, disuniting the United Kingdom that was created in 1707.

All governments struggle with how much power to give subnational units of government and how much to retain in the center. In a democracy, this tension has crucial implications for the power of the majority and the preservation of minority rights, as the case studies of Mexico, India, and Russia demonstrate.

CASE Study

FEDERALISM: MEXICO, INDIA, AND RUSSIA

CASE SYNOPSIS

Mexico, India, and Russia provide us with three distinct models of federalism: each represents differing degrees of centralization, symmetry, and institutionalization. Together, they demonstrate that how federalism works in practice depends more on political context and control over government revenue than on the formal powers granted in constitutions. In Mexico prior to democratization and Russia since democracy's demise, electoral authoritarian regimes have effectively gutted federalism. In India, Congress Party domination and constitutional rules favoring the center made states quite weak. The party system in India, however, has had a role in decentralizing that power, as Congress has become dependent on state-level parties to stay in power. This evolution is an example of the bargaining relationship inherent in all federal systems; how much accountability exists and who can check whom depend on past bargains between governing units and their leaders.

- **CENTRAL VERSUS LOCAL CONTROL** Centralized India and Russia versus somewhat decentralized Mexico

- **SYMMETRY** Symmetrical federalism in Mexico versus asymmetrical in India and Russia

- **POLITICAL CONTEXT** Parties in India; democratization in Mexico; and electoral authoritarian rule in Russia more important than constitutional rules

- **INSTITUTIONALIZATION** Weak institutions and lack of democracy in Russia weaken federalism

The current system of Mexican federalism dates back to the revolutionary-era constitution of 1917. On paper, it is similar to federalism in the United States. The country is divided into thirty-one states and the Federal District (Mexico City, the capital). Each state is governed by a governor and a unicameral legislature, and has power over taxation, police, and education, among other areas. The Mexican Senate, while representing the states, does not have the power of the U.S. Senate; its most important functions are approving presidential appointments and treaties, as in the United States, but it is not as influential in other legislative areas. The reality under the electoral authoritarian regime led by the PRI (1920–2000), though, was quite different from the written constitution. While all the offices existed and officials were duly elected into them, the PRI in fact controlled the entire process. The party, and the president in particular, used power over revenue to punish any states that did not follow central directives and reward those that did. A 1947 law gave the federal government almost all taxation powers in exchange for state governments getting a share of the revenue, though that share was very small. Governors were expected to preserve law and order and follow central party directives. The PRI controlled all governorships from 1929 to 1989, so state governments did not even try to resist central authority.

TABLE 5.1 — Differences in Federalism: Brazil, India, and Russia

	Mexico	India	Russia
Symmetry	Symmetric	Asymmetric	Asymmetric
Centralization	Centralized prior to 1990; growing decentralization since	Centralized; weak upper house in parliament representing states; national government may change state boundaries, dissolve state governments	Very centralized; "federalism" has very little substantive meaning; weak legislature, including upper house representing regions; central control of taxes
Role of ethnicity	Not based on ethnic or religious divisions	Ethnically and linguistically based federalism	Ethnic nationalism posed major recent challenge; ethnically defined regions
Power of states	Growing political power of state governors; weak Senate that only partially represents states	State-level parties gained greater influence for states via participation and bargaining in national-level coalition governments	Regional governors "undisputed bosses" at local level
Reforms	Democratization leads to greater revenue and power to states; continuing problem of state-level authoritarian rule	Reduced ability of central government to dissolve state governments	Greater centralization; president appoints governors

This began to change as the country made a transition to democracy starting in the 1990s (see chapter 9). After the 1994 election, the PRI had lost control of several state governments and faced an economic crisis. It responded with a policy of "New Federalism" that began to decentralize revenue to the states. The president also gave up his power to select PRI candidates for governor; in the newly competitive electoral environment, the party needed locally popular figures as candidates rather than just those loyal to the president. Authoritarian control of several states by PRI governors continued, however; ironically, the weakening power of the PRI at the federal level allowed state-level party machines to repress opposition even after the national party began allowing greater democracy.

The democratization process at the national level was complete when the PRI lost the presidency in 2000. All three major parties controlled some state governments, so some served as opposition to the party in power at the federal level. Governors and state legislatures became much more autonomous and governorships became important stepping-stones to national political leadership in all parties. Governors from all parties created a national association that successfully resisted central government efforts to push responsibility for programs to states without giving them additional revenue (known as "unfunded mandates" in the United States). They also succeeded in getting Congress to reform the fiscal system: by 2004, some 31 percent of the federal budget went to the states and by 2010, the states were providing 21 percent of their own revenue, up from 5 percent a decade earlier (Camp 2014, 209–210). Continued corruption and cronyism plague some states, however.

Russian president Vladimir Putin meets with Ramzan Kadyrov, head of the Chechen Republic, one of the constituent units of Russia's federal system. The Russian army brutally crushed a Chechen rebellion; then Putin imposed Kadyrov as the republic's leader. Putin has greatly centralized power, reducing federalism to little more than a shell, as it was under Soviet rule.

ALEXEI NIKOLSKY/AFP/Getty Images

Several state governors and other leaders were implicated in support of various drug cartels, and the state government and police of Guerrero were infamously implicated in the disappearance of a large group of college students in 2014. Human rights groups claimed several state governments violated basic rights at the local level, one of the biggest problems for Mexico's young democracy. Because of all this, voters in 2016 dealt the ruling PRI (which regained control of the presidency in 2012) a major setback, replacing PRI governors with opposition party candidates in four states that the PRI had controlled since 1929. After the election, the PRI controlled only fifteen of the thirty-one governorships, and analysts viewed the election as a harbinger of a possible PRI loss in the presidential election of 2018. While Mexican federalism remains relatively centralized compared to some others, real democracy has

in CONTEXT

Federalism

Federalism is an unusual institutional choice: only about twenty-five countries have a federal system. Those twenty-five, however, account for over 40 percent of the world's population. In addition,

- seven are among the world's ten geographically largest countries and six are among the world's ten largest countries by population;

- seven of the world's ten largest electoral democracies by area are federal, as are five of the ten largest democracies by population;

- federal countries average 0.52 on an index of ethnic fractionalization, where 0 is perfect homogeneity and 1 is highly fragmented—the world average is 0.48; and

- five federal countries are geographically fragmented, composed of two or more islands or of a peninsula and at least one island.

Sources: Based on data from Forum of Federations 2016 (http://www.forumfed.org); Fearon 2003; and Freedom House 2016 (http://www.freedomhouse.org).

allowed significant decentralization, which has created both benefits and costs to the country's new democratic system.

The origins of India's federalism lie in the colonial era. The British colonial government put modern India together from literally hundreds of separate states, ruling some areas directly and others via various agreements with local rulers. After independence, the new constitution recognized several categories of states and "union territories" with various powers. While most states today have the same basic powers, the central government has bargained with regional groups to create new states to enhance regional loyalty to the center. This has meant giving certain states greater autonomy and power than others. The designers of India's constitution specifically said they were not creating states along linguistic or ethnic lines, but over time that is primarily what has happened. A major commission in the 1950s led to the creation of new states drawn mostly along linguistic lines. While the ruling Congress Party initially resisted the changes, the growing political success of regional parties forced it to yield in order to maintain its electoral strength. In the northeast, six new states were eventually created along ethnic lines as well, and these have greater power and autonomy than do other states, including the freedom to respect local customary law and religious practices. While few new states have been created in recent years, the issue remains very much alive: from 2011 to 2013 protests broke out and several MPs resigned over their demand to create a new state out of a region of Andhra Pradesh in southern India.

India's constitution created an unusually centralized system of federalism. States do not write their own constitutions; each is under the authority of the same central constitution, which includes a parliamentary government with a chief minister who is the state-level equivalent of prime minister. The national government, however, has the right to create, eliminate, or change state boundaries as it pleases. It can also declare President's Rule in a particular state, under which the state government is dismissed and the prime minister in effect governs the state directly until he calls a new state election. The central government's greater taxing power, which has expanded over time, has given it great control over the policies of the states. In 1955–1956, Indian states could finance an average of 69 percent of their expenditures, with the rest coming from the national government; by 2000–2001, this was down to 49 percent (Rao and Singh 2005, 172).

An upper house, the Rajya Sabha, exists to represent states but has limited effect on legislation or the composition of the national government. It did, however, play an important role in 2016 in what could be a very major change to Indian federalism. The government under Prime Minister Narendra Modi came to power promising a new "cooperative federalism," and in 2016 it successfully passed through the Rajya Sabha, which was controlled by the opposition, a constitutional amendment to create a national Goods and Services Tax (GST). This long-standing proposal will replace what critics say is a bewildering array of sales taxes that states can set independently, with goods that cross state lines being taxed multiple times at different rates. The new law will create a GST Council on which each state will get one vote. The council will set a uniform tax on goods and services that cross state lines. Proponents argue that this will enhance economic development by simplifying the tax code for businesses while opponents claim it will severely weaken federalism by reducing individual states' ability to raise revenue (though they will continue to have power to tax goods produced and sold within their states). The GST will be the biggest change in revenue sharing in Indian federalism in decades.

The extent to which Indian federalism has limited majority rule has varied over time, depending mainly on the party system. When the Indian National Congress (INC) was the sole dominant party and controlled the national government between 1947 and 1977, it had tremendous power. Prior to 1967, it controlled virtually all state governments, so they generally did the bidding of the central government, not unlike Mexico under the PRI even though India remained a democracy. Once greater political competition at the state level emerged in the 1970s, Prime Ministers Indira (1966–1977; 1980–1984) and Rajiv (1984–1989) Gandhi used President's Rule for partisan purposes: they would have the president declare President's Rule in states controlled by opposition parties and then call and win new state elections. As we detail in chapter 6, since 1989 India's ethnically based federalism has helped create a number of state-level parties that dominate the politics in their states but have little influence or support elsewhere. Since 1989, India's national governments have always been coalitions between a major national party and several state-level parties. The state parties have used this situation to bargain with the national parties for greater state autonomy, protecting their states' interests vis-à-vis the central government better than the formal rules of the Indian constitution have. Also, a 1994 ruling by India's Supreme Court limited the ability of prime ministers to declare President's Rule. Recent changes in economic policy have also strengthened some state governments: greater market freedoms have allowed certain state governments to attract capital from around the world, enriching those states and their tax base vis-à-vis the national government. Thus, state governments seem to be achieving some degree of institutional autonomy, and horizontal accountability may be increasing vis-à-vis national institutions.

Despite the centralization of the system, India's federalism has managed to keep most ethnic and linguistic conflict within democratic bounds. Atul Kohli (2004) argued that India has used federalism to contain conflict when national leaders have been willing to compromise with regional groups and political institutions were strong. In the 1950s and 1960s, Prime Minister Jawaharlal Nehru used the creation of states to appease movements, such as the Tamils in the south, who demanded greater autonomy for their linguistic groups. In the 1970s and 1980s, Prime Ministers Indira and Rajiv Gandhi were less willing to compromise with regional forces, partly because they had less national political support, resulting in greater religious and ethnic conflict.

Russian federalism dates back to the expanding Russian Empire, but its more recent antecedent is federalism under the Soviet Union. Officially, the Soviets created the largest federal system in the world, consisting of fifteen separate Soviet "republics," of which Russia itself was only one; numerous smaller divisions also existed within the Russian Republic. Soviet federalism was elaborate, but absolute control by the Communist Party gave the republics and smaller political units no real autonomy. Local rulers, appointed by the central party, were able to run their governments more or less as personal fiefdoms, but they could not challenge or question central authority if a conflict between the center and the region arose. Federalism in any real sense cannot exist in an authoritarian system as centrally controlled as Soviet communism. The collapse of the Soviet Union resulted in the separation of the fifteen republics into fifteen sovereign countries. The Russian Republic became a federation, though new and weak institutions made it relatively ineffective in terms of horizontal accountability vis-à-vis the center, one of the reasons why Vladimir Putin was able to create an electoral authoritarian regime that centralized control once again in Moscow.

Ethnic nationalism was a major challenge to post-Soviet Russia. The leaders of former Soviet "ethnic" homelands demanded various degrees of autonomy. Most serious was Chechnya's demand for independence, which resulted in two wars between Russia and Chechen rebels in the 1990s. Today, it remains under Russian rule through the control of a Russian-backed government with little popular support and continued rebel opposition. While Chechnya was the only conflict to produce widespread violence, similar tensions across the country resulted in repeated efforts to amend federalism to recognize ethnically defined governments while preserving the Russian Federation as a whole. The Russian constitution of 1993 created an asymmetrical federal system with eighty-nine subnational units. It gave the greatest powers, however, to the central government, reserving only a handful of powers for joint national-local control, and no powers exclusively for subnational governments. The central government also has the greatest taxation powers: in 2001 it collected 85 percent of all revenue. The status of *republic* is given to areas deemed ethnically non-Russian. The titular ethnic group, however, constituted a majority of the population in only seven of the twenty-one republics. For example, in 2002 Karelians were only 9 percent of the population of the Karelia republic and Khakas only 12 percent of Khakassia. On paper, republics have noticeably more power than do other federal units, including more power over state property and trade.

While the Russian constitution seemed to create a highly centralized system, its operation in the 1990s was "legal chaos" (Graney 2009, 205). Between 1993 and 1998, local demands led President Boris Yeltsin to sign separate bilateral treaties with more than half of the country's eighty-nine subnational governments. In the case of Tatarstan, the republic even gained the power to make separate treaties with foreign powers. Different territories and republics had different governing structures, with at least fifty of their constitutions violating some element of the federal one. Until 2004 each republic was governed by an elected president and elected legislatures; Kathryn Stoner-Weiss (2004) argued that these local officials "[are] the undisputed boss of any given region," suggesting local-level authoritarian rule similar to what Gibson (2013) observed in Latin America. Vladimir Putin came to power with a goal of centralizing power. Critics questioned the constitutionality of some of his early reforms, but they succeeded in bringing subnational governments and laws more in line with the central government's interests. In 2004 Putin moved to gut local autonomy nearly completely, introducing reforms that allowed him to appoint governors and up to half of the upper house of parliament, further centralizing what was already a centralized system of federalism.

President Medvedev briefly restored elections for governor in 2012, but after returning to power Putin passed a new law "allowing" federal units to request that he appoint a governor instead, which is now the norm. Putin's reforms were part of his effort to transform Russia from a weak democracy to an electoral authoritarian regime. While this effort was quite successful, Obydenkova and Swenden (2013) argued that even in this context federalism places some limits on central authority. Ironically, with formal institutions so weak, the most autonomous regional leaders are those in the least democratic regions. Leaders who face no significant opposition rule regions with significant economic resources and have the support of local economic elites so they can bargain with central government authorities for greater autonomy and resources. For weaker local leaders, though, Russian federalism is a shell of what it once was, leaving them with little autonomy.

CASE Questions

1. Comparing our three cases, what is the most important factor in understanding differences in how much accountability federalism provides?
2. What do our three cases suggest about the possible trade-off between accountability and effective policymaking in federal systems?

CONCLUSION

Political institutions clearly have an impact on who has the most power in a society and how they can exercise it. In strong institutions, the formal rules matter because on the whole they are obeyed. A crucial question for a democracy is how the executive power of the state can be effectively limited. The first and most obvious answer is to subject the executive to vertical accountability via elections. That leaves great variation, though, focused mostly on horizontal accountability between elections: Does one set of governing institutions systematically hold executive power more accountable than other types of institutions? The answer in most cases depends not just on the formal governing institutions but on the broader political context in which they operate. The Westminster model seems to provide the weakest horizontal check on executive power, but only when the PM leads a cohesive majority party in parliament. And it arguably provides the clearest vertical accountability: voters know exactly who is responsible for government policy. Coalition governments provide a nearly constant check on the PM, as she must secure coalition partners' agreement to make any significant policy. The judiciary in most democracies is specifically tasked with horizontal accountability via judicial review, but we've seen that courts must assert their independence carefully, given their lack of democratic legitimation via elections and lack of other resources on which to base their power. Japan shows us that even when the elected executive is held accountable, an entrenched bureaucracy may wield great and unelected power and successfully resist reforms to democratize it.

Besides accountability, a second great question in liberal democracy is how to protect minority rights. Accountability is to the majority, which can and often does trample the liberal rights of minorities. Does one set of institutions help preserve minority rights better than others? Most Americans would immediately think of the Supreme Court as fulfilling this role, but political science research indicates that the judiciary upholds the interests of the dominant majority at least as often as it does the minority, and that is likely to be even more true when the judiciary as an institution is relatively weak (Chinn 2006).

More consensual democracies in which a variety of viewpoints are represented within the major governing institutions and compromise is required to make decisions would seem to enhance minority rights. One form of this is federalism, which is often designed specifically to protect ethnic and regional minorities. How well this works depends on how much real power—determined not only by formal rules but by control of revenues—a federal system provides the national and regional governments. Again, the broader political context matters. For example, the strength of federalism in India has varied mainly due to changes in the party system.

A third major question for democracy involves the potential trade-off between representation and effective policymaking: Do some institutions provide more of one or the other, and does a clear optimum balance between them exist? Lijphart's consensual and majoritarian democratic models directly address this question. Majoritarian systems like the Westminster model ought to provide more effective policymaking at the expense of some immediate representation. Institutions that provide more horizontal accountability and require greater consensus, such as the U.S. or Brazilian presidential systems with weak parties and federalism, seem likely to slow down the policy-making process. Lijphart, though, argued that overall consensual models legislate nearly as effectively as majoritarian systems but add much greater representation. While Lijphart favored that balance, the debate is far from concluded. Political context matters here as well: the number and strength of political parties in office will affect how the institutions operate, as Indian history demonstrates—a subject we will examine in detail in the next chapter.

Looking comparatively, we can ask why the same institutions seem to work better in certain places than in others, and why particular countries come to adopt particular institutions in the first place. Our cases suggest that wholesale change of institutions is difficult and unusual. Countries seem prone to follow what they know, as the examples of Britain's former colonies suggest. It is rare for a country to decide, as France did in 1958, that a complete change of institutions is in order, but countries transitioning to democracy face this choice as they write new constitutions. Cultural and historical institutional theories seem to explain best this continuity of institutions. Despite the elegant logic of rational choice arguments about which works best, deeply held values, socialized into the population over time, tend to preserve existing institutions unless they prove exceptionally dysfunctional.

No clear answer to the question of why an institution works better in one place than another is obvious, though certainly social, political, and ethnic contexts matter greatly. A society that is deeply divided by ethnic difference and other past conflicts is likely to benefit from a more consensual set of institutions that requires compromise at every step of the way. A majoritarian system or powerful single office like a presidency is likely to breed distrust, as no political actor in the system is willing to trust the others with such great power. Excessive fragmentation across political parties and local governments, though, may make policymaking nearly impossible or even threaten the continued viability of the state as a whole.

The entire study of democratic institutions is also enmeshed in the theoretical debate between pluralists and elite theorists over who rules. It is about the trade-off between elite power, which might be more effective at making policy, and more dispersed power, which, while slowing down the policy-making process, provides greater representation and accountability. The debate is also about the extent to which pluralism is an accurate depiction of the dispersion of political power in a democracy and how institutions can assist in ensuring that it remains accurate.

KEY CONCEPTS

asymmetrical federal system (p. 266)
bicameral legislature (p. 225)
coalition government (p. 218)
code law (p. 248)
cohabitation (p. 238)
common law (p. 247)
consensus democracy (p. 218)
devolution (p. 267)
executive (p. 216)
federal systems (p. 263)
head of government (p. 220)
head of state (p. 220)
horizontal accountability (p. 216)
institutionalization (p. 215)
iron triangle (p. 261)
judicial independence (p. 249)
judicial review (p. 247)
judiciary (p. 216)
legislative oversight (p. 255)

legislature (p. 216)
majoritarian democracy (p. 217)
member of parliament (MP) (p. 221)
New Public Management (NPM) (p. 256)
parliamentarism (p. 220)
political accountability (p. 215)
political appointees (p. 255)
presidentialism (p. 228)
prime minister (PM) (p. 221)
principal-agent problem (p. 254)
rent seeking (p. 257)
semipresidentialism (p. 238)
separation of powers (p. 228)
symmetrical federal system (p. 266)
unitary systems (p. 263)
vertical accountability (p. 216)
veto player (p. 219)
vote of no confidence (p. 221)

 Sharpen your skills with SAGE edge at **edge.sagepub.com/orvis4e.** **SAGE edge for students** provides a personalized approach to help you accomplish your coursework goals in an easy-to-use learning environment.

WORKS CITED

Amoretti, Ugo M., and Nancy Gina Bermeo, eds. 2004. *Federalism and Territorial Cleavages*. Baltimore, MD: Johns Hopkins University Press.

Applebaum, Benyamin, and Michael D. Shear. 2016. "Once Skeptical of Executive Power, Obama Has Come to Embrace It." *New York Times*. August 13 (http://www.nytimes.com/2016/08/14/us/politics/obama-era-legacy-regulation.html?smprod=nytcore-ipad&smid=nytcore-ipad-share&_r=0).

Baumgartner, Frank R., Brouard, Sylvain, Grossman, E., Lazardeux, S. G., and Moody, J. 2014. "Divided Government, Legislative Productivity, and Policy Change in the USA and France." *Governance* 27: 423–447. doi:10.1111/gove.12047

Bevir, Mark. 2010. *Democratic Governance*. Princeton, NJ: Princeton University Press.

Börzel, T. A., and van Hüllen, V. 2014. State-Building and the European Union's Fight against Corruption in the Southern Caucasus: Why Legitimacy Matters. *Governance* 27: 613–634. doi:10.1111/gove.12068

Camp, Roderic Ai. 2014. *Politics in Mexico: Democratic Consolidation or Decline?* 6th ed. Oxford, UK: Oxford University Press.

Chaisty, Paul, Nic Cheeseman, and Timothy Powers. 2015. *How MPs Understand Coalitional Politics in Presidential Systems.* The Coalitional Presidentialism Project, Research Report, January 2015. Department of Politics and International Relations, University of Oxford (http://www.politics.ox.ac.uk/materials/policy_briefings/CCP_Research_Report_v5.pdf).

Cheibub, José Antonio. 2007. *Presidentialism, Parliamentarism, and Democracy.* New York: Cambridge University Press.

Chinn, Stuart. 2006. "Democracy-Promoting Judicial Review in a Two-Party System: Dealing with Second-Order Preferences." *Polity* 38 (4): 478–500. doi:10.1057/palgrave.polity.2300071

Dahl, Robert. 1957. "Decision-Making in a Democracy: The Supreme Court as a National Policy-Maker." *Journal of Public Law* 6: 279–294.

Diaz-Cayeros, Alberto. 2006. *Federalism, Fiscal Authority, and Centralization in Latin America.* Cambridge, UK: Cambridge University Press.

Ekeh, Peter P. 1975. "Colonialism and the Two Publics in Africa: A Theoretical Statement." *Comparative Studies in Society and History* 17 (1): 91–112. doi:10.1017/S0010417500007659

Elgie, Robert. 2011. *Semi-Presidentialism: Sub-Types and Democratic Performance.* Oxford, UK: Oxford University Press.

_____. 2016. *The Semi-Presidential One* (http://www.semipresidentialism.com).

Fearon, James. 2003. "Ethnic and Cultural Diversity by Country." *Journal of Economic Growth* 8 (2): 195–222. doi:10.1023/A:1024419522867

Ferejohn, John, and Pasquale Pasquino. 2003. "Rule of Democracy and Rule of Law." In *Democracy and the Rule of Law,* edited by José Maria Maravall and Adam Przeworski, 242–260. Cambridge, UK: Cambridge University Press.

Ferejohn, John, Frances Rosenbluth, and Charles Shipan. 2007. "Comparative Judicial Politics." In *The Oxford Handbook of Comparative Politics,* edited by Carles Boix and Susan Carol Stokes, 727–551. Oxford, UK: Oxford University Press.

Filippov, Mikhail, and Olga Shvetsova. 2013. "Federalism, Democracy, and Democratization." In *Federal Dynamics: Continuity, Change, and the Varieties of Federalism,* edited by Arthur Bens and Jorg Broscek, 167–184. Oxford, UK: Oxford University Press.

Gibson, Edward L. 2013. *Boundary Control: Subnational Authoritarianism in Federal Democracies.* Cambridge, UK: Cambridge University Press.

Gibson, James L., Gregory A. Caldeira, and Vanessa A. Baird. 1998. "On the Legitimacy of National High Courts." *American Political Science Review* 92 (2): 343–358.

Graney, Katherine E. 2009. "Ethnicity and Identity." In *Understanding Contemporary Russia,* edited by Michael Bressler, 191–220. Boulder, CO: Lynne Rienner.

Hiroi, Taeko, and Lucio R. Renno. 2016. "Agenda Setting and Gridlock in a Multi-Party Coalitional Presidential System." In *Legislative Institutions and Lawmaking in Latin America,* edited by Eduardo Aleman and George Tsebelis, 61–91. Oxford, UK: Oxford University Press.

Hirschl, Ran. 2009. "The Judicialization of Politics." In *The Oxford Handbook of Political Science,* edited by Robert E. Goodin, 253–274. Oxford, UK: Oxford University Press.

Hood, Christopher, and Ruth Dixon. 2015. *A Government That Worked Better and Cost Less? Evaluating Three Decades of Reform and Change in UK Central Government.* Oxford, UK: Oxford University Press.

Huber, John D., and Charles R. Shipan. 2002. *Deliberate Discretion? The Institutional Foundations of Bureaucratic Autonomy.* Cambridge, UK: Cambridge University Press.

Ingram, Matthew C. 2016. *Crafting Courts in New Democracies: The Politics of Subnational Judicial Reform in Brazil and Mexico.* Cambridge, UK: Cambridge University Press.

Issacharoff, Samuel. 2015. *Fragile Democracies: Contested Power in the Era of Constitutional Courts.* New York: Cambridge University Press.

Johnston, Michael. 2005. *Syndromes of Corruption: Wealth, Power, and Democracy.* New York: Cambridge University Press.

————. 2014. *Corruption, Contention, and Reform: The Power of Deep Democratization.* Cambridge, UK: Cambridge University Press.

Kapiszewski, Diana. 2012. *High Courts and Economic Governance in Argentina and Brazil.* Cambridge, UK: Cambridge University Press.

Kohli, Atul. 2004. "India: Federalism and the Accommodation of Ethnic Nationalism." In *Federalism and Territorial Cleavages,* edited by Ugo M. Amoretti and Nancy G. Bermeo, 281–300. Baltimore, MD: Johns Hopkins University Press.

Landfried, Christine. 1995. "Germany." In *The Global Expansion of Judicial Power,* edited by C. Neal Tate and Torbjörn Vallinder, 307–324. New York: New York University Press.

Lee, Francis. 2014. "American Politics Is More Competitive Than Ever. That's Making Partisanship Worse." Monkey Cage. *Washington Post.* January 9 (https://www.washingtonpost.com/news/monkey-cage/wp/2014/01/09/american-politics-is-more-competitive-than-ever-thats-making-partisanship-worse/).

Leeke, Matthew, Chris Sear, and Oonagh Gay. 2003. *An Introduction to Devolution in the UK.* Research Paper 03/84, November 17. House of Commons Library (http://www.parliament.uk/documents/commons/lib/research/rp2003/rp03-084.pdf).

Lijphart, Arend. 1999. *Patterns of Democracy: Government Forms and Performance in Thirty-six Countries.* New Haven, CT: Yale University Press.

Linz, Juan José. 1990. "The Perils of Presidentialism." *Journal of Democracy* 1 (1): 51–69. doi:10.1353/jod.1990.0011

McCarty, Nolan. 2014. "What We Know and Don't Know about Our Polarized Politics." Monkey Cage. *Washington Post.* January 8 (https://www.washingtonpost.com/news/monkey-cage/wp/2014/01/08/what-we-know-and-dont-know-about-our-polarized-politics/).

Mungiu-Pippidi, Alina. 2015. *The Quest for Good Governance: How Societies Develop Control of Corruption.* Cambridge, UK: Cambridge University Press.

Obydenkova, Anastassia, and Wilfried Swenden. 2013. "Autocracy-Sustaining versus Democratic Federalism: Explaining the Divergent Trajectories of Territorial Politics in Russia and Western Europe." *Territory, Politics, Governance* 1(1): 86–122 (http://www.tandfonline.com/doi/pdf/10.1080/21622671.2013.763733).

O'Donnell, Guillermo. 1999. "Horizontal Accountability in New Democracies." In *The Self-Restraining State: Power and Accountability in New Democracies,* edited by Andreas Schedler, Larry Diamond, and Marc F. Plattner, 29–52. Boulder, CO: Lynne Rienner.

O'Dwyer, Conor. 2006. *Runaway State-Building: Patronage Politics and Democratic Development.* Baltimore, MD: Johns Hopkins University Press.

Oliveira, Vanessa Elias de Dados. 2005. "The Judiciary and Privatizations in Brazil: Is There a Judicialization of Politics? [Judiciario e privatizacoes no Brasil: Existe uma judicializacao da politica?]." *Dados* 48 (3): 559–587.

Pelizzo, Ricardo. 2010. "Fragmentation and Performance: The Indian Case." *Commonwealth and Comparative Politics* 48 (3): 261–280.

Pempel, T. J. 2000. *Regime Shift: Comparative Dynamics of the Japanese Political*

Economy. Ithaca, NY: Cornell University Press.

Pereira, Carlos, Timothy J. Power, and Eric De Raile. 2011. "Presidentialism, Coalitions, and Accountability." In *Corruption and Democracy in Brazil: The Struggle for Accountability,* edited by Timothy J. Power and Matthew M. Taylor, 31–55. South Bend, IN: University of Notre Dame Press.

Powell, G. Bingham, Jr. 2000. *Elections as Instruments of Democracy: Majoritarian and Proportional Visions.* New Haven, CT: Yale University Press.

Power, Timothy J. 2010. "Optimism, Pessimism, and Coalitional Presidentialism: Debating the Institutional Design of Brazilian Democracy." *Bulletin of Latin American Research* 29 (1): 18–33.

Proksch, Sven-Oliver, and Jonathan B. Slapin. 2015. *The Politics of Parliamentary Debate: Parties, Rebels, and Representation.* Cambridge, UK: Cambridge University Press.

Puddington, Arch. 2010. "Freedom in the World 2010: Erosion of Freedom Intensifies" (http://www.freedomhouse.org/).

Rao, M. Govinda, and Nirvikar Singh. 2005. *The Political Economy of Federalism in India.* Oxford, UK: Oxford University Press.

Riker, William. 1964. *Federalism: Origin, Operation, Significance.* Boston: Little, Brown.

Russell, M., and Cowley, P. 2016. "The Policy Power of the Westminster Parliament: The 'Parliamentary State' and the Empirical Evidence." *Governance* 29: 121–137. doi:10.1111/gove.12149

Samuels, David. 2007. "Separation of Powers." In *The Oxford Handbook of Comparative Politics,* edited by Carles Boix and Susan Carol Stokes, 703–726. Oxford, UK: Oxford University Press.

Santiso, Carlos. 2003. "Economic Reform and Judicial Governance in Brazil: Balancing Independence with Accountability." *Democratization* 10 (4): 161–180. doi:10.1080/13510340312331294077

Schleiter, Petra, and Valerie Belu. 2016. "The Decline of Majoritarianism in the UK and the Fixed-Term Parliaments Act." *Parliamentary Affairs* 69 (1): 36–52. doi:10.1093/pa/gsv002

Schleiter, Petra, and Edward Morgan-Jones. 2009. "Review Article: Citizens, Presidents and Assemblies: The Study of Semi-Presidentialism beyond Duverger and Linz." *British Journal of Political Science* 39: 871–892. doi:10.1017/S0007123409990159

Schwindt-Bayer, Leslie A., and Margit Tavits. 2016. *Clarity of Responsibility, Accountability, and Corruption.* Cambridge, UK: Cambridge University Press.

Shankar, B. L., and Valerian Rodrigues. 2011. *The Indian Parliament: A Democracy at Work.* New Delhi, India: Oxford University Press.

Shinoda, Tomohito. 2012. "Japan's Failed Experiment: The DPJ and Institutional Change for Political Leadership." *Asian Survey* 52 (5): 799–821.

Stoner-Weiss, Kathryn. 2004. "Russia: Managing Territorial Cleavages under Dual Transitions." In *Federalism and Territorial Cleavages,* edited by Ugo M. Amoretti and Nancy G. Bermeo, 301–326. Baltimore, MD: Johns Hopkins University Press.

Tate, C. Neal, and Torbjörn Vallinder. 1995. *The Global Expansion of Judicial Power.* New York: New York University Press.

Taylor, Matthew M. 2008. *Judging Policy: Courts and Policy Reform in Democratic Brazil.* Stanford, CA: Stanford University Press.

Thorlakson, Lori. 2013. "Dynamics of Change in Federal Representation." In *Federal Dynamics: Continuity, Change, and the Varieties of Federalism,* edited by Arthur Bens and Jorg Broscek, 229–248. Oxford, UK: Oxford University Press.

Transparency International. 2010. "Corruption Perceptions Index" (http://www.transparency.org/policy_research/surveys_indices/cpi).

Tsebelis, George. 2002. *Veto Players: How Political Institutions Work.* Princeton, NJ: Princeton University Press.

Vanberg, Georg. 2005. *The Politics of Constitutional Review in Germany.* Cambridge, UK: Cambridge University Press.

Watts, J. 2016. *Brazil's Judiciary Faces Scrutiny as Rousseff's Government Teeters. The Guardian.* March 30 (https://www.theguardian.com/world/2016/mar/30/brazil-judiciary-dilma-rousseff-impeachment-corruption).

Williams, Laron K. 2011. "Unsuccessful Success? Failed No-Confidence Motions, Competence Signals, and Electoral Support." *Comparative Political Studies* 44 (11): 1474–1499.

Wolferen, Karel van. 2010. "Japan's Stumbling Revolution." *The Asia-Pacific Journal.* April 12 (http://japanfocus.org/-Karel_van-Wolferen/3341).

Yadav, Vineeta. 2011. *Political Parties, Business Groups, and Corruption in Developing Countries.* Oxford, UK: Oxford University Press.

Yadav, Vineeta, and Bumba Mukherjee. 2014. *Democracy, Electoral Systems, and Judicial Empowerment in Developing Countries.* Ann Arbor: University of Michigan Press.

RESOURCES FOR FURTHER STUDY

Cappelletti, Mauro, Paul J. Kollmer, and Joanne M. Olson. 1989. *The Judicial Process in Comparative Perspective.* Oxford, UK: Clarendon Press.

Cheibub, José Antonio, Zachary Elkins, and Tom Ginsburg. 2014. "Beyond Presidentialism and Parliamentarianism." *British Journal of Political Science* 44 (3): 515–544. doi:http://dx.doi.org/10.1017/S000712341300032X

Frederickson, H. George, and Kevin B. Smith. 2003. *The Public Administration Theory Primer.* Boulder, CO: Westview Press.

Graber, Mark A. 2005. "Constructing Judicial Review." *Annual Review of Political Science* 8: 425–451. doi:10.1146/annurev.polisci.8.082103.104905

Herron, Erik S., and Kirk A. Randazzo. 2003. "The Relationship between Independence and Judicial Review in Post-Communist Courts." *Journal of Politics* 65 (2): 422–438. doi:10.1111/1468-2508.t01-3-00007

Mainwaring, Scott, and Matthew Soberg Shugart, eds. 1997. *Presidentialism and Democracy in Latin America.* New York: Cambridge University Press.

Mulgan, Aurelia George. 2002. *Japan's Failed Revolution: Koizumi and the Politics of Economic Reform.* Canberra, Australia: Asia Pacific Press.

Rosenbluth, Frances McCall, and Michael F. Thies. 2010. *Japan Transformed: Political Change and Economic Restructuring.* Princeton, NJ: Princeton University Press.

WEB RESOURCES

Binghamton University, The Institutions and Elections Project
(http://www.binghamton.edu/political-science/institutions-and-elections-project.html)

International Institute for Democracy and Electoral Assistance (IDEA), Democracy and Development
(http://www.idea.int/development/index.cfm)

Transparency International
(http://www.transparency.org)

Unified Democracy Scores
(http://www.unified-democracy-scores.org/index.html)

University of Bern, Comparative Political Data Sets
(http://www.cpds-data.org/)

6

INSTITUTIONS OF PARTICIPATION AND REPRESENTATION IN DEMOCRACIES

KEY QUESTIONS

- Do some types of institutions in democracies provide better overall representation of and influence for average citizens?
- How do institutions affect the representation of ethnic, gender, religious, and other groups?
- Why do people join political parties and participate in other kinds of political activity?
- How do different electoral and party systems affect political leaders' behavior?
- Are there clear patterns of when and where particular party and electoral systems develop?

This chapter examines the institutions that shape political participation and interest in representation in democracies, the core elements of vertical accountability. Virtually all regimes allow some degree of participation and representation, if only to shore up their own legitimacy or at least the appearance of it. Regimes differ dramatically, however, in the degree to which they seek to control and limit participation and representation. Democratic regimes all claim to value and promote widespread participation and representation, but they differ significantly in how they promote citizen involvement and fair and accurate representation of interests. Because institutions of participation and representation are vital to these regimes, we examine them first. In chapter 8, we examine and compare the same kinds of institutions in authoritarian regimes.

Participation and representation clearly have major implications for answering the question, "Who rules?" Different electoral systems embody different principles of representation and have different effects on accountability. We can demonstrate this by examining how well the systems represent those who seem likely to have less power in the society at large, such as women or racial or ethnic minorities. Given that these groups typically have fewer economic resources, do some systems of representation and participation allow them to have greater influence than do other systems? Elite theorists argue that modern electoral democracies in reality give

Women wait to vote in state-level elections in West Bengal, India, in April 2016. India is the world's largest democracy and holds the world's largest elections in terms of voters and voting places. After long domination by a single party, India now has a multiparty system with two large, national parties and numerous regional ones that compete for voters' support.

Photo by Subhendu Ghosh/Hindustan Times via Getty Images

limited power to those in more marginalized positions; elites dominate the national discourse, control major institutions, and influence voters more than voters influence who is in office. If true, this allocation of influence obviously undermines vertical accountability, a crucial element of democracy.

Another central question regarding participation and representation is, Why do people participate in politics in the first place? We might imagine that the answers would be

obvious: people want to have power or influence, to make a contribution to their community and nation, or to gain recognition and status. While all this is undoubtedly true for some political activists, rational actor theorists long ago explained that for most people most of the time, there is no rational reason to participate in political activity, including voting, because most people cannot significantly influence political outcomes. Expending time or money to work toward any political goal is irrational, given the huge number of citizens and the correspondingly small impact of each individual (Downs 1957). This is an obvious problem in a democracy, and it is exacerbated by the fact that members of the elite, with much greater direct access to key decision makers, have a greater incentive to participate and thus seem more likely to influence policy. Without any ameliorating circumstances, this would suggest that elite theory is correct: "democracies" are really elite controlled.

Democracies must resolve this **collective action problem**: individuals are unwilling to engage in a particular activity because of their rational belief that their individual actions will have little or no effect, yet when they all fail to act, all suffer adverse consequences (in the case of participation in democracy, losing control to the elite). If individuals participate in politics, they may be able to benefit collectively, but it is irrational for each individual to participate in the first place because his individual impact will be negligible. While this is certainly a problem, it is equally clear that millions of people around the world do in fact participate in politics. Besides achieving direct influence over government, which certainly motivates many in spite of the odds against individual influence, some citizens participate because they gain expressive or solidaristic benefits: they find satisfaction in the act of expressing their political beliefs publicly or in being part of a community of like-minded activists. The personal appeal or charisma of a particular leader can also inspire people to engage in the political process (Blondel et al. 2010).

Political institutions, the main focus of this chapter, can also help overcome the collective action problem. Aina Gallego (2015) showed how excessively complex political systems can discourage less educated citizens from participating, even though similar citizens in other political systems do engage. More optimistically, Peter Hall and colleagues (2014) argued that institutions such as political parties and interest groups help citizens identify their interests and then mobilize them to action. Different types of parties, party systems, and interest groups can have great influence over who participates and to what effect.

A final important question is, What influence do institutions—in this chapter, in particular, electoral and party systems—have on political leaders' behavior? What incentives do they give leaders? Do these incentives encourage leaders to promote more participation and representation, or less?

We will see that democracies vary greatly in terms of the three key institutions of representation and participation: electoral systems, parties and party systems, and civil society. A glance at the Country and Concept table shows variation among our case study countries across all the institutions we will define and examine in this chapter. Can we explain these patterns? If certain types of institutions can better represent people than others, where and why have they developed, and can they be replicated elsewhere to the betterment of democracy overall?

THE ELECTORAL SYSTEM

Electoral systems are formal, legal mechanisms that translate votes into control over political offices and shares of political power. Different electoral systems provide distinct incentives to individual voters and political leaders, and affect political parties' strengths and numbers, so they are crucial to understanding what opportunities parties provide for citizen participation.

In almost all elections, enfranchised citizens vote for people who will represent them rather than voting directly on policy. This raises a key issue for electoral systems: How are

collective action problem
Individuals being unwilling to engage in a particular activity because of their rational belief that their individual actions will have little or no effect, yet collectively suffering adverse consequences when all fail to act

electoral systems
Formal, legal mechanisms that translate votes into control over political offices and shares of political power

COUNTRY AND CONCEPT
Parties, Elections, and Civil Society

Country	Electoral system	Party system	Number of significant parties in legislature[1]	Interest-group system
Brazil	Open-list PR	Multiple	19	Pluralist
China	NA	One	1	State corporatist
Germany	Mixed PR	Two and a half	4	Neocorporatist
India	SMD/FPTP	Multiple	8 (in addition to dozens of minor parties)	Pluralist
Iran	Mixed SMD and multimember districts	None	0[2]	Weak
Japan	Mixed PR	Multiple	5	Pluralist
Mexico	Mixed PR	Multiple	3	Neocorporatist
Nigeria	SMD/FPTP	Two	3	Weak
Russia	Mixed PR	Dominant	4	Weak
United Kingdom	SMD/FPTP	Two	3	Pluralist
United States	SMD/FPTP	Two	2	Pluralist

[1] Data on number of parties in legislatures are from *Political Handbook of the World, 2015* (Washington, DC: CQ Press, 2015).

[2] Although political parties are permitted under the constitution, none were recognized following the formal dissolution of the government-sponsored Islamic Republican Party in June 1987, despite Tehran's announcement in October 1988 that such groups would henceforth be welcomed if they "demonstrated commitment to the Islamic system."

votes aggregated and counted? Different systems are based on fundamentally different normative theories of what "good" representation looks like. One common choice is to represent people geographically; a country divides its territory into geographic units, and each unit elects one or more representatives. This system assumes that citizens can best be represented via their membership in geographically defined communities. In contrast, some countries elect their legislatures nationally, or in very large districts. This system assumes that citizens' beliefs as espoused by parties or individual candidates, rather than geographical community, are most important for representation. In rare cases, democratic countries choose to represent specific groups within society rather than or in addition to geographic districts or parties. After an ethnic conflict, for instance, a country may decide it needs to provide special representation for ethnic minorities. Several countries have also legally reserved seats in parliament specifically for women to ensure that they are represented. Ultimately, electoral system choice depends on an answer to the questions, On what basis do we wish to be represented? and, With whom do we share our most important political interests or views?

In addition, electoral institutions often have important effects on governance because they affect the composition of legislatures and the executive branch. Familiar examples of gridlock in American politics or the legendary instability of Italian parliamentary regimes after World War II illustrate this dynamic. These problems do not result from presidential or parliamentary institutions, per se, but rather from the ways in which these institutions interact with the electoral system. Electoral systems help determine as well how majoritarian or consensual a particular democracy is. Systems that encourage many, fragmented parties are more consensual: they provide representation of diverse views in the legislature, but they may make effective government difficult because of the instability of coalition governments in parliamentary systems or the gridlock of different parties controlling the executive and legislative branches in presidential systems. Systems that encourage fewer parties tend to have the opposite effect and therefore are more majoritarian.

Single-Member Districts: "First-Past-the-Post" and Majoritarian Voting

single-member district (SMD)
Electoral system in which each geographic district elects a single representative to a legislature

plurality
The receipt of the most votes, but not necessarily a majority

"first-past-the-post" (FPTP)
An SMD system in which the candidate with a plurality of votes wins

Americans borrowed the **single-member district (SMD)** from Great Britain. In both countries, each geographic district elects a single representative. Two versions of SMD exist: plurality and majoritarian. In a **plurality** system, whoever gets the most votes, even if it's not a majority, wins the election. In a race with more than two contestants, the winner can be elected with a relatively low percentage of the vote total. This system is often called **"first-past-the-post" (FPTP)** because, as in a horse race, the single winner merely needs to edge out the next closest competitor. In a majoritarian system, the winner must gain an absolute majority of the votes (50%, plus one) rather than just a plurality. If no candidate wins an absolute majority, a second election takes place between the top two candidates to produce a winner. Because SMD systems produce one winner per district, they tend to be part of and support the majoritarian model of democracy; a single-party government is more likely to result, and each voter has a specific representative from his electoral district to hold accountable for government actions. Minority voices, however, are less likely to be represented.

Advocates of SMD systems argue they can give constituents a strong sense of identification with their representative. Even if you didn't vote for your representative and you disagree with her, she is still expected to work for you (as U.S. representatives often do by solving Social Security problems for constituents or writing letters of nomination to service academies). Your most vital needs and interests are assumed to have been aggregated into those of your district. Curtice and Shively (2009), however, examined this empirically and found no significant differences between SMD and other systems in terms of voters' level of contact with their representative, their knowledge of who their representative was, or their sense that their representative was representing them well.

Critics of the SMD system make two main arguments against it. First, many votes are "wasted," in the sense that the winning candidate does not represent the views of the voters who did not vote for him. This is especially true in systems with more than two viable parties. Perhaps only 30 or 35 percent of voters actually favored the winner, so the votes of the majority were arguably wasted. This may be one reason why voter participation tends to be lower in countries with SMD than elsewhere. Voters—especially those who prefer minor parties—may find voting a waste of time; the system doesn't encourage them to overcome the collective action problem. Supporters of SMD argue, however, that even voters who have not voted for their representative are represented via **virtual representation**: candidates from their party are elected in other districts and so their views are represented in the legislature, albeit not by their representative.

virtual representation
When voters' views are represented indirectly in the legislature by their chosen party's candidates who have been elected in districts other than their own

Second, this problem can be compounded by the under- or overrepresentation of particular parties. Consider a case in which a third party wins a significant share of the votes in many districts but a plurality in only one or two. The party would win a lot of votes but get only a couple of seats in the legislature. Conversely, if a large number of candidates from a particular party win by a very small plurality in their districts, that party's vote in the legislature will be inflated. The number of its representatives will suggest an overwhelming national consensus, when in fact the party may not even have won a majority of the vote nationwide. Figure 6.1 gives an example from

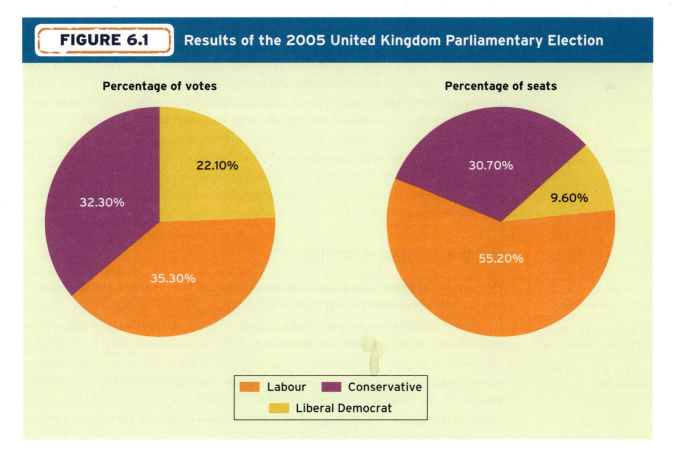

FIGURE 6.1   **Results of the 2005 United Kingdom Parliamentary Election**

Percentage of votes

- 22.10%
- 32.30%
- 35.30%

Percentage of seats

- 30.70%
- 9.60%
- 55.20%

Labour   Conservative   Liberal Democrat

Source: BBC, "Election News, UK Results" (http://www.bbc.com/news/election/2005/results).

Great Britain's 2005 election, in which the two major parties, Labour and Conservative, won similar vote shares but very different numbers of seats, and the third party, the Liberal Democrats, won a far larger share of votes than parliamentary seats. Even when there are only two parties, SMD lends itself to gerrymandering, the drawing of electoral districts to favor a particular party. Both major parties in the United States have done this over the years to varying degrees. Most recently, after the 2010 census, the Republican Party set out to gain control of state legislatures in order to redraw congressional districts in its favor. In the 2012 election, the popular vote for seats in the House of Representatives was a virtual tie but Republicans won thirty-three more seats, and the biggest gaps between the popular vote and seats won were in states where Republicans controlled redistricting. In the ten most imbalanced states, Republicans won 7 percent more votes than Democrats but 76 percent more seats ("Imbalance of Power" 2013). SMD makes the system majoritarian—it may promote efficient, stable policymaking by allowing decisive legislative action—but it may come at the cost of accurate representation of the citizens' preferences.

Proportional Representation

proportional representation (PR)
Electoral system in which seats in a legislature are apportioned on a purely proportional basis, giving each party the share of seats that matches its share of the total vote

Proportional representation (PR) differs from SMD in almost every conceivable way. In PR, representatives are chosen nationally or in large electoral districts with multiple representatives for each district. Thus, either a national legislature is simply divided on a purely proportional basis, or multiple representatives for large districts are allocated proportionally according to the vote in each district. So, for instance, a party that gains 25 percent of the national vote receives a quarter (or very nearly a quarter) of the seats in the legislature. Most PR systems, though, include a minimal electoral threshold—for example, 3 or 5 percent of the vote—a party must cross to gain representation in parliament. Any parties that cross that threshold can be certain that they will be represented. As Figure 6.2 demonstrates for the 2014 Swedish parliamentary elections, a PR system translates each party's share of the votes into almost exactly the same share of legislative seats (in stark contrast to the FPTP system in Britain, as a quick comparison of Figures 6.1 and 6.2 shows). PR systems tend to be part of and support consensus models of democracy; multiple voices via multiple parties are likely to be represented in the legislature, and coalition government is common.

If voters are not choosing among individuals running for a single seat, whom or what are they voting for, and who ends up in the legislature? The answer reflects a very different view of representation from SMD, because in PR systems, the voter is usually voting for a party, not an individual. In **closed-list proportional representation** (the version of PR most dissimilar to SMD), each party presents a ranked list of candidates for all the seats in the legislature. Voters can see the list and know who the "top" candidates are, but they actually vote for the party. If party X gets ten seats in the legislature, then the top ten candidates on the party list occupy those seats.

closed-list proportional representation
Electoral system in which each party presents a ranked list of candidates, voters vote for the party rather than for individual candidates, and each party awards the seats it wins to the candidates on its list in rank order

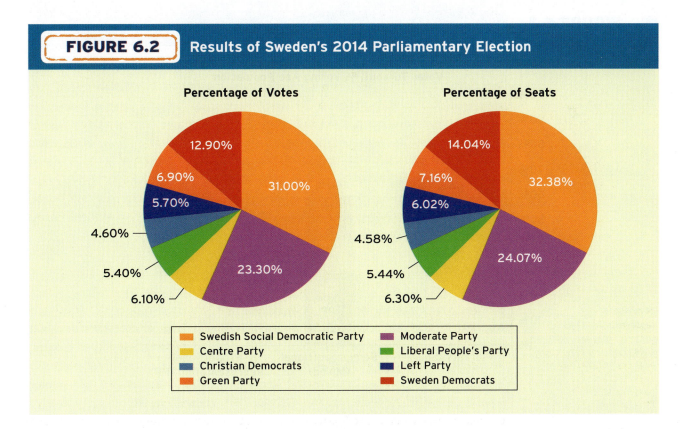

FIGURE 6.2   **Results of Sweden's 2014 Parliamentary Election**

Percentage of Votes

- 31.00%
- 23.30%
- 6.10%
- 5.40%
- 4.60%
- 5.70%
- 6.90%
- 12.90%

Percentage of Seats

- 32.38%
- 24.07%
- 6.30%
- 5.44%
- 4.58%
- 6.02%
- 7.16%
- 14.04%

- Swedish Social Democratic Party
- Moderate Party
- Centre Party
- Liberal People's Party
- Christian Democrats
- Left Party
- Green Party
- Sweden Democrats

Source: Election Resources on the Internet, "Elections to the Swedish Riksdag" http://www.electionresources.org/se/riksdag.php?election=2014

open-list proportional representation
Electoral system in which multiple candidates run in each district, voters vote for the individual candidate of their choice, and the candidates with the most votes in the party get the seats the party wins

Another variant of PR is called **open-list proportional representation.** In this version, voters are presented with a list of candidates and vote for the candidate of their choice. When the votes are counted, each party receives a number of seats proportional to the total number of votes its candidates received. Those seats are then awarded to the top individual vote getters within the party.

PR assumes that voters primarily want their ideas and values represented. Voters are represented by the party they support in the legislature, regardless of the geographic origins of individual legislators. PR has some obvious advantages over SMD. First, there are very few wasted votes, because even very small parties can gain some seats. To the extent that voters feel represented by a party, they can be assured that someone in the legislature is there to give voice to their views—although realistically, smaller parties can usually only impact policy via coalitions with larger parties. Second, perhaps because fewer votes are wasted, participation rates in PR countries are higher, as Figure 6.3 shows. Proponents of PR argue that it is

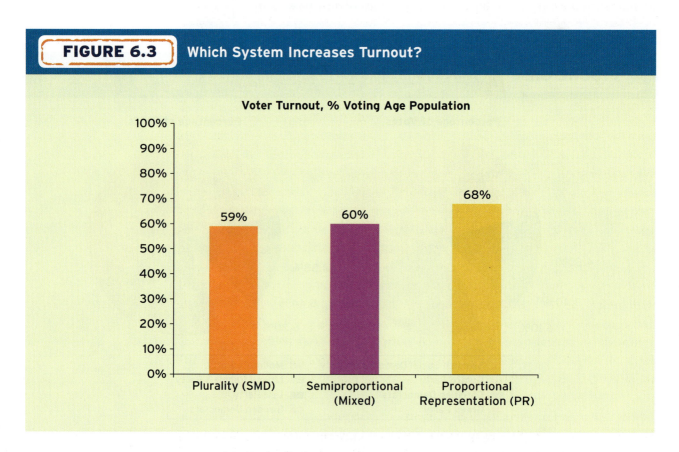

FIGURE 6.3   **Which System Increases Turnout?**

Voter Turnout, % Voting Age Population

- Plurality (SMD): 59%
- Semiproportional (Mixed): 60%
- Proportional Representation (PR): 68%

Sources: Data are from International Institute for Democracy and Electoral Assistance, "What Affects Turnout?" Figure 25 (http://www.idea.int/vt/survey/voter_turnout8.cfm).

therefore more democratic and more broadly representative, since larger percentages of voters participate and virtually all are guaranteed to have their views represented in the legislature. PR systems also tend to elect women and members of ethnic or racial minorities more frequently than SMD systems do, as party leaders often feel compelled (and in some countries are required by law) to include women or minority candidates on their party lists. Salomon Orellana (2014) borrowed theories of small-group decision making to argue that PR systems that produce more parties result in voters having more information available to them and faster changes to policies. He examined New Zealand, which switched from SMD to a partially proportional system, and the UK, which has SMD for its national elections but PR for elections to the European Parliament (the parliament of the EU). He found that the proportional systems in both cases provide a greater range of party positions and information for voters. He also used the World Values Survey to demonstrate that countries with proportional systems were more tolerant of diversity, more likely to adopt policy changes such as same-sex marriage, and more likely to have policies reducing inequality. Mukherjee (2013) used a large-scale quantitative analysis to show that PR systems are associated with higher overall human well-being, arguing that the multiple parties they produce bring more issues into the political arena and create greater competitiveness, giving parties incentives to perform better when in power.

Of course, the PR system has its critics, who point to the "indirect" nature of PR elections: voters don't really choose individual representatives, even in an open-list system. In large, multimember districts, the individual voter does not know that a certain person is "her" unique representative. And in a closed-list system, party officials are the ultimate arbiters of a candidate's fate because they assign the ranking. Because of this, legislators are less likely to open local offices and focus on local issues (Shugart 2005). Proponents of PR argue that in spite of this, voters are represented via the parties that are close to their ideological preferences. Orit Kedar (2009), however, disputed this. Using a rational choice model of voting, she argued that voters use their vote to ensure that their preferred policy would be carried out. In majoritarian, SMD systems, this is straightforward because the winning party will control government and can implement its preferred policy. In consensual PR systems with multiple parties, though, policy is based on negotiated compromises after the election, so voters compensate for this by voting for parties more ideologically extreme than their own positions, assuming negotiations will then result in their preferred and more moderate policy. She found, for instance, that voters in the UK choose the party closest to them ideologically at a much higher rate than do voters in most European countries with PR systems, where voters choose a more extreme party instead. (She used the same theory to explain why voters tend to vote for the party in opposition to the president in legislative elections in presidential systems.)

In addition, opponents of PR argue that having a broad range of parties in a legislature often has negative effects. Small parties, as noted above, often have little voice unless they join coalitions, but small extremist parties may gain inordinate power if they are able to negotiate key roles in ruling coalitions. Coalitions can be hard to form in such a fragmented environment, and where they do form, they may be unstable, as the case of Israel demonstrates.

Because Israel is a country of numerous ideological, religious, and ethnic divisions, multiple parties compete in each election, and coalitions of parties must band together to form a government in its parliamentary system. The country uses a pure, closed-list PR system: the entire country is one electoral district and citizens vote for

CRITICAL inquiry

Women in Power

Americans are used to considering themselves progressive when it comes to women's rights, yet in 2016 only 19.4 percent of representatives in the House and 20 percent of senators were women, slightly below the global average of 22.9 percent. As Table 6.1b shows, in some democracies women constitute nearly half of the legislature, while others fare far worse than in the United States. What explains these disparities in how many women achieve power at the national level?

Table 6.1a suggests an initial hypothesis based on political culture, because regional breakdowns seem to suggest that it plays a role. An alternative hypothesis is that the election of women is a case in which institutions matter. Table 6.1b suggests that PR systems are more conducive to electing women than are SMD systems. Because closed PR systems (most PR systems are closed) require parties to submit lists of candidates, more women are nominated. A party may be under some pressure to include at least some women on its list, since an all-male (or even overwhelmingly male) list could provoke negative reaction. Some PR systems include a quota system: parties must include a certain percentage of women candidates on their lists. A third hypothesis is that the longer a country is democratic, the more women will gain office; democracy provides an opportunity for underrepresented and marginalized groups to gain more influence, and the longer democracy lasts the more likely it will be that such groups will gain influence.

TABLE 6.1a	Percentage of Seats in Lower House Occupied by Women, Regional Averages
Region	**% women**
Nordic countries	41.1%
Americas	27.7%
Europe, OSCE member countries, including Nordic countries	25.8%
Europe, OSCE member countries, excluding Nordic countries	24.3%
sub-Saharan Africa	23.1%
Asia	19.2%
Arab states	18.4%
Pacific	13.5%

Source: Data are from Interparliamentary Union, "Women in National Parliaments" (http://www.ipu.org/wmn-e/world.htm).

Look at the tables carefully. Based on the data, which of the hypotheses seems to be the best explanation for how many women are elected to national legislatures? Why do you come to the conclusion you do on this question? What implications does your answer have for which electoral system is most democratic?

TABLE 6.1b	Women in World Legislatures	

Country	% women in lower house	Type of electoral system	Length of current regime in years
Bolivia	53.1%	Mixed	33
Sweden	43.6%	PR	98
Senegal	42.7%	Mixed	15
South Africa	42.4%	PR	21
Mexico	42.4%	Mixed	18
Finland	41.5%	PR	71
Namibia	41.3%	PR	25
Spain	40%	Mixed	37
Norway	39.6%	PR	70
Mozambique	39.6%	PR	21
Belgium	39.3%	PR	71
Denmark	37.4%	PR	69
Slovenia	36.7%	PR	24
Germany	36.5%	Mixed	25
Argentina	35.8%	PR	32
Portugal	34.8%	PR	39
Serbia	34%	PR	9
Costa Rica	33.3%	PR	96
El Salvador	32.1%	PR	31
Switzerland	32%	Mixed	167
New Zealand	31.4%	Mixed	138
Tunisia	31.3%	PR	1
Italy	31%	PR	67
Austria	30.6%	PR	69
Philippines	29.8%	Mixed	28
United Kingdom	29.4%	SMD	135
Poland	27.4%	PR	24
Israel	26.7%	PR	67
France	26.2%	SMD	46
Peru	26.2%	PR	14
Australia	26%	SMD	114
Canada	26%	SMD	127
Lithuania	23.4%	Mixed	24
Ireland	22.2%	PR	94

Country	% women in lower house	Type of electoral system	Length of current regime in years
Bosnia-Herzegovina	21.4%	PR	0
Albania	20.7%	PR	18
Bulgaria	20.4%	PR	25
Czech Republic	20%	PR	22
Bangladesh	20%	SMD	1
Slovakia	20%	PR	22
Colombia	19.9%	PR	58
Cyprus	19.6%	PR	41
United States	19.4%	SMD	206
Panama	18.3%	Mixed	26
Latvia	18%	PR	24
Montenegro	17.3%	PR	9
Indonesia	17.1%	PR	16
South Korea	17%	Mixed	27
Malawi	16.7%	SMD	21
Uruguay	16.2%	PR	30
Chile	15.8%	Other	26
Paraguay	15%	PR	23
Turkey	14.9%	PR	1
Niger	14.6%	Mixed	4
Mongolia	14.5%	Mixed	23
Guatemala	13.9%	PR	19
Romania	13.7%	Mixed	19
Zambia	12.7%	SMD	14
Sierra Leone	12.4%	SMD	13
India	12%	SMD	65
Ukraine	12%	Mixed	24
Georgia	11.3%	Mixed	24
Ghana	10.9%	SMD	14
Hungary	10.1%	Mixed	25
Brazil	9.9%	PR	30
Botswana	9.5%	SMD	49
Japan	9.5%	Mixed	63
Benin	7.2%	PR	24

Source: Inter-Parliamentary Union, "Women in National Parliaments," World Classification Table (http://www.ipu.org/wmn-e/classif.htm). Based on figures for lower or single house.

their preferred party. The 120 seats in its parliament, the Knesset, are then allocated based on each party's share of the vote. Every party or coalition of parties that receives 3.25 percent of the national vote gets at least one seat in the Knesset. Most elections feature as many as two dozen parties, with at least a dozen winning seats in parliament. While two or three major parties have always existed, almost all governments are coalitions of one major party, which provides the prime minister, and at least three others—sometimes as many as six—who also receive cabinet seats to ensure their support in parliament.

The 2015 election resulted in ten parties (some of which were actually coalitions of smaller parties) winning seats in parliament, with Prime Minister Binyamin Netanyahu's Likud bloc winning the most—one quarter of the total. His governing coalition before the election disintegrated over the country's budget and the issue of whether to define Israel as a "Jewish state," so Netanyahu asked for a dissolution of parliament and an early election. After the election, it took him over six weeks to put together a working coalition government that included five parties in the cabinet, barely gaining him the sixty-one votes he needed to get a majority vote in parliament. With an extremely ideologically diverse cabinet, the prime minister must negotiate policies continuously to keep the government together. Governmental dissolution and the instability that comes with it often lurk right around the corner. Israel demonstrates what critics point to as a weakness of a PR system: government instability. The average government lasts just over two years.

Mixed, or Semiproportional, Systems

Given the plusses and minuses of SMD and PR, it is not surprising that some countries, including our case studies of Germany and Japan, have chosen to combine the two. The resulting hybrid is called a **mixed, or semiproportional,** system. A semiproportional system combines single-member district representation with overall proportionality. Voters cast two ballots: one for a representative from their district, with the winner being the individual who gains a plurality, and a second for a party list.

Under the compensatory mixed system in Germany, the legislature is composed by first awarding seats to all the district representatives, after which the party lists are used to add members until each party gets seats approximately equal to its share of the party list vote. So, for example, a very small party that crosses the 5 percent threshold required to enter parliament might send one or two representatives from its list to the legislature even though none of its candidates for individual district seats were elected. On the other hand, a large party that narrowly sweeps quite a few seats might gain no more from its list when proportional representation is factored in. At the end of the day, the party composition of the legislature looks fairly similar to what it would have if it had been chosen based strictly on PR, but each district is also guaranteed its

mixed, or semiproportional
An electoral system that combines single-member district representation with overall proportionality in allocation of legislative seats to parties; Germany is a key example

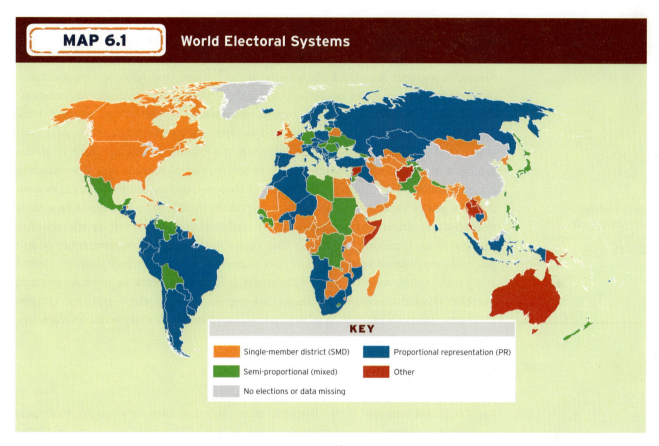

MAP 6.1   **World Electoral Systems**

KEY

- Single-member district (SMD)
- Proportional representation (PR)
- Semi-proportional (mixed)
- Other
- No elections or data missing

Source: International Institute for Democracy and Electoral Assistance (http://www.idea.int/esd/world.cfm). Modified by the authors.

own, individual representative, as in a single-member system. In Japan, the noncompensatory mixed system reserves separate seats for representatives from the individual districts and from the party list vote. Parties get whatever the two seat totals happen to be, making Japan's system less proportional than Germany's.

Mixed systems share some of the advantages of SMD and PR systems. Because they waste fewer votes, participation rates tend to be slightly higher, as in PR (see Figure 6.3), yet citizens are also guaranteed a personal representative to whom they can appeal. In addition, the single-district component of semiproportional systems tends to reinforce the dominance of a couple of large parties that find it easier to win a significant number of individual seats. Small parties also form and are represented, but the dominance of a couple of major parties facilitates coalition formation and stability.

Electoral systems clearly influence the type and extent of representation citizens in a democracy have, and all systems involve trade-offs to some extent. Electoral systems also have an important impact on two other institutions: political parties and party systems.

FORMAL INSTITUTIONS: POLITICAL PARTIES AND PARTY SYSTEMS

American political scientist E. E. Schattschneider wrote that "modern democracy is unthinkable save in terms of parties" (1942/2009, 1). Political parties are associations that seek to formally control government. In democracies, parties seek to control the government via elections and are limited in what they can do once they gain control. They bring together individual citizens and a number of discrete interests into a coalition of broadly shared interests that potentially helps to overcome the collective action problem. The number of parties and their relative institutional strength constitute a **party system.** Parties perform important functions in any democracy, such as mobilizing citizens to participate in the political process, recruiting and training political elites, clarifying and simplifying voter choices, organizing governments, and providing opposition to the current government. Political scientists compare parties and party systems based on parties' ideologies, internal organization and strength, and number. These differences have important implications for where and how citizens can participate in a political system and the extent to which diverse interests are represented in a legislature.

party system
The number of parties and their relative institutional strength

Political Parties

Party organizations and their relationships to their members vary widely. Many parties in Europe began in the nineteenth century as cadre parties, collections of political elites who chose candidates and mobilized voters to support them. They had small memberships and often started among elected politicians who restricted membership to themselves and their closest elite supporters. With the universal franchise and full-scale industrialization, cadre parties became mass parties that recruited as many members as possible who participated actively in the party organization and expected to have some influence over it. Parties thus became important organizations within which political participation takes place; their internal organization and processes of leadership selection help determine how much influence citizens have. Exactly how party members are involved and how much influence they have varies from country to country and over time, as our case studies at the end of the chapter demonstrate.

All parties must mobilize citizens to support them, so how do they overcome the classic collective action problem of convincing the average citizen to participate? Most people would answer that citizens join parties because they agree with their ideas. This is the reason implicit in democratic theory: voters examine available alternatives and support the party that best represents them. Scholars of American politics, in particular, have long noted that the process seems far less rational than that. For most people, party membership and support can become a source of identification that they are socialized into; new voters join and support the party their families "have always supported" without necessarily making a conscious choice. The best predictor of which party any individual will vote for is the party they voted for in the last election; party membership tends to be enduring and crosses generations. It can also come almost automatically from being a member of a particular group, as in the case of ethnically or religiously divided societies in which each group has its own party, or in the case of the Labour Party in Britain, which most union members automatically join via their union membership. Social identities based on ethnicity, religion, region, and work are more important for most people than political loyalties, so the former produce the latter.

People also join or support parties to gain direct material benefits. We defined clientelism in chapter 2 as the exchange of material benefits for political support. It is one of the most widespread of political phenomena; political parties and their candidates practice it regularly. The party machines in early-twentieth-century U.S. cities, for example, offered preferential treatment to party members when allocating jobs or awarding business contracts with city governments. In authoritarian regimes in which formal institutions typically do not allow real citizen participation, individual loyalty to a political leader can be the best means to survive, thrive, and gain influence, as we will discuss in chapter 8. Most political scientists argue that in democracies, clientelism is more common in relatively poor societies and/or in new democracies in which parties are institutionally weak.

In poor and unequal societies, poor people are more likely to need and accept material inducement in exchange for their political support, and a large income gap between political leaders and their potential clients gives the leaders plenty of resources to pass out to clients. Clients provide political support, including votes, in exchange for material help. In new democracies, political parties are typically new as well, and therefore weak as institutions. Without well-established bases of ideological and programmatic support, parties turn to clientelism as an alternative means to mobilize support. In the weakest systems, parties are really just vehicles for key patrons to contest elections; when a patron changes parties, his clients move with him. Loyalty to the patron, not the party, is key. Kitschelt (2014) found that parties use clientelism most frequently in middle-income countries in which the state is typically very involved in the economy; poorer people in these societies will respond to material inducements, and government involvement in the economy gives opportunities for parties to provide public resources to their supporters (see Figure 6.4). Clientelism, though, played an important part in the early growth of many parties that went on to become strong institutions with ideological bases of support, including in the United States. Our case studies show that at least some elements of clientelism exist in all countries.

The relationships among party members, political candidates, and campaign resources (mainly money) are important to a party's institutional strength. Parties that

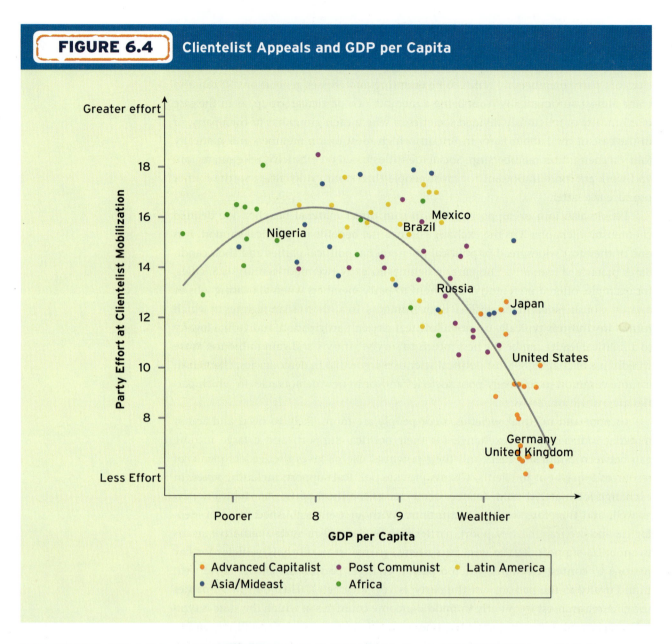

FIGURE 6.4   Clientelist Appeals and GDP per Capita

Comparativist Herbert Kitschelt measured the parties' efforts at using clientelist appeals and compared them to the GDP per capita, finding that parties in middle-income countries use clientelism the most and parties in wealthiest countries use it the least because in those countries programmatic and ideological appeals mobilize most voters.

Source: Figure is modified from Herbert Kitschelt, "Parties and Party Systems," in *Comparing Democracies: Elections and Voting in a Changing World,* edited by Lawrence LeDuc, Richard G. Niemi, and Pippa Norris (Thousand Oaks, CA: Sage, 2014), 32–57.

have internal mechanisms through which registered members select candidates are likely to be stronger than those that select candidates via external processes, such as primaries in the United States. Candidates who are chosen by party members in an internal process like that used in Britain are likely to be very loyal to the interests and demands of the party members who formally select them and who provide the bulk of their campaign resources. Once elected, they are more likely to vote as a block in support of official party positions. In contrast, candidates in the United States raise most of their own campaign funds and gain their party's nomination via a primary election that is open to all voters in the party (or, in some states, to all voters regardless of party), not just formal party members who have paid dues and attended meetings. This means that candidates in the United States are much more independent of party leaders' demands, so they can act more independently once in office. U.S. parties were traditionally less unified and weaker than many of their European counterparts for this reason. A parliamentary system in which top party leaders can aspire to become cabinet members also strengthens parties, as MPs follow their party leaders' wishes in the hope of being selected for the cabinet.

When most people think of parties and their differences, though, the first thing that comes to mind is ideology. Klaus von Beyme (1985) created an influential categorization of European parties based on their origins and ideologies. The most important categories are explained in Figure 6.5. They reflect the social and economic changes that characterized nineteenth- and twentieth-century Europe. For example, conservative parties originated as cadre parties that were interested in defending the traditions and economic status of the landed elite against the liberals, who pressed for expanded rights for the bourgeoisie and the growth of market economies. Socialists and communists, meanwhile, tried to create mass parties to represent the interests of the emerging working class.

The ideological distinctions among the parties and loyalty to them, however, seem to be changing over the past generation. In the last twenty years, political scientists have noted, in particular, a decline of partisan loyalty toward the traditional parties in wealthy democracies. Declining party loyalty has resulted in lower voter turnout in most countries; increased electoral volatility (voters switch parties more frequently from one election to the next); more single-issue voting, especially on postmaterialist issues such as the environment or abortion; more new parties successfully entering the political arena; and greater focus on the personality of individual candidates rather than on parties. Most analysts see the decline of the traditional social divisions of class and religion on which major parties were based as part of the reason for the parties' decline. The extent of this decline varies from one country to another, as Figure 6.6 demonstrates. The United States, where the two-party system is still firmly entrenched, has seen the least decline, while the greatest decline is mostly in European countries with PR electoral systems.

Two schools of thought have emerged to explain these changes and predict where they will lead. Russell Dalton and others saw a fundamental partisan *dealignment*, as voters and parties disconnect, probably for the long term. They argued that major parties used to serve two key functions: educating voters about political issues, and simplifying voters' choices. As voters have become more

FIGURE 6.5 Von Beyme's Categorization of Political Parties

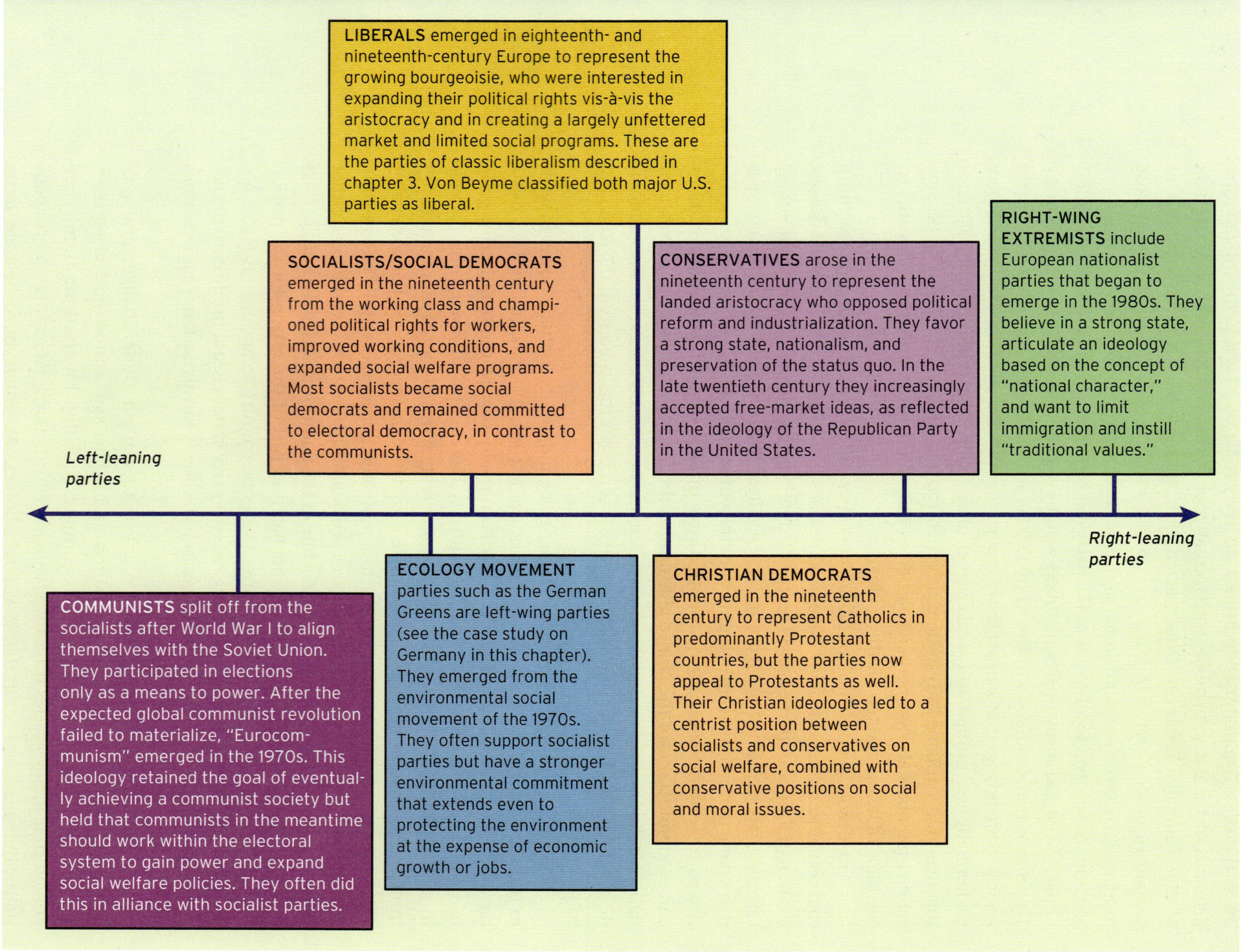

LIBERALS emerged in eighteenth- and nineteenth-century Europe to represent the growing bourgeoisie, who were interested in expanding their political rights vis-à-vis the aristocracy and in creating a largely unfettered market and limited social programs. These are the parties of classic liberalism described in chapter 3. Von Beyme classified both major U.S. parties as liberal.

CONSERVATIVES arose in the nineteenth century to represent the landed aristocracy who opposed political reform and industrialization. They favor a strong state, nationalism, and preservation of the status quo. In the late twentieth century they increasingly accepted free-market ideas, as reflected in the ideology of the Republican Party in the United States.

RIGHT-WING EXTREMISTS include European nationalist parties that began to emerge in the 1980s. They believe in a strong state, articulate an ideology based on the concept of "national character," and want to limit immigration and instill "traditional values."

SOCIALISTS/SOCIAL DEMOCRATS emerged in the nineteenth century from the working class and championed political rights for workers, improved working conditions, and expanded social welfare programs. Most socialists became social democrats and remained committed to electoral democracy, in contrast to the communists.

CHRISTIAN DEMOCRATS emerged in the nineteenth century to represent Catholics in predominantly Protestant countries, but the parties now appeal to Protestants as well. Their Christian ideologies led to a centrist position between socialists and conservatives on social welfare, combined with conservative positions on social and moral issues.

ECOLOGY MOVEMENT parties such as the German Greens are left-wing parties (see the case study on Germany in this chapter). They emerged from the environmental social movement of the 1970s. They often support socialist parties but have a stronger environmental commitment that extends even to protecting the environment at the expense of economic growth or jobs.

COMMUNISTS split off from the socialists after World War I to align themselves with the Soviet Union. They participated in elections only as a means to power. After the expected global communist revolution failed to materialize, "Eurocommunism" emerged in the 1970s. This ideology retained the goal of eventually achieving a communist society but held that communists in the meantime should work within the electoral system to gain power and expand social welfare policies. They often did this in alliance with socialist parties.

Left-leaning parties

Right-leaning parties

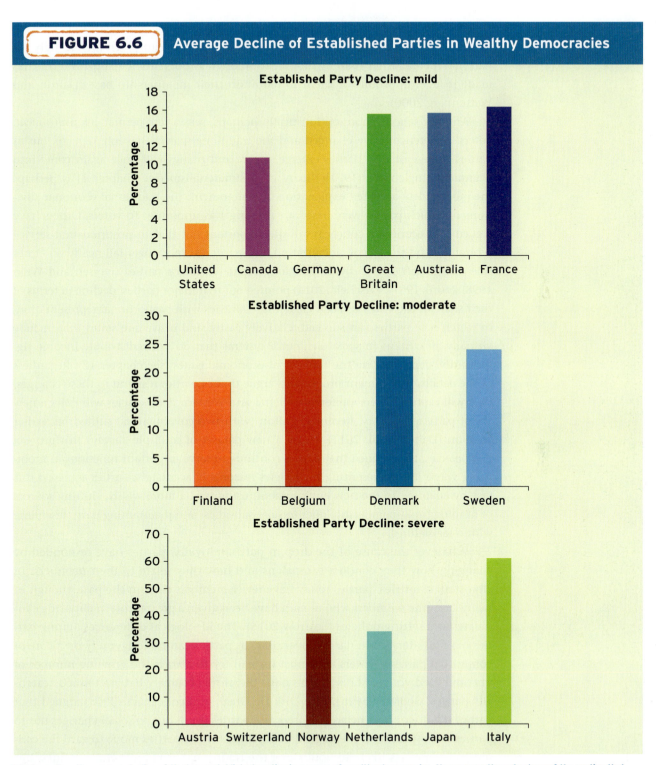

FIGURE 6.6   Average Decline of Established Parties in Wealthy Democracies

The bars show the average decline of the long-established parties in a group of wealthy democracies. It compares the vote share of the parties that were the most important from 1955 to 1965 with those same parties' vote share from 2001 to 2011.

Source: Herbert Kitschelt, "Parties and Party Systems," in *Comparing Democracies: Elections and Voting in a Changing World,* edited by Lawrence LeDuc, Richard G. Niemi, and Pippa Norris (Thousand Oaks, CA: Sage, 2014), 32–57.

educated and media outlets have multiplied, they no longer need parties to educate them. The media changes have also prompted parties to campaign increasingly via national media rather than by mobilization of grassroots membership, and this has made it less important for them to maintain their membership base (Dalton and Wattenberg 2000).

Another school, more optimistically perhaps, sees a less permanent *realignment*: voters' preferences have changed and the traditional parties haven't kept up, but as parties change or new parties emerge, voters and parties will once again come into alignment. Inglehart's (1971) theory of postmaterialism (see chapter 1) is perhaps the most widely accepted explanation of realignment: the traditional economic divisions on which parties were based are no longer as important to voters. Others have argued that economic concerns are still important but that in postindustrial service economies and the age of globalization, those interests no longer fall neatly on either side of the "left–right" divide that long separated major parties (Iversen and Wren 1998; Rodrik 1997). Kitschelt (2014) pointed out that major parties' decline in terms of their share of the vote has been greater in countries with proportional representation, in which new parties can succeed relatively easily, and in welfare states that include virtually all citizens in social insurance systems that do not redistribute income significantly, depoliticizing the traditional economic issues (see chapter 12). Regardless of the details, realignment proponents argue that as parties respond to these changes, they will capture voters' preferences better and Western democracies will enter a new era of partisan stability. Recently, Dalton (with two collaborators) shifted his earlier position (Dalton et al. 2011). Using a new dataset of multiple surveys in thirty-six democracies, they argued that parties continue to serve important functions in mobilizing voters and representing their views reasonably accurately. Parties achieved this task by adapting to the new environment: using media more wisely, shifting sources of funding from membership dues to state subsidies, and maintaining party discipline within legislatures.

Whatever the cause of the drop in partisan loyalty, parties have responded by changing how they conduct campaigns and how they relate to their members. In almost all countries, parties today have fewer members than in the past, though in many cases the members who remain have been given a greater role in choosing candidates and setting policies (Scarrow 2015). The ideological differences among parties have also tended to narrow over time, as parties can no longer rely on a core of committed partisan voters and must instead try to attract the growing number of uncommitted voters. Many parties have therefore become what are termed "catch-all" parties. Geoffrey Evans, Nan Dirk De Graaf, and colleagues (2013) argued that part of the disconnect between voters and parties is not due to social changes but to parties narrowing their ideological distinctions: when parties move toward the center, voters are less likely to vote along the traditional class and religious lines, but when parties give voters distinct ideological choices the traditional voting patterns often still hold. Timothy Hellwig (2014), on the other hand, sees these changes as a rational response to globalization. He used survey research across multiple countries to argue that in countries in which globalization has stronger effects, voters and parties shift away from directly economic issues because they no longer believe their government can influence those areas; instead, voters demand (and parties supply) changes in noneconomic issues over which the government still has control.

Political scientists Mark Blyth and Richard Katz (2005) took this party-focused approach one step further, creating an elite theory of contemporary parties. Using a political economy argument, they suggested that formerly catch-all parties are now becoming what they term "cartel parties." Catch-all parties, they argued, attracted voters by offering more and more government aid and services to them. By the late twentieth century, however, this strategy was meeting budget constraints, in part created by globalization. Governments were no longer able to expand social benefits, so parties could no longer offer more to attract voters. They instead accepted market-oriented economic theories that argued for more limited government services (see chapter 10) and sold those to the electorate, lowering expectations about what was possible. At the same time, changes in media meant elections were won and lost based on access to large amounts of money for successful media campaigns. Mobilizing party members based on ideological passion and commitment was no longer necessary. Competition came to be about "managerial competence" rather than ideological differences or promises of benefits. In effect, major parties formed a cartel to maintain power, using media and money from the government to fund their own activities; all major parties implicitly came to agree on preserving the status quo. Among other things, this hurts citizens' sense of political efficacy, the feeling that their participation can have a political impact (Pardos-Prado and Riera 2016). The only innovative policy alternatives in this context come from minor parties, which is perhaps one reason why their share of votes is increasing in most countries. SMD systems that keep minor parties out of power, then, would seem to be the most elitist under this theory.

Whatever the long-term trends, the growing disconnect between voters and established parties has created an opportunity for new parties. On the left, "green" parties focused on environmental and peace issues emerged across Europe, especially in countries with PR electoral systems. Our case study of Germany is a major example. A more powerful trend, though, has been the emergence of "far-right" parties. While their precise ideologies vary, far-right parties generally espouse a populist nativism that focusses on economic decline and opposes immigration. **Populism** is an amorphous political phenomenon, often referred to as a political "style" rather than ideology, that emphasizes a united and morally superior "people" battling corrupt elites, denies divisions among the "people," and often follows a charismatic leader who claims that once in power he alone will implement the popular will. Nativism is an extreme form of cultural nationalism that sees the nation, or "people," as culturally threatened by outsiders and demands a return to a more culturally pure era.

populism
A political "style" or ideology emphasizing a united "people" pitted against corrupt elites, denying divisions among the "people," and often led by a charismatic leader

The success of far-right parties has varied across Europe, with some gaining as much as a third of the electorate's support while others receive less than 10 percent. The National Front in France is probably the best known example (see chapter 3), but far-right parties have participated in governments in Austria, Italy, the Netherlands, and Switzerland. In our case study of Britain, the United Kingdom Independence Party (UKIP) convinced Britons to vote to leave the European Union in 2016, using a strongly anti-immigrant campaign to do so. And in the United States, Donald Trump's successful campaign for president had many elements of populism and nativism as well (Rahn and Oliver 2016).

Comparativists have sought to explain the rise of the far right mainly as a response to modernization and globalization that has imposed economic costs on certain segments of the population, such as workers in traditional manufacturing. This is often combined with cultural grievances against immigrants. The European refugee crisis in 2015–2016 that saw a million Middle Eastern refugees arrive in Europe in a matter of months significantly strengthened far-right parties, including in our case study of Germany. The nature of the political system, of course, influences far-right parties' success as well; they are more likely to thrive in PR systems, though the passionate commitment of their core supporters allows some to survive even in SMD systems. How established parties respond to the demands of far-right supporters can also influence how successful the new parties are (Golder 2016). David Art (2011) argued as well that who is in the parties themselves is important to explaining their success: where they are able to recruit committed and skilled activists they are able to survive, but where established parties and political activists shun them early on, they are short-lived.

The idea of declining partisan loyalty and the rise of new parties may seem odd to most Americans, who see the two major parties maintaining their share of the national vote and national politics as "too partisan." Compared with most European parties, however, American parties have always been less ideologically divided and more "catch-all" parties without a clear basis in a core social group. America's growing partisan division is often implicitly contrasted to an earlier era of bipartisan respect and cooperation. Political science research shows that partisanship has indeed risen in the United States, but also that it is a return to long-standing patterns. The relative bipartisanship of the New Deal consensus from World War II through the 1970s was an anomaly in U.S. history. Furthermore, although the United States may be returning to greater partisanship, American parties are still no more, and in many cases less, ideologically distant from one another than are European parties (Dalton et al. 2011, 132–137).

Frances Lee (2009) argued that ideological differences do not fully explain the partisan divisions and "gridlock" that characterize U.S. politics. Looking at the Senate, where the requirement of sixty votes to pass major legislation creates a significant veto player, Lee analyzed roll-call votes to argue that senators have a joint electoral interest in opposing one another, even when they do not disagree ideologically. This is especially true when parties can block an opposing president's goals and control the congressional agenda to assert their electoral message. American partisanship, she suggested, is as much about gaining electoral advantage as it is about real ideological differences.

Before these recent changes, the European ideologies that arose in the nineteenth and early twentieth centuries influenced parties throughout the world, though many countries have parties based on social divisions and ideas other than those derived in Europe. In Latin America, as in Europe, cadre parties emerged in the nineteenth century that pitted some type of conservative party favoring the landholding elite against liberals favoring reforms in the interest of industry and urbanization. Later, socialist parties championing workers' interests emerged as well. With industrialization, parties expanded their mass membership to some extent, though in many countries they remained rather weak due in part to authoritarian interruptions to the democratic process. Populism was a common phenomenon as well, best exemplified by President Juan Perón (1946–1955) of Argentina. Latin American populists' policies were often based on a form of clientelism—they rewarded urban supporters with government services and infrastructure. Military governments in the 1960s and 1970s banned or severely limited the freedom of political parties. Parties had to reemerge and rebuild whenever democracy was restored.

Parties emerged as part of the nationalist movements in Asia and in Africa opposing colonial rule. These were mass parties from the start but often remained very weak, in part because they were so new. In addition, their primary ideology was anticolonialism, and their members often did not agree on much else. Many, in reality, were collections of disparate leaders, each with a following based on patronage and ethnic or religious identity. After independence, many of these parties fragmented, inviting military intervention. Alternatively, one faction would gain control, create a one-party state, and eliminate democracy. Either outcome eliminated real party competition by destroying or emasculating most parties. Parties would eventually reemerge in the 1990s as very weak institutions in new democracies, a subject to which we turn in chapter 9. In these situations, high levels of uncertainty about the stability of the regime and its institutions make it extraordinarily difficult for parties to organize and mobilize voters the way they do in more established democracies (Lupu and Reidl 2013).

Party Systems

Individual parties exist in party systems, which are categorized by the number of parties and their relative strength. By definition, democratic party systems include at least two parties, but they vary beyond that. At one extreme is the **dominant-party system,** in which multiple parties exist but the same party wins every election and governs continuously. In this system, free and (more or less) fair elections take place following the electoral rules of the country, but one party is popular enough to win every election. In South Africa, for instance, the African National Congress (ANC), Nelson Mandela's party that led the struggle for liberation from apartheid, has won

dominant-party system
Party system in which multiple parties exist but the same one wins every election and governs continuously

two-party system
Party system in which only two parties are able to garner enough votes to win an election, though more may compete; the United Kingdom and United States are key examples

multiparty systems
Party systems in which more than two parties could potentially win a national election and govern

all five national elections easily. (It garnered 62 percent of the vote in the 2014 election, a drop of 4 percent from 2009.) Numerous opposition parties exist, have some seats in the legislature, and are allowed to compete openly in the elections. The ANC remains dominant, however, though it lost several important local elections in 2016, leading some analysts to predict an end to the dominant-party system there. The line can be thin between a dominant-party system and an electoral authoritarian regime; in the latter, a dominant party maintains power not only via its popularity but also via manipulation of the electoral system, control of government resources, and intimidation of other parties.

In a **two-party system,** only two parties are able to garner enough votes to win an election, though more may compete. The United States is a classic case of a two-party system: no third party has had significant representation in government since the Republicans emerged in the 1850s. Third parties, such as H. Ross Perot's Reform Party during the presidential campaigns of the 1990s, arise to compete in particular elections, but they never survive more than two elections as a political force of any significance.

Finally, **multiparty systems** are those in which more than two parties could potentially win a national election and govern. In some of these, such as Italy for most of its post–World War II history, two of the parties are quite large but one of them almost always has to form a coalition with one or more of the smaller parties in order to gain a majority in parliament and govern. In still other multiparty systems, three or four relatively equal parties regularly contend for power, with a legislative majority always requiring a coalition of at least two of them.

How and why did these different party systems emerge and change over time in different countries? The main explanations are sociological and institutional. Sociological explanations posit that a party system reflects the society in which it emerges. Parties arise to represent the various interests of self-conscious groups in particular societies. In nineteenth-century Europe, two major conflicts emerged: an economic one between capital and labor, and a religious one either between Protestants and Catholics or between church supporters and more secular voters. The economic conflict became universal as industrialization expanded. All countries eventually had some sort of party defending business interests (usually called "liberal") and a socialist or social democratic party championing workers' concerns. Religious divisions, on the other hand, existed in some places but not everywhere. For instance, Germany has a Christian Democratic Party that originally represented the Catholic minority, but France, which was all Catholic, does not. Where economic and religious divisions were politically salient, multiparty systems emerged; where only the economic division was important, two-party systems emerged.

Institutionalists, on the other hand, argue that the broader institutional setting, especially a country's electoral system, shapes both the number and strength of parties. Political leaders will respond rationally to the institutional constraints they face by creating the types of parties that will help them gain power in the system in which they operate. One classic institutionalist argument is **Duverger's Law,** named after French political scientist Maurice Duverger. He contended that the logic of competition in SMD electoral systems results in the long-term survival of only two parties. Multiple parties are unlikely to survive because all political parties must gain a plurality (or a majority, if required) in a particular district to win that district's legislative seat. The successful parties will be those whose members realize that their parties must have very broad appeal to gain majority support. Relying on a small, ideologically committed core group will yield no legislative seats. Parties without any legislative seats are less appealing to voters, who don't want to "waste" their vote. Over time, ambitious politicians realize that the way to electoral victory is through the already established major parties rather than the creation of new ones. Duverger's native France is one of the clearer examples of his law at work (see box).

In contrast, PR systems create an incentive for small, focused parties to emerge. The German environmental movement was able to create a successful Green Party because even with a narrow focus, the party could get enough votes to cross the minimum threshold and gain seats in parliament. Conversely, the United Kingdom does not have a strong Green Party because it could not compete for a meaningful number of seats with the Labour Party and the Conservatives. PR systems tend to create more parties and parties that are more ideologically distinct than SMD systems.

The debate between sociological and institutional theories of party systems creates something of a "chicken and egg" question: Did political leaders create electoral systems to match the number and kinds of parties they led, or did the electoral systems provide incentives to create particular kinds of parties? The logic in both directions seems strong. In a society with multiple viable parties, party leaders seem likely to favor a proportional system if given the opportunity to choose. No one or two parties are dominant, so all would fear they would lose out in an SMD electoral system. Conversely, in a two-party system like that in the United Kingdom in the late nineteenth century, the two dominant parties would logically prefer to create or preserve an SMD system, which strongly favors them over newer and smaller rivals.

Carles Boix (2007) presented a historical analysis to try to bring the two approaches together. He argued that in almost all of Europe, parties began as cadre parties—one

Duverger's Law
Institutionalist argument by French political scientist Maurice Duverger that SMD electoral systems will produce two major parties, eliminating smaller parties

liberal and one conservative—among the elite, with tiny electorates in SMD systems. Where religious divisions grew, religiously based parties challenged and sometimes split the two established parties. With the rise of the working class and its enfranchisement in the late nineteenth century, socialist parties emerged as well. Where SMD systems were well entrenched, such as in the United Kingdom, the socialists tended to displace one of the prior parties, and both the two-party and SMD systems survived. Where religious divisions had already split the two parties—or in newer democracies in the early twentieth century that did not have well-institutionalized electoral systems— the socialists and other smaller parties successfully demanded a proportional system. Amel Ahmed (2013) made a slightly different argument: both SMD and PR were products of efforts by conservative parties to contain workers' parties. Where conservative parties did not face a serious threat from a workers' party with socialist leanings, they would preserve SMD; where they faced a greater threat from workers, they created a PR system to accept but limit the electoral potential of the working class. Heather Stoll (2013) combined institutional and sociological factors to explain how new social groups such as women and ethnic or racial minorities were incorporated into party systems: Did they form their own parties, or were they absorbed into existing ones? She found that while the electoral system matters, more important is the prior homogeneity of the society, the size and type of the new group, its level of politicization, and the response of existing parties; on the whole, sociological factors mattered more than institutional ones.

The debate between sociological and institutional understandings of party development also raises the question of whether the institutionalist argument about the effects of electoral systems on parties really reflects the logic of the institutions or the underlying society in which the institutions operate: Does SMD really lead to only two parties, or does that electoral system happen to exist in societies with only one major cleavage that would produce two parties no matter what electoral system you used? Comparativists Robert Moser and Ethan Scheiner (2012) found a way to examine this question by focusing on countries with semiproportional systems. By comparing election results for the SMD and PR seats within the same country, they were able to see the effects of the two different electoral systems in a single sociological context. Scientifically speaking, this allowed them to control for sociological and other variables, isolating the effects of the institutions. They found that SMD and PR systems had the effects institutionalists claim in long-established democracies such as those in western Europe. In newer democracies with less-institutionalized party systems, however, the electoral systems did not have any effect. In newer democracies, SMD did not tend to produce two parties because voters were not very strategic in their voting; for instance, they might have loyalty for a particular party because it represents their ethnic group, and they will not change that allegiance regardless of whether their party wins or not. Leaders of such parties know they can count on that support, so they have less incentive to compromise. In this situation, FPTP produces a winning candidate with only 20 to 30 percent of the vote in some cases because

France and the Shift toward a Two-Party System

France provides a classic case of Duverger's Law, though the country's two-round system and multiparty heritage has meant that even there the law has not worked perfectly. France's Third (1871–1940) and Fourth (1946–1958) Republics had parliamentary governing structures with PR electoral systems, which facilitated the election of numerous parties into parliament and unstable coalition governments. A crisis at the end of the Fourth Republic led to the creation in 1958 of the Fifth Republic, whose semipresidential system was designed to end the instability.

The constitution of the Fifth Republic created an SMD two-round, majoritarian electoral system. For both legislative and presidential elections, a first-round election is open to all registered parties. If a candidate for a legislative district (or nationally, for the presidency) wins a majority of the votes in the first round, she is elected. If not, a runoff election is held two weeks later between the top two candidates in the first round, producing a majority winner. This allows all of France's numerous parties to contest the first-round election. When a second round takes place, the losing parties usually support the candidate who is ideologically closest to them.

This system resulted in the creation of two "families" of ideologically similar parties, one on the left and one on the right, which were pledged to support each other in the second-round elections. By the 1970s, each party family consisted of two significant parties, the Communists and the Socialists on the left and the Gaullists (political descendants of the Fifth Republic's founder, Charles de Gaulle) and Centrists on the right. Within each family, the two major parties were almost equally represented in the National Assembly, thus producing four major parties.

Further movement toward a two-party system came in the 1980s and 1990s. The Communists became less popular with the end of the Cold War, and the Socialists won the presidency for the first time in 1981. By 1988, the Socialists held nearly 90 percent of the seats won by the left as a whole. On the right, the two main parties survived longer, but once the Gaullist Jacques Chirac became president in 1995, his movement also became dominant, gaining nearly 90 percent of the seats controlled by the right. By 2012, the two largest parties, the Socialists on the left and the Gaullists on the right, controlled 82 percent of the seats in the National Assembly, compared with only 56 percent in 1973. While the smaller parties continue to exist and gain some legislative seats, Duverger's Law has worked in his own country; the shift from PR to a majoritarian system has come close to producing a two-party system. This has provided much greater political stability, but some would argue that it has diminished representation of the country's ideologically diverse citizenry.

---

many candidates are competing, but the number of parties does not drop over time. The ultimate question, perhaps, is whether the institutional logic will start having an effect over a longer time period as the democracies endure and parties become more institutionalized.

Parties and party systems have important implications for democratic rule. The number of parties influences the type of parties that exist, the choices voters have, and the stability of governments. SMD tends to encourage two-party systems rather than the multiparty systems that are more likely under PR (at least in well-established democracies). Most analysts have argued that an SMD system with only two broad parties makes governing easier and policy more coherent. Multiparty systems, on the other hand, give more formal voice to diverse opinions in the legislature but can produce unstable coalition governments. Lorelei Moosbrugger (2012), however, questioned the claim that SMD systems make governing easier. She argued that because politicians in SMD systems must appeal to a broad coalition of voters, they are vulnerable to the threatened loss of even a small group in their electoral coalition. By threatening to vote against incumbents, small groups can veto policy changes they oppose,

CRITICAL **in**quiry

What Explains Government Effectiveness?

This chapter and the last have discussed at length the relationship between the type of political system and the effectiveness of policymaking. The data below allow us to examine this relationship ourselves. Table 6.2 lists a large set of electoral democracies. The first column is a measure of "government effectiveness" created by the World Bank. It assesses the quality of public services and the quality of policy formulation and implementation. The other columns identify key elements of the political systems: the electoral system, the executive-legislative system, and the number of "effective" political parties (a measure of the number and share of legislative seats of parties). Look closely at the table. Can you develop hypotheses for which elements of the political system produce more effective governance? Does a particular type of electoral system or executive-legislative system seem to be associated with more effective government? Do more parties or fewer create government effectiveness? Do you need to combine the variables to explain why some countries achieve more effective government than others? Finally, look at the list of countries and think about where they are in the world. Do other hypotheses emerge about government effectiveness that have nothing to do with the type of political system? What is your overall conclusion based on the table?

TABLE 6.2	Measures of Government Effectiveness		
Country	**Effectiveness (2014)***	**Electoral system**	**Executive-legislative system**	**Number of effective parliamentary parties**
Finland	2.02	PR	Parliamentary	6.47
New Zealand	1.93	Mixed	Parliamentary	2.96
Switzerland	2.13	Mixed	Presidential	5.57
Canada	1.76	SMD	Parliamentary	2.41
Netherlands	1.83	PR	Parliamentary	5.70
Norway	1.81	PR	Parliamentary	4.39
Liechtenstein	1.68	PR	Semipresidential	3.31
Australia	1.59	SMD	Parliamentary	3.23
Iceland	1.50	PR	Parliamentary	4.42
United Kingdom	1.62	SMD	Parliamentary	2.57
Germany	173.0	Mixed	Parliamentary	3.51
Ireland	1.60	PR	Parliamentary	3.52
United States	1.46	SMD	Presidential	1.96
France	1.40	SMD	Semipresidential	2.83

Country	Effectiveness (2014)*	Electoral system	Executive-legislative system	Number of effective parliamentary parties
Japan	1.82	Mixed	Parliamentary	2.42
South Korea	1.18	Mixed	Presidential	2.28
Israel	1.16	PR	Parliamentary	6.94
Chile	1.14	Other	Presidential	2.09
Spain	1.15	Mixed	Parliamentary	2.60
Czech Republic	1.02	PR	Parliamentary	6.12
Portugal	1.01	PR	Semipresidential	2.93
Slovak Republic	0.87	PR	Parliamentary	2.85
Mauritius	1.13	SMD	Parliamentary	2.0
Hungary	0.53	Mixed	Parliamentary	2.01
Latvia	0.97	PR	Parliamentary	5.13
Lithuania	0.99	Mixed	Parliamentary	5.28
Poland	0.82	PR	Parliamentary	3.0
Uruguay	0.48	PR	Presidential	2.65
Croatia	0.69	PR	Parliamentary	2.59
Georgia	0.48	Mixed	Semipresidential	1.97
Botswana	0.32	SMD	Presidential	1.95
Greece	0.40	PR	Parliamentary	3.09
Italy	0.38	PR	Parliamentary	3.47
Turkey	0.38	PR	Parliamentary	2.34
South Africa	0.33	PR	Presidential	2.60
Costa Rica	0.40	PR	Presidential	4.92
Mexico	0.19	Mixed	Presidential	2.80
Jamaica	0.14	SMD	Parliamentary	1.8
Montenegro	0.28	PR	Parliamentary	3.18
Panama	0.27	Mixed	Presidential	3.01
Namibia	0.20	PR	Presidential	1.54

(Continued)

(Continued)

Country	Effectiveness (2014)*	Electoral system	Executive-legislative system	Number of effective parliamentary parties
Tunisia	−0.13	PR	Semipresidential	4.62
Bulgaria	0.09	PR	Parliamentary	5.06
Brazil	−0.15	PR	Presidential	13.22
India	−0.20	SMD	Parliamentary	3.45
Ghana	−0.27	SMD	Presidential	2.04
El Salvador	−0.02	PR	Presidential	3.31
Macedonia, FYR	0.15	PR	Parliamentary	2.86
Serbia	0.09	PR	Parliamentary	4.87
Peru	−0.28	PR	Presidential	3.97
Argentina	−0.18	PR	Presidential	6.49
Albania	−0.07	PR	Parliamentary	2.78
Romania	0.00	Mixed	Semipresidential	2.12
Indonesia	−0.01	PR	Presidential	8.16
Bolivia	−0.59	Mixed	Presidential	1.91
Senegal	−0.39	Mixed	Semipresidential	1.57
Benin	−0.50	PR	Presidential	8.83
Mozambique	−0.73	PR	Presidential	2.16
Moldova	−0.38	PR	Parliamentary	4.80
Niger	−0.74	Mixed	Semipresidential	4.64
Bosnia and Herzegovina	−0.47	PR	Parliamentary	7.60
Ukraine	−0.38	Mixed	Semipresidential	3.3
Paraguay	−0.92	PR	Presidential	2.39
Sierra Leone	−1.22	SMD	Presidential	1.9
Liberia	−1.37	SMD	Presidential	6.34

Sources: Government effectiveness data are from the World Bank, Worldwide Governance Indicators, "Government Effectiveness" (http://info .worldbank.org/governance/wgi/index.asp [http://info.worldbank.org/governance/wgi/wgidataset.xlsx]). Data for the degree of institutionalization of democracy are from Polity IV (http://www.systemic peace.org/inscr/inscr.htm). Data for number of effective parties are from Michael Gallagher, 2015, Election indices dataset at http://www.tcd.ie/Political_Science/staff/michael_gallagher/ElSystems/index.php, accessed August 2016. These indices: data for electoral family are from IDEA (http://www.idea.int/uid/fieldview.cfm?id=156&themeContext=4). 350.

*Estimate of governance (ranges from approximately −2.5 [weak] to 2.5 [strong] governance performance).

even if the policies have majority support. In PR systems with multiple parties, on the other hand, politicians are less threatened by the loss of a particular, small group upset over one issue. She demonstrated that farmers were able to prevent widely supported environment policies more effectively in SMD than in PR systems. By bringing organized interest groups into the analysis, she was able to conclude that the conventional wisdom about which type of party system is more effective at governing may be incorrect. We turn, then, to the important role of interest groups in modern democracies.

CIVIL SOCIETY

A great deal of participation and representation occurs in civil society, the sphere of organized citizen activity between the state and the individual family or firm that we discussed in chapter 3. As that chapter delineated, civil society arose in Europe with capitalism, industrialization, and democracy. It provides a space within which groups of citizens organize to influence government. As with parties, we ask questions about how well organizations in civil society enhance democracy: Are their internal rules democratic? Do they represent their constituents accurately? Do they gain undue influence? Do they have beliefs and foster policies that enhance democracy or harm it?

Our definition of civil society is a very broad one. It includes every conceivable organized activity that is not focused on individual self-interest and is not controlled by the government. Do all of these necessarily enhance democratic participation and representation? Does a parent–teacher organization or a local Little League matter to democracy? More troubling, does the Ku Klux Klan (KKK)? Is it a viable member of civil society? The KKK is clearly an organized group of citizens that provides a venue for participatory activities that could certainly include trying to influence governmental policy. Its core beliefs, however, violate the basic tenets of liberal democracy, so we could liken it to a political party that runs on a platform that questions the legitimacy of democracy (as the Islamic Front did in Algeria in the early 1990s). Should democracies allow such organizations to exist, and does their existence contribute positively or negatively to participation and representation in democracy?

The internal structure of organizations in civil society and the reasons why their members join them can matter as well. These issues come up, in particular, with organizations focused on propagating ethnic or religious ideologies. Often, though certainly not always, membership in such organizations requires being born into the broader group that it represents. Ethnic and religious organizations are therefore typically different from groups in which individual citizens choose to come together based on a shared concern. Ethnic and religious groups also often view any internal dissent as a threat to the group's sense of identity, resulting in an undemocratic internal organizational structure. As more and more different kinds of countries become democratic, more and more varied types of civil society organizations arise, making the study of their impact on democracy increasingly important.

Timeline
Political Institutions

Country	Institution development
18th Century	
United Kingdom	Cadre parties
Early 19th Century	
Europe	Rudimentary social movements begin to emerge
United Kingdom	Beginnings of liberal parties
United States	Beginnings of liberal parties
United States	Cadre parties
Mid-19th Century	
United States	Expansion of voting rights to all white men
United States	Beginnings of mass parties
United States	Origins of modern Republican and Democratic Parties
Late 19th Century	
Brazil	First Republic with cadre parties controlled by rural elites
Germany	Corporatist tradition begins under Bismarck
India	Indian National Congress formed
Europe	Mass parties and parties of the left emerge, including Germany's SDP
Russia	Communist Party origins
United States	Tammany Hall and the heyday of patronage
United Kingdom	Expansion of voting rights to all men
United Kingdom	Emergence of socialist parties, beginnings of mass parties, including the Labour Party

(Continued)

In most long-standing democracies, though, the term *civil society* typically connotes interest groups. These associations of individuals attempt to influence government, and most claim to represent clearly defined interests that their members share, such as protecting the environment, advancing civil rights, or representing various industries. They are formally organized, though their degree of institutionalization varies widely. They also are often regulated by the government and have to follow certain rules and procedures if they wish to be recognized as legitimate. Ideally, well-institutionalized interest groups are visible, have relatively large and active memberships, and have a significant voice on the issues in which they are interested. Less-institutionalized groups are less effective, and their legitimacy as representatives on various issues is often questioned. Similar to parties, interest groups bring together like-minded individuals to achieve a goal, but interest groups do not seek formal political power. If they are effective in carrying out their functions, the political system becomes more responsive and inclusive.

Modern interest groups emerged in the nineteenth century alongside mass electoral democracy. Labor, business, and agriculture became the key "sectoral" categories of interest groups; that is, they represented the three key sectors of the economy. As the bulk of the citizenry became more involved in the political process, other interest groups emerged as well, including groups focused on expanding participation rights for women and racial minorities. In postcolonial countries, similar groups emerged. In Latin America, unions and business associations arose with the beginning of industrialization in the late nineteenth century. In Asia and Africa, trade unions developed under colonial rule as colonial subjects began to work for wages and started to organize. Unions became important in the nationalist struggles for independence in most countries. In ethnically and

religiously divided societies, though, ethnic or religious organizations are often more politically important than unions or other sectoral groups. In these societies, the questions we ask above about which types of groups should be included in civil society loom large: Do strong ethnic group organizations into which a citizen must be born serve to strengthen democracy?

As is true for political parties, analysts have grown increasingly concerned about the strength of civil society even in well-established democracies. Robert Putnam (2000) decried a decline in **social capital**—that is, social networks and norms of reciprocity that are crucial to democratic participation. Even apparently "nonpolitical" organizations in civil society, he argued, create social networks and mutual trust among members, which can be used for political action. In the United States, in particular, Theda Skocpol (2003) argued that the system of mass-membership organizations that arose in the nineteenth century declined in the late twentieth century. They were replaced with what she called "managed advocacy" groups that rely on members for financial support and for occasional phone calls, e-mails, or presence at rallies, but no longer have active local branches that bring members together on a regular basis. Van Deth, Maloney, and colleagues (2012) note that many citizens seem willing to "contract out" political participation to professionals in interest groups, supporting them via "chequebook" participation. The question they ask is, What effect does this have on the quality of democracy?

> **social capital**
> Social networks and norms of reciprocity that are important for a strong civil society

Other scholars, however, point out that some types of political activity have held steady or even increased. They argue that while levels of trust and membership in formal organizations have declined, involvement in political activities has not. Rather, it has shifted to new and different organizations and forms. Citizens may participate in these new groups and perhaps influence government successfully, but they move relatively quickly among different issues and movements and may not develop strong ties with any particular group. Americans also volunteer more than ever before and join small groups such as self-help groups at higher rates than in the past. These scholars argue that new forms of activity have arisen to replace, at least in part, those that have declined. Much of this activity takes place via social movements and involves the use of social media, both of which we address in chapter 7.

Government–Interest Group Interaction: Two Models

No matter their origin, cause, or relative strength, the formal and informal relationships that interest groups have with government are crucial to how they operate and how effective they can be. The two major democratic models of government–interest group interaction are known as "corporatist" and "pluralist."

Interest-Group Pluralism   We used the word *pluralist* in chapter 1 to describe one of the major theories that attempts to answer the question "Who rules?"; here, however, **interest-group pluralism** means a system in which many groups exist to

> **interest-group pluralism**
> Interest-group system in which many groups exist to represent particular interests and the government remains officially neutral among them; the United States is a key example

Early 20th century

Brazil	Populist political leaders and parties
China	Origins of Chinese Communist Party
Germany	Origins of National Socialist (Nazi) Party
Japan	Taisho Democracy with electoral competition, 1912–1926
Russia	Russian Revolution; Soviet Communist Party becomes ruling party
United Kingdom	Labour replaces Liberals as second major party
United States	Progressive movement (social movements such as temperance, women's suffrage); early interest groups such as Sierra Club, League of Women Voters

Mid-20th century

Brazil	New Republic; rapid industrialization and expansion of labor unions
Brazil	Military rule and state corporatism with limited party competition, 1964–1985
Germany	Electoral system created
Germany	New social movements, including Greens, antinuclear, women's movements
India	Mass nationalist parties and independence
Iran	Competitive elections; Mossaddeq elected prime minister in 1951, later overthrown
Japan	Electoral system created
Japan	Origins of Japan's LDP
Nigeria	Mass nationalist parties and independence
United States	New social movements, including civil rights, antiwar, women's; new interest groups arise, including NOW, EarthFirst!, PETA

(Continued)

represent particular interests and the government remains officially neutral among them. Under a pluralist system in this sense, many groups may exist to represent the same broad "interest," and all can try to gain influence. The government, at least in theory, is neutral and does not give preferential access and power to any one group or allow it to be the official representative of a particular interest. The United States is the primary model of this pluralist system. The Chamber of Commerce exists to represent business interests, but so does the National Association of Manufacturers, the National Association of Realtors, and myriad other groups. Washington, D.C., contains literally thousands of interest groups, sometimes dozens organized around the same issue, all vying for influence over decision makers. This is repeated, on a smaller scale, in all fifty state capitals. The government of the day may listen more to one than another of these groups on a particular issue, but no official and enduring preference or access is given to one over others. Even when one large organization speaks on behalf of most of a sector of society—such as the AFL-CIO for labor—it is a loose confederation of groups whose individual organizational members can and do ignore positions and policies of the national confederation. Alternative groups have the right to organize as best they can. Figure 6.7 depicts this often confusing system, with multiple groups interacting directly with the government as well as forming various loose affiliations (such as the AFL-CIO) that also interact with the government.

Corporatism The major alternative to interest-group pluralism is corporatism. Unlike pluralism, which exists only in democracies, corporatism has more democratic (societal or neocorporatist) and less democratic (state corporatist) variants. We discuss the latter in chapter 8. **Neocorporatism**, also known as societal corporatism, is most common in northern Europe, where strong **peak associations**

represent the major interests in society by bringing together numerous local groups, and government works closely with the peak associations to develop policy. Figure 6.7 depicts this more hierarchical system, in which government tends to interact with fewer, larger, and more highly institutionalized peak associations than under pluralism. Germany is a key example, examined in greater detail below. In a neocorporatist system, peak associations maintain their unity and institutional strength via internal mechanisms that ensure local organizations will abide by the decisions of the national body. By negotiating binding agreements with them, the state in effect recognizes the peak associations as the official representatives of their sectors. Unlike **state corporatism**, however, no individuals or groups are required to belong to these associations, and they maintain internal systems of democratic control. Dissatisfied members may try to change the association's policies or found alternative organizations, but most do not pursue the latter option because membership in the main body provides direct access to government.

Pluralism and Neocorporatism Compared

Both pluralist and neocorporatist models have strengths and weaknesses. Pluralism allows greater local control and participation because any individual or group is free to start a new organization. National organizations have limited control over their local affiliates, so local members can work internally to move their local organization in whatever direction they wish. Because the state does not officially recognize any one group, there are fewer incentives for large organizations to maintain unity. This decentralization may limit the institutional strength and overall power of organizations in national politics. France is well known for its weak labor unions, for instance, in part because its two largest unions (one communist and one Catholic) are deeply divided over ideology.

neocorporatism
Also called societal corporatism; corporatism that evolves historically and voluntarily rather than being mandated by the state; Germany is a key example

peak associations
Organizations that bring together all interest groups in a particular sector to influence and negotiate agreements with the state; in the United States, an example is the AFL-CIO

state corporatism
Corporatism mandated by the state; common in fascist regimes

A boy practices target-shooting via a video game at the National Rifle Association's Youth Day in 2013. The NRA is one of the most powerful interest groups in the United States. The pluralist U.S. system gives interest groups exceptional access to legislators, in particular. Critics argue these "special interest groups" unduly influence policy and help create the "gridlock" familiar to Americans.

AP Photo/Houston Chronicle, Johnny Hanson

Late 20th/early 21st century

Brazil	Transition to multiparty democracy, 1985-1989
Brazil	Presidential victory of strong, programmatic party, the PT, in 2002
China	Emergence of very limited civil society under state corporatism
Germany	Reunification of East and West Germany, rise of Green Party, and expansion of number of parties from three to five
India	Rise of religious parties
India	End of Congress Party dominance, replaced by coalition governments from 1989 onward
India	Rise of lower-caste movements and parties
Iran	Elections, some with parties, under Islamic Republic, from 1980 onward
Japan	Electoral reform from SNTV to semiproportional system in 1993; watershed defeat of long-ruling LDP in 2009
Nigeria	Transition to multiparty democracy in 1999, though with seriously flawed elections; rise of dominant party, the PDP, by 2007; first change of party in power via election in 2015
Russia	Fall of communism and birth of new parties, 1991
Russia	Reduction of party competition under Putin from 2000 onward; shift from mixed to PR electoral system in 2005
United Kingdom	Continued dominance of centrist, mass parties; first coalition government in sixty years after 2010 election
United States	Continued dominance of centrist, mass parties; growing electoral volatility from one party to the other

Interest groups gain power vis-à-vis the state due to the resources they can bring to bear on the government. More centralized organizations have more resources and can legitimately claim to speak on behalf of more citizens. These factors increase their potential clout, although critics point out that no government treats each kind of group equally, at least in a market economy. Business interests are crucial for the well-being of the economy; therefore, the government in any market economy, even in the most pluralist systems, will pay more attention to business interests than to others, no matter how effectively others organize. Critics of the pluralist model contend that groups such as workers are better off under neocorporatist systems, in which they are united in large, strong organizations that have a better chance of countering the always strong influence of business.

Because neocorporatist associations are so large and united, they typically have more direct influence on government than does any single national association in a pluralist system. The disincentives to creating new organizations, however, and the power that government recognition provides to the elite leadership of the peak associations, make neocorporatist associations seem less participatory. The incentives against starting alternative organizations are so strong that the vast majority of relevant constituents remain in the confines of already established entities rather than starting new ones, no matter how dissatisfied they may be. A crucial question in these systems, then, is the degree of democratic control *within* the peak associations. If the association has strong mechanisms of internal democracy, such as open elections for leadership positions and constituent participation in setting organizational policies, its leaders can legitimately claim to represent members' views. If the association does not, it may have significant access to government and influence, but it may not really represent its members' views.

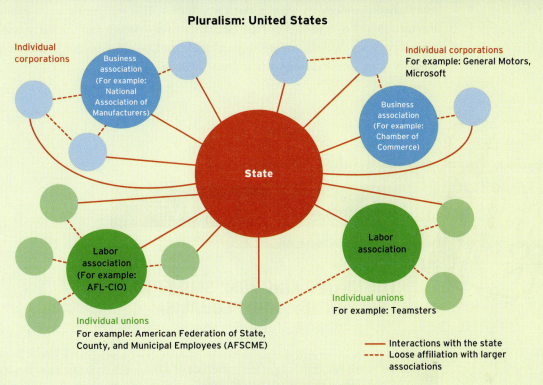

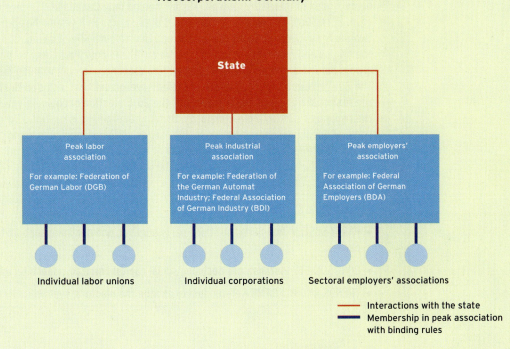

FIGURE 6.7 — Contrasting Models of State-Interest Group Interaction

CASE STUDIES IN PARTICIPATION AND REPRESENTATION

We now turn to an examination of participation and representation in several of the established democracies among our case studies. This will allow us to examine the interaction and overall effect of the electoral system, parties and the party system, and civil society on citizens' ability to participate and be represented. It will illustrate as well the questions and trade-offs addressed above.

CASE Study

THE UNITED KINGDOM: SMD/FPTP, TWO PARTIES, AND PLURALISM

CASE SYNOPSIS

The United Kingdom is a paradigmatic case of a two-party, SMD system with a pluralist interest-group system. Of thirty-six long-established democracies, Britain ranked third on an "index of interest-group pluralism," behind only Canada and Greece (Taylor et al. 2014, 196). As Duverger's Law would predict, its FPTP system has produced a two-party system, but there are indications that this may be evolving. Due to both the origins and more recent internal battles of the Labour Party, a third party has always survived, though the electoral system prevented it from winning many seats. The 2010 election produced a rare coalition government that included the third party, the first coalition since World War II, but the 2015 election once again gave one of the two major parties a clear majority. Britain nonetheless is part of a European trend of declining support for the major parties, with new parties gaining ground in recent elections as well. A similar decline of traditional interest-group influence has occurred. What exactly this portends of the country's political system in the longer run remains uncertain.

- ELECTORAL SYSTEM SMD and FPTP
- PARTY SYSTEM Two-party, but third-party survival, and declining support for major parties
- CIVIL SOCIETY Pluralist, but declining social capital and traditional interest groups
- TRENDS AND REFORMS Referendum to change the electoral system

In 2016 the long-standing British two-party system looked to be in disarray. Having lost the referendum on leaving the European Union (EU), Conservative prime minister David Cameron resigned only a little more than a year after winning an outright majority in Parliament and was replaced as PM by one of his cabinet ministers, Theresa May. The other major party, Labour, was under the leadership of Jeremy Corbyn, a leftist popular with the party's core supporters but so unpopular with his own MPs that they forced an unusual party leadership election in 2016 to try to unseat him. Despite Labour MPs' opposition, party members easily reelected Corbyn as leader. The perennial third party, the Liberal Democrats, who had been in an unusual coalition government with the Conservatives from 2010 to 2015, saw its share of the vote collapse from 23 percent in 2010 to 8 percent in 2015. Meanwhile, the Scottish National Party (SNP), which favored the secession of Scotland, swept almost all the Scottish seats in Parliament in 2015, decimating Labour's vote there, and the nationalist United Kingdom Independence Party (UKIP), which favored leaving the EU, quadrupled its share of the vote (see Figure 6.8). The leadership of both major parties supported staying in the EU, though the Conservative Party was split on the issue; the voters, however, supported "Brexit," responding to a populist, anti-immigration campaign led by UKIP and the maverick Conservative mayor of London. In spite of the seeming decline of the major parties, though, opinion polls in 2016 showed about two-thirds of Britons still planned to vote for one of the two major parties in the next general election. Despite the turmoil, the SMD system still seems likely to favor the two major parties.

British parties began in the nineteenth century as cadre parties within Parliament, divided primarily over how much power they thought should be reserved for the long-ruling aristocracy. As the reforms of the later nineteenth century (see chapter 3) expanded the franchise, the two major parties, the Conservatives and the Liberals, slowly built mass parties to incorporate and appeal to the growing number of (male) voters. In 1900 trade unions and socialist societies founded the Labour Party. Throughout the world, parties formed or evolved to represent workers as industrialization expanded,

Jeremy Corbyn, leader of the Labour Party, speaks to supporters in August 2016. Corbyn was elected by party stalwarts as party leader, but the party's MPs held a vote of no confidence in him after Britain voted to leave the EU, forcing a second party election in late 2016. In the 2015 general election, Labour lost badly, leading to Corbyn's selection as the new party leader, but opinion polls in 2016 suggested that under him the party would lose the next election as well.

Photo by Rob Stothard/Getty Images

but only in Britain did labor unions successfully create their own party. By the 1920s, Labour had replaced the Liberals as the second major party and had led its first government. The Liberals survived as a third party, but until the 1970s they received a small fraction of the vote and only a handful of seats in Parliament. In terms of seats and votes, the United Kingdom for all intents and purposes had a two-party system. The SMD system that relies on simple FPTP to determine the winner of each election usually translates modest electoral victories into significant parliamentary seat majorities, as Figure 6.8 demonstrates for 2015, ensuring that one of the two dominant parties can form a single-party government.

The origins of British parties show clearly why British elections were long influenced by exceptionally strong class-based voting. The Conservative Party is historically the party of the aristocracy, long proclaiming what it termed "Tory paternalism": the upper class would take good care of the rest of society. Liberals arose originally as the class of the new entrepreneurs of the industrial era, favoring free enterprise and reduction in aristocratic privilege. Both gained support mainly from the middle and upper classes by the mid-twentieth century. Labour, of course, was literally the party of trade unions, the vast majority of whose members supported it. This class-based voting broke down, as it did all over Europe, as manual workers' share of the total population shrank and their interests diverged. In response, the Labour Party in particular shifted its ideology under party leader and PM Tony Blair in the 1990s, moving to a more centrist position to attract more middle-class voters. Evans and Tilley (2013) argued that Britons' class-based ideologies had not shifted that much; instead, the main party's ideologies had moved to the center, leaving voters on both sides without parties to support. On the right, the success of the nationalist UKIP may reflect that. On the left, the election of a much more leftist Labour leader, Jeremy Corbyn, in 2015 may augur well for the party's future, though opinion polls in 2016 suggested just the opposite.

As elsewhere in Europe, the decline of class-based voting also resulted in the decline of the two major parties' share of the vote. Between 1974 and 2010, the Liberal Party (renamed the Liberal Democratic Party in 1988) won between 15 and 25 percent of the vote but always a much smaller share of seats, thanks to the FPTP electoral system. In 2010 neither major party was very popular in the context of the Great Recession. The election (see Figure 6.8) denied the Conservatives a majority of seats, necessitating a coalition government for the first time since World War II. The Conservative PM, David Cameron, invited the Liberal Democrats to join his government to form a parliamentary majority. The two major parties' combined share of the vote fell to just over 65 percent, the lowest total in decades. The thirty-year slide of support for the two major parties finally went far enough to deny either party a parliamentary majority, even given the effects of FPTP.

The 2015 election, though, returned the country to its traditional status of a two-party system, as the incumbent Conservatives secured a majority in Parliament and the Liberal Democrats' share of the vote collapsed. It was clear that the Liberal Democrats' support had been in part a "protest vote" against both major parties; once they were part of government, that support evaporated. As the traditional third party lost votes, though, two others gained, the SNP and UKIP, as Figure 6.8 demonstrates. Figure 6.8 also shows the effects of the FPTP system. While UKIP and the Liberal Democrats gained a larger share of the vote than had the SNP, the latter got far more seats in Parliament because its support was regionally concentrated in Scotland, where it won virtually all the seats. UKIP's 12.6 percent of the vote was unprecedented in the nationalist party's history, but because it was spread throughout England it gained only one seat in Parliament. The Green Party (not shown in Figure 6.8) won 3.8 percent of the vote—almost as much as the SNP—but won only one parliamentary seat, as opposed to SNP's fifty-six.

The disproportionality of Britain's elections stems from the combination of its FPTP system and the continuing presence of smaller parties that collectively gained close to a third of the popular vote in recent elections. Clearly, institutional logic alone cannot explain this outcome; instead, we must turn to sociological explanations. The traditional third party, the Liberal Democrats, was long the party ideologically positioned between Labour and the Conservatives, and it was a haven for those unhappy with the two major parties; its historical legacy and a split in Labour in the 1980s allowed it to survive for decades. The SNP has arisen with Scottish nationalism. It has controlled the government in Scotland most of the time since devolution gave the region its own parliament. Although it lost the 2014 referendum on Scottish independence, its membership swelled dramatically after that loss and it subsequently swept Scotland's seats in the UK Parliament in 2015. UKIP's popularity, heavily based in England, has grown in recent years based on its primary focus: anti-immigration and leaving the EU. Its longtime leader, Nigel Farage, was a leader of the successful campaign for "Brexit" in the 2016 referendum, as he and the party rode a wave of populist support for anti-immigration policies that affected much of Europe and the United States that year. When Duverger's Law does not work for sociological reasons, the result is extreme disproportionality in the electoral system. The Liberal Democrats recognized this and demanded a most unusual referendum on a new and more proportional electoral system as a price for joining the coalition government in 2010, but Britons voted a year later to keep the FPTP system they have had for so long.

The internal organization of British parties has evolved as the parties' electoral fortunes have shifted. As is true for much of Europe, the major parties have tried to increase the role of individual members as the number of members has plummeted. Britain had no tradition of primary elections like those in the United States. Parties selected their MP candidates for each constituency and presented them to the voters. Like most European parties, sitting MPs had long controlled most real decision making in the Conservative Party. That changed after 1997, when a new party leader proposed direct election of the leader by all dues-paying party members. Candidates for individual seats are selected by dues-paying members in each constituency but are still subject to approval from national headquarters.

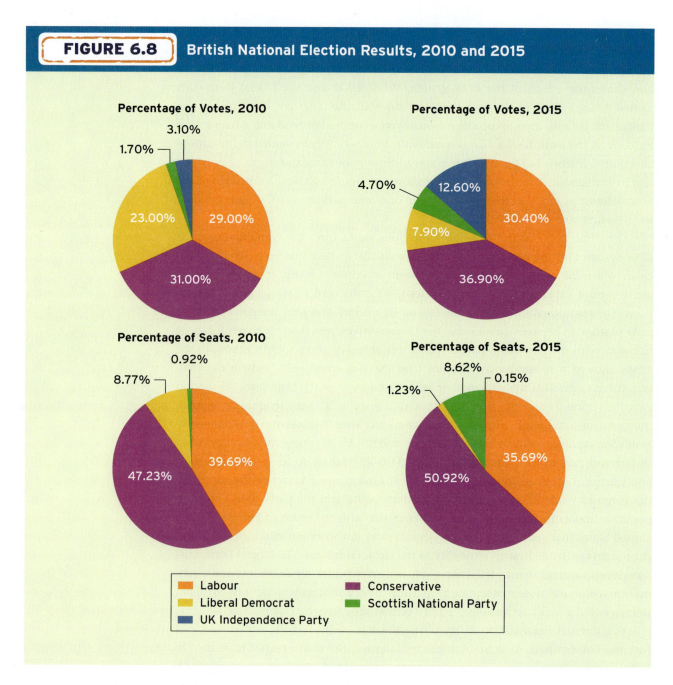

FIGURE 6.8   British National Election Results, 2010 and 2015

Percentage of Votes, 2010
- Labour 29.00%
- Conservative 31.00%
- Liberal Democrat 23.00%
- Scottish National Party 1.70%
- UK Independence Party 3.10%

Percentage of Votes, 2015
- Labour 30.40%
- Conservative 36.90%
- Liberal Democrat 7.90%
- Scottish National Party 4.70%
- UK Independence Party 12.60%

Percentage of Seats, 2010
- Labour 39.69%
- Conservative 47.23%
- Liberal Democrat 8.77%
- Scottish National Party 0.92%

Percentage of Seats, 2015
- Labour 35.69%
- Conservative 50.92%
- Liberal Democrat 1.23%
- Scottish National Party 8.62%
- UK Independence Party 0.15%

Legend:
- Labour
- Liberal Democrat
- UK Independence Party
- Conservative
- Scottish National Party

Source: BBC, "Election 2010" (http://news.bbc.co.uk/2/shared/election2010/results/); BBC, "Election 2015" (http://www.bbc.com/news/election/2015/results).

The Labour Party's initial organization was most unusual, having been created by unions rather than coming out of Parliament. Union members were automatically party members via their union membership, whatever their individual party preference. Initially, unions controlled 90 percent of the voting power in the party, so they could set the party platform, while the party's MPs selected the party leaders. Pressure from new social movements and party leaders wanting to distance the party from the declining labor unions led to reforms in the 1980s that gave equal voting weight for both the platform and leadership to three separate groups: (1) paid-up individual members, (2) unions, and (3) party MPs. In 2014 the system was changed again, giving each member one vote, thus requiring unions to have their members register as individual party members; the special role of trade unions in the party was over. While membership of both major parties is a fraction of what it was a half century ago, internal rules make both appear more "democratic" to the broader electorate.

First Past the Post

- In 2016, some fifty-six countries used "first-past-the-post" rules for their legislative elections
- These countries included the Bahamas, Canada, Jamaica, Kenya, Malaysia, Yemen, and Zambia
- The vast majority of countries using FPTP are former British colonies
- In 2016 no country in continental Europe used FPTP

Source: International Institute for Democracy and Electoral Assistance, Table of Electoral Systems Worldwide (http://www.idea.int/esd/world.cfm).

The most important players in Britain's pluralist interest-group system have long been somewhat more centralized than are interest groups in most pluralist systems because the peak associations have greater control over their members. However, the system was never as centralized as corporatist systems, as our case study of Germany below shows. Business and labor are each represented by one major peak association: the Confederation of British Industry (CBI) for business and the Trades Union Congress (TUC) for labor. In the 1960s and 1970s, Labour Party governments even created quasi-corporatist arrangements in which the party consulted regularly and formally with both groups in an attempt to set wages and other economic policies. The limited ability of the groups to control their members, though, resulted in widespread strikes in the 1970s, culminating in the "winter of discontent" in 1978–1979 and Labour's electoral defeat in 1979 at the hands of Margaret Thatcher, the new Conservative leader. Thatcher immediately ended the corporatist arrangements and largely shunned not only the TUC but also the CBI, preferring the advice and support of various conservative think tanks and ideological pressure groups.

Because decision making in Britain's parliamentary system is centralized in the cabinet, interest groups focus much more on lobbying the executive than the Parliament. Indeed, they lobby MPs primarily as a conduit to gain access to cabinet members. How much influence particular groups have, then, depends very much on which party is in power and with which groups the prime minister, in particular, is willing to work. Of course, all groups still have other means of influencing policy, such as petitioning, gaining media attention, contributing to campaigns, etc. Moosbrugger (2012) demonstrated that British interest groups can certainly have a powerful influence. The main farmers' union worked with relevant ministries to block several significant environmental policies that would hurt farmers, in spite of the fact that the vast majority of the British public favored the changes. British civil society has seen the same evolution that we noted earlier throughout Western societies: a decline in the support of traditional interest groups and the rise of new social movements. This was spurred in part by Thatcher's preference for working with smaller groups that shared her conservative ideology and her aggressive anti-union policies in the 1980s, which made organizing and striking much more difficult. Environmental, women's, antinuclear, and racial groups became important in the struggle for reorganization of the Labour Party in particular. The number of these groups has exploded since the 1960s. At the same time, the TUC in particular has declined as its membership base has contracted.

CASE Questions

1. Britain's FPTP electoral system and party structure (particularly for the Labour Party) are unlike those in most European countries, yet it has faced several of the same trends of other European countries. What might explain this?
2. What explains the survival of a viable, if small, third party in spite of Britain's FPTP electoral system? What does this suggest for the theoretical debate over sociological versus institutional explanations of the development and evolution of political parties?

GERMANY: TWO-AND-A-HALF-PARTY SYSTEM AND NEOCORPORATISM UNDER THREAT

Germany's democracy had been viewed as an unusual and exceptionally stable "two-and-a-half-party" system, with a semiproportional electoral system and a neocorporatist interest-group system. Changes in the class structure, the rise of new social movements, and the decline of religious observance have eroded the major parties' bases of support, following the trends noted for Western democracies

CASE SYNOPSIS

in general. Globalization and European unification also threatened Germany's neocorporatist system. Declining support for and power of the peak associations have made the neocorporatist institutions ever more difficult to maintain. Germany's semiproportional electoral system has allowed these changes to result in the rise of significant new parties that influence elections, most recently via the rise of a new, anti-immigrant conservative party.

- **ELECTORAL SYSTEM** Mixed proportional
- **PARTY SYSTEM** "Two-and-a-half-party," becoming multiparty
- **CIVIL SOCIETY** Neocorporatist
- **TRENDS AND REFORMS** Weakening peak associations and neocorporatism; weakening support for major parties; rising right-wing populist party and anti-immigrant movements

In the 2013 parliamentary election, Germany's two major parties gained only 67 percent of the vote, though this was better than their share of the vote in 2009 (57%), their lowest combined total ever. Chancellor Angela Merkel of the Christian Democratic Union (CDU/CSU) scored a personal victory, with her party receiving more votes than either major party had in years. Nonetheless, the decline of the long-dominant parties was clear, as were its causes: the waning significance of long-standing class and religious divisions and the partial unraveling of Germany's neocorporatist system. The 2013 election also heralded the demise of Germany's traditional third party; support for the Free Democrats Party (FDP), which had been the junior coalition party in most of Germany's post–World War II governments, fell so low that it failed to gain representation in parliament for the first time in its history. Leftist parties, the Left Party and Green Party, gained some seats, while a new anti-immigrant party, Alternative for Germany (AfD), just missed getting enough votes to enter parliament, suggesting Germany has shifted definitively to a multiparty system.

The instability of Germany's first democracy, the Weimar Republic (1918–1933), and subsequent rise of Adolf Hitler profoundly influenced the post–World War II system the Allies helped create in West Germany. Parties were central to the new democracy and were explicitly recognized and regulated in the Basic Law, West Germany's constitution. The major parties that developed were the Christian Democrats and the Social Democrats (SPD). The third or "half" party was the liberal FDP, which, as in Britain, lies ideologically between the two major parties. The key difference with Britain is that in Germany's mixed PR system the FDP regularly participated as a junior partner in coalition governments, as neither major party won enough seats to govern alone. The German electoral system also requires that a party must receive 5 percent of the national vote to win seats in parliament, thus excluding the very smallest parties from power. This produced the stable, "two-and-a-half-party" system that continued through the end of the twentieth century. Since 1969, power has shifted back and forth between the two major parties, almost always in coalition with the FDP or, more recently, the Green Party (in a coalition with the SPD). The two major parties increasingly became catch-all parties, competing for the most votes via expanded government programs but having limited ideological differences.

At the same time that the stable party system flourished, German neocorporatism reached its zenith. The German Trade Union Federation claimed to represent 85 percent of the unionized workforce. Business is represented by three peak associations, each representing different-sized firms. From the 1950s through the 1970s, these peak associations worked closely with the major political parties and the government to set wages and social policies. Most MPs on key committees were members of one of the peak associations, and many had worked professionally for them before entering parliament. SPD MPs often had strong union backgrounds, and CDU/CSU MPs had business connections, though labor and business associations had members in and maintained close contact with both parties.

Political scientists saw this model of stability and neocorporatism as a great success into the 1970s. Underlying it, however, were trends that would raise serious questions. Popular discontent became quite apparent by the late 1960s. A strong student movement arose that was opposed to the Vietnam War, German rearmament, the consumer culture, and Germany's strong support for the United States in the Cold War. Growing unemployment affected would-be middle-class college students and working-class young adults alike. All of this discontent culminated in widespread protests in 1968, which the government forcefully put down. The demise of this movement led young political activists to pursue several different paths. Some founded feminist, antinuclear, and environmental groups, while others formed what came to be known as "civil action groups." These were small, local groups of

German chancellor Angela Merkel meets with cabinet ministers and leaders of Germany's peak labor and business associations in 2015. Under Germany's neocorporatist system, the peak associations and government leaders regularly set economic policies collectively. In recent years, globalization has weakened the power of the peak associations and governments have had repeated problems negotiating agreements to guide economic policy.

ADAM BERRY/AFP/Getty Images

usually not more than thirty people that were focused on petitioning local government on issues such as building new schools or cleaning up pollution. By 1979, some 1.5 million Germans were participating in at least fifty thousand such groups. In the mid-1970s, some of the groups that focused primarily on the environment came together to form a national association. By 1980, this association helped create the Green Party, and in 1983 it became the first new party since 1949 to break the 5 percent barrier and gain seats in parliament, taking votes mainly from the SPD. In 1998 it joined a coalition government with the SPD, creating what came to be called the "Red–Green Alliance" (*Red* referring to socialism), which ruled until 2005. The semi-proportional system allowed the environmental movement to become a successful political party, in contrast to Britain, where a Green Party exists but has never gained significant representation.

The second major shift in the German party system came with the reunification with East Germany in 1990. With reunification, the West German electoral system and constitution covered the entire reunited country, and initially, the major parties in the west reached out and worked with like-minded parties in the east. Ultimately, they absorbed many of the eastern parties. The former ruling Communist Party rebranded itself as the Party of Social Democracy (PDS) and positioned itself ideologically left of the SPD to champion causes particularly relevant to the poorer and heavily unemployed regions in eastern Germany. While initially receiving little support, it slowly expanded its appeal, winning 21 percent of the eastern vote by 1998. In 2007 it merged with some former members of the SPD to create the Left Party and became the third-largest party in parliament after the 2013 election, winning 8.6 percent of the national vote.

At the same time that the new social movements, new parties, and reunification were altering the landscape of party politics, economic problems were threatening neocorporatism. The ability of the peak associations to enforce collective wage agreements was key to their power and influence. In the 1980s, these key associations began to weaken as unemployment rose and unions allowed greater flexibility in setting working conditions within firms. As control of working conditions became more localized, however, local unions had less reason to obey the dictates of the peak associations, thereby weakening their role. Facing rising costs from exporters elsewhere in the world, smaller businesses began leaving the employers' associations as well. The decline of traditional manufacturing, meanwhile, caused union membership to plummet by four million during the 1990s. The peak associations for both business and labor were speaking for and able to enforce central agreements on a shrinking share of the private sector, further weakening neocorporatism.

Politicians responded to these trends by distancing themselves from the peak associations. Far fewer members of parliament from both parties were members of or worked in the key associations. In the face of these changes and continuing high unemployment, neither the CDU/CSU government prior to 1998 nor the SPD/Green government from 1998 to 2005 was able to negotiate new binding agreements with business and labor for fundamental economic reforms. The result was the closely divided 2005 election that led to an unusual "grand coalition" government that included both major parties. The new chancellor, Angela Merkel, was the leader of the CDU, and the first woman and first East German to lead the country. Although the CDU/CSU won the 2009 election, the major parties' share of the total vote dropped to an all-time low of 57 percent, largely due to an 11-point decrease in support of the SPD. As Figure 6.9 shows, the vote share of all three minor parties increased, with each surpassing 10 percent. The elimination of the FDP from parliament in the 2013 election forced Merkel once again to form a "grand coalition" with the SPD in order to form a government.

Most union members still support the SPD and religious voters support the CDU/CSU, but economic changes and secularization have meant fewer voters in both categories. In 2011 the Green Party reached a new milestone by winning control of a *Land* (state) government for the first time and coming in second (ahead of the CDU/CSU) in another. In 2013 a new right-wing populist party opposed to Germany's policies on the euro crisis (see chapter 10) almost gained enough votes to enter parliament. The Alternative for Germany (AfD), founded in April 2013, garnered 4.7 percent of the national vote in the September 2013 elections. The party initially focused on economic issues, criticizing Chancellor Merkel's policies toward Greece and other bankrupt "Eurozone" countries. While the party continued to gain attention, it also had to contend with internal strife—one faction focused on economic issues and another on immigration. This increased attention on immigration coincided with the rise of an anti-immigrant movement, Patriotic Europeans Against the Islamization of the West (PEGIDA), which held weekly rallies of up to 10,000 people by December 2014.

In 2015 tensions within AfD grew and by mid-year the party split, with a majority supporting Frauke Petry, who shifted the party's focus to immigration, arguing that too many immigrants, particularly Muslims, were threatening national identity. While AfD and PEGIDA remain separate entities, AfD nonetheless began championing the anti-immigrant cause; by 2016 it gained representation in nine (of sixteen) German state parliaments. The most notable elections were held in September 2016 in Chancellor Merkel's home state, Mecklenburg–West Pomerania, where the AfD won 21 percent of the regional election vote and outpolled the Christian Democrats, and in Berlin, where the CDU suffered its worst defeat since World War II and the AfD entered the legislature for the first time. Although the CDU led in many public opinion polls in September 2016 (31% support), fewer than 50 percent of respondents agreed that Merkel should run for reelection as chancellor (DW.com 2016). Much of the AfD support, and disagreement with Frau Merkel, comes as a reaction

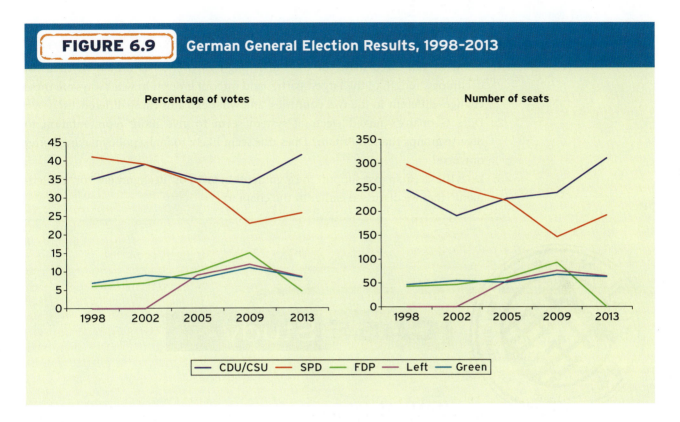

FIGURE 6.9   **German General Election Results, 1998-2013**

Percentage of votes

Number of seats

CDU/CSU — SPD — FDP — Left — Green

Source: Election Resources on the Internet, "Elections to the German Bundestag" (http://electionresources.org/de).

to her and the government's response to the 2015–2016 refugee crisis in which the chancellor welcomed over 1.1 million Syrian and other refugees. While initially supportive, popular opinion quickly turned against her policies, with people fearing that the country could not absorb that many immigrants that quickly. While Germans are not as anti-immigrant as many other European countries, 61 percent in 2016 believed that Muslim immigrants increased the possibility of a terrorist attack and that Muslims did not want to integrate culturally into Germany (Wike, Stokes, and Simmons 2016).

These trends of declining older parties and the rise of several new ones have been strong enough that Thomas Poguntke (2012) argued that Germany's "two-and-a-half-party" system has fundamentally changed to a multiparty system similar to what Italy used to have, with two large parties vying for control but likely to require the support of at least one of several minor parties to form coalition governments. If true, this change has the potential to reduce Germany's famed political stability.

CASE Questions

1. Germany has faced many of the same long-term trends as Britain in terms of declining strength of the largest parties and interest groups. In what ways are these changes different in the two countries, and what explains those differences?

2. Does Germany's mixed electoral system seem to give more representation to diverse groups than in Britain? Does this seem likely to make policymaking better or worse?

3. Does the German case support the arguments in favor of "dealignment" or "realignment" that we discussed earlier in the chapter?

JAPAN: FROM DOMINANT-PARTY TO TWO-PARTY SYSTEM?

CASE SYNOPSIS

A 1994 electoral reform in Japan was one of the biggest systemic changes in established democracies of the last generation. It created a mixed electoral system that showed the distinct differences between SMD and PR elections in the same country. By 2009, an opposition party defeated the long-ruling Liberal Democratic Party (LDP) and took the reins of government for the first time. The fifteen-year history since the reform appeared to provide a textbook example of Duverger's Law at work, as a new electoral system seemed to transform Japan into a two-party system. The LDP's return to power in late 2012, though, raised questions about whether that transformation would really occur. The electoral change also resulted in internal strengthening of Japan's parties. Participation is increasing in what had been a very weak civil society, though voter turnout has hit historic lows.

- ELECTORAL SYSTEM Mixed
- PARTY SYSTEM Dominant-party system, shifting to two-party system?
- CIVIL SOCIETY Weak interest groups, but signs of growing strength
- TRENDS AND REFORMS Electoral reform from SNTV to mixed system; shift to two-party system?; low voter turnout

On August 30, 2009, the Democratic Party of Japan (DPJ) swept into power, winning 308 of the 480 seats in the lower and more powerful house of the Diet, Japan's parliament. It unseated the LDP that had ruled nearly continuously since 1955. Many analysts saw the 2009 election as the dawning of a new era in Japan. The LDP had dominated Japanese politics from the first election in 1955. Despite its name, it was a conservative party that supported the interests of business and economic growth. The party guided the creation of Japan's phenomenally successful development model (see chapter 10), winning a majority of the legislative seats in every election to the Diet from 1955 to 1993 and always gaining a plurality (though, after 1963, rarely a majority) of the national vote. Its great economic success until 1990 allowed it to provide benefits to large segments of the population, including the rapidly growing urban middle class. It was a relatively weak party in terms of internal organization, with strong factions, but the electoral system allowed those factions to share power and keep the party from splitting.

Japan's unusual single, nontransferable vote (SNTV) electoral system prior to 1993 was crucial to the LDP's success. SNTV has large, multimember districts, but each voter votes for only one candidate. The candidates who receive the most votes win. Each party, therefore, runs several candidates in each district, and the winning candidates often receive only 15 to 20 percent of the votes in their district. Like SMD, the system gave the winning party a larger share of seats in the legislature than its share of votes, so even as the LDP's popularity declined, it maintained majority control of the Diet. In addition, district lines were intentionally gerrymandered to overrepresent rural areas, the LDP's main support base.

The multimember districts under SNTV allowed several factions within the dominant party to run candidates and potentially win seats in each district. Most campaigns were battles among the LDP factions rather than between the LDP and other parties. LDP factions were based not on ideology but rather on clientelist networks. Under SNTV, a winning party had to run several candidates in each district who would draw support from different groups of voters so as not to dilute the support of other candidates in the party. To gain the resources to compete, potential candidates would become loyal members of a faction. A patron who was a leading national party (and often government) official led each faction and provided campaign funds as well as patronage to his followers. To make sure no single candidate took too many votes away from the party's other candidates in the same district, each candidate also developed a local voter-mobilization machine, called *koenkai,* which consisted of area notables who could deliver votes. A candidate then promised the factional leader that he could use his *koenkai* to deliver a certain percentage of the vote in a district if the patron would provide campaign financing. Locally, a *koenkai* could transfer its loyalty from a retiring candidate to a new one, sometimes the original candidate's son. As in any other dominant-party systems, several small opposition parties continued to exist, but they never threatened the LDP's grip on power.

An economic crisis in 1990 and growing corruption scandals inspired the 1994 reform of the electoral system. Patronage politics in the LDP took the form of governmental largesse such as infrastructure improvements (and awarding the associated construction contracts to local supporters). Although this is common in many countries, Japanese politicians were also expected to attend local events, such as the weddings and funerals of their supporters, and provide generous gifts. Japanese elections, not surprisingly, became the most expensive in the world, in spite of the fact that candidates were not allowed to advertise on television and the length of campaigns was strictly limited. Patrons had to raise huge sums via corrupt deals that provided kickbacks from large businesses in exchange for government contracts or exemptions from governmental regulations. As the economy and therefore the popularity of the LDP slipped, citizens and the media began to question this system, leading to the revelations of major corruption we discussed in chapter 5. The economic crisis was the final straw. Perceiving imminent electoral disaster, several major LDP leaders left the party in 1993 to form new opposition parties. Some formed a coalition government after the 1993 election that would briefly exclude the LDP from power for the first time since its founding.

The new government passed a fundamental reform of the electoral system, creating a mixed system in which 300 seats in the Diet would be elected in single-member districts and 180 would be elected via closed-list PR. A crucial difference between this new system and Germany's is that Japan's is noncompensatory, meaning that the SMD and PR votes are completely separate (though candidates can simultaneously run in both elections). Because there are far more SMD than PR seats, the system overall is more majoritarian than proportional. This is reinforced by the practice of both major parties awarding PR seats to candidates who perform well but do not win SMD seats. This gives candidates an incentive to campaign hard in an SMD election even if they

Prime Minister Shinzō Abe, second from left, and other LDP leaders smile at party headquarters during the 2016 vote for Japan's upper house of parliament. The LDP won handily, giving it a two-thirds majority in both houses of parliament and therefore the ability to change the constitution, which it might do to remove the "pacifism" rule imposed by the United States after World War II.

David Mareuil/Anadolu Agency/Getty Images

have little chance of winning. Reformers believed this new system would reduce the role of money (and therefore corruption) in the electoral system, limit the power of the LDP, and lead to the emergence of a two-party system.

As Figure 6.10 demonstrates, until the 2012 election Japan seemed to be a model of the power of Duverger's Law. By the 2000 election, the DPJ had emerged as the primary opposition to the LDP. Smaller parties survived, but over the first five elections after the reform, the two largest parties' share of both votes and parliamentary seats rose, mainly due to the SMD seats. The difference between votes and seats in the SMD results demonstrates once again the disproportionality of the SMD system. At the district level, the trend was toward two candidates per district, and increasingly those contests are between the two largest parties (Reed 2005, 283). The DPJ's failure to revive the economy in the wake of the Great Recession and respond well to the devastating *tsunami* in 2011, however, caused it to fragment, as dozens of the party's MPs defected to other parties or created new ones; it

in CONTEXT

SNTV

- The SNTV voting system used in Japan prior to 1993 is one of the world's rarest electoral systems

- Currently, only two countries use SNTV: Afghanistan and the Pitcairn Islands

- SNTV systems have the lowest average turnout of any electoral system: just 54 percent

- SNTV encourages better representation of minority parties and independent candidates than do simple SMD systems because SNTV elects multiple candidates in the same district

Source: International Institute for Democracy and Electoral Assistance, Table of Electoral Systems Worldwide (http://www.idea.int/esd/world.cfm).

suffered a huge loss in popularity. Forced to hold an early election in December 2012, it lost at the hands of the LDP, which regained majority control of the Diet and therefore the government.

Reed and colleagues (2012) argued that the 2012 election resulted in "the at least temporary disappearance of Japan's Duvergerian two-party system." The LDP landslide resulted not from the party's renewed popularity but from the collapse of the DPJ, which allowed a significant third party to arise and split the anti-LDP vote. Voter turnout in 2012 plummeted to 59 percent from 69 percent in 2009, and the vast majority of the abstentions were former DPJ voters who were alienated but did not support the LDP either. The LDP won only 2 more PR seats than it did in 2009, but the divided opposition vote allowed it to claim a whopping 173 additional SMD seats (see Figure 6.10).

In December 2014 victorious LDP PM Shinzō Abe called a "snap election" just two years after winning office in order to secure a new term while he was still popular. The 2014 election largely replayed 2012, with the LDP garnering almost exactly the same share of the vote and parliamentary seats. The opposition, though, seemed to start to learn the lesson of 2012 and the logic of Duverger's Law. The DPJ and smaller opposition parties coordinated their campaigns much more in 2014, with only one party running a candidate in many constituencies where that particular party or candidate seemed most likely to win (Scheiner, Smith, and Thies 2016). In 2016 the DPJ merged with a smaller party to form the new Democratic Party to contest elections to Japan's weaker upper house of parliament. While the electoral results did not improve for the opposition, coordination and then merger among opposition parties showed the logic of SMD elections. As of 2016, though, the LDP and its coalition partner commanded a two-thirds majority in both houses of parliament, allowing Abe to reform the constitution single-handedly if he could gain his party's support. He hoped to use that power to end Japan's pledge never to have a military, imposed by the American occupation after World War II.

The electoral reform induced internal changes to parties as well: all have become more centrally controlled. With the advent of the closed-list PR system, party endorsement became more important, enhancing party leaders' influence over local politicians in all parties. The combined effect of the rise of charismatic leader, PM Junichirō Koizumi and the end of multimember districts greatly reduced the power of factions within the LDP. They still matter for gaining certain party and bureaucratic posts but no longer dominate the electoral process as they once did. Politicians still have and use their *koenkai* to campaign and raise funds, but their share of total campaign expenditures has dropped relative to central party money, and the overall cost of campaigns has declined as well (Carlson 2007). Kabashima and Steel (2010) found that *koenkai* also became less important to voters; they increasingly shifted their attention during campaigns from local leaders to national media and the prime ministerial candidates.

Political scientists have always considered Japan's civil society rather weak. Business was certainly very well represented and served during the period of LDP dominance. Most major business interests were represented in the *Keidanren*, a single organization closely associated with and supported by the ruling party in a neo-corporatist manner. At least as important, though, were the connections among key bureaucrats, major political leaders, and individual businesses. A major business interest, a relevant bureaucratic agency, and key members of the Diet would form an iron triangle. They allowed privileged business interests, especially the large conglomerates known as *keiretsu* (see chapter 10), personal access to and influence over governmental decisions, but they excluded other interests. They also fuelled the corruption for which Japan would become famous in the 1980s and 1990s. As globalization rose, larger businesses became increasingly active in global trade and therefore needed less from the government in terms of special favors and regulations. Accordingly, they reduced their unquestioned support of the LDP, a factor that led to the LDP splits in the early 1990s. Even with all of these changes, however, business remains the organized interest with the greatest access to and influence over the central government.

Japan's rate of unionization has always been lower than that found in most of Europe and, as in other wealthy nations, has declined in the face of globalization.

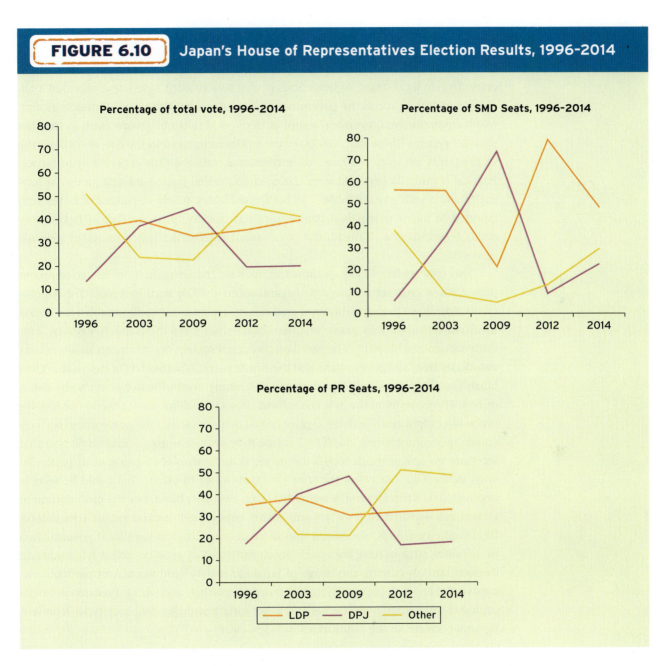

FIGURE 6.10   Japan's House of Representatives Election Results, 1996–2014

Percentage of total vote, 1996–2014

Percentage of SMD Seats, 1996–2014

Percentage of PR Seats, 1996–2014

LDP — DPJ — Other

Source: Election Resources on the Internet, "Parliamentary Elections in Japan" (http://electionresources.org/jp).

Two major union organizations existed until their merger in 1989. The group actually fielded its own candidates in the first elections after the merger, arguing that no major party could defend workers adequately. By the mid-1990s, though, its members increasingly supported the LDP or the DPJ. Throughout this process, unions never gained great influence over government policy.

Japan has a pluralist interest-group system, but one tightly regulated by the bureaucracy. To gain legal status, organizations in civil society must have the approval of a relevant ministry, a process the government has used to limit the scope of interest groups. Many environmental, women's, senior citizens', and religious groups exist, as in other pluralist systems (more than 400,000 were legally recognized in the late 1990s), but the vast majority are local and have few professional staff and little expertise or influence. Political scientist Robert Pekkanen (2006) characterized Japan's interest groups as having "members without advocates." In the United States, nearly 40 percent of all research reported in major newspapers comes from civil society organizations; in Japan, only about 5 percent does. Instead, the government itself is the major source of reported research.

This civil society weakness, however, may be changing. In 1999 the government passed a law creating a nonprofit organizations (NPOs) legal category. This significantly liberalized the regulations on civil society organizations and provided tax breaks for financial support to many of them. More than forty thousand NPOs were officially recognized by 2011. The new law gives civil society organizations much greater autonomy from the government and the ruling party. Whether NPOs' new status gives Japan's civil society significantly greater autonomy and influence is yet to be determined. The majority of the new NPOs focus on social welfare issues that do not involve much direct "political" activity. Ogawa (2009) contended that the government actively encourages volunteerism via NPOs because they provide unpaid social services so that the state no longer needs to. Furthermore, volunteerism is encouraged in particular areas that are supportive of the state's needs but not in others that could be seen as oppositional or threatening. Martin (2011), on the other hand, saw the proliferation of groups as a sign that civil society and citizen engagement are increasing. Focusing on local women's groups, she found that since decentralization gave local governments more power, citizens have engaged in more participatory activity such as referenda and demonstrations, belying the image of Japanese society (and women in particular) as passive. Greater volunteer activity is certainly occurring, and with it presumably social capital is increasing, but whether this is creating a stronger civil society to represent Japanese citizens in the political realm is less clear.

CASE Questions

1. What does the complex history of the effects of electoral reform in Japan since 1994 teach us about Duverger's Law?
2. The recent rise of civil society in Japan has been primarily at the local level. Can such activity have a major impact on how well a democracy functions, or are national-level changes essential?

INDIA: FROM DOMINANT-PARTY TO MULTIPARTY DEMOCRACY

CASE SYNOPSIS

Institutionalists would expect India's FPTP electoral system to create a two-party system. In India, however, great social and cultural diversity, a federal system, and FPTP have combined to produce numerous state-level two-party systems (following Duverger's Law). These forces have collectively created a multiparty national system, with two large national parties competing for power, usually leading multiparty coalitions. Both major parties have lost support to the growing numbers of regional and state-level parties. This history is partly explained by the expansion of civil society, as excluded groups have organized and begun demanding greater access and participation. A pluralist interest-group system looks quite different in a country where the most important divisions are based not on industrialization but on region, ethnicity, caste, and religion. While often corrupt and sometimes violent, India's democracy has nonetheless kept interest groups and parties mostly operating within institutionalized bounds. It has also been a system in which participation and representation have expanded over the decades.

- ELECTORAL SYSTEM SMD/FPTP in a federal system

- PARTY SYSTEM Dominant party, 1947–1977; multiparty since

- CIVIL SOCIETY Language, caste, and religious groups more important than sectoral groups

- TRENDS AND REFORMS Shift to multiparty system and coalition government, but SMD produces two-party contests in many states; single-party government since 2014

The Indian National Congress party (commonly called the "Congress") led India to independence. The charismatic leaders Mahatma Gandhi and Jawaharlal Nehru created a party that dominated Indian politics for four decades. Nehru served as prime minister until his death and was succeeded two years later by his daughter, Indira Gandhi, who led the country from 1966 to 1984 (except for 1977–1980); she in turn was succeeded by her son, Rajiv, from 1984 to 1989. To achieve this dominance, Congress became a very broad-based party. While proclaiming a transformative ideology of social democracy, it mobilized support primarily via local Brahmin landowners, who effectively controlled the votes of millions of peasants. Ziegfeld (2016), among others, termed India a "clientelistic democracy" because clientelism is the primary (though not only) way parties mobilize support. Because India uses an

FPTP electoral system (adopted from its British colonizers), Congress never had to win an outright majority of the vote to control a majority of seats in parliament, typically winning a little over 40 percent of the vote. As in any dominant-party system, the most important political battles were among factions within the ruling party.

Opposition to Congress initially came from two ideological alternatives: communism and Hindu nationalism. The larger of two communist parties controlled two state governments for many years. It was sometimes part of a Congress-led coalition government at the national level and maintained a steady share of parliamentary seats until a precipitous drop in 2009. **Hindu nationalism** dates back to the late nineteenth century. Hindu nationalists call for a Hindu conception of the Indian nation, one based on the three pillars of geographical unity of all of India, racial descent from Aryan ancestors, and a common culture with Hindu roots, as we discussed in chapter 4. In the 1980s, the Bharatiya Janata Party (BJP) emerged as the primary Hindu nationalist party and the largest rival to the Congress, with its greatest strength in the northern, Hindi-speaking region of the country, where both Hinduism and caste identities are strongest.

The first opposition victories over Congress came at the state level in 1967. In many states, elections became essentially two-party races between Congress and a local, state-level party (or the communist party in a couple of states). With the rise of the BJP in the 1980s and 1990s, the Hindu nationalists came to compete with state-level parties, especially in the north, to the exclusion of Congress. The importance of regional parties increased notably after the 1989 election that produced a coalition government; prior to then they typically gained about a quarter of the total vote, but after 1989 they averaged about 45 percent. Zeigfeld (2016) argued that regional parties gained such support not because Indian voters supported appeals to regional interests but because Indian elites found it beneficial to create regional parties. All parties, whether national or regional, rely primarily on clientelist means of mobilizing voters, so voters care more about the benefits they might receive from a party than its ideology or identity. Because clientelism requires local connections, creating nationwide parties is difficult, Zeigfeld argued, and India's federal and FPTP electoral system provides an institutional context in which it is easy to create regional parties. In the era of coalition government after 1989, regional politicians could potentially benefit greatly by controlling a regional party with which they could bargain for a place in the coalition government. Hence, after 1989, the number of regional parties increased significantly. What emerged, then, was a system with two major national parties (Congress and the BJP) and numerous regional parties. Each regional party that competed against a national party successfully at the state level sent a handful of MPs to the national parliament. In the process, the total number of parties has exploded, from only 50 in 1952 to 342 in 2009 (Hasan 2010, 245). The number of "effective parties" in parliament increased from 4.8 in 1989 to 7.7 in 2009 (Palshikar 2013, 95).

Every election from 1989 to 2014 resulted in a coalition government, since neither of the major parties has been able to win a majority of parliamentary seats. Anti-Congress coalitions ruled from 1989 to 1991 and 1996 to 2004, while Congress led coalition governments from 1991 to 1996 and again from 2004 to 2014. By the late

Hindu nationalism
In India, a movement to define the country as primarily Hindu; the founding ideology of the BJP

1990s, as political leaders realized coalitions were essential, they began forming them before elections, led by a national party and supported by numerous state-level allies, so that elections came to be contests among two major alliances and one or two smaller ones. Electoral losses were the result not only of receiving fewer votes but also of parties' shifting alliances. The alliances were based more on practical considerations, such as geographic interests and striking deals with the national parties, than on ideological affinities among coalition partners.

In 2014, the BJP became the first party besides Congress to win an outright majority in parliament since independence. The Congress-led coalition that had been in power for a decade became increasingly unpopular, as economic growth slowed, corruption scandals grew, and Prime Minister Manmohan Singh seemed ineffectual. Both parties entered the campaign under unusually prominent leaders. Rahul Gandhi, scion of the Nehru–Gandhi dynasty, led Congress, while Chief Minister (the equivalent of governor) Narendra Modi of Gujarat led the BJP. Modi had become a charismatic leader who grew up in poverty and was seen to have instituted effective economic reforms in his home state. The BJP emphasized economic reforms over its traditional Hindu nationalism (though the latter did not disappear entirely) and successfully tailored its campaign message to the interests of voters in differing states (Mitra and Schöttli 2016).Voter turnout set an all-time record and the BJP increased its share of the vote from 19 percent in 2009 to 31 percent, with Congress dropping from 29 percent to 19 percent. It was a historic loss for Congress. In India's SMD system, the BJP's 31 percent of the vote was widespread, so it captured 52 percent of parliamentary seats, giving it sole control of the government—the first time any party had achieved that since 1989. While it was a historic victory, subsequent BJP losses in state elections in 2015 and 2016 still suggested that Indian politics would remain competitive for years to come.

These fundamental electoral changes played themselves out at the same time major changes in Indian civil society were taking place. As in most postcolonial, primarily rural countries, the most important groups in civil society are not trade unions and business associations. Both certainly exist, but they are relatively weak. Most workers are in the informal sector and are typically not members of unions. They do organize, however, and in India women in the informal sector in particular have formed associations to demand greater social services from the state, rather than the traditional labor rights that typically interest unions (Agarwala 2013). Indeed, in September 2016, Indian trade unions called what became one of the biggest strikes in human history, as tens of millions of public-sector employees walked off the job to protest the Modi government's market-oriented economic reforms. In response, the government increased the minimum wage, among other reforms. An important farmers' movement is probably the strongest formal-sector organization.

While these class-based groups certainly mattered, they are ultimately overshadowed in civil society by groups championing ethnic, religious, or caste interests. These groups came out of and appeal to the poor, rural majority but ultimately have come to speak for many urban citizens as well. Numerous movements initially arose around ethnic identity, based primarily on language. This was particularly true in the non-Hindi-speaking south of the country, where groups demanded greater recognition and autonomy in India's federal system. In the end, a major government commission created additional states, drawn largely along linguistic lines, to appease these groups (see chapter 5).

Movements based on religion proved much more explosive. A Sikh movement in the 1970s ultimately turned violent. The government defeated it, but a Sikh nationalist subsequently assassinated Prime Minister Indira Gandhi. The largest religious movement is Hindu nationalism. Muslims and Sikhs vociferously oppose Hindu nationalists' emphasis on the Hindu cultural heritage of all Indians. The primary organization of Hindu nationalists is the Rashtriya Swayamsevak Sangh (RSS), founded in 1925. It became a militaristic—many say neofascist—organization that trained young men for nationalist struggle, rejecting Mahatma Gandhi's nonviolence and his mobilization of the lower castes. After being fairly quiescent during the period of Congress dominance, the RSS reemerged strongly in the 1980s and helped found the BJP. Its greatest cause became the destruction of a mosque and construction of a Hindu temple in its place in the northern city of Ayodhya. Occasional violent conflicts between Hindus and Muslims have occurred ever since, as religion has replaced language as the most volatile basis of political divisions in India. Modi was the chief minister of the state of Gujarat in 2002, when India's worst religious violence this century took place there, as Hindus massacred Muslims after the latter attacked a train of Hindu pilgrims returning from Ayodhya. While he has never been formally charged, many believe Modi at a minimum allowed the anti-Muslim pogrom to take place, and some believe he encouraged it. Since the BJP gained control of the national government under Modi, the RSS has expanded its membership dramatically.

The most common elements of Indian civil society, however, have been based on caste. The Indian caste system is an exceptionally complex social hierarchy that has changed dramatically over the past century. At an abstract level, virtually the entire society is divided into four large *varna,* or castes; in reality, there are literally thousands

Members of the Rashtriya Swayamsevak Sangh (RSS) meet at a rally in 2009. The RSS is a Hindu nationalist organization that supports the Bharatiya Janata Party (BJP). Critics argue the RSS is neofascist because of its demands that India reject its long-standing secularism and embrace a more Hindu identity.

AP Photo/Aijaz Rahi

of *jati*, localized castes with more specific identities. Traditionally, most of the distinctions among castes were based on occupation, with certain castes performing certain types of work. Along with these economic distinctions came strict social practices, such as not eating with, drinking from the same well as, or marrying a member of a caste beneath you. At the bottom of this hierarchy were the so-called untouchables, now known as *dalit*s.

Technological change, increased access to education, urbanization, and employment/education quotas for lower castes have changed the economic basis for caste divisions. Brahmin landlords no longer control land as completely and thoroughly as they once did; many of the lower-caste occupations no longer exist; and growing numbers of people of all castes have moved to cities, taking up new occupations at various levels of education and compensation. Nonetheless, caste remains very important. A 1999 survey found that 42 percent of Brahmins worked in "white-collar" professional positions or owned large businesses, as opposed to only 17 percent of middle castes and 10 percent of *dalit*s. Conversely, less than 4 percent of Brahmins worked as agricultural laborers, as opposed to 35 percent of *dalit*s.

Although the Indian constitution legally banned "untouchability" at independence, the data show that *dalit*s' position in society remains rather poor. They started associations in the colonial period, which developed rapidly after independence, and have expanded further since the 1980s. The colonial government started what Americans would call an "affirmative action" program (Indians refer to it as "positive discrimination") for *dalit*s, which gives them preferential access to education and government employment. The Indian government substantially expanded these programs starting in the 1970s. *Dalit* groups have also successfully championed the reservation of parliamentary seats exclusively for *dalit*s and "other backward castes and tribes"; these seats now constitute 120 of the nearly 600 seats in parliament. In Uttar Pradesh, a northern state, a party led by and championing *dalit*s became the BJP's chief rival for control of the state in the 1990s. Developing these caste associations has involved shifting the social construction of caste identity. Traditionally, specific caste identities were very localized, and people mainly thought of themselves in relation to other local castes above and below them. Leaders of caste-based movements, associations, and parties have helped create a more "horizontal" understanding of caste, forging common identities among similar castes with different names in different locales. These movements created a new type of caste identity to which major parties had to respond if they wanted to win elections.

Identity-based groups, however, were not the only players in Indian civil society. Movements arose shortly after independence to champion a variety of environmental issues and women's concerns. These have been quite influential. Most recently, a social movement has arisen around the issue of battling the extensive corruption that plagues India. Symbolically led by Kisan Baburao "Anna" Hazare, movement members demanded that the government pass a bill creating an anticorruption agency designed in a way they believed would produce a real reduction in corruption. Hazare went on hunger strikes in April 2011 and August 2012 that captured national and international attention and brought out tens of thousands of protesters demanding passage of the anticorruption bill. His supporters, without his approval, created a political party, Aam Aadmi, dedicated to reducing corruption. They swept into power in New Delhi, the capital, in the local elections of 2015, capturing 95 percent of the vote, but a subsequent split among their leadership hurt their ability to battle corruption in the nation's capital.

CASE Questions

1. What does the history of India's electoral and party systems teach us about the debate between institutional and sociological explanations of the evolution of political parties?
2. The "civic culture" argument we outlined in chapter 1 argued that democracy requires a certain type of culture to survive, one that characterizes the United Kingdom and the United States in particular. Comparing political participation in the Indian and the United Kingdom cases, what is your assessment of that argument?

CASE Study

BRAZIL: PARTIES AND CIVIL SOCIETY IN A YOUNG DEMOCRACY

CASE SYNOPSIS

Brazil's still-young democracy is an example of a successful transition to democracy, though it certainly has continued problems. The institutions created in the 1988 constitution satisfied the various interests involved, though they perhaps did not create the most coherent political system imaginable. Most important are weak parties, which have made policymaking difficult and accountability limited. Party strength seems to have started rising recently, though weak institutions and corruption remain serious problems. Participation is undoubtedly greater than at any time in Brazil's history, and the prominence of the PT until 2016 allowed poorer citizens more access to government

CASE SYNOPSIS

than ever before. When economic growth was strong and poverty dropping, the government was quite popular. Once economic decline set in and the PT was embroiled in a massive corruption scandal, millions turned against it, protesting in the streets, supporting the president's impeachment in 2016, and creating the greatest political crisis in the Third Republic's history.

- ELECTORAL SYSTEM Open-list PR
- PARTY SYSTEM Multiple and weak
- CIVIL SOCIETY Strong democracy movement; 2013 demonstrations
- TRENDS AND REFORMS Parties getting stronger; less clientelism

Brazil has long been one of the world's most unequal societies. From the *coronelismo* of the nineteenth century to the populism of the more industrialized twentieth century, Brazil's elite has kept the masses under its control. Given this history, January 1, 2003, was not your average day for poor Brazilians. On that day, they celebrated the inauguration of President Luiz "Lula" Inácio da Silva, a trade-union leader who grew up in poverty with a fourth-grade education. The inauguration of the leader of the social democratic Workers Party (PT) seemed to herald the fruition of Brazil's new democracy. His party, born out of the workers' struggle to gain the right to form their own unions and end military rule, was a new type of political organization. It had been created from the bottom up rather than from the top down. The popularity of Lula's innovative social welfare program (see chapter 12) and rapid economic growth (see chapter 11) gave him approval ratings of 75 percent in 2010, prompting U.S. president Barack Obama to call him "the most popular politician in the world." It came as a shock, then, when support for the PT began to collapse in 2013, and the vast majority of the country supported the impeachment of Lula's hand-picked successor in 2016.

After twenty-five years of military rule, Brazil became a full democracy again in 1989. Its long but successful shedding of military rule was a classic transition to democracy. The 1988 constitution created the presidential system we outlined in chapter 5. The most interesting and controversial element of the new democratic constitution, however, was the electoral system that has helped produce the extremely fragmented party system. Brazil uses an open-list PR system for the Chamber of Deputies, which is the lower and more powerful house of the National Congress. Each state is an electoral district that has a number of seats based loosely on its population. *Open-list* means that the individual candidates are listed on the ballot and voters can vote either for the party or an individual candidate. Within each district, a party is allotted a number of seats that is proportional to its total share of the vote, and then the individual candidates from that party who receive the most votes get those seats.

This system gives candidates an incentive to garner as many individual votes as possible to place them as high as possible among their party's candidates. It provides no incentive for candidates within the same party to cooperate with one another.

Given the long-standing role of patronage in Brazilian politics and the decentralized federal system, candidates understandably focused primarily on local issues. Most were really representatives of particular areas or particular social groups, rather than party stalwarts. They were dependent on their own ability to mobilize supporters in their home areas and on important local leaders such as mayors and governors, but they were not dependent on national parties. Indeed, national parties were dependent on locally popular candidates to garner votes that add to the party's total tally in a state.

The obvious result is weak parties. In fact, parties were so weak that between 1989 and 1995, one-third of legislators switched parties while in office. With the exception of a few major parties, most parties (like most candidates) are really local. They represent one region or sometimes are just vehicles for a particular local candidate. The electoral system has no minimum threshold of votes a party must get to gain representation in the chamber, so a locally popular candidate with a tiny fraction of the national total may well end up in office. And yes, this produces many parties in the legislature—twenty-eight after the 2014 election—though these were grouped into three broad coalitions: one supporting the PT-led government and two opposing it.

Forged in the massive strikes of 1978–1979, the PT was different from other parties in Brazil. From its first election in 1982, it refused to play by the rules of "politics as usual," insisting instead that it would recognize only those candidates whom it vetted as supporting its ideology. Because of its scathing critique of the corruption of the Brazilian political elite, it refused to cooperate with any other party. It also refused to use patronage to gain political support. Its longtime leader, Lula, began as a union leader who campaigned wearing blue jeans and using the working-class vernacular. The party's discipline and success by the 1990s led other parties to become somewhat more disciplined in imitation. Lula ran for president and came in second in the elections of 1989, 1994, and 1998, finally winning the presidency in 2002. In the end, the PT did have to make compromises to win. Most important, it dropped its opposition to forming coalitions, a crucial factor in Lula's eventual election. A scandal in 2005 involving the PT government bribing members of Congress to vote for its policies revealed that once in office it had also fallen into long-standing patterns of clientelism and patronage in order to rule.

The degree and effect of party weakness has been the subject of significant debate among scholars of Brazil. Initial assumptions in the 1990s were that such weak parties inhibited the system's ability to pass coherent legislation, thereby threatening the effectiveness of the new democracy. Legislators seemed to vote as they pleased, ignoring party leaders' positions and instructions. Political scientist Barry Ames (2001) suggested that when legislators did vote with their parties they did so not because of party loyalty but instead because they could gain patronage and resources for their home areas in exchange for their votes.

Research by Brazilian scholars Argelina Figueiredo and Fernando Limongi (2000), however, showed that legislators voted with their parties to a higher degree than had been assumed, suggesting that party leaders were able to marshal their troops in favor of their preferred policies. In the 2000s, legislators were increasingly voting as a bloc, party switching had dropped to half of what it was in the early 1990s, and electoral volatility (voters switching parties from one election to the next) was down (Hagopian et al. 2009; Santos 2008). Frances Hagopian and colleagues (2009) used a rational choice analysis of politicians' incentives to argue that changes in economic policies reduced the amount of government "pork" available to legislators. This made politicians more dependent on parties' "brands" to secure office, which in turn led them to support their party leadership more faithfully in legislative votes, stick to one party longer, and campaign on the party's platform. And though they are quite vague, the major Brazilian parties can loosely be grouped into "right," "center," and "left" parties (with several in each category). In recent elections, parties have formed coalitions to support the most popular candidates. In 2007 Brazil's top court imposed a rule that legislators could not switch parties after being elected and retain their seat, further reducing party switching; the court argued that under the PR system, legislative seats belong to the party, not the individual. Brazilian parties have gained some strength, even if they remain weak compared with parties in older democracies.

Hagopian (2016) argued that the political crisis of 2013–2016 was in part a reflection of parties' greater but still limited strength. Economic growth and improved social programs cut both inequality and poverty substantially in Brazil in the new millennium. Poor voters had greater access to formal social programs and less need for the clientelist favors politicians traditionally offered. Surveys showed that party support was increasingly based on voters' assessment of how well the parties ruled rather than their distribution of patronage. In a relatively young democracy, though, partisan loyalty remains weak. When the PT and its allies were successful, voters supported them readily, but once economic performance dropped and the party was implicated in a massive corruption scandal involving the national oil company, that support collapsed. What had been the strongest party in the Brazilian political system for two decades dramatically lost support, as Brazilians cheered the impeachment of PT president Dilma Rousseff in August 2016.

Brazil's civil society has long been active. It was instrumental in the transition to democracy, and massive street protests were a regular part of the pressure that forced the military to leave power. Lula and his supporters helped create independent trade unions that broke the monopoly of state corporatism imposed by the military government; women's movements and Catholic organizations based around liberation theology also became active participants demanding democracy. Ironically, once achieved, democracy has led to concern about the effectiveness of participation. The country's exceptional social inequality, many argue, affects participation in the same way that it affects the rule of law: the poor, who are often black, are left out. The PT was innovative in trying to overcome this problem. Starting in the city of Porto Alegre under a PT government, the party instituted a "participatory budgeting" (PB) system in which citizens in neighborhoods meet to set their priorities for the annual government budget. These groups elect representatives who meet at higher levels to produce a set of budget proposals for the city's officials to consider and enact. The system gives local citizens a voice and serves as a means of higher-level participation for more active citizens, who typically are members of local social movements or NGOs. The PB process has provided an avenue for greater participation for local civil society organizations (Avritzer 2009), though it's not clear that this was also effective at changing policy (Montero 2011). Once in power, the PT initially tried to institute national-level versions of participatory democracy, but these were ultimately criticized by participants as being only advisory and having little real impact (Goldfrank 2011).

An economic slowdown hit the country in 2011, just as it agreed to host both the 2014 World Cup and the 2016 Olympics. By 2013, it had turned into a full-blown recession, with the economy shrinking every year from 2013 to 2016. In that context, when the government announced rate hikes to the crucial urban public transportation sector in June 2013, massive demonstrations broke out. A group called "Free Fare" called a demonstration in São Paulo, the country's largest city, and was overwhelmed by thousands of people heeding the call to take to the streets in a peaceful protest. The police responded with force, and within a week, demonstrations of thousands—in some cases, hundreds of thousands—of people had spread to at least one hundred Brazilian cities. Showing it clearly was a democracy, if a flawed one, the government responded with announcing reduced transit fares and more spending of oil revenues on schools.

Widespread protests erupted again in March 2015, continuing off and on through Rousseff's impeachment in 2016. The massive "Car Wash" scandal (so called because of the use of car washes in laundering money) pursued by the increasingly independent and aggressive judiciary we discussed in chapter 5 resulted in hundreds of arrests, including the Speaker of the National Assembly and prominent PT officials. In the midst of a recession and the expenses associated with the upcoming Olympics, millions of Brazilians took to the streets demanding justice and the president's ouster. At one point, protests were held simultaneously in all twenty-six states and over 200 cities. By March 2016, protests had spread to over 300 cities, with one protest in São Paulo, the largest city, drawing an estimated 1.4 million people. The government introduced anticorruption legislation, but far too late to matter:

Rousseff's approval rating barely topped 10 percent, and she was duly impeached by the end of August.

Civil society in Brazil in the form of protests at the time of crisis seems alive and well, but Alfred Montero (2011) argued that while Brazil's civil society includes numerous active groups, their effectiveness is limited. Long-standing clientelism continues to be the predominant relationship between political leaders and citizens, as the latter vote for local politicians who provide services and infrastructure, regardless of their party, ideology, or level of corruption. The weak parties created by the electoral system reinforce these tendencies. Thus, in spite of an active civil society, Brazil's citizens may not have much influence. The question is whether the massive mobilizations of the last few years will mark a significant change, strengthening civil society's voice permanently.

CASE Questions

1. What would you say are the strengths and weaknesses of Brazil's open-list PR system? How does it compare with closed-list PR systems? Do you think it should be changed? If so, why and how? If not, why not?
2. The outbreak of massive demonstrations in Brazil in 2013 is an interesting case of a social movement in formation. What does the episode teach us about how social movements form and expand?

CONCLUSION

Citizen participation and representation are at the heart of democracy, which ideally gives each citizen equal voice and power. The reality, of course, is that no set of institutions can translate participation into representation and power in a way that treats everyone perfectly equally. Different electoral, party, and interest-group systems channel participation and provide representation in different ways. These institutions also interact with the governing institutions we outlined in chapter 5, creating yet more variation as we seek to understand who rules and what affects political behavior in democracies.

The most fundamental question about institutions of participation and representation is which system, if any, facilitates greater participation and better representation. Those systems that are more open to diverse organizations and viewpoints seem to create greater participation: multiparty systems, PR electoral systems, and pluralist interest-group systems. Whether they provide greater representation, however, depends on whether representation means only giving a set of people a voice or actually giving them influence. If the latter is a concern, then some would argue that a neocorporatist interest-group system that is based on stronger interest groups is better. While they may limit the ability to form new interest groups, neocorporatist systems arguably provide the greatest influence for recognized groups. Similarly, fewer and larger parties may provide less representation but more influence for their constituents than more numerous and smaller parties would.

This discussion raises the trade-off that Powell (2000) discerned between opportunities for participation and representation on the one hand and accountability on the other. Institutions that allow much representation of diverse interests often make it more difficult for citizens to know exactly whom to hold accountable for government action. More majoritarian systems, with a single ruling party at any given time, arguably provide less representation of diverse voices but make accountability more clear. Similarly, institutions of participation and representation influence the trade-off we discussed in chapter 5 between participation and effective governance. PR electoral systems that allow numerous, small parties to gain legislative representation arguably allow more distinct viewpoints to be expressed. The party coalitions that are then necessary to govern may make governing a challenge, though some political science research has questioned this conclusion.

Institutions affect the representation and participation of marginalized groups even more than they do average citizens. Ethnic or racial minorities and women are often unrepresented in large, catch-all parties or interest groups controlled primarily by the dominant groups in a society. One of the most robust findings in comparative politics is that PR systems provide greater representation of women in parliament. India is an example of going even further to ensure representation of minorities, reserving a specific share of legislative seats for them. While India does this on the basis of caste, several countries do it for women as well, as we discussed in chapter 4. Such laws implicitly assume that members of these groups can only be truly represented if members of their own groups are their official representatives. An SMD system without reservations, such as in the United States or the United Kingdom, assumes that people will be adequately represented by whomever voters collectively choose, regardless of the individual's own characteristics. In a two-party system, though, the choices are limited and disproportionately exclude women and racial or ethnic minorities.

The ultimate "Who rules?" question goes back to the classic debate between pluralist and elite theorists: Do modern democracies really provide government in which average citizens have effective power, or do elites' abilities to gain direct access to decision makers, shape the political agenda, and influence (or control) key institutions mean that they really rule? In the elite model, voters occasionally get a limited choice among a handful of alternatives, all of them led by elites and all typically within a relatively narrow ideological debate. Declining partisan loyalty and social capital in recent decades simply strengthen these trends of elite control. Pluralists counter that institutions can and do make a difference in who is represented and in how much meaningful participation average citizens, and especially more marginalized citizens, can have. Regardless of institutional differences, liberal democracies ultimately provide all voters with the ability to organize and sanction leaders via the ballot box.

Most political participation happens within institutions. When citizens find that available parties, interest groups, and other institutions fail to represent them adequately, though, they may choose to make demands outside institutions' bounds, the realm of what comparativists refer to as "contentious politics," to which we turn next.

KEY CONCEPTS

closed-list proportional
  representation (p. 289)

collective action problem (p. 284)

dominant-party system (p. 305)

Duverger's Law (p. 307)

electoral systems (p. 284)

"first-past-the-post" (FPTP) (p. 286)

Hindu nationalism (p. 340)

interest-group pluralism (p. 315)

mixed, or semiproportional (p. 294)

multiparty systems (p. 306)

neocorporatism (p. 317)

open-list proportional
  representation (p. 290)

party system (p. 296)

peak associations (p. 317)

plurality (p. 286)

populism (p. 303)

proportional representation (PR) (p. 288)

single-member district (SMD) (p. 286)

social capital (p. 315)

state corporatism (p. 317)

two-party system (p. 306)

virtual representation (p. 287)

 **for CQ Press** Sharpen your skills with SAGE edge at **edge.sagepub.com/orvis4e.** **SAGE edge for students** provides a personalized approach to help you accomplish your coursework goals in an easy-to-use learning environment.

WORKS CITED

Agarwala, Rina. 2013. *Informal Labor, Formal Politics, and Dignified Discontent in India.* Cambridge, UK: Cambridge University Press.

Ahmed, Amel. 2013. *Democracy and the Politics of Electoral System Choice: Engineering Electoral Dominance.* Cambridge, UK: Cambridge University Press.

Ames, Barry. 2001. *The Deadlock of Democracy in Brazil.* Ann Arbor: University of Michigan Press.

Art, David. 2011. *Inside the Radical Right: The Development of Anti-Immigrant Parties in Western Europe.* Cambridge, UK: Cambridge University Press.

Avritzer, Leonardo. 2009. *Participatory Institutions in Democratic Brazil.* Baltimore, MD: Johns Hopkins University Press; Washington, DC: Woodrow Wilson Center Press.

Beyme, Klaus von. 1985. *Political Parties in Western Democracies.* Aldershot, UK: Gower.

Blondel, Jean, Jean-Louis Thiebault, with Katarzyna Czernicka, Takashi Inoguchi, Ukrist Pathmanand, and Fulvio Venturino. 2010. *Political Leadership, Parties and Citizens: The Personalisation of Leadership.* New York: Routledge.

Blyth, Mark, and Richard Katz. 2005. "From Catch-all Politics to Cartelisation: The Political Economy of the Cartel Party." *West European Politics* 28 (1): 33–60. doi:10.1080/0140238042000297080

Boix, Carles. 2007. "The Emergence of Parties and Party Systems." In *The Oxford Handbook of Comparative Politics,* edited by Carles Boix and Susan Carol Stokes. Oxford, UK: Oxford University Press.

Carlson, Matthew. 2007. *Money Politics in Japan: New Rules, Old Practices.* Boulder, CO: Lynne Rienner.

Curtice, John, and W. Phillips Shively. 2009. "Who Represents Us Best? One Member or Many?" In *The Comparative Study of Electoral Systems,* edited by Hans-Dieter

Klingemann, 171–192. Oxford, UK: Oxford University Press.

Dalton, Russell J., David M. Farrell, and Ian McAllister. 2011. *Political Parties and Democratic Linkage: How Parties Organize Democracy.* Oxford, UK: Oxford University Press.

Dalton, Russell J., and Martin P. Wattenberg. 2000. *Parties without Partisans: Political Change in Advanced Industrial Democracies.* New York: Oxford University Press.

Downs, Anthony. 1957. *An Economic Theory of Democracy.* New York: Harper and Row.

Duverger, Maurice. 1969. *Political Parties, Their Organization and Activity in the Modern State.* London: Methuen.

Dw.com. 2016. *Nationwide German Poll: Merkel's Popularity Dips to Five-Year Low* (http://www.dw.com/en/nationwide-german-poll-merkels-popularity-dips-to-five-year-low/a-19521704).

Evans, Geoffrey, and Nan Dirk De Graaf, eds. 2013. *Political Choice Matters: Explaining the Strength of Class and Religious Cleavages in Cross-National Perspective.* New York: Oxford University Press.

Evans, Geoffrey, and James Tilley. 2013. "Ideological Convergence and the Decline of Class Voting in Britain." In *Political Choice Matters: Explaining the Strength of Class and Religious Cleavages in Cross-National Perspective,* edited by Geoffrey Evans and Nan Dirk De Graaf, 87–113. New York: Oxford University Press.

Figueiredo, Argelina Cheibub, and Fernando Limongi. 2000. "Presidential Power, Legislative Organization, and Party Behavior in Brazil." *Comparative Politics* 32 (2): 151–170.

Gallego, Aina. 2015. *Unequal Political Participation Worldwide.* New York: Cambridge University Press.

Golder, Matt. 2016. "Far Right Parties in Europe." *Annual Review of Political Science.* Vol 19, 477–497.

Goldfrank, Benjamin. 2011. "The Left and Participatory Democracy: Brazil, Uruguay, and Venezuela." In *The Resurgence of the Latin American Left,* edited by Steven Levitsky and Kenneth M. Roberts, 162–183. Baltimore, MD: Johns Hopkins University Press.

Hagopian, Frances. 2005. "Chile and Brazil." In *Assessing the Quality of Democracy,* edited by Larry Diamond and Leonardo Morlino, 123–162. Baltimore, MD: Johns Hopkins University Press.

Hagopian, Frances. 2016. "Brazil's Accountability Paradox." *Journal of Democracy* 27 (3): 119–128. July.

Hagopian, Frances, Carlos Vervasoni, and Juan Andrés Moraes. 2009. "From Patronage to Program: The Emergence of Party-Oriented Legislators in Brazil." *Comparative Political Studies* 42 (3): 360–391.

Hall, Peter A., Wade Jacoby, Jonah Levy, and Sophie Meunier, eds. 2014.*The Politics of Representation in the Global Age: Identification, Mobilization, and Adjudication.* New York: Cambridge University Press.

Hasan, Zoya. 2010. "Political Parties in India." In *The Oxford Companion to Politics in India,* edited by Niraja Gopal Jayal and Pratap Bhanu Mehta. Oxford, UK: Oxford University Press.

Hellwig, Timothy. 2014. *Globalization and Mass Politics: Retaining the Room to Maneuver.* New York: Cambridge University Press.

"Imbalance of Power." 2013. *New York Times.* February 2 (http://www.nytimes.com/interactive/2013/02/03/sunday-review/imbalance-of-power.html?ref=sunday&_r=0).

Inglehart, Ronald. 1971. "The Silent Revolution in Europe: Intergenerational Change in Post-Industrial Societies." *American Political Science Review* 65 (4): 991–1017. doi:10.1017/S0003055406392568

Iversen, Torben, and Anne Wren. 1998. "Equality, Employment, and Budgetary

Restraint: The Trilemma of the Service Economy." *World Politics* 50 (4): 507–546.

Kabashima, Ikuo, and Gill Steel. 2010. *Changing Politics in Japan.* Ithaca, NY: Cornell University Press.

Kedar, Orit. 2009. *Voting for Policy, Not Parties: How Voters Compensate for Power Sharing.* New York: Cambridge University Press.

Kitschelt, Herbert. 2014. "Parties and Party Systems." In *Comparing Democracies: Elections and Voting in a Changing World.* 4th ed., edited by Lawrence LeDuc, Richard G. Niemi, and Pippa Norris, 32–57. Thousand Oaks, CA: Sage.

Krauss, Ellis S., and Robert J. Pekkanen. 2011. *The Rise and Fall of Japan's LDP: Political Party Organizations as Historical Institutions.* Ithaca, NY: Cornell University Press.

Lee, Frances E. 2009. *Beyond Ideology: Politics, Principles, and Partisanship in the U.S. Senate.* Chicago: University of Chicago Press.

Lupu, Noam, and Rachel Beatty Riedl. 2013. "Political Parties and Uncertainty in Developing Democracies." *Comparative Political Studies* 46 (11): 1339–1365.

Martin, Sherry L. 2011. *Popular Democracy in Japan: How Gender and Community Are Changing Modern Electoral Politics.* Ithaca, NY: Cornell University Press.

Mitra, Subrata K., and Jivanta Schöttli. 2016. "India's 2014 General Elections: A Critical Realignment in Indian Politics?" *Asian Survey* 56 (4): 605–628. July/August. doi:10.1525/as.2016.56.4.605

Montero, Alfred P. 2011. "Brazil: The Persistence of Oligarchy." In *The Quality of Democracy in Latin America,* edited by Daniel Levine and Jose Molina, 111–136. Boulder, CO: Lynne Rienner.

Moosbrugger, Lorelei K. 2012. *The Vulnerability Thesis: Interest Group Influence and Institutional Design.* New Haven, CT: Yale University Press.

Moser, Robert G., and Ethan Scheiner. 2012. *Electoral Systems and Political Context: How the Effects of Rules Vary across New and Established Democracies.* New York: Cambridge University Press.

Mukherjee, Nisha. 2013. "Party Systems and Human Well-being." *Party Politics* 19 (4): 601–623.

Ogawa, Akihiro. 2009. *The Failure of Civil Society? The Third Sector and the State in Contemporary Japan.* Albany, NY: SUNY Press.

Orellana, Salomon. 2014. *Electoral Systems and Governance: How Diversity Can Improve Policy-making.* New York: Routledge.

Palshikar, Suhas. 2013. "Regional and Caste Parties." In *Routledge Handbook of Indian Politics,* edited by Atul Kohli and Prema Singh, 91–104. New York: Routledge.

Pardos-Prado, Sergi, and Pedro Riera. 2016. "The Attitudinal Implications of the Cartel Party Thesis: Ideological Convergence and Political Efficacy in Contemporary Democracies." In *Party Politics and Democracy in Europe: Essays in Honour of Peter Mair,* edited by Ferdinand Muller-Rommel and Fernando Casal, 83–100. New York: Routledge.

Pekkanen, Robert. 2006. *Japan's Dual Civil Society: Members without Advocates.* Stanford, CA: Stanford University Press.

Poguntke, Thomas. 2012. "Towards a New Party System: The Vanishing Hold of the Catch-All Parties in Germany." *Party Politics.* October.

Powell, G. Bingham. 2000. *Elections as Instruments of Democracy: Majoritarian and Proportional Visions.* New Haven, CT: Yale University Press.

Putnam, Robert D. 2000. *Bowling Alone: The Collapse and Revival of American Community.* New York: Simon and Schuster.

Rahn, Wendy, and Erik Oliver. 2016. "Trump's Voters Aren't Authoritarians, New Research Says. So What Are They?" Monkey Cage. *Washington Post.* March 9 (https://www.washingtonpost.com/news/monkey-cage/wp/2016/03/09/trumps-voters-arent-authoritarians-new-research-says-so-what-are-they/?tid=a_inl).

Reed, Steven R. 2005. "Japan: Haltingly toward a Two-Party System." In *The Politics of Electoral Systems,* edited by Michael Gallagher and Paul Mitchell, 277–294. Oxford, UK: Oxford University Press.

Reed, Steven R., Ethan Scheiner, Daniel M. Smith, and Michael Thies. 2012. "The Japanese General Election of 2012: Sometimes, Lucky Is Better Than Popular." Monkey Cage. *Washington Post.* December 27 (http://Themonkey cage.Org/2012/12/27/The-Japanese-General-Election-Of-2012-Sometimes-Lucky-Is-Better-Than-Popular/#Comments).

Rodrik, Dani. 1997. *Has Globalization Gone Too Far?* Washington, DC: Institute for International Economics.

Santos, Fabiano. 2008. "Brazilian Democracy and the Power of 'Old' Theories of Party Competition." *Brazilian Political Science Review* 2 (1): 57–76 (http://www.bpsr.org.br/english/arquivos/BPSR_v2_n3_jun2008_03.pdf).

Scarrow, Susan E. 2015. *Beyond Party Members: Changing Approaches to Partisan Mobilization.* New York: Oxford University Press.

Schattschneider, Elmer Eric. 2009. *Party Government.* 3rd ed. New Brunswick, NJ: Transaction. (Originally published 1942 in New York by Holt, Rinehart and Winston.)

Scheiner, Ethan, Daniel M. Smith, and Michael F. Thies. 2016. "The 2014 Japanese Election Results: The Opposition Cooperates but Fails to Inspire." In *Japan Decides 2014: The Japanese General Election,* edited by Robert J. Pekkanen, Steven R. Reed, and Ethan Scheiner, 22–40. New York: Palgrave Macmillan.

Shugart, Matthew Soberg. 2005. "Comparative Electoral Systems Research: The Maturation of a Field and New Challenges Ahead." In *The Politics of Electoral Systems,* edited by Michael Gallagher and Paul Mitchell, 22–55. Oxford, UK: Oxford University Press.

Skocpol, Theda. 2003. *Diminished Democracy: From Membership to Management in American Civic Life.* Norman: University of Oklahoma Press.

Stoll, Heather. 2013. *Changing Societies, Changing Party Systems.* New York: Cambridge University Press.

Taylor, Steven L., Matthew S. Shugart, Arend Lijphart, and Bernard Grofman. 2014. *A Different Democracy: American Government in a Thirty-One-Country Perspective.* New Haven, CT: Yale University Press.

van Deth, Jan W., and William A. Maloney, eds. 2012. *New Participation Dimensions in Civil Society: Professionalization and Individualized Collective Action.* New York: Routledge.

Wike, Richard, Bruce Stokes, and Katie Simmons. 2016. *Europeans Fear Wave of Refugees Will Mean More Terrorism, Fewer Jobs: Sharp Ideological Divides across EU on Views about Minorities, Diversity and National Identity.* Pew Research Center, July 11 (http://www.pewglobal.org/2016/07/11/europeans-fear-wave-of-refugees-will-mean-more-terrorism-fewer-jobs/).

Ziegfeld, Adam. 2016. *Why Regional Parties? Clientelism, Elites, and the Indian Party System.* New York: Cambridge University Press.

RESOURCES FOR FURTHER STUDY

Aldrich, John H. 1995. *Why Parties? The Origin and Transformation of Political Parties in America.* Chicago: University of Chicago Press.

Art, David. 2011. *Inside the Radical Right: The Development of Anti-Immigrant Parties in Western Europe.* New York: Cambridge University Press.

Green, Michael J. 2010. "Japan's Confused Revolution." *Washington Quarterly* 33 (1): 3–19. doi:10.1080/01636600903418637

Levendusky, Matthew. 2009. *The Partisan Sort: How Liberals Became Democrats and Conservatives Became Republicans.* Chicago: University of Chicago Press.

Norris, Pippa. 2002. *Democratic Phoenix: Reinventing Political Activism.* New York: Cambridge University Press.

Pharr, Susan J., and Robert D. Putnam, eds. 2000. *Disaffected Democracies: What's Troubling the Trilateral Countries?* Princeton, NJ: Princeton University Press.

Putnam, Robert D., ed. 2002. *Democracies in Flux: The Evolution of Social Capital in Contemporary Society.* New York: Oxford University Press.

Rosenbluth, Frances McCall, and Michael F. Thies. 2010. *Japan Transformed: Political Change and Economic Restructuring.* Princeton, NJ: Princeton University Press.

Thomas, Clive S. 2001. *Political Parties and Interest Groups: Shaping Democratic Governance.* Boulder, CO: Lynne Rienner.

Tocqueville, Alexis de. 1969. *Democracy in America.* Garden City, NY: Doubleday Anchor. (Originally published in two volumes in 1835 and 1840, respectively, in London by Saunders and Otley.)

Ware, Alan. 1996. *Political Parties and Party Systems.* New York: Oxford University Press.

Wren, Anne, and Kenneth M. McElwain. 2007. "Voters and Parties." In *The Oxford Handbook of Comparative Politics,* edited by Carles Boix and Susan Carol Stokes, 555–581. Oxford, UK: Oxford University Press.

WEB RESOURCES

Constituency-Level Elections Archive (CLEA)
(http://www.electiondataarchive.org)

Golder, Matt, "Democratic Electoral Systems around the World, 1946–2011"
(http://mattgolder.com/elections)

Hyde, Susan, and Nikolay Marinov, National Elections across Democracy and Autocracy (NELDA)
(http://www.nelda.co/#)

International Foundation for Electoral System, ElectionGuide
(http://www.electionguide.org)

International Institute for Democracy and Electoral Assistance (IDEA)
(http://www.idea.int)

Inter-Parliamentary Union, PARLINE Database on National Parliaments
(http://www.ipu.org/parline-e/parlinesearch.asp)

Johnson, Joel W., and Jessica S. Wallack, "Electoral Systems and the Personal Vote"
(http://thedata.harvard.edu/dvn/dv/jwjohnson/faces/study/StudyPage.xhtml?globalId=hdl:1902.1/17901)

University of California, San Diego, Lijphart Elections Archive
(http://libraries.ucsd.edu/resources/data-gov-info-gis/ssds/guides/lij/)

7 CONTENTIOUS POLITICS
SOCIAL MOVEMENTS, POLITICAL VIOLENCE, AND REVOLUTION

KEY QUESTIONS

- How and why are people mobilized to participate in contentious politics?

- How do social movements and other forms of contentious politics function?

- What effects do contentious politics have on governments and policies?

- What effects have globalization and the advent of Internet-based communications and social media had on contentious politics?

- Why does contentious politics sometimes turn violent and take the forms of terrorism, civil war, or revolution?

2011 was a banner year for political protest; from the "Arab Spring" to the "Occupy" movement to protests against economic policies in Spain, Greece, and Italy, citizens everywhere seemed to mass in the streets demanding change. While not all of those protests succeeded, they gave new impetus to a long-standing area of interest in comparative politics, what most scholars refer to as "contentious politics." **Contentious politics** is political activity that is at least in part beyond institutional bounds. Groups form over grievances and demand change; they may work via elections and other institutions as well, but the hallmark of contentious politics is extra-institutional activity: petitions, protests, riots, violence, civil war, and revolution. Decades ago, political scientists often viewed such activity as a dangerous threat to political order (Huntington 1968). In the last several decades, most have come to see contentious politics, at least in nonviolent forms, as an important part of civil society and political participation, whether in a democracy where such activity is usually legal or an authoritarian regime where it is not.

The last chapter examined political participation within institutions; in this chapter we will explore participation that goes beyond institutions, the realm of contentious politics. We will examine social movements and protests; political violence, including ethnic conflict, terrorism, and civil war; and revolution. The Country and Concept table (page 359) shows

#WeCantBreathe

how widespread contentious politics is. While relatively few regime-threatening acts of political violence take place, hundreds and often thousands of protests occurred in our case study countries over a fifteen-year period, including in both democratic and authoritarian regimes. Terrorist actions have also been common, and far more common in some poor countries like India and Nigeria than in the United States and other wealthy democracies. How regimes respond to violence varies greatly as well, with some engaging in far more repression than others. Finally, as a sign of the impact of globalization and technological change, the table also shows the ubiquity of cell phones around the world.

Despite all this activity, participation outside institutional bounds faces the same collective action problem we outlined in the previous chapter. While many people may have grievances against their government, what incentives do they have to join a group, protest in the street, or throw a rock? Indeed, politics outside institutional channels is often more risky and in some cases illegal; the collective action problem may be even greater than what we discussed earlier. One of the key questions we ask, then, is, How and why are people mobilized to participate in contentious politics?

contentious politics
Political activity that is at least in part beyond institutional bounds, involving extra-institutional activity such as petitions, protests, riots, violence, civil war, and revolution

Once they are, we ask, How do social movements and other forms of contentious politics function, and what effects do they have on governments and policies? We will also ask, What effects have globalization and the advent of Internet-based communications and social media had on contentious politics, a phenomenon highlighted in the 2011 protests? Then we will turn to the question, Why do politics sometimes turn violent and take the form of terrorism or civil war? Finally, we will ask, Why do revolutions—contentious political episodes that change regimes—arise? We will start, however, with a brief examination of the role of contentious politics, particularly in its nonviolent forms.

FRAMING CONTENTIOUS POLITICS

Political scientists have studied contentious politics for years, most commonly examining **social movements,** organizations that have a loosely defined organizational structure and represent people who perceive themselves to be outside the bounds of formal institutions, seek major socioeconomic or political changes to the status quo, or employ noninstitutional forms of collective action.

What we now call social movements arose at least a century ago, but they have become much more common since the 1960s. In that decade in much of the Western world, growing numbers of citizens, particularly young "baby boomers," came to feel that their governments, political parties, and interest groups were not providing adequate forms of participation or representation. They viewed all major political institutions as organs of elite rule. Established institutions were overwhelmingly controlled by white men. In response, "new social movements" led by racial minorities, women, antiwar activists, and environmentalists arose, challenging the status quo. These groups have since been joined by many others, such as the antiglobalization movement that proclaimed itself to the world in 1999 in protests in Seattle, the more recent "Occupy" movement that arose in 2011 in New York, and the "Black Lives Matter" movement in response to police violence against African Americans that began in Florida and Missouri.

While they exist throughout the world, and have had significant impact especially in the process of democratization of authoritarian regimes (which we examine in chapter 9), social movements are most common and have arguably had the greatest impact in wealthy democracies. Social movements helped women enter public life to a degree never before seen. Racial minorities united to get many segregationist and discriminatory policies overturned and were able to enter public life to a much greater degree. Gay rights activists have succeeded in getting a number of governments to redefine marriage and international organizations to think of gay rights as part of universal human rights. And in the age of global climate change, environmentalists have put their concerns on the agenda of national and international institutions.

Social movements are generally seen as pursuing a "progressive" agenda, meaning an agenda of social change based on new ideas favored by those who consider

COUNTRY AND CONCEPT
Contentious Politics

Country	Political protests (1990–2004)	Episodes of political violence focused on regime change since 1945	Level of state repression (average response to violent episodes; 0 = none, 3 = severe)	Number of terrorist incidents since 2000	Access to social media (mobile cellular subscriptions per 100 people [2016])
Brazil	797	2	0.5	22	139
China	898	15	1.8	127	92
Germany	2,012 (including East and West Germany)	2*	2.5*	118	120
India	1,451	78	2.77	6,900	74
Iran	408	22	2.77	134	88
Japan	719	0	NA	39	120
Mexico	902	15	2.77	95	82
Nigeria	456	27	2.1	2,807	78
Russia	1,160 (including USSR and Russian Federation)	20	2.6	1,776	155
United Kingdom	3,029	0	NA	826	124
United States	5,722	0	NA	337	110

Sources: Data for political protests are from J. Craig Jenkins, Charles Lewis Taylor, Marianne Abbott, Thomas V. Maher, and Lindsey Peterson, *The World Handbook of Political Indicators IV* (Columbus, OH: Mershon Center for International Security Studies, The Ohio State University) (https://sociology.osu.edu/worldhandbook). Data for episodes of political violence and response to violence are from Erica Chenoweth and Orion A. Lewis, *Nonviolent and Violent Campaigns Outcomes Dataset,* Vol. 2.0 (http://www.du.edu/korbel/sie/research/chenow_navco_data.html). Data for terrorism are from the Global Terrorism Database (https://www.start.umd.edu/gtd/). Data for cell-phone penetration are from World Bank, "Mobile Cellular Subscriptions (per 100 People)" (http://data.worldbank.org/indicator/IT.CEL.SETS.P2/).

Note: For the column "response to violent episodes (level of state repression)," 0 = none; 1 = mild repression; 2 = moderate repression; 3 = extreme repression.

*Data for Germany are for East Germany to 1990 only.

themselves on the "left" of the political spectrum, usually in the name of the less powerful members of society. The rise of the Tea Party in the United States., however, demonstrates that social movements can come from the conservative side of the political spectrum as well. The Tea Party possesses all of the elements of a social movement: loose organization and leadership, opposition to what its members see as the status quo in both political parties and established interest groups, self-perception of its members as outsiders, and demands for fundamental change. It is a conservative movement, though, in the sense that it calls for a return to an earlier era (based on what its members see as the original meaning of the U.S. Constitution). This would mean a rollback of many major policies of the last half-century. Similar movements have arisen in Europe as well, most recently in response to increased immigration from Muslim countries.

Given this history, comparativists have taken great interest in social movements, and contentious politics more broadly. At one time or another, scholars have used almost all of the theoretical approaches we outlined in chapter 1 to try to understand contentious politics. The oldest theories are psychological or structural. Various psychological theories can explain why people choose to act on grievances by joining groups, or engaging in violence. Scholars have also used both economic and political structural arguments to explain protest. More recently, they have looked at strategic interactions based loosely on rational actor models to analyze the dynamics of how movements emerge and evolve. Finally, cultural theories have helped explain why and how movements gain supporters and effect change. We will examine this theoretical debate in this section, then turn to related debates about why people turn to violent political action in the next section.

Why Contentious Politics Happen

The first question we must address is why contentious politics happen. Why do people mobilize to demand change and engage in protest or other actions beyond

Members of the "Tea Party" movement protest at the U.S. Capitol in June 2013. Social movements typically form on the "left" or "progressive" side of issues, but the Tea Party is a social movement from the "right" or conservative side that has had a significant impact on U.S. politics since 2009.

AP Photo/J. Scott Applewhite

the day-to-day politics of elections and lobbying? The oldest theories are mostly psychological, focusing on why people develop grievances against their government. The best known is based on the concept of **relative deprivation,** a group's or individual's belief that they are not getting their share of something of value relative to others. Social psychology research suggests that relative deprivation produces demands for change especially when it is group-based: a sense that members of a self-identified group are not getting what they deserve in part because of who they are (Klandermans 2015, 220). Thus, the identities we discussed in chapter 4—race, ethnicity, gender, etc.—can be powerful sources of contentious politics. More recently, comparativists have looked at emotions as sources of grievances. A situation that transgresses people's core values or sense of fairness and produces moral outrage and anger can lead people to demand change just as relative deprivation can (Flam 2015).

Christian Welzel (2013) argued that people's values, not just their grievances or emotions, can lead them to participate in contentious politics. Using data from the World Values Survey, covering nearly ninety countries and 200,000 people, he found that what he and colleagues call "emancipative values" enhance participation in nonviolent social movements in particular. Emancipative values (see chapter 9 for more on this) are values favoring greater individual freedom and equality of opportunity. He found that as both individuals' and entire societies' emancipative values increased, so did participation in social movements. Following the postmaterialist thesis we outlined in chapter 1, he argued these values rise as people's basic needs are satisfied. Hence, social movements have been strongest and most effective in relatively wealthy countries, and even in those countries, support often comes not from the most deprived segments of society but from those at least somewhat better off and more educated.

Most scholars, though, argue that individual motivations—whether grievances, emotions, or values—do not fully explain contentious politics. People with grievances will not necessarily create or join a movement, protest, or rebel; they may instead feel disempowered, unhappy but feeling unable to do anything about it. Overcoming the collective action problem requires something more. Scholars of contentious politics have pointed to several factors that explain how grievances lead to political mobilization. First, they examined what came to be known as "resource mobilization": What resources do groups and organizations have to effect change? These resources could include organizational capacity, money, or educated and effective leadership, among other things. The existence of seemingly strong organizations that at least appear to have the potential to succeed encourage people with grievances to join and support them.

A second group of scholars argued that resources alone are not enough. They added a structural argument based on political opportunity. The **political opportunity structure** is the extent to which a regime is open to influence from social movements and other extra-institutional groups. Consensual democracies are likely to be more open than majoritarian ones, and both are generally more open than authoritarian

relative deprivation
A group's or individual's belief that they are not getting their share of something of value relative to others

political opportunity structure
The extent to which a regime is open to influence from social movements and other extra-institutional groups

regimes. Multiple and independent centers of power, openness to new actors, instability in political alignments, influential allies within the regime, and regime willingness to facilitate collective action all enhance the political opportunities social movements have (Tilly and Tarrow 2015, 59). Greater opportunities to succeed encourage people with grievances to mobilize to demand change.

Another group of scholars, mainly in sociology, have argued that networks are crucial to explain why contentious politics happen. Networks provide potential group members personal connections to a group and direct information on the group's goals and activities, and can serve as direct channels of recruitment into groups. Network connections to a relevant group thus encourage overcoming the collective action problem. Networks can also be closely related to identity, a powerful source of contentious politics: if you already identify with a particular ethnic or racial group, for instance, you are likely to have personal networks established within that group, both of which increase the likelihood of your engaging politically in what can be high-risk activities.

How Contentious Politics Happen

Once we have some ideas of why contentious politics happen, we can ask, What do social movements and other groups engaged in contentious politics actually do, and how can we understand variation in their behavior? Doug McAdam, Sidney Tarrow, and Charles Tilly, in their influential book, *Dynamics of Contention* (2001), argued that we need to analyze contentious politics as a process involving multiple actors and mechanisms. Social movements and other groups have particular resources and act within a particular political opportunity structure and cultural context. As they act, however, other political actors and institutions respond and the context can shift as a result, leading to changes in the way the social movements respond. This iterative process plays itself out in what they term "contentious episodes" of varying lengths.

Strategies and Repertoires   Social movements and other groups engage in a variety of strategic actions to demand change, from peaceful protest to acts of civil disobedience such as the sit-ins at lunch counters or the "Black Lives Matter" movement's blocking roadways more recently. Violent actions, which we discuss in more detail below, can also be strategic actions, even if they are typically condemned more quickly than other options. All of these are examples of "repertoires of action" that groups use in political performances to gain attention to their cause and demand change. Which repertoires a group chooses and which are more likely to be successful depend very much on context. Successful repertoires usually draw on meaningful past examples, often within a given society, though not always. The Mahatma Gandhi's repertoire of civil disobedience (refusing to obey what he believed to be unjust laws), for instance, was consciously adopted by leaders of the American civil rights movement in the 1950s and 1960s (e.g., blacks riding in the "white" section of a bus), then taken up by the movement against the Vietnam War (e.g., burning draft cards). Sidney Tarrow

(2013) argued that the language movements use as part of their repertoires needs to have "symbolic resonance" in a particular context to be effective.

Political Opportunity Structures These can strongly influence how social movements engage in contentious politics. Consensual democracies with multiple-party systems are more likely to produce major candidates and/or parties that champion a social movement's demands, leading the latter to engage in electoral politics more readily. At the other extreme, repression under authoritarian regimes leads groups to engage in "repressive repertoires": often "underground" actions to preserve their group and plan for more overt action when the opportunity arises (Johnston 2015).

Discourse and Identity Scholars examining cultural influences, often using a postmodern approach, analyze how social movements create meaning via discourses and constructing identities. Constructing stigmatized identities—such as identities based on ethnic, racial, or religious minorities—is particularly powerful in mobilizing support. These scholars often argue that constructing an identity, as we discussed in chapter 4, and giving the group political voice can be important ends in themselves (Scholl 2014). This was a key element of the "new social movements" that arose in the 1960s in Western countries, giving voice to women, gays and lesbians, and racial minorities.

New Communications Technology The rise of new communications technology in the last twenty years, and especially social media in the last decade, has provided new repertoires for use in contentious politics, and set off a debate about the effects of the new technology on movements' strength. As part of the debate over social capital we outlined in the previous chapter, some observers fear online communications isolate individuals, thereby limiting their likely participation in social movements, and threatening the continued existence of the movements themselves. Other skeptics see online activity as "slacktivism"—low-cost, low-commitment activism that has little impact. At the other extreme, scholars such as Manuel Castells argue that "the networked social movements of the digital age represent a new species of social movement" (2012, 15). Social media, in particular, allows activists to bypass their traditional reliance on "mainstream media" to disseminate their ideas. It also allows all individuals, regardless of their past involvement or leadership, to express their grievances to larger audiences and find like-minded people with whom to form networks. This, supporters argue, means social media creates a more horizontal and potentially democratic "public space" in which social movements can form and act.

Activists and social movements can use social media and other web-based communications in various ways. Long-standing social movements can use the web to disseminate their ideas, new movements can form first via social media and then organize real-world actions (the model of many of the movements of 2011), or activism can remain purely online. Jennifer Earl and Katrina Kimport (2011) argued that the web has two transformative elements: lowering the costs of creating and organizing movements, and aggregating individuals' actions into collective actions without requiring the participants to act in the same time and place. When movements are able to harness these benefits, they create new and powerful models of contentious politics; when they do not do that, the effects of the web are far less important. Lowering the costs of communication can help mobilize people in the first place. If a potential activist reads social media posts from people with similar grievances, she may be more likely to translate her grievances into activism rather than free ride on others' actions; if she knows via social media that many people support the cause and say they will show up to protest in the square, she will be more likely to overcome her fear and show up herself. Eliminating the need for activists to be in the same time and place can reduce organizational costs dramatically, perhaps even allowing the elimination of expensive infrastructure such as offices and paid staff. Paolo Gerbaudo (2012, 5), however, suggested that "influential Facebook admins and activist tweeps become 'soft leaders' or choreographers, involved in setting the scene, and constructing an emotional space within which collective action can unfold." Social media does not eliminate the need for organizations and leaders, and must be used wisely to be effective. These authors thus argue that how transformative social media will be depends on how it is used; the nature of the technology alone does not determine its impact on contentious politics.

The role of social media was most famously illustrated in the "Arab Spring." As 2011 began, the world watched as seemingly out of nowhere tens of thousands of Tunisians took to the streets, demanding the ouster of the country's long-ruling president, Zine Ben Ali, in what came to be known as the Jasmine revolution. As this revolt unfolded, Egyptians began flooding the main square in Cairo, demanding the ouster of their even longer-ruling president, Hosni Mubarak. In just six weeks, two of the oldest and seemingly most stable authoritarian regimes of the Arab world had fallen. Protests quickly followed in most Arab countries, with varying outcomes. We examine those outcomes in chapter 9, but here we look at how the protests arose in the first place.

The Arab Spring, particularly the seminal cases of Tunisia and Egypt, illustrates much of what we have learned about contentious politics. Social media certainly had an important role but was far from the only element of importance. Ricardo Larémont (2014) argued that relative deprivation explains much of the grievances behind the protests. Economic growth was significant in most Arab countries prior to the uprising but was unequally distributed; those left out felt they were promised more than they received. They also saw evidence of massive corruption among the elite that denied the rest of the population the benefits of booming economies. Mobilization for protest, though, takes more than grievances. Earlier and less dramatic protests took place in both Tunisia and Egypt, starting in 2008 and 2005, respectively. In Tunisia, these began in the relatively poor hinterland among underemployed youth; in Egypt, the protests were around lack of political reforms in the 2005 and 2010 elections. These protests helped create social movement organizations with a set of repertoires and networks with which to mobilize people. In both countries, survival under authoritarian rule required people to have extensive social networks (see chapter 8) that they used to mobilize politically.

It is not as clear that an obvious political opportunity existed in either country going into 2011; while open resistance to both regimes was growing, neither seemed under extreme pressure. It began in Tunisia, where a university-educated street vendor (who couldn't get a better job) set himself on fire in a small, poor town in the interior, to protest harassment from the local government. Protests, building on those from several years earlier, began there and spread to nearby towns. News of his death from his wounds a few weeks later, and the regime's repression of the early protests, was spread via social media, especially in urban areas. What had been a series of local revolts became a national movement, culminating in tens of thousands of people marching in the capital. After initial reluctance, the national labor union joined the effort, mobilizing its long-standing membership to join the young, social-media-driven activists. After further regime repression, the movement demanded, and got, the long-ruling president's resignation. As David Patel et al. (2014) argued, Tunisia created a portable model: it achieved its goal relatively quickly and with minimal loss of life, and established a set of repertoires that could be copied throughout the region.

News of the Tunisian president's resignation spread rapidly via "mainstream" media—in particular the relatively new, regional television network, Al Jazeera—and social media throughout the Arab world. Activists from earlier protest movements in Egypt called for a national day of protest, and used a repertoire similar to the one in Tunisia: occupation of a central square in the capital. A relative handful of social media activists who had been involved in the protests of 2005 and 2010 mobilized a massive group using Facebook and other online tools. The long-standing Muslim Brotherhood did not officially endorse the protest but told its massive membership (it was by far the largest opposition group in the country) that they were free to join the protest. Over a million people took over the iconic Tahrir Square on January 25, 2011, and within weeks, Hosni Mubarak, a dictator of thirty years' duration, had resigned.

Digital media played an important role throughout the Arab Spring. Tunisia and Egypt were among the countries with the highest levels of connectivity, particularly via mobile phones, which had become nearly universal, especially in urban areas. Philip Howard and Muzammil Hussain (2013) found that social media was particularly important in helping activists share and spread their grievances, plan the protest itself, and ignite the spark that got people into the streets. Wendy Pearlman (2013) argued that shifting emotions played a crucial role in overcoming what seemed to be a lack of political opportunity: the regime's initial repression and the strength in numbers gained via social media spread transnationally from Tunisia to Egypt to other Arab countries, turning fear into anger, a powerful mobilizing emotion. While the outcomes varied widely—from electoral democracy in Tunisia to a return to military rule in Egypt to civil war in Syria and Libya—contentious politics affected the entire region. But the protests were not as spontaneous as they seemed; long-standing social movements used social media, their preexisting networks, and a common set of repertoires to mobilize people for effective action.

Transnational Activism   The Internet is but one aspect of the broader phenomenon of globalization, which has had multiple effects on contentious politics. As global communication has become easier and a growing number of issues (e.g., trade, human rights, environmental protection) seem to require global action, transnational social movements have arisen. One estimate counted 183 such groups in 1973 and over 1,000 in 2003 (Tarrow 2012, 187). Virtually all of these groups operate at both the national and global level. Some groups, such as the global justice movement (GJM), launched in the "battle for Seattle" in 1999, explicitly target international organizations, while others simply use global resources to fight domestic battles. The Seattle protest at the 1999 meeting of the World Trade Organization (WTO) was the first of a series of protests targeting global organizations such as the WTO, World Bank, International Monetary Fund, and G8 (an annual meeting of the heads of government of eight of the largest economies in the world). These actions brought together traditional movements like labor unions with "new" transnational networks of activists around issues of fair labor, environmental destruction, and indigenous rights, all connected together by a concern for the effects of globalization. Conflicts among the groups—between the older hierarchical organizations such as labor unions and the newer "horizontal" networks of activists, and between violent and nonviolent groups—was a continuing problem, but these protests nonetheless represented a new level of global organizing and action (Fominaya 2014).

The GJM is only the best known of a set of new "transnational advocacy networks" of activists working together to use global resources to force policy change (Keck and Sikkink 1998). Transnational activism has created new political opportunity structures

An Egyptian woman uses her cell phone to take a photo during a demonstration in Tahrir Square, Cairo, in January 2011. Mobile phone technology was a crucial tool used by organizers of the "Arab Spring," especially in Egypt, where the rate of cell phone usage is quite high. On the ground, demonstrations were organized partially via social media, and documented with cell phones for the world to see.

Marco Vacca / Contributor

and new resources: groups can target international organizations instead of or in addition to national governments, and wealthy and more experienced groups can share their knowledge and resources with younger and weaker groups in other countries. Groups can also share repertoires of action across borders much more easily, as global norms around issues such as human rights create a sense of collective purpose. These changes have been particularly important for groups in poorer countries and under authoritarian regimes; their ability to appeal to, and borrow repertoires and resources from, groups in wealthier countries can be crucial to their survival and success. Entire networks of like-minded organizations have formed to engage in parallel actions around the world, as the Occupy movement briefly demonstrated in 2011.

What Effects Does Contentious Politics Have? Scholars have explained why and how contentious politics occurs at great length, but the ultimate question may be, Does it matter? What effects has all this difficult political action had? Oddly, political scientists have examined this question far less than the questions above. On the one hand, it seems obvious that contentious politics has mattered a great deal. For anyone living in "the West," the new social movements arising in the 1950s to the 1970s clearly have had an impact: attitudes and policies about racial minorities, women, and the environment—just to name a few—have changed dramatically. Similarly, authoritarian regimes around the world have fallen over the last thirty years as their citizens mobilized, demanding democracy. On the other hand, how do we know that these changes were a result of the social movements' actions? Outcomes of contentious politics are particularly difficult to discern because many factors influence government policy, social attitudes, and cultural changes. And if we can figure that out, can we then determine why some forms of contentious politics are more successful than others?

Most social movements focus on changing government policy, but many outcomes are possible. In addition to policy changes, contentious politics can affect access to the political system, the political agenda, policy output (resources for and implementation of policy), policy impact on people's lives, and more fundamental structural changes (Giugni 2004, 7). Contentious politics can also have indirect effects on policy by changing social or cultural attitudes and opinions, or the practices of other important institutions such as large corporations. Finally, particular episodes or groups can affect future contentious politics, as social movements evolve or give rise to new ones. Thus, the study of the outcome of contentious politics is exceptionally complex.

Scholars are divided over what explains the outcomes of contentious politics. Some, following the political opportunity structure approach, argue that the context in which particular movements act is crucial. In particular, a state's capacity to respond by changing policy efficiently and effectively and the presence of political allies within the state affect groups' ability to effect policy change. If a state cannot adapt new policies with relative ease, no amount of pressure is likely to change policy. Marco Giugni

Are Nonviolent Movements More Successful Than Violent Ones?

The table below gives some examples of the cases on which Chenoweth and Stephan (2011) based their argument that nonviolent movements tend to be more successful than violent ones. What other hypotheses about why movements succeed or fail can you generate from the table? The table includes the years of the movement, so you can think about the era in which it took place and its length, as well as whether it used new media in the digital age and the level of repression it faced from the state.

Country	Group	Years	Violent?	Use of new media	Repression	Success
Afghanistan	Taliban	1992–1996	Yes	No	Extreme	Yes
Burma	Karens	1948–2006	No	No	Extreme	No
China	Democracy Movement	1976–1979	No	No	Moderate	No
Colombia	FARC	1964–2006	Yes	Yes	Extreme	No
Czechoslovakia	Velvet Revolution	1989–1990	No	No	Mixed	Yes
Egypt	Kifaya	2000–2005	No	Yes	Moderate	No
Ethiopia	Eritrean Secession	1974–1991	Yes	No	Extreme	Yes
Georgia	Rose Revolution	2003	No	Yes	None	Yes
Great Britain	IRA	1968–2006	Yes	No	Extreme	No
India	Kashmir Separatists	1988–2006	Yes	Yes	Extreme	No
Indonesia	East Timorese Independence	1988–1999	No	No	Extreme	Yes
Kenya	Democracy Movement	1990–1991	No	No	Moderate	Yes
Mexico	Democracy Movement	1987–2000	No	Some	Moderate	Yes
Romania	Ani-Ceausescu	1987–1989	Yes	No	Extreme	Yes
Russia	Chechen Independence	1994–2006	Yes	Yes	Extreme	No
Spain	Basque Separatist	1968–2006	Yes	No	Moderate	No
Sri Lanka	Tamil Separatist	1972–2006	Yes	No	Extreme	No
West Papua	Anti-Occupation	1964–2006	No	Yes	Extreme	No

Source: Data are from Erica Chenoweth and Orion A. Lewis, *Nonviolent and Violent Campaigns Outcomes Dataset*, Vol. 2.0 (http://www .du.edu/korbel/sie/research/chenow_navco_data.html).

(2004) argued that the presence of allies within the state and public opinion in support of a movement's goals are crucial to success.

Other scholars, however, argue that factors internal to movements themselves are crucial. Those following the resource mobilization school argue that only sufficient resources of all types will allow a group to succeed. In addition to resources is the question of which strategies are most effective. William Gamson (1990), and many scholars since, argued that disruptive tactics and even violence produce successful change; groups engage in these tactics because they work. Some scholars have suggested more recently that this argument applies to terrorism as well, a subject we address below. On the other hand, Erica Chenoweth and Maria Stephan (2011) used a quantitative analysis of a large data set covering the past century to examine movements demanding regime change. They argued that nonviolent civil resistance is more effective than violence in all cases except secessionist movements, primarily because nonviolent movements are more effective at mobilizing widespread popular support for their cause. Nonviolent movements that could not mobilize widespread support tended to fail, while the relatively few successful violent movements were those that did mobilize widespread support. This was true even when facing authoritarian regimes and active repression.

Beyond policy and regime changes, social movements and their individual members evolve in response to their past activities, another set of potentially important outcomes. Some of their members go on to found or join formal interest groups, such as the National Organization of Women, or even political parties, such as the German Green Party. The nature of the electoral system can profoundly affect these trajectories; proportional representation in Germany provided an opportunity for the environmental movement to form a party that doesn't exist in the first-past-the-post system in the United States. When successful social movements cross over into the sphere of formal institutions, new groups often emerge to replace them with new and more challenging

Activists take part in the International Day of Climate Action in Sydney, Australia. The event was organized by 350. org, a group working to bring attention to climate change around the world. It organizes primarily via the Internet and, while based in the United States, has spread throughout the world, an example of a transnational social movement using modern technology to coordinate contentious political action across time and place.

Janie Barrett/The Sydney Morning Herald/Fairfax Media via Getty Images

agendas. In the U.S. environmental movement, for example, the institutionalization of groups like Friends of the Earth as interest groups has left the role of social movements open to new challengers like EarthFirst! and 350.org. Sabine Lang (2013) argued the fate of many social movements has been what she and others have termed "NGOization." As social movements become more institutionalized, they become NGOs (nongovernmental organizations), developing organizational imperatives to find funding and hire professional staff. In the process, they adapt both their goals and strategies to work within institutionalized political systems rather than challenging those systems more directly, and, she argued, speak for rather than engage with the citizens whom they claim to represent. Carew Boulding (2014), on the other hand, suggested that where the quality of democratic representation is low—where parties and elections do not represent popular opinion well—NGOs can have an important role in mobilizing protest; once again, the political opportunity structure matters.

Scholars of contentious politics have drawn from a wide array of political science theories—institutional, structural, and cultural—to try to understand why, how, and to what effect contentious political movements occur. Many of these theories were first developed in the context of iconic examples of contentious politics such as the American civil rights movement but can be applied to more contemporary contentious politics as well, as our case study of the Occupy and Tea Party movements in the United States demonstrates.

THE UNITED STATES: REACTING TO ECONOMIC DECLINE—OCCUPY AND THE TEA PARTY

CASE SYNOPSIS

Movements of the right and left—the Tea Party and the Occupy movement, respectively—seemed to announce a new era of contentious politics in the United States. Both movements arose in reaction to the effects of the Great Recession of 2008–2009, and the Occupy movement was also inspired by the Arab Spring. Their grievances, however, differed greatly, from a focus on inequality in Occupy to a desire to restore an earlier version of America in the Tea Party. Like most conservative social movements, the Tea Party entered electoral politics relatively quickly and had a significant impact within the Republican Party. The Occupy movement, on the other hand, joined other, recent progressive social movements in using a new repertoire of action involving long-term encampments and very active use of social media. Neither movement was sustained as a prominent organization, though the Tea Party arguably continues to have more influence than Occupy. Both, however, influenced American public opinion greatly, which the 2016 presidential campaign clearly illustrated.

- WHY Economic downturn and Obama's election produce grievances, against inequality on the left and against Obama and his policies on the right
- HOW Repertoire of "occupying" public space on the left versus more traditional protests and electoral action on the right
- OUTCOMES Changing public opinion and changing American political debate; electoral success on the right; weak long-term organizations

In response to President Barack Obama's plan of relief for homeowners affected by the mortgage crisis during the Great Recession, CNBC commentator Rick Santelli proposed on air a "Chicago Tea Party" on February 19, 2009, to oppose taxpayers' money being used to "pay your neighbor's mortgage." Two weeks later, the first "Tea Party" protests took place across the country, mostly drawing a few hundred protestors. By April, an estimated 300,000 people had attended at least one of several hundred Tea Party actions across the country. By the 2010 congressional elections, nearly forty new members of Congress who identified with the Tea Party were elected to office, returning control of the House of Representatives to Republicans.

A little over two years after the first Tea Party call went out, on September 17, 2011, approximately a thousand activists descended on the little-known Zuccotti Park near Wall Street. In the name of "occupying Wall Street," they set up a camp in which they remained for two months, drawing international attention. "Occupy" groups quickly

Protestors converge during "Occupy Los Angeles" in October 2011. In response to Occupy Wall Street, Occupy protests occurred all over the United States and around the world. While the movement was not sustained in the longer term, in part due to its decentralized organization, it brought great prominence to the issue of economic inequality in the United States and elsewhere, and arguably led to Sen. Bernie Sanders's surprisingly successful challenge to Hillary Clinton for the Democratic Party's presidential nomination in 2016.

Kevork Djansezian/Getty Images

emerged in other American cities and around the world, including a very large one in front of St. Paul's Cathedral in central London. Occupy actions, by and large copying the repertoire of the original, ultimately took place in 951 cities in eighty-two countries (Rogers 2011). In the aftermath of the economic crisis of 2008–2009, the largest and most energetic social movements the United States had seen in years emerged on both the right and left side of the political spectrum, some of which spread around the world.

Why did these dramatic examples of contentious politics explode in 2009–2011? The websites of the various "Tea Party" groups stated their ideology as restoring the government to the role they claimed the Constitution envisioned by reducing its involvement in the economy. Tea Party activists particularly opposed the government "bailout" of the financial industry in the wake of the Great Recession and Obama's proposed health care reform (what came to be known as "Obamacare"). They called for a balanced budget with lower taxes and spending, reduced environmental regulations, and an end to "pork barrel" spending in Congress. This was a conservative social movement aimed at restoring a previous era in American politics, or in their words, to "take back our country." A number of political scientists, however, argued that other grievances were at work as well. The Great Recession coincided with the election of the first African American president. Surveys showed that Tea Party members and supporters were disproportionately older men, with slightly above-average incomes, and almost exclusively white. Christopher Parker and Matt Barreto (2013), among other scholars, used survey research to demonstrate that what particularly distinguished Tea Party supporters and activists from the general population and from other conservatives were (1) their expressed fear of Obama—many believed him to be a socialist, a secret Muslim, and not really an American; (2) their negative views of other races and homosexuals; and (3) their belief in a strong social hierarchy in which people "know their place." They certainly were conservative, but they did not personally feel greater economic anxiety than other Americans and on some issues were less traditionally "conservative" than other self-proclaimed conservatives. Rory McVeigh (2014) argued that a "power devaluation model" best explains the rise of the Tea Party: its supporters believed their position in society was threatened by the relative rise of other groups and they reacted with a movement aimed at restoring an earlier time when their power was greater.

The Occupy movement two years later gained support from a different group of people. While still heavily white (though not quite as much as the Tea Party), its supporters were disproportionately young and highly educated, and had somewhat higher than average incomes; but they also had disproportionately experienced a recent job loss, home loss, or high level of debt. Many were unemployed or underemployed (Milkman et al., n.d.). Their grievances centered on the political and economic inequality that seemed to increase significantly after the recession. The initial focus of the movement was on the "economic crimes" in the financial industry that allegedly caused the recession, but a more general critique of inequality emerged, including reducing income inequality overall, reducing corporate political influence, providing greater regulation of the financial sector, and reducing student debt. The slogan "We are the 99%" emerged as the rallying cry, criticizing the wealthiest one percent who, the movement argued, had disproportionate political influence in American democracy and controlled far more economic wealth than they believed was fair.

With vastly different ideologies and bases of support, the two groups used quite different repertoires of action, with differing results. They did share one element common to social movements: very loose organizational structure. The "Tea Party" was not a political party at all, of course, and it wasn't even a single organization. Several—sometimes competing—groups emerged and established websites and blogs using the Tea Party name, the best known of which was the Tea Party Patriots. The websites typically enunciated the group's general beliefs, had space for blogs and other online forums, and most crucially provided advice and support for local activists to start their own Tea Party groups, hundreds of which sprang up around the country. Similarly, the Occupy movement never became a single organization. Indeed, organizers declared it a new kind of movement based on a "horizontal" model of organizing and a new conception of participatory democracy. They in fact denied that any real "leaders" existed, though a key group of people organized the general assembly that planned the main events and ran key social media sites. Debate was largely based on an "open mic" model in which everyone was invited to share their views.

Conservative social movements are almost always distinguished from the more common "progressive" movements by two elements: greater resources and a greater willingness to engage in electoral politics. While the Tea Party was initially suggested by a news commentator, and hundreds of thousands of supporters quickly emerged across the country, it was also financially supported by long-standing conservative political groups. Early on, the Tea Party Patriots received a million-dollar donation from a well-known conservative group, and several similar groups organized many of the protests over the first two years. These protests were the first repertoire the Tea Party used. In the summer of 2009, in particular, older conservative groups joined forces with newer Tea Party organizations to sponsor debates about "Obamacare" in congressional districts across the country, many of which became "contentious" in the clearest sense of the world, descending into shouting matches if not violence. A Tea Party Express bus tour across the country also took place. The movement's leaders, though, quickly entered the electoral arena. They helped recruit, fund, and work for insurgent candidates in Republican Party primaries in 2010.

The Occupy movement engaged in a very different and much newer repertoire of action involving long-term occupation of space and active use of social media. Inspired by the Arab Spring and the massive movement of *Indignados* (the indignant) in Spain (who protested the economic policies imposed on Spain by the European Union in the European debt crisis), they sought to establish a long-term encampment, like those in Tahrir Square in Cairo and Puerta Del Sol in Madrid. In July, the Canadian magazine *Adbusters* put out a call for twenty thousand of its readers to "occupy Wall Street" in September. Initially, it attracted limited attention, until local political activists in New York met to discuss the idea in August and created a "general assembly" to discuss and plan the event. Ultimately, the initial call fell far short of the twenty thousand protestors; for most of the two months of the encampment, a few hundred people were there. Prior to the encampment, activists primarily used Twitter to spread their message, eschewing Facebook as not trustworthy and too corporate. Their tweeting efforts, though, inspired relatively few followers, until the police reacted harshly to the initial encampment and other activists created Facebook pages and a Tumblr blog that quickly gained "likes" and support. Gerbaudo (2012, 113–117) argued that the Twitter efforts had little effect because they did not make an appeal to people's emotions. Once the "99%" slogan crystallized and an online campaign of photos of people holding signs saying "I am the 99%" went viral, support spread rapidly. Occupy groups sprang up across the country and around the world, occupying city squares, university campuses, prominent government headquarters, and financial institutions.

Arguably, neither movement has had a long-term organizational impact in its own name. Both still existed in 2016, but with significantly reduced public attention. Both, however, impacted American politics in significant ways. In opinion polls at the height of its influence, nearly one-quarter of Americans said they were supporters of the Tea Party, though a tiny fraction of those actively participated. The group's electoral efforts ultimately nominated over one hundred congressional candidates and elected thirty-nine to Congress in 2010. Quite a few incumbent members of the House and Senate also declared their allegiance to the Tea Party as its electoral clout became clear. This new group, joined by others in subsequent elections, gave the Republican Party control of Congress and set much of its subsequent agenda. Its budgetary demands led to a brief shutdown of the federal government in 2013 and the ouster of the incumbent Speaker of the House in 2015. By the 2016 presidential primaries, several major Republican candidates had emerged from or were open supporters of the Tea Party. All were defeated, however, by Donald Trump, who did not have a direct organizational tie to the movement but was the chief spokesman for the claim, popular within the Tea Party, that President Obama was not born in the United States and therefore ineligible to be president. Few candidates in 2016, though, were publicly proclaiming their loyalty to the Tea Party in the manner they had in the 2010–2014 elections. The movement had had a profound impact on the rhetoric and ideology of the Republican Party, though, even if relatively few people mouthed the words *Tea Party* in 2016.

The Occupy movement's "We are the 99%" slogan gained support from people from a wide array of backgrounds and was the first class-based social movement in many years in the United States (Winlow et al., 2015). This model, though, ultimately led those in the encampment to decide against making any specific demands of political leaders; they produced a critique but were so skeptical of established political institutions that they had no wish to negotiate with anyone in power, and they certainly did not engage in electoral politics. Any specific list of demands would inevitably leave some people's demands out, undermining the consensual, participatory organizing model. Critics contended that this was a strategic mistake, preventing the group from creating a forward-looking vision to rally people in the future (Winslow et al., 2015). Some even contended that it left New York City mayor Michael Bloomberg little choice but to remove the protestors, since the city could not respond to specific demands.

On November 15, 2011, Mayor Bloomberg ordered the New York police to disperse the encampment in Zuccotti Park, citing public health concerns as justification. While it had inspired similar protests around the world, as an organized activity, Occupy largely ceased to exist by the end of 2012. A small group of activists tried but failed to recreate the encampment on New Year's Eve of 2011 and leaders held a major rally in New York City on May 1, 2012, supported by many mainstream political organizations such as labor unions, but further efforts to resuscitate the movement met with little success.

Milkman et al. (n.d.), however, noted that the movement raised the issue of inequality in the United States in a lasting way. A survey at the time found nearly half of Americans supported the basic ideas Occupy espoused. In 2016 inequality continued to be a major political issue: the Occupy movement inspired much of the subsequent effort to raise the minimum wage to $15 per hour, which became law in a number of American cities and states, including New York state; and political and economic inequality was the main thrust behind Sen. Bernie Sanders's surprisingly successful insurgent campaign for the Democratic presidential nomination. Occupy also influenced a generation of activists. It initially brought together older, experienced political activists with younger "millennials" who had little political experience; many of the

The Tea Party Caucus's website, now defunct, featured original Tea Party candidates Rep. Michele Bachmann, R-Minn. (right), and Sen. Ted Cruz, R-Tex. (center), who went on to run in the 2016 presidential race in the United States.

Source: Tea Party Caucus (https://web.archive.org/web/20141205195335/http://teapartycaucus-bachmann.house.gov/).

latter have remained politically active in various ways, including supporting the "Black Lives Matter" movement that began in 2014.

Many observers saw the Tea Party and Occupy movement, followed by the Black Lives Matter movement, as ushering in a new era of contentious political activity in the United States. Certainly, both the Sanders and Trump 2016 campaigns often felt like "insurgent" movements rather than traditional electoral campaigns within mainstream parties. On the left, inequality gained attention as a problem to be solved to an extent that had not been true for decades. On the right, Trump's campaign upset most "conventional wisdom" about Republican Party politics. While Trump did not foreground the Tea Party rhetorically, and his policies (such as support for maintaining Social Security and Medicare as is) were sometimes at odds with the Tea Party's original agenda, survey data showed his supporters displayed the same types of resentment of Obama, other races, and immigrants that Tea Party supporters did five years earlier (Klinkner 2016).

CASE Questions

1. Which theories of contentious politics best explain why the Occupy and Tea Party movements arose and were successful when they were?
2. What do the outcomes of the two movements suggest for the debate over the impact of contentious politics in general?

POLITICAL VIOLENCE

Many people have sympathy for social movements that engage in peaceful protest but very different feelings toward groups that engage in violence. This is especially true in liberal democracies, where peaceful protest is a well-established action within the bounds of civil society but violence is seen as illegitimate; but even when opposition groups face authoritarian regimes, many people question whether violence is justified. Scholars of contentious politics, however, see violence as simply one more repertoire of action in which movements might engage. Rather than asking whether violence is ethically justifiable, comparativists in the field of contentious politics instead ask why and how groups choose to engage in violence. They note that many groups shift from nonviolent to violent tactics and back again, and assert that the contentious politics framework we outlined above can help us explain why violence happens.

Scholars working in other subfields of comparative politics—such as security studies, ethnic conflict, terrorism studies, and revolution—of course, also try to explain why violence occurs. Violence also takes many forms, from small-scale protests using physical force to terrorism to ethnically divided conflict or genocide to full-scale civil war. These categories overlap and merge into one another at times, as particular situations evolve. Often, the distinctions among these categories of violence do not involve the intent of violent groups in society but whether a regime splits in response to their actions and a transfer of power is possible (Tilly and Tarrow 2015, 172–175). We examine all of these situations briefly, using multiple perspectives from comparative politics.

Theories of Political Violence

Political violence is the use of physical force by nonstate actors for political ends. We include the term *nonstate* in this definition simply to distinguish political violence from war undertaken by states. We make no assumption or argument here about the ethical superiority or justification of political violence vis-à-vis war, but it is analytically useful to distinguish the terms. Donatella della Porta (2013) used the contentious politics framework to explain why groups choose to engage in violence. She highlighted the interactive processes between social movements and the state, and among competing movements. The political opportunity structure that groups face, she argued, is a key element. Scholars have long noted that social movements are likely to be more peaceful in democracies, where they have greater opportunity to achieve their goals. Repression, under whatever type of regime, can produce violent responses. It is likely to undermine the influence of or radicalize moderates within opposition groups, leading the groups in a more radical direction. If police escalate their response to protest, and especially if protestors see that response as excessively brutal vis-à-vis nonviolent demonstrators, a violent response is more likely. Competition among protest groups can also produce violence, as they compete for attention and support by engaging in ever more dramatic actions. Repertoires of action, however, also matter; past political violence in a society can serve as a model of acceptable and/or effective tactics, while certain forms of violence may be seen as beyond the bounds of moral acceptability, regardless of their effectiveness. Finally, emotions can be a powerful force as well; Seferiades and Johnston (2012) argue that violence can help turn emotions into a sense of meaning and purpose for activists. For della Porta and others using the contentious politics framework, we cannot explain violence by looking at the nature of the groups or individuals involved or their ideology. Rather, we have to understand the dynamic process that unfolds as groups engage in contentious actions, and the state and other groups react, all within an evolving political system and cultural setting.

Conflicts among ethnic or other identity groups, as we discussed in chapter 4, are a particularly common source of political violence. Identity groups, like other social movements, may pursue their grievances in nonviolent ways initially and then choose to become violent. Comparativists studying ethnic and other types of identity conflicts, though, have developed several other theories for why these conflicts seem to generate so much violence. Probably the oldest explanation is the primordialist argument of "ancient hatreds": some groups of people have grievances dating back centuries, hatreds they pass from one generation to the next, and they will attack one another when they get the chance. As we argued in chapter 4, though, primordialism

political violence
The use of physical force by nonstate actors for political ends

ignores the historical variation and modern origins of most ethnic identities and fails to explain why violence breaks out at certain times and not others. Indeed, in a recent comparative analysis of several African cases, Scott Straus (2015) argued that the way in which the political community was socially constructed along lines of identity is central to understanding when the most horrific form of ethnic violence, genocide, happens:

> [G]enocide [is] more likely in those places where founding narratives establish a primary identity-based population whom the state serves. Such narratives thereby construct a group or groups within a territorial space that should not be dominant and in whose hands power should not reside. In a crisis, political elites are more likely to take actions that conform to the protection of the group that defines the nation and to construct the excluded group as having interests that are inimical to the primary group. (2015, 64)

He noted that genocide only happens in times of war: when faced with an extreme threat, elites follow the logic of socially constructed identities, protecting "their own" at the expense of "the other" when groups have been constructed in the manner he describes above.

The perception of threat is a long-standing explanation for a wide variety of ethnic violence via the concept of the **security dilemma.** This is a situation in which two or more groups do not trust and may even fear one another and do not believe that institutional constraints will protect them, often because the state is weak. In that context, the fear of being attacked leads people to attack first, believing that doing so is necessary to protect themselves. Stanley Kaufman (2001) joined the security dilemma and leaders' manipulation of ethnic symbols, arguing that violent ethnic conflict arises when the two combine in a vicious spiral. Straus's (2015) study of genocide reaffirms this general approach, arguing that it explains even the worst types of violence.

The security dilemma can be especially explosive when the boundaries of identity groups overlap other social, political, or economic cleavages. If an ethnic group, for instance, believes that it as a group is not getting its fair share of land, income, or political power, violence is often possible. The perception of injustice based on the unequal distribution of resources or power is reinforced by the symbolic importance of an identity group vis-à-vis others. Psychological theorists note experiments that regularly show any time people are grouped distinctly, over time an "us versus them" attitude develops. Combined with perceived unfairness or inequality, this attitude can be explosive. Emotions can play an important role as well. Roger Petersen (2002) posited three emotions that lead to violence: fear, hatred, and resentment. Fear is a response to situations like the security dilemma in which a group's primary motivation is safety. Hatred is a motivation when an opportunity arises for violence against a group that has been frequently attacked in the past. Resentment motivates violence after a sudden change in status hierarchies among ethnic groups.

security dilemma
A situation in which two or more groups do not trust and may even fear one another, and do not believe that institutional constraints will protect them, increasing the likelihood that violence will break out between them

One of the most difficult tests of these theories in recent history is the genocide in Rwanda in 1994. In one hundred days, thousands of Hutu slaughtered 800,000 of their Tutsi compatriots in the worst genocide since the Holocaust. Genocide, the attempt to completely eliminate a people, is perhaps the most difficult political phenomenon to understand: why would large numbers of people, even when horrific leaders are encouraging them, slaughter people en masse based on who they are? In most cases of genocide, including Rwanda, people had been living together more or less peacefully (though not without resentment and memories of past violence) when, seemingly overnight, large numbers of one group started slaughtering people in a different group. While many people view Africa as full of "ancient tribal" animosities, no situation shows the inaccuracy of this primordial argument better than Rwanda. Hutu and Tutsi spoke the same language, lived in the same communities and neighborhoods, had the same customs, followed the same religions, and had lived for centuries in the same kingdom. Cultural differences between them don't exist. What did exist were several other elements commonly involved in political mobilization and violence: a potential battle over a key resource (land), a sense of relative deprivation, fear of attack in a situation of extreme political uncertainty, and an elite using a racist ideology to mobilize hatred of the "other" as part of an effort to build a strong state that it could control.

The Tutsi dominated the precolonial kingdom, but a Hutu-led government controlled the country from independence in 1960 to the genocide. Tutsi exiles who had long lived in neighboring Uganda invaded the country in 1990. By 1993 a ceasefire had been established, and democratic elections were planned. Elements on both sides, however, feared the results. Hutu leaders enjoyed the privileges of power and wanted to maintain them, and some Tutsi rebel leaders seemed unwilling to allow the majority (overwhelmingly Hutu) to rule, even via democratic means. A group of Hutu extremists in the government began propagating an anti-Tutsi ideology.

A soldier stands at a checkpoint in Rwanda in 1994. Like all genocides, Rwanda's was planned in advance and led by a militia created for the purpose. Roadside checkpoints were a key location where Hutu militia members found and killed Tutsi.

Scott Peterson/Liaison/ Hulton Archive via Getty Images

They continuously told their followers that the Tutsi were trying to regain complete power, take away Hutu land, and kill them. In a very densely populated country dependent on agriculture, the threat to land ownership was particularly explosive. The Hutu extremists also created private militia of unemployed and desperate young Hutu men, and when the Hutu president's plane was shot down on April 6, 1994, the extremists and their armed militia swung into action. Barriers went up across streets all over the capital, and the militia began systematically executing "moderate" Hutu who might oppose the genocide (lists of the first to be killed had been prepared in advance), as well as any Tutsi they found. The extremist hate-radio directed much of the effort, telling the militia where Tutsi were hiding. Members of the militia demanded that other Hutu join them in identifying and killing Tutsi; those who refused would themselves be killed. The killing didn't stop until the Tutsi-led rebellion swept into the capital, took over the country, and stopped the genocide—but only after three-quarters of the entire Tutsi population had been killed. Leaders took advantage of a situation of fear (the security dilemma) and relative deprivation to mobilize people around a socially constructed identity tied to claims on both sides that they should rightfully rule the nation. While crimes of this magnitude are still impossible to comprehend fully, we can see some patterns that help us find a rational explanation based on past theories.

Civil War

The Rwandan genocide took place at the end of a three-year civil war. While not all civil wars occur along ethnic lines, many, as the Rwandan example suggests, do. **Civil war,** whether tied to ethnicity or not, has been a particularly common form of political violence in recent decades. It is distinguished from other forms of political violence by the nature of the conflict: two or more armed groups, at least one of which is tied

civil war
Two or more armed groups, at least one of which is tied to the most recent regime in power, fight for control of the state

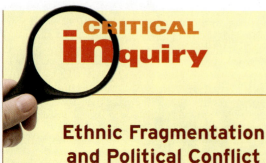

CRITICAL inquiry

Ethnic Fragmentation and Political Conflict

Collier and Hoeffler (2004) claimed that ethnicity has little to do with violent conflict; it is simply a way to justify conflict and mobilize supporters. Cederman et al. (2013), on the other hand, argued that ethnically based political exclusion and inequality do produce conflict. Map 7.1 provides measures of ethnic fragmentation and violent political conflict around the world. Comparing the two maps, what patterns do you see? Does it seem that countries with greater ethnic fragmentation also have a lot of violent political conflict? What hypotheses can you develop from the map to explain why political violence occurs more in some places than others? What do the maps suggest for the debate over what explains ethnically based violence?

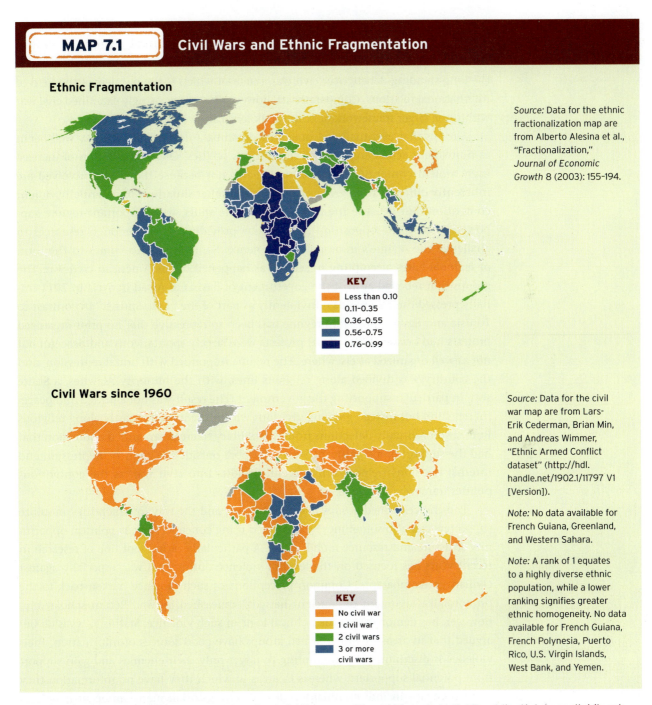

MAP 7.1 — Civil Wars and Ethnic Fragmentation

Ethnic Fragmentation

KEY
- Less than 0.10
- 0.11–0.35
- 0.36–0.55
- 0.56–0.75
- 0.76–0.99

Source: Data for the ethnic fractionalization map are from Alberto Alesina et al., "Fractionalization," *Journal of Economic Growth* 8 (2003): 155-194.

Civil Wars since 1960

KEY
- No civil war
- 1 civil war
- 2 civil wars
- 3 or more civil wars

Source: Data for the civil war map are from Lars-Erik Cederman, Brian Min, and Andreas Wimmer, "Ethnic Armed Conflict dataset" (http://hdl.handle.net/1902.1/11797 V1 [Version]).

Note: No data available for French Guiana, Greenland, and Western Sahara.

Note: A rank of 1 equates to a highly diverse ethnic population, while a lower ranking signifies greater ethnic homogeneity. No data available for French Guiana, French Polynesia, Puerto Rico, U.S. Virgin Islands, West Bank, and Yemen.

A comparison of the level of ethnic fragmentation and the outbreak of civil wars around the world demonstrates that the relationship between ethnicity and violent conflict is more complicated than people usually assume. While some countries with the highest levels of ethnic fragmentation have suffered from multiple civil wars (such as Congo, Angola, and Nigeria), others have had none (Kenya, Kazakhstan, Canada).

to the most recent regime in power, fight for control of the state (Tilly and Tarrow 2015, 180). Since 1960, civil wars have constituted a significant majority of all wars worldwide (Tilly and Tarrow 2015, 182). This chapter cannot present all elements of the long-standing debate over civil war, much of which is the purview of the field of international relations. Comparativists, however, have increasingly examined civil war within the larger framework of political violence and contentious politics.

Groups that eventually become armed combatants in civil wars may well begin as nonviolent actors engaging in contentious politics. Often, a situation of increasingly violent contention becomes a civil war not because the groups involved are inherently different from groups competing in other situations of potentially violent contention, but because the incumbent regime splits, with important regime supporters joining the opposition and thereby providing it with enough resources to challenge the regime's monopoly on violence. Sometimes, this comes in the form of regional elites attempting to secede, as happened in the American civil war. The groups that rebelled against the government of Bashar al-Assad in Syria in 2011 initially pressed their demands nonviolently as part of the "Arab Spring." In contrast to Tunisia and Egypt, the Syrian regime had been so repressive that no prior organized protests had occurred; the initial protests were largely spontaneous and peaceful but not as well organized as elsewhere. The regime responded with brutal repression, and the country was divided along religious lines, with the minority Alawites, a Shiite sect, in particular supporting the government. The result was not a united and peaceful rebellion but instead growing divisions within the military, partly along religious lines, and eventually defections from the military to create an armed opposition that had the support of a significant Syrian diaspora outside the country. Repression and internal divisions helped turn peaceful protests into civil war, as the contentious politics framework suggests.

The choices armed groups make during war and the way in which they mobilize supporters can also sometimes be explained using concepts such as political opportunity structure and resource mobilization. A particularly prominent line of research in recent years has focused on the level of violence during civil war, especially against civilian noncombatants. Common perceptions of such violence harken back to the primordialist argument of "ancient hatreds" unleashed by war. Recent scholarship, however, has demonstrated the political logic of such violence. Stathis Kalyvas (2006) argued that in areas in which armed groups have good sources of information, their violence is discriminating, attempting to target only their enemies and gain support from potential supporters, whereas in areas in which they have no information they tend to engage in indiscriminant violence, willing to kill many innocent people to ensure they get their enemies. Jeremy Weinstein (2007) examined resource mobilization, finding that groups that can rely on external sources of funding such as access to natural resources are more violent vis-à-vis the civilian population because they do not require local support, whereas groups that depend on the local population for resources are far less violent.

Scholars of security studies and ethnic conflict have also contributed to the debate over civil war, especially what causes it in the first place. Analysts long assumed a close connection between ethnic difference and civil war: groups forced to live together, typically in postcolonial states, had profound cultural, social, and political differences, and this inevitably led to secession and civil war. A group of economists led by Paul Collier, however, conducted a large, quantitative examination of all civil wars since 1960, finding that greed and opportunity were the key factors that led to violence, not ethnic difference (Collier and Hoeffler 2004; Collier, Hoeffler, and Rohner 2009). Where valuable resources such as minerals were available for groups to fight over and reap the rewards of, civil war was more likely, indicating greed is a major driving force. Civil war is also more likely in societies with large numbers of young men, available to join ethnic militia, and in societies with mountainous terrain in which rebels can hide, suggesting opportunity is also a major factor. In contrast, societies with greater ethnic fragmentation were not more likely to have civil wars, indicating these wars really weren't about identity politics at all, even if their leaders claimed that was what they were fighting over.

Recently, political scientists Andreas Wimmer (2013) and Lars-Erik Cederman et al. (2013) used new data to challenge the economists' arguments. Their data measured not just the existence of ethnic difference but the degree to which ethnic groups were excluded from political power and the degree of economic inequality among groups. Wimmer (2013) argued that civil wars typically occur in the first few decades after the formation of a nation-state, when political institutions are often weak and ethnically divided elites cannot compromise on shared governance, and some may be excluded entirely. Cederman et al. (2013) found that both an ethnic group's political exclusion and relative poverty increased the likelihood of civil war. Thus, ethnic grievances do cause civil war, but not just because different ethnic groups exist (which is what Collier and colleagues measured) but because certain groups are excluded from power and what they perceive to be their fair share of society's resources. These situations lead to mobilization of opposition as outlined in the contentious politics framework, which can and often does turn violent.

Terrorism

While civil war is unquestionably the form of political violence that has produced the most fatalities in recent decades, the most closely studied type of violence in the last fifteen years, of course, has been **terrorism**: "political violence or the threat of violence by groups or individuals who deliberately target civilians or noncombatants in order to influence the behavior and actions of targeted publics and governments" (Nacos 2012, 32). The key distinction between terrorism and other forms of political violence is who is targeted. Radical groups that become violent in opposition to some government typically target that government directly: the African National Congress in South Africa battled apartheid primarily by attacking the symbols and infrastructure

terrorism
Political violence or the threat of violence by groups or individuals who deliberately target civilians or noncombatants in order to influence the behavior and actions of targeted publics and governments

of the state, such as police stations and the power grid. In civil war, the goal is to target and defeat the government, even if civilians are killed in the process. Terrorists, on the other hand, target civilians who are not directly responsible for the targeted state's policies; they try to sow fear in a general population via seemingly random acts of violence in order to influence a particular government or population. Terrorist groups are almost always clandestine, while other groups engaging in political violence are typically more public.

Since the attacks by Al Qaeda on September 11, 2001, the field of "terrorism studies" has exploded. About fifty books were published on the subject in the 1990s and over three thousand in the 2000s (della Porta 2013, 11). Like most forms of political violence, terrorism is a tactic, not a type of unchangeable group. Many groups that engage in terrorism began using other means to address their grievances, and some ceased using terrorism at some point. Many types of groups can and have used terrorism; one of the longest-standing "terrorist groups"—now no longer using violence at all—was the Irish Republic Army (IRA), which fought to free Northern Ireland from British rule. Today, of course, most attention is focused on religious terrorists, and Islamist ones in particular.

Scholars working in "terrorism studies" explain the decision to use terrorism primarily by looking at characteristics of individuals or groups who engage in it. After the 2001 attacks, many observers asserted that terrorism ultimately stems from the poverty and lack of education in many Muslim societies, particularly among young men. In fact, numerous studies have shown that neither factor is associated with the decision to join a terrorist group; some have found that more education is associated with more terrorism, not less (Nacos 2012, 103). Others have argued that emotions such as fear and humiliation motivate terrorism, particularly in the Middle East, where Muslim societies have gone from perceiving themselves as being the most "advanced" societies in the world a millennium ago to being colonized and exploited by the West over the last century. No single factor, though, has been found to be systematically associated with individuals' decisions to engage in terrorism.

Ideology, of course, is another possible cause of terrorism; religious terrorism justifies acts of violence against what most people would see as "innocent" civilians in the name of God (or Allah) and His dictates. The leadership of Al Qaeda was heavily influenced by the Salafi form of Islam prominent in Saudi Arabia, in particular, which looks back to the founding of the religion as the golden age to which Muslims should adhere. Motivated by opposition to Israel and Western support for it, the Iranian revolution (though that was Shiite), and the Soviet invasion of Afghanistan, some radical Salafis developed a "jihadist" version of Islam that justified terrorism in the name of ridding the *umma* (the Muslim community as a whole) of Western and Jewish influence. They look to the eventual re-creation of the caliphate, or single Muslim theocratic rule across the entire Muslim world. As we discussed in chapter 2, the Islamic State in Iraq and Syria (ISIS) tried to put that caliphate in place. Some scholars see religious terrorism as qualitatively different from older, secular forms, arguing that religiously inspired groups seem to desire to kill as many people as possible, apparently without limits.

Scholars using the contentious politics framework, though, question the utility of explaining terrorism via the traits of individuals or groups. They point out that even Al Qaeda evolved over time in response to its political context, like many other episodes of contentious politics. Osama bin Laden and others officially founded Al Qaeda in 1988 as an offshoot of a broader jihadist movement whose main purpose was supporting the Taliban in its fight against the Soviet occupation of Afghanistan. The United States and Saudi governments, among others, actively supported the jihadists, including bin Laden, in their fight against the Soviets. Once the Soviets withdrew from Afghanistan, many jihadists, mostly from Saudi Arabia and Egypt, tried to return home to continue Islamist political activity, both peaceful and violent. They, for instance, were active in fighting in Yemen and Bosnia in the early 1990s in defense of what they saw as Western or Soviet attacks on Muslims. Many of their governments, however, viewed the returning jihadists as threats to domestic stability; Egypt actively repressed them, while the Saudi government initially tried to co-opt them. When the Saudi government allowed U.S. troops into the kingdom in response to the Iraqi invasion of neighboring Kuwait in 1990, bin Laden broke with his government. By 1992, he had been forced into exile in Sudan and then in 1996 to Pakistan. It was in this period, facing repression, financial constraints, and competition for followers among competing Islamist groups, that Al Qaeda issued two key *fatwas*, or commands, in 1993 and 1996, identifying the United States as the primary enemy of the Islamic *umma* and instructing the faithful to kill all Americans. Al Qaeda's ideology had evolved from fighting to defend Muslim territory from direct invasion to indiscriminate terrorism on a global scale, in response to political opportunity structures, resources, and competition within the larger Islamist movement (Alimi, Demetriou, and Bosi 2015).

"Subcommandante Marcos," in ski mask, speaks with representatives of Mexican political parties in 1994. Marcos's erudition, anonymity, and effective use of Internet communication made him and the Zapatista movement a global phenomenon, drawing support from around the world for an indigenous movement in a small, poor state in southern Mexico.

GERARDO MAGALLON/AFP/Getty Images

Political violence takes many forms and has many consequences, not all of which we can illustrate easily with our case study countries. Two recent examples of groups engaging in differing kinds of political violence, and with differing effects, are the Zapatista rebellion in Mexico that began in 1994 and the terrorism of Boko Haram in Nigeria that started in 2009. While the two cases illustrate some commonalities in the economic and political context in which political violence occurs, they also illustrate how different organizations with different ideologies can use violence to very different effect.

MEXICO: THE ZAPATISTA REBELLION

CASE SYNOPSIS

A rebellion of indigenous peasant farmers in 1994 in southern Mexico initially looked like a rather typical example of localized political violence in Latin America. It occurred in Chiapas, the poorest state in the country, where postrevolution land reform essentially never happened. But it became most unusual; via the group's charismatic leader, careful choice of language with which to express demands, and adroit appeal for national and international support via the new technology of the Internet, the movement became one of the earliest major examples of transnational activism. Its initial goal of overthrowing the government was never achieved. Instead, a long military stalemate set in, but one that allowed the movement to control and mostly govern some of its own territory. The movement's national and global appeal, though, helped spur Mexican democratization and improve indigenous rights, as well as goad the government into finally carrying out significant land reform in Chiapas. Rather than a nonviolent movement choosing to use violence strategically, the rebellion was an example of an armed group using political violence initially to gain enough attention to pursue its goals via a later shift to mostly nonviolent means.

- WHY Long repression, poverty, and end of land reform

- HOW Initial political violence, followed by first major Internet-based transnational activism, protests, and semiautonomous control of territory

- OUTCOMES Land reform; helped spur democratization; improved indigenous rights

On January 1, 1994, the day the North American Free Trade Accord (NAFTA) officially took effect, two thousand, mostly indigenous, armed rebels wearing ski masks took control of several cities in Chiapas, Mexico's southernmost and poorest state. A nonindigenous spokesman who called himself Subcommandante Marcos announced that the Zapatista Army of National Liberation, or EZLN (Ejército Zapatista de Liberación Nacional), had taken over the state. Its first communiqué called for social justice and democracy and asked for a national uprising to remove the long-ruling, electoral authoritarian PRI government. The government's response was the traditional one: it sent in ten thousand troops to quell the uprising. Within two weeks, the rebels returned to the jungle hideouts from which they came, but the military situation would remain at a standstill for years. Failing to gain military victory, the Zapatistas quickly pivoted to other repertoires of action to advance their claims, some quite successfully.

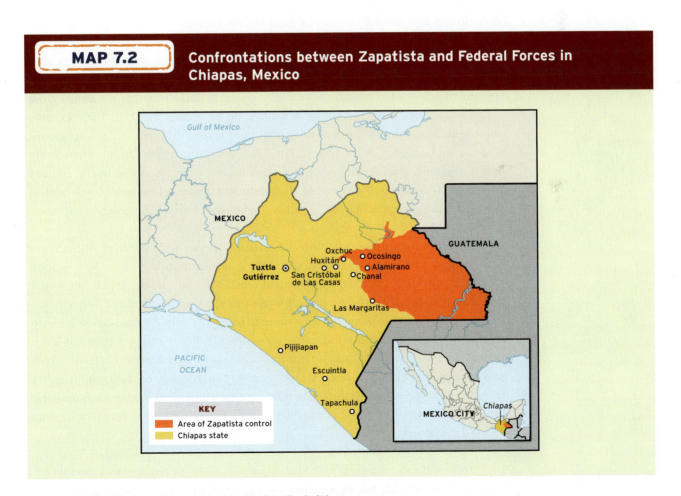

MAP 7.2   **Confrontations between Zapatista and Federal Forces in Chiapas, Mexico**

Source: George A. Collier, *Basta! Land and the Zapatista Rebellion in Chiapas.*

Behind the uprising lay a history of repression in Chiapas. The indigenous population was in turn enslaved or treated as feudal peasants throughout the prerevolutionary history of Mexico. The changes experienced in the rest of the country following the 1910–1920 revolution barely touched Chiapas. Most important, the land reforms of the 1930s that gave peasant farmers control of land via the *ejido* system never really happened in Chiapas, where large landowners and corrupt governments were able to prevent any serious reform. In significant parts of the state, the federal government had very little role, relying on local strongmen to keep order in support of the ruling party. In this sense, it was a situation of a weak state ruling over an oppressed people. The state ranked at the bottom of numerous indicators of well-being compared to other Mexican states.

In this context, social movements demanding change arose in the 1970s and 1980s throughout the state, focusing on various local concerns. They were met with repression by a particularly corrupt and brutal state government. When the federal government announced the end of land reform nationwide in 1992, before it had really ever begun in Chiapas, the situation was ripe for conflict. In addition, prices for key commodities grown in the state, such as coffee, had fallen significantly amid fears that NAFTA would cause further drops. A national leftist organization had sent a handful of activists to Chiapas in the 1980s to start to build a clandestine armed group for an unspecified future rebellion. It focused on an area of the state that was unoccupied jungle terrain until recent in-migration of several different indigenous groups, who carved farms out of the jungle. The EZLN was formed from among these indigenous migrants, with several nonindigenous leaders from elsewhere in the country. In 1993 the government discovered the group and engaged in a small battle with it. Afterward, the group decided the rebellion had to start soon or the government would wipe out all its efforts.

The Zapatista uprising was unusual in that it began with political violence and then shifted partly to nonviolent repertoires, rather than the other way around. Although only about two thousand armed rebels took part in the actual uprising, it was clear that they had the support of tens of thousands of others in Chiapas. Their initial call for overthrow of the government focused solely on class-based issues of social justice such as land reform. The government's heavy military response led to the rebels' military retreat and a shift in language use and repertoire. Their second and subsequent communiqués increasingly used the language of "indigenous rights" in addition to class-based claims. The military repression of an "indigenous uprising" caught the attention of activists and NGOs around the world, via a very new medium called the Internet:

> This swarming by a large multitude of militant NGOs in response to a distant upheaval—the first major case anywhere—was no anomaly. It drew on two to three decades of relatively unnoticed organizational and technological changes around

the world that meant the information revolution was altering the context and conduct of social conflict. Because of this, the NGOs were able to form into highly networked loosely coordinated, cross-border coalitions to wage an information-age social netwar that would constrain the Mexican government and assist the EZLN's cause. (Fuller et al., 1999, 3)

One of the first major cases of transnational activism was underway. Todd Eisenstadt (2011) argued the shift from class-based to indigenous claims was crucial to this success. Also crucial were the erudition, lucidity, and charisma of Subcommandante Marcos, who quickly became the anonymous (always behind his ski mask) international face of the movement. The international attention may have kept the government from pursuing the rebels militarily into the jungle. Instead, a military standoff and multiyear negotiation took place. An agreement was initially reached in 1996, but the government failed to pass the legislation to put it into effect and the standoff continued. Only after democratization in Mexico in 2000 did the national government finally approve some of the demands the Zapatistas had included in the 1996 accord.

Even with this limited success on the ground, though, the Zapatistas were very successful nationally and internationally. They hosted two significant conferences in the 1990s in the territory they controlled, inviting national and international activists to attend. While nothing concrete came of these efforts, they kept global attention on the movement. Political violence continued off and on through 1999, though little has occurred since. Their repertoire expanded in the new century. After initial optimism about improvements under the new government after 2000, the movement was disappointed by limited policy changes. Subcommandante Marcos and others led a caravan demanding indigenous rights around the country in 2001, culminating in Mexico City. The opposition party that gained control of the Chiapas state government in 2000 has informally taken a position of tolerance of the Zapatista presence; in areas under Zapatista control the organization runs some social services such as health clinics and schools in lieu of the government, while the government still maintains other services. In 2003 the group announced the formation of "Good Government Committees" to try to provide improved services in the areas of Chiapas still under their control, trying to replace the government altogether. Zapatistas were also active in protests demanding provision of water in particular areas of Chiapas in 2004.

The Zapatista rebellion produced neither civil war nor revolution. It did have a significant impact on the democratization of Mexico, though; the long-ruling party was seen as corrupt and brutal in its handling of the rebellion, increasing the pressure on them to yield to real political competition. Many credit the Zapatistas for amendments in 2001 that enshrined indigenous rights in the national constitution, even though the movement itself rejected them as inadequate. The state government, belatedly, also carried out extensive land reform in Chiapas in response to the rebellion in the mid-1990s, transferring 1,100 square miles of land to peasant farmers, and significantly increased social spending (Eisenstadt 2011, 36). A Catholic bishop in Chiapas said in 2014 that "[t]he EZLN remains alive, not as a military option, but as a social and political organization that fights for a dignified life. . . . It is an effort to demonstrate that autonomy is possible; you don't have to depend on the government" (*USA Today* 2014).

CASE Questions

1. What does the Zapatista rebellion suggest about the debate over why political violence arises and how effective it is?
2. What does it suggest about the debate over the role of the Internet and other new media on contentious politics?

NIGERIA: BOKO HARAM AND TERRORISM

CASE SYNOPSIS

Boko Haram in northeastern Nigeria exhibits many classic characteristics of contemporary terrorism. Its leadership emerged in an area and time of ongoing Islamist reform movements, influenced by the Salafi sect of Saudi Arabia. It began with at least slightly less violent tendencies and a stated desire to create an Islamic state separate from secular Nigeria. The military's brutal tactics in battling against it led the group to adopt terrorist tactics, targeting not only government installations but innocent civilians in schools and churches in increasingly brutal attacks. In a marginalized region with exceptionally weak presence of the national state, it briefly thrived. By 2016, it was losing ground but continued to terrorize remote areas of the region.

- WHY Regional poverty and marginalization; widespread political violence; Islamist movements locally and globally

- HOW Shift from violence targeted at state infrastructure to terrorism, partly in response to military repression

- OUTCOME Declared caliphate and joined ISIS in 2014–2015, but declining by 2016

Most Westerners first heard of "Boko Haram" in northeastern Nigeria in April 2014, when members kidnapped 276 secondary school girls from the town of Chibok. An international Twitter campaign ensued demanding the girls' return to their families, and Western governments vowed to do all they could to secure their release. As of late 2016, most were still missing, though the Nigerian government negotiated the release of twenty-one of the girls in October. The kidnapping happened in the fifth year of the group's violent struggle with the Nigerian and neighboring states, with 2014–2015 seeing the group's greatest military strength. Lying behind the insurgency, though, is a long history of poverty, political marginalization, other forms of political violence, and Islamic reform movements in the region.

Boko Haram was founded in 2002 as *Jamā'at Ahl as-Sunnah lid-Da'wah wa'l-Jihād* (Groups of the People of Sunnah for Preaching and Jihad) and changed its name to *Wilāyat Gharb Ifrīqīyyah* (Islamic State West Africa Province) when it pledged allegiance to the Islamic State of Iraq and Syria (ISIS) in March 2015. The name Boko Haram, which means "Western education is sinful," is actually a pejorative term that local detractors used to describe the group, but it has become the common name by which it is known around the world. It began in the most northeastern state of Nigeria, Borno, and operates primarily there and in two neighboring states, plus the neighboring countries of Niger, Chad, and Cameroon. As we noted in chapter 4, Nigeria has a long and difficult history of regional and ethnic conflict. In spite of the predominantly Muslim, northern region producing most of the country's military and civilian presidents, the northeastern states where Boko Haram arose remain among the poorest and most economically unequal in the country. Nigerian political scientist Abdul Raufu Mustapha (2014) argued that this economic context, combined with the local political context, are crucial for understanding the group's rise. He pointed to the extreme weakness and corruption of the Nigerian state in the region as a key initial factor. Furthermore, Nigeria's democracy since 1999 has seen a great deal of political

Nigerian school girls in Maiduguri in northern Nigeria stand next to the remains of their school after a Boko Haram attack. Boko Haram arose in a poor, marginalized area of Nigeria that was undergoing great Islamic religious ferment. It ultimately turned violent and affiliated itself with the Islamist State, though its military strength had declined by 2016.

PIUS UTOMI EKPEI/AFP/GettyImages

violence of all types, including violent campaigns for governor in Borno that involved a temporary alliance of the winning candidate and Mohammed Yusuf, Boko Haram's founder. Finally, much-heralded development schemes to reduce youth unemployment were poorly and unfairly implemented, creating great resentment among poor, young men in the region.

Boko Haram arose in this political and economic context. Northern Nigeria has a history of Islamic reformist movements dating back two centuries. Boko Haram can be traced directly to religious fervor in the 1970s and 1980s. Yusuf was youth leader of an Islamic sect that had broken off of earlier ones, heavily influenced by the Salafi version of Islam originating in Saudi Arabia, which also inspired Al Qaeda leaders. Yusuf ultimately broke with the earlier group and founded Boko Haram over the issue of how much a "true" Muslim could compromise with the secular Nigerian state. Although Borno and other northern states had already adopted *sharia* as their source of civil law under Nigeria's democracy, the Salafi sects did not think they implemented it in a pure enough form. Yusuf further argued that true believers should not work with the secular state in any way. In 2003 he and about two hundred followers created their own community in a remote area, where they dedicated themselves to living under their own version of *sharia*. They launched a series of attacks on police stations and other government offices, and Yusuf went into self-imposed exile in Saudi Arabia to avoid arrest. A rapprochement with the state government allowed him to return in 2005, when he created a mosque in the state capital, Maiduguri, and gathered followers via his charismatic preaching and provision of social services.

In 2009 police stopped a caravan of the group allegedly because it was ignoring a new motorcycle helmet law, and a firefight ensued. This led to larger battles, with the Nigerian police ultimately killing hundreds of Boko Haram supporters, capturing its headquarters, and summarily executing Yusuf without a trial. Remnants of the group quickly reformed under the leadership of one of Yusuf's assistants, Abubakar Shekau, and began a much larger-scale campaign of violence, targeting Christian churches, schools, and state institutions such as police stations and prisons. It was at this point that the group began to engage in actual terrorism, targeting innocent civilians rather than just government institutions. The group has killed several thousand people and the fighting has displaced several million, though most observers believe the Nigerian military's counterattacks have actually killed more people than Boko Haram has. The country's president declared states of emergency in 2011 and 2013, eliminating civil rights in the key northeastern states. In 2013 the military was widely reported to have gone on a rampage, indiscriminately killing hundreds of civilians in one village, in response to a Boko Haram attack that killed some soldiers.

Under its new leadership, Boko Haram's violence grew more horrific; in 2015 it was declared the most violent terrorist group in the world, killing more people than

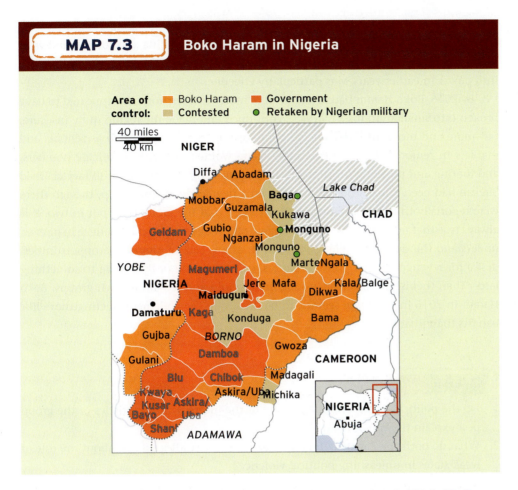

MAP 7.3   **Boko Haram in Nigeria**

Area of control: ■ Boko Haram ■ Government ■ Contested ● Retaken by Nigerian military

Boko Haram controlled significant territory in the northeastern corner of Nigeria in 2014–2015. By 2016, the Nigerian military, with the help of neighboring countries, had reduced its presence greatly, but it continued to operate as a mobile terrorist organization throughout the region.

any other. A spiral of vengeful attacks began between the group and the Nigerian military. The military's corruption and lack of resources were widely blamed for its failure to stop the group. At one point, soldiers and their wives went on strike over being sent into battle unprepared and underequipped (Mustapha 2014). Some in Nigeria believed the president at the time, who hailed from the south, was not truly interested in ending the conflict that was ripping through his political enemies' base of support. By August 2014, the group controlled significant territory in Nigeria, and Shekau declared it an independent Islamic caliphate, pledging allegiance to ISIS a few months later. The election of a new Nigerian president, a northern Muslim and former military dictator, in 2015 helped turn the tide of the battle. He reorganized the military and cracked down on some of the corruption. The neighboring states of Chad and Cameroon, which had increasingly seen violence tied to Boko Haram as well, were allowed to join the battle in Nigeria. Local citizens' militia also formed and were instrumental in helping defeat the group. Chad's military, which had fought its way into power in earlier years, was particularly effective.

By 2016, Boko Haram had lost control of most of its territory and appeared to have broken into smaller groups. Its attacks continued and made the region quite insecure, but more and more involved suicide bombings of "soft targets" such as schools and markets in remote villages, increasingly using women and girls as suicide bombers, and looting and pillaging for supplies. In August 2016, the Nigerian military claimed Shekau had been killed, and ISIS recognized a new leader of the group, though there were reports both that Shekau was still alive and that the group had split in two. It is always true that not all followers of an organization like Boko Haram believe in or even understand the declared theology behind it; often, lack of alternative opportunities, desire for revenge in local political battles, or just a sense of belonging to something larger than themselves motivate young men to join and remain in such groups. Boko Haram in 2016 increasingly seemed to be driven by these elements, acting more like bandits than jihadists.

CASE Questions

1. Do the political and economic context or the internal characteristics of the group best explain the rise of Boko Haram?
2. What do both the Zapatista and Boko Haram case studies suggest about the role of weak states in unleashing political violence?

REVOLUTION

The Zapatistas in Mexico initially hoped to foment a revolution, overthrowing the electoral authoritarian regime and replacing it with a democracy. That didn't happen. What Charles Tilly (1978) called a "revolutionary situation" seemed to exist in Chiapas, but no revolution occurred. Revolutions are a form of contentious politics, but with a difference: they involve not just a mobilized group demanding change but the successful overthrow of a regime, and in some cases an entire social order. The impetus behind revolutionary movements is often similar to the causes of other types of contentious movements, but the outcome—regime change—requires additional explanation. Social movements and other forms of contentious politics could become revolutionary movements demanding regime change, though only a handful do, and even fewer succeed. Here, we address why revolutions occur, and save their outcomes for chapter 9, where we discuss regime change more broadly.

Types of Revolution

As with so many terms in political science, scholars have debated endlessly how to define and classify *revolutions*. One way is to classify them by the ideologies that inspire them: the liberal revolution of France, the communist revolutions of Russia and China, and the Islamic revolution of Iran, for example. These ideological differences would seem to be crucial, yet most scholars of revolution argue just the opposite, that the ideological motivations and pronouncements of key leaders do not explain very much about revolutions. Typically, only the top leadership thoroughly understands and believes in the ideology in whose name the revolution is fought. As is true for all forms of contentious politics, many participants have other motivations for joining a revolution, and specific political circumstances must exist for revolutions to succeed. Ideology helps more to explain the outcomes of revolutions in that the subsequent regimes, as we discussed in chapter 3, arise out of the ideological commitments of the revolutionary leadership. However, ideology usually does not tell us much about why the revolutions happened in the first place.

We find it most useful to think of two key types of revolutions: political revolutions and social revolutions. A **political revolution** is the fundamental transformation of an existing regime, instigated and primarily carried out by a social movement or armed group. The key difference between a political revolution and a military coup or regime transition negotiated among elites (see chapter 9) is the role of at least one major social movement or armed group. Political revolutions are relatively rare, but much more rare are **social revolutions**: fundamental transformations of a regime and social structure, instigated and primarily carried out by a social movement or armed group. Social revolutions are so rare they are often historically important events not only for their country but the world, such as in France (1789), Russia (1917), China (1911–1949), Cuba (1959), Iran (1979), and eastern Europe (1989–1990).

political revolution
The fundamental transformation of an existing regime, instigated and primarily carried out by a social movement or armed group

social revolution
A fundamental transformation of a regime and social structure, instigated and primarily carried out by a social movement or armed group

Lech Walesa, the trade union leader who became the chief leader of the anticommunist movement in Poland, campaigns for president in 1989. The collapse of communism in eastern Europe from 1989 to 1990 is the most recent example of social revolution: not only the regime but also the social and economic structures of society fundamentally changed. Some countries, like Poland, became fully democratic, while others did not; but they all profoundly changed via revolutions, the rarest form of regime change.

AP Photo/Czarek Sokolowski

Many revolutions, particularly social revolutions, are violent, though they need not be by definition. For many years, analysts believed that violent movements were more likely to result in revolution, particularly social revolutions. The presumed scenario was an armed group overwhelming a weak and illegitimate regime, militarily removing them from power: storming the *bastille* in France is the classic image. Since the end of the Cold War, some theorists have reassessed that position. As we noted earlier, Chenoweth and Stephan (2011) found that nonviolent movements are actually more successful at achieving regime change than are violent movements. Not all regime changes are revolution, though, as we will discuss further in chapter 9. Using a comparative case method, Sharon Nepstad (2011) argued that nonviolent movements achieve political revolutions when they convince a section of the regime's security forces to abandon the regime. It seems the state's monopoly over the use of violence has to be eliminated one way or the other, either by overwhelming it with an alternative force or by splitting it into factions.

Why Do Revolutions Happen?

Comparativists have developed several theories to explain why revolutions occur, using the full range of political science theory: Marxist analyses of the economic structure of the old regime, structural arguments focused on political opportunity structures and movements' resources, psychological theories of the motivation to revolt, and analyses of the process of modernization.

Scholars using the contentious politics framework have claimed that grievances, mobilization, resources, and political opportunity can all be important in producing a revolution. Using social-psychological theories, James Davies (1962) argued that revolutions occur at periods of rising expectations: people don't revolt when they are at their lowest point but rather when things have started to get better and they want more. This is closely related to Ted Robert Gurr's (1970) theory of relative deprivation, which can explain the motivation for revolution just as it can other contentious political actions. Nepstad (2011, 5–6) noted the factors involving grievances and mobilization that produce a revolutionary situation: widespread grievances against the state, some elites shifting allegiance from the state to the opposition, enough anger over regime injustices to motivate popular action, a unifying ideology of rebellion, and a mobilizing organization with adequate resources to coordinate and mobilize people.

Many argue, however, that a revolutionary situation will result in revolution only when the political opportunity and/or economic structures are supportive. Theda Skocpol (1979) noted that a crucial ingredient for successful revolution is a state in crisis, often one that has been weakened by international events. She pointed to the effects of World War I on Russia as an example. A revolution can only happen where a state faces a severe crisis and lacks the resources to respond, creating a political opportunity. Jeff Goodwin (2001) also focused on the state but argued that certain types of states are prone to revolution: those with weak, neopatrimonial regimes that exclude

Was the American Revolution Really a Revolution?

The careful reader might note that we have not mentioned the United States in our discussion of revolutions. This may come as a surprise to American students who are accustomed to thinking of the "American Revolution" as a pivotal historical event. It certainly was that, but whether it was a revolution in the sense that comparativists use the term has been subject to extensive debate. Barrington Moore (1966) argued that the real revolution in the United States was the Civil War, which ended slavery as an economic system and established the dominance of industrial capitalism. He was clearly thinking of a social revolution in arguing that the American Revolution did not qualify. Like any successful anticolonial movement based on a popular uprising, the American Revolution seems to qualify as a political revolution, in that the colonial regime was destroyed and a fundamentally new one put in its place. The crux of the debate over the place of the America Revolution in the broader understanding of revolutions is the question of whether it fundamentally transformed not just political institutions but the social structure as well.

One school of thought argues that the American War of Independence was led primarily by the colonial elite, who did not envision or implement a major redistribution of wealth. Granted, they eliminated British rule and created a new republic based on the republican ideal of equality of all citizens, but they defined citizens very consciously and deliberately as white male property owners. Wealth was actually distributed less equally after the war than it had been before—and, arguably, slavery was more entrenched (Wood 1992). Not only was slavery codified in the Constitution, but it expanded for several more decades. Indeed, the Constitution as a whole can be seen in part as an effort to limit the effects of egalitarianism in that it created an indirectly elected Senate to represent state governments rather than citizens and an indirectly elected president with the power to veto laws passed by the directly elected House of Representatives.

The chief proponent of the view that the "American Revolution" really was a social revolution is historian Gordon Wood. Wood argued that the American Revolution "was as radical and as revolutionary as any in history" (1992, 5). Though he readily conceded most of the points mentioned above, he argued that the egalitarian ideals of republicanism created not just a political but also a social and cultural revolution during and after the war. Republican thought did not deny the existence of all forms of superiority but instead argued that superiority should not come from birth but from talent and reason. Some men (women were not included) would rise to the top as leaders of the new society based on their abilities, their hard work, and the willingness of others to elect them to positions of leadership. Government was therefore to serve the public interest in a way that a monarchy never did or could.

This egalitarian ideal spread throughout society, Wood contended, leading to further questions about the prerogatives of rank and privilege. He noted numerous changes to social and cultural norms, such as pressure to end many private clubs, the taking of the titles "Mr." and "Mrs." that were previously reserved for the landed gentry, and the shift from reserving the front pews in churches for select families in perpetuity to selling rights to those pews to the highest bidders. As the latter suggests, the revolution caused commerce to expand rapidly as well; wealth became even more unequally distributed, but many new men gained it. This revolution of ideas and in the way men treated other men (the treatment of women changed little and wouldn't for well over a century) helped to create a new society never before seen in which inherited status was considered illegitimate and leadership and high status were to be based solely on merit and election.

In the long term, the American Revolution clearly had a profound effect, especially due to its notion of equal citizenship. As Wood rightly noted, its ramifications went far beyond what its original Founders intended. But most of the political and social elite before the War of Independence remained the elite after the war. As for the grand ideals of equality, they applied only within the very restricted realm of white, male property owners for another generation. As Crane Brinton (1965) noted in his classic study of revolutions, the American Revolution (which he included as one of his cases) is also quite peculiar in its evolution and result: no reign of terror occurred, as is so common in violent revolutions, and an authoritarian state did not ultimately result. While arguably beneficial, the absence of these elements, along with the other points above, raises questions about whether the first war of independence against European colonialism was also a social revolution.

major groups from a share of power. These regimes are not capable or willing to allow political opposition a role in politics, which forces the opposition to turn to revolution as the only option for change, and the states' weakness means it cannot resist revolutions once started.

The earliest theorist of revolution in the modern era was Karl Marx. As we explained briefly in chapter 3, Marx believed that social revolution was the necessary transition from one mode of production to another, and that the most important transition would be from capitalism to communism. Therefore, he thought the major revolutions of the future would be communist and would occur in the wealthiest, most advanced capitalist countries. Events would show that he was clearly wrong about where, and therefore why, revolutions would occur. Many social revolutions have been communist-inspired, but they have not happened in wealthy capitalist societies or democracies. Instead, they have occurred in relatively poor countries with authoritarian regimes, most notably in Russia and China. Marx explained revolutions as the result of a particular economic structure. More recently, numerous scholars have viewed revolutions more specifically as part of the modernization process. Samuel Huntington (1968) saw them as being most likely to occur after economic development has raised popular expectations and political demands, but state institutions have not developed adequately to respond to them. Steven Pincus (2007) argued more narrowly that state modernization is the key: revolutions are most likely when the old regime is attempting to modernize the state, which brings new groups into contact with the state and expands its activities. If, in this process, it becomes apparent that the state may lack a full monopoly on the use of violence, revolutionary leaders will try to take advantage of the situation. Perhaps the most influential modernization approach, though, was Barrington Moore's *Social Origins of Dictatorship and Democracy* (1966). Moore set out to answer not only why revolutions occur but also why democracies emerge in some places and dictatorships (sometimes via revolutions) in others. He focused on the transition from agricultural to industrial society, arguing that if the landed elite commercializes agriculture by removing the peasants from the land and hires labor instead, as happened in Britain, the landed elite would ultimately become part of the bourgeoisie and demand liberal rights, putting the country on the path to liberal democracy. In contrast, if the peasantry remained on the land into the modern era, as in Russia and China, they continued to be affected by the commercialization of agriculture in ways that harmed them. In response, they provided the basis for revolutionary communist movements.

As with many areas of comparative politics, the theoretical debate over the cause of revolutions will undoubtedly continue. Some scholars see revolutions as products of particular historical epochs or transitional periods, which could help explain why there seem to be fewer of them now than in the past. Others see them as the result of forces and circumstances not tied to a particular era: rising expectations or particular political opportunities such as a severely weakened state. We can see the interplay of these various causes in our case studies of two classic social revolutions in China and Iran.

REVOLUTION: CHINA AND IRAN

CASE SYNOPSIS

The revolutions in China and Iran both came out of societies in which a sense of relative deprivation was widespread and the state had been noticeably weakened. The Chinese people had seen massive social dislocation and economic decline for at least fifty years prior to the revolution, while Iranians had witnessed a growing economy that precipitated growing inequality. Both felt a sense of relative deprivation. Both states were weakened and appeared vulnerable, creating political opportunities, though China's decline was much more severe. The political organization that took advantage of the revolutionary opportunity in China was much more united and organized than the mix of forces that overthrew the shah of Iran, resulting in a more united, but also more ruthless, postrevolutionary regime in China.

- WHY Relative deprivation, weakened state, political opportunity; differing strength and unity of revolutionary movement

- HOW Prolonged armed uprising in China; mostly nonviolent mass mobilization in Iran

- OUTCOMES Communist regime (China) and Islamist theocracy (Iran)

The revolution in China in 1949 resulted from a combination of a sense of relative deprivation on the part of the peasant majority, the creation of a political organization (the Communist Party) that could mobilize popular discontent, and an extremely weak state. The first Chinese political revolution arguably occurred in 1911 when the *ancien empire* finally fell. The peasantry, which constituted the great majority of the population, had long-standing grievances and a tradition of revolting against local landlords who became too repressive. During the late nineteenth and early twentieth centuries, though, the peasantry faced greater impoverishment than usual as the empire declined and lost control of much of its territory to Japanese and Western interests. A younger generation of elites increasingly questioned the traditions of and justifications for the old empire. In the first decade of the twentieth century, the Empress Dowager Cixi tried to respond to this growing disenchantment and rebellion with a series of reforms. Reformers, however, wanted far more radical change; many wholly rejected Confucian traditions and argued for a liberal society. Young military leaders in the provinces shared these sentiments and were the local leaders of the 1911 rebellion that created Sun Yat-sen's nationalist Republic of China.

The new republic failed to establish a democracy or hold the country together; regional warlords took over provinces and preyed on the local population while

battling one another for territory. The plight of the peasantry only got worse. Chiang Kai-shek managed to reunite the country in 1927, but under a repressive authoritarian regime led by a group who referred to themselves as Nationalists. A new generation of people still clamored for change inspired by Western models, not only liberal ones but also communist. Members of the same young, educated elite who had championed nationalism and liberalism were the initial adherents of communism, with support from the newly established Soviet Union. The Communist Party became the principal military and political rival to the Nationalists in the 1920s. During the famous Long March (1934–1935), Mao Zedong gained control of the party and began implementing his major revision of Marxist revolutionary doctrine by focusing on the peasantry as a potentially revolutionary group.

At the end of the Long March, the Communists established themselves in Yenan in northern China, creating in effect a state within a state. They began implementing their new society, and for the first time in a century peasants saw their situation in life at least stabilize, if not improve. They became the backbone of Communist Party support. Mao also built up the party, welcoming intellectuals, elites, and peasants. It became the central authority in the "liberated" territory, an early version of the state he would create after 1949. The Communists' guerrilla tactics also proved effective against the Japanese occupiers during World War II and popular with the Chinese public, giving the Communists the mantle of defenders of the beleaguered nation.

After World War II, the final phase of the revolution broke out: a four-year battle that the Communists won based on expanding support from the peasantry against Western-supported Nationalist forces. Communist victory ushered in a new state that completely changed Chinese society; a full social revolution from below had occurred. Like most social revolutions, it resulted in an authoritarian state. Those who had supported the revolution but were not Communists, and even Communists who argued for alternatives to Mao's preferred policies, were quickly eliminated, making the People's Republic of China a full-scale dictatorship.

The 1949 revolution certainly was based on grievances among the peasantry, but success also required political resources—a mechanism through which local peasant grievances and revolts could be channeled into a broader movement—and the Communist Party became that mechanism. It successfully overthrew a regime that had been weak from its inception in 1911 and had been weakened further by its humiliation at the hands of the Japanese in World War II. Deprivation, state weakness, and political mobilization had to combine to produce the Chinese revolution.

The Iranian revolution of 1979 that created the Islamic Republic contrasted starkly with the Chinese Communist revolution in terms of ideology, but it emerged from roughly similar circumstances. A sense of relative deprivation arose among many segments of the population despite a growing economy; the old regime was weakened by at least the perception of a loss of international (especially U.S.) support; and a religious leader became the charismatic symbol of revolution. The movement, though symbolically led by the Ayatollah Khomeini, was not united under one organization like the Chinese Communist Party. After the revolution, therefore, numerous groups with differing ideologies competed for power. Khomeini and his religious followers simply proved to be the most popular and were able to outmaneuver other groups to assume complete control during the first year of the new regime.

The shah of Iran's government had seemed to be a classic case of a modernizing authoritarian regime during the 1960s and 1970s. The shah consciously sought to modernize society by encouraging foreign investment, greater mechanization of agriculture, access to higher education, and secularism. These policies, however, did not benefit everyone equally. Instead, they favored larger over smaller enterprises, foreign over domestic investors, and urban over rural interests. While economic growth and personal incomes rose noticeably on average, what the poor saw was the elite's conspicuous consumption, which they compared with their own very meager gains. The 1973 quadrupling of world oil prices brought Iran a glut of wealth but skewed its distribution even further. Modernization of agriculture drove rural migrants to the cities, and there they joined the long-standing *bazaari* groups (petty traders in Iran's traditional bazaars). *Bazaari*s felt threatened by modernization as well, as the shah encouraged Western shops and banks to open in Iran to cater to the growing urban middle class, reducing the *bazaari*s' market opportunities (Clawson and Rubin 2005).

The *bazaari*s and recent urban migrants, along with students and workers, became key supporters of the revolution. Opposition to the shah had survived underground ever since the early 1950s but was divided along ideological lines among nationalists who wanted greater democracy, Marxists, and religious groups. Secular intellectuals wrote anonymous letters and circulated pamphlets calling for the overthrow of the shah. The Islamic clergy opposed the shah's Westernization policies as a threat to Islam. Exiled radical cleric Ayatollah Khomeini increasingly became the chief symbol of opposition to the regime, and even though the opposition groups supported varying ideologies, they all united in opposition to the shah.

A perception that the shah's regime was weak was a crucial element in igniting the actual revolution. U.S. president Jimmy Carter enunciated a new foreign policy based on human rights and noted the shah's regime as one that did not adequately protect such rights. The United States had strongly supported the regime for decades, so even the hint of U.S. willingness to consider regime change inspired the opposition to act. In January 1978, the government wrote a newspaper article attacking Khomeini. The following day, theology students organized a large demonstration in protest in the holy city of Qom. The shah's police responded with violence, and at least seventy people were killed. The religious opposition, joined by students and the *bazaaris*, then used the traditional mourning gatherings for those killed to organize greater demonstrations. By September, a demonstration of more than a million people took place in Tehran, and the shah once again reacted with the use of force: more than five hundred people were killed. The government declared martial law shortly afterward, shutting down universities and newspapers. This only led to greater opposition as the urban working class joined the movement by organizing strikes, including in the country's crucial oil sector.

By December, the shah had tried to respond to the rising revolt by replacing his prime minister, but this was not nearly enough to satisfy the growing opposition. In January 1979, the new prime minister managed to get the shah to leave office "temporarily" and began dismantling his hated secret police. The opposition, though, demanded Khomeini's return from exile, a demand the government continued to resist until finally giving in on February 1. Khomeini immediately declared one of his supporters the "real prime minister," a claim the government rejected. The opposition mobilized its followers to invade prisons, police stations, and military bases on February 10 and 11 to take them over in the name of the revolution. After two bloody days in which hundreds more people were killed, the revolutionaries succeeded in gaining power.

Unlike the Chinese revolution, however, no single political organization had control of the movement. Khomeini was the charismatic and symbolic leader, but one who also pledged to work with other forces. The revolutionary forces that came to power included religious groups that followed Khomeini, secular liberal nationalists who argued for democracy, and Marxists of various sorts. Over the course of the first year, however, Khomeini systematically put his supporters in charge of key institutions and called for an early referendum on the creation of an Islamic republic. The population overwhelmingly approved this move, and the new constitution discussed in chapter 8 was put in place. Over the next few years, Khomeini and his religious supporters increasingly repressed the other factions of the revolutionary movement to take firm control and create Iran's authoritarian theocracy.

CASE Questions

1. We argued that relative deprivation and political opportunity were the primary causes of the revolutions in China and Iran. Look back at our discussion of the causes of revolution. Can you use some of the other theories to explain these two cases as well? Which theory do you find ultimately most convincing, and why?

2. What similarities and differences do you see in these cases of revolution and the earlier cases of other forms of contentious politics in the United States, Mexico, and Nigeria?

CONCLUSION

The study of contentious politics has helped transform our understanding of political action outside formal institutional bounds. Political leaders and political scientists alike had earlier seen demonstrations, riots, sit-ins, and rebellions as nothing but threats to political stability. Starting in the 1960s, both activists and scholars began to argue that such contentious political acts could enhance democracy. At least in their nonviolent forms, they could express legitimate grievances that were not being met institutionally in a democracy, and they could seriously threaten authoritarian regimes. The original focus of the contentious politics framework was on social movements in Western societies, but scholars have expanded its use to examine various forms of political violence and even revolution. The study of both violence and revolution, though, includes scholars using other theoretical frameworks such as security studies.

Comparativists have examined individual motivations; internal group characteristics and dynamics; and the larger political, economic, and cultural context to try to understand contentious politics. Psychological theories are the primary means by which scholars try to explain individual motivation, focusing on why and how people form grievances and then choose to act on them. The latter, however, usually involves something beyond the psychological level. A relatively recent theory that is closely related to psychological theories focuses on emotion, particularly how anger arises. Beyond that, though, theorists have examined how and why aggrieved and angry people overcome the collective action problem. In this context, internal characteristics of mobilizing groups such as their resources and networks can be important, but so can the political and economic context. Political opportunities can lower the threat of repression from the state and increase the perceived odds of success, leading people to act. Groups' effective use of key cultural symbols and language can also help motivate action.

While nonviolent forms of contentious politics are widely accepted as legitimate in democracies and as legitimate opposition to authoritarian regimes, political violence is not. Indeed, since the September 11, 2001, terrorist attacks in the United States, political violence is most often associated with the killing of innocent civilians. In fact, other types of political violence have long existed and are far more common than terrorism. Ethnic and other types of identity movements can be particularly susceptible to becoming violent, in part because of the powerful connection between individuals' grievances and their identity. Where such violence leads—to small-scale armed rebellion, civil war, or revolution—depends as much or more on the context as it does the ideological motivations of the group in question. Groups often change repertoires, from nonviolent to violent and among violent options, depending on what is strategically advantageous and perhaps morally justified in their minds. Most scholars even see terrorism as a repertoire rather than a permanent characteristic of a group, though some groups such as ISIS seem to have placed terrorism at the heart of their ideology.

Revolutions are the rarest form of contentious politics, meaning a particular set of circumstances must account for them, but it is not always easy to determine what those circumstances are. A weakened old regime and state seem essential, as strong states can resist revolution no matter how many people are involved. A strong revolutionary organization that unites and mobilizes people's grievances also seems vital. Revolutions are known by their leaders' ideologies, but that does not always explain the motivations of the masses supporting them. The masses are often motivated by the failure of the old regime as well as a sense of relative deprivation, whether due to declining economic circumstances or rising expectations that have not been met.

The full range of political science theories have been employed to explain contentious politics. Theories focusing on individual motivation, both psychological and rational actor, try to understand the individual motivations behind contentious politics. Rational actor theorists have also looked at the strategic dynamics between the state and political movements to explain the evolution of particular episodes of contentious politics. Structural theories have long been used as well, looking at the economic structure of a society, the political opportunity structure, and the distribution of resources among groups to explain why some succeed while others fail. Finally, theorists using cultural models have sought to understand why particular symbols and language embedded in groups' repertoires are successful at mobilizing support, and how these repertoires shift over time and place.

We turn next to political institutions and participation in authoritarian regimes. While scholars initially studied contentious politics mainly in wealthy democracies, many have done so in authoritarian regimes in recent years. With institutionalized participation severely limited, scholars have recognized the growing role of contentious politics, both in expressing citizens' grievances within authoritarian regimes and in demanding the end of those regimes, a subject to which we turn in chapter 9.

KEY CONCEPTS

civil war (p. 380)

contentious politics (p. 357)

political opportunity structure (p. 361)

political revolution (p. 395)

political violence (p. 377)

relative deprivation (p. 361)

security dilemma (p. 378)

social movements (p. 358)

social revolution (p. 395)

terrorism (p. 383)

Sharpen your skills with SAGE edge at **edge.sagepub.com/orvis4e.** **SAGE edge for students** provides a personalized approach to help you accomplish your coursework goals in an easy-to-use learning environment.

WORKS CITED

Alimi, Eitan Y., Chares Demetriou, and Lorenzo Bosi. 2015. *The Dynamics of Radicalization: A Relational and Comparative Perspective.* Oxford, UK: Oxford University Press.

Boulding, Carew. 2014. *NGOs, Political Protest, and Civil Society.* Cambridge, UK: Cambridge University Press.

Brinton, Crane. 1965. *The Anatomy of Revolution.* New York: Vintage Books.

Castells, Manuel. 2012. *Networks of Outrage and Hope: Social Movements in the Internet Age.* Cambridge, UK: Polity Press.

Cederman, Lars-Erik, Kristian Skrede Gleditsch, and Alvard Buhaug. 2013. *Inequality, Grievances, and Civil War.* Cambridge, UK: Cambridge University Press.

Chenoweth, Erica, and Maria J. Stephan. 2011. *Why Civil Resistance Works: The Strategic Logic of Nonviolent Conflict.* New York: Columbia University Press.

Clawson, Patrick, and Michael Rubin. 2005. *Eternal Iran: Continuity and Chaos.* New York: Palgrave Macmillan.

Collier, Paul, and Anke Hoeffler. 2004. "Greed and Grievance in Civil War." *Oxford Economic Papers* 56 (4): 563–595. doi:10.1093/oep/gpf064

Collier, Paul, Anke Hoeffler, and Dominic Rohner. 2009. "Beyond Greed and Grievance: Feasibility and Civil War." *Oxford Economic Papers* 61 (1): 1–27. doi:10.1093/oep/gpn029

Davies, James C. 1962. "Toward a Theory of Revolution." *American Sociological Review* 27 (1): 5–19.

della Porta, Donatella. 2013. *Clandestine Political Violence.* Cambridge, UK: Cambridge University Press.

Earl, Jennifer, and Katrina Kimport. 2011. *Digitally Enabled Social Change: Activism in the Internet Age.* Cambridge, MA: MIT Press.

Eisenstadt, Todd A. 2011. *Politics, Identity, and Mexico's Indigenous Rights Movements.* Cambridge, UK: Cambridge University Press.

Flam, Helena. 2015. "Micromobilization and Emotions." In *The Oxford Handbook of Social Movements*, edited by Donatella della Porta and Mario Diani, 264–276. Oxford, UK: Oxford University Press.

Fominaya, Cristina Flesher. 2014. *Social Movements and Globalization: How Protests, Occupations and Uprisings Are Changing the World.* Basingstoke, UK: Palgrave Macmillan.

Fuller, Graham, David Ronfeldt, and John Arquilla. 1999. *Zapatista Social Netwar in Mexico.* Santa Monica, CA: RAND Corporation.

Gamson, William. 1990. *The Strategy of Social Protest.* 2nd ed. Belmont, CA: Wadsworth.

Gerbaudo, Paolo. 2012. *Tweets and the Streets: Social Media and Contemporary Activism.* London: Pluto Press.

Giugni, Marco. 2004. *Social Protest and Policy Change: Ecology, Antinuclear, and Peace Movements in Comparative Perspective.* New York: Rowman and Littlefield.

Goodwin, Jeff. 2001. *No Other Way Out: States and Revolutionary Movements, 1945–1991.* Cambridge, UK: Cambridge University Press.

Gurr, Ted Robert. 1970. *Why Men Rebel.* Princeton, NJ: Princeton University Press.

Howard, Philip N., and Muzammil M. Hussain. 2013. *Democracy's Fourth Wave? Digital Media and the Arab Spring.* Oxford, UK: Oxford University Press.

Huntington, Samuel P. 1968. *Political Order in Changing Societies.* New Haven, CT: Yale University Press.

Johnston, Hank. 2015. "'The Game's Afoot': Social Movements in Authoritarian States." In *The Oxford Handbook of Social Movements*, edited by Donatella della Porta and Mario Diani, 619–633. Oxford, UK: Oxford University Press.

Kalyvas, Stathis N. 2006. *The Logic of Violence in Civil War.* Cambridge, UK: Cambridge University Press.

Kaufman, Stanley J. 2001. *Modern Hatreds: The Symbolic Politics of Ethnic War.* Ithaca, NY: Cornell University Press.

Keck, Margaret, and Kathryn Sikkink. 1998. *Activists beyond Borders.* Ithaca, NY: Cornell University Press.

Klandermans, Bert. 2015. "Motivations to Action." In *The Oxford Handbook of Social Movements*, edited by Donatella della Porta and Mario Diani, 219–230. Oxford, UK: Oxford University Press.

Klinkner, Philip. 2016. "The Easiest Way to Guess if Someone Supports Trump? Ask if Obama Is a Muslim." Vox (http://www.vox.com/2016/6/2/11833548/donald-trump-support-race-religion-economy). June 2.

Lang, Sabine. 2013. *NGOs, Civil Society, and the Public Sphere.* Cambridge, UK: Cambridge University Press.

Larémont, Ricardo René. 2014. "Revolution, Revolt and Reform in North Africa." In *Revolution, Revolt and Reform in North Africa: The Arab Spring and Beyond,* edited by Ricardo René Larémont, 1–14. Abingdon, UK: Routledge.

McAdam, Doug, Sidney Tarrow, and Charles Tilly. 2001. *Dynamics of Contention.* New York: Cambridge University Press.

McVeigh, Rory. 2014. "What's New about the Tea Party Movement?" In *Understanding the Tea Party Movement*, edited by Nella Van Dyke and David S. Meyer, chapter 1. Burlington, VT: Ashgate.

Milkman, Ruth, Stephanie Luce, and Penny Lewis. n.d. "Changing the Subject: A Bottom-up Account of Occupy Wall Street in New York City" (https://assets.documentcloud.org/documents/562862/changing-the-subject-2.pdf).

Moore, Barrington. 1966. *Social Origins of Dictatorship and Democracy: Lord and Peasant in the Making of the Modern World.* Boston: Beacon Press.

Mustapha, Abdul Raufu. 2014. "Understanding *Boko Haram.*" In *Sects and Social Disorder: Muslim Identities and Conflict in Northern Nigeria,* edited by Abdul Raufu Mustapha, 147–198. Woodbridge, UK: James Currey.

Nacos, Brigitte L. 2012. *Terrorism and Counterterrorism.* 4th ed. New York: Longman.

Nepstad, Sharon Erickson. 2011. *Nonviolent Revolutions: Civil Resistance in the Late 20th Century.* Oxford, UK: Oxford University Press.

Parker, Christopher S., and Matt A. Barreto. 2013. *Change They Can't Believe In: The Tea Party and Reactionary Politics in America.* Princeton, NJ: Princeton University Press.

Patel, David, Valerie Bunce, and Sharon Wolchik. 2014. "Diffusion and Demonstration." In *The Arab Uprisings Explained: New Contentious Politics in the Middle East,* edited by Marc Lynch, 57–74. New York: Columbia University Press.

Pearlman, Wendy. 2013. "Emotions and the Microfoundations of the Arab Uprisings," *Perspectives on Politics,* 387–409. June.

Petersen, Roger. 2002. *Understanding Ethnic Violence: Fear, Hatred, and Resentment in Twentieth-Century Eastern Europe.* New York: Cambridge University Press.

Pincus, Steven. 2007. "Rethinking Revolutions: A Neo-Tocquevillian Perspective." In *The Oxford Handbook of Comparative Politics,* edited by Carles Boix and Susan Carol Stokes, 397–415. Oxford, UK: Oxford University Press.

Rogers, Simon. 2011. "Occupy Protests around the World: Full List Visualized." *The Guardian.* October 17 (http://www.theguardian.com/news/datablog/2011/oct/17/occupy-protests-world-list-map).

Scholl, Christian. 2014. "The New Social Movement Approach." In *Handbook of Political Citizenship and Social Movements,* edited by Hein-Anton van der Heijden, 233–258. Northampton, MA: Edward Elgar.

Seferiades, Seraphim, and Hank Johnston. 2012. "The Dynamics of Violent Protest: Emotions, Repression, and Disruptive

Deficit." In *Violent Protest, Contentious Politics, and the Neoliberal State*, edited by Seraphim Seferiades and Hank Johnston, 3–18. Burlington, VT: Ashgate.

Skocpol, Theda. 1979. *States and Social Revolutions: A Comparative Analysis of France, Russia, and China*. New York: Cambridge University Press.

Straus, Scott. 2015. *Making and Unmaking Nations: War, Leadership, and Genocide in Modern Africa*. Ithaca, NY: Cornell University Press.

Tarrow, Sidney. 2012. *Strangers at the Gates: Movements and States in Contentious Politics*. New York: Cambridge University Press.

———. 2013. *The Language of Contention: Revolutions in Words, 1688–2012*. Cambridge, UK: Cambridge University Press.

Tilly, Charles. 1978. *From Mobilization to Revolution*. New York: McGraw-Hill.

Tilly, Charles, and Sidney Tarrow. 2015. *Contentious Politics*. 2nd ed. Oxford, UK: Oxford University Press.

USA Today. 2014. "Mexico's Zapatista Rebel Movement Marks 20 Years." January 2 (http://www.usatoday.com/story/news/world/2014/01/02/mexicos-zapatista-rebel-movement-marks-20-years/4284461/).

Weinstein, Jeremy M. 2007. *Inside Rebellion: The Politics of Insurgent Violence*. Cambridge, UK: Cambridge University Press.

Welzel, Christian. 2013. *Freedom Rising: Human Empowerment and the Quest for Emancipation*. New York: Cambridge University Press.

Wimmer, Andreas. 2013. *Waves of War: Nationalism, State Formation, and Ethnic Exclusion in the Modern World*. Cambridge, UK: Cambridge University Press.

Winlow, Simon, Steve Hall, James Treadwell, and Daniel Briggs. 2015. *Riots and Political Protest: Notes from the Post-Political Present*. New York: Routledge.

Wood, Gordon. 1992. *The Radicalism of the American Revolution*. New York: Knopf.

RESOURCES FOR FURTHER STUDY

della Porta, Donatella. 2015. *Social Movements in Times of Austerity*. Cambridge, UK: Polity Press.

della Porta, Donatella, and Mario Diani, eds. 2015. *The Oxford Handbook of Social Movements*. Oxford, UK: Oxford University Press.

Sadiki, Larbi, ed. 2015. *Routledge Handbook of the Arab Spring: Rethinking Democratization*. Abingdon, UK: Routledge.

Van der Heijden, Hein-Anton, ed. 2014. *Handbook of Political Citizenship and Social Movements*. Cheltenham, UK: Edward Elgar.

WEB RESOURCES

Global Terrorism Database
(https://www.start.umd.edu/gtd/)

The Nonviolent and Violent Campaigns and Outcomes (NAVCO) Data Project
(http://www.du.edu/korbel/sie/research/chenow_navco_data.html)

The World Handbook of Political Indicators
(https://sociology.osu.edu/worldhandbook)

8 AUTHORITARIAN INSTITUTIONS

KEY QUESTIONS

- Some authoritarian regimes disperse power more widely than others. How can comparativists determine "who rules" and what limits executive power in an authoritarian regime?

- Authoritarian regimes come in several different subtypes: military, one-party, theocratic, personalist, and electoral authoritarian. In what ways do differences across these subtypes explain differences in leaders' actions, levels of repression, and types of popular participation?

- Why is clientelism so prevalent and important in authoritarian regimes? In what types of authoritarian regimes does it seem most important, and what might explain this?

- Some authoritarian regimes allow at least some institutionalized limits on rulers' power. What explains where and why this happens, or doesn't happen?

The spread of democracy in the aftermath of the Cold War led some to believe that democratic rule was irreversible; dictators were historical relics, soon to be relegated to the "dustbin of history." Many eastern European and African societies that threw off or severely challenged their authoritarian regimes, however, ended up creating new ones, albeit less repressive than their predecessors. Electoral authoritarian regimes, in which some opposition and participation were allowed but a key ruler or party firmly held onto power, became more common. In other cases, especially in the Middle East, the winds of democratic change did not blow strongly enough to seriously challenge authoritarian regimes until the sudden outburst of popular opposition in the "Arab Spring" of 2011. Abandoning the study of authoritarian regimes at the end of the Cold War was clearly premature, and in the new millennium comparativists have taken renewed interest in the subject. The Country and Concept table on page 410 shows how common and how varied authoritarian regimes are, just within our eleven case studies.

The answer to the question "Who rules?" seems like it ought to be particularly obvious in authoritarian regimes: the dictator does. In fact, discerning who really has power and how much power they have is not always obvious. In chapter 3, we noted that in modernizing authoritarian

A man walks by a portrait of Syrian president Bashar al-Assad near the Syrian capital of Damascus. The Syrian civil war shows the potential conflagration that can occur when an authoritarian regime starts to lose control. Assad met a peaceful uprising as part of the "Arab Spring" in 2011 with violence and clung to power. The Syrian civil war ensued and five years later continued, provoking one of the biggest humanitarian disasters of the new millennium, sucking in international actors including both the United States and Russia, and producing a refugee crisis of such magnitude that it rocked the foundations of the EU.

(YOUSSEF KARWASHAN/AFP/Getty Images)

and personalist regimes, neither ideology nor formal institutions necessarily explain who rules or how a particular regime functions. Authoritarian regimes tend to arise in relatively weak states that have weak formal institutions, and therefore informal institutions and processes are more important. This makes determining who has how much power particularly difficult.

The prevalence of important informal institutions in authoritarian regimes also makes explaining political behavior challenging. In chapter 3 we outlined several subtypes of authoritarian regimes based on their origins and formal institutions: one-party, military, personalist, theocratic, and electoral authoritarian. These subtypes clearly have somewhat different governing institutions, but given that formal institutions in authoritarian regimes tend to be weak, how much does this really explain? Are one-party regimes as a group different in distinctive ways from military regimes? Does one subtype always provide greater levels of institutionalized limits on executive power? Is one subtype always more repressive? It is clear as well that clientelist networks are important in virtually all authoritarian regimes. Why is this the case, and does this also vary across the subtypes of authoritarian regimes?

COUNTRY AND CONCEPT
Authoritarian Rule

Country	Twentieth-century authoritarian rule since independence (years)	Authoritarian regime type	Number of supreme leaders	Average length of leader's rule (years)	Cause of regime demise
Brazil	1930–1945	Modernizing authoritarian	1	15	Democratization
	1964–1985	Military	5	4	Democratization
China*	1927–1949	Modernizing authoritarian	1	22	Revolution
	1949–	Communist/modernizing authoritarian	6	11	NA
Germany	1871–1918	Modernizing authoritarian	2	23	War loss
	1933–1945	Fascist	1	12	War loss
India	None	–	–	–	–
Iran	1921–1979	Modernizing authoritarian	2	27	Revolution
	1979–	Theocratic	2	18	NA
Japan	1867–1945	Modernizing authoritarian	3	26	War loss
Mexico	1924–2000	Modernizing authoritarian	15	4.5	Democratization
Nigeria	1966–1979	Military	4	3	Democratization
	1983–1998	Military	3	5	Democratization
Russia	1917–1991	Communist	7	10	Democratization
	2000–	Electoral authoritarian	1	16	NA
United Kingdom	None	–	–	–	–
United States	None	–	–	–	–

*China's republic (1912–1927) never consolidated an effective state.

A key difference among authoritarian regimes that will help us answer these questions is the regimes' level of institutionalization, which we defined in chapter 5 as the degree to which government processes and procedures are established, predictable, and routinized. In the least-institutionalized personalist regimes, decisions truly can be made and implemented at the whim of the dictator. In other authoritarian regimes, the leader's power is still extensive, but it is somewhat curtailed by institutionalized checks. For example, the Brazilian military regime in the latter part of the twentieth century institutionalized a rotating presidency, with each branch of the military designating a president for an established term. Communist regimes have politburos and other mechanisms of high-level party consultation that may force some discussion and consensus building among the party elites. Trying to explain variations in institutionalized limits in authoritarian regimes is another important question that we examine in this chapter.

All modern states, including those with authoritarian regimes, have executive branches and bureaucracies and provide some sort of judiciary, though how much the judiciary is independent of the executive is a major question. Some authoritarian regimes also develop institutions such as legislatures and even hold elections to provide some degree, however small, of citizen participation, though not enough to threaten the power of the key rulers. We therefore examine the same sets of institutions in this chapter that we did in chapters 5 and 6 for democracies, but the distinct context and logic of authoritarian regimes require somewhat different foci and theoretical lenses to understand those institutions.

AUTHORITARIAN RULE AROUND THE WORLD

While not the promised land of universal democracy that some analysts thought it would be, the era after the end of the Cold War certainly had a significant effect on authoritarian regimes. Their numbers declined, particularly in the 1990s, and their institutions changed. The result was a decline in the number of purely authoritarian regimes and the rise of electoral authoritarian regimes. With the expansion of democracy as a global ideal, more regimes attempted to legitimize their rule through the creation of elections and legislatures but kept those institutions limited enough to maintain authoritarian control overall. The ultimate control that authoritarian rulers—whether individuals, groups, or parties—preserve even in electoral authoritarian regimes means that we can analyze the latter with many of the same concepts we will use to analyze all authoritarian regimes, as we discuss below.

The total number of authoritarian regimes in the world peaked in the late 1970s, though the decline was much more rapid after the end of the Cold War. Authoritarian regimes ruled about 75 percent of all countries in the 1970s, but by 2008 that number was down to about 40 percent (Svolik 2012, 25), many of which were electoral authoritarian regimes. Map 8.1 shows this transformation around the world and over time.

The changing nature of the institutions in contemporary authoritarian and electoral authoritarian regimes is clear in Figures 8.1 and 8.2. Most dramatic is the precipitous drop (Figure 8.1) in single-party systems among authoritarian regimes at the end of the Cold War and their replacement with multiple-party systems. This clearly shows the sharp rise in electoral authoritarian regimes, the product of liberalization of older authoritarian regimes or (as we will discuss in chapter 9) failed transitions to democracy. Figure 8.2 demonstrates that these regimes now allow opposing parties some voice via legislatures as well. Over 80 percent of current regimes have elected legislatures of some sort, and about 60 percent allow multiple candidates per legislative seat, a good indicator of an electoral authoritarian regime. In about 40 percent, the ruling party controls less than three-quarters of the legislative seats, indicating it has allowed the opposition a significant (though still firmly minority) position. Today, most authoritarian regimes allow some sort of legislature and opposition parties to exist and participate in some form. A key question is why.

GOVERNING INSTITUTIONS IN AUTHORITARIAN REGIMES

supreme leader
Individual who wields executive power with few formal limits in an authoritarian regime; in the Islamic Republic of Iran, the formal title of the top ruling cleric

Virtually all authoritarian regimes recognize one supreme leader, even if he leads a larger ruling group, such as the politburo in a communist system or the ruling junta in a military government. This **supreme leader** typically wields executive power with few formal limits. He is likely to consult with other top leaders and may be chosen by them, but he nonetheless contends with few formal constraints on his power. In many regimes, the top leaders each informally control an important source of power—an institution or a faction within the government—and the supreme leader must make sure that he has sufficient support from these other leaders before he makes major decisions. In some more personalist regimes, even these informal limits may not exist.

All supreme leaders rule through some combination of repression, co-optation, and efforts at legitimation. *Repression* is the popular image that pops into people's minds when they think of dictators, but it is an expensive way to rule. Even the most ruthless dictator needs to find other means by which to ensure citizens' loyalties. *Co-optation* via material inducements and official positions (which often go hand in hand with corruption) is the most obvious alternative means of securing support. Most regimes also expend resources to try to instill loyalty in the citizenry to secure some actual *legitimacy*; if citizens believe in the regime, they will obey it without the costs of repression or co-optation. Communist parties use their well-developed ideology for this purpose to a greater extent than do most authoritarian regimes, but virtually all authoritarian regimes try to gain legitimacy in some way.

Security is certainly all regimes' top priority, and this is especially true for authoritarian regimes, which often have limited legitimacy. All types of authoritarian regimes, not just military ones, spend generously on military security, typically aimed more at internal than external threats. The loyalty of the military is, of course, crucial. One-party states either incorporate key military leaders into the party leadership or make sure that loyal party leaders have control of the military, or both. For example, after the 1979 revolution that overthrew Anastasio Somoza's personalist regime in Nicaragua, the new Sandinista regime insisted that the new military (which replaced the Somoza-created National Guard) remain under the control of the Sandinista army that had

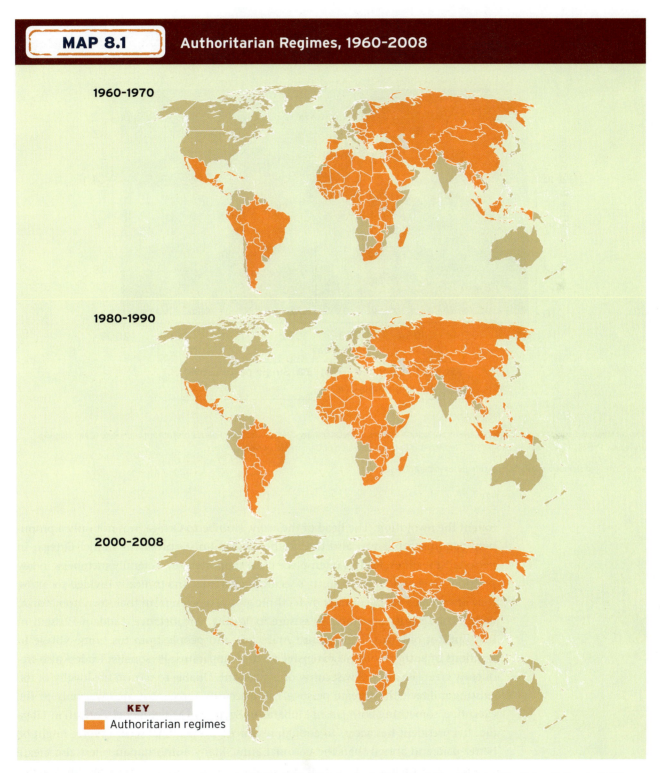

MAP 8.1   **Authoritarian Regimes, 1960–2008**

1960–1970

1980–1990

2000–2008

KEY

Authoritarian regimes

Source: Data for the map are derived from Milan W. Svolik, *The Politics of Authoritarian Rule* (Cambridge, UK: Cambridge University Press), 45–50.
© Milan W. Svolik 2012.

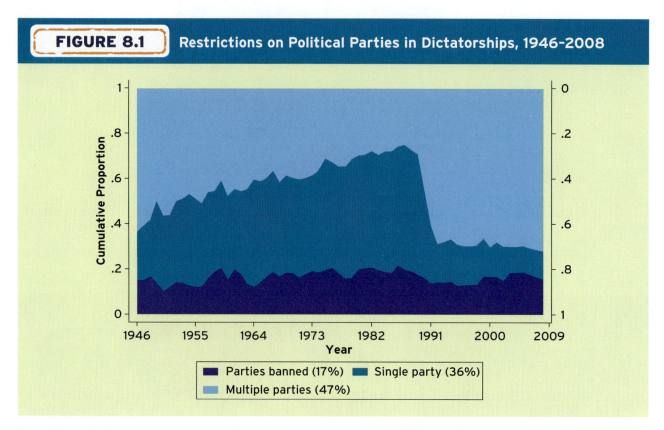

FIGURE 8.1   Restrictions on Political Parties in Dictatorships, 1946-2008

Legend:
- Parties banned (17%)
- Single party (36%)
- Multiple parties (47%)

Source: Milan W. Svolik, "Figure 2.4, Restrictions on Political Parties in Dictatorships, 1946-2008," *The Politics of Authoritarian Rule* (Cambridge University Press), 35. © Milan W. Svolik 2012. Reprinted with the permission of Cambridge University Press.

Note: Overall distribution of individual categories in parentheses.

fought the revolution. The head of the army, Humberto Ortega, was not only a prominent Sandinista but was also the brother of Sandinista president Daniel Ortega. In personalist regimes, leaders often place close supporters, even family members, in key positions in charge of the country's security apparatus. In ethnically divided societies, they often place people of their own ethnic group, or even from their own hometown, within the security apparatus to ensure its loyalty. For instance, Saddam Hussein in Iraq put not only his fellow Sunni Arabs but also people from his home village in positions of authority in his extensive security apparatus. Personalist leaders also frequently create entirely new security organizations. Unable to rely on the loyalty of the existing military, they create personal, elite security forces that are loyal only to the executive, something both Hosni Mubarak in Egypt and Muammar el-Qaddafi in Libya did. If a president has access to enough resources, his personal security force might be better paid and armed than the national army. Many authoritarian rulers also create vast networks of spies, both civilian and military, whose job is to gather intelligence on regime opponents.

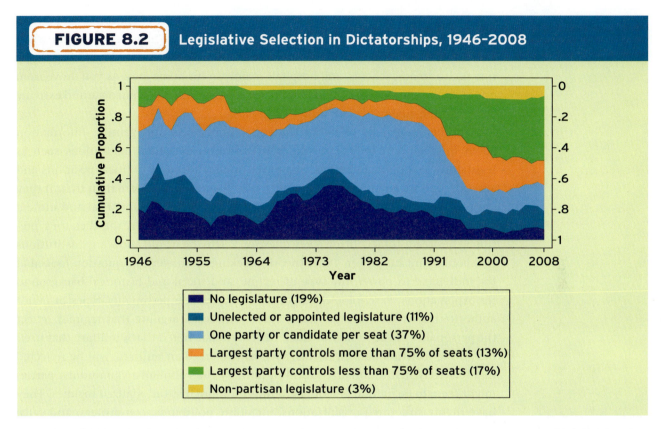

FIGURE 8.2   Legislative Selection in Dictatorships, 1946–2008

Source: Milan W. Svolik, "Figure 2.6, Legislative Selection in Dictatorships, 1946–2008," *The Politics of Authoritarian Rule* (Cambridge, UK: Cambridge University Press, 2012), 36. © Milan W. Svolik 2012. Reprinted with the permission of Cambridge University Press.

Note: Overall distribution of individual categories in parentheses.

Ronald Wintrobe (1998) used a rational choice approach to argue that all authoritarian leaders face what he termed the **dictator's dilemma**: because of the repression they practice, they lack accurate information on how much political support they actually have. Repression breeds fear, which in turn breeds misinformation; the greater the repression, the greater the dictator's dilemma. Uncertain of their position, dictators try to co-opt potential rivals by purchasing their loyalty. They can never be certain, however, of how much they need to spend to purchase the loyalty they require, so they tend to overspend, lavishing resources on key sectors from which they believe threats may emanate. Various elements in the military often receive such attention. This is especially true in military regimes that came to power via coups d'état themselves. They are acutely aware that potential rivals within the military may well overthrow them. Milan Svolik (2012) argued also that authoritarian regimes that rely on the military for repression risk being overthrown by the military; the regime's reliance on the military gives the latter greater power and resources and therefore the ability to intervene. In ethnically divided societies, dictators may focus spending on their own ethnic group

dictator's dilemma
An authoritarian ruler's repression creates fear, which then breeds uncertainty about how much support the ruler has; in response, the ruler spends more resources than is rational to co-opt the opposition

to maintain their core base of support. In a number of African authoritarian regimes in the 1970s and 1980s, you could tell who was in power by how well paved the roads were in different regions of the country. The current dictator would build infrastructure such as roads, schools, and hospitals mainly in his home area. As you drove from one region to another, you could literally see who ruled by the immediate and extreme change in the quality of the roads.

Another means of co-opting potential opponents and gaining information about their support for the regime is the creation of formal institutions such as legislatures and political parties. These can provide lucrative political positions and access to patronage to co-opt opponents, but they may offer more than that. If they create a credible and safe means of voicing opposition, even if partial and muted, institutions can help overcome the dictator's dilemma. Given the dictator's presumed desire for total control, a key question is why he would allow any institutions that could limit his power. Older theories seeking to answer this question looked at the individual in power, the type of regime, and social and historical background for explanations. Psychological theorists examined the personality types of major authoritarian leaders such as Hitler, Stalin, and Mao, arguing that regimes reflect the personality of the supreme leader. Other scholars noted that a military that itself has strong institutionalized norms, such as the Brazilian military, will be reflected in a relatively institutionalized form of military rule. Similarly, Communist parties might seem to be natural breeding grounds for more institutionalized regimes. They have highly structured organizations, including politburos, committees, and cells, in addition to consultative and decision-making mechanisms. Both political culture theorists and historical institutionalists looked to broader societal factors and history. An authoritarian regime in a country with some historical experience with democracy may well be more likely to adopt or recreate some limited formal institutions like a legislature. Citizens are accustomed to these institutions, and the regime leaders therefore believe they can gain legitimacy by at least appearing to adhere to these institutional norms.

More recently, most scholars of authoritarian rule have used rational choice theory to explain the rise of institutions, focusing on the supreme leader's need to make credible commitments vis-à-vis other important political actors. Dictators fear potential opponents, often including their alleged allies, who have access to arms and could overthrow them. This can be especially important when an authoritarian ruler first comes to power. No one does so single-handedly; whether via a coup, a rebellion, or a single party winning an election and then taking absolute control, all dictators gain power with a group of supporters. Initially, at least, those supporters are likely to fear the new dictator usurping all power, and they are the group most capable of overthrowing him. The new leader can use institutions to try to make credible commitments that limit his power somewhat, or even provide means for his possible removal, in order to convince these other important actors that they will be safe from an uncontrollable personalist regime.

Svolik (2012) argued that institutions are most likely to arise when a balance of power exists between a dictator and his closest allies. As a dictator tries to usurp more power for himself, his allies' only way to resist is a credible threat to overthrow him. The allies, however, face a collective action problem: any individual who commits to an unsuccessful rebellion faces likely imprisonment or death. If the dictator can amass great personal power, his allies' credibility to resist him drops, and the collective action problem gets worse, meaning he can usurp even more power. The result is a personalist dictatorship. If a balance of power exists between the dictator and his allies at the outset, however, the allies are more likely to be able to credibly threaten a rebellion against him and he is less likely to attempt to usurp power. Some formal institutions are therefore more likely.

Jennifer Gandhi (2008) applied a similar logic to the dictator's opponents: when the opposition is united, formal institutions are more likely to arise. Where the regime controls extensive mineral wealth, on the other hand, institutions are less likely because the dictator can use mineral wealth to co-opt segments of the opposition. Legislatures and opposition parties are also more likely, she argued, in civilian dictatorships than in either monarchies or military regimes. The latter have independent power bases— the monarchy in its family and traditional legitimacy and the military in its control of repression—that provide them greater power vis-à-vis the opposition and therefore less need for legislatures or opposition parties. Where the opposition is united, though, and the regime does not have other sources of legitimacy or support, it is more likely to allow legislatures and political parties, thus explaining why electoral authoritarian regimes arise. Legislatures and political parties, however, may do more than simply help dictators make credible commitments to ward off overthrow. They can actually provide a space in which policy compromise can occur: "Within these institutions, leaders of religious organizations, business and labor associations, and various other groups can express demands that do not appear as acts of public resistance to the regime. The dictator, in turn, uses legislatures and parties as a way to control dissent and to make concessions while appearing to be magnanimous rather than weak" (Gandhi 2008, 137). Gandhi demonstrated that regimes with legislatures and parties spend less money on the military and have greater respect for human rights, both of which are classic demands of opposition forces. Similarly, Yadav and Mukherjee (2016) found that the presence of both a small and medium business association and a multiparty legislature induced authoritarian regimes to reduce corruption, a common demand of opposition groups. These findings indicate that policy compromise and a degree of horizontal accountability are greater in electoral authoritarian regimes than other types of authoritarian rule.

The ability of regime opponents in legislatures to influence policy, though, depends on how much they are able to negotiate a set of institutions that allows them real voice. Our case study of Brazil provides an example of a highly restricted legislature and opposition party. The military (in power from 1964 to 1985) recreated an elected legislature but limited participation to two parties, one officially supporting the regime and one officially opposing it. The opposition, however, was severely restricted in what it was allowed to say or do in the legislature, whose powers were fairly nominal in any case. Nevertheless, the legislature served as a forum in which the opposition party could voice its views and the government could respond. In Kenya's one-party state in the 1960s and early 1970s, individual legislators within the sole, ruling party were able to voice limited criticisms of the government, work on behalf of their constituents to gain resources for their home areas, and use their access to government to gain direct benefits for themselves and their closest associates via corruption. The parliament clearly served as a mechanism of co-optation and, occasionally, of limited policy discussion. When MPs criticized the dictator too much, though, they faced repression: several sitting MPs were detained and tortured in the mid-1970s when their criticisms of the regime became too strident, and the most popular member of their group was assassinated. This effectively ended all vestiges of legislative independence, moving the regime closer to a personalist one.

Some authoritarian regimes also allow for a degree of rule of law and autonomy for the judiciary, though this is always limited. Typically, judicial autonomy is permitted only in nonpolitical cases. Providing the political good of basic personal security to citizens who do not oppose the regime allows the regime to gain a degree of legitimacy. Allowing this type of limited judicial autonomy can also help top leaders gain information about how effectively their state functions on the ground, reducing the dictator's dilemma. Citizens can go to court to attempt to get local government to carry out its functions properly, revealing to leaders potential local problems. Allowing courts to enforce property rights and contracts encourages domestic and foreign investment, which improves economic growth and therefore government revenue, potentially strengthening the regime. Using our case study of China, Yuhua Wang (2015) found that authorities allowed judicial autonomy on economic issues when organized investors were strong enough to demand it, threatening to take their assets elsewhere if their demands were not met. Authoritarian leaders, however, do not allow the rule of law to limit them in any fundamental way: when necessary, they use the judicial system to repress their opponents and remove judges to ensure that the leader's will is done. In many authoritarian regimes, especially personalist ones, the judiciary becomes quite corrupt as well. Regime leaders and other wealthy people often bribe judges to rule in their favor; once this begins, more and more people recognize what "justice" actually requires, and corruption expands.

All states, regardless of regime type, require a bureaucracy, and all leaders face the principal-agent problem we identified in chapter 5. In an authoritarian regime, though, the question is how strong and independent a bureaucracy the supreme leader wants and opponents can demand. A less-institutionalized bureaucracy, while not serving citizens' interests well, may have distinct advantages to the leader in the form of patronage opportunities that it offers regime supporters. Bureaucratic positions provide opportunities for corruption. The top leaders can thus maintain loyalty by allowing officials to use their positions to their own benefit, weakening the

The "Politics of Survival" in Mobutu's Zaire

Zaire (now the Democratic Republic of the Congo) under the dictatorship of Gen. Mobutu Sese Seko (1965–1997) was a classic case of a corrupt, personalist regime in a weak state. His long rule shows the ability of a personalist dictator to survive, especially when he has external support, but it also demonstrates that the means he must use to survive continuously weaken institutions, ultimately undermining his rule.

Mobutu came to power via a U.S.-supported military coup in the midst of a civil war and created the formal structures of a one-party state, but his rule was very personalist. All power and all major decisions went through him, and personal loyalty and patronage were the key elements of his political power. To maintain personalist rule, he had to severely weaken virtually all institutions by following the logic of what political scientist Joel Migdal (1988) termed "the politics of survival."

Strong institutions can be sources of regime strength and longevity if the supreme leader is willing to or is forced to allow them. A personalist regime is one in which the leader has managed to avoid that, perhaps to his short-term advantage of maintaining total power. In the long term, though, he comes to fear any potential source of opposition, including from those who control whatever institutions exist. Subordinates who lead state agencies that can solve people's problems or provide valuable resources thereby gain political support, potentially threatening the supreme leader. Personalist leaders thus do not follow the logic of allowing some institutionalization in order to co-opt opposition within limited bounds. Instead, they undermine institutions via such practices as frequently shuffling subordinates so that none of them becomes entrenched in any one position and appointing people who are personally loyal to them but who may have little competence in their positions.

Mobutu was a master of this kind of politics. He ruled first and foremost by patronage, creating a regime that many referred to as a "kleptocracy," or rule by theft. A government appointment was a license to steal. He also shuffled personnel frequently. If he saw an important official as a rival, he would remove him and then return him to power shortly afterward. A famous case involved Nguza Karl-i-Bond. He was foreign minister and then head of the ruling party in the mid-1970s, but after being mentioned as a possible successor to Mobutu he was accused of treason in 1977, imprisoned, and tortured. A year later, Mobutu forgave him and restored him to the prominent

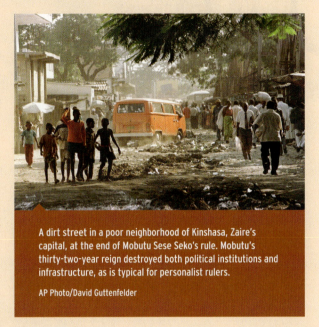

A dirt street in a poor neighborhood of Kinshasa, Zaire's capital, at the end of Mobutu Sese Seko's rule. Mobutu's thirty-two-year reign destroyed both political institutions and infrastructure, as is typical for personalist rulers.

AP Photo/David Guttenfelder

office of state commissioner. Then, in 1981, Nguza fled into exile in Belgium, denounced Mobutu for his corruption and brutality, and even testified against him before the U.S. Congress. In 1986, however, Mobutu once again forgave him, and Nguza returned to Zaire to a hero's welcome; shortly afterward he was named to the prestigious position of ambassador to the United States. Examples like this proved to all that Mobutu could take people from a top position to prison and back again in the blink of an eye.

"The politics of survival" (along with generous Western support during the Cold War) kept Mobutu in power for three decades but weakened all institutions in Zaire. Even basic infrastructure declined as the state's resources and capabilities collapsed. When Mobutu's neighbor and ally, Rwandan president Juvénal Habyarimana, was facing an armed insurrection in the early 1990s, Mobutu is alleged to have told him, "Your problem is you built roads. They are coming down those roads to get you." Mobutu did not make that mistake: Zaire's road network deteriorated to almost nothing under his rule. Nonetheless, rebel forces eventually forced the aging Mobutu out of power, after the end of the Cold War deprived him of Western support.

What Explains the Rise and Fall of Authoritarian Regimes?

We have now become familiar with several of the leading theories of why authoritarian rulers do or do not create institutions and allow some opposition to have a voice. Map 8.1 and Figures 8.1 and 8.2 on pages 413–415 showed us the broad patterns of when and where authoritarian regimes have arisen and disappeared and shifts in their use of particular institutions. Looking again at the map and figures, can the theories we've just discussed explain the patterns you see? What other hypotheses can you create that would explain the patterns you see in the map and figures?

institutions of the state but rewarding the loyalty of potential rivals. If this behavior is informally institutionalized, it can become somewhat predictable: lesser officials will remain loyal because they believe they can rise to higher and more rewarding positions, which can lead to somewhat predictable career paths within key institutions.

Where stronger institutions are created and survive, they can lengthen the life of an authoritarian regime. Opponents and allies of the leader are less likely to attempt to overthrow the regime if they gain some combination of personal reward and influence that is regularized via institutions. Svolik (2012, 111) created a dataset of authoritarian regime longevity that showed that those with legislatures lasted much longer than those without. Similarly, Albertus and Menaldo (2016) found that in Latin America, authoritarian regimes that instituted new constitutions survived longer than similar regimes that did not write constitutions. Institutions make political life more predictable, helping to overcome antiregime opposition, and may make the question of leadership succession more predictable as well, a key concern all authoritarian regimes face.

The Problem of Succession

Authoritarian regimes are plagued by the question of succession. Electoral democracies provide a means of changing leadership on a regular basis; authoritarian regimes have no such procedure readily at hand. Each regime must create its own system for choosing new leaders. Again, the degree of institutionalization matters greatly. Communist regimes, for instance, generally chose new leaders from among key contenders within the politburo. While the exact process was usually hidden from the general public, both regime leaders and citizens knew that should a leader die, resign, or be forced from office, a pool of successors was available and top party leaders would collectively choose one from among their own. China continues to follow this model today, as we discuss below. The Country and Concept table on page 410 illustrates the institutionalization of succession in the Soviet regime (listed under Russia in the table); it had seven different leaders over seventy-four years, while many less-institutionalized authoritarian regimes typically have no succession system and fail to survive their founders' demise.

Personalist leaders often rule for life or until they are forced out of office. Many will groom a successor as they age, all the while working to make sure that the successor does not become a threat before the time to pass the baton arrives. In the most personalist regimes, the leader grooms his own son to be his successor. The Somoza dynasty in Nicaragua (1936–1979) began with Anastasio senior, who was succeeded by his son Luis, who in turn was succeeded by his brother, another Anastasio. This was also the case in the regimes of "Papa Doc" (1957–1971) and "Baby Doc" Duvalier (1971–1986) in Haiti. Baby Doc was only nineteen years old when his father died and he became head of state. Should a personalist ruler die without clearly identifying a successor, a battle among key elites can emerge that can cause the regime to crumble. Sometimes, as in the case of Nigeria, the death of a personalist ruler can be the opportunity for democracy to emerge anew. Erica Frantz and Natasha Ezrow (2011) found that leaders of military and one-party regimes are more likely to be removed from office than are leaders of personalist regimes, but that when personalist leaders are overthrown, the entire regime is likely to collapse.

Some authoritarian regimes do have modest institutionalized limits on executive power, a form of limited horizontal accountability among key elites. In electoral authoritarian regimes, legal opposition and a legislature are allowed, which can allow some predictability to the regime and modest policy influence for the opposition, but ultimate power is kept firmly in the hands of the key rulers. Vertical accountability, the ability of the citizenry to hold leaders directly accountable, is extremely limited. We will take up this subject after examining authoritarian governing institutions in our case studies of China, Russia, and Iran.

CHINA: FROM COMMUNIST TO MODERNIZING AUTHORITARIAN RULE

CASE SYNOPSIS

China has transformed itself from a communist regime with strong personalist overtones under Mao into a modernizing authoritarian regime that has substantially institutionalized its rule. In the process, it has become much more stable and predictable, though it continues to use repression when necessary and faces a grave threat from corruption. Corruption, though, demonstrates that co-opting potential opposition is an important survival strategy for the Chinese regime, just as it is for most authoritarian regimes. Despite these continuing problems, the regime has presided over the fastest-growing economy in the world and has found a solution to one of the

CASE SYNOPSIS

chief problems of authoritarian rule: succession. Since 2012, President Xi Jinping has increased repression of dissent, anticorruption efforts, and the party's ideological propaganda to gain greater control over the party and attempt to gain greater legitimacy. Some fear that the charismatic president is also personalizing power, possibly reversing some of the successful institutionalization of the last decades.

- REGIME TYPE One-party, modernizing authoritarian
- REPRESSION Primarily aimed at major regime opponents
- CO-OPTATION Patronage and corruption opportunities within party and government
- INSTITUTIONALIZATION Greatly increased in top leadership, judiciary, civilian control of military; possibly increased personalization under President Xi
- SUCCESSION Regularized and signaled in advance from within ruling party elite

In November 2012, the Chinese Communist Party (CCP) held the biggest event on its calendar, the Party Congress, which happens once every five years. It anointed Xi Jinping as the new supreme leader, electing him general secretary of the party and head of the military commission; he was duly appointed president of the country a few months later. Xi's rise to the top was not a surprise; the prior Party Congress in 2007 clearly signaled Xi's position as the next leader by appointing him vice president, among other posts. The long process demonstrated the full maturation of an opaque but nonetheless predictable succession process that has emerged over the last two decades. It represents an institutionalization of the authoritarian regime that is part of the reason why it has survived so long and so well. The Party Congress on the surface is all about uniformity, with nearly unanimous votes on every issue and leader. But the united face shown to the public is the product of months of jockeying among key leaders to get their people into top positions. Xi's ascension was a carefully orchestrated compromise between the two prior supreme leaders and their followers; his vice president is from the opposing faction. Institutionalization co-opts all major political elites to maintain unity.

China's communist regime has been in power since 1949 but has changed profoundly since Mao's death in 1976. Though communist in name, in practice China has become a modernizing authoritarian regime by successfully encouraging state-led, capitalist development while maintaining a firm one-party hold on political power via greater institutionalization and a mix of repression and co-optation. This is a far cry from the early days of the regime. Communist rule under Mao developed into a full-blown personality cult by the late 1960s. Mao's rule, especially during the Cultural Revolution (1966–1976), undermined most institutions; the regime was increasingly personalist and obedient to the whims of the aging Mao.

Upon Mao's death, the new leader, Deng Xiaoping, (1978–1989) joined others in trying to reestablish order and stable governing institutions under the authority of the CCP. The leaders seem to have deliberately set out to create a more-institutionalized system of rule. These reforms were embodied in a new constitution in 1982, which was significantly amended in 1999. Authority remains vested first and foremost in the ruling party, which fuses executive and legislative functions. As Figure 8.3 shows, each key governing institution has a parallel party institution. The National Party Congress is the official decision-making body of the party, and the National People's Congress is the equivalent of the legislature. Both institutions are ostensibly elected by provincial and local bodies, but in reality the higher organs ensure that only candidates loyal to the ruling party are selected. Real power lies in the party's politburo and even more so in the smaller Politburo Standing Committee (PSC). The State Council and its Standing Committee are in effect the cabinet that actually runs the government, overseen by the politburo and PSC.

Like all communist regimes, China has struggled with the relationship between the party and state institutions. Under Mao, membership in the top parallel institutions was nearly identical; today, overlapping membership continues but is by no means universal. The regime under recent leaders has tried to distinguish between the governing role of the State Council and the political oversight role of the politburo and the PSC. The ultimate authority of the party organs and their top leadership, however, remains unchallenged; party entities oversee every level of the state throughout the country.

Greater institutionalization is perhaps most apparent in leadership succession. Upon Mao's death in 1976, a two-year battle among factions ensued that created a period of great uncertainty. Ultimately, Deng and his allies emerged victorious, launching China on its current path. Deng anointed Jiang Zemin as his successor and systematically began transferring power to him in 1989, though the process took several years. In 2003 the transfer of power became regularized as Jiang chose Hu as his successor, though Jiang continued to be influential, including having a substantial role in choosing the new politburo and getting his protégé, Xi, appointed as supreme leader a

Chinese president Xi Jinping, center, speaks during a meeting of the Chinese Community Party's politburo. Since Mao's death, China has created an increasingly institutionalized, modernizing authoritarian regime. By all accounts, the politburo rules somewhat collectively, though Xi has amassed more power and personal following than his recent predecessors, leading some analysts to fear a personalization of power that could undermine institutionalization.

(Xinhua/Li Xueren via Getty Images)

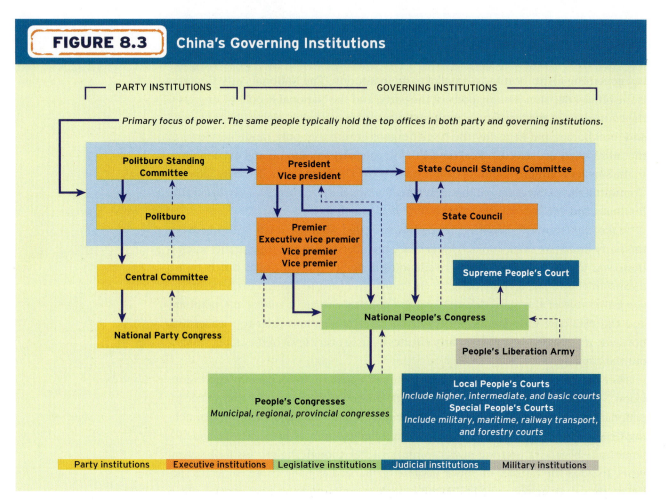

FIGURE 8.3 | **China's Governing Institutions**

Note: Dashed arrows indicate formal selection process or direction of authority. Bold arrows indicate actual selection process or direction of authority.

decade later. Generational change in the broader leadership has also come to be a hallmark of Party Congresses: the Central Committee elected at each Party Congress now routinely includes about 60 percent new members, with each Party Congress seeing a significant shift toward younger and more highly educated members (Shambaugh 2008, 153). Xi is the first supreme leader born after the 1949 revolution. China seems to have institutionalized a form of leadership succession both for the very top posts and more broadly that, while still opaque to outsiders, promises some predictability and stability.

There has always been one supreme leader who is simultaneously president, general secretary of the party, and chair of the Central Military Commission, though he does not rule alone. While the workings of the politburo and the PSC are secret, all reports suggest that a great deal of open discussion occurs within these highest organs of power, and their members represent all major factions among the top elite. With Hu's elevation to the top leadership, two major factions emerged: those with backgrounds in the party's youth league, through which Hu rose and who are supported by leaders from inland and poorer regions, and those from the wealthier, coastal areas, collectively known as the "Shanghai gang" (Li and White 2006). The two factions have split power very evenly since 2007 in terms of membership in the top decision-making organs. Li Cheng (2010) saw the factional balance serving as an informal system of checks and balances on the top rulers as they limit one another's power and, therefore, the power of the supreme leader. The succession of Hu to replace Jiang, and Xi (a member of the Shanghai faction) to replace Hu, may also be establishing a norm of shifting the leadership between the factions. As the charismatic President Xi gained power and popularity, however, some analysts argued he was amassing greater personal power than any leader since Deng, potentially threatening the collective leadership (Minzner 2015). Reports circulated in late 2016 that Xi was planning on delaying the announcement of

The Decline of Communism

Number of one-party communist states in 1975: sixteen

Albania	North Korea
Bulgaria	Poland
China	Romania
Cuba	South Yemen (People's
Czechoslovakia	Democratic Republic of Yemen)
East Germany	Soviet Union
Hungary	Vietnam
Laos	Yugoslavia
Mongolia	

Number of one-party communist states in 2016: five

China (in name only)	North Korea
Cuba	Vietnam (in name only)
Laos	

Source: "One-Party State" (Wikipedia (http://en.wikipedia.org/wiki/Single-party_state#Former_single-party_states/) and (http://en.wikipedia.org/wiki/List_of_Communist_States).

his successor until after the 2017 Party Congress, breaking with past precedent and increasing speculation that he might try to hold power longer than the two terms that have become the norm.

In addition to the party leadership, the military has long been a crucial faction in Chinese politics but also has been subordinate to the civilian leadership of the party. The vast majority of the army, and certainly all of its top leaders, are ruling party members, trained to support the party and its ideals. Both Mao and Deng retained great military loyalty because of their personal roles during the revolution. Even Deng, however, had to appease the armed forces at times. For example, when the top commander in Beijing refused to use his troops to disperse the student demonstrators in Tiananmen Square in June 1989, Deng had to call a meeting of all seven regional commanders and persuade the other six to back the move before the army would act. After that, Deng initiated major reforms of the military that have significantly professionalized it as well as improved its funding. No military leaders have been in the top organs of the country's leadership since the 1990s, and while the military does have channels to let its voice be heard, it does so primarily in areas of direct relevance to it such as defense and foreign policy. The army remains an important faction behind the scenes, but for the moment the top leadership seems to have institutionalized effective civilian control over it, eliminating a potential threat to survival that is common in authoritarian regimes.

The judiciary has also seen significant institutionalization in the past two decades. Under Mao, virtually no criminal justice system existed; little in the way of codified law existed, and what law did exist was not followed with any regularity. Significant changes have occurred since 1980, though the Chinese legal system still does not include the basic rights familiar to Western citizens. The Supreme People's Court, the country's highest court, has the right to interpret the law and the constitution but not to overturn decisions of the National Congress. As always, the party remains supreme over all. Trials are now supposed to be open to the public, and most are, but the government still prevents the public from attending high-profile political cases. The trial of the popular regional leader Bo Xilai on corruption charges in 2013 included the public release of edited transcripts, the highest level of transparency in a major political trial up to that time.

Civil and economic law have been liberalized more extensively than criminal law, as the government has had to protect private property rights and contracts to attract foreign investment. A 1989 reform of administrative law increased the ability of citizens to take local government agencies to court for not doing their job properly. An average of 100,000 such cases were filed annually in the 1990s, with a success rate estimated at 15 to 20 percent (Ginsburg 2008). A broad survey found rapidly growing use of and trust in courts among Chinese citizens in the new millennium, especially for handling civil disputes (Landry 2008). By the early 2000s, the courts became overwhelmed and the central government issued an order to reduce the number of cases accepted; therefore, Chinese citizens with complaints against local government took petitions directly to authorities rather than trying to sue. A proposed change in 2016 would take control of local courts away from the local party branch and give it to the provincial branch higher up, raising hopes that the courts would be more willing to address grievances against local governments if they have support from higher-level authority. Wang (2015) examined where and why courts have been strengthened in China, arguing that stronger courts and rule of law exist primarily for civil and economic law involving property rights and contracts. His quantitative analysis found that local governments strengthened the rule of law in these areas in response to demands from foreign investors who did not have the political connections to gain special treatment and therefore demanded fair treatment via the courts.

China has significantly institutionalized its regime, but the government is certainly still willing to use repression when necessary. Bruce Dickson (2016) argued that China has a long history of easing and tightening repression as needed to control problems at minimal cost. The latest tightening, he argued, began in the lead up to the 2008 Olympics and accelerated once Xi became president. Crackdowns

against human rights activists and others increased significantly as the Olympics approached. The government also increased restrictions in Tibet, a region whose populace desires greater autonomy or independence, after five hundred monks protested continued Chinese rule. A similar response met protests by ethnic Uyghurs demanding greater freedoms and social services. Fearing a public reaction to the "Arab Spring" in 2011, the government cracked down again on journalists and dissidents and censored Internet sites related to the uprising, including all references to the word *jasmine* because of the "Jasmine revolution" in Tunisia. Xi cracked down more harshly on dissent beginning in 2013, including within the press. In 2016 the international NGO Reporters without Borders ranked China the fifth-worst country in the world on press freedom.

Under Xi, the party has also returned to an active effort at mandating an official ideology. Jiang and Hu made little attempt to enunciate an official ideology beyond following in Deng's path and pursuing economic growth. Xi, on the other hand, began making major ideological pronouncements shortly after gaining power. He has tried to rehabilitate Mao's image by saying that both Mao's and Deng's era were equally important in understanding China today. He has mandated ideological training for journalists and in universities and arrested many professionals who dared to criticize the regime, including university faculty, lawyers, and editors (Zhao 2016). Xi has also expanded the role of nationalism and Confucianism as ideological supports for the regime, pursuing a more aggressive foreign policy to establish China clearly as a major superpower and the unquestioned leader of Asia.

One of the biggest threats to the CCP does not come from protesters or dissidents but from within: corruption. The government's legitimacy is now heavily based on its economic performance, which corruption directly damages. Dickson (2016) found via an extensive public opinion survey that rising personal incomes increased the regime's popular support while personal experiences with corruption lowered it. Zhou (2015, 122) reported that corruption costs the country an estimated 13–17 percent of GDP every year. With the rise of a market economy, opportunities for corruption have multiplied rapidly. State and party officials are in positions to receive bribes because of their control over regulation of financial services, key licenses for business activities, land-use rights, infrastructure contracts, and government procurement. A new practice since the 1990s is *maiguan maiguan,* the buying and selling of government positions, especially at the local level in less-developed regions. Joseph Fewsmith (2013) argued that the CCP faces a classic principal-agent problem. The party leadership demands that local officials achieve economic growth while maintaining social stability. In the world's largest country, however, much authority is left in the hands of local party leaders. As long as they "deliver" on the key items of growth and stability, they will please their superiors and earn promotions; otherwise, they are free to pursue their own interests. This has produced corruption, personalization of power in the hands of local leaders who control promotions, and an expansion of local government.

The party's Central Commission for Discipline Inspection is charged with ferreting out corruption within the party, and the Chinese leadership is emphasizing corruption eradication more strongly than in the past. Pei (2007) reported that while 130,000 to 190,000 party members were disciplined between 1982 and 2007, only 6 percent were prosecuted, and only half of those have been convicted. President Xi launched a massive anticorruption crusade in 2013, which reached higher into the ruling elite than ever before and helped him purge potential internal opponents. By 2016, an estimated 300,000 people had faced corruption charges, including close to 150 high-level elites. The very top leadership itself had long been beyond accountability, until the case of Bo Xilai, a provincial party secretary and a rising star in the party. In 2012, one of Bo's top aides was accused of massive corruption and Bo's wife was ultimately implicated in a murder that Bo may well have been trying to cover up. His very public removal from office exposed high-level intrigue and corruption in the party like nothing the country had yet witnessed.

Subsequently, former PSC and top military officials were convicted on corruption charges as well, as the elite increasingly worried that almost no one was safe from Xi's campaign. Reducing corruption, though, poses risks itself. To the extent the regime relies on co-opting elites via corruption opportunities for support, it will only go so far in eliminating those opportunities. The anticorruption drive has made Xi personally very popular. Combined with his ideological campaign, perhaps he will be able to maintain personal and regime power with less need for corruption. The anticorruption efforts seem to be having some effect: in 1995 Transparency International ranked China the fourth most corrupt country in the world, while in 2015 it was ranked seventy-fifth, in the middle of the global spectrum.

CASE Questions

1. What does China's succession system suggest about the relationship between personal power, succession, and regime survival in authoritarian regimes?
2. What does China's battle with corruption teach us about how well authoritarian regimes can reduce corruption, and what corruption's implications are for regime survival?

CASE Study

RUSSIA: CREATING AN ELECTORAL AUTHORITARIAN REGIME

CASE SYNOPSIS

Vladimir Putin transformed what was a chaotic electoral democracy into an electoral authoritarian regime. While Russia was rated only as "Partly Free" by Freedom House in the 1990s, it shifted to "Not Free" in 2005, where it has remained. Putin manipulated the formal rules of a weakly institutionalized semipresidential system to cement his power. Crucial to this, though, was the loyalty of the security apparatus out of which he arose, and his ability to use growing state revenue from mineral exports to co-opt opponents and reward allies. Until his return to the presidency in 2012, he seemed to have great popular support, based on the growing economy and his use of an ideology of state strength, order, and nationalism.

- REGIME TYPE Electoral Authoritarian

- REPRESSION FSB security apparatus key to Putin's power

- CO-OPTATION Oil wealth, state-owned companies, and ruling party as sources of patronage

- INSTITUTIONALIZATION Regular though fraudulent elections, manipulation of constitution to ensure executive power, selective use of anticorruption laws

- SUCCESSION Putin observed two-term limit as president, but retained informal power and returned to presidency after one term as prime minister

In the 2016 U.S. presidential campaign, Russia's autocratic leader, Vladimir Putin, became a significant source of debate. He had increased Russia's role in world affairs significantly, often in ways the U.S. government opposed; Russian hackers had allegedly stolen and released Democratic Party e-mails; and Republican candidate Donald Trump openly admired him as a "strong leader," while Democratic candidate Hillary Clinton portrayed him as a brutal tyrant. To many, it appeared that a "new Cold War" was developing, with an authoritarian Russia once again a nemesis of the United States. Putin gained this international notoriety by creating an electoral authoritarian regime after being elected president in 2000.

Putin inherited the semipresidential system depicted in Figure 8.4. As discussed in chapter 5, the Russian version of semipresidentialism gave exceptional power to the president. The parliament, or Duma, had to reject the president's nominee for

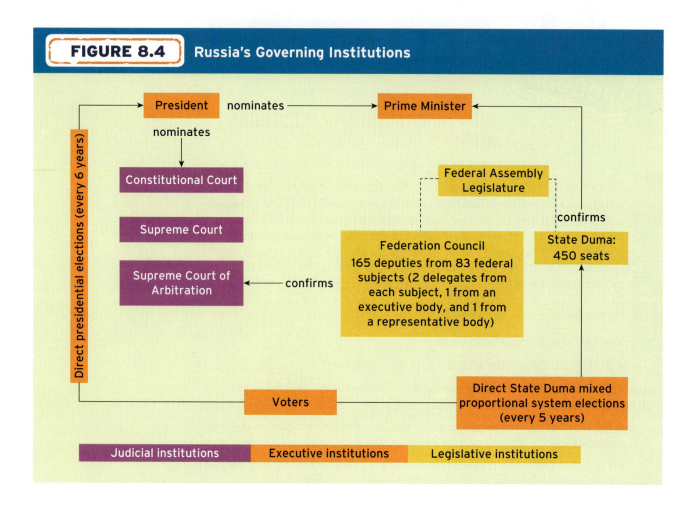

FIGURE 8.4   Russia's Governing Institutions

prime minister three times before it would be official, at which point parliament would be dissolved and new elections held, a clear incentive to support the president's choice. Beyond that, the president and prime minister had nearly unchecked powers of appointment of cabinet ministers and other key officials and could issue laws by decree when parliament did not pass a piece of legislation. Putin's predecessor, Boris Yeltsin, ultimately became a very weak president in spite of his formal powers. As we will outline in more detail in chapter 9, Russia's transition to democracy in the 1990s was quite chaotic. Yeltsin never managed to secure majority support in parliament for his major policies, in part because he refused to engage in party politics, preferring to stay "above the fray." Instead, he ruled largely via his decree powers, and he was informally dependent on the wealthy "oligarchs" who captured control of major companies during the chaotic transition from a state-planned to a market economy. By the end of the decade, Yeltsin had virtually no popular support and was increasingly ill and ineffective. Facing a destabilizing battle for his succession among several close aides, in 1999 Yeltsin anointed the relatively unknown Vladimir Putin as his successor and resigned from office so Putin could run as an incumbent in the 2000 presidential election.

Putin, a former KGB agent who led the security apparatus under Yeltsin, would prove to be a much stronger president than his predecessor. He came to office in auspicious times. The transition to a market economy in the 1990s caused years of economic decline and hardship until a full-blown crisis in August 1998. In the aftermath of that, however, and supported by a rapid rise in the price of oil, Russia's top export, the economy started to stabilize and by 2000, economic growth reached 5 percent; for the first time in a decade at least, the average Russian's income was going up, not down. Putin was mainly known to the Russian people as a war hero from the first war in the breakaway region of Chechnya (see chapter 5), and the successful prosecution of the second war in Chechnya (1999–2004) added to his military luster. Upon assuming office, he announced goals of establishing order, increasing the strength of the state, and furthering market-oriented economic reforms. After a decade of chaos and weakness, the public was ready for order and strength, and Putin won the 2000 election with 53 percent of the vote in the first round.

From there, Putin rapidly put in place an electoral authoritarian regime, though he referred to it as "managed democracy," saying he supported democracy but only as long as it did not produce disorder and weakness. He put the new regime in place by (1) relying on his tight control of the security apparatus; (2) an initial agreement with the "oligarchs" to minimize their political influence, followed by stripping them of their assets; (3) the creation of a dominant, ruling party; (4) greater centralization of Russian federalism (discussed in chapter 5); and (5) an ideology of order and strength that became increasingly nationalist. The economic boom gave Putin vast resources to expend in co-opting support to make all this happen.

Putin replaced Yeltsin's "family" that had wielded informal influence in the 1990s with a group of former agents of the Federal Security Bureau (FSB), the successor to the KGB where he had spent most of his career. Over several years, he placed members of this group in key ministries and agencies throughout the executive branch, appointed them governors of regions, and gave them control of many important companies (Hesli 2007). They were his closest allies on whom he could rely. As they gained power and positions at the expense of the oligarchs of the 1990s, their loyalty was also cemented via the opportunities for corruption they received, with many becoming very wealthy.

While Putin began with loyal support within the security apparatus, he faced powerful potential enemies in the oligarchs. They had gained wealth via the corrupt and chaotic privatization of state-owned companies in the 1990s. The wealthiest and most influential were in the energy and media sectors. In his first year in office, Putin met with the most important oligarchs and made a frank bargain with them: he would not question or investigate the way in which they gained their wealth or their current economic activities, as long as they did not oppose him politically. They readily agreed.

Some, however, later resisted. Most famous was Mikhail Khodorkovski, head of the giant Yukos oil firm. By 2003, he was courting Western investment in his company and becoming increasingly open about his plans to enter politics against Putin. As he did with a number of other oligarchs before and after, Putin used selective enforcement of anticorruption laws to eliminate Khodorkovski. He was charged with corruption and ultimately jailed by a compliant judiciary whose judges Putin mostly appointed. Many other oligarchs fled the country to avoid the same fate. The government was able to buy Yukos stock and take control of it, placing it firmly in the hands of the state oil company, led by loyal Putin supporters from the security apparatus. After the "Yukos affair," Putin turned against other oligarchs, primarily in the energy sector so that the state could regain direct control of the most important sector of the economy, and in the media, to eliminate any critical voices.

Putin successfully emasculated the power of both the parliament and regional governments in his first few years in power. Creating a dominant, ruling party that was loyal to him was a crucial element of both efforts. We discuss the party directly in the case study below on participation. It started, though, as a bargain with the Communist Party, the largest in the Duma when Putin became president. He formed a working coalition with it until he was able to co-opt the leaders of other, smaller parties, at which point he turned against the Communists, who have been a weak opposition ever since. Once it was established, the dominant party, United Russia, could get candidates elected in regional governments rather easily across the country. This helped him reduce resistance to the changes he made to federalism that we outlined in chapter 5: replacing elected governors with ones appointed by him; creating "presidential representatives" overseeing seven, large regions across the country; and gaining complete control of the upper chamber of the parliament, which became a rubber stamp for his proposals. As the economy boomed, revenue poured into the central states' coffers as well, which Putin distributed to regions based on their political loyalty, also removing any opposition to his gutting of federalism.

President Vladimir Putin meets with MPs from his ruling party, United Russia, in the Kremlin. The party is a key institution in Russia's electoral authoritarian regime.

Mikhail Klimentyev\TASS via ImagesMikhail Klimentyev\TASS via Getty Images

Finally, Putin used ideology to cement popular support. Initially he focused on increasing state strength and establishing order, which was welcomed by a weary populace at the turn of the millennium. Over time, Putin increasingly used nationalist appeals to gain support, including aligning himself with the Russian Orthodox Church and "traditional Russian values." This turn to nationalism increased when the Russian-backed president in neighboring Ukraine was overthrown in 2014. Shortly afterward, Russia invaded and annexed Crimea, a region that had historically been Russian and was populated largely by Russian speakers but was officially part of Ukraine. He then supported, with a covert military invasion, Russian speakers in eastern Ukraine who rejected the change of government in Ukraine and wanted to become part of Russia. These policies were wildly popular with the Russian people, garnering him great, though short-lived, popularity at home. Subsequent forays into international affairs, most prominently in the Syrian civil war, also gained him support as a strong nationalist building a strong state.

Facing a constitutional limit of two terms as president, Putin anointed Dmitry Medvedev as his successor, who was duly elected president in May 2008. Putin himself became head of his ruling party in the Duma and PM and unofficially remained the chief leader of the country. While some observers thought Medvedev might gain real power and chart a more liberal path than Putin's, after one term as prime minister, Putin and Medvedev "agreed" to switch roles, with Putin running for and winning the presidency again in 2012 and Medvedev returning to the prime minister position. While Medvedev did institute some liberalizations, most notably restoring the election of governors, it became clear that he ultimately remained dependent on his mentor's power, based in Putin's control of patronage via the growing state sector and the loyalty of the security apparatus. Indeed, another "reform" Medvedev instituted was extending the president's term to six years, meaning Putin is legally eligible to stay in office until 2024. After Putin became president, the Duma amended the rules on electing governors in a way that gave Putin renewed power over their selection (see chapter 5).

CASE Questions

1. How did Putin use the tools of dictatorial rule as outlined earlier to create an electoral authoritarian regime?
2. Why has Putin preserved the trappings of democracy rather than creating a purely authoritarian regime? Can you use the theories of why dictators allow institutions to survive to explain Putin's actions?

IRAN: A THEOCRATIC, ELECTORAL AUTHORITARIAN REGIME

CASE SYNOPSIS

Iran's formal system of government combines theocratic institutions with quasi-democratic ones, producing a theocratic version of an electoral authoritarian regime. The "democratic" elements are intended to provide some space for participation and for popular voices to be heard, but the constitution ensures that the supreme leader and the institutions he directly controls can dominate when they need to. They have used repression when necessary, clientelism, and efforts to combine theocratic and democratic claims to legitimacy to remain in power. In the 1990s, the regime allowed reformist politicians who wanted to reduce strict adherence to Islam to gain elected office, but then it effectively blocked them from enacting significant changes. By 2005, the conservative clerical leadership and the increasingly powerful Revolutionary Guard had regained control. As in other authoritarian regimes, succession of the supreme leader looms large. While Iran has an institutionalized process of succession, it has not been tested since the revolutionary leader, Khomeini, personally appointed his heir apparent.

- REGIME TYPE Theocracy and electoral authoritarian

- REPRESSION Supreme leader able to eliminate political opposition when necessary via Guardian Council, Revolutionary Guard, and judiciary

- CO-OPTATION Patronage via Islamic foundations and Revolutionary Guard

- INSTITUTIONALIZATION Theocratic institutions always more powerful than quasi-democratic ones

- SUCCESSION Selection process for supreme leader amended to allow politically astute choice; president elected to four-year term

The Islamic Republic of Iran created a unique set of political institutions that are based on the theocratic principles we outlined in chapter 3, but with significant participatory elements. The regime mixes appointed and elected offices to maintain the central control of the leading clergy while allowing some voice to other political forces, though within strict limits. Figure 8.5 provides an overview of these institutions. Elected officials are allowed to pass laws and voice some public criticism, but the authority of the Shiite clergy is final. So despite its unique institutions, the Iranian government rules like many other authoritarian regimes, through a combination of repression and co-optation but with a greater than usual effort to gain legitimacy via Islamic ideology and electoral authoritarian institutions.

Khomeini's contribution to Islamic political thought is the position of supreme leader, which is always filled by a respected member of the clergy. He is both legal and spiritual guide of the country. First occupied by Khomeini himself, and then (since Khomeini's death in 1989) by Ayatollah Ali Khamenei, the office has the power to appoint the heads of all the armed forces, the head of the judiciary, six of the twelve members of the all-important Guardian Council, and the leaders of Friday prayers at mosques. These powers mean that very little of significance can occur in Iran without at least the supreme leader's tacit consent. An Assembly of Experts composed entirely of clergy but that is popularly elected by citizens appoints the supreme leader and at least theoretically has the right to remove him, though so far it seems that the position has a lifetime term of office.

The supreme leader shares formal executive power with a directly elected president in a theocratic version of a semi-presidential system. The supreme leader has broader powers than the president and is the legal head of state. The elected president appoints a cabinet, which the parliament must approve and can remove, and runs the daily affairs of government. The president is selected via a majoritarian election and can serve two four-year terms, which the last four presidents have done. The dual executive creates the possibility of tension between the supreme leader and president similar to tensions between the president and prime minister under cohabitation in semipresidential systems. When an avowed reformist was president from 1997 to 2005, he clashed regularly with the supreme leader and the institutions like the Guardian Council that limit the president's power. When Mahmoud Ahmadinejad was elected president in 2005 and reelected in 2009, he had the supreme leader's support but lost it in 2011. Ahmadinejad was using increasingly secular nationalist rhetoric that threatened to go against the Islamist basis for the regime's legitimacy, and he had built up an independent base of support in the government via appointments of supporters to many positions. Ayatollah Khamenei ultimately opposed him, and the president's influence declined drastically. His supporters subsequently lost both the parliamentary election in 2012 and the presidential election in 2013. While analysts had wondered if Ahmadinejad's growing power would prove to be a real challenge to Khamenei, the episode demonstrated that the supreme leader remains truly supreme in Iran's power structure.

As in other semipresidential systems, laws must be passed by the parliament and approved by the president. The Iranian system, however, strictly limits the freedom of these elected offices. The Guardian Council, consisting of six clergy appointed by the supreme leader and six lay leaders nominated by the head of the judiciary and

Iran's supreme leader, Ayatollah Ali Khamenei, waves to worshippers in 2005. Khamenei has increasingly centralized power in his hands, repressing virtually all political leaders who want to reform the Islamic Republic's governing structure or moderate its policies. The moderate president, Hassan Rouhani, elected in 2013, has had limited success in changing domestic policies, due in large part to Khamenei's opposition.

© RAHEB HOMAVANDI/Reuters/Corbis

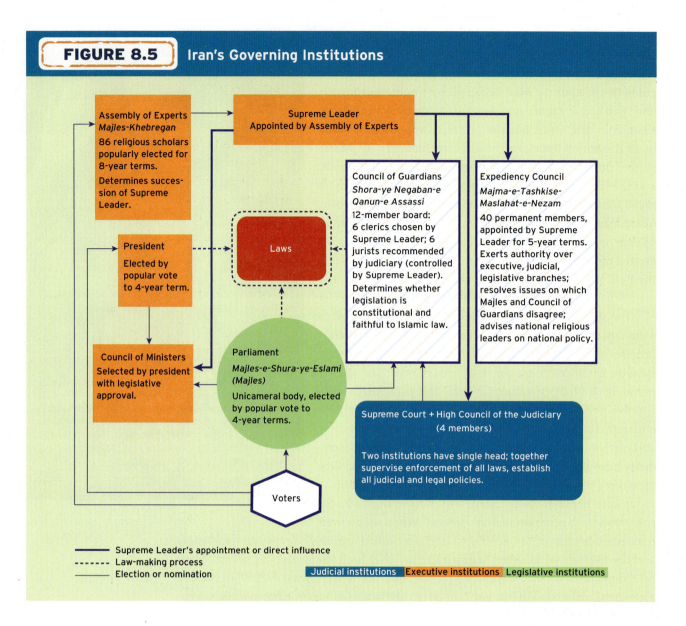

FIGURE 8.5 Iran's Governing Institutions

Assembly of Experts
Majles-Khebregan
86 religious scholars popularly elected for 8-year terms.
Determines succession of Supreme Leader.

Supreme Leader
Appointed by Assembly of Experts

Council of Guardians
Shora-ye Negaban-e Qanun-e Assassi
12-member board: 6 clerics chosen by Supreme Leader; 6 jurists recommended by judiciary (controlled by Supreme Leader). Determines whether legislation is constitutional and faithful to Islamic law.

Expediency Council
Majma-e-Tashkise-Maslahat-e-Nezam
40 permanent members, appointed by Supreme Leader for 5-year terms. Exerts authority over executive, judicial, legislative branches; resolves issues on which Majles and Council of Guardians disagree; advises national religious leaders on national policy.

President
Elected by popular vote to 4-year term.

Laws

Council of Ministers
Selected by president with legislative approval.

Parliament
Majles-e-Shura-ye-Eslami (Majles)
Unicameral body, elected by popular vote to 4-year terms.

Supreme Court + High Council of the Judiciary (4 members)

Two institutions have single head; together supervise enforcement of all laws, establish all judicial and legal policies.

Voters

——— Supreme Leader's appointment or direct influence
- - - - - Law-making process
——— Election or nomination

Judicial institutions   Executive institutions   Legislative institutions

approved by parliament, must also agree to all legislation. Given that all of its members are either appointed directly by the supreme leader or nominated by his appointed judiciary, the Council of Guardians is a bastion of clerical authority that preserves the will of the supreme leader. It also must approve all candidates for election and has repeatedly banned candidates it has deemed unacceptable for president, parliament, and local government councils. A second body, the Expediency Council, was added via constitutional amendment in 1989 to be an advisory body to the supreme leader. It has the power to resolve disputes between parliament and the Guardian Council, and its rulings are final. The supreme leader appoints all of its members, so it is an additional way for him to control elected officials.

The dual executive has control over the bureaucracy, judiciary, and armed forces. Like many authoritarian systems, Iran has more than one army. The Revolutionary Guard was formed as the armed wing of the revolution. Khomeini maintained it after the revolution because he didn't trust the regular national army, which was an institution of the prior regime. The Guard has become the most important military organization. After the Iran–Iraq War (1980–1988), the government encouraged the Guard to fund itself by starting its own companies to help rebuild the country. This was the start of the Guard's expanding business empire, which now includes the largest contractor in the country and numerous other companies in many fields, as well as rumored large-scale smuggling of illegal products into the country. Hen-Tov and Gonzalez (2010, 21) estimated that the Guard's business empire constituted at least 25 percent of Iran's economy. The government takes good care of the large and ideologically loyal Guard as well—its annual budget is larger than those of all but a handful of government ministries.

The Guard began to play a more direct political role after 1997, when a reformist won the presidency and later reformist candidates took control of the elected legislature. The supreme leader and his allies turned to nonelected institutions to thwart the reform movement's policies. First, the Guardian Council turned against the reformers, banning many of them from running in the 2004 legislative elections. Then, former Guard member Mahmoud Ahmadinejad won the 2005 presidential election, and two-thirds of the people he appointed to his cabinet were also former Guard members. The Guard and its civilian counterpart, the Basij militia, infamously led the attacks against the street protesters after the disputed June 2009 election, effectively repressing the largest demonstrations since the revolution and preserving the fraudulent reelection of Ahmadinejad. Many analysts wondered if the Guard's support for Ahmadinejad created a power base that was independent of the supreme leader, but by 2011 it was clear that most of the Guard retained its loyalty to Khamenei; when he split with Ahmadinejad, the Guard remained loyal to the supreme leader, one of the reasons why he was able to stifle his opponent so successfully. Since the election of President Rouhani, the Guard has clearly been a bastion of support for the supreme leader; its economic clout seems likely to limit the effects of any major changes in economic policies that Rouhani attempts.

The supreme leader appoints the head of the judiciary, who in turn appoints all of the judges under him. The Guardian and Expediency Councils perform functions somewhat akin to judicial review in democracies, but the judiciary's role is strictly that of interpreter and enforcer of the Islamic legal code, *sharia,* for criminal and civil cases. Other than nominating half of the Guardian Council, the judiciary has no formal political role. The supreme leader, though, has used it repeatedly to repress political opponents; numerous political activists, journalists, and students were prosecuted on charges such as treason after the 2009 demonstrations and sentenced to long prison terms.

In contrast to the absolute authority of the supreme leader, the autonomy and strength of the parliament (the *majlis*) are severely circumscribed, even though its formal powers look significant. In addition to passing all legislation, the *majlis* has approval authority over cabinet nominees and half the nominees to the Guardian Council, and it can investigate the executive's implementation of the law. It has used these powers repeatedly, exposing corruption in the bureaucracy and opposing many of Ahmadinejad's legislative initiatives after the split between the president and supreme leader. The power of the appointed clerics, however, always lurks behind the actions of the *majlis.* When the clerics disapprove of significant legislation, they don't hesitate to use their power to veto it via the Guardian Council and rewrite it in the Expediency Council. When the reformists gained control of the *majlis* in 2000, the Guardian Council vetoed virtually all of their significant reform legislation.

The Iranian regime, like virtually all authoritarian regimes, also uses clientelism to maintain its control. The Iranian bureaucracy has expanded by as much as 50 percent since the revolution. Because of Iran's massive oil revenue, government spending is a majority of the country's economy. This gives the top leadership significant patronage opportunities. Government and quasi-governmental foundations (called *bonyads*) have also become key venues through which the nation's oil wealth is shared with regime supporters. The foundations often receive government funding, and some engage in commercial activity as well. One of the largest, the Imam Charity Committee, receives private donations in addition to the fourth-largest share of the government's annual budget. It is controlled by conservative supporters of the clergy, who use it to mobilize poor voters in favor of conservative candidates. The Revolutionary Guard also controls one of the largest *bonyads,* which provides income support to millions of people, giving the Guard its own independent basis for patronage. Some of these foundations and their leaders engage in outright corruption as well, stealing oil revenues and accepting bribes in return for access to key officials.

The importance of the supreme leader and his de facto life term leaves Iran with one of the classic problems of authoritarian rule: succession. Khomeini's popularity and power were based not only on the traditional legitimacy he enjoyed as a Grand Ayatollah, one of a handful of the highest religious authorities in Shiite Islam, but also on his charismatic legitimacy as the leader of the revolution. Khomeini and other leaders did not believe that any of the other Grand Ayatollahs could fully replace him as the supreme leader, so to avert a potential crisis, a constitutional amendment eliminated the requirement that the supreme leader come from only among their ranks. This allowed the regime to select then-president Ali Khamenei as the new supreme leader. He was only a midlevel cleric, and in fact was raised overnight to the rank of Ayatollah (still below Grand Ayatollah) in an effort to give him greater religious authority. Khomeini and his advisers chose someone who understood politics rather than an icon of religious authority. The other Grand Ayatollahs did not fight Khamenei's ascendance because they had become increasingly disillusioned with the regime; while initially in favor of the revolution, most had taken an increasingly traditionalist position during the 1980s, divorcing themselves from active politics. Still, lack of clerical support raised questions about Khamanei's legitimacy as supreme leader, which was one of the factors that led him to strengthen the power of the Revolutionary Guard, a military force loyal to him.

CASE Questions

1. Recent trends have suggested that the quasi-democratic elements of Iran's governing institutions are relatively weak. Nonetheless, how might they help the top Iranian leadership overcome the "dictator's dilemma" that all authoritarian regimes face?

2. What does Iran's history suggest about the relative importance of repression, co-optation, and legitimacy for the survival of authoritarian regimes?

ELECTIONS, PARTIES, AND CIVIL SOCIETY IN AUTHORITARIAN REGIMES

Elections, parties, and civil society are important to democracies in part because they help to overcome the collective action dilemma: they encourage participation and channel and promote democratic representation. It should not come as a great shock that authoritarian regimes are not particularly interested in overcoming the collective action problem. Many authoritarian regimes nonetheless create or allow institutions that at least superficially resemble elections, parties, and interest groups, but these differ greatly from their more democratic counterparts in both form and function.

As we noted above, supreme leaders cannot rule by repression alone. They must care about gaining the support of potentially rival elites and, ideally, some legitimacy from the general populace. Many authoritarian regimes, both more and less institutionalized, use elaborate public displays of support to try to gain this legitimacy, a form of involuntary political participation. For example, they hold massive independence day celebrations, complete with throngs of cheering supporters and displays of military might to show their popularity and power. Participants typically have little choice but to participate and are often paid in some form. When Mexico's Partido Revolucionario Institucional (PRI) ruled as an electoral authoritarian regime, supporters would be trucked in from the countryside to rallies in the cities, where they would enjoy free food, drink, and entertainment. Cameroonian scholar Achille Mbembe (1992) called such huge but empty displays the "banality of power." Svolik (2012), however, argued that these displays are not banal but serve a clear purpose: they arise after a regime has consolidated its power and serve as a warning to potential rivals who might think about rebelling.

In the most extreme cases of personalist rule, such public demonstrations become a **personality cult** that constantly glorifies the ruler and attempts to turn his every utterance into not only government fiat but also divine wisdom. Personality cults have arisen in an array of regimes, from communist North Korea under "Great Leader"

personality cult
Phenomenon that occurs in the most extreme cases of personalist rule in which followers constantly glorify the ruler and attempt to turn his every utterance into not only government fiat but also divine wisdom

Kim Il-Sung, to Zaire under Western-supporting dictator Mobutu Sese Seko, to "President for Life" Saparmurat Niyazov in post-Soviet Turkmenistan. Regimes with more elaborate ideological justification for their rule, such as communist and theocratic regimes, also make extensive use of their founding ideologies to try to gain popular legitimacy, as the case of Iran below demonstrates.

Elections and Parties

Beyond these massive demonstrations of support, most authoritarian regimes encourage carefully monitored and limited political participation. Even some one-party regimes hold regular elections. Communist regimes usually allow direct elections at the most local level. The general electorate may get to participate in local block, neighborhood, or town elections, but then those representatives elect the next layer of representatives above them and so on up to the national parliamentary level. In addition, although nonparty candidates may be permitted at the local level, all candidates typically have to be cleared by the Communist Party before they can run. This system is consistent with the ideological perspective of communism because it permits popular participation while also preserving the guiding role of the Communist Party, the only legitimate representative of the people according to communist doctrine.

More common now are electoral authoritarian regimes in which a ruling party wins major elections easily, with some opposition parties winning a small share of power. The ruling party creates the system to ensure its continued rule. The more sophisticated and institutionalized systems do not usually require outright voter fraud for the ruling party to remain in power, though rulers will certainly engage in that too if necessary. Usually, the type of electoral system (typically a majoritarian one that favors the already large ruling party), gerrymandering constituency boundaries, vote buying, controlling access to the media, restricting civil liberties, using government resources for partisan purposes, and jailing opponents serve to keep the opposition under control. In Kenya in the 1990s, government civil servants openly campaigned for the ruling party during work hours, candidates handed potential voters gifts of cash or food, and opposition party rallies were denied permits or harassed by police. In Rwanda's 2010 presidential election, three opposition candidates ended up in jail by election day, allowing President Paul Kagame (in power since the genocide in 1994) to win 93 percent of the vote. In Mexico under the PRI's long rule, the government systematically spent money before each election to purchase political support in areas where the PRI needed votes (Magaloni 2006).

Given that authoritarian rulers can hold power without any opposition or elections at all, an obvious question is, Why do they bother creating these systems? A long-standing answer has been that elections serve as a façade of democratic legitimacy, both domestically and internationally. The ascendancy of liberal democracy in the post–Cold War era makes this more important than it was earlier. Recently, scholars have come to believe that elections in authoritarian regimes serve other purposes as well. As we discussed above, Gandhi (2008) argued that both legislatures and multiple parties co-opt the opposition and provide a space for some policy compromise. Using our case study of Mexico, Beatriz Magaloni (2006) argued that in addition to co-opting opposition within the system, elections provided the ruling party with information on who opposed it (helping overcome the dictator's dilemma), allowed power sharing among leaders within the ruling party, and deterred opponents by showing (via large election victories) the ruling party's ability to mobilize support. She suggested that elections in electoral authoritarian regimes demonstrate to elite opponents that the ruling party continues to enjoy significant support, thereby discouraging opponents from openly challenging the system. Lisa Blaydes (2011) argued that elections during Hosni Mubarak's reign (1981–2011) in Egypt also helped resolve conflicts over the distribution of resources, particularly access to rents and other opportunities for graft; offices below the top echelon of key rulers go to the winners of elections without the ruler having to distribute them directly. Authoritarian elections, then, can provide the regime clear benefits. The danger always exists, of course, that somehow the opposition will find a way to actually gain power. This is rare, and when it happens, the ruling party may openly "steal" the election via voter fraud to remain in power. This happened in Kenya in December 2007, setting off two months of ethnically based violence that killed 1,500 and displaced hundreds of thousands. In other cases, however, such elections can be part of a transition from an authoritarian to a democratic regime, a subject we explore in the next chapter.

Authoritarian elections are coupled with very limited party systems. Most important and strongest is always the ruling party, whether in a one-party or electoral authoritarian system. Using a historical institutionalist perspective, Jason Brownlee (2007) argued that strong ruling parties emerge early in an authoritarian regime if the supreme leader is able to repress and co-opt potential opposition to create an elite coalition within the party. If he is unable to do this, a weak ruling party (or none at all) will develop, and the regime will be less stable and more likely to be overthrown. Svolik (2012) demonstrated statistically that since World War II, single-party authoritarian regimes have lasted much longer than regimes that either banned parties or allowed multiple parties (i.e., electoral authoritarian regimes). He argued that by requiring service to the party early in a potential leader's career and benefits (from top party positions) only later in a career, parties create "sunk" investments for politicians that will only pay off in the long term via loyalty to the regime. Combined with a party's control over a wide array of political and economic positions, this creates very strong incentives for would-be leaders to remain loyal to a regime rather than attempt to oppose it.

The ruling party is nearly always a vehicle for access to goods and jobs and thus a key mechanism for large-scale patronage. In Alfredo Stroessner's Paraguay, for instance, membership in the ruling Colorado Party was compulsory for government employees, and nearly a quarter of the population belonged to it. Mexico's PRI politicians operated on the basis of patronage, and citizens in rural regions in particular understood that votes for the PRI could result in material benefits for their communities. Similarly, membership in the Communist Party is usually a prerequisite for many jobs in any communist regime. Communist parties also promote political socialization of young people through party youth organizations and serve as ideological watchdogs for the leaders. Party cells exist in all government agencies, communities, and major organizations, such as state-run companies. While ruling parties in electoral authoritarian regimes do not fulfill all of these socialization and watchdog functions, they nonetheless provide incentives that keep potential opponents within the system. The availability of institutionalized alternatives in the form of opposition parties, though, helps explain why Svolik (2012) found that regimes with multiple parties were not as long-lived as single-party regimes; the alternative parties provide a possibility of resistance to the regime that doesn't exist in single-party regimes.

Civil Society

Because participation must go through approved regime channels, civil society in authoritarian regimes is extremely circumscribed and repressed. Indeed, often it hardly exists at all. Communist regimes such as the Soviet Union and China at their height were totalitarian, as North Korea remains today. Totalitarian regimes completely eliminate civil society; the ruling party "represents" all interests that it believes deserve representation. Trade unions or youth or women's groups often nominally exist in communist countries, but these "mass organizations" are always part of the Communist Party. They cannot be said to be truly part of civil society, which by definition is autonomous from the state.

Noncommunist regimes often use state corporatism to control interest groups. Remember that corporatism is the idea that each component (or interest) in society should be represented by one organization. When a government legally mandates this, it is referred to as state corporatism because the state controls the interest groups and chooses the ones it wishes to recognize. Mexico's electoral authoritarian regime under the PRI was a classic example. The PRI recognized and included within the party a single labor organization, a single peasant association, and a single association for "popular groups"—small businesses, women's interests, and various others. These organizations were to represent their constituents within the party. Over time, however, they became increasingly corrupt and controlled by the elite at the top of the party hierarchy. The workers' organization, in particular, was very powerful within the party, and real wages rose for most of the PRI's long rule, even though the unions rarely contradict official party policies. In most of Asia and Africa, unions and other major interest groups arose with and were part of nationalist movements for independence. After independence, however, authoritarian regimes emasculated these organizations, often creating state corporatist systems in their place.

Often, observers assume that civil society, when not obviously controlled by a ruling party, will inherently resist authoritarian rule, but this is not always the case. Organizations in civil society need to survive if they hope to benefit their members, and cooperating with the regime even when not legally required to may be the best way to achieve that aim. Accepting regime patronage, and therefore supporting the regime, may gain organizations access to resources for their members, while a principled opposition in the name of democracy may prevent them from achieving anything (Jamal 2007). Religious organizations, for instance, often cooperate with authoritarian regimes to gain regularized status and material rewards; authoritarian leaders may be willing to cooperate with them in order to gain prestige and possible legitimacy by association, especially when a particular religion has deep social roots, such as the Russian Orthodox Church (Koesel 2014).

Using our case study of China, Jessica Teets (2014) argued that this dynamic is producing a new model of state–civil society relations—"consultative authoritarianism"—that combines elements of liberal autonomy and state corporatism. Authoritarian regimes, she argued, increasingly allow civil society groups to operate to improve overall governance by helping overcome the dictator's dilemma and by providing services directly. On the other hand, the regimes must ensure civil society stays within certain bounds to maintain regime control, so they use a combination of positive and negative incentives to do so, minimizing repression to the extent possible. The result is improved governance for citizens on a daily basis but little chance that civil society will foster regime change toward democracy.

The emergence of truly independent social movements within authoritarian regimes is often one of the first signs of a democratic opening. In Latin America in the 1970s, labor-based social movements outside the confines of the official corporatist unions began challenging the status quo and ultimately forced authoritarian regimes to move toward democratization. Other social movements arose as well. Brazil, for instance, has active gay-rights, Afro-Brazilian, and women's movements, many of which originated during the military regime. Indigenous movements also emerged in much of Latin America in the 1980s and 1990s, challenging authoritarian control of rural areas. With the spread of more electoral democracy since the end of the Cold War, interest groups and civil society more broadly have reemerged in most of these countries, but they face a legacy of weakness and regime repression.

Clientelism

With civil society very weak and parties and elections mainly aimed at ensuring elite cohesion and regime survival, clientelism is often the primary means through which average citizens can participate in politics in authoritarian regimes. The weaker the formal institutions, the more this is likely to be true. Strong ruling parties and small but accepted opposition parties in electoral authoritarian regimes provide some institutionalized means of participation. In more personalist regimes, or regimes in which parties are weak institutions that command little loyalty, even these avenues are mostly cut off. By becoming a client of a powerful patron, citizens can gain access to some resources, power, or influence. This occurs behind closed doors, of course, but as the patron gains power and position in the system, the clients gain also through special privileges and access to resources.

Such relationships are the primary means of political participation in virtually all sub-Saharan African countries. While myriad formal institutions exist, most citizens participate by attaching themselves to a patron. In Kenya's one-party regime (1963–1992), the ruling party consisted of ethnically and regionally based factions that were headed by major patrons. The system allowed very limited public political debate, so political leaders gained support by directing government resources toward their home areas and providing individual support to their myriad clients. Clients got jobs in government or influence in local politics by attaching themselves to patrons who could offer them these benefits.

In the absence of other effective means of participation and representation, following a patron may be the best available option. A patron can represent a client's most immediate interests vis-à-vis the state. The problems in this type of system, though, are numerous. First, its informality means that no client is ever guaranteed anything. Each individual has a unique and largely private relationship with a patron, who will try to maintain the client's loyalty in the long term but who will not respond to every demand. Clients have no recourse unless an alternative patron is available. This is sometimes the case, but transferring loyalty is never easy or quick. Second, clientelism discourages citizens from organizing on the basis of collective interests. As long as citizens believe that following a personal patron is the most effective route to obtaining what they need from government, they have little incentive to organize collectively to change the government and its policies more broadly. This is especially true in authoritarian regimes that violently repress any significant organized political activity.

Participation in authoritarian regimes is extremely limited. More institutionalized regimes have allowed some formal participation, including elections with limited choices. With the spread of electoral authoritarian regimes in the last two decades, tightly controlled elections have become more common. Their main purpose, however, is elite cohesion and regime support. Citizens are rarely content with these limited choices in the long term because they give voters little real influence. Less-institutionalized regimes typically grant little or no opportunities for participation. Given this, many citizens "participate" on a daily basis simply to survive and prosper individually through the use of individual clientelist relationships. This allows the leadership of a regime to use co-optation to maintain adequate support, or at least prevent outright rebellion.

Rebellion, however, can and does happen. Social movements often arise in these situations outside the limited formal boundaries of legal participation. Larger movements for change that bring an entire regime into question also can emerge and produce fundamental regime change, a subject we examine in the next chapter. But first, we look at participation in three authoritarian regimes in our case study countries.

CASE Study

CHINA: GROWING PARTICIPATION BUT NOT DEMOCRACY

CASE SYNOPSIS

China has evolved from a communist to a modernizing authoritarian regime. As it has, it has adjusted its communist system of forced participation in a way that attempts to legitimize the regime. The opening of the market economy has required the party to allow some greater participation, but it has nonetheless kept demands for fundamental reform effectively repressed. The co-opting of key elites into the ruling party, the creation of state corporatist regulation of civil society, and the use of repression when necessary have kept large-scale protest to a minimum since the Tiananmen Square protest in 1989. Semicompetitive elections have allowed some real participation at the local levels of government, but nothing on a larger scale. Democracy advocates hope that the initial expansion of participation will ultimately yield greater pressure toward real democratic reform, though the regime under current president Xi seems to be moving decisively in the opposite direction.

- ELECTIONS Competitive local elections help overcome dictator's dilemma
- PARTIES Continued one-party rule, but changing party membership; technocrats, entrepreneurs, and lawyers
- CIVIL SOCIETY Expansion, but under state corporatism; growing local protests, labor unrest, online activism, and NGOs; growing repression since 2013
- CLIENTELISM *Guanxi* personal networks
- LEGITIMATION Based on growing *economy* and service provision; renewed ideological efforts under Xi

China's Communist regime under Mao included ritualistic "participation" by the public in the form of token elections, but it also initiated spurts of greater participation as Mao attempted to overcome the inertia of bureaucratic control of his "revolution." For the average citizen, though, influencing government was much more informal and individual. CCP membership was the essential and only formal route into the political process beyond the most local level. Party membership was also the sole road ambitious citizens could travel to political, social, or economic success. Yet fewer than 10 percent of citizens were party members, which meant that most people who wanted to influence the government had to do so in informal ways. With the complete ban on any independent organizations, citizens had little ability to demand changes in government policy or to petition the government about issues of concern. As with most authoritarian regimes, clientelism often took the place of institutionalized means of participation. In China, networks of personal supporters, including but not exclusively family, are known as *guanxi*. Before, during, and since the Mao era, the Chinese have used their *guanxi* to survive and attempt to prosper. At the height of the communist system, the state controlled virtually the entire economy, including the allocation of jobs, houses, and other services. Appearing loyal to the regime was crucial to one's success in the system, but *guanxi* helped a great deal as well. Relatives and friends in the system could help get you a better job or apartment or keep you out of trouble with local authorities. For the more ambitious, participation included becoming a member of and taking an active role in the local CCP apparatus in addition to using *guanxi* to help career advancement.

The rapid expansion of the market economy has forced the regime to open up the system of participation and representation at least slightly, making some political accommodations in terms of who can participate and how. This has involved co-opting new elites, allowing semicompetitive elections at the local level, and implementing elements of state corporatism to manage relations with the still limited civil society. One change has been the Communist Party itself. Throughout the Communist era, a debate raged over the role of "reds" and "experts." On one side were leaders, including Mao, who argued that those properly committed to revolutionary ideals (that is, loyal to Mao and the CCP) and from the proper "revolutionary classes" (the peasantry and proletariat) should constitute the core of the party and be given preference in participation. On the other side were those who favored party membership and participation for experts—that is, intellectuals, scientists, and engineers who, presumably, could help modernize the country. Since the country's opening to the world market, the CCP has shifted significantly in the direction of the experts. Farmers' and workers' share of party membership dropped from 63 percent in 1994 to 44 percent in 2003. Large numbers of scientists, engineers, and other intellectuals have joined the party.

A candidate for a village committee stands in front of a blackboard displaying his vote total. The Chinese ruling party has allowed some competition in local-level elections, though how much real competition has happened varies from place to place.

REUTERS/Jason Lee

By 1997, technocrats made up about three-quarters of top Chinese leaders, a share that has since shrunk as they have been replaced by the two newest additions: lawyers and entrepreneurs. In 2001 the party leadership decided to allow private entrepreneurs into the party—this was the ultimate irony, including successful capitalists in the Communist Party (Dickson 2003). By 2011, an estimated 40 percent of Chinese entrepreneurs were party members. With the booming economy, it has become quite clear as well that party membership is highly correlated with wealth: "90 percent of China's millionaires are the children of high-ranking officials" (Saich 2013, 110).

The political implications of the changes are not clear. Given the development of liberalism in the West, we might expect that allowing intellectuals and especially entrepreneurs to enter the political system would expand democracy; the bourgeoisie, after all, was the class that helped create liberalism in Europe. Market economies, in precisely this way, are supposed to help produce and sustain liberal democracy. Dickson (2003), however, surveyed China's new entrepreneurs and found that their political attitudes do not suggest they will help create greater democracy. In fact, they share the concerns of other party officials about limiting participation to the elite in order to maintain stability. Fewsmith (2013) reported that local business associations find it much easier to use connections and corruption to secure what they need from the state rather than champion the "rule of law." Chen and Lu (2011) surveyed middle-class citizens more broadly and found similar results: they did not have a particularly strong preference for democracy, and the more economically dependent they were on the state the less support they showed for democracy. China's middle class remains relatively small and is heavily employed by institutions related to the state, so it has yet to press for democracy as much as democratization theory would predict (Nathan 2016). The CCP so far seems to have opened up the party to the intellectual and business elite without risking its continued control.

Changes to the electoral system for local-level congresses have provided opportunities for voter participation and representation within the strict confines of an authoritarian regime. Following typically Communist practices, China long had direct elections for the most local level of government—village committees—but with only one party-approved candidate for each position. Since 1980, the government has revised the electoral law several times to allow greater participation by nonparty members. The first election after minimum reforms included candidates actively campaigning for fundamental changes, which threatened the regime and resulted in new rules that increased party oversight of candidate selection and campaigning. Today, candidates can be nominated by the party, other local organizations, or any group of ten citizens. Studies have shown that how this system actually works in practice varies greatly because local officials often severely limit the level of competition. Recent estimates are that the elections are actually competitive in about half of the country. Hundreds of thousands of candidates have lost village elections since 1999, and 48 percent of elected village officials are not Communist Party members (Landry, Davis, and Wang 2010, 766). One survey in the late 1990s found that more than half of voters had attended a campaign event and nearly 20 percent had participated in nominating a candidate (Shi 2006, 365). Nonetheless, so-called "independent candidates"—those nominated by individual voters—remain rare and are successful even less frequently. Electoral turnout has varied widely but in some places has been as high as 30 percent, a higher turnout than in most local elections in the United States. Melanie Manion (2015) surveyed members of local congresses and voters and argued that while local congresses remain firmly under the control of the ruling party, local representatives nonetheless are able to provide the party with knowledge of local concerns, and local party leaders are often responsive to these concerns because their career advancement requires maintaining social stability; any local concerns that result in larger and more public demands can threaten an official's career. Voters attempt to choose candidates they think will honestly represent local interests and help bring government investment to the area. The Chinese ruling party has clearly tried to use local elections to help resolve the dictator's dilemma, providing them with information about local concerns without undermining their continued rule.

Along with greater openness in local elections have come some of the problems that plague new democracies elsewhere: corruption, kinship-based politics, and sexism. Candidates in some village elections have engaged in vote buying—handing out gifts in exchange for votes. The candidates earn a return on this investment via corrupt land deals after they take office. Local village politics are often divided not by policy questions but by competition among local kinship groups for political control. Initially, semicompetitive local elections reduced the number of women in rural village committees. The government responded with a law requiring that at least 20 percent of local congressional representatives must be women. Even limited democracy allows local social mores and customs to have full expression in the political process, for better or for worse.

Civil society has expanded greatly over the past two decades, though it remains tightly circumscribed. Under full Communist rule, the party completely controlled all interest groups. The All-China Federation of Trade Unions (ACFTU), for instance, was the sole legal union, with mandatory branches in any enterprise with more than one hundred employees. The rapid expansion of private enterprises has made it difficult for the party to maintain its monopoly on union organization, but the ACFTU remains tightly controlled by and supportive of the government. A revised labor law enacted in 2008 made arbitration and court cases by workers easier. The number of such cases more than doubled, and in the most industrialized regions the system is overwhelmed with cases. Lee and Friedman (2009) argued that, as in other countries around the world, the opening of the economy to globalization has reduced workers' ability to secure the growing rights that the government has formally granted them. Forty percent of urban workers are part-time, casual, or temporary employees who have great difficulty demanding better treatment; nearly half of them report not receiving wages on time. In 2010, however, several major strikes erupted, most notably at Honda and Toyota plants. As the Chinese economy rebounded after the Great Recession, it became clear that its seemingly endless stream of cheap labor was running out: employers were starting to face labor shortages, and wages were rising in some areas, giving some workers the economic strength to strike and demand more. At the Honda plant in Foshan, workers unsuccessfully demanded the right to form their own independent union.

The number of officially registered NGOs more than tripled between 2000 and 2012, to about half a million (Dickson 2016, 125). To control these organizations, the government created a registration system for NGOs and approved only one organization of a particular type in each administrative area, in effect beginning a system of state corporatism. As the government became more comfortable with its ability to control NGOs, it dropped this rule and allowed more than one focused on the same issue to register in an area and eliminated the requirement that each one have a government agency as sponsor. Teets (2014) saw these as key signs of the emergence of her new model of state–civil society relations, consultative authoritarianism. Under President Xi, though, the government has cracked down further, particularly on NGOs with a political role. A new law in 2016 required the seven thousand foreign NGOs to register with the government and reveal their funding sources, giving the government the potential to deny legal status to those it believed may threaten regime stability. It also restricted contact between foreign and Chinese NGOs and made it virtually impossible for the latter to get international funding. A similar law regulating religious organizations was passed in late 2016, limiting their contact with like-minded foreign groups and trying to ensure they register with the state. The state has also created its own organizations for the policy issues in which it is particularly interested; these are referred to by the Orwellian name "government-organized nongovernmental organizations" (GONGOs).

Bruce Dickson (2016) and others divide Chinese civil society into Civil Society I and Civil Society II. The former include the many NGOs focused on economic, cultural, sports, and charitable work; the latter are the more directly "political" groups that seek changes the regime sees as threatening. The former are often welcomed by local government and at times influence the direction of government policy, though mostly at the local level. Local branches of the ACFTU have successfully supported workers' strikes on a number of occasions, and the national organization helped to get a five-day workweek approved. Lu Yiyi (2009) studied urban NGOs providing social services and found that despite financial and informational dependence on the state, the NGOs can achieve a degree of autonomy, in part through their personal relationships with local bureaucrats who can protect them from the more draconian demands of the state. Indeed, she found that GONGOs actually achieve greater autonomy than citizen-initiated NGOs. NGOs, of course, cannot voice any significant political criticisms of the regime as a whole. Hildebrandt (2013) argued that NGO leaders limit their own demands to what they find politically acceptable in a particular locale and issue area in order to preserve their organizations and have what impact they can. Local governments often welcome NGOs that receive international funding for charitable purposes; they serve as supplements to the government's limited social welfare programs. Sometimes, however, charitable organizations can raise political issues. For instance, many seek to serve the needs of urban immigrants who are not officially registered as urban residents and therefore cannot receive government services. The local government, on the other hand, may want to discourage those immigrants, so providing them support goes against government policy (Dickson 2016, 130–131).

The Chinese media, though tightly controlled, expanded dramatically in the past generation. In the aftermath of economic reform, media outlets are mostly private and must be profitable. Government restrictions remain, however, and have tightened since Xi came to power. While criticisms of local officials' malfeasance are tolerated, political criticism of the regime is strictly prohibited. Daniela Stockman (2012) argued that, like the role of the courts, the media's criticism of local government helps the regime overcome the "dictator's dilemma" by providing it information about what is happening "on the ground." On the other hand, she found that commercialization did not provide a greater diversity of political viewpoints in the media; indeed, citizens' opinions are more likely to be influenced in the direction of supporting the regime by unofficial media outlets than by the state-owned media. This is because citizens trust unofficial sources more, but these sources still must report only news that stays within the bounds of the state's informal but tight censorship. Under Xi, the government has cracked down on the media more severely, replacing editors who criticized the regime too much and requiring journalists to attend ideological indoctrination workshops; press criticism of the government seems to have dropped markedly under Xi's leadership (Zhao 2016).

The biggest venue for criticism of the regime has been the Internet, and the government has created the so-called "Great Firewall of China" to prevent Internet users from accessing information on sensitive topics. The regime employs tens of thousands of cyberpolice and sophisticated security programs to constantly monitor Internet use and has eliminated virtually all of the major global Internet providers such as Google, Facebook, and YouTube, replacing them with more controlled Chinese alternatives. Nonetheless, Chinese "netizens" created active online communities and techniques to evade censorship. The latter included new Chinese-language characters that can make it past filtering systems, websites based on foreign servers, and meetings held in secret chat rooms. Online activism became a major source of criticism of the regime, most dramatically with the "Charter 08" manifesto that called for democracy (Yang 2009). As in other areas, though, the government under President Xi has repressed online activity more severely than before, reducing activists' ability to coordinate their activities and effectively keeping threatening topics out of the public's view. The regime kept the release of the "Panama Papers" in 2016, for instance, out of both traditional and online media because they showed that several top officials, including President Xi, had offshore bank accounts.

Even though elections and civil society now offer opportunities for greater participation than in the past, pressure for more fundamental changes have continually arisen. The most famous case is the Tiananmen Square protest in 1989. What started as a few hundred students mushroomed within a week to daily protests by 200,000 students. They demanded the government reevaluate the career of the reformist leader Hu Yaobang (who had just died), free jailed intellectual dissidents, publicly account for party leaders' finances, permit freedom of the press, and provide greater funding for education (note that they did not demand full democracy with competitive national elections, as is often asserted). A hunger strike garnered massive public support, as more than a million Beijing residents turned out to defend the hunger strikers, who finally got some minor concessions from the government. After making these concessions, the government declared martial law in the city and called in the army. At least a million citizens poured into the streets and erected barricades to try to prevent the army from entering, but it overcame the populace and moved into Tiananmen Square. In the middle of the night it opened fire on the remaining student dissidents, killing between 1,000 and 3,000 students and civilians. The military action sparked worldwide condemnation, but the regime survived.

More recently, the government cracked down on Falun Gong, a religious sect founded in 1997. It was legally registered as a religious organization, but in April 1999 the group organized a silent march of 10,000 followers in Beijing to protest a government article critical of the movement. After that, the government banned the organization and has since jailed thousands of its supporters. Large-scale protests in the outlying regions of Tibet and Xinjiang in 2008 met similar repression. Under President Xi, the government has also arrested large numbers of human rights activists and lawyers.

This history of repression has successfully eliminated most large-scale protests for the time being, but many local protests continue. An estimated 8,700 protests (what the Chinese government calls "mass incidents") took place in 1993; by 2010, the number had risen to 180,000 (Fewsmith 2013, 26–27). A key organizational tool for protesters and petitioners is to get the ear of the central government via the media or dramatic acts, often referred to as "troublemaking." The central government is often more willing to make concessions to the protesters than is local government because the central authorities are more concerned about the overall legitimacy of the system. Xi Chen (2012) argued that the Chinese state actively facilitated "troublemaking" to gain citizen input and pressure on local government that did not threaten the party's rule more broadly.

How far and how fast all of the political reforms will go is probably the major question that political scientists looking at China ask. Teresa Wright (2010) used a political economy approach to argue that the regime has been more successful than many assume at maintaining its legitimacy. China's economic policy, while creating much greater inequality than in the past, has nonetheless favored many segments of society. First and foremost, the regime has earned the support of budding entrepreneurs and professionals, who have gained great wealth under the reforms. In addition, workers in the private sector, and even workers in the declining state-owned sector who still have some social welfare protections from the state, fear that they would be worse off if the ruling party were no longer in power. Comparativist Tony Saich (2012) conducted surveys from 2003 to 2011 on satisfaction with government. In 2011 overall satisfaction with the central government stood at well over 80 percent, slightly down from 2009 but about where it has been across the decade. Respondents consistently reported higher levels of satisfaction with the central government than with local governments; satisfaction with the most local level of government, though, increased markedly from just over 40 percent in 2003 to over 60 percent in 2011. The still low level of satisfaction with local government may both reflect and explain the massive number of protests aimed locally. For a regime that has staked its legitimacy mainly on its ability to "modernize" the country, however, 80 percent approval ratings suggest a higher level of legitimacy than many outsiders might assume is the case. In 2012 and 2013, protests over the closing of a newspaper and ever worsening pollution raised questions about whether the regime was still maintaining its performance-based legitimacy (Wong 2013). Meanwhile, China's new president, Xi Jinping, started a campaign within the party in 2013 to warn members about key ideas that would undermine the party's grip on power; at the top of the list were "constitutional democracy" and "universal human rights." Clearly, the current leadership has no intention of yielding to demands for democracy anytime soon.

CASE Questions

1. The Chinese government has allowed participation and criticism at the local level in various ways but repressed it firmly at the national level. Can you use the idea of the "dictator's dilemma" to explain this pattern of behavior?
2. China often seems to be pursuing a contradictory set of policies that alternatively allow and then repress participation. What does this mean for the possibility of democracy emerging over the long term?

CASE Study

RUSSIA: WEAK OPPOSITION IN AN ELECTORAL AUTHORITARIAN REGIME

Under Vladimir Putin's electoral authoritarian regime, elections have occurred regularly. The degree of competition within them, though, continually dropped, at least until 2011 when the opposition's share of the vote increased notably. Putin created a dominant, ruling party that has been a key vehicle through which he maintains power and rewards loyal allies with government positions. Co-optation and manipulation of the electoral rules, and increasingly outright fraud, have given him a secure majority in parliament

CASE SYNOPSIS

since 2003. Coming out of the Soviet era of Communist domination, civil society has been relatively weak. While many organizations exist, few have sustained memberships and funding. Protests, however, have increased over the last decade, culminating in a huge demonstration in 2011–2012, the largest since the end of the Soviet Union. In spite of these, the regime has held onto power while granting relatively few concessions.

- **ELECTIONS** Regular for parliament and president, but limited competition and growing fraud; shift from mixed PR system to pure PR and then back to mixed
- **PARTIES** Dominant ruling party with weak opposition parties
- **CIVIL SOCIETY** Weak organizations but growing protests
- **CLIENTELISM** State use of oil revenue and ruling party to co-opt support
- **LEGITIMATION** Ideology of state strength, order, and nationalism

When tens of thousands of people poured into the streets of Moscow and other major cities in December 2011 to protest what they saw as outright voter fraud, Putin was as surprised as most observers. The Russian public had long been quiescent and Putin's popularity seemed secure. He built his support by creating a dominant party through which to gain parliamentary support and manipulating electoral rules as needed to ensure the party's victories. The party, United Russia, was created by the state, rather than growing out of society, as most parties do. Shortly after becoming president, Putin got a couple of smaller parties in the Duma to merge to create United Russia. He then brokered a deal with the Communist Party to achieve a working majority, which allowed him to rule via legislation rather than decree, as Yeltsin had. Once he was able to use patronage to co-opt a couple of other small parties, he jettisoned the alliance with the Communists. He used his popularity (throughout his first two terms, his popular approval ratings rarely dipped below 70 percent) and his control over patronage to ensure that United Russia won handily. In the 2003 Duma election, United Russia easily won control of parliament and proceeded to pass every major bill Putin submitted. The "party of power" has retained majority control ever since. By controlling most seats not only in the Duma but in legislatures in virtually all eighty-nine regional governments, United Russia provides Putin a vast array of offices to give to loyal supporters. As in other electoral authoritarian regimes, elections also allowed a rotation of elites in office, rewarding newly loyal supporters and punishing those who prove disloyal or ineffective.

Putin manipulated the electoral system as needed to his party's advantage. Under the mixed electoral system he inherited, his most significant opposition came from independent MPs and regional parties elected in the single-member districts, so he changed the electoral system to a purely closed-list PR system to eliminate independent candidates, and passed a law banning purely regional parties. This reduced the number of parties from forty in 2003 to fourteen in 2008. By 2012, only four parties remained in the Duma, all of whom supported Putin (the only token opposition came from the long-standing Communist Party).

Civil society in Russia has long been considered relatively weak. While Russia has a long tradition of protests in the street, it has much less of a tradition of sustained organization of groups in civil society. Indeed, under Soviet rule, civil society was effectively eliminated by the Communist Party's monopoly on all public organizations. One of the reforms of the Soviet system in the late 1980s was allowing independent groups to emerge for the first time, and thousands did. This trend continued in the 1990s, but most groups had little funding and very limited support. The government itself under Putin has tried to create civil society groups to control. Putin made clear early on that the oligarchs and other businesses would receive favorable treatment if they joined particular, regime-approved business associations, so most did. The government also created GONGOs in several sectors, as the Chinese government had a decade earlier. The best known of these was a Putin-supporting youth group called *Nashi* (Ours) that staged mass rallies in support of the president, complete with its own pamphlets, other propaganda, and uniforms. For many Russians, the resemblance to the Soviet-era Communist Youth League was striking.

Protests were common in the 1990s, but many of them were instigated by regional elites as part of their implicit bargaining with Moscow, not by independent organizations (Robertson 2011). Early in Putin's reign, the number of protests dropped significantly. Beginning in 2005, however, protests escalated again. The first major protest since Putin became president was in response to a government proposal to end a variety of benefits that primarily supported elderly pensioners, replacing them with a cash payment worth far less. Largely spontaneous protests arose in the biggest cities and spread to virtually every region of the country, and the government responded with modest compromises. Failure to create sustained organizations, however, meant the protests petered out within a few months. More localized protests, focused on specific

Police arrest a protestor in December 2011 during the protests against fraud in the parliamentary election. The protests were the largest since the end of the Soviet Union, but Russia's electoral authoritarian regime withstood the opposition and continues to rule.

Sovfoto/UIG via Getty Images

local grievances, continued through the end of the decade; the government typically made modest compromises and the protests died down (Evans 2013). In urban areas, activists tried to stage protests supporting civil rights and other pro-democracy concerns but met with very limited support.

The massive protests that broke out in December 2011, then, took everyone, including the regime, by surprise. Economic decline since the global recession of 2008–2009 and the subsequent drop in world oil prices had tarnished the regime's popularity by 2011. When Putin and Medvedev announced that Putin would once again run for president, politically aware citizens in the growing middle class felt that the choice of president was already made for them. The parliamentary elections in December 2011 included widespread fraud, some of it captured on video and posted on the Internet. After years of relative quiescence, Russian civil society awoke; protests of tens of thousands of people demanding fairer elections took place repeatedly from December 2011 to March 2012, organized largely online. The regime did not respond with force. Instead, it made limited concessions, promising cleaner elections in the future and approving the election of regional governors. This did not appease most of the protestors, who continued, but the regime successfully outlasted them and Putin was duly elected president (again, partly via fraudulent elections) in March 2012.

The 2011–2012 elections, though, were not the overwhelming victory that the 2004 and 2008 elections had been; Putin won only 65 percent of the vote, even though he had legally eliminated most serious opposition contenders, and his party's parliamentary majority was reduced from 70 to 53 percent of the seats in the Duma, even with the widespread fraud. The opposition debated in advance how to engage in the Duma elections, with some urging a boycott of what they believed would be fraudulent polls. Ultimately, opposition forces united on a plan to vote for any party but United Russia and propagated that online, successfully reducing the party's vote substantially (Gel'man 2015, 117). After the presidential election a few months later, though, Putin cracked down, passing laws that massively increased penalties for unauthorized gatherings, arresting organizers of the protests, and requiring NGOs who received foreign funding to register as "foreign agents" with the government.

Despite hanging on, Putin did not seem to have the unquestioned domination he had when the economy was stronger. Elections for mayor in several large cities in 2014, in which opposition candidates polled surprisingly well, raised concerns inside the government. With another Duma election looming in 2016, Putin reversed course on the electoral system, recreating the mixed system, though with a 5 percent threshold to keep out smaller parties. This was widely seen as a plan to strengthen the power of United Russia even further. With the elimination of so many parties and the ban on regional ones, United Russia was the only party able to field winning candidates across the nation. Two years of severe recession, caused mainly by declining oil prices, reduced his popularity by 2016, and a poll showed support for United Russia at only 45 percent (Stratfor 2016). Nonetheless, the electoral changes worked: United Russia won a supermajority of the Duma—343 of 450 seats—allowing it to change the constitution at will. As predicted, it won virtually all single-member seats, as well as 54 percent of the PR vote. While there were clear examples of fraud, it seemed much less than in 2011 and no major protests occurred; Putin was able to win the election through more subtle forms of manipulation.

CASE Questions

1. What are the benefits and costs to Putin's regime of continuing to allow some opposition to exist and holding elections? Why has he continued to do this in spite of the potential threat it could hold for him?
2. What do recent trends suggest for the future stability and success of Putin's regime?

IRAN: FROM PARTICIPATION AND REFORM TO RENEWED REPRESSION

CASE SYNOPSIS

Iran is the only fully developed Islamic theocratic regime in the world today. This gives it an unusual ideological justification and, at least initially, gave it revolutionary and ideological legitimacy. After more than three decades, however, the regime shows attributes of many other electoral authoritarian regimes in that it rules via repression, co-optation, efforts at legitimation, and limited electoral institutions. The clerical elite have proven willing to repress opponents who step beyond what they are willing to tolerate. A 2009 crisis over what was clearly a sham presidential election badly damaged the legitimacy of Iran's quasi-democratic institutions. The successful repression of the reform movement that year led many to believe the population had grown quiescent, if not supportive of the regime, but the surprise victory of the moderate candidate in the 2013 presidential election showed that Iran's people were still willing to support any movement for change, no matter how small and limited. While the population lacks organizational strength or a public voice in the face of severe repression, it may be waiting for an opening to reemerge even more forcefully.

- ELECTIONS Presidential and legislative, but Guardian Council control of candidate selection
- PARTIES Banned for many years; allowed now, but very weak

- CIVIL SOCIETY Weak but growing until post-2005 repression; Green Movement of 2009
- CLIENTELISM Islamic foundations and Revolutionary Guards
- LEGITIMATION Tension between Islamist and democratic claims

On June 12, 2009, Iran's president Mahmoud Ahmadinejad faced reelection. Early on, he was predicted to win easily, but he fared poorly in a televised debate, and suddenly his opponents and their supporters believed he was vulnerable. Interest in the election skyrocketed, and predictions shifted to a possible opposition victory. The morning after the election, the government announced the results with only two-thirds of the votes counted, claiming the president had won 62 percent of the vote, clearly a fraudulent outcome. The number-two candidate, reformist Mir-Hossein Mousavi, called on his supporters to protest, and within a day more than one million people marched through the streets of Tehran in the largest demonstration since the 1979 revolution. After weeks of demonstrations, the government finally and effectively cracked down, arresting as many as five thousand protesters, putting over one hundred on televised trials on trumped-up charges, and allegedly torturing and raping some in prison. In the next presidential election in June 2013, however, the supreme leader was thwarted, as the closest thing to a reformist candidate won. It was, however, a far cry from 2009: the victor, Hassan Rouhani, was seen as a moderate but nonetheless a regime insider who was unlikely to challenge the supreme leadership. Despite this, people poured into the streets to celebrate the election victory of the candidate who was most distant from the supreme leader, once again showing that Iranian voters were willing to use the democratic elements of Iran's theocracy to show their displeasure with the regime.

Iranian twins dressed in the teal headscarves that are a symbol of the reform movement pass out leaflets during the 2016 election. President Hassan Rouhani's moderate coalition won majority control of parliament, but only after the Guardian Council had refused to allow at least 1,500 reformist candidates to enter the race. Whether the moderates' control of parliament would allow them to change the government's policies, though, remained to be seen, in that the Guardian Council can veto any legislation it finds is "against the revolution."

Photo by Scott Peterson/Getty Images

The dramatic events of 2009 were perhaps the zenith of a long battle between conservative supporters of the regime who wished to preserve the power of the clergy and Revolutionary Guard, and reformist elements who wanted to strengthen the quasi-democratic institutions, reduce the role of Islamic law, and more fully open the society to the world. Citizens demanding change have put reformers into office off and on over the history of the Islamic Republic, most notably during the Khatami presidency (1997–2005). The supreme leader and his allies, however, effectively blocked reformers' efforts and forced them out of office via Ahmadinejad's first election in 2005.

Majlis elections in Iran are majoritarian in single-member districts. They are held every four years, and while none has been truly free and fair, the Guardian Council at times has allowed significant competition. The council is pivotal to the process because of its power to ban candidates from running, a power it has used increasingly to thwart reform candidates. In the 1997 presidential election, Mohammad Khatami, a reformist cleric, won a sweeping victory that many observers saw as the start of a major liberalization of the political system. Until 2000, however, conservatives in parliament were numerous enough to block major reforms. In the 2000 *majlis* election, the Guardian Council did not prevent reformist candidates from running because of Khatami's popularity, and reformists won 80 percent of the vote. The new *majlis* passed reforms involving greater freedoms of expression, women's rights, human rights in general, and market-oriented economic policies. The Guardian Council, however, vetoed many of these, arguing that they violated *sharia*. By the 2004 *majlis* election, the Guardian Council once again felt it was safe to ban thousands of reformist candidates. Conservatives won the election, but turnout dropped from nearly 70 percent to 50 percent. Since then, the council has repeatedly banned reformist candidates, leading the major reformist party to boycott the 2012 *majlis* election altogether.

The 2013 presidential election once again showed the power of the Guardian Council to enforce the interests of the supreme leader. Forty candidates put their names forward, but the council approved only eight, six of whom were conservative supporters of the clerical leadership. Both President Ahmadinejad's preferred candidate and the leading reformist candidate, former president Hashemi Rafsanjani, were banned. As the campaign developed, Rafsanjani endorsed Rouhani as the closest thing to a true reformist candidate, and he won with just over 50 percent of the vote. The election showed both the continuing popular demand for change and the clerical leadership's ability to limit reformers' efforts.

Since coming to office, President Rouhani has had limited success, especially on domestic policy. He supported the successful nuclear accord with the United States that many hardliners opposed, which resulted in a partial lifting of economic sanctions. His initial efforts at opening up the economy to outside influences more fully were resisted by opponents in parliament and the Revolutionary Guard, whose economic influence is huge. Rouhani's moderate reformist coalition won majority control of the *majles* in 2016, though the Guardian Council prevented hundreds of more radical reformist candidates from running for office. His parliamentary majority should nonetheless allow him to pursue more changes in domestic policy. The Guardian Council, though, can always veto any change the supreme leader opposes, and the Revolutionary Guard and other economic forces in favor of preserving the current, closed economy can resist many changes even if Rouhani is successful at getting official policy changed.

Political parties are weak institutions in contemporary Iran, but given the severe restrictions on the power of elective offices, this is understandable. The prerevolutionary regime of the shah was modernizing authoritarian and rarely allowed significant participation, so the country has no major history of political parties. Despite the Islamic constitution's guarantee of a right to form parties, Khomeini banned them in 1987, claiming they produced unnecessary divisions. Reformist president Khatami successfully legalized parties again in 1998, which helped make the 2000 *majlis* election the most open and competitive ever. Khatami's reformist supporters coalesced into a party called the Khordad Front that won the huge victory that year. Parties continue to exist, but as loose coalitions around individual leaders, not as enduring organizations with which citizens identify. In spite of this weakness, the government banned the two leading reformist parties after the 2009 election.

In the absence of stronger parties, ideological factions are central to understanding Iranian political shifts over time. Iranian political scientist Payam Mohseni (2016) delineated two key factional dimensions: theocracy versus republicanism and left versus right. The latter is the familiar division between those who favor economic policies emphasizing greater market forces versus those who favor a greater role for the state (see chapter 10). The theocratic versus republican division is unique to Iran; it distinguishes those who believe in the nearly absolute power of the supreme leader and legitimacy coming solely from Allah versus those who see legitimacy as coming from the populace via the regime's democratic elements. Mohseni analyzed each major political era in Iran's turbulent history as a result of an alliance between two of these factions. The reformists who supported President Khatami in the 1990s, for instance, were an alliance among republicans, both left and right, while President Ahmadinejad, a key leader of the theocratic left, ruled in an alliance with the theocratic right. This coalition, while united in its support for theocracy, showed significant internal contradictions over economic policies, such as using more oil money to fund social programs for the poor, which members of the theocratic right in the *majles* resisted.

Like political parties, civil society is not particularly strong in Iran, but the period of reformist ascendancy—1997 to 2004—saw an explosion of civil society activity when government restrictions were temporarily relaxed. Of particular note were media, women's, and student groups. Whenever the government has allowed it, the media have expanded rapidly. Leading up to the 2000 *majlis* election, many newspapers emerged, and an exceptionally open political debate occurred. Since that time, religious authorities have again repressed newspapers, closing them down for criticizing the government too harshly and drastically reducing public debate. Civil society groups once again emerged in the 2009 protests until they met with overwhelming repression. Since 2009, numerous political activists and journalists have been arrested

in CONTEXT

Iran and the Middle East

In spite of its reputation as a "pariah state" in much of the West, Iran was about average in its region in terms of the level of freedom and social well-being enjoyed by its population, at least until the controversial 2009 election and its aftermath moved the country in a less democratic direction.

	Iran	Middle East/North Africa average*
Freedom House civil liberties score	6	5.27
Freedom House political rights score	6	5.53
Democracy Index 2008	2.83	3.54
Democracy Index 2015	2.16	3.48
Human Development Index 2015	0.766	0.686
Literacy rate	86.8%	89.85%

Sources: Data are from Freedom House, 2016 (https://freedomhouse.org/report/freedom-world/freedom-world-2016); *CIA World Factbook*; Human Development Index (http://hdr.undp.org/en/composite/HDI); and Democracy Index, 2015 (Economist Intelligence Unit) (http://www.yabiladi.com/img/content/EIU-Democracy-Index-2015.pdf).

*Averages exclude North Africa. For Human Development Index, use "Arab States."

and jailed, and key journalistic and legal associations were banned. The government created a new "cyberpolice force" to monitor the Internet and disrupt bloggers and social media sites critical of the regime, and it officially banned Facebook and Instagram. These restrictions, however, have had modest effects; forty-five million Iranians have Facebook accounts, including, ironically, Supreme Leader Khamenei and President Rouhani (Milani 2015, 58). Clearly, a debate on how to deal with social media is ongoing within the regime, or the Iranian state does not have the strength to implement the regime's rules with the effectiveness of the Chinese state.

Women have become an important organized force over the last decade. Ironically, in terms of women's position in society, the Islamic regime may well have been more "modernizing" than the earlier modernizing authoritarian regime of the shah. Women now constitute 62 percent of university students, and a birth control policy has lowered childbearing and population growth rates dramatically (see chapter 4). Conservative clergy have resisted changes to laws regarding divorce, clothing, and other issues associated with religious observance, but they have allowed significant socioeconomic changes in women's lives. These changes have fostered the growth of women's organizations calling for even further change. All major politicians now court the women's vote during elections.

The Green Movement that emerged in response to the fraudulent 2009 election showed both the strength and weakness of Iran's incipient civil society. It brought at least a million people onto the streets of Tehran and reached beyond its middle-class base, but it did not have much effect in the countryside. Though initiated in response to an appeal from the losing candidate, it had no clear formal organization. A decentralized organizing system using Twitter and Facebook became the main means of communication, aided by public statements and occasional public appearances by reformist leaders. Protests continued for weeks and showed the youthful participants that change was possible, but the government successfully repressed them in spite of widespread international condemnation. Moussavi, the leading reformer, called for demonstrations again in February 2011 in support of the "Arab Spring" movements in Egypt and Tunisia. Tens of thousands of Iranians turned out, but the government responded with force, disbanding the demonstrations and arresting its leaders once again, in spite of the fact that the regime itself was in favor of the "Arab Spring." Seven years after the huge demonstrations and in spite of the partial victory in the 2013 presidential election and 2016 parliamentary election, the reform movement is severely limited. Reformers have supported the more moderate forces around President Rouhani, but those demanding more fundamental changes in the regime have been effectively silenced.

Given the weak formal institutions of participation and the government's repeated repression of them, it is not surprising that clientelism is a crucial form of political activity as well as a key way to gain support for the government. Clientelist factions long predate the Islamic regime in Iran, and the regime has done little to eliminate them. Indeed, many scholars argue that such factions are essential to the regime's continued rule. The ruling elite consists of numerous patrons in key government or *bonyad* positions, informally leading large numbers of clients who provide them with political support. These factions are crucial venues through which political participation occurs. Indeed, President Khatami's reforms in the late 1990s and early 2000s were aimed in part at strengthening civil society to weaken the networks that clerics and their supporters use as tools of co-optation. Under President Ahmadinejad, factions and networks of former Revolutionary Guards expanded their power and position dramatically. They are now among the strongest opponents to President Rouhani's reform agenda.

CASE Questions

1. What does the history of the 2009 and 2013 presidential elections and Green Movement suggest about the possibility of democratic change in Iran in the near future?

2. Given the role of the Guardian Council in controlling candidates for elections when it so chooses, do the democratic elements of Iran's regime really make any difference to how it is ruled?

CONCLUSION

By the dawn of the new millennium, it was clear that while democracy had expanded, authoritarianism was not about to disappear entirely. Since the end of the Cold War, electoral authoritarian rule has expanded, and more "closed" authoritarian rule that allows no formal opposition has been on the wane (with China clearly being the world's biggest exception to the trend). The differences between fully authoritarian and electoral authoritarian rule, though, aren't as great as they might at first appear. Understanding the opaque political dynamics of authoritarian and electoral authoritarian regimes will continue to be a concern for comparative politics for the foreseeable future.

On the face of it, dictators seem to control virtually everything in authoritarian regimes. The executive would seem to be all-powerful. As we've seen, though, this is often not the case, which makes figuring out who rules rather difficult. The key question is not just what formal institutions exist but how institutionalized they are. Ultimately, in authoritarian regimes the supreme leader or a small coterie of leaders (such as a politburo) has final authority to decide as they will. Ruling by fiat and repression alone, however, is both difficult and expensive. Holding a gun to every citizen's head, as well as maintaining the loyalty of those holding the guns, is not easy. All regimes, therefore, seek to gain some sort of legitimacy or at least to buy support via co-optation. A means to achieve both legitimacy and support is to limit the supreme leader's power in order to give others, especially key elites, some influence. Institutionalized and therefore predictable governing and limited participatory institutions can accomplish this. Examining those institutions and how strong they are can thus be a key means to understanding who really rules and how much influence they have. Even in the most personalist regimes with little institutionalization, patron-client relationships are important for co-opting opposition. More powerful individuals control more patronage, and on the other side, some clients are more powerful and thus more likely to have their requests attended to than others. Comparativists attempt the difficult task of understanding these informal networks and relationships to determine who rules in countries where institutions matter little.

Comparativists have long catalogued authoritarian regimes into various subtypes. It's clear, however, that certain commonalities exist in all authoritarian regimes. For instance, all dictators face the dictator's dilemma, though they attempt to solve it in different ways. All dictators also rule through some combination of repression, co-optation, and attempts at legitimation, but again in differing ways and amounts. Some of this variation is systematic across subtypes: different subtypes display consistent and distinct behavior. One-party and of course electoral authoritarian regimes provide opportunities for greater participation via formal institutions. Military regimes are less likely to do so, as political participation and open dissent are foreign to professional military culture. Following the logic of the dictator's dilemma, regimes that allow less participation are likely to require more repression and co-optation. Military regimes seem likely to use repression, given their inherent control of force. Personalist regimes that have weak institutions across the board focus mostly on co-optation via patronage, using repression as well but often in less institutionalized and therefore less effective ways. Such a personalist regime might have, for example, multiple and competing military agencies that are informally loyal to individual leaders rather than to the regime as a whole. The splits within the military in response to the 2011 uprising in Libya show the possible effects of this aspect of personalist rule.

The earliest theoretical approaches to understanding authoritarian regimes focused mainly on individual leaders or national cultures. Individual leaders are clearly crucial in such regimes, so scholars used psychological theories to understand their personal influences and motivations. Other scholars, looking beyond the individual, used political culture theories to argue why such regimes emerged in the first place and how they operated. Authoritarian regimes emerged in countries with political cultures that had authoritarian traits such as lack of interpersonal trust, lack of belief in core democratic principles, lack of popular interest in participation in politics, or a popular desire to follow a perceived "strong" leader. For example, the lack of any lengthy democratic experience in postcolonial Africa created regimes that eliminated virtually all democratic trappings.

More recently, scholars have used rational choice or historical-institutionalist models to understand authoritarian regimes. Dictators face a common set of governing problems. To overcome these, they engage in a combination of repression, co-optation, and legitimation. This action pattern, rational choice theorists argue, is determined by the dictators' and their opponents' or allies' rational responses to their conditions, the most important of which are the relative strengths of the actors and the resources at their disposal. Historical institutionalists agree with much of this, but assert that the creation of key institutions, such as strong ruling parties, happens at particular historical junctures and heavily influences regime strength and longevity; institutions cannot be created at any time the dictator comes to believe he needs them. As with many arguments in comparative politics, institutionalist theories are at the forefront of the debate today but have not definitively proven their case. We turn next to another set of difficult questions about regimes: why and how they change from one type to another via military coup, revolution, or democratization.

KEY CONCEPTS

dictator's dilemma (p. 415)
personality cult (p. 439)

supreme leader (p. 412)

 Sharpen your skills with SAGE edge at **edge.sagepub.com/orvis4e.** **SAGE edge for students** provides a personalized approach to help you accomplish your coursework goals in an easy-to-use learning environment.

WORKS CITED

Albertus, Michael, and Victor Menaldo. 2016. "The Political Economy of Autocratic Constitutions." In *Constitutions in Authoritarian Regimes*, edited by Tom Ginsburg and Alberto Simpser, 53–82. Cambridge, UK: Cambridge University Press.

Blaydes, Lisa. 2011. *Elections and Distributive Politics in Mubarak's Egypt.* Cambridge, UK: Cambridge University Press.

Boroumand, Ladan. 2009. "Civil Society's Choice." *Journal of Democracy* 20 (4): 16–20 (http://www.journalofdemocracy.org/articles/gratis/Boroumand-20-4.pdf).

Brown, Kerry. 2013. "The CCP and the On-Party State." In *Handbook of China's Governance and Domestic Politics,* edited by Chris Ogden, 3–11. New York: Routledge.

Brownlee, Jason. 2007. *Authoritarianism in an Age of Democratization.* Cambridge, UK: Cambridge University Press.

Chen, Jie, and Chunlong Lu. 2011. "Democratization and the Middle Class in China: The Middle Class's Attitudes toward Democracy." *Political Research Quarterly* 64: 705–719. September.

Chen, Xi. 2012. *Social Protest and Contentious Authoritarianism in China.* Cambridge, UK: Cambridge University Press.

Dickson, Bruce J. 2003. *Red Capitalists in China: The Party, Private Entrepreneurs, and Prospects for Political Change.* New York: Cambridge University Press.

_____. 2016. *The Dictator's Dilemma: The Chinese Communist Party's Strategy for Survival.* Oxford, UK: Oxford University Press.

Evans, Alfred B., Jr. 2013. "Civil Society and Protest." In *Return to Putin's Russia: Past Imperfect, Future Uncertain,* edited by Stephen K. Wegren, 103–104. 5th ed. Lanham, MD: Rowman and Littlefield.

Fewsmith, Joseph. 2013. *The Logic and Limits of Political Reform in China.* New York: Cambridge University Press.

Frantz, Erica, and Natasha Ezrow. 2011. *The Politics of Dictatorship: Institutions and Outcomes in Authoritarian Regimes.* Boulder, CO: Lynne Rienner.

Gandhi, Jennifer. 2008. *Political Institutions under Dictatorship.* Cambridge, UK: Cambridge University Press.

Gel'man, Vladimir. 2015. *Authoritarian Russia: Analyzing Post-Soviet Regime Changes.* Pittsburgh, PA: University of Pittsburgh Press.

Ginsburg, Tom. 2008. "Administrative Law and the Judicial Control of Agents in Authoritarian Regimes." In *Rule by Law: The Politics of Courts in Authoritarian Regimes,* edited by Tom Ginsburg and Tamir Moustafa, 58–72. Cambridge, UK: Cambridge University Press.

Hen-Tov, Elliot, and Nathan Gonzalez. 2010. "The Militarization of Post-Khomeini Iran: Praetorianism 2.0." *Washington Quarterly* 34 (1): 45–59. doi:10.1080/0163660X.2011.534962

Hesli, Vicki L. 2007. *Government and Politics in Russia and the Post-Soviet Region.* Boston: Houghton Mifflin.

Hildebrandt, Timothy. 2013. *Social Organizations and the Authoritarian State in China.* Cambridge, UK: Cambridge University Press.

Jamal, Amaney A. 2007. *Barriers to Democracy: The Other Side of Social Capital in Palestine and the Arab World.* Princeton, NJ: Princeton University Press.

Koesel, Karri. J. 2014. *Religion and Authoritarianism: Cooperation, Conflict, and the Consequences.* Cambridge, UK: Cambridge University Press.

Landry, Pierre F. 2008. "The Institutional Diffusion of Courts in China: Evidence from Survey Data." In *Rule by Law: The Politics of Courts in Authoritarian Regimes,* edited by Tom Ginsburg and Tamir Moustafa, 207–234. Cambridge, UK: Cambridge University Press.

Landry, Pierre F., Deborah Davis, and Shiru Wang. 2010. "Elections in Rural China: Competition without Parties." *Comparative Political Studies* 43 (6): 763–790. doi:10.1177/0010414009359392

Lee, Ching Kwan, and Eli Friedman. 2009. "The Labor Movement." *Journal of Democracy* 20 (3): 21–24.

Li, Cheng. 2010. "China's Communist Party-State: The Structure and Dynamics of Power." In *Politics in China: An Introduction,* edited by William A. Joseph, 165–191. Oxford, UK: Oxford University Press.

Li, Cheng, and Lynn White. 2006. "The Sixteenth Central Committee of the Chinese Communist Party: Emerging Patterns of Power Sharing." In *China's Deep Reform: Domestic Politics in Transition,* edited by Lowell Dittmer and Guoli Liu, 81–118. Lanham, MD: Rowman and Littlefield.

Lu, Yiyi. 2009. *Non-Governmental Organizations in China: The Rise of Dependent Autonomy.* New York: Routledge.

Magaloni, Beatriz. 2006. *Voting for Autocracy: Hegemonic Party Survival and Its Demise in Mexico.* Cambridge, UK: Cambridge University Press.

Manion, Melanie. 2015. *Information for Autocrats: Representation in Chinese Local Congresses.* Cambridge, UK: Cambridge University Press.

Mbembe, Achille. 1992. "Provisional Notes on the Postcolony." *Africa: Journal of the International African Institute* 62 (1): 3–37. doi:10.2307/1160062

Migdal, Joel S. 1988. *Strong Societies and Weak States: State-Society Relations and State Capabilities in the Third World.* Princeton, NJ: Princeton University Press.

Milani, Abbas. 2015. "Iran's Paradoxical Regime." *Journal of Democracy* 26 (2): 52–60. April.

Minzner, Carl. 2015. "China after the Reform Era." *Journal of Democracy* 26 (3): 129–143. July.

Mohseni, Payam. 2016. "Factionalism, Privatization, and the Political Economic of Regime Transformation." In *Power and Change in Iran: Politics of Contentions and Conciliation*, edited by Daniel Brumberg and Farideh Farhi, 37–69. Bloomington: Indiana University Press.

Nathan, Andrew J. 2016. "The Puzzle of the Chinese Middle Class." *Journal of Democracy* 26 (2): 5–19. April.

Pei, Minxin. 2007. "Corruption Threatens China's Future." Carnegie Endowment for International Peace, Policy Brief 55. October (http://carnegieendowment.org/files/pb55_pei_china_corruption_final.pdf).

Robertson, Graeme B. 2011. *The Politics of Protest in Hybrid Regimes: Managing Dissent in Post-Communist Russia.* Cambridge, UK: Cambridge University Press.

Saich, Tony. 2012. *The Quality of Governance in China: The Citizens' View.* Cambridge, MA: John F. Kennedy School of Government. Harvard University: Faculty Research Working Paper, RWP12-051. November.

_____. 2013. "Political Representation." In *Handbook of China's Governance and Domestic Politics,* edited by Chris Ogden, 109–119. New York: Routledge.

Shambaugh, David. 2008. *China's Communist Party: Atrophy and Adaptation.* Washington, DC: Woodrow Wilson Center Press.

Shi, Tianjian. 2006. "Village Committee Elections in China: Institutionalist Tactics for Democracy." In *China's Deep Reform: Domestic Politics in Transition,* edited by Lowell Dittmer and Guoli Liu, 353–380. Lanham, MD: Rowman and Littlefield.

Stockman, Daniela. 2012. *Media Commercialization and Authoritarian Rule in China.* Cambridge, UK: Cambridge University Press.

Stratfor. 2016. "A Subtle Manipulation of Russian Elections." March 29 (https://www.stratfor.com/analysis/subtle-manipulation-russian-elections).

Svolik, Milan W. 2012. *The Politics of Authoritarian Rule.* Cambridge, UK: Cambridge University Press.

Teets, Jessica C. 2014. *Civil Society under Authoritarianism: The China Model.* Cambridge, UK: Cambridge University Press.

Wang, Yuhua. 2015. *Typing the Autocrat's Hands: The Rise of the Rule of Law in China.* Cambridge, UK: Cambridge University Press.

Wintrobe, Ronald. 1998. *The Political Economy of Dictatorship.* Cambridge, UK: Cambridge University Press.

Wong, Edward. 2013. "In China, Widening Discontent among the Communist Party Faithful." *New York Times,* January 19

(http://www.nytimes.com/2013/01/20/
world/asia/in-china-discontent-among-
the-normally-faithful.html?emc=eta1).

Wright, Teresa. 2010. *Accepting Authoritarianism: State-Society Relations in China's Reform Era*. Stanford, CA: Stanford University Press.

Yadav, Vineeta, and Bumba Mukherjee. 2016. *The Politics of Corruption in Dictatorships*. Cambridge, UK: Cambridge University Press.

Yang, Guobin. 2009. "Online Activism." *Journal of Democracy* 20 (3): 33–36. doi:10.1353/jod.0.0094

Zhao, Suisheng. 2016. "Xi Jinping's Maoist Revival." *Journal of Democracy* 27 (3): 83–97. July.

Zhou, Jinghao. 2015. *Chinese vs. Western Perspectives: Understanding Contemporary China*. New York: Lexington Books.

RESOURCES FOR FURTHER STUDY

Clapham, Christopher S. 1982. *Private Patronage and Public Power: Political Clientelism in the Modern State*. New York: St. Martin's Press.

Clapham, Christopher S., and George D. E. Philip, eds. 1985. *The Political Dilemmas of Military Regimes*. Totowa, NJ: Barnes and Noble.

Jahanbegloo, Ramin, ed. 2012. *Civil Society and Democracy in Iran*. New York: Lexington Books.

Mbembe, Achille. 2001. *On the Postcolony*. Berkeley: University of California Press.

McFaul, Michael. 2005. "Chinese Dreams, Persian Realities." *Journal of Democracy* 16 (4): 74–82. doi:10.1353/jod.2005.0068

WEB RESOURCES

Quality of Government Institute, University of Gothenburg, The QoG Data
(http://www.qog.pol.gu.se/data)

World Bank, Database of Political Institutions
(http://go.worldbank.org/2EAGGLRZ40)

World Justice Project, Rule of Law Index
(http://www.worldjusticeproject.org/rule-of-law-index)

World Values Survey
(http://www.worldvaluessurvey.org)

9 REGIME CHANGE

KEY QUESTIONS

- Why does the military intervene in politics in certain countries and not in others?

- How can civilians maintain effective control over the military? When the military takes power, what explains how it rules and how much power, if any, it shares with civilians?

- What best explains why some new democracies survive while others revert to authoritarianism?

- Can a democracy survive in any country, or does it require a certain type of society, culture, or economy?

Regime change is the high drama of comparative politics. Many of our most iconic political images are of regime change, from the "shot heard 'round the world" signaling the start of the American Revolution in 1776, to Nelson Mandela taking the oath of office in South Africa in 1994, to protesters in Tahrir Square in Egypt in 2011. They are images of popular and charismatic leaders backed by the mobilized masses demanding a better world. There can also be less positive images, though, like that of a general seizing power as tanks roll into the capital, as happened in Egypt in 2013. Comparativists analyze all of these events, whether positive or negative, as **regime change**, the process through which one regime is transformed into another.

Comparativists have long studied regime change. Initially focused on military coups d'état and revolutions, since the 1980s we have concentrated primarily on what Samuel Huntington (1991) called the "third wave" of democratization. All types of regime change remain important, however, as the Country and Concept table on page 471 illustrates. While democratization has been the most widespread type of regime change in the last two decades, military coups are the most common type of regime change in the longer term. Coups took place in Guinea and Mali in this decade and a failed coup attempt in Turkey in July 2016 made world headlines. The "Arab Spring," and the recent history of Egypt in

particular, shows that it's often not clear in the short term what kind of regime change is taking place as it happens. Understanding all three types remains essential. Since we examined revolutions in detail in chapter 7, in this chapter we only address the outcomes of revolutions—the type of regime change they typically produce.

The study of regime change raises several fundamental questions in comparative politics: Why do revolutions or military coups happen in some countries and not in others? When the military stages a coup, what explains how it rules and how much power, if any, it shares with civilians? Why does democratization succeed or fail? Can democracy survive in any country or in only certain types of countries, and why? We address all of these questions in our examination of regime change, starting with the historically most common type: military coups d'état.

regime change
The process through which one regime is transformed into another

THE MILITARY IN POLITICS: COUPS D'ÉTAT

Military force is central to the modern state. All states must have a military and maintain effective control over it to maintain sovereignty. Americans generally view the military as an organization that is firmly under civilian control and that should stay out of politics. In reality, no military is completely apolitical. When President Barack Obama decided that he wanted to get the U.S. military out of Iraq and reduce its presence in Afghanistan, various military leaders made it clear they disagreed with those decisions. When congressional committees consider the U.S. defense budget, they hold hearings and listen to the advice of top military leaders, among others. These are both examples of the military engaging in political activity. The key is that a regime with effective control over the military, whether democratic or authoritarian, keeps such activities within institutionalized limits: the military does not go beyond the bounds set by the civilian leadership. When it does, a constitutional or political crisis can arise. We now examine the most flagrant military intervention in politics, the **coup d'état,** in which the military forcibly removes the existing regime and establishes a new one.

coup d'état
When the military forcibly removes an existing regime and establishes a new one

When American students are asked why the military does not stage a coup in the United States, the first answer is usually that the Constitution prevents it. The elected president is commander in chief, and the military must obey him. But given that the Constitution is a piece of paper and the president is one unarmed person, whereas the U.S. military is arguably the most powerful force on the planet, there must be more to it than that. And there is. A civilian regime, whether democratic or authoritarian, goes to great lengths to ensure that the military is loyal to the regime's ideals and institutions. Civilian leaders try to inculcate the appropriate values in the military leadership, either professional values specific to the military or more general values that are supportive of the regime and that reflect the broader political culture. Well-established democracies train military leaders carefully in military academies, such as West Point in the United States or Sandhurst in Britain, to instill professional values that portray the military as prestigious and apolitical. Since military personnel come out of society as a whole, a strong system of political socialization throughout the society that ingrains respect for the major political institutions also helps to ensure that military leaders have those same values. Communist systems attempted to achieve the same ends via direct Communist Party involvement in the military, mandatory party membership for the military leadership, and, like democracies, political socialization in the broader society.

Less-institutionalized authoritarian regimes often lack these types of generally effective and systematic mechanisms. Instead, they rely on the creation of multiple military institutions (as mentioned in chapter 8), so that no single one becomes too powerful, or on informal ties of loyalty such as ethnic affiliations between the ruler and military personnel. Many African personalist rulers created a well-equipped and well-paid presidential guard from the same ethnic group or region as the president, which was personally loyal to the president as an individual patron. The job of this presidential guard was, in part, to protect the president from his own army.

COUNTRY AND CONCEPT
Regime Change and Outcome

Country	Date	Type of regime change (20th century)	Outcome: type of regime	Length of new regime (years)
Brazil	1930	Military coup	Neofascist	15
	1945	Democratization	Democracy	19
	1964	Military coup	Modernizing authoritarian	21
	1985	Democratization	Democracy	31+
China	1911	Political revolution	State collapse/warlord rule	16
	1949	Social revolution	Communist	67+
Germany	1918	Democratization	Democracy	15
	1933	Fascist putsch	Fascist	12
	1950	Democratization	Democracy	66+
	1990	Democratization (end of East German state)	Democracy (expanded)	NA
India	1947	Democratization (end of colonial rule)	Democracy	69+
Iran	1921	Military coup	Modernizing authoritarian	58
	1979	Social revolution	Theocratic	37+
Japan	1950	Democratization	Democracy	66+
Mexico	1920	Political revolution	Electoral authoritarian	74
	1994	Democratization	Democracy	22+
Nigeria	1960	Democratization (end of colonial rule)	Democracy	6
	1966	Military coup	Modernizing authoritarian	13
	1979	Democratization	Democracy	4
	1983	Military coup	Personalist	16
	1999	Democratization	Democracy	17+
Russia	1917	Social revolution	Communist	74
	1991	Democratization	Democracy	9
	2003	Democratic decay	Electoral authoritarian	16+
United Kingdom	None	NA	NA	NA
United States	None	NA	NA	NA

Why Do Military Coups Happen?

Military coups occur when all efforts to keep the military loyal to (or at least under the control of) the regime fail. Three major schools of thought attempt to explain why coups happen. In the 1960s, when coups became quite common in postcolonial countries, the dominant explanation focused not on the military itself but instead on the societies and political systems in which the coups occurred. Samuel Huntington, focusing on the weakness of institutions, contended that "the most important causes of military intervention in politics are not military . . . but the political and institutional structure of the society" (1968, 194). Samuel Finer, in his classic 1962 work *The Man on Horseback*, made a political-culture argument: countries with political cultures that do not highly value nonmilitary means of transferring power and civil society are more prone to coups. Weak institutions and corrupt rule under early postcolonial leaders created political instability and often violence. The military, these theorists argued, intervened to restore order when civilian leaders had weakened the civilian regime via corrupt and incompetent rule. Most of these early students of military coups were modernization theorists who argued that the military, with its training and hierarchical organization, was one of the few modern institutions in postcolonial societies. They believed that the military could rule in the national interest, reestablishing order and restarting development. This thinking was in line with the theories of modernizing authoritarianism prominent at the time (see chapter 3).

More recently, Africa scholar Chris Allen (1995) argued that military coups in Africa in the 1960s and 1970s happened in states in which civilian elites could not resolve the "clientelist crisis" that resulted from decolonization. He argued that African political parties mobilized voters via clientelism in the elections before and right after independence. The parties that won the first elections gained enormous advantages by gaining control of state expenditures to use as patronage; those who lost used whatever means they could to battle against the incumbent advantage. The losers appealed more strongly to ethnic loyalty and used violence as necessary to try to regain power. Politics became an unregulated "spoils" game of growing ethnic divisions, corruption, and violence. Some leaders managed to avoid the worst of this by negotiating agreements among key elites and thereby creating more stable, one-party regimes with a powerful central ruler who limited political competition (Tanzania and Kenya are classic examples). Regimes that could not achieve this spiraled into crisis, with military coups a common result (our case study of Nigeria is a prime example). While not sharing modernization theorists' belief in the positive aspects of military rule, Allen does concur with their understanding of coups as coming from failures of civilian leadership.

A second school of thought looked not at society but within military organizations themselves. These theorists argued that a military engages in a coup to advance its own institutional interests, such as getting larger budgets, higher pay, or better equipment (Huntington 1964; Janowitz 1964). When military leaders perceive civilian rulers as not adequately considering the military's needs, they may intervene, not in the national interest, but rather to improve their own position. They may also instigate a coup in response to what they perceive as unjustified civilian intervention in military matters, such as the appointment of top officers without the military's approval or the assignment of inappropriate duties. Recently, Kristen Harkness (2014) used a quantitative study in Africa to argue that military coups happen when leaders attempt to manipulate security forces along ethnic lines, either imposing their ethnic kin in the military or removing their predecessors' or opponents'. Military leaders may see a coup in these situations as a defense of their professional status vis-à-vis civilian leaders. In effect, the military in this theory is just another interest group clamoring for power and position within the government, but one with guns.

Samuel Decalo developed the third major explanation for coups by drawing on the ideas of neopatrimonialism. Focusing on Africa, he argued that the first two schools of thought misunderstood the nature of many African (and perhaps other postcolonial) militaries and therefore failed to recognize the true motivations for coups. The typical African military, he said, was "a coterie of distinct armed camps owing primary clientelist allegiance to a handful of mutually competitive officers of different ranks seething with a variety of corporate, ethnic and personal grievances" (1976, 14–15). He believed that prior theorists mistakenly viewed the military as a united and professional body concerned with either national interests or its own interests. Instead, he saw African armies as riven by the same regional, ethnic, and personal divisions that characterize neopatrimonial rule in general. Decalo argued that most coups occurred because particular military leaders wanted to gain power for their own interests, those of their ethnic group or region, or those of their faction within the military. Coups were about gaining a greater share of power and resources for the coup leaders and their clients, not about the interests of society as a whole or even "the military" as an institution.

None of these theories differentiates between coup attempts and coup successes, however. Naunihal Singh (2014) recently pointed out that only about half of all coups succeed, leading him to investigate why some succeed and others fail. Using a large quantitative analysis of all coup attempts from 1950 to 2000 and a detailed case study of Ghana (which has had ten attempts and six successes), he found that the key explanations of success are the rank of the leadership of the coup attempt and whether the country has seen successful coups in the past. Coups from the top of the military hierarchy succeeded about two-thirds of the time, those led from the middle ranks succeeded 42 percent of the time, and those from the lower ranks only 28 percent of the time (Singh 2014, 71). He argued that this is because the key elements are dynamics within the military; once a coup is launched, civilian action makes little difference to the outcome. He used a rational choice model to show that coups are "coordination games": military leaders are most likely to support a coup if they think it will be successful, regardless of their personal opinions.

CRITICAL inquiry

Coups and Coup Attempts around the World

Naunihal Singh (2014) argued that coups are more likely to succeed when they are led by top military leaders and in countries that have had successful coups in the past. Map 9.1 shows coups and coup attempts around the world since World War II.

The maps use categorized data, but the detailed data show Iraq leading the world with sixteen coup attempts but only one success; Sudan is second with eleven attempts and four successes. Other countries, such as Algeria, have had only one attempt, but it was successful. Also note the countries that are gray, meaning they have had no attempts or no successes. Compare the two maps for specific countries, especially those that have had more attempts than successes. What trends do you see in terms of where and when coups have happened and their success rates? Can you formulate hypotheses other than Singh's to explain these trends? How would you try to determine which hypothesis best explains why coups occurred and when, where, and why they succeeded or failed?

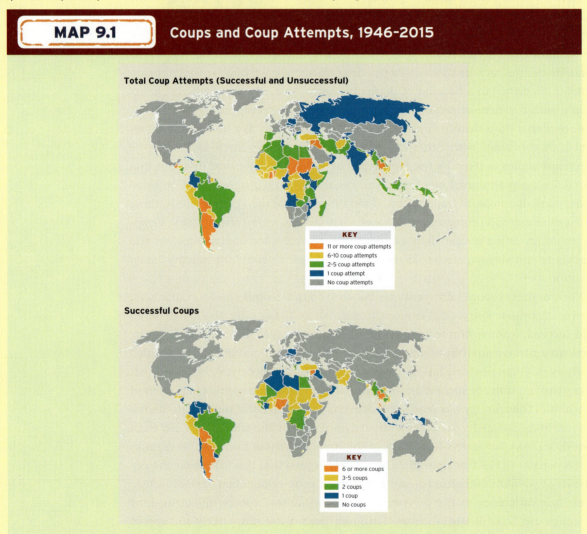

MAP 9.1   Coups and Coup Attempts, 1946–2015

Total Coup Attempts (Successful and Unsuccessful)

KEY
- 11 or more coup attempts
- 6–10 coup attempts
- 2–5 coup attempts
- 1 coup attempt
- No coup attempts

Successful Coups

KEY
- 6 or more coups
- 3–5 coups
- 2 coups
- 1 coup
- No coups

Source: Data for the maps are from Monty Marshall and Donna Ramsey Marshall, "Coup d'État Events, 1946–2015," Center for Systemic Peace (http://www.systemicpeace.org/inscrdata.html).

Past successful attempts, especially recent ones, will lead them to believe the new attempt will succeed. Communication is also crucial; if military leaders not initially involved believe the coup has widespread support within the military and the coup leaders can seize and hold key broadcast media sites and other symbolic buildings like presidential palaces and parliaments, they will believe the coup is succeeding and will join in, bringing their forces with them. All of this is easier to achieve for leaders at the top of the military ranks and most difficult for those at the bottom, who are rebelling against not just the government but the entire military hierarchy. Once things like socialization of the military fail and a coup attempt occurs, its success, Singh showed, depends on the actions of military leaders themselves.

The coup attempt in Turkey in 2016 illustrates this dynamic. The country has seen numerous coups over the years, most recently in 1997. Typically, the military has seen itself as defender of the secular tradition established by the country's founder, Kemal Atatürk, after World War I. Whenever an Islamist-oriented group gained too much power, the military would step in to remove it and restore democracy relatively quickly, after suppressing Islamist groups. The top of the military hierarchy led most of the coups so they were both successful and bloodless; little opposition was possible. The Islamist party in power since 2003, however, managed to avoid military intervention, initially by being more moderate than past Islamists and then by a successful purge of much of the military leadership, replacing its secular opponents with those more willing at least to tolerate the moderate Islamist government. As the party's leader, Tayyip Erdoğan, became more autocratic, secularists became increasingly concerned.

While the exact leadership and intent of the coup attempt in July 2016 is unclear, it was clear that the top military leadership did not take part. Middle and lower-level officers were leading the rebellion and were met with armed opposition from other military forces loyal to the president. The government reportedly knew in advance of the coup plot, so the rebels were forced to launch the coup earlier than planned.

Military Coups in Africa by Decade

Nigeria's history of military coups and regimes from the 1960s into the 1990s was part of Africa's continuing pattern of coups and military rule in the region. Coups in the first decade of the twenty-first century were down 43 percent from the average of twenty-one coups per decade from the 1960s to the 1990s.

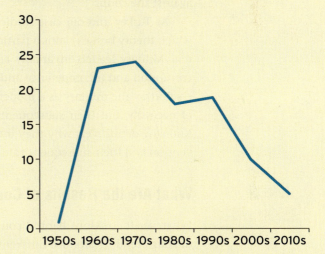

Source: George K. Kieh and Pita O. Agbese, *The Military and Politics in Africa: From Engagement to Democratic and Constitutional Control* (Aldershot, UK: Ashgate, 2002). Updated by the authors.

They failed to capture Erdoğan or all of the media outlets, allowing Erdoğan to speak with the media initially via FaceTime on his cell phone. He urged his civilian supporters to pour into the streets to oppose the coup and was able to communicate with top generals as well. Within less than twenty-four hours, the coup was defeated and at least fifty thousand government employees—in the military, judicial system, and education system—were arrested within a week, with an estimated eighty thousand eventually losing their jobs. Erdoğan blamed supporters of a former ally who were known to hold positions throughout the government, including the military. Indeed, some of the rebellious military leaders rose in the ranks after Erdoğan's earlier removal of more secular officers he didn't trust (Arango and Yeginsu 2016). Whatever the motives for the coup, though, the rebels severely failed at the "coordination game": Erdoğan was able to communicate strength rather than the rebels doing so, and most of the military and civilians (including opposition parties) supported the government against the coup.

As Turkey and our case studies below demonstrate, it is often difficult to discern which theory best explains a particular coup, especially what motivates the coup plotters. Military leaders invariably claim that they intervened to save the nation from corruption and incompetence and to provide unity to pursue development. The leaders portray the military as a modern and national institution that intervenes only out of necessity, but their subsequent rule often betrays them as having other motives. Knowing definitively why they intervened is often difficult because motives for intervention and their subsequent rule are not always connected.

What Are the Results of Coups?

Whatever the reasons behind coups, different kinds of militaries and different kinds of coups tend to produce different kinds of military regimes. Among coups that succeed, the factor that is probably of greatest importance in determining the kind of

Turkish prime minister Tayyip Erdoğan attends a ceremony with his top military leadership in 2010. After the failed July 2016 coup attempt, led mostly by midlevel officers, Erdoğan conducted a major purge of the military. He detained as many as ten thousand military personnel and dishonorably discharged nearly two thousand in the first two weeks after the coup attempt. Turkey has the second largest military in NATO after the United States and has been actively involved in the Syrian civil war, making instability in its military and government of great concern around the world.

ADEM ALTAN/AFP/Getty Images

subsequent military regime is the institutional strength of the military itself, as we noted in chapter 8. A military that maintains a strongly hierarchical organization is less likely to produce a coup that is driven by individual or sectional interests. Rather, an institutionalized military might instigate a coup to try to create order out of political chaos or a coup that is in the narrow interests of the military as an institution. The military regime resulting from the coup is likely to be relatively institutionalized, predictable, and stable, if not necessarily legitimate. In addition, a coup carried out primarily in the interests of the military as an institution is likely to result in a shift of governmental resources toward military spending, which usually has deleterious economic effects overall. A more personal coup is likely to produce a more personalist regime that is far less institutionalized than other types of authoritarian regimes and is more subject to countercoups in the future. Nikolay Marinov and Hein Goemans (2014) found a significant change in the outcome of coups since the end of the Cold War: they are far more likely to result in transitions to democracy than was true during the Cold War. They argued that stronger international pressure in favor of democracy explains this, and this outcome in turn explains why coups happen less frequently than they did in the past. A failed coup, on the other hand, is likely to usher in a period of greater strength for the incumbent government and often repression of its enemies, as the attempted coup in Turkey in 2016 showed.

CASE Study

COMPARING COUPS: BRAZIL AND NIGERIA

CASE SYNOPSIS

In both Brazil and Nigeria, understanding the precise motives for coups is difficult because while all coup leaders claim to intervene in the national interest, the subsequent governments, especially in the case of Nigeria, belie those intentions. Therefore, motives other than protecting the national interest seem at least equally plausible. The biggest difference between the two countries is probably the level of institutionalization of their militaries. Brazil's more institutionalized military entered politics with a clear ideology and was a strong enough institution to implement its vision, for better or worse, and it preserved some very limited civilian political participation in the process. Nigeria's far less institutionalized military reflected the country's ethnic and class conflicts, and it ruled in a far less institutionalized manner that ultimately undermined Nigeria's political institutions. It also engaged in at least as much corruption as the civilian officials it overthrew.

- INSTITUTIONALIZATION Brazil's military more institutionalized; Nigeria's less so
- CAUSES OF COUPS Societal versus military for Brazil; societal versus personal for Nigeria

Political scientists have used both societal and institutional (within the military) arguments to explain Brazil's 1964 coup, which ushered in a modernizing authoritarian state, a crucial milestone in the country's political and economic development. The Brazilian military was involved in politics since the founding of the republic in 1889. It was instrumental in the governments of the first decade and emerged again as central under the neofascist Estado Novo in the 1930s. Even during the country's democratic periods, the military has been politically influential. Elected officials regularly consulted with military leaders on a variety of policy issues, and the military leaders were quite willing to get involved in politics when they thought necessary, at least until the consolidation of Brazil's new democracy in the 1990s.

The origins of Brazil's 1964 coup can be traced to the creation of an elite military academy after World War II, the Escola Superior de Guerra (ESG), or Superior War College, which came to play an influential role in the Brazilian military and elite politics in general. Its faculty developed what came to be known as the National Security Doctrine in the 1950s. This doctrine was then taught to ESG students, who were not only high-ranking military officers but also selected senior civilian officials. Essentially, it envisioned national security as including not just protection from foreign aggression but also economic development and prevention of domestic insurrection. At the height of the Cold War, the ESG military intellectuals saw domestic communist insurrection as a primary threat and strong economic development as essential to national security. The ESG's National Security Doctrine laid the intellectual roots for the 1964 coup and subsequent military regime.

In 1961 leftist vice president João Goulart became president when his elected predecessor abruptly resigned. Goulart seemed intent on reforming Brazil's very unequal society: strengthening labor unions, redistributing land, and providing greater benefits to the urban working classes. He clashed with both the military elite and the conservative majority in the National Congress, both of whom saw him as trying to move the country in the direction of socialism, and perhaps even communism. As Goulart failed to get his policies passed through the National Congress and faced growing opposition within the military, he became more populist. To try to gain greater military loyalty, he replaced several senior military officers who opposed him with others who were more supportive, thus dividing the military itself. Finally, in March 1964, he dramatically called for fundamental reforms that the conservative elite, both civilian and military, opposed. When junior navy officers revolted against their superiors, demanding the right to unionize, Goulart supported them.

The night after Goulart proclaimed his support for the naval officers, the military moved to take over the reins of government in a largely bloodless coup it dubbed the "Revolution." The coup clearly was led from the top as a united effort, and with quiet U.S. support, meaning coordination of its efforts was easy. The regime it subsequently created was strongly institutionalized and based heavily on the National Security Doctrine. It attempted to keep a veneer of civilian rule by preserving most of the prior constitution, but it also issued Institutional Acts, which gave the military president the power to overrule the legislature and revoked many basic rights. Eventually, the party system was restricted to two tightly controlled parties, one that supported the regime and one that was allowed to oppose it within strict limits. When popular opposition from students, workers, and the rural poor arose, the military leadership did not hesitate to use force against them. Brazil's military government was far less brutal than many in Latin America at the time, but it nonetheless jailed and killed opponents when necessary.

Several explanations for the 1964 coup have been put forward. The best known is Guillermo O'Donnell's (1979) argument that the coup came about because of economic contradictions that the democratic government could not resolve. While not a modernization

João Goulart, Brazil's civilian president who was overthrown by the country's military in 1964. Goulart's leftist policies and intervention in the military hierarchy helped provoke the U.S.-backed coup that initiated twenty years of military rule.

Dick DeMarsico, Library of Congress

theorist, O'Donnell nonetheless saw the origins of the coup in the society as a whole. If capitalist industrialization was to continue, it required a repressive government to force it on an increasingly restless population. Industrialization and populism, the dominant way of mobilizing support in Brazil's democracy, had produced a growing working class that demanded a greater share of the benefits of economic growth. The elite realized that this would reduce the resources available for further investment. Additional industrialization would require investment in heavier industry, and that in turn would require lower wages. An elected government could not do this politically, so the military stepped in, under the auspices of its National Security Doctrine, to take the necessary steps.

Other analysts, however, have noted that the coup itself was caused just as much by Goulart's direct threat to the military hierarchy. By removing military officers who opposed him, and especially by supporting junior officers who wanted to unionize, Goulart was interfering with the autonomy of the military itself. Riordan Roett (1978)

Military Coups in Latin America by Decade

Brazil's military coups and regimes (1930–1945 and 1964–1985) were part of a broader trend of coups and military rule in the region that has declined over time.

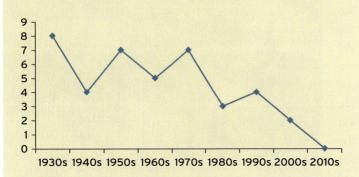

Source: Data are from *Political Handbook of the World 2015* (Washington, DC: CQ Press, 2015).

contended that the military remained divided over Goulart's economic policies but united in opposition to him because it saw him as undermining the autonomy of both the military and Congress. It is entirely possible, of course, that these two sets of factors (economic pressures plus threats to the autonomy of the military) dovetailed, coming together to give the military the incentive and justification to intervene and set Brazilian politics on a fundamentally different course.

Nigeria's military is very different from Brazil's because it is far weaker as an institution. Nevertheless, Nigeria's history of regime changes once again demonstrates the difficulty of understanding the motives for military coups. The country has had six successful coups (see the timeline in chapter 8) and at least two failed coup attempts. Without exception, each of the military leaders came to power promising to serve only in a "corrective" capacity to end corruption, restore order, and revive the economy before handing power back to elected civilians. In reality, the military ruled for two very long periods (1966–1979 and 1983–1999) under multiple leaders and returned the country to democratic rule only after much domestic and international pressure. Analysts have identified both societal and individual motives behind the actions of Nigeria's military. We focus here primarily on two of the six coups: those that overthrew democratic governments.

The first two military interventions happened six months apart in 1966. Nigeria's First Republic, its initial postcolonial democracy, had very weak institutions and grew increasingly chaotic from independence in 1960. The democratic government and subsequent military governments were riven by increasingly intense ethnic rivalries. Numerical advantage gave the northern region control of the government at independence. After the government manipulated two elections, citizens in the western region, who felt the northern-dominated government had stolen control of the country, turned violent. By late 1965, the national government had lost effective control of the western region, and general lawlessness was spreading throughout the country.

In January 1966, five army majors led a rebellion in an attempt to overthrow what they saw as an illegitimate national government. Most of the leaders, including Gen. Johnson T. U. Aguiyi-Ironsi, who ultimately took over as the military ruler, were ethnic

Igbo from the eastern region. This ethnic homogeneity may have made the coordination game of the coup easier because the leaders trusted one another. In carrying out the coup, they killed several important northern and western political and military figures but no eastern ones. Ironsi abolished all parties and ethnic associations, and soon declared the end of Nigeria's fractured federalism, creating a unitary state instead. Many analysts viewed Ironsi as genuinely interested in national well-being, but northerners saw the coup and Ironsi's elimination of federalism as an attempt by the eastern, Igbo military elite to centralize all power for themselves. Six months later, the northerners responded with a countercoup that brought army chief of staff Yakubu Gowon to power. Gowon was backed by northern military leaders and the coup clearly came primarily from the top of the military. They were intent on removing what they saw as an "Igbo" government. Gowon immediately recreated a federal system, with twelve states replacing the former three regions. Eastern military leaders rebelled, proclaiming themselves the leaders of the independent Republic of Biafra. A three-year civil war ensued. Gowon received much credit for winning the war and helping reconcile the nation afterward. As all of Nigeria's military leaders would do, he had from the start promised a return to democracy. By the mid-1970s, however, he and the military governors of the states were seen as increasingly corrupt, stealing from Nigeria's rapidly growing oil revenues and continually delaying the promised return to democracy. Ultimately, other northern military leaders overthrew him and returned the country to democracy in 1979.

That democracy would last until 1983, and in many ways, the events of that year can be seen as a repeat of those of 1965, though without the same ethnic conflict. The Second Republic government that was elected in 1979 and reelected in 1983 was again dominated by the northern region, and by 1983 it was both corrupt and malfeasant. Nigeria's economy was declining as the level of corruption seemed to be skyrocketing and world oil prices were plummeting. Consequently, the 1983 election in which incumbent president Shehu Shagari was reelected was widely seen as fraudulent.

The coup weeks later came with little opposition. At first glance, one could say that the coup leaders were motivated by the weakness and chaos of the civilian regime. William Graf, a leading scholar of the era, argued differently (1988). In contrast to the first coup in 1966, the coup leaders were not junior officers but rather the top military officials in the country, primarily from the north. This means that the coup was not ethnically motivated, in that both the perpetrators and the main victims were northerners. Graf went on to say that, instead, the main motivation for the coup was the desire of top officers to maintain their access to government resources and preserve the social status quo. He suggested that the top military officers took control because they saw the corruption of the civilian elite as excessive. The officers believed that corruption threatened to provoke an uprising within the military and perhaps within the broader society. Indeed, rumors abounded that junior officers, with a more radical interest in fundamentally changing the Nigerian regime, were about to stage a coup. In the subsequent regime (1983–1999), power remained in the hands of northern military leaders, and the regime became increasingly corrupt and brutal as time went on, until the untimely death of the last military dictator led to a return to democracy (see below).

Nigeria's two coups that directly overthrew democratic rule can be explained by societal factors, which include the weakness of prior political institutions and increasing political and economic chaos. In both cases, the argument goes that the military stepped in to restore order in a situation in which stable democracy no longer existed. However, the leaders of the coups may have had other motives, and both faced subsequent countercoups. These brought to power northern military leaders who ruled for extended periods during which corruption grew and institutions weakened. Personal, ethnic, and regional interests in gaining power and resources seem at least as likely an explanation for the coups as the political problems the military allegedly stepped in to resolve.

CASE Questions

1. What does the comparison of military coups in Brazil and Nigeria teach us about the utility of the theories of why coups occur? Is one particular theory more convincing than the others in explaining coups in both countries? If not, why not?
2. What are the connections between why the coups happened in the two countries and the characteristics of the subsequent military regimes? (You might want to look back on the case studies of Nigeria and Brazil in chapter 3 to help you answer this question.)

REVOLUTION

Military coups change governments and regimes, while revolutions can change the entire social order. Revolutions are rare events that mark major turning points not only in the lives of the countries in which they occur but often in world history as well. On the continent of Africa alone there have been more than eighty military coups since 1960, whereas only a small number of revolutions have occurred anywhere in the world. Social revolutions that overturn the entire social order are extremely rare, but even political revolutions, which only change regimes, are infrequent. We examined why revolutions occur in chapter 7, so here we briefly address only the question of regime change: What types of regimes do revolutions produce?

Aside from some of the former Communist countries of eastern Europe, the general outcome of social revolutions has been fairly consistent: authoritarian rule and the creation of stronger states. Political revolutions' outcomes vary a little more; some lead to democracy, though that is by no means certain, even though it is often the stated goal of the key revolutionary groups. Postrevolutionary governments have taken various forms, based in part on the ideological beliefs of their revolutionary leaders, but few have become enduring democracies directly after the revolution. This was true even in countries such as France, where many of the revolution's leaders were liberals.

Theda Skocpol (1979) argued convincingly that all major revolutions, which were caused in part by the weakness of the *ancien régime,* ultimately created stronger states than had previously existed in those countries.

Scholars account for these outcomes by pointing out the extremely difficult political circumstances facing postrevolutionary governments. The entire regime and sometimes the social structure have been overthrown, so new ones must be created. Many revolutions are at least partly violent and the new regime must recreate the state's monopoly on the use of force. Postrevolutionary societies are almost by definition deeply divided along ideological lines; the new leadership is committed to a particular ideological blueprint of what the new regime should look like, while many followers do not fully share this commitment. All of these factors lead postrevolutionary leaders to brook little dissent and to view any opposition as a threat to the revolution. The immediate postrevolutionary situation often includes a diversity of viewpoints, but those who do not share the vision of the key leadership are quickly eliminated, and with them go the prospects for democracy, at least in the short to medium term. As revolutionary leaders consolidate their power and eliminate their enemies, they create stronger states as well, at least in the short to medium term. Eventually, as the case of the Soviet Union attests, those states might weaken, but after the revolution is consolidated, the new state will be stronger than the old one. This process is clear in our case studies of the postrevolutionary governments in China and Iran in chapter 8.

A significant set of exceptions to this rule are some of the postcommunist revolutions, such as in the Czech Republic, Hungary, and Poland. The complete collapse of communism in the early 1990s led to a widespread perception in eastern Europe that communist regimes were illegitimate; thus, postrevolutionary divisions were not nearly as great as in earlier revolutions. The populaces were also not as mobilized, and the revolutions were largely nonviolent. All of these elements made the compromises necessary for democracy more possible, though the failure to establish democracy in some of the postcommunist countries indicates that a democratic outcome was by no means guaranteed (Sanderson 2005).

Political revolutions have more mixed results than do social revolutions. The former do not overthrow the entire social order and are often less violent, so many postrevolutionary divisions are not as difficult to overcome. New political institutions nonetheless often have to be put in place quickly, making regime outcomes uncertain. The "color revolutions" that peacefully replaced several sitting governments between 2000 and 2005, most famously in Ukraine and Georgia, are good examples. In Ukraine, the "Orange Revolution" averted what appeared to be a deterioration of a minimally democratic regime and installed a more popular leader. It also eventually resulted, however, in a Russian annexation of the disputed region of Crimea and "soft invasion" of a larger section of the eastern part of the country, instigating a war of secession that crippled the state in that region. The "Rose Revolution" in Georgia seemed more successful, helping to move Georgia from what had become an electoral authoritarian regime to a flawed but nonetheless democratic one, including making significant constitutional changes. It also, however, lost effective sovereignty in part of its territory to Russian-backed separatists.

DEMOCRATIZATION

In 1972 Freedom House, a nongovernmental organization (NGO) that analyzes the level of political and civil rights in countries around the world, classified forty-four countries as "free," meaning that they were fully functioning liberal democracies. In 1990 the number of "free" countries rose to sixty-one, and in 2016 it had grown to eight-six. The third wave of democratization (the first two waves having followed each of the world wars) was a dramatic process. It included the "People Power" movement that overthrew the corrupt and brutal dictator Ferdinand Marcos in the Philippines, the fall of the Berlin Wall in Germany, and the election of Nelson Mandela in South Africa. It seemed that the world's people were arising en masse to demand democratic rights. In the new millennium, though, progress has slowed or even reversed. Freedom House data indicated that 2016 was the tenth straight year in which the number of countries that became less free was greater than the number that became more free. Figure 9.1 shows the impact of the third wave, as the percentage of fully authoritarian regimes plummeted starting in the late 1980s, while the number of democracies and electoral authoritarian regimes increased markedly.

Without a doubt, democracy has expanded, but reversal is clearly possible, and the image of global mass rebellion overwhelming dictators and establishing lasting democracy was, alas, overly simplistic. As we discussed in chapter 7, political revolutions in which popular uprisings overwhelm a dictator happen but are rare. The fall of Marcos in the Philippines in 1986 and Nicolae Ceaușescu in Romania three years later are classic examples that captured the world's imagination. Much more common, though, are negotiated changes from an authoritarian to a democratic regime, like the four-year process in South Africa from Mandela's release from prison in 1990 to his election as president in 1994. Comparativists have tried to understand the expansion of democracy and its more recent stagnation by asking why countries become democratic, how they become democratic, what obstacles they face, how democratic they are, how likely they are to stay democratic, and how they can become more democratic.

TRANSITIONS TO DEMOCRACY

transition to democracy
A regime change typically involving a negotiated process that removes an authoritarian regime and concludes with a founding election of a new, democratic regime

pact
In a transition to democracy, a conscious agreement among the most important political actors in the authoritarian regime and those in civil society to establish a new form of government

A **transition to democracy** is a regime change typically involving a negotiated process among major political actors in an authoritarian regime and their opponents who demand democracy, resulting in the removal of the old regime and the birth of a new democracy. In what many theorists consider an ideal model, the process of negotiation results in a **pact,** an explicit agreement among the most important political actors in the regime and civil society to establish a new form of government. The pact would ideally

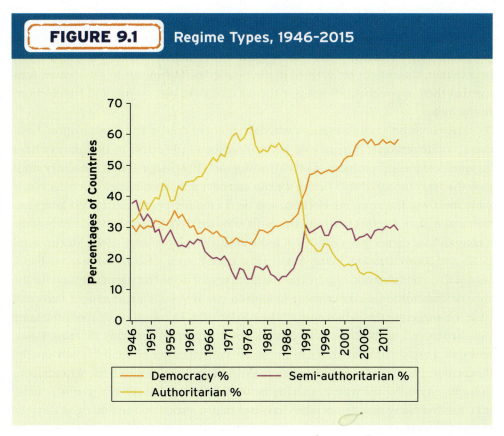

FIGURE 9.1   **Regime Types, 1946–2015**

Source: Data are from the Polity Project's Polity IV dataset, Center for Systemic Peace (http://www.systemicpeace .org/polityproject.html).

Note: Electoral authoritarian regimes are regimes with scores between –5 and 5. Authoritarian regimes score between –10 and –6 and democracies rate between .6 and 10. The labels shown above have been modified from the original by the authors to conform to terminology used in this book. Polity IV's label of "anocracy" we referred to as "electoral authoritarian," and Polity IV's label of "autocracy" is labeled here as "authoritarian."

produce a new democratic constitution and be followed by a **founding election,** the first democratic election in many years (or ever) that marks the completion of the transition process.

 Creating a democracy is one thing; sustaining it over the long term is another. Political history is littered with democracies that reverted to authoritarian rule, from the Nazi takeover of Germany in 1932, to the end of electoral democracy in most of sub-Saharan Africa in the 1960s, to the military coups that overthrew democracy repeatedly in Pakistan and Turkey. Transition theorists developed the concept of **democratic consolidation** to help answer the question of the sustainability of democracy, but much dispute over the definition and utility of the concept has arisen. Intuitively, democratic consolidation is simply the idea that democracy has become widely accepted as the permanent form of political activity in a particular country. It has become "the only game in town," and all significant political elites and their

founding election
The first democratic election in many years (or ever), marking the completion of a transition to democracy

democratic consolidation
The widespread acceptance of democracy as the permanent form of political activity; all significant political elites and their followers accept democratic rules and are confident everyone else does as well

followers accept democratic rules and are confident that everyone else does as well. This is important, because democracy requires faith that in the future, any significant party or group might gain power via an election. If some major political actors do not believe that, they might be tempted to use nondemocratic means to gain power, fearing that their opponents will not give them a chance to win via free and fair elections in the future.

Knowing when a country has reached the point of democratic consolidation, however, is quite difficult: How can we know whether all the actors in the country have accepted democracy unquestionably? Huntington (1991) argued that a country must pass the "two-turnover test" before we can consider it a consolidated democracy: one party must win the founding election, and then a different party must win a later election and replace the first party. By this strict standard, West Germany did not become a consolidated democracy until 1969, India until 1980, Japan until 1993, Mexico until 2012, and South Africa still does not qualify. Luca Tomini (2014), on the other hand, argued that consolidation requires both legitimacy for democracy generally and for the specific constitutional arrangement in a given country. Looking at eastern European cases, he suggested that while most of the countries had a transition at about the same time at the end of the Cold War, consolidation happened at widely differing times, and that a rapid consolidation can mean the consolidation of relatively low-quality democracy. Those that consolidated more slowly sometimes resolved more fundamental problems along the way, producing better democracy. Whatever measure is used, it's clear that many new democracies have not fully consolidated and doing so can take not just years but decades.

Transition theorists look for evidence of democratic consolidation because they fear democratic breakdown—that is, a return to authoritarian rule. During the third wave of democratization and since, few countries that have completed a transition to democracy have reverted to full-scale authoritarian rule. Some hold reasonably free and fair elections but do not abide by the full array of liberal rights and the rule of law, while others become electoral authoritarian regimes in which a ruling party rigs elections as necessary to stay in power. For democracies that avoided a reversion to authoritarian or electoral authoritarian rule and seem to have become more or less consolidated, the next logical consideration is the quality of democracy, including the extent of participation, the rule of law, and vertical and horizontal accountability. These issues, of course, apply to all democracies, even those that are two hundred years old. Attempts to measure the quality of democracy have shown the third wave to produce distinctly mixed results (Levine and Molina 2011; Morlino 2011; Roberts 2010).

EXPLAINING DEMOCRATIZATION, CONSOLIDATION, AND BREAKDOWN

Political scientists have used the full array of theories we outlined in chapter 1 to try to explain why democratization happens and whether new democracies will succeed in the long run. As is so often the case, we can usefully divide the theoretical debate into approaches based on structures, culture and beliefs, and individual action.

Structures Prior to the third wave, all but a handful of democracies were wealthy, Western countries. In the 1950s and 1960s, political scientists understandably followed the ideas of modernization theory in both its economic and cultural senses, arguing that democracy could be sustained only in certain types of societies. Seymour Martin Lipset (1959) saw economic structure as the most important element, arguing that democracies arise only in countries with reasonably wealthy economies and a large middle class that is educated and has its basic needs securely met. In these societies, political competition is not too intense and therefore compromise, an essential component of democracy, is easier. In *The Civic Culture* (1963, 1989), Gabriel Almond and Sidney Verba argued that democracy can thrive only in countries that have democratic political cultures (what they called "civic cultures") in which citizens value participation but are willing to defer to elected leaders enough to let them govern. Other scholars argued that political developments must occur in a particular sequence. For instance, a strong state and sense of national identity must emerge before a democracy can.

The third wave seemed initially to wreak intellectual havoc on modernization theories; democracy began breaking out in all the "wrong" places. First, southern European and then Latin American military dictatorships became democratic. Then the end of the Cold War unleashed a new round of democracy creation, first in the former Communist countries of eastern Europe and then in Africa and parts of Asia. These were countries that were far too poor, that still faced questions about the strength of their state and national identity, and that seemed not to have democratic cultures, yet here they were writing constitutions, holding elections, and establishing democracies. The limited success of many of these new democracies, however, led comparativists in the new millennium to revisit some of the ideas of modernization theory, using new and much more sophisticated research methods. Others looked at additional structural variables, such as a country's position in the international system, level of inequality, or the strength of political institutions.

Adam Przeworski and colleagues (2000) created a data set of 141 countries from 1950 to 1990, revisiting the key structural arguments: Did socioeconomic development predict whether countries have transitions to democracy and how long those new democracies survive? They found a strong statistical relationship between development and the sustainability of democracy, arguing that "democracy is almost certain to survive in countries with per capita incomes above $4,000" (Przeworski et al. 2000, 273), but a very weak relationship between development and the likelihood that a country would have a transition. They concluded that in terms of predicting transitions, "modernization theory appears to have little, if any, explanatory power" (Przeworski et al. 2000, 137). Carles Boix and Susan Stokes (2003) challenged these findings. They used the same data but removed some countries from it: states during the Cold War that were tightly controlled by the Soviet Union and countries heavily dependent on oil wealth. They argued that both of these factors would prevent democracy from occurring and therefore should not be included in a test of modernization theory overall. Removing these countries from the data, they concluded that for the countries on which the theory focuses—poor and middle-income countries—development does indeed make transitions to democracy more likely.

Many postcolonial countries going through transitions to democracy simultaneously went through market-oriented economic reform (see chapter 11), which in the short term often causes economic decline before it brings benefits. So a new question based on economic structure arose: Perhaps, rather than the overall level of economic development, sudden changes in economic well-being influence whether new democracies can survive? Theorists feared that negative economic effects might undermine popular support for democracy after a transition. Nancy Bermeo (2003) examined this hypothesis, looking at the breakdown of democracy in Europe before World War II and in Latin America in the 1960s. She found that the populace as a whole did not reject democracy in times of economic crisis, but instead key elites did. The military in Latin America, for instance, feared economic instability and put an end to democracy without widespread popular support for their action.

Other modernization theorists debated not just the effects of economic growth on democratization but also the effects of inequality. One school of thought argued that relatively unequal societies were unlikely to democratize because elites fear that if the impoverished majority gains the vote, they will use it to redistribute income, so the elites will fight to maintain authoritarian rule. In more equal societies, the elite will fear redistribution less, so they will be more willing to allow democratization (Acemoglu and Robinson 2006; Boix 2003). Ben Ansell and David Samuels (2014), however, pointed out that little evidence supports the thesis that inequality prevents democracy or that democracies redistribute income. Instead, they argued that democratization happens when a newly wealthy but disenfranchised group demands democracy to protect their property from arbitrary rule, following classical liberal thought (see chapter 3). They provided an extensive quantitative analysis covering 1820 to 2004 to support their claims.

The type of prior authoritarian regime and strength of political institutions are additional possible structural sources of democratic transition or breakdown. Since World War II, military regimes are twice as likely to collapse as personalist regimes, and three times as likely to collapse as one-party regimes. About two-thirds of transitions from military regimes have produced democracies (rather than new authoritarian regimes), as opposed to just over half of transitions from one-party regimes and only a third of transitions from personalist regimes. Part of the explanation for these patterns is the domestic support the differing regimes typically have, their coercive ability, and the likely result they face if they leave office; personalist leaders, for instance, are far more likely to face death, jail, or exile after a transition and therefore cling to power as long as possible (Escriba-Folch and Wright 2015, 42–64).

Lucan Way (2015) used a comparative case study in eastern Europe to argue that weak authoritarian state institutions, a weak ruling party, and the presence of two relatively equal identity groups facilitated transitions to weak democracies or electoral authoritarian regimes in which minimal competition occurs but democracy is not fully consolidated. Political competition in these states emerged "by default" because the authoritarian regime wasn't strong enough to hold onto power exclusively. Similarly, Michael Bratton and Nicholas van del Walle (1997) argued that Africa's neopatrimonial regimes result in transitions that typically do not lead to democracies. In neopatrimonial regimes with exceptionally weak institutions, political competition remains primarily about securing access to government resources for patronage. Pacts almost never happen because parties are little more than temporary vehicles for shifting coalitions of patrons trying to gain power, so parties neither have sufficient ideological disagreements nor enough stability to provide the credible commitments that pacts require. In the absence of pacts, incumbents typically do not liberalize their regimes completely, instead holding elections that are only partially free and fair. More often than not, they win those elections, and even when the opposition wins, it is likely to create an electoral authoritarian regime in order to maintain its access to key resources. Freedom House ratings reflect this outcome: while almost all African countries have experienced at least an attempted transition, only seven were rated as "free" in 2016, while nineteen were "partly free" and eighteen were "not free."

The growing number of electoral authoritarian regimes has led scholars to ask whether and when these regimes might give way to greater democracy. Levitsky and Way (2010) argued that whether these regimes move toward democracy, move away from it, or remain stable electoral authoritarian regimes depends on Western linkage (economic, political, and social ties and cross-border flows with the West) and leverage (vulnerability to Western pressure), as well as the strength of the state and ruling party vis-à-vis the opposition. Strong Western influence raises the costs of authoritarian crackdown, since those regimes face greater external pressure to move toward democracy. Strong states and ruling parties in the absence of Western influence, though, tend to produce more fully authoritarian regimes, as the opposition cannot counter the regime's power and external pressure is weak. Grigore Pop-Eleches and Graeme Robertson (2015) looked only at domestic structural factors in electoral authoritarian regimes—income level, ethnic and religious cleavages, and state capacity—and found that those with structural advantages on these key dimensions (more wealth, ethnic and religious homogeneity, and state capacity) are more likely to transition to democracy while those with structural disadvantages will more typically oscillate between democracy and some type of authoritarian rule over time.

Barbara Wejnert (2014) also argued that the international context and linkages were crucial to understanding democratization. Using a large statistical modeling approach, she examined democratization around the world since 1800, arguing that diffusion from one country to another was more important than any characteristics of individual countries. Particularly in poorer countries, proximity to other democracies and interactions with neighboring countries significantly increased the likelihood of countries becoming democratic. International structure matters more, she argued, than domestic structures or culture.

Culture and Beliefs A similar debate arose among those examining the effects of culture. Many scholars assumed that ethnic fragmentation in particular is likely to harm the chances of democracy; they argued that ethnically divided societies have a weaker sense of national unity that often results in bitter political competition for control of the state and therefore threatens to undermine democratic norms and institutions. Given the ethnic diversity of many of the countries in the third wave of democratization, these theorists predicted the new democracies were unlikely to last. A study by Steven Fish and Robin Brooks (2004) across approximately 160 countries, though, found no correlation between ethnic diversity and the strength of democracy. Christian Houle (2015), however, found that economic inequality between ethnic groups, especially when each is relatively equal internally, harms democratic consolidation.

Ronald Inglehart and Christian Welzel (2005) used data from a global survey of citizen beliefs to examine the effect of culture on democracy. They found that what they call "emancipative values"—values that emphasize freedom of expression and equality of opportunities—helped sustain democracy. Even controlling for earlier experience with democracy and prior economic development, countries with higher emancipative values in the early 1990s were much more likely to have stronger democracies after 2002. Hadenius and Teorell (2005), however, criticized Inglehart and Welzel's measure of democracy, arguing it combined a real measure of democracy (Freedom House scores) with an unrelated measure of corruption. Using only the Freedom House measures, Hadenius and Teorell found no relationship between emancipative values and levels of democracy. More recently, based on new survey data, Welzel (2013) argued that emancipative values matter to democracy via their effect on people's understanding of democracy. Higher emancipative values are associated with a more fully liberal understanding of democracy, which leads people to be critical of governments that don't fully respect liberal rights; where people have these values, governments face more pressure to provide full democracy and are more likely to do so. Clearly, the debate over modernization theory in both its structural and cultural forms remains unresolved.

Individual Action As the third wave of democratization took place from the 1970s to the 1990s and made modernization theory seem less relevant, a new generation of democratization theorists influenced by rational choice theory argued that democracy could emerge in any country if the major political elites came to see it as a set of institutions that could serve their interests, whether they or the citizenry actually believed in democratic principles or not. Well-institutionalized democracy provides all major political actors with a degree of participation, protection from the worst forms of repression, and the possibility that they can gain power at some point. These features led self-interested political leaders to create democracies in countries that comparativists previously had seen as bound to be autocratic for years to come. While theorists did not dispute the idea that democracy would be easier to sustain in countries that were wealthier and had prior democratic experience, the new "transition paradigm" provided a model for how democracy was possible anywhere.

They argued that the typical transition begins when an authoritarian regime faces a severe crisis of some sort—economic downturn or succession were common crises out of which democracy could emerge—and its leadership then splits internally into hardliners and softliners. The former believe in repressing any opposition and preserving the status quo, while the latter are willing to consider compromising with opponents as a means to survive the crisis. Simultaneously, the crisis would produce a surge in the activity of civil society, typically led by unions, religious authorities, or middle-class professionals who demanded fundamental political reforms. Civil society subsequently would often divide between radicals, who wanted immediate and complete democratization, and moderates, who were willing to compromise with the authoritarian government to make some gains. A successful transition to democracy would be most likely if the softliners in the regime and the moderates in civil society could each gain the upper hand over their internal opponents and then negotiate with one another to establish new rules of the game. Some form of democracy, though often with limits, would become a compromise on which both sides could agree (Huntington 1991).

How this process unfolded in individual countries depended a great deal on the relative power of the major political actors involved. Most theorists argued that the regime and civil society have to be of roughly equal strength for the transition process to produce a full democracy. If the regime, and especially the hardliners within it, were very strong, it would control the process, and any democracy that resulted from the transition would have significant limitations. In Chile, for instance, the military under dictator Augusto Pinochet wrote a democratic constitution that reserved seats in the Senate and control of the central bank for the army. On the other hand, if civil society, especially its more radical elements, were too strong, it would demand full democratization with no protection for members of the old regime, and the resulting hardliner backlash would crush the nascent democratization. In the case of political revolutions, when the revolution actually succeeds—radicals in the popular uprising overwhelm the hardliners and the old regime falls suddenly—no new institutions have been put in place, and major actors who shared their opposition to authoritarian rule but agree on little else have to find a way to create a new regime. The result is often a great deal of political instability and the possibility of a very weak or flawed democracy emerging. For instance, in 2016

Freedom House rated two countries that had well-known political revolutions, the Philippines and Romania, as "partly free" (the Philippines) and "free" (Romania), but with one of the weaker democracies in Europe.

Sujian Guo and Gary Stradiotto (2014) recently examined the effects of the type of transition the country went through on the quality and durability of the subsequent democracy over its first ten years. Undertaking a quantitative analysis of all transitions since 1900, they found that those that they term "cooperative"—those that involved pacts and in which the opposition had enough power to influence the outcome of the pact—were of significantly higher quality and more likely to survive. This was due, they argued, to these transitions being more inclusive of all significant political actors, leading more of them to support the subsequent democratic system. They found that neither the type of prior authoritarian regime nor the region of the world (and therefore culture) in which the country was located had any influence on democracy in the long term. The only other factor that did improve the quality and endurance of democracy was level of wealth, as modernization theorists would assert.

South Africa's transition to democratic rule in 1994 is a classic case of the transition process unfolding in a way the transition paradigm saw as ideal (our case study of Brazil is a similar example). The apartheid regime was besieged internally and externally in the 1980s. It faced widespread international sanctions and an increasingly violent and radical uprising on the streets of the black townships. It had tried modest liberalizations such as allowing mixed-race people some minimal political participation, but this was met with simply more resistance. Upon coming to power in 1990, President F. W. de Klerk shocked the nation and the world by quickly announcing that he was freeing Nelson Mandela from prison and lifting the ban on Mandela's party, the African National Congress (ANC). Faced with a crisis he did not believe his government could contain, de Klerk became a softliner who, after secret negotiations before the public announcement, came to see Mandela as a moderate with whom he could negotiate. Three years of negotiations for a new constitution ensued, with white hardliners and black radicals frequently and sometimes violently attacking the process and both parties involved. Ultimately, though, Mandela and de Klerk held majority support of their respective communities and agreed on a pact, a new constitution that was then ratified by the population. On April 27, 1994, Nelson Mandela was elected president, ending the world's last bastion of legal racial segregation. The ANC has ruled ever since, though, which has raised questions about how fully democratic the society has really become. Nonetheless, Freedom House has continuously rated it as "free."

South Africa's successful transition was not completely surprising, in that it was a middle-income country; its level of socioeconomic development seemed to make democracy plausible. A much more surprising African success story was Ghana, a country with a history of military coups and a Gross National Income per capita of only

$1,590 in 2016. As the third wave of democratization washed over Africa, Ghanaian military ruler Jerry Rawlings agreed to allow multiparty competition based on a new constitution that he and his aides wrote. It created a presidential system that gave the president great powers, and Rawlings won the subsequent election. Domestic and international electoral observers saw significant electoral fraud, and many feared Ghana's democracy might be stillborn. After that founding election, however, the electoral commission brought the major political leaders together to discuss what electoral rules they would use in the future. With the support of external aid, the leaders helped strengthen the national election commission itself, which helped the opposing leaders gain some trust in one another and in the political process in general. The greater fairness of the next election in 1996 reinforced this trust. While Ghana did not have a full pact, the major leaders did agree on a set of electoral rules that they came to accept and believed would work. In 2000 Rawlings was constitutionally barred from running for a third term. He did not resist leaving office, and without Rawlings leading the ticket his party lost the election; power changed hands from one elected leader to the next for the first time in Ghana's history. In 2008 Rawlings's party won the presidency again, by less than one-half of 1 percent of the vote. The losing party ultimately accepted the outcome of what was called Africa's closest election ever, and for the second time, power was peacefully transferred from one party to another. Ghana's democracy is certainly not perfect, but in contrast to our case study of Nigeria and many other African countries, democracy is functioning well; Freedom House has long rated it as fully "free."

The type of political institutions that are adopted during the transition can also affect success. Juan Linz (1990) argued that the "perils of presidentialism" (see chapter 5) are particularly important in new democracies. Because new democracies are often deeply divided and competing elites do not fully trust one another or the new democratic institutions, consensus democracies with power-sharing mechanisms such

African National Congress (ANC) supporters await the start of a campaign rally in 2016. South Africa's transition to democracy from 1990 to 1994 is seen as a model of the transition paradigm. Nelson Mandela's party, the ANC, has remained in power ever since, though, raising concerns about limited democracy in a dominant-party system. Opponents criticize the ANC for placing limits on political competition and for allowing corruption, but Freedom House still rates the country as "free," and so far South African voters have been unwilling to give up their allegiance to the party that they credit with ending apartheid.

JOHN WESSELS/AFP/Getty Images

The Arab Spring: Revolution, Democratization, or None of the Above?

In chapter 7, we briefly discussed the Arab Spring as a case of contentious politics, trying to explain why and how protests suddenly exploded across the region. Here we look at the outcomes of those protests: What regime changes did they produce, and why? As of 2016, Tunisia was seen as the "success story" in that it had an elected government; Freedom House rated it as "partially free" and Polity IV scored it as a democracy, though barely. Egypt initially appeared to be following a similar, though less certain, path until the military coup of 2013 created a new authoritarian regime that Freedom House rated as "unfree" and Policy IV as an electoral authoritarian regime (though just one point from fully authoritarian). Syria, Libya, and Yemen descended into civil wars. Protests broke out in other Arab countries as well, but as the table shows, none saw a regime change or war; instead, the old regime successfully repressed the protests. How can we explain the different trajectories regime change took in these countries?

Outcomes Since 2011

	Freedom House score, 2016	Polity IV democracy score, 2016*	Regime transition since 2011
Algeria	Not free	3	None
Bahrain	Not free	0	None
Egypt	Not free	0	Electoral democracy (2011–2013)
			Electoral authoritarian (2013–)
Iran	Not free	0	None
Iraq	Not free	6	None
			None
Jordan	Not free	2	None
Kuwait	Partly free	0	None

	Freedom House score, 2016	Polity IV democracy score, 2016*	Regime transition since 2011
Lebanon	Partly free	6	None
Libya	Not free	Interregnum	Civil war
Morocco	Partly free	1	None
Oman	Not free	0	None
Qatar	Not free	0	None
Saudi Arabia	Not free	0	None
Sudan	Not free	0	None
Syria	Not free	0	Civil war
Tunisia	Free	7	Electoral democracy (2013)
Turkey	Partly free	4	None
United Arab Emirates	Not free	0	None
Yemen	Not free	Interregnum	Civil war

*Higher number means more democratic.

A key element was the role of negotiations and the ability of opposing political forces to create a pact. Key actors in most of the countries of the Arab Spring included the military, secular opposition forces, and Islamist groups who, to varying degrees, seemed willing to participate in a democratic process. The transition in Tunisia came to be known as the Jasmine revolution, and could certainly be considered a political revolution, in that a movement from within society forced fundamental regime change. But, in fact, negotiations were crucial to establishing a democracy. While the dictator did flee in the face of a massive uprising, democracy emerged from a subsequent pact creating a new constitution. Stepan (2012) noted that exiled secular and Islamist opposition leaders had been meeting secretly in Europe for several years and therefore knew and trusted one another. This allowed them to negotiate a pact with the military that created the new regime relatively seamlessly, creating a PR electoral system that ensured all significant parties would be well represented in parliament. While the process had tense moments, it ultimately produced a new constitution and democracy in which elections have been free and fair, though not all individual rights are fully respected and the rule of law remains weak.

In Egypt, military leaders initially took full control after the dictator was forced out. The military pushed through enough constitutional changes to hold elections but preserved significant control for themselves. The secular and Islamist forces (the Muslim Brotherhood) had not worked together at all and did not trust one another or the military. The single-member district (SMD) elections gave the Muslim Brotherhood dominant power in the elected bodies, but the military still retained great autonomy, and the judiciary—still full of the appointees from the old regime—ruled important elements of the new constitution illegal. Crucially, the Supreme Constitutional Court annulled the initial parliamentary election and forced the parliament to disband. In response, President Mohamed Morsi, a member of the Muslim Brotherhood, declared in November 2012 that he would rule by decree until the new constitution was fully implemented and new elections held. The Brotherhood's opponents ultimately walked out of the negotiations for a permanent constitution, which the Morsi government nonetheless completed and the citizenry ratified via a referendum.

At this point, the legitimacy of all political institutions was seriously questioned by at least some major political actor, and a deep chasm had clearly developed between the Muslim Brotherhood and more secular political forces. In response to Morsi's pushing through a new constitution, the military intervened in July 2013, ousting Morsi from power and severely constricting civil and political rights, including banning the Muslim Brotherhood and arresting most of its leaders. The secular forces that initiated the original uprising in 2011 at least initially supported the coup, fearing the Muslim Brotherhood more than they did the military.

Clearly, the military was a crucial player in both countries. Both Egypt's and Tunisia's authoritarian regimes were relatively institutionalized, with coherent militaries that had major stakes in the stability of the society and economy. In both cases, the old rulers gave up power not when the protesters went into the streets, but when the military decided to support the protesters to protect its own interests vis-à-vis the regimes' top leaders. A united military forced the old dictators out of office and took an active part in the transition to a new regime. The willingness or ability of the military to negotiate a pact with opposition forces ultimately determined the different outcomes in the two cases.

The regimes in Libya and Syria were both much more personalist and divided. When protests broke out in Libya the regime responded with repression, but in the eastern region, which had never supported the dictator Muammar el-Qaddafi, protesters took over the major city and essentially declared themselves free of the regime. The military, like society at large, was divided by regional and kinship loyalties. Qaddafi responded with military force, knowing he had the personal support of at least some of the military, but other elements of the military broke off and formed independent militia, igniting the civil war. With Western support, the militia eventually gained control of the entire country. A new government was put in place and elections held, but it remained extremely weak, ultimately descending into renewed civil war, in large part because many of the militia remained independent; the state had not fully restored its monopoly on the legitimate use of force.

The Syrian regime responded forcefully to protesters as well, which led to the creation of independent militia and the start of the civil war. Syrian society was divided along sectarian lines and some military personnel broke with the regime but most did not, enabling the regime to hold out much longer than in Libya (and the West, for strategic reasons, chose not to intervene). In still other countries, such as Bahrain, the military held firm with the regime and was united, so protests were crushed.

The Arab Spring produced different outcomes in different places in part because of the nature of the authoritarian regimes and particularly the militaries at the heart of them. The rather modest differences in the socioeconomic and cultural characteristics of the countries in the region lend little support to modernization theory as an explanation of the different types of regime change. The distinct paths taken by the transitions to new regimes in Tunisia and Egypt, though, demonstrate key elements of the transition paradigm, particularly the importance of a pact to establish a new order to which all major political forces could agree.

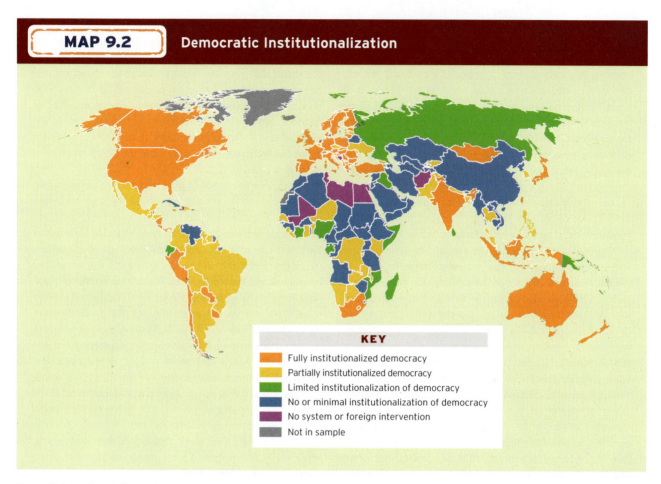

MAP 9.2   **Democratic Institutionalization**

KEY

- Fully institutionalized democracy
- Partially institutionalized democracy
- Limited institutionalization of democracy
- No or minimal institutionalization of democracy
- No system or foreign intervention
- Not in sample

Source: Data are from Polity IV, The Polity Project, Center for Systemic Peace (http://www.systemicpeace.org/polityproject.html).

as coalition governments in parliamentary systems are likely to help preserve democracy. Others disagree, suggesting instead that presidential systems can provide both democratic legitimacy and stability by having a single head of state directly elected by a majority of the nation. Kapstein and Converse (2008) argued that the issue of whether a new democracy is presidential or parliamentary is less important than how effective the limits on the executive are. Steven Fish (2006) supported this argument, using a new data set that measured the strength of the legislative branch to show that a strong legislature is the most important institutional ingredient in maintaining democracy, regardless of the kind of political system in place.

More than just the executive and legislature, though, are important in democracies. Chapter 6 demonstrated the importance of political parties to any democracy. In new democracies, strong parties can form the basis of coherent and powerful opposition to the ruling party, before and after an initial transition. In Africa (Lebas 2011) and eastern Europe (Gherghina 2015; Tavits 2013), historical legacies and conscious choices party leaders make to build their organizations made a difference to how strong parties were during and after a transition. Ironically, in Africa, stronger authoritarian leaders who were able to control the democratization process more fully provided incentives for opponents to form more institutionalized parties to compete against the incumbent, resulting in greater accountability and stability (Reidl 2014). Legal scholar Samuel Issacharoff (2015), on the other hand, argued that the creation of separate constitutional courts, common in code law countries, has been crucial in preserving young and fragile democracies. Finally, Edward Gibson (2012) warned that even when national politics are democratized, "subnational authoritarianism" can survive as local leaders in federal systems are able to monopolize power, a problem we examine in our case study of Mexico below.

After the initial attempted transition, whether successful or not, political institutions, especially elections, may have an impact of further democratization. Staffan Lindberg (2009) showed how in Africa, elections can shift the balance of power between the ruling party and opposition. Even quite limited elections allow the opposition to win some share of power and give dissidents within the ruling party a viable alternative and thus an incentive to defect to the opposition. When political leaders think an opposition coalition has a real chance to win, they become even more likely to join it, further strengthening its chances until a "tipping point" is reached at which a large opposition coalition emerges to win an election in spite of the incumbent's manipulation of the system (van de Walle 2006). Pippa Norris (2014) showed that poor-quality elections can undermine regime legitimacy, especially in a new democracy, though opposition protests of electoral manipulation can sometimes result in real reforms and greater democratization when they are supported by important international actors (Beaulieu 2014). On the other hand, successful electoral manipulation by incumbents can convince opponents that it would be foolish to continue to oppose those in power, and show rulers' allies that none of them is indispensable, strengthening the rulers' bargaining power vis-à-vis both supporters and opponents (Simpser 2013).

The 1990s were the halcyon days of democratization, when it seemed that democracy was spreading to nearly every corner of the globe. It has certainly spread significantly, with most Latin American countries making apparently long-term transformations toward consolidated democracy. Some Asian and African countries, as Ghana demonstrates, have also made successful transitions. In many other cases, though, initial transitions have produced electoral authoritarian regimes. These mixed outcomes have meant the debates about democratic transitions, consolidation, and breakdown are far from settled. Our case studies of Mexico, Russia, and Nigeria demonstrate the diverging processes and outcomes of the "transition era."

CASE Study

MEXICO: TRANSITION FROM AN ELECTORAL AUTHORITARIAN REGIME

CASE SYNOPSIS

Mexico completed a transition to democracy in 2000. Consolidation, in the sense of all major political actors (save the drug cartels) accepting the electoral process as "the only game in town," seems well established, at least at the national level; the country passed the "two-turnover test" in 2012. Modernization certainly may have provided the backdrop that helped this democracy come into being, but economic crisis, loss of the ruling party's legitimacy, and elite divisions were necessary to make it happen when it did. This young democracy, though, is plagued by the problems of a still-weak state, the most important of which are endemic corruption, continued clientelism, and drug-related violence that seem beyond the state's ability (or desire) to stop. The return of the long-ruling PRI to power in 2012 and its subsequent actions have raised questions about its commitment to abide by the rule of law and ensure political rights for all.

- **TRANSITION** Modernization lays backdrop; split within ruling party and reforms of electoral system

- **CONSOLIDATION** Exists at national electoral level; not certain at local level

- **QUALITY** Weak institutions, weak rule of law, corruption, drug-cartel violence, continuing clientelism

- **FREEDOM HOUSE RATING IN 2016: 3.0 = "partly free"**

On July 30, 2006, Andrés Manuel López Obrador, the center-left candidate of the Party of the Democratic Revolution (PRD), spoke before hundreds of thousands of supporters in Mexico City's main square, the Zócalo. Less than one month prior, Felipe Calderón of the center-right National Action Party (PAN) had been declared president by a margin of one-half of 1 percent. In his speech, López Obrador called on his partisans to stage a sit-in at the Zócalo as they awaited a ruling by the Federal Election Tribunal over the veracity of the vote. He dramatically told the crowd that without the proper channels of democracy, only "submission or violence" remained as viable alternatives for his movement.

Ultimately, the tribunal held Calderón to be the legitimate victor, but the summer of 2006 was a difficult test for Mexico's young democracy. The PRI's electoral authoritarian regime (see chapter 3) ruled from 1929 to 2000, when for the first time in seventy years another party was allowed to win a national election and take over the reins of government. The contention surrounding Calderón's victory now threatened to plunge the country into disarray. But this never materialized, as the majority of the public soon turned its back on López Obrador, preferring to accept the official results as declared by Mexico's democratic institutions. In response to the crisis, Congress passed electoral reforms that further leveled the playing field between the incumbent party and challengers, and in 2012 the PRI itself regained the presidency in an election that was not nearly as controversial. In terms of credible national elections and the two-turnover test, Mexico is a consolidated democracy; in other ways, though, serious challenges remain.

Modernization theorists might have expected Mexico to democratize as early as the 1950s, but Sebastián Garrido de Sierra (2011) argued that three factors combined to delay democratization until the 1990s. First, prior to electoral reforms in the 1990s, Mexican elites did not have viable avenues to defect and form an opposition. Second, urbanization by the 1990s finally moved enough Mexicans away from the reach of the PRI's rural clientelistic networks and into areas where other forms of political mobilization were more easily achieved. Last but not least, a historic split in the leadership of the PRI created the necessary impetus for opposition.

The seeds of change, though, were sown much earlier. The PRI had maintained its authoritarian rule via large-scale clientelism, using state resources as patronage; repression when needed; and some legitimacy, mostly based on the relative success of the economy and the party's efforts to distribute wealth more widely than many governments do. A series of economic crises in the 1970s and 1980s undermined the PRI's main claims to legitimacy. The crises forced the PRI to shift toward more market-oriented economic policies (see chapter 11) that undermined their sources of patronage and hurt the incomes of poor and rural people, two of their key constituencies. The spark that led to visible political change was a split in the ruling party. The shift in economic policies created divisions between PRI leaders loyal to the party's traditional

Enrique Peña Nieto, left, stands with outgoing president Felipe Calderón at Peña Nieto's inauguration in December 2012. Peña Nieto's victory returned the PRI, Mexico's ruling party during the electoral authoritarian regime, back to power, but this time via a fully democratic election. The transfer of power from the PRI to Calderón's PAN in 2000 and then back to the PRI in 2012 meant Mexico passed the "two-turnover test," a sign of democratic consolidation.

LatinContent/Getty Images

claims to egalitarianism and newer leaders who favored the reforms. When one of the latter was chosen as the presidential candidate in 1988, Cuauhtémoc Cárdenas, a PRI insider, revolted and ran as an opposition candidate. Son of the legendary president Lázaro Cárdenas (1934–1940), Cuauhtémoc was heir to his father's political reputation and thus was able to galvanize leftist segments in the PRI to join his cause.

The 1988 election was hotly contested, with PRI candidate Carlos Salinas de Gortari officially garnering just over 50 percent of the vote, Cárdenas 31 percent, and conservative PAN candidate Manuel Clouthier 17 percent. Cárdenas denounced the election as a fraud and claimed to be the legitimate victor, a claim many analysts and Mexican citizens believed. Whether true or not, the PRI's legitimacy suffered a significant blow. Following the election, the PRI tried to reform the system to restore some legitimacy, and opposition forces took advantage of the ruling party's weakness. First, constitutional changes created newly independent agencies to administer future elections and adjudicate electoral disputes. Second, the media shed many of their self-imposed limits on expression. Newspapers and television stations began taking an increasingly fair approach to political coverage, exposing the country's leaders to criticism and even ridicule. Third, Cárdenas formed the PRD in 1989 as a permanent home for disaffected PRI activists who sought both further democracy and a greater commitment to the radical heritage the PRI had once claimed. The PRD helped turn Mexico into a three-party system. Finally, the long-established but previously weak opposition party, the PAN, also became an increasingly powerful force. The PAN began to attract a larger following, and for the first time since its founding in 1939, it won a governorship in 1989. The PRI allowed the PAN victories as part of an implicit pact between the two parties. The pro-business PAN agreed with the PRI's economic policies and both wanted to limit the success of the more anti-market PRD (Hamilton 2011, 146–149). The ruling party (softliners within the regime) compromised with the moderate PAN in an effort to keep the more radical PRD out of power, following the logic of the transition paradigm.

By the time of the 1994 election, political contestation was open enough that the winner, the PRI's Ernesto Zedillo, is generally considered to be the first democratically elected president of Mexico. But Zedillo's government still faced serious questions of legitimacy. The government had reacted harshly to the Zapatista uprising that began in January 1994 in the southern state of Chiapas (see chapter 7) and never overcame the economic crisis it inherited. Even though it pursued further electoral reforms to try to rebuild its legitimacy, in 1997 the PRI lost control of the National Congress for the first time in its history.

The final act of the long transition came with the election of conservative Vicente Fox Quesada, a member of the PAN, as president in 2000. His victory brought wild, unrealistic hopes about what democracy would mean for Mexico, and Fox himself did little to tamp down expectations. Many of his election promises fell short, as Mexico experienced increasing inequality, greater criminal violence, and general political gridlock, making the Fox presidency among the least popular in recent history. Ironically, one of Fox's biggest difficulties was negotiating with members of Congress to pass legislation, a necessity now that Congress was no longer subservient to the president but instead represented a wider array of Mexican political forces. Indeed, since 1997, no party has had a majority of seats in Congress, requiring coalitions of parties to pass legislation. The ability of Congress to limit the president's power and the strength of three, ideologically distinct parties became one of the strongest elements of Mexico's young democracy. Members of Congress successfully initiate legislation, regularly amend the president's legislative initiatives, and are able to form coalitions of at least two parties to pass legislation (Casar 2016). By 2016, though, the leftist PRD had split into two parties, while independent candidates and several smaller parties significantly increased their share of congressional seats; the stability of Mexico's three-party system became less certain.

Other aspects of Mexico's democracy remain fragile. Claudio Holzner (2011) pointed to weak institutions as the core problem that in turn produces weak rule of law, continuing clientelism, continuing corruption, local-level authoritarianism, and near loss of sovereignty to drug lords in some states. Clientelism and corruption allow the wealthy to continue to enjoy disproportionate political power. Drug gangs became so powerful in some states that the police were entirely corrupted and drug lords financed their own candidates for governor, mayor, and other offices. The PAN government after 2006 tried to battle the drug lords with increased military action, which produced tens of thousands of deaths and six thousand detentions but actually increased drug-related violence. Institutional weakness was infamously demonstrated by the 2014 disappearance of forty-three students from a teachers' college who were on their way to a political protest. The government investigation claimed that the local mayor had handed them over to a criminal gang, believing they were members of a drug gang. A subsequent report by an international body concluded that this scenario could not have happened and the case remained unresolved in 2016, though it's clear all the students were killed. Insecurity became so great that in one state, residents formed illegal "self-defense" groups to try to protect themselves (Magaloni and Razu 2016). Julio Rios-Figueroa (2013) argued that the judiciary at the top had become effective at resolving high-level political disputes but was still ineffective at upholding individual rights, at least until recent reforms, the effects of which are not yet fully known.

Even in states without significant drug gangs, some local leaders were able to use control of state resources as patronage to preserve "subnational authoritarian" rule, and Mexican presidents supported those efforts when it provided them political advantages (Giraudy 2015). Since 2011, however, a series of public scandals and judicial charges have come forward against former governors, usually after they lose an election to an opposing party, which is happening more frequently as opposition parties are able to use the electoral system to overcome entrenched rulers. Thus, while national politics increasingly appear to represent a consolidated democracy, the quality of that democracy, especially at the local level, is far from ideal.

By the 2012 campaign, Mexico had not fully recovered from the effects of the global recession: economic growth was slow, unemployment high, and poverty

Freedom House Scores: Mexico and Latin America

Mexico's transition to democracy was a belated part of a broader move toward democracy across Latin America. In 1990 Mexico lagged behind its regional neighbors in terms of democracy, but the transition in 2000 meant it had caught up. Growing problems with the quality of its democracy by 2016, though, once again meant it lagged behind other democracies in the region.

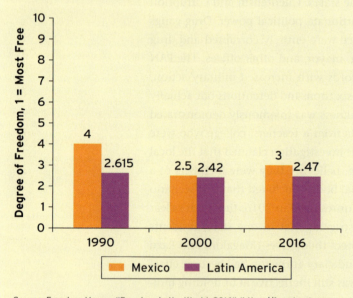

Source: Freedom House, "Freedom in the World, 2016" (https://freedomhouse .org/report/freedom-world/freedom-world-2016).

increasing. President Calderón's use of the military to battle drug gangs increased the death rate dramatically but was seen as achieving little. In this context, Mexicans voted the PRI candidate, Enrique Peña Nieto, into office as president. While the election was deemed "free and fair" and less controversial than the 2006 vote, surveys estimated that anywhere from 5 to 20 percent of voters (higher in some states) received direct gifts from political parties to try to buy their vote, and a large majority of these came from the PRI. Clientelism, while not determining the outcome of the election, continued to play an important role (Nichter and Palmer-Rubin 2014). The return of the PRI to power raised other questions about Mexican democracy. The PRI continued to enjoy authoritarian control of a number of state governments via entrenched and corrupt governors, and it had disproportionate support from the country's two major television networks. It proclaimed itself committed to democracy, though, and did not have majority control of Congress, so it required support from one other party to pass legislation.

Halfway through Peña Nieto's term, however, signs of further restrictions on democracy were apparent. Corruption continued to be a major problem, though slightly improved in recent years: the country fell from 57th place (out of 180 countries and territories) in the Corruption Perceptions Index in 2008 to 105th place (out of 176) in 2012, but rose slightly to 95th place (out of 168) in 2015. Peña Nieto's wife was caught in a corruption scandal, illegally buying a house from a government-affiliated contractor, for which the president ultimately apologized. A law to try to rein in corruption came to Congress via a citizen petition. Although no member of Congress wanted to sponsor it, if enough citizens sign a petition Congress must consider a proposal; it got five times the signatures required. In mid-2016 Congress, facing massive public pressure, passed the law, but President Peña Nieto vetoed key elements of it that would have required people or firms who receive government funding to disclose their assets and taxes.

The PRI government also reacted increasingly harshly to it critics. Numerous teachers who protested against the government's controversial educational reform plans were beaten and/or arrested, and the country became notorious as one of the most dangerous places in the world for journalists. One particularly fierce but highly regarded and popular journalistic critic of the government was summarily fired, allegedly to improve his company's relationship with the Peña Nieto government. Another was killed by drug gangs. It was not clear how much the Mexican populace would demand further reforms, either: in 2015 only 48 percent believed democracy to be the best form of government, and less than 20 percent thought Mexican democracy was working well, one of the lowest figures in Latin America (Latinobarometro 2015).

CASE Questions

1. Given the discrepancy between national electoral politics and local politics, can we say that Mexico has truly become a consolidated democracy? What evidence is most important in answering this question?
2. Does Mexico suggest that modernization theory or the "transition paradigm" is correct in terms of where and when democratization is likely to occur?

RUSSIA: TRANSITION TO AN ELECTORAL AUTHORITARIAN REGIME

CASE SYNOPSIS

Initially, newly independent Russia seemed to be on a path to democracy, though a chaotic one. President Boris Yeltsin and his supporters chose to establish a weak legislature to enable a strong presidency; the result was extremely weak parties. Limited economic reform and massive oil production led to large-scale corruption and gave the executive the ability to co-opt much opposition via distributing patronage. When Vladimir Putin succeeded Yeltsin in 2000, he was able to use these powers to transform Russia from a weak democracy to an electoral authoritarian regime in a few short years. Democratic breakdown occurred in one of the world's most important countries. Putin justified his actions in terms of building a strong state, improving the economy, and achieving national glory. His economic and nationalist successes made him popular in spite of his undermining democracy, but when economic growth dropped, so did his support. Protests against electoral fraud in 2012 showed that many Russians still desired at least a freer and fairer electoral system, but Putin and his United Russia Party seemed firmly in control in 2016.

- **TRANSITION** Initially to democracy with weak institutions, then to electoral authoritarian regime
- **CONSOLIDATION** None
- **QUALITY OF DEMOCRACY** Weak legislature and parties in 1990s; not a democracy since 2000
- **FREEDOM HOUSE RATING IN 2016:** 6.0 = "not free"

As Russian president Boris Yeltsin climbed atop a tank in Moscow to stop a coup attempt in August 1991, it seemed that freedom was on the rise in Russia. The coup was the last-gasp effort of hardliners in the old Communist regime of the Soviet Union. The reforms of softliner Soviet president Mikhail Gorbachev in the late 1980s had significantly opened the Soviet political system and economy, but demands for far greater reforms were in the air. With Gorbachev on vacation, elements in the military tried to roll the tanks into Moscow to restore the old system and prevent the reconfiguration of the Soviet Union as a smaller, more decentralized federation. It was a classic case of hardliners within the regime trying to repress political liberalization. Popular and international opposition, led by Yeltsin, forced the military to back down. By December, the Soviet Union was dissolved. Fifteen new countries emerged, with Russia being by far the biggest and most important, and each was expected to transition to democracy. The world's number-two superpower appeared to be starting an unprecedented transition from a Communist regime to one that was democratic and capitalist.

Russia's transition, however, has not been to democracy but instead to electoral authoritarian rule. This has been a result of the effects of partial and poorly institutionalized economic reform, weak political institutions, an exceptionally strong presidency, and the perverse effects of Russia's abundant natural resources. The full effects of this shift to electoral authoritarian rule would be clear only after Vladimir Putin, Russia's second president, consolidated his rule in the first few years of the new millennium. While he abided by the constitutional limit of two terms as president, he handpicked his successor, who dutifully chose Putin for the number-two position of prime minister. In 2012 Putin once again ran and won the presidency in an election many saw as fraudulent. He is likely to hold onto power at least until 2024.

Russia's transition started long before Putin rose to power. Gorbachev's most dramatic reform was ending the Communist Party's claim to absolute power in February 1990. This was followed in March by Russia's legislative elections and Yeltsin's election as Russian president a year later. At the time, Russia was still just one of fifteen constituent republics of the Soviet Union, and these were the first elections to include non-Communist candidates since the Communist revolution. The military backlash destroyed the possibility of a negotiated pact and led to the dissolution of the Soviet Union. The provincial Russian institutions became those of the newly independent state, with Yeltsin as president. The transition from a state-controlled to a market economy began immediately and was very difficult, making the new government unpopular early on. Yeltsin claimed that the benefits of the new capitalist economy would be widespread, but the immediate effect was a dramatic increase in prices that left Russians with little means of support. More often than not, former Communist factory managers became the owners of newly privatized businesses. To the average worker, it looked like not much had changed, until the owners had to fire much of the bloated workforce to compete in the new market economy. The economy shrank 14.5 percent, and inflation ballooned to more than 1,500 percent in 1992. Unemployment tripled from 1992 to 1998. A few spectacularly successful businessmen, especially in Russia's huge oil sector, emerged to control vast swaths of the economy. Key allies of Yeltsin, they formed a group that came to be known as the "family," and in effect ran the economy and the government.

The early years of an independent Russia were as chaotic and difficult politically as they were economically. While the elected legislature included non-Communist members, the Communist Party still held a majority of seats. Yeltsin feared holding new elections because of the unpopularity of the economic changes. Faced with an increasingly hostile parliament, he ruled primarily by decree. He proposed the creation of the semipresidential system with an exceptionally strong presidency that we outlined in chapter 5. The legislature refused to ratify his ideas, leading him to disband it in September 1993. Legislators barricaded themselves in the parliament building, determined not to leave, and voted to impeach Yeltsin. After a weeklong standoff, Yeltsin called in the army to lay siege to the parliament building, forcibly ending the Soviet-era parliament. Once again, a moment when a negotiated pact might have

Russian president Vladimir Putin speaks at the Congress of his United Russia Party in June 2016. In contrast to Boris Yeltsin, the first president of post-communist Russia, Putin has been fully involved in the party process, using United Russia as a vehicle to control the increasingly compliant parliament. While several small opposition parties have seats in parliament, none has any significant power in the electoral authoritarian regime that ultimately emerged from Russia's failed transition to democracy.

Mikhail Svetlov/Getty Images

been possible ended instead with violence. Yeltsin subsequently held a referendum on the constitution, which passed by a narrow margin, and then an election for a new legislature. In spite of these successes, he still faced opposition to many of his reforms and continued to rule by decree without legislative support. Citizens also blamed him for the unpopular, brutal, and ineffective war in the breakaway region of Chechnya. He narrowly won reelection in 1996, but neither his popularity nor the economy ever fully recovered.

A primary reason why Yeltsin lacked support in the legislature was that he refused to join a political party, trying instead to appear "above" partisan politics. His refusal to participate, in addition to the very weak powers of the Duma, resulted in the creation of weak parties. The mixed electoral system (similar to Germany's) in the 1993 constitution was part of the problem. Half the Duma's seats were elected via closed-list proportional representation (PR) and the other half via single-member districts. Unlike in Germany, few parties could compete effectively in both types of elections; the few national parties won most of the PR seats, and independent candidates with no party affiliation but strong local bases of support won many of the SMD seats. Power resided overwhelmingly in the executive branch, in any case. Therefore, most parties were of limited consequence, rising and falling with the popularity and shifting allegiances of major politicians. Across four elections from 1993 to 2005, anywhere from twelve to seventeen parties were in parliament, and fewer than half of them in one parliament continued to hold seats in the next one. Ironically, the biggest exception was the Communist Party, which had the clearest ideology and still has an estimated 160,000 members.

Political scientists Hans Oversloot and Ruben Verheul (2006) argued that the most important party in Russia is the "party of power, the party that those around the president create to win as many seats as they can in the *duma,* insuring support for the president's proposals." This party has changed from one election to the next; it was called Russia's Choice in 1993, Our Home Is Russia in 1995, Unity in 1999, and United Russia since 2003. Putin chose to help foster his party of power, United Russia, to a degree Yeltsin never did. He used his greater popularity (throughout his first two terms, his popular approval ratings rarely dipped below 70 percent) and his control over patronage to ensure that United Russia won handily. Since 2003, United Russia has easily dominated the Duma, meaning the Duma has rubber-stamped everything Putin has proposed. Not surprisingly, this domination has reduced the number of parties in the Duma; after the 2011 election, only four had representation in the legislature, with United Russia controlling 53 percent of the seats. The Communist Party became a "loyal opposition," giving Putin legislative support in exchange for his allowing them to continue to enjoy the perks of office.

In constructing an electoral authoritarian regime, Putin significantly centralized power in the executive and eliminated almost all vestiges of real democracy. In addition to increasing the powers of the presidency vis-à-vis the regions, he harassed and closed down most independent media, undermined independent civil society groups with new regulations, and broke the informal power of the oligarchs who had arisen under Yeltsin. He replaced Yeltsin's "family" with a group of former agents of the Federal Security Bureau (FSB), the successor to the KGB where he had spent most of his career. Members of this group sit in key ministries and agencies throughout the executive branch, have been appointed as governors, and control many important companies (Hesli 2007).

Putin also manipulated the electoral system. Under the mixed electoral system, his most significant opposition came from independent MPs elected in the single-member districts, so he changed the electoral system to a purely closed-list PR system to eliminate independent candidates. This reduced the number of parties from forty in 2003 to fourteen in 2008. If real electoral competition existed, this could be seen as enhancing democracy, since fewer and larger parties give voters clearer and more credible options. But in the context of Putin building his party of power, repressing civil society and the media, and using oil wealth as patronage to buy off opponents, the drop in the number of parties was simply part of a broader process of centralizing control. In 2014 Putin reversed course, recreating the mixed system, though with a 5 percent threshold to keep out smaller parties. Because United Russia was the only party capable of running candidates in all SMD constituencies, the new system allowed it to win a record 343 of 450 seats without resorting to the blatant electoral fraud that set off protests in 2011–2012. It won 54 percent of the PR vote but virtually all the SMD seats.

Putin used economic growth (based on high oil revenues) and improved security to gain much popular support through 2009 (Rose et al. 2011), but economic decline had damaged that by 2011. The parliamentary elections in December 2011 included widespread fraud, some of it captured on video and posted on the Internet. After years of relative quiescence, Russian civil society awoke; protests of tens of thousands of people demanding fairer elections took place repeatedly from December 2011 to March 2012. The regime successfully resisted the protesters' demands, however, and Putin

Freedom House Scores: Russia and Central Europe

In the aftermath of communism in central Europe, democracy spread rapidly, as seen in the region's improved Freedom House scores. Russia, though, reversed course in the new millennium as Putin consolidated an electoral authoritarian regime.

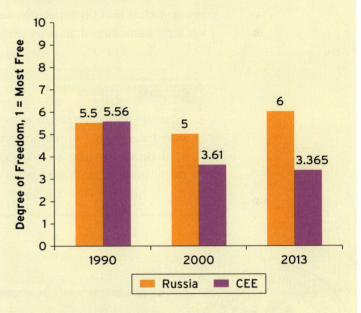

Source: Freedom House, "Freedom in the World, 2016" (https://freedomhouse.org/report/freedom-world/freedom-world-2016).

was duly elected (again, partly via fraudulent elections) president in March 2012. He quickly instituted new laws that dramatically increased the fines for unauthorized demonstrations, put greater legal restrictions on NGOs, and reversed slight liberalizations President Dmitry Medvedev had made to Russian federalism (see chapter 5). Putin also increased his use of Russian nationalism to gain support, sharpening his opposition to the West in foreign policy and aligning himself more tightly with the Russian Orthodox Church. His nationalist appeal increased after Russia's invasion and annexation of the Crimea in 2014. The Crimea historically was a region of Russia but became part of Ukraine under Soviet rule and, hence, part of independent Ukraine in 1991. Putin took advantage of the weak Ukrainian government during an uprising in its capital to annex the territory, a wildly popular move at home. His popularity rating was estimated at 75 percent shortly thereafter. Two years of severe recession, caused mainly by declining oil and other mineral prices, reduced his popularity by 2016. While economic decline hurt his popularity, his firm control of an electoral authoritarian regime left little doubt he and his party would continue to rule for the foreseeable future.

CASE Questions

1. What are the key problems in Russia's transition to democracy that ultimately produced an electoral authoritarian regime?
2. Look back at Levitsky and Way's theory of when an electoral authoritarian regime might make a transition toward democracy (page 489). What would they predict for the future of Putin's regime in Russia, and why?

NIGERIA: NEOPATRIMONIAL TRANSITION

The Nigerian case demonstrates the potential to establish democracy in a poor country, as well as the severe problems that can arise when politics is based on neopatrimonialism. The competition for office becomes all-consuming and often violent, undermining democratic norms of the "free and fair" choice of candidates. Corruption continues throughout the country, with only slight improvement, weakening all state

CASE SYNOPSIS

institutions and popular faith in democracy. Yet the fragile democratic regime in Nigeria seems to have brought the military under control. A few other key institutions—term limits and judicial independence—have been strengthened as well. In 2015 even the much-criticized electoral process seemed to improve and power changed hands from one party to another via an election for the first time in the country's history. Advocates of democracy in countries like Nigeria hope that these institutional gains will be the basis for further improvement and the slow establishment of a consolidated and relatively high-quality democracy, though the latter seems quite far off in Nigeria.

- **TRANSITION** Led by civil society; electoral democracy, but with dominant-party system until 2015

- **CONSOLIDATION** Tension over regional, ethnic, and religious political rivalries; civilian control of the military; power turnover via election for first time

- **QUALITY** Electoral fraud and corruption, but strengthened judiciary and limits on presidential power

- **FREEDOM HOUSE RATING IN 2016: 4.5 = "partly free"**

On April 1, 2015, incumbent president Goodluck Jonathan of the long-ruling People's Democratic Party (PDP) did something a Nigerian president had never done before: he publicly congratulated his opponent for winning the election and conceded defeat. This regular occurrence in well-established democracies was a milestone for Nigeria. Just eight years earlier, the country changed presidents via an election for the first time in its history, though both presidents were from the PDP, which had won every election since the democratic transition in 1999. Domestic and international observers saw each of three successive national elections (1999, 2003, and 2007) as further from democratic norms than the one that preceded it. Though the 2011 election was improved, it seemed that a dominant-party system had emerged that limited democratic competition. A split in the ruling party led to the 2015 electoral turnover and the hope that Nigeria was a little closer to a consolidated democracy, even though a violent Islamist movement threatened sovereignty in the north, ethnic and regional voting remained the norm, and corruption was still a serious problem.

The election of 1999 marked Nigeria's second return to democratic rule. The first created the Second Republic in 1979, which ended in a military coup in 1983 discussed above. A failed transition in 1993, in which the military dictator annulled the presidential election because his candidate did not win, gave rise to a vociferous democracy movement. As in much of Africa, democratic transition in Nigeria began with grassroots protests. The annulment of the long-awaited election in 1993 motivated many new groups to join the democracy effort; in 1994 they formed the National Democratic Coalition (NADECO), which included former politicians, union members, students, and human rights campaigners. NADECO's breadth allowed it to put greater pressure than ever before on Nigeria's military government. In its first campaign, "Babangida Must Go," it demanded that military dictator Ibrahim

Babangida be replaced by the rightful winner of the election. Babangida did go but was replaced by the even more repressive and corrupt dictator, Sani Abacha (see chapter 3). The real transition began only after Abacha's death in 1998. His successor recognized how discredited the military had become under Abacha's rule and immediately agreed to a transition. The subsequent elections in 1999 were far from perfect, but most observers deemed them minimally adequate to start Nigeria's new democracy. The military elite put together what became the ruling party, the PDP, and chose the military dictator who had shepherded the 1979 transition, retired general Olusegun Obasanjo, as its presidential candidate.

In Nigeria's ethnically and religiously divided society, Obasanjo benefited from being a Yoruba from the southwest. The long dominance of northerners under military rule led all Nigerians to recognize that it was time for a president from the country's southern region. So the "Kaduna mafia," a group of Muslim military leaders from the north that has controlled most of Nigeria's governments, picked as their candidate a southerner, a retired general whom they trusted. Ironically, Obasanjo won handily in most of the country but not in his home area among the Yoruba, who saw him as having sold out to northern military interests. By the 2003 election, Obasanjo and his party won more easily than in 1999, and his handpicked successor, Umaru Yar'Adua (a northerner), won 72 percent of the vote in 2007. Throughout, the PDP also maintained control of the legislature. It seemed the country had established a dominant-party system, to the detriment of real democratic competition and turnover.

Often, one of the most democratizing events possible in a dominant-party system is a split in the ruling party. In regionally, ethnically, and religiously divided Nigeria, the PDP became dominant in part by agreeing that the presidency would alternate between a northerner and a southerner (hence from Obasanjo to Yar'Adua). President Yar'Adua, however, became gravely ill shortly after taking power and died in March 2010. He was succeeded by his vice president, Jonathan, who was from the southeast.

Outgoing president Goodluck Jonathan (left) presents a gift to newly elected president Muhammadu Buhari. The transfer of power between them in 2015 was the first time in the country's history that the party in control of the government changed via an election. This was a historic moment for the young democracy.

REUTERS/Afolabi Sotunde

This inadvertently violated the principle of north–south alteration, in that Yar'Adua only completed part of his term. Initially, northern party leaders resisted Jonathan's desire to run for a full term of office in 2011, arguing the north deserved the presidency after Yar'Ardua's death. After extensive behind-the-scenes campaigning, which allegedly included funneling oil money to key governors to gain their support, the ruling party allowed Jonathan to stand for office, effectively ending the policy of alternating the presidency between north and south. Muhammadu Buhari, the major opposition candidate and also a northerner, gained support because of this but the PDP held together and won the 2011 election, albeit with a reduced majority in the legislature.

In 2013, however, the PDP split as a former vice president and seven state governors stormed out of the party convention, objecting to the fact that their candidates were not given key party positions. Most of those who left were from the north and opposed President Jonathan's planned reelection bid in 2015. They believed he was moving to gain greater control of the party to ensure another term as president. Ultimately, they helped craft an opposition coalition with several smaller parties that nominated Buhari as its presidential candidate, setting up the 2015 election as the most competitive in the country's history. The newly united opposition party, the All Progressives Congress (APC), took advantage of the fact that President Jonathan was increasingly unpopular, largely due to his inability or unwillingness (as some northerners alleged) to defeat Boko Haram in the north (see chapter 7), continuing massive corruption, and a declining economy that suffered from the dramatic drop in world oil prices. Buhari won 54 percent of the popular vote nationwide, sweeping all northern and most southwestern states, leaving Jonathan with only his native southeast and a few other states. The APC also won secure

Freedom House Scores: Nigeria and Africa

Nigeria's mixed record of democratization is not unusual for Africa. While Freedom House rated it slightly above average for sub-Saharan Africa in 2016, the difference is not substantial. After the initial wave of transitions in the early 1990s, improvements to democracy in the region have been slow and difficult to achieve. A handful of countries such as Ghana have created fully "free" democracies, but most regime change has resulted in electoral authoritarian regimes.

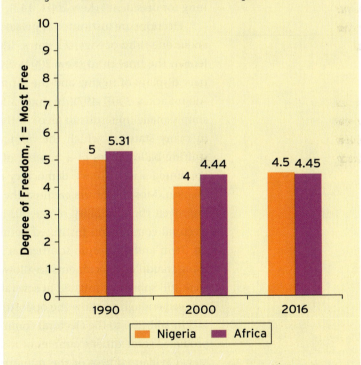

Source: Freedom House, "Freedom in the World, 2016" (https://freedomhouse.org/report/freedom-world/freedom-world-2016).

majorities in both houses of the National Assembly. International and domestic observers deemed the election credible. While some PDP leaders wanted to resist handing over power, with one leader even going to the electoral commission with his personal security force to try to stop the counting of ballots when it became clear the PDP was losing, international governments and civil society demanded the results be respected, and Jonathan ultimately made his historic concession (Lewis and Kew 2015).

Despite the hopefulness the electoral turnover produced, Nigeria's democracy faces several enduring problems. Political parties in Nigeria are not strong institutions with loyal supporters based on party ideology and symbols; instead, they are based mainly on the support of key "Big Men" and their use of patronage. The neopatrimonialism that characterized military rule has continued under the new democracy. While the two leading parties captured 99 percent of the 2015 presidential vote, dozens of parties were legally registered and fourteen fielded presidential candidates, "but most parties consisted primarily of the office staff at the national headquarters . . . and were typically centered on a Big Man who was funding the operations and running for president" (Kew 2004, 147).

Elections are institutionally weak as well. In 2003 the elections were free and fair in about one-third of Nigeria's states, "dubious" in another third, and completely fraudulent in the final third (Kew 2004). By 2007, "the elections were marred by extraordinary displays of rigging and the intimidation of voters in many areas" (Rawlence and Albin-Lackey 2007, 497). In quite a few states, no elections took place at all: officials simply made up results in favor of the ruling party. Voter turnout was grossly inflated in many states in which the ruling party won, and observers saw officials openly stuffing ballot boxes in a number of cases. After assuming the presidency, Jonathan appointed a well-known democracy advocate and scholar to head the electoral commission. Most observers credited the electoral commission with having substantially improved the credibility of the 2011 and 2015 elections. For the 2011 election, the electoral commission instituted permanent voters' cards with biometric information on them and electronic scanners at all polling places to try to prevent parties from using fraudulent documents to allow supporters to vote multiple times. While results were still somehow inflated in several states, especially where the PDP won, fraud was reduced enough to allow the opposition victory (Lewis and Kew 2015).

In addition to the electoral commission, Nigeria's experiment with democracy has produced some other examples of institutionalization that have strengthened democracy. Civilian control of the military has been key. Military leaders of the "Kaduna mafia" backed Obasanjo for president in 1999 because they assumed they could control him after he took office. After becoming president, however, he quickly removed the most politically active northern generals and replaced them with less politically active and more southern officers. Several years later, when Yar'Adua's prolonged illness left him incapacitated and the country's government very uncertain for nearly three months, rumors of military intervention were rife but the armed forces remained in their barracks. Some observers believe the reason why elections have become so hotly contested is the stakes are so high. No one expects military intervention, so election is the sole means for gaining political power.

A second institution that has been strengthened is the judiciary. The new constitution created a National Judicial Council that has helped insulate the judiciary from pressures from elected officials. The Supreme Court has made several important rulings that demonstrated its autonomy. In the area of federal versus state control over oil revenues, it ruled in some key cases in favor of the oil-producing states and in others in favor of the federal government, indicating a certain degree of autonomy from political pressure from either side. After the faulty 2007 election, the courts also ruled several gubernatorial victories invalid and required new elections.

Perhaps the two most important tests of institutional strength for Nigerian democracy went against incumbent presidents, indicating some institutionalization of limits on personal rule. The first came when President Obasanjo launched a campaign to revoke the two-term limit for the presidency. Amending the constitution to allow Obasanjo a third term required Senate approval. Reportedly, he and his supporters were trying to bribe senators to vote in favor of the amendment with offers as high as $750,000. It became crystal clear, though, that the population overwhelmingly opposed the move, and the Senate voted it down despite all the pressure and inducements Obasanjo brought to bear. Some observers also argue that many of the elite quietly opposed Obasanjo as well. In a patronage-based system with oil revenue available, the presidency is very powerful and lucrative. The political elite do not want one individual to remain in office too long so that other leaders and groups have a chance to gain its benefits.

The second major institutional challenge began in 2009, when President Yar'Adua became gravely ill and left the country for treatment in Saudi Arabia. An incapacitated president is supposed to turn over his powers to his vice president, but Yar'Adua refused. His wife and closest aides did not let any Nigerians see him and released no information about his health. For two months, the country was without even an acting president. Amid growing domestic and international pressure to clarify the situation, Yar'Adua gave a radio interview in which he said in a weak voice that he hoped to return to work soon. The National Assembly took that as a public statement that he was incapacitated and appointed Vice President Jonathan as acting president. Once again, the sitting president and his closest aides were rebuffed in an illegitimate attempt to retain power.

The country also remains deeply divided along regional, ethnic, and religious lines. In the northeast, of course, Boko Haram has wreaked havoc since 2013, though President Buhari reorganized the military and, working with neighboring countries, had greatly reduced Boko Haram's territory by 2016 (see chapter 7). In the southeast, the battle over control of oil revenues has been both violent and tied to ethnic demands. The Movement for the Emancipation of the Niger Delta (MEND) shocked the nation when bombs exploded in the capital during the celebration of the fiftieth anniversary of independence in 2010, killing at least sixteen people. While an amnesty offered to armed rebels in the oil areas reduced the level of violence for several years, the underlying issues of environmental problems, inequality, and unemployment in the region remain. Indeed, by 2016, a movement for the re-creation of an independent Biafra (the name chosen by the leaders of the rebellion in the southeast that tried to secede in 1967, setting off a civil war) was gaining support.

A controversy over the role of *sharia* in the Muslim north has also raised regional and religious tensions. The 1999 constitution allows states to set their own legal codes within national law, and Nigeria has long allowed dual civil law codes based on religion. Immediately after the transition to democracy, twelve northern states adopted *sharia* for both civil and criminal law, setting off confrontations with Christian minorities in several of these states and opposition from the south in general. Long-standing northern and Muslim control of national politics has left southerners and Christians fearful of any further Islamic movements. Because of federalism, each state's version of *sharia* is slightly different; some states apply some Muslim laws to non-Muslims and other states don't, while some include the harshest penalties such as stoning and others don't. So far, national courts have neither revoked states' rights to implement *sharia* nor insisted on a uniform version across all states.

All of these institutional problems are related to the overall weakness of the state. Not surprisingly in a country where neopatrimonial authority continues to be important, corruption is rampant. Transparency International's 1999 Corruption Perception Index ranked Nigeria as the second most corrupt country in the world, with a score of 1.6. In 2015 it was number 136 of 168 countries, with a score of 2.6, showing modest but noticeable improvement. This is due in part to an anticorruption drive Obasanjo launched that received great praise in its early years. Jonathan appointed a new head of the Central Bank who won praise for removing some corrupt officials, as well as appointing the successful new head of the electoral commission. The greatest corruption is in the oil sector, however. Government reports found that approximately $1.5 billion of oil revenue failed to reach the treasury in 2012–2013, and as much as $16 billion has been missing since. President Buhari, who initiated a harsh anticorruption campaign when he ruled as a military dictator in the 1980s, has promised to battle corruption, including plans to break up the national oil company into smaller companies that, he hopes, will be easier to control. Continued corruption has made all state institutions weak, harmed the ability of the electoral commission to conduct proper elections (though this is the area of greatest improvement, it seems), prevented people in the oil-producing states from benefiting from their oil, and led northerners to turn to *sharia* in the hope that it will be less corrupt and more just than secular courts.

CASE Questions

1. Comparing all three of our case studies of democratization, what effects do weak institutions have on the democratization process? Are the effects similar in all three countries? Which of the three suffered the greatest effects of weak institutions, and why?

2. Nigeria's transition juxtaposes some very serious problems against some notable successes in creating democratic limits on the executive. Given this, what do you think are the most important changes that would likely improve the quality of its democracy?

CONCLUSION

Regime change is a difficult process to understand and predict. By definition, it lies outside the realm of "normal" politics. Instead, it is a period of intense politicization and rapidly unfolding events. This makes it an exceptionally fascinating area of comparative politics to study, and many comparativists have done so. Many questions remain, however.

Regime change affects who rules, but not only in the ways that might be expected. At least in theory, democratization produces regimes in which citizens rule. How true that is, of course, depends on the quality of the democracy that emerges. Not infrequently, though, a democracy does not emerge at all. Similarly, a seemingly united revolutionary front in the interests of the people can result in leaders imposing their own vision on society and demobilizing popular participation in the new regime. In politics, those who fight for change do not necessarily get what they seek. The military holds the guns on which the state and regime rely and therefore can intervene directly if it chooses, putting itself in power. But militaries, even highly institutionalized ones, are not designed to rule. Every military regime relies on civilian support to some extent, especially within the state itself.

The often chaotic process of regime change continues to limit comparativists' predictive powers. Some cases, such as Ghana, defy the odds, producing democracy where theorists would least expect it. Consolidating a new democracy is an extremely challenging process. Partly for this reason, comparativists for years believed that democracy would only survive in very specific kinds of countries. That position was challenged by the "transition paradigm," which argued that democracy could survive anywhere. More careful recent scholarship suggests that while democracy can arise anywhere, its chances of survival are definitely higher in favorable cultural and economic contexts. The process can be easily undermined by institutional breakdowns of all sorts. An increasingly common result of these breakdowns, especially in the former Soviet Union and much of Africa, seems to be electoral authoritarian regimes, whose future will have a major impact on the future of democracy around the world.

Military coups are the most common and quickest form of regime change. When civilian efforts to socialize and thereby control the military fail, troops seize the capital for a variety of reasons. These can range from the military's sense that the nation needs to be "rescued," to the military's own interests as an organization, to the more particular interests of individual leaders or groups within the military. Which explanation is most useful often depends on the nature of the military itself, especially its degree of institutionalization, and is often far from obvious. Military intervention does not always lead to military rule, either, as the case of Tunisia demonstrates.

Regime change is such a large and important topic that virtually all major theories of comparative politics have been used to explain it. Political-culture theorists long argued that attributes of particular cultures set the stage for particular kinds of regimes. Some analysts of democratic transition argued as well that individual actors' belief in democracy matters. Influenced by rational choice theory, the transition paradigm argues that neither culture nor ideology is particularly important in understanding when a transition will occur; transitions take place when political elites see the acceptance of democratic institutions to be in their rational self-interest. Modernization theorists have responded, with growing evidence, that even if transition is possible, either culture or a structural condition—such as economic development—is necessary to preserve democracy in the long run.

KEY CONCEPTS

coup d'état (p. 470)

pact (p. 484)

democratic consolidation (p. 485)

regime change (p. 469)

founding election (p. 485)

transition to democracy (p. 484)

Sharpen your skills with SAGE edge at **edge.sagepub.com/orvis4e. SAGE edge for students** provides a personalized approach to help you accomplish your coursework goals in an easy-to-use learning environment.

WORKS CITED

Acemoglu, Daron, and James A. Robinson. 2006. *Economic Origins of Dictatorship and Democracy*. New York: Cambridge University Press.

Allen, Chris. 1995. "Understanding African Politics." *Review of African Political Economy* 22 (65): 301–320.

Almond, Gabriel A., and Sidney Verba. 1963. *The Civic Culture: Political Attitudes and Democracy in Five Nations*. Princeton, NJ: Princeton University Press.

———. 1989. *The Civic Culture Revisited*. Newbury Park, CA: Sage.

Ansell, Ben W., and David J. Samuels. 2014. *Inequality and Democratization: An Elite-Competition Approach*. New York: Cambridge University Press.

Arango, Tim, and Ceylon Yeginsu. 2016. "With Army in Disarray, A Pillar of Modern Turkey Lies Broken." *New York Times*. July 29 (http://www.nytimes.com/2016/07/29/world/europe/turkey-military-coup.html?smprod=nytcore-ipad&smid=nytcore-ipad-share&_r=0).

Beaulieu, Emily. 2014. *Electoral Protest and Democracy in the Developing World*. New York: Cambridge University Press.

Bermeo, Nancy Gina. 2003. *Ordinary People in Extraordinary Times: The Citizenry and the Breakdown of Democracy*. Princeton, NJ: Princeton University Press.

Boix, Carles. 2003. *Democracy and Redistribution*. New York: Cambridge University Press.

Boix, Carles, and Susan Carol Stokes. 2003. "Endogenous Democratization." *World Politics* 55 (4): 517–549. doi:10.1353/wp.2003.0019

Bratton, Michael, and Nicholas van de Walle. 1997. *Democratic Experiments in Africa: Regime Transitions in Comparative Perspective*. New York: Cambridge University Press.

Casar, Ma. Amparo. 2016. "Parliamentary Agenda Setting in Latin America: The Case of Mexico." In *Legislative Institutions and Lawmaking in Latin America*, edited by Eduardo Aleman and George Tsebelis. Oxford, UK: Oxford University Press, 148–174.

Crenshaw, Martha. 1981. "The Causes of Terrorism." *Comparative Politics* 13 (4): 379–399.

Decalo, Samuel. 1976. *Coups and Army Rule in Africa*. New Haven, CT: Yale University Press.

Escriba-Folch, Abel, and Joseph Wright. 2015. *Foreign Pressure and the Politics of Autocratic Survival*. Oxford, UK: Oxford University Press.

Finer, Samuel E. 1962. *The Man on Horseback: The Role of the Military in Politics*. New York: Praeger.

Fish, M. Steven. 2006. "Stronger Legislatures, Stronger Democracies." *Journal of Democracy* 17 (1): 5–20. doi:10.1353/jod.2006.0008

Fish, M. Steven, and Robin S. Brooks. 2004. "Does Diversity Hurt Democracy?" *Journal of Democracy* 15 (1): 154–166.

Freedom House. "Freedom in the World" (http://www.freedomhouse.org/template.cfm?page=15).

Garrido de Sierra, Sebastián. 2011. "Eroded Unity and Clientele Migration: An Alternative Explanation of Mexico's Democratic Transition." Paper presented at the annual meeting of the Midwest Political Science Association, Chicago, March–April.

Gherghina, Sergiu. 2015. *Party Organization and Electoral Volatility in Central and Eastern Europe*. New York: Routledge.

Gibson, Edward L. 2012. *Boundary Control: Subnational Authoritarianism in Federal Democracies*. Cambridge, UK: Cambridge University Press.

Giraudy, Agustina. 2015. *Democrats and Autocrats: Pathways of Subnational Undemocratic Regime Continuity within Democratic Countries*. Oxford, UK: Oxford University Press.

Graf, William. 1988. *The Nigerian State: Political Economy, State Class, and Political System in the Post-Colonial Era*. London: J. Currey; Portsmouth, NH: Heinemann.

Guo, Sujian, and Gary A. Stradiotto. 2014. *Democratic Transitions: Modes and Outcomes*. New York: Routledge.

Hadenius, Axel, and Jan Teorell. 2005. "Cultural and Economic Prerequisites of Democracy: Reassessing Recent Evidence." *Studies in Comparative International Development* 39 (4): 87–106.

Hamilton, Nora. 2011. *Mexico: Political, Social, and Economic Evolution*. Oxford, UK: Oxford University Press.

Harkness, Kristen. 2014. "The Ethnic Army and the State: Explaining Coup Traps and the Difficulties of Democratization in Africa." *Journal of Conflict Resolution* 60 (4): 587–616. doi:10.1177/00220027145453

Hesli, Vicki L. 2007. *Government and Politics in Russia and the Post-Soviet Region*. Boston: Houghton Mifflin.

Holzner, Claudio A. 2011. "Mexico: Weak State, Weak Democracy." In *The Quality of Democracy in Latin America*, edited by Daniel H. Levine and José E. Molina, 83–110. Boulder, CO: Lynne Rienner.

Houle, Christian. 2015. "Ethnic Inequality and the Dismantling of Democracy: A Global Analysis." *World Politics* 67(3): 469–505. doi:http://dx.doi.org/10.1017/S0043887115000106

Huntington, Samuel P. 1964. *The Soldier and the State: The Theory and Politics of Civil-Military Relations*. New York: Random House.

_____. 1968. *Political Order in Changing Societies*. New Haven, CT: Yale University Press.

———. 1991. *The Third Wave: Democratization in the Late Twentieth Century.* Norman: University of Oklahoma Press.

Inglehart, Ronald, and Christian Welzel. 2005. *Modernization, Cultural Change, and Democracy: The Human Development Sequence.* New York: Cambridge University Press.

Issacharoff, Samuel. 2015. *Fragile Democracies: Contested Power in the Era of Constitutional Courts.* New York: Cambridge University Press.

Janowitz, Morris. 1964. *The Military in the Political Development of New Nations: An Essay in Comparative Analysis.* Chicago: University of Chicago Press.

Kapstein, Ethan B., and Nathan Converse. 2008. "Why Democracies Fail." *Journal of Democracy* 19 (4): 57–68. doi:10.1353/jod.0.0031

Kew, Darren. 2004. "The 2003 Elections: Hardly Credible, but Acceptable." In *Crafting the New Nigeria,* edited by Robert I. Rotberg, 139–173. Boulder, CO: Lynne Rienner.

Kieh, George Klay, and Pita Ogaba Agbese. 2002. *The Military and Politics in Africa: From Engagement to Democratic and Constitutional Control.* Aldershot, UK: Ashgate.

Latinobarometro. 2015 (http://www.latinobarometro.org/latOnline.jsp).

Lebas, Adrienne. 2011. *From Protest to Parties: Party-Building and Democratization in Africa.* New York: Oxford University Press.

Levine, Daniel H., and José E. Molina, eds. 2011. *The Quality of Democracy in Latin America.* Boulder, CO: Lynne Rienner.

Levitsky, Steve, and Lucan Way. 2010. *Competitive Authoritarianism: Hybrid Regimes after the Cold War.* New York: Cambridge University Press.

Lewis, Peter, and Darren Kew. 2015. "Nigeria's Hopeful Election." *Journal of Democracy* 26 (3): 94–109.

Lindberg, Staffan I. 2009. "The Power of Elections in Africa Revisited." In *Democratization by Elections: A New Mode of Transition,* edited by Staffan I. Lindberg, 25–46. Baltimore, MD: Johns Hopkins University Press.

Linz, Juan. 1990. "The Perils of Presidentialism." *Journal of Democracy* 1 (1): 51–69. doi:10.1353/jod.1990.0011

Lipset, Seymour Martin. 1959. "Some Social Requisites of Democracy: Economic Development and Political Legitimacy." *American Political Science Review* 53 (1): 69–105. doi:10.2307/1951731

Magaloni, Beatriz, and Zaira Razu. 2016. "Mexico in the Grip of Violence." *Current History* 115 (778): 57–62. February.

Marinov, Nikolay, and Hein Goemans. 2014. "Coups and Democracy." *British Journal of Political Science* 44 (4): 799–825. doi:http://dx.doi.org/10.1017/S0007123413000264

Morlino, Leonardo. 2011. *Changes for Democracy: Actors, Structures, Processes.* New York: Oxford University Press.

Nichter, Simeon, and Brian Palmer-Rubin. 2014. "Clientelism, Declared Support, and Mexico's 2012 Campaign." In *Mexico's Evolving Democracy: A Comparative Study of the 2012 Elections,* edited by Jorge I. Domínguez, Kenneth F. Greene, and Chappell H. Lawson. Baltimore, MD: Johns Hopkins University Press.

Norris, Pippa. 2014. *Why Electoral Integrity Matters.* New York: Cambridge University Press.

O'Donnell, Guillermo A. 1979. *Modernization and Bureaucratic-Authoritarianism: Studies in South American Politics.* Berkeley: Institute of International Studies, University of California Press.

Oversloot, Hans, and Ruben Verheul. 2006. "Managing Democracy: Political Parties and the State in Russia." *Journal of Communist Studies and Transition Politics* 22 (3): 383–405. doi:10.1080/13523270600855795

Pérez Silva, Ciro. 2004. "*Colosio Fernández Dirige Sospechas contra Salinas.*" *La Jornada.* February 11 (http://www.jornada.unam.mx/2004/02/11/008n1pol.php).

Pop-Eleches, Grigore, and Graeme B. Robertson. 2015. "Structural Conditions and Democratization." *Journal of Democracy* 26 (3): 144–156 (http://www.journalofdemocracy.org/article/structural-conditions-and-democratization).

Przeworski, Adam, Michael E. Alvarez, José Antonio Cheibub, and Fernando Limongi. 2000. *Democracy and Development: Political Institutions and Well-Being in the World, 1950–1990.* Cambridge, UK: Cambridge University Press.

Rawlence, Ben, and Chris Albin-Lackey. 2007. "Briefing: Nigeria's 2007 General Elections; Democracy in Retreat." *African Affairs* 106 (424): 497–506. doi:10.1093/afraf/adm039

Reidl, Ruth Betty. 2014. *Authoritarian Origins of Democratic Party Systems in Africa.* New York: Cambridge University Press.

Rios-Figueroa, Julio. 2013. "Effectiveness and Accessibility of Justice System Institutions in Mexico's Transition to Democracy." In *Representation and Effectiveness in Latin American Democracies: Congress, Judiciary and Civil Society,* edited by Moira B. MacKinnon and Ludovico Feoli, 143–159. New York: Routledge.

Roberts, Andrew. 2010. *The Quality of Democracy in Eastern Europe: Public Preferences and Policy Reforms.* New York: Cambridge University Press.

Roett, Riordan. 1978. *Brazil: Politics in a Patrimonial Society,* rev. ed. New York: Praeger.

Rose, Richard, William Mishler, and Neil Munro. 2011. *Popular Support for an Undemocratic Regime: The Changing Views of Russians.* New York: Cambridge University Press.

Sanderson, Stephen K. 2005. *Revolutions: A Worldwide Introduction to Political and Social Change.* Boulder, CO: Paradigm.

Simpser, Alberto. 2013. *Why Governments and Parties Manipulate Elections: Theory, Practice, and Implications.* New York: Cambridge University Press.

Singh, Naunihal. 2014. *Seizing Power: The Strategic Logic of Military Coups.* Baltimore, MD: Johns Hopkins University Press.

Skocpol, Theda. 1979. *States and Social Revolutions: A Comparative Analysis of France, Russia, and China.* New York: Cambridge University Press.

Stepan, Alfred. 2012. "Tunisia's Transition and the Twin Tolerations." *Journal of Democracy* 23 (2): 89–103.

Tavits, Margit. 2013. *Post-Communist Democracies and Party Organization.* New York: Cambridge University Press.

Tomini, Luca. 2014. "Reassessing Democratic Consolidation in Central and Eastern Europe and the Role of the EU." *Europe–Asia Studies* 66 (6): 859–891. August.

van de Walle, Nicolas. 2006. "Tipping Games: When Do Opposition Parties Coalesce?" In *Electoral Authoritarianism: The Dynamics of Unfree Competition,* edited by Andreas Shedler, 77–92. Boulder, CO: Lynne Rienner.

Way, Lucan. 2025. *Pluralism by Default: Weak Autocrats and the Rise of Competitive Politics.* Baltimore, MD: Johns Hopkins University Press.

Wejnert, Barbara. 2014. *Diffusion of Democracy: The Past and Future of Global Democracy.* New York: Cambridge University Press.

Welzel, Christian. 2013. *Freedom Rising: Human Empowerment and the Quest for Emancipation.* New York: Cambridge University Press.

RESOURCES FOR FURTHER STUDY

Ackerman, Peter, and Jack Duvall. 2000. *A Force More Powerful: A Century of Nonviolent Conflict.* New York: St. Martin's Press.

Casper, Gretchen. 1995. *Fragile Democracies: The Legacies of Authoritarian Rule.* Pittsburgh, PA: University of Pittsburgh Press.

Dahl, Robert. 1971. *Polyarchy: Participation and Opposition*. New Haven, CT: Yale University Press.

Diamond, Larry, and Leonardo Morlino. 2005. *Assessing the Quality of Democracy*. Baltimore, MD: Johns Hopkins University Press.

Fish, M. Steven. 2005. *Democracy Derailed in Russia: The Failure of Open Politics*. New York: Cambridge University Press.

Haggard, Stephan, and Robert R. Kaufman. 1995. *The Political Economy of Democratic Transitions*. Princeton, NJ: Princeton University Press.

Mainwaring, Scott, and Aníbal Pérez-Liñán. 2013. *Democracies and Dictatorships in Latin America: Emergence, Survival, and Fall*. New York: Cambridge University Press.

Moore, Barrington. 1966. *Social Origins of Dictatorship and Democracy: Lord and Peasant in the Making of the Modern World*. Boston: Beacon Press.

Morgenstern, Scott, and Benito Nacif, eds. 2002. *Legislative Politics in Latin America*. New York: Cambridge University Press.

O'Donnell, Guillermo. 1999. "Horizontal Accountability in New Democracies." In *The Self-Restraining State: Power and Accountability in New Democracies,* edited by Andreas Schedler, Larry Diamond, and Marc F. Plattner, 29–51. Boulder, CO: Lynne Rienner.

O'Donnell, Guillermo A., and Phillipe Schmitter. 1986. *Transitions from Authoritarian Rule: Tentative Conclusions about Uncertain Democracies*. Baltimore, MD: Johns Hopkins University Press.

Pinkney, Robert. 2003. *Democracy in the Third World*. Boulder, CO: Lynne Rienner.

Przeworski, Adam. 1991. *Democracy and the Market: Political and Economic Reforms in Eastern Europe and Latin America*. Cambridge, UK: Cambridge University Press.

Reynolds, Andrew. 2002. *The Architecture of Democracy: Constitutional Design, Conflict Management, and Democracy*. New York: Oxford University Press.

Schedler, Andreas. 2006. *Electoral Authoritarianism: The Dynamics of Unfree Competition*. Boulder, CO: Lynne Rienner.

Van Inwegen, Patrick. 2011. *Understanding Revolution*. Boulder, CO: Lynne Rienner.

Webb, Paul, and Stephen White, eds. 2007. *Party Politics in New Democracies*. Oxford, UK: Oxford University Press.

Wegren, Stephen K., and Dale R. Herspring, eds. 2010. *After Putin's Russia: Past Imperfect, Future Uncertain*. New York: Rowman and Littlefield.

Zakaria, Fareed. 2003. *The Future of Freedom: Illiberal Democracy at Home and Abroad*. New York: W. W. Norton.

WEB RESOURCES

Freedom House, Freedom in the World, 2016
(https://freedomhouse.org/report/freedom-world/freedom-world-2016)
Global Integrity
(http://www.globalintegrity.org/)
Polity IV Project, 2016, "Global Trends in Governance, 1800–2014"
(http://www.systemicpeace.org/polityproject.html)
Transparency International, Corruption Perceptions Index
(http://www.transparency.org/research/cpi/overview)
Unified Democracy Scores
(http://www.unified-democracy-scores.org)

REUTERS/Amr Abdallah Dalsh

10 POLITICAL ECONOMY OF WEALTH

KEY QUESTIONS

- How and why should states intervene in the market economy?
- In what ways do economic policies reflect the relative power of different groups in a society?
- How important is globalization in determining the economic policies of individual countries?
- Why have some wealthy states intervened in the market economy more than others?

The "Great Recession" that began in the United States in 2007 and spread across the globe in 2008–2009 caused not only massive economic upheaval but major political changes as well. Between 2008 and 2016, governments changed hands in France, Greece, Iceland, Ireland, Italy, Japan, Portugal, Spain, the United Kingdom, and the United States, among other countries. And in all of those contests, the state of the economy was a major factor in the incumbent party's loss. With the global economy still not recovering all that strongly in 2016, the British voted, in an unprecedented move, to leave the European Union, and Americans elected Donald Trump president, whose campaign focused heavily on severely restricting trade. As Bill Clinton's 1992 presidential campaign put it, "It's the economy, stupid!" Political leaders in democracies across the globe rise and fall on the basis of citizens' perceptions of the economy and their own economic well-being.

Market economies have become nearly universal since the end of the Cold War. In these economies, the state does not control the economy as the communist governments did in the past, but governments can and do intervene in the economy to try to encourage economic growth and influence how economic benefits are distributed. Therefore, the relationship between the state and the market and the debates surrounding it are crucial to understanding modern politics virtually everywhere. This is the

realm of political economy, which we introduced in chapter 1 as the study of the interaction between economics and politics. We will examine it in detail in this and the next two chapters. As the Country and Concept table (page 525) demonstrates, even though virtually all countries are now market economies, they have achieved widely varying levels of economic success. Different histories, positions in the global economy, and economic policies produce dramatically different levels of wealth, economic growth, unemployment, inequality, and poverty.

This chapter examines the fundamental economic concepts that will help us understand the enduring relationship between the state and the market and the long-standing debates over that relationship. We ask how, why, and to what effect states intervene in market economies. We also examine various models of state-market relationships in wealthy democracies. Finally, we examine how the forces of globalization have challenged long-established models and theories, and how wealthy states are responding. We will return to these themes in chapter 11, where we look at economic issues in middle- and low-income countries.

THE MARKET, CAPITALISM, AND THE STATE

market economy
An economic system in which individuals and firms exchange goods and services in a largely unfettered manner

A **market economy** is an economic system in which individuals and firms exchange goods and services in a largely unfettered manner. This includes not only the exchange of finished products but also inputs into the production process, including labor. To most people, this seems like a natural state of affairs, but until fairly recently it was the exception, not the norm. In many preindustrial societies, people subsisted on the fruits of their own labor and engaged in very limited trade. In feudal Europe, most people were legally bound to a particular lord and manor and could not exchange their labor for a wage anywhere they pleased. The creation of the modern market economy required that feudal bonds restricting labor be broken so that most people would become dependent on market exchanges. In modern industrial and postindustrial societies, virtually the entire population depends on earning a wage or receiving a share of profit via the market.

Capitalism

capitalism
The combination of a market economy with private property rights

Capitalism is not exactly the same thing as a market economy, though the terms are typically used interchangeably. Rather, capitalism is the combination of a market economy with private property rights. In theory, one can imagine a market economy without individual property rights. For example, collectively owned firms could be free to produce whatever they could for a profit in an unfettered market. Yugoslavia under the communist rule of Josip Tito attempted but never fully implemented a modified version of such a system in the 1960s and 1970s.

Virtually all countries have some form of a capitalist economy today, although the degree to which the market is unfettered and the precise nature of private property rights vary widely. There is no absolute law in economics about how "free" market exchanges or private property must be for a capitalist economy to function. The debates over the extent to which the state should intervene to limit and shape market exchanges and property rights are at the core of many of the most important political issues around the globe. The end of the Cold War eliminated the communist **command economy**—an economic system in which most prices, property, and production are directly controlled by the state—as a viable political economic model, but it did not end the debate over what ought to be the relationship between the market and the state.

command economy
An economic system in which most prices, property, and production are directly controlled by the state

Because people tend to see the capitalist market economy as somehow natural, they also see it as existing independently of government. Nothing could be further from the truth. Command economies were ultimately of limited efficiency, but they proved that a state can exist for a long time without a market economy. Capitalism, on the other hand, cannot exist without the state. In a situation of anarchy—the absence of a state—the market would be severely limited; without state provision of security, property and contract rights, and money, exchange would be limited to bartering and would require extensive provision of private security forces. Mafias are examples of

COUNTRY AND CONCEPT
States and Markets

Country	Average GDP growth (annual %) 1980–2015	Average unemployment (% of total labor force), 1980–2014	Average inflation (% change), 1980–2015	Absolute poverty, 2002–2015 (% of population below $1.25 per day)[4]	Inequality (Gini coefficient), 2005–2013[5]
Brazil	1.08	6.44	311.23	3.8	52.7
China	8.68	3.25	4.81	6.3	37.0
Germany	1.59	7.58	1.82	N/A	30.6
India	4.38	3.5	8.49	23.6	33.6
Iran	0.45	11.3	19.84	N/A	38.3
Japan	1.73	3.46	1.12	N/A	32.1
Mexico	0.91	4.02	25.79	1.0	48.1
Nigeria	1.03	12.83	17.75	62.0	43.0
Russia	0.67	8.02	81.73	N/A	39.7
United Kingdom	1.77	6.56	2.65	N/A	38.0
United States	1.62	7.8	3.39	N/A	41.1

[1] World Bank, GDP per capita growth (annual %) (http://data.worldbank.org/indicator/NY.GDP.PCAP.KD.ZG); data for Iran 2015 not available; data for Russian Federation between 1980 and 1990 not available.

[2] World Bank, World Development Indicators, average total unemployment (% total labor force) (http://databank.worldbank.org/data/views/reports/tableview.aspx). Data between 1988 and 1989, 2002 and 2003 missing for all countries. Data missing for: Brazil (1980, 1991, 1994, 2000, 2010); Germany (1980, 1981, 1982); India (1980–1993, 1999, 2001, 2004, 2006–2009, 2011); Iran (1980–1985, 1987, 1988, 1992–1995, 1997–2001, 2006, 2011 and 2012; Mexico (1980–1990); Nigeria (1980–1985, 1987–2005), Russia (1980–1991), and United Kingdom (1980–1982).

[3] World Bank, World Development Indicators, inflation (% change), (http://databank.worldbank.org/data/views/reports/tableview.aspx). Data between 1988 and 1989, 2002, and 2003 are missing for all countries. Data missing for: Brazil (1980); China (1980–1986); Germany (1980–1991); Russian Federation (1980–1992); United Kingdom (1980–1987).

[4] Human Development Reports, "Multidimensional Poverty Index" (http://hdr.undp.org/sites/default/files/2015_human_development_report_1.pdf).

[5] Human Development Reports, "Gini coefficient" (http://hdr.undp.org/en/media/HDR_2010_EN_Table3_reprint.pdf).

this kind of capitalism, which arises where states are weak or absent; they provide their own security and enforce their own contracts. While this can create some productive economic activity, the uncertainty of property rights and contracts, and the costs of private security, limit economic growth and create a society in which few would like to live. This points to the first of several *essential roles* the state must play in a capitalist economy: providing security. In addition to certain roles that are essential to capitalism, the modern state also often plays important roles that are not essential but are either *beneficial* or *politically generated*.

Essential Roles

The state's essential roles are providing security, establishing and enforcing property and contract rights, and creating and controlling currency. Most essential roles, and many of the beneficial ones as well, involve the provision of **public goods**: goods or services that cannot or will not be provided via the market because their costs are too high or their benefits are too diffuse. National security is an excellent example of a public good. Individual provision of security is extremely expensive, and if any one company could pay for it, the benefits would accrue to everyone in the country anyway, not allowing the company to generate revenue sufficient to cover the costs. The state must provide this service if the market economy is to thrive.

Protection of property and contract rights is also an essential state function in a market economy. Capitalism requires investing now with the expectation of future gains. Some uncertainty is always involved, but if potential investors have no means of ensuring that the future gains will accrue, no one will invest. Property rights protect not only property legally purchased in the market but also future property—the profits of current investment and productive activity. Similarly, profits require honest market exchanges: if a ton of cotton is promised for delivery at a set price, it must actually be delivered at that price. Details can vary significantly, but some legal guarantee that current and future property and exchanges will be protected is essential to achieving the productivity associated with modern market economies.

The modern state must also provide a currency to facilitate economic exchanges. States did not always print or control currency. Prior to the American Civil War, for instance, private banks printed most currency in the United States (hence the old-fashioned term *banknote*). When the state took over this process and created a uniform currency, exchanges across the entire country were eased. This happened transnationally as thirteen countries adopted the euro as the single currency of the European Union (EU) in 2002, greatly easing exchange across much of the continent.

Beneficial Roles

Several other roles the state commonly plays in the modern market economy are not absolutely essential, but most analysts consider them beneficial. These include providing infrastructure, education, and health care, and correcting market failures. The first three are all examples of public goods. Roads are a classic example of infrastructure as a public good. Private roads can and sometimes do exist, but governments build the bulk of all highway systems. Public provision of a road network lowers the cost

public goods
Goods or services that cannot or will not be provided via the market because their costs are too high or their benefits are too diffuse

of transporting goods and people, which improves the efficiency and profitability of many sectors of the economy.

Similarly, most economists and business leaders see an educated populace as beneficial to economic efficiency. Workers who can read, write, and do arithmetic are far more productive than those who cannot. Companies could provide this education themselves, but because education is a lengthy process, because children learn many things more efficiently and effectively than do adults, and because workers can switch jobs and take their company-provided education with them, providing basic education is not a profitable endeavor and is therefore a nearly universal function of the state.

In most countries, the provision of basic health care is seen in similar terms. Obviously, a healthy workforce is more productive than an unhealthy one, and investment in health is most productive in the early stages of life; the economic benefits of high-quality prenatal and early childhood health care are far greater than the benefits of health care for the elderly. Most countries, therefore, consider health care a public good. At the very least, the government aggressively intervenes in the health care market to ensure that such care is provided to all.

Today, vigorous debates about the state's role in providing public goods and services continue in many countries. While virtually all agree that basic education is beneficial and ought to be provided by the state (the United Nations has officially endorsed education as a right for all), that still leaves a great deal open to dispute: How much secondary and higher education should the state provide? Should the government pay for all or most of a person's higher education, as is the case in most of Europe, or should the individual pay a substantial share, as in the United States? Health care is even more controversial. While most agree that a healthy workforce enhances a market economy, how to achieve such a healthy population is the subject of near-constant debate. These issues are analyzed in greater depth in chapter 12.

The fourth beneficial economic function of the modern state is intervention to correct market failure. **Market failure** occurs when markets fail to perform efficiently. The primary justification for a market is efficiency: a well-functioning market maximizes the efficient use of all available resources. Three common causes of market failure are **externalities** (transactions that do not include the full costs or benefits of production in the price), imperfect information, and monopolies in which one seller can set prices. Advocates of an unfettered market recognize market failures as something governments should try to correct, but exactly when such intervention is justified and how governments should respond remain controversial.

Market externalities occur when a cost or benefit of the production process is not fully included in the price of the final market transaction, thereby reducing efficiency. Environmental damage is a common externality. If a factory pollutes the air as it makes a product, costs are incurred at least by local residents. The factory owners, however, do not have to pay those costs as they make and sell their products, and the price charged customers doesn't include those costs. The factory will pollute more than it would if it and its customers had to pay the costs of that pollution. Many economists

market failure
Phenomenon that occurs when markets fail to perform efficiently or fail to perform according to other widely held social values

externality
A cost or benefit of the production process that is not fully included in the price of the final market transaction when the product is sold

argue, therefore, that the state should intervene to make the producers and consumers of the product bear its full costs.

Markets can also only maximize efficiency when buyers and sellers know the full costs and benefits of their transactions. Economists call this having "perfect information." In our financially and technologically complex societies, market actors often lack perfect information. The financial collapse that caused the 2008–2009 recession resulted in part from a set of transactions in which consumers and investors did not fully know what they were purchasing. The first breakdown in information came as many Americans purchased homes during the housing boom earlier in the decade. Potential buyers were desperate to purchase as home prices rose rapidly. Some lenders, especially in the "hottest" markets, offered buyers variable-rate mortgages with payments and interest that were low in the short term but that increased dramatically later. Many buyers seemed not to understand how high the payments would go, and some lenders used aggressive or fraudulent techniques to sell mortgages to uncreditworthy buyers, seeking to earn loan-processing fees and interest in the short term and not caring whether the borrowers would be able to pay back the loans in the long term (a practice known as predatory lending).

The second set of transactions in which buyers lacked perfect information occurred on Wall Street, where major banks sold investments called "mortgage-backed securities" (MBS), which were basically bundles of these high-risk mortgages. Theoretically, these investments helped to spread out the risks of these high-risk mortgages across many investors. Banks tried to reduce risk further by selling MBS investors a kind of insurance called credit default swaps (which are part of a broader investment category called derivatives), which would compensate them if the mortgage holders defaulted on their loans. However, the Wall Street banks selling these investments and the companies that rate the risks did not fully disclose or realize the level of risk in the mortgages, so investors did not fully understand the risks involved in their investments. Once housing prices began to fall significantly in 2008, the most heavily involved Wall Street banks, most notably Lehman Brothers, faced bankruptcy as their investors tried to sell the MBS as quickly as possible but found no buyers, so the value of those investments collapsed. Even worse, the banks had to pay off those investors who had bought credit default swaps. Bankruptcy ensued for some of the banks, and investors in the United States and around the world (often unknowingly via instruments like pension funds) faced a massive loss of wealth. The result was the biggest economic downturn since the Great Depression. The market failure embedded in this series of transactions in which buyers of all sorts lacked "perfect information" led to renewed debate over how much government regulation is necessary in the mortgage and financial markets.

monopoly
The control of the entire supply of a valued good or service by one economic actor

The third common market failure is **monopoly**—the control of the entire supply of a valued good or service by one seller. In a market economy, competition among alternative suppliers is a key incentive for efficiency. Because monopolies eliminate this incentive, the state may intervene to prevent them. It may do so in three ways:

by making the monopoly government owned and therefore (in theory) run in the interest of the general public, by regulating the monopoly to ensure that its prices are closer to what they would be in a competitive market, or by forcing the breakup of the monopoly into smaller, competing entities.

Some monopolies are considered **natural monopolies**; these occur in sectors of the economy in which competition would raise costs and reduce efficiency. Where a natural monopoly exists, it makes more sense to regulate or take control of it rather than force a breakup. A good example of a natural monopoly is the history of telephone service. A generation ago, every phone had to be hardwired into a land line, and all calls traveled over wires; this meant that competition would have required more than one company to run wires down the same street. This obviously would have been prohibitively expensive and inefficient. Britain, like many other countries, chose the first option to deal with this natural monopoly: it created the government-owned company, British Telephone. The United States, by contrast, chose to heavily regulate a privately owned monopoly, and all services were provided by "Ma Bell" (as AT&T was nicknamed). By 1984, however, new ways to deliver voice and high-speed data transmission reduced the "natural" quality of the monopoly. A lawsuit led to the breakup of AT&T, spawning several local phone companies. With the advent of satellite and wireless technology, the natural monopoly evaporated; around the world, governments have privatized or deregulated phone services, and consumers now have a choice of providers.

natural monopoly
The control of the entire supply of valued goods or services by one economic actor in a sector of the economy in which competition would raise costs and reduce efficiency

A worker stands in a construction site for a new sewage processing facility in St. Petersburg, Russia. Without facilities treating sewage, companies and households will dump their waste into rivers and lakes, destroying the environment, likely sickening people who live near the waterways, and harming fishing. The people polluting the water, however, may well not pay the cost of the damage they are causing. Externalities like this are a primary justification for state intervention in a market.

Peter Kovalev/TASS (Photo by Peter Kovalev\TASS via Getty Images)

Politically Generated Roles

All the economic functions of the state discussed to this point are economically required or at least beneficial to the market. The final category of state functions in a market economy are those that are politically generated by citizens demanding that a state take action. Most economists do not see these functions as essential or perhaps even beneficial to creating an efficient market, but states have taken on these roles because a large section of the populace has demanded them. Karl Polanyi argued in his 1944 book, *The Great Transformation,* that the rise of the modern industrial economy produced political demands to limit what many people saw as the negative effects of the market. This led to what is now termed the "modern welfare state." Through the democratic process in European countries and the United States, in particular, citizens demanded protection from the market, and governments began to provide it to a greater or lesser extent. Primary examples of these politically generated state functions are government regulations requiring improved working conditions and policies that redistribute income.

Because these state interventions are the results of political demands, they remain very contentious and vary greatly from country to country. In wealthy industrial economies, modern working conditions— including a minimum wage, an eight-hour workday, and workers' health and safety standards—are largely the product of labor union demands. Yet, as the case studies at the end of this chapter show, labor policies in wealthy countries vary significantly, particularly in areas such as the length of the workweek, job security, the length of maternity leave, and the amount of paid vacation time that employers are required to give. In countries that have begun industrializing more recently, such as Brazil and China, labor unions are recent creations that have not had the opportunity to successfully champion the same reforms that are now taken for granted in countries that industrialized much earlier. Minimum wages may be low or nonexistent, workdays may be as long as twelve hours, and paid vacations are rare. This disparity between wealthier and poorer countries is at the core of the controversies surrounding globalization.

Similar controversy and variation exist around income redistribution policies. Typically referred to as "welfare" in the United States (though Social Security, which is not usually seen as "welfare," is also an income redistribution policy), these policies exist to mitigate the effects of unequal income distribution that markets generate. Markets can provide great economic efficiency and growth, but they have no rules for how wealth is distributed. As social and economic inequality expanded in the late nineteenth and early twentieth centuries, reformers began to demand that the state take action to help those who were gaining little or nothing in the market. For reasons we explore in chapter 12, the extent to which the early industrializing countries in Europe and the United States pursued income redistribution and poverty amelioration varied considerably. As with proper and regulated working conditions, income redistribution policies barely exist at all in the poorest countries; the poorest people are left to survive in the market as best they can.

Overall, the symbiotic relationship between the modern state and the market economy provides a means to analyze state interventions in modern economic life. The state must carry out certain roles if capitalism is to survive and thrive. Political leaders know that much of their popularity rests on the ability to generate goods and services, jobs, and government revenue. In the modern economy, states pursue various policies and market interventions beyond those that are the bare essentials for the survival of capitalism. Some of these are widely recognized as beneficial to contemporary economies, though the details of how and how much to pursue them remain controversial. Other policies, however, are generated primarily by political demands emanating from society, especially in democracies. These policies remain the most controversial and vary the most from state to state, as we will see in chapter 12.

KEY ECONOMIC DEBATES

Understanding political economy and the relationship between the state and the market requires the application of both political science and basic economics. Major economic theories lie behind the debates over how governments should intervene in the market. The first, central debate that must be understood is between Keynesian and neoliberal theories of when, why, and how the state ought to attempt to guide the economy. Prior to the Great Depression, Western governments engaged in minimal intervention in the economy. Economists and government officials recognized that during economic downturns, unemployment rose and people suffered, but they

The Role of the State in the Market

Essential functions of the state	Beneficial functions of the state	Politically generated functions of the state
Provide national and personal security: Failure to do so produces anarchy or the creation of a mafia.	**Provide public goods:** These are goods or services not provided via the market because their costs are too high or their benefits are too diffuse, such as public education.	**Improve working conditions:** Examples include health and safety standards, eight-hour workday, minimum wage.
Protect property and contract rights: These are essential for investments to produce profits over time.	**Mitigate market failures:** These are interventions when the market fails to allocate resources efficiently. Examples include environmental regulations and laws limiting monopolies.	**Redistribute income:** Examples include retirement benefits, unemployment compensation, welfare.
Provide a currency: Facilitates widespread exchange.		

believed that in the longer term, unemployment lowered wages until labor was cheap enough that businesses started to invest and employ people again, thus creating a new cycle of economic growth. Therefore, during economic downturns, government should do little but wait.

Keynesianism

Keynesian theory
Named for British economist John Maynard Keynes, who argued that governments can manage the business cycles of capitalism via active fiscal policy and monetary policy, including deficit spending when necessary

fiscal policy
Government budgetary policy

deficit spending
Government spending more than is collected in revenue

monetary policy
The amount of money a government prints and puts into circulation and the basic interest rates the government sets

John Maynard Keynes, after whom **Keynesian theory** is named, revolutionized economics after watching his native Britain enter the Great Depression in the 1930s. Keynes argued that the state could, and should, do more to manage economic crises. In an economic downturn like the Great Depression, the main problem was a lack of demand for goods and services, and he believed that through **fiscal policy,** or management of the government budget, government could revive demand and stimulate the economy. He suggested that the government could and should engage in **deficit spending**; that is, it should spend more than it collected in revenue to stimulate demand. To do this, it would borrow money. By creating new programs and hiring people, the government would put that money into people's hands; they in turn would start to buy other goods and services, and the economy would start to rebound. Similarly, **monetary policy**—the amount of money a government prints and puts into circulation and the basic interest rates the government sets—can stimulate the economy. Central banks (called the Federal Reserve in the United States) should lower interest rates to stimulate borrowing in an economic downturn. When the downturn is over, the government can reduce spending to pay off the debt it had taken on and raise interest rates. These policies would slow demand in the economy, as too much demand can cause inflation. Keynes believed that in this way the state could manage the economy, smoothing out the cycle of economic expansion and contraction—known as the business cycle—that seemed inherent in unchecked capitalism. Done properly, such management might even achieve continuous full employment.

Keynesians also recognized market failures and believed that governments had an important role to play in correcting them. This combined with growing political demands in areas like environmental pollution to produce a more activist state that regulated a variety of economic activity. From the 1940s to the 1970s in the United States, for instance, numerous regulatory agencies were created to protect consumers from harmful food and drugs, reduce pollution, and protect workers' safety. The state also regulated monopolies or oligopolies in areas like telephone communications and airlines. Fearing financial collapses like the one that produced the Great Depression, governments also regulated the banking industry more tightly; in the United States, rules required banks serving average consumers to remain entirely separate (and insured their deposits against bank failure) from banks engaged in stock market transactions. David Kotz (2015) termed this era "regulated capitalism."

Keynesianism (and the onset of World War II) offered governments a way to help their economies out of the Depression, and most Western governments adopted it either explicitly or implicitly. Growth rates and average incomes rose significantly throughout the Western world in the 1950s and 1960s. The power of the economic theory alone, however, was not the only reason why Keynesian policies became so popular. Deficit spending allowed elected politicians to create programs to benefit their constituents without having to raise taxes to pay for them. The appeal for politicians facing reelection is obvious. In Europe, Keynesianism also gave social democratic parties economic justification for a significant expansion of social spending and welfare policies after World War II. This political logic led to frequent distortion of pure Keynesian policies—deficit spending continued in many countries even in times of economic growth in contradiction to Keynes's idea that when the economy improved, a government would pay off its debt.

By the 1970s, Keynesian policies came under sustained questioning, first by economists and then in the political arena. Due partly to the quadrupling of oil prices in 1973, most Western countries faced a new economic situation: stagflation, meaning simultaneous high inflation and high unemployment. Keynes's prescription of more government borrowing to reduce unemployment was seen as potentially disastrous in this situation because it was likely to produce more inflation. Growth slowed, unemployment grew, and incomes stagnated.

Neoliberalism

In this context, an alternative economic theory gained popularity. What came to be known as **neoliberalism** (the "liberalism" refers back to nineteenth-century liberal ideas in favor of individual freedom and open markets rather than modern, American liberalism associated with the Democratic Party) argued that government intervention to steer the economy was at best ineffective and often harmful. Instead, neoliberal economists such as Milton Friedman and Friedrich Hayek argued that government should minimize intervention in the free market so that the market can allocate resources as efficiently as possible to maximize wealth generation. They believed market failures are rare and most government regulation is therefore harmful. Friedman argued that fiscal policy does not stimulate economic growth. Rather, government borrowing and deficit spending simply "crowd out" private-sector borrowing, impeding the ability of businesses to invest and thereby reducing long-term growth. The key to economic growth, Friedman argued, is simply monetary policy. Inflation, he and other neoliberals asserted, is caused chiefly by excessive government printing of money, and low growth is due in part to government borrowing. Achieving continuous full employment, they claimed, was impossible and produced inflation. Defeating stagflation and restoring growth would therefore require reducing the amount of money in circulation, raising interest rates, and reducing deficit spending.

Because they believe market failure is relatively rare and government spending harms the ability of businesses to invest, neoliberal theorists also favor cutting back most government regulations. Government efforts to reduce pollution, protect

neoliberalism
An economic theory that argues government should balance its budget and minimize its role in the economy to allow the market to allocate resources to maximize efficiency and thereby economic growth

consumers' and workers' safety, and regulate business activities such as banking put constraints on businesses' ability to invest wisely and waste precious resources. They call for a reduction in regulations and the overall size of government, in addition to balancing government budgets by eliminating deficit spending.

Neoliberalism became the theoretical justification for the economic policies of U.S. president Ronald Reagan and British prime minister Margaret Thatcher. Both set out to radically reduce the size and scope of government intervention in the economy in the early 1980s. The economic boom that followed was seen as a vindication of neoliberalism more broadly, which became the "conventional wisdom" in economic theory, at least until the recession of 2008–2009. Even when the Democratic and Labour Parties came to power in the United States and United Kingdom in the 1990s, they continued to pursue mostly neoliberal policies: deregulation of the financial sector in the United States, for instance, was completed by Democratic president Bill Clinton in 1999. Neoliberal ideas and policies spread, with varying levels of adoption, to many other countries. They became particularly powerful in poorer countries, a subject to which we turn in chapter 11.

Keynesianism versus Neoliberalism: An Ongoing Debate

The 2008–2009 Great Recession and its aftermath led to the most significant debate on economic policy in a generation. As the economy collapsed, most states, including the previously neoliberal United States, first turned to Keynesian policy to try to restart economic growth; governments engaged in significant deficit spending to stimulate the economy. Neoliberal restrictions on government spending collapsed in the face of the highest unemployment rates since the Great Depression and the political pressures that they had produced. As a slow recovery set in, however, governments on both sides of the Atlantic returned to greater fiscal austerity; fear of excessive debt became greater than desire for more short-term growth. Keynesian economists lambasted this move as happening far too early, pointing to similar policies in the mid-1930s that are believed to have lengthened the Great Depression. Neoliberals, on the other hand, saw the move back in their direction as a wise reversal after the Keynesian panic of 2009. By 2016, U.S. growth was over 2 percent annually compared to about 1.5 percent in the EU, while U.S. unemployment had dropped to about 5 percent versus 10 percent in the EU. The United States pursued somewhat more aggressive deficit spending in response to the crisis in 2009 and did not reverse it until 2012, a year after the EU did. Similarly, the U.S. Federal Reserve cut interest rates more quickly than did the European Central Bank (ECB), and began "quantitative easing"—a means of pumping money into the economy—earlier as well. While the debate continues, by 2016 it seemed that the more aggressive stimulus in the United States had resulted in a somewhat stronger recovery, though even in the United States the recovery was slower than in past recessions.

The recession also initiated a renewed debate about government regulation, especially of the financial sector. Neoliberal economist Alan Greenspan, chair of the U.S.

Federal Reserve from 1987 to 2006, believed that private competition in the market for investments like mortgage-backed securities and credit default swaps would produce better security than would government rules. Investors could be counted on not to take on more risk than was prudent, meaning the government would be wasting money if it were constantly watching over investors' shoulders. Many Keynesians, on the other hand, believe regulation to be especially appropriate in the financial sector, since they see it as unusually prone to irrational and inefficient booms and busts. In the years following the crisis, both the United States and ECB put in place new regulations to monitor the largest banks considered "too big to fail" and reduce the risks they could take.

Crises such as the Great Recession can be moments when societies move in entirely new directions, what institutionalists call "critical junctures." Many initially believed the Great Recession would be such a critical juncture: after three decades of the dominance of neoliberal economic theory, governments rapidly shifted toward Keynesian policy in response to the crisis. Some analysts saw a potential shift back to the "golden age" of Keynesianism, while others wondered if a new model of economic policy might emerge (Kotz 2015). Nearly everyone saw a stronger role for the state as a likely outcome. By 2016, expanded regulations on finance were in place but were modest, and governments were reducing deficit spending around the world, suggesting they had not abandoned neoliberalism yet. The financial system was saved, though growth remained sluggish and unemployment high in many countries; average people's incomes remained below where they had been before the crisis. Several scholars argued that neoliberalism, strongly supported by the political power of the finance sector in wealthy countries, had survived the crisis, even if modestly greater government intervention had become the norm (Panizza and Philip 2014).

Key Economic Theories

	Keynesianism	Neoliberalism
Architect	John Maynard Keynes	Milton Friedman/Friedrich Hayek
Role of governments	Governments should actively manage business cycles	Governments should play diminished role in economy; open economies to global trade
Key instruments	Fiscal policy, including deficit spending; regulation; looser monetary policy	Monetary policy; deregulation; privatization
Criticisms	Deficit spending reduces private investment and growth and causes inflation; regulation limits business investment	Neoliberal restrictions on government spending slow growth during recession; deregulation creates boom and bust; increases inequality

TYPES OF CAPITALIST ECONOMIES

Now that we have outlined the fundamental relationships between states and markets, and the economic theories that guide government policies, we can examine the various models of capitalism among wealthy countries. While the state must perform certain core functions to sustain capitalism, this leaves much possible variation. As our case studies at the end of the chapter will demonstrate, wealthy countries have created distinct models of capitalism that involve significant differences in how the state intervenes in the market. A recent, influential school of thought known as the **varieties of capitalism (VOC)** approach attempts to analyze these differences systematically. It focuses primarily on business firms and how they are governed in terms of their interactions with government, one another, workers, and sources of finance such as banks and stock markets. Proponents of this approach distinguish between two broad types of economies among wealthy capitalist countries: liberal market economies (LMEs) and coordinated market economies (CMEs).

Liberal Market Economies (LMEs)

Liberal market economies (LMEs), such as the United States and the United Kingdom, rely more heavily on market relationships, meaning that firms interact with other firms and secure sources of finance through purely market-based transactions. They know little about one another's inner workings, which leads them to focus primarily on short-term profits to enhance stock prices, a key source of finance. Such firms' relationship to workers is also primarily via open markets: rates of unionization are low and labor laws are flexible, allowing firms to hire and fire employees with ease. The government's role in such economies is relatively minimal and is focused simply on ensuring that market relationships function properly through, for instance, fairly stringent antimonopoly laws and rules governing stock exchanges that guarantee that all buyers are privy to the same information.

Coordinated Market Economies (CMEs)

Coordinated market economies (CMEs), by contrast, involve more conscious coordination among firms, financiers, unions, and government. Many firms and banks hold large amounts of stock in one another's operations, which gives them inside information on how the others operate. This, in turn, encourages firms to coordinate their activities and establish long-term relationships in terms of finance and buying inputs. Firms are able to focus on longer-term initiatives because financiers have inside information about the potential for long-term gains. CMEs tend to have stronger unions and higher levels of unionization, and worker training is focused within sectors of the economy and within related firms. The government is involved in negotiating

varieties of capitalism (VOC)
School of thought analyzing wealthy market economies that focuses primarily on business firms and how they are governed; divides such economies into liberal market economies and coordinated market economies

liberal market economies (LMEs)
In the varieties of capitalism approach, countries that rely heavily on market relationships to govern economic activity; the United States and United Kingdom are key examples

coordinated market economies (CMEs)
In the varieties of capitalism approach, capitalist economies in which firms, financiers, unions, and government consciously coordinate their actions via interlocking ownership and participation; Germany and Japan are key examples

agreements among firms and between firms and unions, and it allows or even encourages the close relationships that might be termed "insider trading" or quasi-monopoly situations in an LME. Germany is a prime example of a CME. Japan's "developmentalist state" that we outline in the case study in this chapter is usually classified as a CME as well, though with a smaller role for unions than is found in European CMEs.

The logic of the VOC approach also suggests that LMEs and CMEs are likely to pursue distinct fiscal and welfare policies. At first glance, it might seem that CMEs, with their high levels of government involvement in coordinating the economy, would be likely to pursue more interventionist, Keynesian fiscal policies, but VOC theorists argue exactly the opposite. Because CMEs have built-in ways to stabilize the labor market to maintain employment, they are less likely to need or want to pursue fiscal stimulation. LMEs, on the other hand, have far more flexible labor markets; therefore, unemployment is likely to go up more quickly in a recession, and their governments will need to pursue more Keynesian stimulation to reduce unemployment.

Scholars also noted a relationship between varieties of capitalism and the two types of democracies we outlined in chapter 5: majoritarian and consensus. Majoritarian democracies tend to have LMEs, while consensus democracies have CMEs. Japanese political scientist Masanobu Ido (2012), among others, argued that in consensus democracies, mostly with PR electoral systems, parties representing business interests must negotiate policies with parties representing labor so businesses become more adept and willing to negotiate with labor generally in CMEs. Consensus democracies also provide greater policy stability because of the many veto points in the system. This makes workers more willing to invest in the sector-specific skills typical of a CME; they are assured that government support for the particular sector—and therefore their skills—will continue. In majoritarian democracies, on the other hand, policy can change more quickly and workers will be reluctant to invest heavily in a particular sector. Businesses in majoritarian democracies, meanwhile, prefer to gain majority control of the government via the parties that represent them and create policies they favor, rather than negotiating with labor, thus creating an LME.

The distinct models of capitalism in different wealthy countries developed after World War II and arguably came to full fruition by the 1970s and 1980s. They then faced what many analysts saw as a set of forces that threatened each model's ability to maintain its distinctive qualities, and even the states' powers to set economic policy generally: globalization.

GLOBALIZATION: A NEW WORLD ORDER, OR DÉJÀ VU ALL OVER AGAIN?

There is no doubt that the 2008–2009 recession showed the negative elements of globalization clearly: a financial crisis based in the United States quickly spread around the world. Major European investors had stakes in the high-risk securities that collapsed on Wall Street, causing European banks to face possible bankruptcy and Cyprus, Greece, Ireland, Italy, Portugal, and Spain to come close to default. Export markets for developing economies like China and India plummeted, and a brief era of economic growth in Africa was nipped in the bud. These global effects all started with average people in places like Arizona and Florida buying homes with risky, variable-rate mortgages.

Globalization has become perhaps the most frequently used, and abused, term in political economy. It first gained prominence in the 1990s, and since then hundreds of books and countless articles have been written about it. It has cultural as well as economic and political implications, but we will focus on the latter two in order to understand its effects on the relationship between the state and the market. That economic activity across borders has increased over the last generation is beyond question: between 1980 and 2010 trade as a share of global GDP increased from 30 percent to 56 percent, foreign direct investment more than quadrupled, and annual minutes of international phone calls from the United States went from two billion to seventy-five billion (Dadush and Dervis 2013).

globalization
A rapid increase in the flow of economic activity, technology, and communications around the globe, and the increased sharing of cultural symbols, political ideas, and movements across countries

Globalization has many definitions. We define it as a rapid increase in the flow of economic activity, technology, and communications around the globe. Three key questions have arisen about globalization: (1) Does it represent a brave new world in which the fundamental relationship between the state and the market has changed forever, or is it simply the latest phase in that relationship—something new and interesting but not fundamentally different? (2) What caused it in the first place? (3) What can and should be done about it, if anything?

A Brave New World?

Globalization's earliest adherents saw it as a portent of fundamental change. Japanese scholar Kenichi Ohmae, writing in 1995, argued that globalization would result in the "end of the nation-state." He focused on economic aspects of globalization, but others have broadened this general argument, claiming that the rapid flow of money, goods and services, ideas, and cultural symbols around the globe will eventually make the nation-state irrelevant. Regional, if not global, management will have to fill the role currently played by the state. The flow of ideas and culture will severely weaken national identity, as the Internet in particular will allow people to form identities not linked to territories and their immediate local communities. All of these changes ultimately will require political responses in the form of strengthened international organizations for global governance and a new global civil society to respond to global problems with global solutions.

Since the initial separation of the economic and political spheres in early modern Europe, capital's greatest weapon has been its mobility: business can usually threaten to move if it does not receive adequate treatment from a state. The state, in sharp contrast, is tied to a territory. Ohmae and other prophets of change are right that globalization has significantly increased capital mobility so that businesses can credibly threaten to leave a country much more easily now than they could a generation ago. This mobility has increased capital's power in relation to states. In trying to manage their economies, policymakers must be actively concerned about preserving the investments they have and attracting new ones, and with business able to move relatively easily, states increasingly must compete to attract it.

Similar changes in global finance—the flow of money around the world—also have weakened the state. Most countries now allow their currencies to be traded freely. Electronic communications have made currency transactions nearly instantaneous. For a government trying to pursue sound monetary policies through control of its money supply and interest rates, this new world of global currency flow can be problematic. The collapse of many Southeast Asian economies in 1997 was caused at least in part by currency speculators, traders who purchase a country's currency not to buy goods in that country but simply to try to buy it at a low valuation and sell it later at a higher valuation. When the speculators, led by international financier George Soros, found the Southeast Asian economies were weaker than they had believed, they began to sell the currencies. This led to a classic market panic in which virtually all international traders sold those currencies, causing immense economic loss and political instability in the region and, ultimately, in developing countries worldwide. States, especially in small and poor countries, must base monetary and fiscal policy not only on domestic concerns but also on how "global markets" might react.

The rapid flow of all sorts of economic transactions across state borders has no doubt shifted the relative power of capital and the state. States do still have an important role to play; however, their power varies significantly. Political scientist

Workers sit in protest in Italy, demanding the reopening of an Alcoa (an American company) aluminum plant. Globalization has shifted manufacturing jobs around the world in particular, leading to workers in some areas losing jobs while large numbers are hired elsewhere. Those on the losing end often fight politically against the changes, reflected in this kind of protest as well as the "Brexit" vote in the United Kingdom.

Photo by Andrea Ronchini/Pacific Press/LightRocket via Getty Images

Geoffrey Garrett (1998) argued that European countries can maintain policies favoring labor unions and related groups if they provide long-term stability and predictability for business. The Great Recession raised questions about this argument, as many European governments felt the dramatic effects of international bond markets no longer having faith in them; the result was intense pressure to reduce social welfare spending and regulations protecting labor. Poor countries are in an even weaker position. Investments in Europe mostly involve hiring highly trained labor for which business is willing to pay more to ensure long-term stability. Businesses in Europe also have the advantage of the EU, a huge and wealthy market in which to sell products. El Salvador, by contrast, has none of these advantages. Investments there are in agriculture and "light manufacturing," which involve a large amount of cheap, unskilled, and easily replaceable labor. The Salvadoran government is in a significantly weaker bargaining position vis-à-vis likely international investors than is the German government.

In the new millennium, the scholarly consensus has moved away from Ohmae's view of globalization toward a more modest assessment of its effects. Certainly all of the trends described above exist, and most agree that globalization is likely to weaken the nation-state, but few now believe that globalization will destroy it. While the fundamental relationship between states and business has not been transformed into something entirely new, there has been a shift in their relative power. Any state interested in the economic well-being of its populace must negotiate the rapidly expanding global markets as well as possible, bargaining for the best "deal" for its people. Knowing how to do this effectively is not easy, as some of the case studies in this and the next chapter illustrate.

Causes of Globalization

What factors facilitated this weakening of the state vis-à-vis capital? The causes of globalization are undoubtedly multiple, but two major answers to this question have competed for attention. The first one is that technology is the driving force of globalization. The costs of communication and transportation have dropped dramatically. Air travel, once a luxury good for the elite, is now a common practice for citizens of wealthy countries. Advances in containerization and just-in-time manufacturing have allowed more rapid and efficient shipment of goods. And, as we all know, the personal computer, the mobile phone, and the Internet have created instantaneous global communications capabilities while reducing costs. All of this has allowed businesses to expand across national borders at unprecedented rates. Those arguing that globalization does represent a new era point out that this communications and transportation revolution allows transnational corporations to coordinate complex production processes for both goods and services across multiple countries in a manner that is entirely new. Shoes may be designed in Portland, Oregon, but produced in Malaysia using Bangladeshi labor and material inputs from Vietnam and China, all coordinated by "just-in-time" manufacturing to deliver just the number of shoes that are likely to sell in your local shopping mall this month.

A second school of thought argues that while technology was necessary for globalization, government policies made globalization a reality. The shift to neoliberal economic policies significantly reduced the role of most governments in regulating economic transactions, especially across their borders. The creation of the World Trade Organization (WTO) in 1995 accelerated a process, started after World War II, of lowering tariffs on imports and exports. Removing government controls on exchange rates allowed money to travel around the world without limit, seeking the best return at the least risk.

It is difficult to disentangle technological and policy changes to find a single cause of globalization. The different answers, though, have important implications. If technology is the primary cause, then globalization is inevitable and irreversible. If policies play an important role as well, then globalization may be subject to change. Both technology and policy seem crucial to the ultimate outcome, and they are interrelated. As technological change opened new areas of potential profit for international businesses, the leaders of those businesses became a source of powerful political pressure to liberalize economic policies so that they could take advantage of the new opportunities. Once policy shifted in a more liberal direction, more businesses were able to benefit from the changes, demand increased for more new technology to facilitate global communications and transportation, and the political pressure in favor of liberalized economic policies expanded that much further.

Political Responses to Globalization

The expanded global market and capital mobility also raise questions about the level at which political responses to economic problems can and should occur. As we noted above, individual states are still important, as they navigate global markets the best they can via their economic policies. More and more analysts argue, however, that new global problems require global political solutions. An obvious example is the ultimate global environmental problem: climate change. If pollution is an externality that should cause states to intervene in the market to protect the environment, then climate change is a global externality that only global agreement can remedy. Future generations, one way or another, will pay the costs of this externality that businesses and their consumers are not paying today, but no single state—even the largest and wealthiest—can solve the problem alone. Similarly, individual governments acting alone cannot solve the problem of poor states keeping their labor costs low and working conditions poor in an effort to attract foreign investment. Individual governments that change their policies will simply lose out to the competition. A uniform global policy on wages and working conditions, though extremely difficult to achieve, would be needed to reduce this competition.

As we discussed in chapter 7, many groups in civil society are not waiting for states to implement globally coordinated policies on their own. Citizens' groups are actively organizing across borders to put pressure on governments or international bodies such as the WTO, the International Monetary Fund (IMF), and the World Bank to enact global measures to address global problems. To the extent that non-governmental groups are successful, individual states may be weakened because, as citizens focus their political organization and pressure at the international level, they make individual states less relevant. Many core economic problems, including most of those discussed in this chapter, remain at the national level, however, particularly in large and wealthy countries. So while the state is weakened vis-à-vis capital, it is far from dead.

This has become particularly clear in the extended aftermath of the Great Recession. As unemployment rates remained stubbornly high, especially in Europe, and middle- and lower-class incomes stagnated, opposition to globalization grew. Growing numbers of citizens blamed trade and immigration (aspects of the reduced border controls of globalization) for their problems. This took the form of the populist, far-right parties and movements across Europe that we discussed in chapter 6, as well as the campaign of Republican presidential candidate Donald Trump in the United States. In the presidential campaign, both major candidates opposed the Trans-Pacific Partnership, the latest international agreement to further open up trade. Numerous analysts saw these trends as a political backlash against globalization. They pitted those whose education, skills, and income allowed them to benefit from globalization against those who could not benefit, and at least perceived themselves to be harmed by it. These movements focused very much on the level of the nation-state and on the most visible signs of globalization: trade and immigration.

Globalization and the European Union

"Brexit"—the vote to remove Britain from the EU—was also a part of this backlash against globalization. By voting to leave the EU, a majority of British voters asserted their sovereignty vis-à-vis a transnational entity they no longer trusted. The creation of the EU and especially of its common currency, the euro, raised fundamental questions about globalization and state sovereignty over economic policy. On the one hand, the existence of the EU could be argued to limit globalization because it creates a regional market as an alternative. On the other hand, EU member states have given up far more economic sovereignty to a transnational organization than have any other modern states.

Initially, EU member states did not yield substantial sovereignty because each state retained an effective veto over Europe-wide policies. That changed with the Single

European Act of 1987, which limited a single state's veto power; not even Germany, the biggest state, can veto decisions. Instead, several states must vote together to block a decision, which means that individual states have given up their individual sovereign right over key economic decisions. The next and biggest step was the Maastricht Treaty of 1992, which created the euro, controlled by a new European Central Bank (ECB). The seventeen states that have so far agreed to participate (the EU has twenty-seven members, but only seventeen have adopted the euro so far) gave up their ability to control their own monetary policy and agreed to limits on their fiscal policy, severely limiting their ability to set their own economic policies. The ECB controls the money supply and therefore monetary policy for these states. Crucially, however, each state continues to control its own fiscal policy; the disjuncture between monetary and fiscal policy, and limited EU power over the latter, was at the center of the "euro crisis" that began in 2009.

The Great Recession hit the EU and especially the euro extremely hard. Maintaining the limits on debt required by euro rules has always been hard, even for the healthier economies such as Germany and France. In the economic boom that preceded the crisis, several of the weaker economies ran up debts and deficits, using the strength of the euro to help them borrow money cheaply. Others, such as Spain and Ireland, had fiscal surpluses before the crisis, but the recession hit the countries' banking sector so hard that their tax revenue plummeted, creating a fiscal crisis. In some countries, such as Ireland and Cyprus, the banking sector constituted a huge share of the entire economy, setting off a severe recession when the financial crisis hit. The crisis revealed the problems created by EU control of monetary policy while fiscal policy remained at the national level and member countries' economic strength varied greatly. In 2010 private international creditors began to doubt the weaker states' ability to repay their debts and, therefore, started refusing to buy their government bonds. The worst hit were Greece and Ireland, followed by Portugal, Italy, Spain, and Cyprus. Usually, countries in this situation would allow the value of their currencies to drop to encourage exports and restart growth. This was not an option, however, because the countries use the euro and its value is tied to the strength of the entire EU. The value of the euro was not dropping fast enough to spur exports because of the continuing economic strength of the larger countries—especially Germany, which, as the strongest exporter in the region, had long been advantaged by the euro.

Without the ability to lower the value of their currencies or the willingness of the wealthier EU countries to provide bailouts, the debt-ridden governments had to institute severe fiscal policies to reduce their deficits, cutting government employment and raising taxes, which led to widespread protests. Even these measures failed to convince international creditors of the countries' economic soundness. Bailout packages funded by the ECB and IMF were put in place in 2010 for Greece and Ireland, with Greece requiring two more in 2012 and 2016. The bailouts gave those countries new funds

MAP 10.1	**The European Union**

European Union:
- Member
- Non-member
- Candidate
- Exiting

Seventeen countries in the EU have adopted the euro as their official currency: Austria, Belgium, Cyprus, Estonia, Finland, France, Germany, Greece, Ireland, Italy, Luxembourg, Malta, the Netherlands, Portugal, Slovakia, Slovenia, and Spain.

Source: Adapted from European Union (http://europa.eu/about-eu/countries/index_en.htm).

to pay their debt and reduced Greece's overall debt but required continued and more severe deficit reduction. Alternatives, such as raising taxes on banks and the wealthy across Europe to help fund the weaker governments, were proposed by groups such as trade unions but never seriously considered by the ECB or IMF (Cafruny and Talani 2013). The policies that Greece and other countries had to accept put most of the cost of recovery on them. Widespread protests turned violent in Greece and toppled the governments in Ireland and Italy. Critics contended, however, that even further measures to strengthen the union by moving toward a truly transnational fiscal policy may ultimately be needed (Cafruny and Talani 2013).

By 2013, the ECB had agreed to buy member government bonds if necessary (thereby protecting them from the worst effects of the markets) and had placed one hundred to two hundred of the largest European banks under its direct supervision to help ensure their integrity; the EU had created a permanent fund to support countries in financial crisis; and it had initiated policies to give stronger incentives to governments to stick to the official limits on their debts and deficits. All of this was an effort to reassure investors about the long-term stability of the euro. In 2015, facing popular opposition to the severe spending cuts and tax increases, the Greek prime minister called a "snap" election and a new, leftist party won on the promise of ending austerity and renegotiating the bailouts. After taking office, however, it had no choice but to negotiate a new bailout and, while still clinging to power in 2016, was widely seen as having betrayed its voters. The agreements to bail out the countries in crisis were unpopular in the wealthier countries such as Germany as well, whose citizens saw them as having to pay for the economic mistakes of other countries. The agreements still failed to resolve the worst crises in Greece, where unemployment stood at 23 percent in mid-2016 and the economy was nearly a third smaller compared to before the crisis.

For the first time since the creation of the euro, the crisis produced open discussion (especially in Greece) about whether continuing to use the common currency was wise. Critics of the EU have long opposed the fiscal and monetary policies required to join the euro, seeing them as forcing every member country to follow the neoliberal economic orthodoxy that they believe is undermining European social welfare policies. The crisis reinforced these arguments, calling into question the benefits that a single currency was supposed to provide while requiring even more unpopular fiscal policies. By 2016, Italy was leading calls to demand that the EU reduce its focus on austerity to stimulate more growth, something Germany continued to oppose.

Britain had long only partially participated in the EU. It never adopted the euro and in 2015 refused to accept new rules on fiscal policy. Nonetheless, a long-standing movement led by the right-wing UKIP (see chapter 6) called for leaving the EU entirely. This ultimately succeeded in a 2016 referendum, as "Brexit" passed with 52 percent of the vote and Britain began to prepare for the complicated process of leaving the European Union. The immediate economic effect was a large drop in the value of both the British pound and the euro. The latter, ironically, may help stimulate the weakest economies, like Greece. EU supporters, however, feared that Brexit might encourage other countries to consider leaving as well, potentially threatening the EU's bold experiment of yielding economic sovereignty to a transnational organization.

State Responses to Globalization

The biggest economic effect of globalization in the wealthy countries has been *deindustrialization*. As transportation and communication improved and neoliberal trade policies allowed industries to take advantage of lower production costs in developing countries, corporations began moving manufacturing plants out of wealthy countries and exporting products back to their home markets. Hundreds of thousands of workers, long reliant on relatively well-paying and secure jobs in such industries as automobile manufacturing and steel, faced unemployment and bleak prospects.

Two schools of thought have debated how wealthy governments should or must respond. According to the **convergence** thesis, the distinctions among different models of capitalism that we discussed above will tend to disappear as all governments are forced to conform to the logic of attracting global capital. In effect, they must pursue even more neoliberal policies. They must keep inflation low so prices are stable, which requires restraining government spending and the money supply. They must keep corporate taxes low so that businesses will want to invest, but if taxes are low, then spending must be low as well, meaning that social welfare programs also have to be cut. They must ensure that labor is flexible and relatively compliant, and they must do what they can to keep labor unions from making too many demands because rigid contracts and rules that guarantee jobs or benefits for long periods discourage investment. And, of course, they must keep tariffs and other barriers to the entry and exit of capital at a minimum.

Comparativists using the varieties of capitalism approach outlined above, on the other hand, suggest that while globalization applies pressure toward convergence, long-established political and economic institutions heavily influence how each country can and will respond, with different effects on their long-term economic well-being. Peter Hall and David Soskice (2001), who created the VOC approach, coined the term **comparative institutional advantage** to help explain how these different kinds of economies respond to the pressures of globalization. They argued that the various institutionalized relationships in each kind of economy are complementary: the institutions work together to provide greater benefits than any single institution could alone. It is difficult, they argued, to change one particular institution, such as corporate finance, without changing many others. Consequently, firms have interests in maintaining the institutions in which they operate, and they will be reluctant to change them in response to globalization. Firms in CMEs benefit from the various institutions that help them coordinate their activities, train their workers, and secure the services of employees over the long term. A more rigid labor market that does not make it as easy for workers to move from firm to firm, for instance, complements a training system in which firms invest in educating their workers for specific tasks. If workers could quickly move from job to job, the firms would lose the benefits of their investment in training. In LMEs, by contrast, more flexible labor markets give firms little incentive to train employees. Workers and the public education system therefore invest in more general skills that workers can transfer from firm to firm, meaning that firms don't have to invest directly in employee training.

convergence
Argument that globalization will force similar neoliberal policies across all countries

comparative institutional advantage
Idea in the varieties of capitalism school of thought that different kinds of capitalist systems have different institutional advantages that they usually will try to maintain, resulting in different responses to external economic pressures

FIGURE 10.1 Globalization's Effects on Economic Policies: Two Views

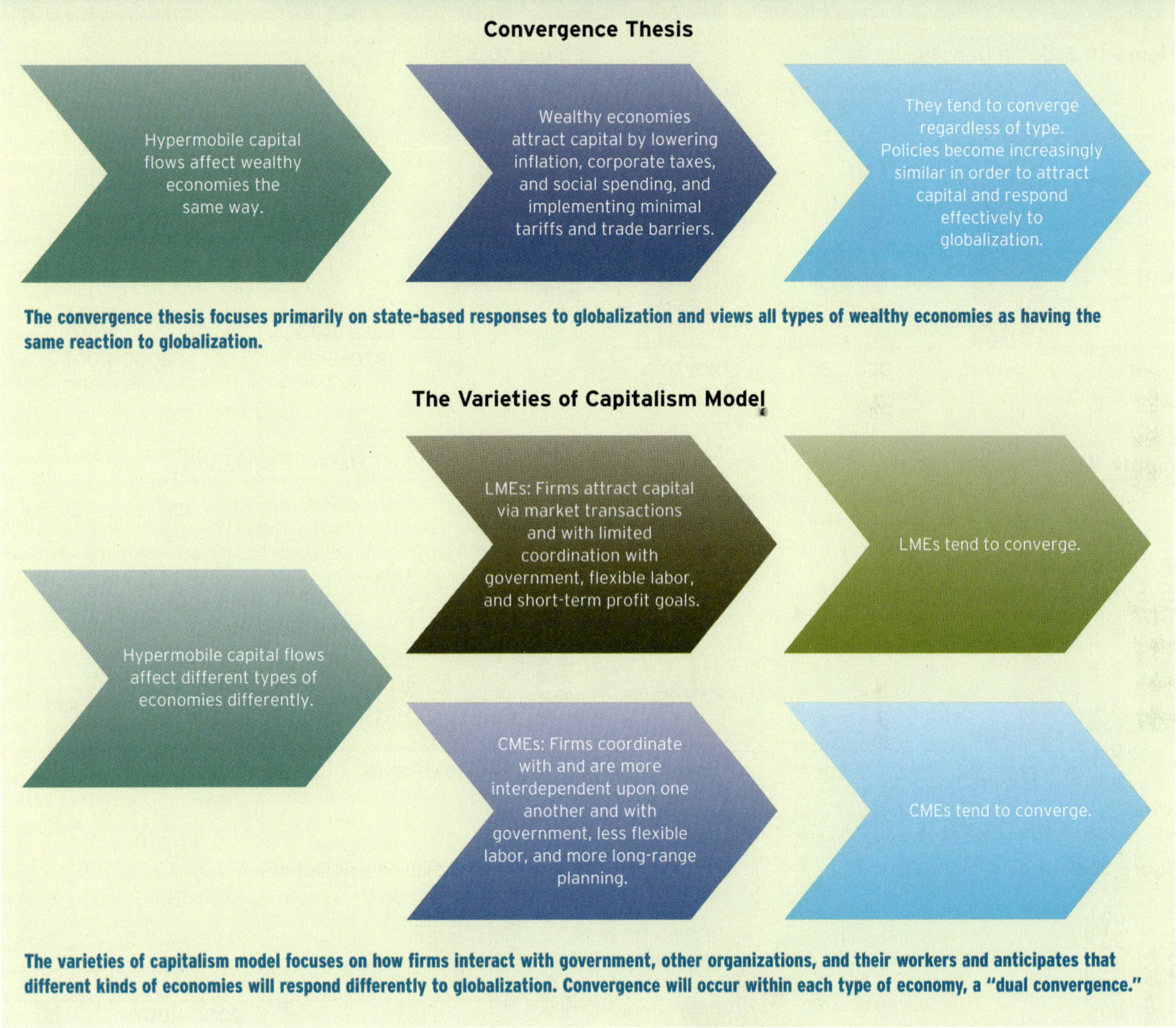

Convergence Thesis

Hypermobile capital flows affect wealthy economies the same way.

Wealthy economies attract capital by lowering inflation, corporate taxes, and social spending, and implementing minimal tariffs and trade barriers.

They tend to converge regardless of type. Policies become increasingly similar in order to attract capital and respond effectively to globalization.

The convergence thesis focuses primarily on state-based responses to globalization and views all types of wealthy economies as having the same reaction to globalization.

The Varieties of Capitalism Model

Hypermobile capital flows affect different types of economies differently.

LMEs: Firms attract capital via market transactions and with limited coordination with government, flexible labor, and short-term profit goals.

LMEs tend to converge.

CMEs: Firms coordinate with and are more interdependent upon one another and with government, less flexible labor, and more long-range planning.

CMEs tend to converge.

The varieties of capitalism model focuses on how firms interact with government, other organizations, and their workers and anticipates that different kinds of economies will respond differently to globalization. Convergence will occur within each type of economy, a "dual convergence."

The comparative institutional advantage of LMEs is in their flexible market relationships. In response to globalization, they tend to strengthen market mechanisms even more. Governments work to decrease union influence, provide broad-based education for an ever more flexible workforce, and increase the variety and efficiency of open-market sources of finance such as stock markets. Their typical majoritarian

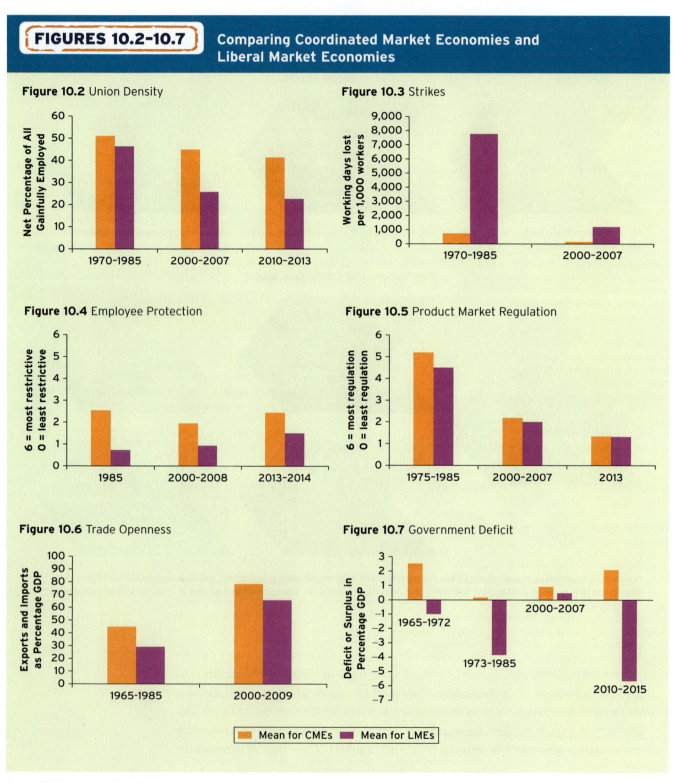

FIGURES 10.2–10.7 Comparing Coordinated Market Economies and Liberal Market Economies

Figure 10.2 Union Density

Figure 10.3 Strikes

Figure 10.4 Employee Protection

Figure 10.5 Product Market Regulation

Figure 10.6 Trade Openness

Figure 10.7 Government Deficit

Mean for CMEs   Mean for LMEs

Source: All data are from the Organisation for Economic Co-operation and Development (OECD).

democracies help ruling parties institute these changes relatively quickly. LMEs, advocates argue, are more adept at making radical innovations in response to new opportunities. Management and workers all have few reasons for caution, as their long-term futures are not tied to a specific firm.

The comparative institutional advantage of CMEs is in their ability to adjust but maintain their coordination mechanisms in response to globalization. Firms do not abandon countries with CMEs because doing so would cause them to give up the institutional advantages they have there, advantages in which they have long invested. Their consensus democracies mean that policy change is slower. CMEs are better at marginal innovation than at radical innovation because they can and must coordinate activities across a number of firms and sectors, including training workers in specific skills. Management and workers have incentives to make marginal changes to improve the performance of the firms in which they have a long-term interest. CMEs tend to be more innovative in older industries, such as pharmaceuticals, than in newer industries, such as high-tech sectors. Indeed, firms in CMEs tend to transfer their branches that engage in more radical innovations to LMEs, where they benefit from the comparative institutional advantages that LMEs offer.

Assessing whether the convergence or VOC approach best explains wealthy countries' response to globalization is complicated. Figures 10.2 to 10.7 provide a broad comparison of CMEs and LMEs over time, as globalization unfolded since the 1970s. What stands out immediately is the difference in the relationship between workers and the state in the two models. Union density (the percentage of workers who are in unions) has dropped, as would be expected in the face of globalization, but unionization remains much higher in CMEs. Strikes have always been much less frequent in CMEs, which set wages with union participation, but have dropped precipitously everywhere, again as convergence theorists might expect. Laws protecting employees in the labor market have not changed that much over time, and they actually increased in LMEs. This seems to be a convergence, but in the opposite direction of what convergence theory would expect. Convergence appears stronger in regulations on business (product market regulation) and trade openness. Finally, deficit spending has been much greater in LMEs, both before and since the Great Recession, as VOC theory would predict. Overall, CMEs and LMEs appear to remain distinct in terms of how they treat workers and fiscal policy, but they have converged substantially in terms of business regulations, openness to the global economy, and fiscal policy.

Hall and Gingerich (2009) tested the VOC approach with a series of extensive statistical techniques. They found that the patterns outlined by the approach held up empirically. Each type of economy (LME and CME) can be discerned by a set of complementary practices across a variety of statistical measures. Comparative institutional advantage holds up as well, in the sense that countries that more closely conform to one of the two models achieved higher growth rates. Countries with more mixed systems, and therefore less reinforcing comparative institutional advantages, grew more slowly. Across a variety of measures, however, they also found that most wealthy economies are moving in the direction the forces of globalization would suggest: protection of labor is down, social spending is down, and flexibility has increased. Hall and Gingerich point out, though, that the differences between LMEs and CMEs persist; while both types of economies have moved in the same direction, CMEs remain quite distinct from LMEs.

Kathleen Thelen (2014), however, argued that while coordination may be continuing, it is not necessarily resulting in the same outcomes. In particular, she noted that inequality is increasing in some CMEs but not in others. She suggested that VOC scholars have often conflated coordination and egalitarianism and that CMEs can preserve the former (as indicated by Hall and Gingerich's finding above) without the latter. Understanding the differences among CMEs requires understanding the rise of the service sector, decline of manufacturing, and entry of women into the labor force. Workers in the service sector do not require the specific skills that are needed in manufacturing but instead need more general skills. This makes coordination less crucial and more general education more important. In some CMEs, especially in Scandinavia, women were encouraged to enter the workforce early, and the extensive social welfare system created a large public sector as well. These workers did not demand, and business was not interested in providing, sector-specific skills, but they did need broad training to respond to an increasingly flexible labor market. Coordination has been reduced, but relative social equality has been maintained. In other CMEs, including our case study of Germany, women did not enter the workforce as early. As manufacturing shrank as a share of the economy, the service sector demanded more flexible labor. Service-sector workers and women were not part of the coordinated system that benefitted manufacturing and were not powerful enough to demand changes; coordination in the CME continued, but its scope shrank as it applied to fewer and fewer workers. Those workers in traditional sectors such as manufacturing continued to benefit, but workers in the newer sectors—who are disproportionately women and immigrants—did not, so inequality increased. Thus, CMEs as a group have not responded in identical ways to the forces of economic change and globalization.

Scholars have also found little evidence that CMEs and LMEs responded differently to the Great Recession. Jonas Pontusson and Damian Raess (2012) looked at fiscal policy and argued that there is no discernible difference in how major, wealthy countries responded to the Great Recession; all initially pursued Keynesian policies to stimulate the economy, then reduced those. While the amount of stimulus varied, CMEs and LMEs did not pursue distinctly different policies. Nancy Bermeo and Jonas Pontusson (2012), while not rejecting the VOC approach entirely, noted that the longer-term effects of globalization produced a narrower range of responses to the Great Recession than to prior crises. In particular, deindustrialization, the decline of labor unions, and the rise of the financial sector meant it was difficult to mobilize workers to demand protection for particular industries (the auto industry was the only exception to this), as happened in some countries in the past. While this effect was strongest in LMEs, it existed in many CMEs as well.

FIGURES 10.8–10.13   Economic Overview

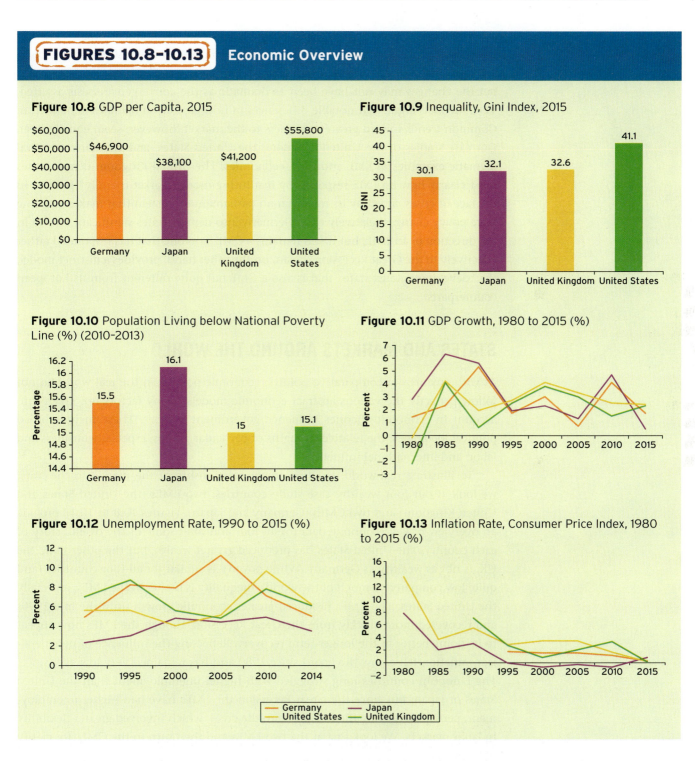

Figure 10.8 GDP per Capita, 2015

Figure 10.9 Inequality, Gini Index, 2015

Figure 10.10 Population Living below National Poverty Line (%) (2010–2013)

Figure 10.11 GDP Growth, 1980 to 2015 (%)

Figure 10.12 Unemployment Rate, 1990 to 2015 (%)

Figure 10.13 Inflation Rate, Consumer Price Index, 1980 to 2015 (%)

Sources: Figure 10.8: *CIA World Factbook*, Country Comparison: GDP per Capita, 2015 Estimates (https://www.cia.gov/library/publications/the-world-factbook/fields/2004.html#ni); Figure 10.9: World Bank, Gini Coefficients—Most Recent Measures per Country (http://data.worldbank.org/indicator/SI.POV.GINI); Figure 10.10: *CIA World Factbook*, "Population below Poverty Line" (https://www.cia.gov/library/publications/the-world-factbook/fields/2046.html#ni); Figure 10.11: World Development Indicators from World Bank, GDP Growth (annual %) (http://data.worldbank.org/indicator/NY.GDP.MKTP.KD.ZG); Figures 10.12 and 10.13: World Bank (http://databank.worldbank.org/data/reports.aspx?source=2&series=SL.UEM.TOTL.ZS&country=).

The logic of globalization seems clear. Capital's greater mobility ought to give it greater power vis-à-vis immobile states and less-mobile workers. Virtually all scholars agree that this has happened to some extent over the past thirty to forty years, but the changes may not have been as dramatic as the convergence thesis asserted. VOC theorists argue that notable differences in how capitalism operates remain clear. Common trends toward greater openness to the market, however, seem equally clear. Our case studies of the United Kingdom, the United States, and Germany are paradigmatic examples of LME and CME economies. The United Kingdom demonstrates most clearly how an LME responds by instituting more "market-friendly" policies in the face of crises, aided by its majoritarian parliamentary system that makes enacting large policy changes relatively easy. Germany also demonstrates significant reform in the direction of an LME, but it still remains a CME, and one that has responded rather effectively to the Great Recession. Japan, on the other hand, provides a distinct model, the "developmentalist state" that is also a CME but quite different from its European counterparts.

STATES AND MARKETS AROUND THE WORLD

As with any area of comparative politics, economic policies in the real world do not follow perfectly the various abstract economic models. Many factors not taken into account in economic theories influence government policies. These include broad political ideologies; the relative strengths of particular groups, especially business and labor; and international influences.

To illustrate real-world variation in the relationship of the market to the state, we look at our four wealthy case study countries: two LMEs (the United States and United Kingdom) and two CMEs (Germany and Japan). Figures 10.8 to 10.13 provide an overview of key economic data for all four and offer some of the overall story of each country. The United States has produced greater wealth, but the other LME, the UK, is not as wealthy as Germany. While poverty is similar for all four countries (and quite low compared to much of the world), inequality is higher in the LMEs, especially the United States. The CMEs produced greater economic growth until the mid-1990s and recovered more quickly from the Great Recession, though the LMEs now appear to be doing better in the longer-term recovery. Reflecting the influence of neoliberalism, inflation fell across the board since 1980 and has remained very low ever since. The European countries long struggled with higher unemployment than the United States or Japan, but since the Great Recession the LMEs have had higher unemployment, perhaps reflecting their response to the crisis, which involved greater flexibility in labor markets. We look first at the two LMEs and then turn to the CMEs for clarity of comparison.

THE UNITED STATES: THE FREE-MARKET MODEL

CASE SYNOPSIS

The United States has long been the greatest exemplar of the free-market, or *laissez-faire*, model of economic development and capitalism, a classic LME. Not until the Great Depression and the New Deal of the 1930s did the government begin to attempt to guide the economy to increase growth and employment and to redistribute income. From the New Deal through the 1960s, the government more or less followed Keynesian policies. As predicted by the LME model, though, in the face of globalization it pursued strong, neoliberal policies starting in the 1980s. Its neoliberalism came into question, though, with the start of the Great Recession. Indeed, it responded initially to the recession with a stronger Keynesian stimulus than most countries, but reduced that rapidly. While it has produced great wealth, the American LME has also produced a dramatic increase in inequality while leaving middle-class incomes stagnant. By 2016, this seemed to cause a growing political backlash.

- **ECONOMIC MODEL LME**

- **ECONOMIC MILESTONES** Great Depression and New Deal; 1980s shift to neoliberalism

- **GLOBALIZATION EFFECTS** Manufacturing job loss; financial sector gain; growing inequality

- **RESPONSE TO GREAT RECESSION** Keynesian stimulus followed by neoliberalism again; slow but better recovery than most countries

The 2008–2009 "Great Recession" that began in the United States shook the foundations of the leading economic model in the world and led the government under newly elected president Barack Obama to engage in the largest Keynesian deficit spending in a generation to stimulate the economy. By the 2012 election, a fundamental debate over the proper role of government in the economy became the centerpiece of the campaign. The Republican Party, long a champion of limited government intervention, followed neoliberal theory in insisting on reduced government deficits, which would require massive spending cuts rather than tax increases because greater taxes would hurt business and therefore growth. Democrats countered with a Keynesian argument that in a recession the government needed to help stimulate the economy in the short term and worry about deficit reduction only after growth is well underway. By the 2016 presidential campaign, the debate had shifted even more broadly, to the benefits of globalization amid growing demands for restricting its effects.

The modern U.S. economy emerged in the late nineteenth and early twentieth centuries as rapid industrialization transformed the country from a primarily agricultural and rural society into a rapidly growing urban and industrial economy. With industrialization also came the rise of labor unions. The government actively and often violently opposed the increasingly frequent strikes in the late nineteenth and early twentieth centuries but by the 1930s acquiesced and accepted the presence of unions. The government's nearly complete lack of involvement in the economy up to that point had to change. Its initial policies, however, were aimed primarily at ensuring that the market would remain as free as possible by eliminating or regulating monopoly control of key sectors of the economy. This started with regulation of the railways and then expanded with the landmark Sherman Antitrust Act of 1890. In 1913 it addressed other crucial needs of a modern economy, creating both the nation's first central bank, the Federal Reserve (the "Fed"), and the income and corporate tax systems. The Fed, modeled after the British and German central banks, was given a monopoly on printing legal currency and charged with regulating the nation's money supply. Since industry had come to generate the bulk of the nation's wealth and employment, the government began taxing business profits and personal incomes to provide a stronger revenue stream.

The Great Depression, which produced 25 percent unemployment at its peak in 1933, shook the foundations of the nation's belief in the free market. During this

A supporter waits to hear Republican presidential candidate Donald Trump speak during the 2016 campaign. Trump based his campaign heavily on opposition to two key components of globalization in the United States: immigration and trade. He promised to renegotiate major trade deals in order to bring back the many manufacturing jobs that had left places like Ohio over the last decades.

(Phil Masturzo/Akron Beacon Journal/TNS via Getty Images)

time of rapidly rising union membership and radical political demands, Franklin Roosevelt won the presidency in 1932 with a promise of a "new deal." The fruition of this promise was an ambitious program of unprecedented government spending on public works projects that employed large numbers of workers to improve the nation's infrastructure. It also created a federally mandated eight-hour workday, collective bargaining rights for workers, a minimum wage, protection against unfair labor practices, federal subsidies for farmers, a pension plan for the elderly (Social Security), and federal income support for poor single mothers. With government acquiescence, union membership doubled between 1925 and 1941, reaching its peak in the 1960s.

Central Banks

A central bank or some other monetary authority is a crucial institution of economic policy. Many central banks were started in part to create a unified national currency. In most wealthy countries today, central banks are independent institutions, supposedly free of political influence, that establish currency stability and monetary policy. The U.S. Federal Reserve System was a relative latecomer among wealthy countries at establishing a central bank, as the timeline demonstrates.

The New Deal era was one of unprecedented growth in government involvement in the economy, a period of Keynesian economic policy in which the government actively worked to improve economic growth and expand employment. In the 1960s, Lyndon Johnson's administration initiated the "Great Society" to complete the goals of the New Deal. The pillars of this effort were the creation of Medicare, medical insurance for Social Security recipients; Aid to Families with Dependent Children (AFDC), a much-expanded welfare program for poor mothers; and Medicaid, health care for AFDC and other welfare recipients. These programs, along with the earlier Social Security system, helped reduce poverty from 25 percent of the population in 1955 to 11 percent by 1973. However, slower economic growth and waning political support subsequently led the government to reduce the real value of these antipoverty programs, contributing to a rise in the poverty rate to around 14 percent by the 1990s.

Sustained economic growth and Keynesian policies continued through the mid-1960s. By the late 1960s, continued deficit spending caused by the cost of the Vietnam War and the Great Society programs helped produce rising inflation. The quadrupling of world oil prices in 1973 further slowed economic growth and spurred more inflation, producing "stagflation" by the late 1970s that the government seemed incapable of reversing. Ronald Reagan won the presidency in 1980 on a platform that emphasized the need to reduce the size and scope of government by embracing neoliberalism's prescriptions for reduced government spending, accepting a "natural rate of unemployment," and freeing the market to restart growth. Reagan deregulated industry; reduced the power and reach of unions, whose membership had been declining throughout the 1970s; cut spending on social programs; and cut taxes to spur economic growth. At the same time, the Federal Reserve embraced neoliberal policies, raising interest rates and reining in the money supply to reduce inflation. Although the tax cuts resulted in unintended government deficits, the 1980s as a whole saw a reversal of the Keynesian effort of the New Deal–Great Society period, marking the most dramatic shift in economic policy since the 1930s. Neoliberalism continued to be the accepted economic theory through the 1980s and 1990s: the U.S. government removed most of the restrictive New Deal–era regulations on banking, and by the mid-1990s had produced a budget surplus.

After a brief recession in 1981–1983, the economy expanded nearly continuously from 1983 to 2000, though growth slowed in the new millennium. The era also saw greater economic inequality and poverty. The Gini index, an overall measure of inequality, was at about 37 in the United States in the late 1940s. It dropped (meaning greater equality) to 35 by the late 1960s, but by 1994 it had risen to 41, where it has remained ever since. As the Country and Concept table (page 525) shows, this is a much higher level of inequality than in other wealthy countries. In the late 1960s, the wealthiest fifth of the U.S. population had 40.6 percent of all income; by 2001, that figure had risen to 49.6 percent. The poorest fifth's share of income, on the other hand, dropped from 5.6 percent to 3.5 percent. The ratio of wages between the wealthiest and poorest 10 percent of full-time workers had been relatively high in the United States in the 1970s, but by the 2000s it had jumped from 3.8 to 4.8, by far the highest of any wealthy country.

The Great Recession seems to have expanded inequality further. The richest 1 percent of all Americans "captured about 95 percent of the income gains since the recession ended," giving them about 20 percent of total income—one of the highest levels ever recorded (Lowrey 2013). From 1980 to 2011, the wealthiest 1 percent of the population saw its incomes increase an average of 115 percent, while the fiftieth percentile (the middle of the income distribution) saw its incomes increase by only an average of 11 percent. Until the Great Recession, growth and consumption remained high in spite of growing inequality and stagnant incomes for the lower half of the population because debt expanded rapidly; as housing prices rose, consumers believed they had great wealth and willingly went into debt, stimulating the economy. Unfortunately, the bottom fell out of the housing market starting in 2007.

When the Wall Street firm Lehman Brothers went bankrupt in September 2008, a full-scale financial crisis began. Banks virtually ceased all lending for several months, afraid that any loans they made would not be repaid. At the same time, the slump in housing prices led to foreclosures of high-risk mortgages, which in turn caused a rapid drop in the values of investments based on those mortgages. Without access to credit, businesses could not invest and began firing workers. The nation's GDP plunged 8.4 percent in the second half of 2009, and unemployment rose from 4.9 to 10 percent by the end of the year.

In response to Lehman Brothers' collapse, the George W. Bush administration and Congress created the Troubled Asset Relief Program (TARP), under which the government agreed to purchase or guarantee bank-owned investments tied to the plummeting housing market in exchange for a substantial share of the banks' stock. The government, in effect, became a substantial owner of a number of American banks. The new Obama administration in 2009 implemented more "bailouts," as they came to be known, this time for the troubled auto industry. While the credit market remained very weak until the middle of the year, ultimately credit began to flow again, and the economy began to recover by the end of 2009. In spite of fears that the taxpayers would never get their money back, most major banks and auto companies repaid the government, repurchasing government-owned stock by mid-2010. The Obama administration also pushed through Congress an unprecedented stimulus plan of $787 billion in early 2009 in a clear attempt to use Keynesian policy to "jump-start" the economy. Simultaneously, the Federal Reserve reduced interest rates to nearly zero, where they stayed through 2016.

In late 2010, continued high unemployment led both Congress and the Federal Reserve to take further stimulus measures. First, the Federal Reserve announced a policy of "quantitative easing," essentially printing new money and using it to buy $600 billion of U.S. Treasury bonds, thus effectively pumping that amount of money into the economy via the banking system. At the end of the year, the Obama administration and Congress compromised on a tax bill that preserved tax cuts that had been passed a decade earlier, reduced Social Security taxes for 2011, and extended unemployment benefits. The president and Congress paid for all of this by expanding the deficit in classic Keynesian style.

Even though the American stimulus packages were significantly larger than any in Europe, many Keynesian economists believed they did not go far enough. Edward Ashbee (2014) notes that the Obama administration initially planned on a larger package but reduced it to gain support of Republicans in Congress; the veto players in the U.S. political system made modest policy response essential. By 2011, arguments against further stimulus gained strength as the recovery remained lethargic. The newly elected Republicans in the House of Representatives set out to reduce budget deficits substantially in 2011, locking horns with Democrats who still controlled the Senate and with President Obama; implicitly, this was a classic battle over which economic theory to pursue. A compromise raised taxes on the wealthiest 1 percent

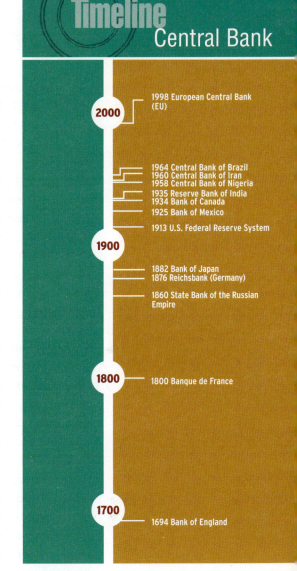

Timeline
Central Bank

1998 European Central Bank (EU)
2000

1964 Central Bank of Brazil
1960 Central Bank of Iran
1958 Central Bank of Nigeria
1935 Reserve Bank of India
1934 Bank of Canada
1925 Bank of Mexico

1913 U.S. Federal Reserve System

1900

1882 Bank of Japan
1876 Reichsbank (Germany)

1860 State Bank of the Russian Empire

1800   1800 Banque de France

1700   1694 Bank of England

of the population but also imposed across-the-board cuts to federal spending starting in 2013. By 2015, the federal deficit was half of what it had been in 2012. Moody Analytics and several other private-sector economic analysts argued that the spending cuts would reduce economic growth by 1.2 percent and keep unemployment about 0.5 percent higher than it would have been without the cuts (Calmes and Weisman 2013).

The economic recovery, which saw the stock market rise dramatically from its low point in March 2009, did not provide much relief for the average person until 2016. The bailout of the banks, widespread publicity about bank managers' high bonuses in spite of the recession, and the continuing high unemployment rates and stagnant incomes left many Americans angry that the government seemed to have saved Wall Street but ignored "Main Street." This sentiment helped produce both the Occupy and Tea Party movements we discussed in chapter 7 and demands for a large increase in the minimum wage, the real value of which had fallen since the late 1960s. The recovery finally seemed to start improving people's lives only in 2015. Unemployment dropped slowly after the recession, and finally went below 5 percent in 2016. Median household income rose 5.2 percent in 2015, the first increase since 2007, and poverty dropped to 13.5 percent (from 14.8 in 2014). Inflation remained low, which prevented the Federal Reserve from increasing interest rates from their historically low levels.

With the worst of the recession over (at least in the financial and housing sectors) by 2010, the U.S. government turned its attention to measures designed to prevent future crises. After the Great Depression, the government had regulated banks rather strictly, treating commercial banks that people use on a daily basis differently than investment banks on Wall Street. In the 1990s, however, President Bill Clinton and a Republican-dominated Congress, influenced by neoliberal arguments, lifted many of those restrictions. Simultaneously, investment bankers created new kinds of investments that the government regulated only lightly or not at all, including derivatives like the credit default swaps that would be part of the 2008–2009 financial crisis.

In the aftermath of the Great Recession, few economists or policymakers repudiated neoliberal policies entirely, but many argued that the crisis had demonstrated the need for more regulation of the financial sector. Some wanted to prevent banks from getting "too big to fail," others wanted to re-create the earlier separation of commercial and investment banks, and still others simply argued that the investment products themselves needed closer government regulation. As is the case when monopolies arise, the state's interest in preserving a healthy and growing capitalist economy may require it to enact policies against the immediate interests of particular capitalists—in this case, major investment banks whose unchecked search for profits seemed to threaten the stability of the system as a whole. In July 2010, Congress passed and President Obama signed the largest financial regulatory bill since World War II. While it neither fully returned banks to the pre-1980s regulations nor limited their size, it did the following: institute regulation of the derivatives markets; establish a council to monitor the largest banks (those considered "too big to fail"); institute regulations to ensure that if such banks did fail, their stockholders—rather than tax-payers—would pay the costs; and restrict banks from making speculative investments with their own money. By 2015, only about three-quarters of the necessary regulations had been implemented, however, in part due to the finance industry's active opposition to many of them. Debate continued among Keynesians who thought the act would succeed in applying reasonable regulations, others who feared it was too little to matter, and neoliberals who argued it would strangle the growth potential of the finance industry.

In spite of the signs of improvement in the economy, the 2016 presidential campaign featured major debates over economic policy. Growing inequality helped fuel the populist presidential campaigns of Bernie Sanders and Donald Trump. The Republican Party had long been the champion of neoliberal ideas to give businesses incentives to invest, while Democrats were generally more willing to engage in Keynesian policies to stimulate demand by increasing employment and wages directly. The 2016 campaign, though, showed that the perceived effects of globalization may well be reorienting the economic debate. Republican candidate Donald Trump championed a dramatic reduction in two key areas of globalization, trade and immigration, promising to "tear up" trade agreements in order to restore manufacturing jobs lost to developing countries, China in particular. He also promised to preserve and expand government spending, especially on the military, without raising taxes, a difficult feat. Democrat Hillary Clinton, while still championing Keynesian expansion, was much more sympathetic to continued openness to the global economy. Among white voters, she gained the support of the majority of those with a college education while Trump won heavily among those without a college degree. Analysts increasingly saw this as a battle between those who had the education and skills to benefit from globalization and those who didn't.

CASE Questions

1. The United States has shifted economic policy between neoliberalism and Keynesianism several times. Overall, which seems to be the most effective policy option, and why?
2. While the United States has long championed the "free-market model," the government has in fact intervened in the market in various ways. What are the main impetuses behind those interventions? Are they primarily essential, beneficial, or politically generated interventions?
3. How does the United States demonstrate the classic elements of an LME, how does it differ from the LME model, and why?

CASE Study

UNITED KINGDOM: RADICAL REFORM IN A LIBERAL MARKET ECONOMY

CASE SYNOPSIS

The United Kingdom, like the United States, is a classic example of an LME. Prior to the 1980s, however, it had exceptionally large and active trade unions, and since World War II has had a far more extensive welfare state than the United States. Nonetheless, twice in the last generation, the UK has pursued some of the most radical neoliberal reforms of any major Western country, first in the 1980s under Prime Minister Margaret Thatcher and again beginning in 2010 under newly elected prime minister David Cameron. The first reforms reduced the power of unions, privatized state-owned companies, and cut government spending and debt to encourage new investment. Thatcher's reforms resulted in a more flexible labor market with more competitive wages in which a higher percentage of employees worked at part-time jobs and far fewer were unionized. The initial result was a booming economy accompanied by growing inequality, but one that was highly exposed to the very global markets most severely affected by the financial crisis of 2008–2009. The second reforms under Cameron in 2010 dramatically cut the budget in response to the crisis. In 2016 Britain began a third, bold experiment when it voted for "Brexit," promising to leave the EU within two years.

- TYPE OF ECONOMY LME

- ECONOMIC MILESTONES Postwar consensus and Keynesian policies; entry into the EU; radical neoliberalism in 1980s; "Brexit"—leaving the EU

- GLOBALIZATION EFFECTS Manufacturing job loss; financial sector gain; integration with EU

- RESPONSE TO GREAT RECESSION First stimulus under Labour government, then austerity under Conservative government; very little recovery

The United Kingdom is an LME like the United States, but from World War II to the 1970s, the government was significantly more prominent in Britain. This was largely due to the influence of the union-led Labour Party. Prior to World War II, the UK was a more typical LME. The Bank of England, the second-oldest central bank in the world and the one after which most others are modeled, was privately owned even though it had control over currency, until it was nationalized by the Labour government after World War II. In the 1940s, and following its long-held belief that the largest industries should be publicly owned and therefore work for the benefit of the people rather than solely profits, the Labour government nationalized several major industries in addition to the central bank, such as airlines, mining, automobile

British commuters in the City of London, Britain's financial district. Under the country's LME, London's financial sector is second only to New York's. The "Brexit" vote to leave the EU in 2016, though, threatened that success. A number of large banks were considering moving to somewhere in Continental Europe to stay within the EU.

Richard Baker / In Pictures via Getty Images

manufacturing, and telephone service. Simultaneously, it created the National Health Service (see chapter 12) and built government-owned housing for millions of working-class people. All of this was in keeping with the party's platform and gained popular support after the war out of a sense of shared sacrifice in the war effort; most citizens believed the country needed a less class-based, more egalitarian society.

A strong economy in the global boom after World War II fell apart in the 1970s, a period of unparalleled economic crisis in the United Kingdom. Rising oil prices and global recession hit the country particularly hard, reducing growth and increasing inflation. Both the Conservative and Labour governments tried but failed to improve the economy. As inflation grew, unions demanded that wage increases keep up, which fueled more inflation. About half of the British labor force belonged to a union, an unusually high level even by European standards. The government tried voluntary agreements like those common in a corporatist system to get unions to restrain their demands and thereby slow inflation. Unfortunately, the peak labor association, the Trade Unions Congress (TUC), did not have the power over its members that unions in corporatist systems do, and local unions repeatedly ignored the voluntary restraints negotiated by the TUC leadership. In an LME such as the United Kingdom, neither unions nor businesses have a history of or an incentive to negotiate lasting agreements to moderate wage increases, so the result was a growing number of strikes. These culminated in the "winter of discontent" in 1978–1979, when the Labour government lost control and massive strikes occurred.

Out of this crisis rose a new, neoliberal manifestation of the Conservative Party, which Thatcher led to victory in the 1979 election. She won on promises of implementing a completely new approach to economic policy, unions, and the welfare state, along the same lines as the approach adopted by Ronald Reagan, who was elected U.S. president a year later. Her first target was the power of unions, which she sought to reduce to create a more flexible labor force, in line with the LME model. She passed legislation that made it far more difficult for unions to strike and reduced their organizational power. By 1995, union membership had dropped from half of all employees when Thatcher was elected to only a third. As the LME model suggests, when facing global economic pressure, LMEs look to reduce labor costs and increase flexibility to compete more effectively. This is precisely what Thatcher did.

The second area of major reform under Thatcher was privatization of state-owned companies. Many of these were far from profitable when Thatcher took power. She began selling off the state-owned companies to private investors, ultimately privatizing 120 corporations. Some became profitable private-sector companies; others simply went bankrupt. One immediate effect was increased unemployment as the unprofitable companies laid off workers in large numbers; unemployment rose from an average of 4.2 percent in the late 1970s to 9.5 percent in the 1980s (Huber and Stephens 2001, A11). She also privatized a great deal of Britain's publicly owned housing for the working class, selling much of it to the tenants.

In the early 1980s, Thatcher's neoliberal government successfully reduced inflation by reducing the money supply and budget deficit. This deepened the ongoing recession but made clear that fighting inflation was her top priority. She also shifted the source of taxation, reducing individual and corporate income taxes and compensating by raising Britain's national sales tax (the value-added tax, or VAT). The net result was an increased tax burden on lower-income groups and a lower burden on the wealthy. She was less successful in changing fiscal policy, failing to reduce significantly the overall size of the government's budget and social spending.

Despite the fact that social spending did not drop, inequality increased more in Britain under Thatcher than in any other wealthy country: the share of the population living on less than half of the average national income increased from 9 to 25 percent under Thatcher and has since dropped only slightly (Ginsburg 2001, 186). Regional inequality increased a great deal as well. Many of the unprofitable state-owned companies and older manufacturing firms were in the northern half of the country. Deindustrialization combined with Thatcher's reforms to hurt that region severely, causing increased unemployment and poverty, while the southern part of the country, especially London, became one of the wealthiest regions in Europe.

Thatcher's reforms reshaped the British economy by making it a purer LME. The reforms were particularly dramatic not only because of the crisis the country faced at the time but also because Britain's majoritarian parliamentary system allows a government great power to reorient policy. The comparison with Ronald Reagan in the United States is interesting in this regard. While Reagan reoriented American economic policy in a neoliberal direction, his changes were not nearly as sweeping as Thatcher's reforms. The U.S. presidential system, with Democrats controlling Congress for most of his presidency and a federal system that reserves considerable power for the states, limited what Reagan could accomplish.

Subsequent British governments have not fundamentally changed Thatcher's policies. The Labour government (1997–2010) took its most dramatic action immediately after coming into office: it gave autonomy to the Bank of England to set monetary policy, much as the Federal Reserve does in the United States. In the past, the PM and the cabinet had controlled monetary policy, so giving the bank autonomy clearly signaled that the new Labour government would value macroeconomic stability at least as much as its Conservative predecessors. The Labour government presided over a period of unprecedented economic well-being until the financial crisis of 2008–2009. GDP growth, averaging 2.6 percent annually, was well above that of other European countries; inflation averaged only 1.5 percent; the deficit was kept low; and Britain was the favored location for foreign investment in Europe (Faucher-King and Le Galès 2010). After 2002, the government invested more heavily in education and job training in a successful effort to lower the unemployment rate, which dropped to only 5.5 percent. A successful anti-child-poverty policy removed over one million children from poverty between 2005 and 2007, though overall inequality was reduced only slightly. Labour, however, did not reverse the policies that had weakened trade unions or the basic neoliberal orientation of British macroeconomic policy, thus preserving the fundamentals of the British LME.

The exceptional British economic success up to 2007 was based in part on growing financial, stock, and real estate markets, all of which were heavily hit by the global financial crisis. The economy shrank nearly 5 percent in 2009, and unemployment hit 8 percent (up from 4.5 percent a couple of years earlier). As in most Western economies, sluggish growth resumed in 2010, though unemployment dropped only slightly. Gordon Brown's Labour government initially responded similarly to the U.S. government, first with large infusions of cash to ailing banks and then with a stimulus program, primarily via tax cuts, that dramatically increased the government deficit. The failure of these measures in the short term led to a Labour route in the May 2010 election, which brought an unusual Conservative-led coalition government to power (see chapter 6). The new government quickly reversed course on economic policy, arguing that the government's growing debt threatened to undermine Britain's financial standing in the global economy, as was happening to both Greece and Ireland. The government's first budget instituted draconian cuts in spending, averaging 19 percent. The goal was to reduce the budget deficit from 11 percent of GDP in 2010 to under 3 percent in 2015. While not completely successful, by 2015 the deficit was down to just over 4 percent of GDP. The government also raised the retirement age, required those on long-term unemployment benefits to seek work actively, and capped those benefits at one year. Protests erupted several times after the announcement of the new budget, primarily among university students reacting against major tuition increases. The only sectors spared the ax were the National Health Service (see chapter 12) and primary and secondary education. A year later, though, the government increased austerity further, including raising the value-added tax—the biggest tax average citizens pay—to reduce the deficit.

While the government pursued austerity, the central bank pursued expansion, dropping interest rates all the way to 0.5 percent and using "quantitative easing," as the Fed did in the United States, to pump money into the economy. Though the economy slipped into a second recession in 2012, by 2014 growth was up to about 3 percent and in 2016 unemployment was down to 5 percent. With inflation still just above zero, the central bank did not change its policies, until the "Brexit" vote to leave the EU. The immediate response to the vote was a rapid drop in the value of the British pound, which hit a thirty-year low. Forecasts predicted growth dropping to about 1.5 percent for 2016, with further drops in the following years. In response, the central bank lowered interest rates to 0.25 percent, with speculation it would go even lower. The new Conservative government that took over after the "Brexit" vote immediately declared it would increase government spending on infrastructure, recognizing that continued fiscal austerity could not be sustained. Longer-term fears over "Brexit" were that the vast financial sector (London is second only to New York in global banking) would shrink as banks shifted their activities to countries within the EU and that Britain's extensive trade with the rest of Europe would drop significantly as well. The extent to which these long-term trends would come to fruition would depend very much on the lengthy negotiations that must occur between Britain and the EU over the details of "Brexit."

CASE Questions

1. Britain provides one of the most dramatic examples of reform in an LME. Overall, does its experience suggest the LME model is a viable path to negotiate the globalized economy?
2. Why did Britain decide to pursue an austerity policy, reducing its government budget deficit, after the Great Recession? Does this fit with the LME model, and what are the implications of it for Britain's recovery?
3. Britain's majoritarian democracy allows ruling parties to implement policies pretty much as they please, at least in the short run. Has this been beneficial or harmful to the country's economic well-being?

CASE Study

GERMANY: STRUGGLING TO REFORM A COORDINATED MARKET ECONOMY

Over the course of the twentieth century, Germany created a much-admired model of regulated capitalism known as the social market economy, its particular version of a CME. This model combined a highly productive market economy that became the world's leading industrial exporter with an extensive and generous welfare state, as

CASE SYNOPSIS

well as unusually active involvement of both business and labor associations in setting and implementing economic policy. It was termed the economy of "high everything"—high productivity, high-quality goods, high wages, high taxes, high benefits. Globalization raised significant questions about the viability of the social market economy, though, as Germany faced high unemployment in the 1990s and early years of the new millennium, much slower economic growth, difficulty financing its generous social welfare benefits, and trouble maintaining the strict limits on deficit spending that the euro requires. These problems forced reforms that liberalized both finance and labor. They reduced wages, social welfare benefits, and workers' bargaining positions. While it was hit heavily by the recession of 2008–2009, it recovered more quickly than many countries. Some analysts were once again talking about a "German miracle" because, despite a large drop in GDP, unemployment went up only slightly during the recession. This left it the strongest economy in Europe, and playing a central role in trying to resolve the financial crisis affecting the weaker economies within the "euro zone." While German policies have clearly moved in the direction of the LME model, the question is how fundamental these changes are. Cox (2002) argued that most reforms have been "tinkering" rather than "transformative," but Streeck (2009) suggested that the cumulative changes across an array of economic sectors demonstrate that fundamental changes are in process.

- TYPE OF ECONOMY CME
- ECONOMIC MILESTONES Reunification; growing unemployment; costs of social spending
- GLOBALIZATION EFFECTS Neoliberal reforms
- RESPONSE TO GREAT RECESSION Relatively successful, continuing problems of large debt and aging population

T he modern German economy first developed under Otto von Bismarck in the 1860s and 1870s. Bismarck set out to build German national strength via economic growth, so he pursued policies that protected industry and produced rapid industrialization and urbanization to catch up with early industrializers like Britain and France. This came at the expense of workers, who faced horrific working conditions, social dislocation in the expanding cities, and low wages. These conditions helped produce the Social Democratic Party (SDP) in 1875 to work for socialism via nonviolent means. Bismarck, worried about the socialist threat, committed the state to some beneficial and politically generated market roles. He created extensive (for its time) social policy for workers while simultaneously outlawing socialist parties and labor unions. The new policies included the world's first national health insurance system, accident insurance, and old-age and widows' pensions subsidized by the federal government.

After Germany's loss in World War I the influence of labor unions increased rapidly as their numbers increased, and by the mid-1920s, employers had agreed to establish an eight-hour workday and a forty-eight-hour workweek. Social expenditures leapt from 19 percent of government spending in 1919 to 40 percent by 1930, and wages rose as employers and unions agreed to mandatory collective bargaining (Crew 1998). Adolf Hitler interrupted this process, but after his defeat, the new government of West Germany extended the social welfare system again. The Christian Democratic Union (CDU) under Konrad Adenauer governed West Germany from its first election in 1949 until 1966. Though a "conservative" party, the CDU officially coined the term **social market economy** and fully developed the model. Christian Democrats generally saw protection of workers as part of their Christian ideology. The SDP often wanted social spending to expand even more rapidly, but both major parties agreed with the basic premises of the system. The social market economy created a form of capitalism in which close relationships and interpenetration between the private and public sectors have shaped economic and social policies, creating a classic CME.

Unions were crucial in negotiating binding wage agreements with employers' associations, which all employers in a given sector had to follow. Unions are also represented on the supervisory boards of all German firms with more than two thousand employees. This system, known as *codetermination*, was created in 1976 and gives unions power to influence employers' policies. Codetermination creates an element of democracy within the management of business enterprises, though ultimately businesses are still privately owned and must answer to their stockholders and lenders, as in any other capitalist economy.

This economic model made West Germany one of the most successful economies in the world from the end of World War II until the 1980s. All of this began to change, however, with the end of the Cold War and the acceleration of globalization, as can be seen in Figure 10.8 (page 551). Reunification required the economic absorption of the much poorer East Germany into the social market economy. Privatization of formerly government-owned industries in East Germany created massive unemployment. West Germans had to fund huge social programs, infrastructure construction, and job training programs as they worked to integrate the eastern economy into the western. The biggest single problem resulting from this was unemployment, which had hovered around 1 percent for decades in West Germany but hit nearly 12 percent in reunified Germany by 1998 and stayed as high as 9 percent through 2005.

As these internal changes were occurring, Germany was also feeling the effects of globalization. The biggest impact in Germany's CME has been in corporate finance. Following the CME model, German banks, rather than the stock market, long provided the bulk of corporate finance. With the rise of new global financial opportunities, large German businesses and the German government have pushed for financial reform, including legal reforms to open the stock market up to global investors and the listing of German firms on global markets. Manufacturers have looked to

social market economy
In Germany, a postwar economic system that combines a highly productive market economy with an extensive and generous welfare state, as well as unusually active involvement of both business and labor in economic policy

these changes as providing new sources of finance, and banks see them as new areas of profit. The net effect from 1996 to 2002 was a reduction of over 50 percent in the share of firms' capital that was controlled by the banks that lent them money (Streeck 2009, 80). This means that German firms, like firms in LMEs, have had to become more concerned about anonymous shareholders' short-term interests in profits. Codetermination, unions' participation in corporate management, still exists, but it has been reduced significantly due to increased concern for shareholders' short-term returns.

For banks, globalization provided new profit opportunities but exposure to high risk as well. German banks began investing heavily in securities, including mortgage-backed securities and derivatives based on the risky U.S. mortgages that were the source of the Great Recession. These investments provided significant profits, but the banks suffered severe losses when the bubble burst in 2008. The German government responded by creating a fund that troubled banks could voluntarily draw on, as well as essentially nationalizing the banks in the worst trouble. The government subsequently passed legislation that tightened up regulations to limit the practices that had gotten the banks into trouble in the first place and to increase the assets that banks were required to keep on hand in case of a crisis (Hardie and Howarth 2009).

Globalization has also affected wages and collective bargaining between employers and unions in Germany, though key elements of neocorporatism remain and have helped Germany weather the Great Recession relatively well. Germany's neocorporatist model was always based on peak associations of employers and unions being able to make and stick to wage agreements. Globalization, though, has created divisions among German companies. The largest manufacturing companies have created globally linked production processes that are very sensitive to disruption. Because

A truck moves a container at the port in Duisburg, Germany. Germany's CME has long been one of the world's leading exporters. Since the Great Recession, the country has become more dependent on exports than it was before, a cause for concern should there be another global downturn.

Krisztian Bocsi/Bloomberg via Getty Images

of this, they have become more willing to agree to high wages to avoid strikes or lockouts and have defended continued coordination with unions. Smaller businesses, especially in the service sector, cannot afford these higher wages, and they increasingly ignore agreements set between unions and the largest employers. Unions respond with more strikes at the local level against the smaller firms. Simultaneously, changes in labor laws encouraged more temporary, low-paid workers, whose share of the workforce increased substantially. The result has been a fragmentation of the neocorporatist agreements that used to govern wages. In 1995 some 53 percent of all workplaces had wage agreements negotiated by industry-wide collective bargaining; by 2006, this number had dropped to 37 percent (Streeck 2009, 39; Streeck and Hassel 2003, 112). Greater flexibility has also allowed firms to increase their use of temporary workers. While those workers are covered by union agreements in the large manufacturing firms, they are not in the service sector. These trends coincided with the steep decline in membership in employers' associations and unions that we discussed in chapter 6. The end result has been growing inequality, as workers in the more protected manufacturing sector continue to enjoy the benefits of Germany's traditional CME arrangements, while other workers earn far less (Thelen 2014, 130–141).

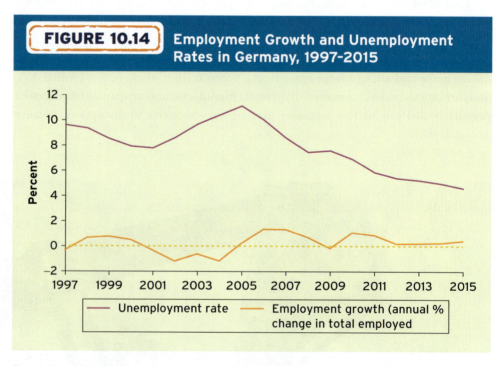

FIGURE 10.14 Employment Growth and Unemployment Rates in Germany, 1997-2015

Unemployment rate

Employment growth (annual % change in total employed)

Sources: Unemployment rate: unemployed as proportion of the economically active population (persons in employment + unemployed); employment growth data: labor force survey (microcensus), Statistisches Bundesamt, Wiesbaden, 2016 (https://www-genesis.destatis.de/genesis/online).

German banks' heavy international investments and the economy's dependence on exports meant that the Great Recession hit Germany hard: the economy shrank by 5 percent in 2009. Exports, long the mainstay of German manufacturing, also dropped nearly 20 percent. Germany, however, bounced back rapidly, growing by 3.7 percent in 2010 and 3 percent in 2011. Despite a long history of fiscal austerity, the German government initially turned to Keynesian stimulus to respond to the recession. After the stimulus, though, the government passed a constitutional amendment requiring a bal-

Government and Growth in the EU

The government in Germany and in the Eurozone as a whole consistently takes in a larger share of economic production as taxes than does the United States (see chart A). Neoliberal economists predict that this will hurt economic growth in Germany and the Eurozone. Chart B, however, shows that the Eurozone grew faster than the United States at the dawn of the new millennium, though the United States started to recover from the Great Recession sooner.

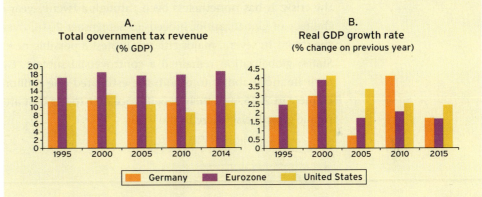

Sources: All data are from World Bank and OECD indicators: (http://data.worldbank.org/indicator/GC.TAX.TOTL.GD.ZS) and (http://data.worldbank.org/indicator/NY.GDP.MKTP.KD.ZG).

anced budget. The stimulus plan and recession caused the government's budget deficit to soar to 4.5 percent of GDP by 2010, but by 2014 the balanced budget amendment and renewed growth had produced a surplus, some of which the government was spending on the Syrian refugee crisis in 2016. Growth slowed to virtually nothing in 2012 and 2013 but rose to a little over 1.5 percent for 2014–2016. Germany's famous export sector roared back as well: the country had the largest trade surplus (money earned from exports minus money spent on imports) in the world in 2014.

Remarkably, the recession only raised unemployment by about 1 percentage point, a far less dramatic drop than most countries saw. Indeed, since 2010, unemployment has been below 7 percent, its lowest level since 1992; in 2015 it dropped to

6.4 percent. When the recession hit, the social market economy tradition of working cooperatively with unions allowed many employers to negotiate with their unions to accept cuts in wages and hours to avoid layoffs. The government gave incentives for this with adjustments to its *Kurzarbeit* (short time) program, which subsidized agreements that retained workers at reduced hours rather than firing them. The government introduced the country's first minimum wage, at about $11 per hour, in 2015. In the social market economy, wage agreements kept wages relatively high with no legal minimum; the government's acquiescence to demands for a legal minimum was another step in the direction of an LME. Indeed, unions in the protected manufacturing sector initially opposed the minimum wage, fearing it would drive down the wages they have gained via bargaining, while service-sector workers without such protections strongly supported it.

By 2016, some eight years after the Great Recession, the German economy had rebounded relatively well. While growth remained low, unemployment hit historic lows and exports rose. The largest economy in the EU, it was also the strongest after the crisis. It has nonetheless been through a twenty-year effort to reform its CME in the face of globalization. Indeed, in September 2016, over 300,000 Germans took to the streets in several major cities to protest a possible new trade deal with the United States; globalization remained a controversial subject. Germans also worried about their financial ability to absorb the estimated one million refugees who entered the country in 2015, and their dependence on exports that are vulnerable to slowing economic growth elsewhere in the world.

CASE Questions

1. Why was the social market economy such a success story from the 1960s to the 1980s? What changed to make it seem less successful, and what does that teach us about the prospects for more extensive government intervention in the economy in the future?
2. Germany has clearly instigated reforms that have moved it some distance away from the pure CME model and toward the LME model. How fundamental do these changes seem to be? Do they suggest the varieties of capitalism approach is still applicable, or is Germany a case in which globalization is forcing convergence?

CASE Study

JAPAN: THE DEVELOPMENTAL STATE AND ITS CRISIS

CASE SYNOPSIS

Postwar Japan created a distinct version of a CME, called the developmental state, which proved spectacularly successful at transforming the country into a global power and one of the wealthiest countries in the world. Even more than in Germany, the state guided economic growth, encouraging what a more laissez-faire model would see as excessive collaboration among large conglomerates and between them and the government. The mechanisms through which the state achieved this, however, proved to have negative effects when faced with the pressure of globalization. Since 1990, the Japanese economy has been stagnant. The Great Recession ended the first economic growth in over a decade, and the government changed hands twice. The new government bet on Keynesian policies starting in 2013, which had limited but positive effects by 2016.

- TYPE OF ECONOMY CME

- ECONOMIC MILESTONES Rapid Growth, 1950–1990; 1990 collapse and two decades of stagnation and deflation

- GLOBALIZATION EFFECTS Decline of developmental state's ability to influence economy

- RESPONSE TO GREAT RECESSION Political upheaval and promises of bold reform

Japan was the first non-Western society to industrialize successfully and create a fully modern and wealthy economy. This process began under Japan's first modern state, the Meiji regime, which led the country from 1868 until World War II. The government actively intervened in economic activity, directly investing not only in infrastructure but also in key industries. Once the government started an industry, it often sold it to private investors at bargain prices and actively encouraged industrial mergers to create larger and more internationally competitive firms. This produced a very concentrated business class, at the heart of which were the *zaibatsu*, three family-dominated industrial conglomerates that controlled key areas of the economy and had close relations with the government. In contrast to standard practice in capitalist economies, the government helped create business cartels in order to control specific sectors of the economy, and it helped create trade associations in order to coordinate development efforts among firms in the same industry.

After World War II, the United States dethroned not only the emperor but also the *zaibatsu*. While the Meiji government saw the conglomerates as part of a deliberate

Pedestrians walk past the Tokyo Stock Exchange. Japan's developmental state produced rapid growth, propelling the country to become the second-largest economy in the world by the 1980s. Since 1990, though, it has struggled through a long period of stagnation and has found no policy alternative that can restart more rapid growth in the face of globalization.

KAZUHIRO NOGI/AFP/Getty Images

industrialization strategy, the United States objected to them on political and economic grounds. Politically, they were part of the fascist Japanese past and therefore needed to be replaced by a more "democratic" business class. Economically, they were antithetical to healthy competition in a market economy. The United States therefore wrote antimonopoly legislation into Japanese law that disbanded the *zaibatsu*. But a shortage of capital for investment forced the American occupation to allow Japanese banks to own stock in industrial companies and to allow the companies to own stock in one another.

By the 1960s, the fully developed result of all this was the *keiretsu:* complex networks of firms that work together closely (see Figure 10.15). Some are direct descendants of the *zaibatsu*. At the center of most *keiretsu* is a major bank, which lends money on favorable terms to its *keiretsu* members and typically sends representatives to work in the firms to which it has lent money to ensure that its loans are being used wisely. Firms in a *keiretsu* own stock in one another's companies and therefore give one another orders for products. "Vertical" *keiretsu* like Toyota and Nissan involve a major manufacturer tied to hundreds of favored suppliers. While ownership of capital is not as concentrated as it was under the Meiji regime, the system nonetheless encourages long-term relationships among firms and limits the ability of firms outside the *keiretsu*, including foreign firms, to do business. Much of the coordination in Japan's CME takes place within *keiretsu*.

What Chalmers Johnson (1982) termed the **developmental state** emerged along with the rise of the *keiretsu*. A developmental state consciously seeks to create national strength in particular economic areas, taking an active and conscious role in the development of specific sectors of the economy. The Japanese government did this via two key bureaucratic agencies, the Ministry of Finance (MOF) and the Ministry of International Trade and Industry (MITI). Until liberalization in the 1970s, the MOF had extensive influence over the banking sector via its control over interest rates and over the role of banks in the *keiretsu*. By guaranteeing the key bank loans, the MOF had substantial influence of where and how they lent.

MITI influenced industrial policies more specifically through extensive licensing of technology and "administrative guidance," the bureaucracy's practice of informally

developmental state
A state that seeks to create national strength by taking an active and conscious role in the development of specific sectors of the economy

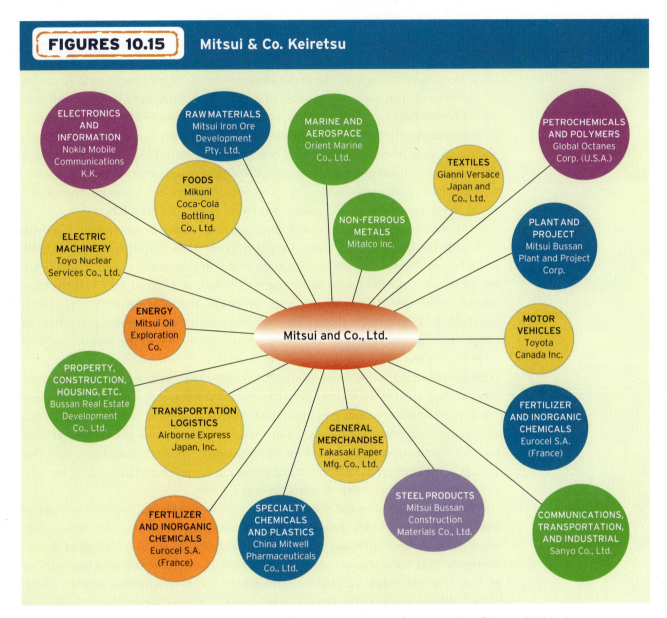

FIGURES 10.15 Mitsui & Co. Keiretsu

ELECTRONICS AND INFORMATION
Nokia Mobile Communications K.K.

RAW MATERIALS
Mitsui Iron Ore Development Pty. Ltd.

MARINE AND AEROSPACE
Orient Marine Co., Ltd.

PETROCHEMICALS AND POLYMERS
Global Octanes Corp. (U.S.A.)

FOODS
Mikuni Coca-Cola Bottling Co., Ltd.

TEXTILES
Gianni Versace Japan and Co., Ltd.

NON-FERROUS METALS
Mitalco Inc.

PLANT AND PROJECT
Mitsui Bussan Plant and Project Corp.

ELECTRIC MACHINERY
Toyo Nuclear Services Co., Ltd.

ENERGY
Mitsui Oil Exploration Co.

Mitsui and Co., Ltd.

MOTOR VEHICLES
Toyota Canada Inc.

PROPERTY, CONSTRUCTION, HOUSING, ETC.
Bussan Real Estate Development Co., Ltd.

TRANSPORTATION LOGISTICS
Airborne Express Japan, Inc.

GENERAL MERCHANDISE
Takasaki Paper Mfg. Co., Ltd.

FERTILIZER AND INORGANIC CHEMICALS
Eurocel S.A. (France)

FERTILIZER AND INORGANIC CHEMICALS
Eurocel S.A. (France)

SPECIALTY CHEMICALS AND PLASTICS
China Mitwell Pharmaceuticals Co., Ltd.

STEEL PRODUCTS
Mitsui Bussan Construction Materials Co., Ltd.

COMMUNICATIONS, TRANSPORTATION, AND INDUSTRIAL
Sanyo Co., Ltd.

Source: FundingUniverse.com, "Mitsui & Co., Ltd. History" (http://www.fundinguniverse.com/company-histories/mitsui-co-ltd-history).

and successfully suggesting that an industry or firm pursue a particular endeavor. MITI was able to use this informal system to guide industrial growth because of the licensing, financial, and other powers it held over business and because of the close relationship that developed among key industries, bureaucracies, and the ruling party. Leaders in all three of these sectors would move from one to the other over the course of their careers; for instance, former bureaucrats frequently became members of parliament.

T. J. Pempel (2000) argued that Japan's development state was fundamentally a "conservative regime" in the sense that it favored business and governing elites over labor. In contrast to most European CMEs, labor unions are relatively weak and do not have an important role in the coordination process in Japan. This is due in part to what has been termed "lifetime employment" at major Japanese firms; each member of the core, "permanent" workforce of a major company has (or at least had) a near guarantee of employment. This was made possible in part by the existence of a large, flexible, and mostly female force of part-time workers that firms could hire and fire as market conditions warranted. The full-time male workforce received nearly guaranteed employment and was assured health and retirement benefits via the firm. Therefore, many of them chose to remain loyal to the same firm for life and were uninterested in unionization. At the height of this labor system, workers with "lifetime employment" constituted about 30 percent of the entire Japanese workforce (Kingston 2013, 83).

The developmental state created the "Japanese miracle," the sustained growth that made the Japanese economy six times larger in 1975 than it had been in 1950. Japan became the world's second-largest economy (it is now third or fourth, depending on the year, behind China and sometimes India), and "Japan Inc." was the chief economic rival to the United States in the 1970s and 1980s. As Figure 10.9 (page 551) and Table 10.1 (page 575) show, Japan has also maintained a relatively low level of inequality and only moderate levels of poverty, mainly due to the lifetime employment system and the extensive benefits that large companies provided workers, what Japanese political scientist Mari Miura (2012) called the "welfare through work" system. Workers at large firms typically get a substantial lump-sum payment upon retirement, and some also receive pensions after that. The retirement payment and the fact that many companies pay a substantial share of annual wages via occasional large bonuses have helped make Japan's savings rate one of the highest in the world. This savings helped fuel rapid investment and growth in earlier years, but arguably hurt the country's ability to move out of recession in the 1990s.

Table 10.1 illustrates the sharp difference between the last twenty-five years in Japan and earlier decades. Economic growth has dropped substantially, unemployment has risen, and prices fell nearly continuously for fifteen years, a sign of serious economic stagnation. The economic miracle ended in 1990; on the first business day of that year, real estate and stock prices, which had been climbing rapidly, plummeted and the bubble burst. There had been warning signs: productivity growth had been slowing since the 1970s, as had the government's ability to influence the direction of economic activity. Acquiescing to international pressure, the government had slowly begun to reduce its power to control flows of money and financing in the late 1970s. In the 1980s, the system of guaranteeing bank loans led Japanese corporations to take on excessive debt, which they invested in real estate and other unproductive areas. Simultaneously, the more successful Japanese companies such as Toyota and Nissan fully entered the age of globalization, investing elsewhere in the world so that instead of exporting cars from Japan, they began building them in the United States and Europe. This reduced Japan's key source of growth: exports. All of this reduced the extent to which *keiretsu* members continued to coordinate their activity,

TABLE 10.1	Profile of Japan's Economy, 1970-Most Recent Available					
State	**1970**	**1980**	**1990**	**2000**	**2011**	**Most recent**
GDP growth (annual %)	10.7	2.8	5.2	2.9	-0.7	0.6% (2015)
Social expenditures (total, as % of GDP)	..	10.3	11.2	16.1	23.1	23.1 (2011)
Gross national savings (as % of nominal GDP)	..	..	33.2	27.5	22	21 (2015)
Share of income or consumption, ratio of richest 20% to poorest 20%	..	..	4.3	3.4	3.4	N/A

Sources: Data are from World Bank Indicators, OECD, UNDP Human Development Reports, and CountryWatch.

as the corporate structure of the Japanese economy in the 1990s and 2000s moved perceptibly toward a more "American" model of vertically integrated, globally active corporations (Lincoln and Shimotani 2009). The economic base of Japan's CME was profoundly shifting.

When the bubble burst, the government had difficulty responding. Over time, it tried both Keynesian and neoliberal policies, engaging in deficit spending and lowering official interest rates all the way to zero, but nothing seemed to revive economic growth. A key problem was massive bad bank debt from all the poorly invested loans. Government spending went to paying off the bad loans and bailing out the banks that had made them. Corporations cut their permanent workforces and shifted to more part-time workers, reducing worker benefits and real wages. Up to a third of the labor force was now in temporary positions, many of which would be lost in the global recession in 2008–2009. The more flexible labor market increased both inequality and poverty, even before the global recession (Miura 2012).

The Great Recession destroyed the modest gains in economic growth the country had achieved in the mid-2000s. Japan was hit exceptionally hard because of its dependence on exports, particularly to the United States. In 2009 the Japanese economy shrank by more than 5 percent, and deflation worsened significantly. The government responded with a Keynesian economic stimulus that increased its already high fiscal deficit and once again reduced interest rates to zero. Modest economic growth returned in late 2009 and in 2010 hit 4 percent. The massive earthquake and tsunami in March 2011, however, cut growth to 0.4 percent for 2011. The earthquake, the fourth biggest in recorded history, killed twenty thousand people, displaced hundreds of thousands more, and resulted in an expensive cleanup of a damaged nuclear reactor; the total costs were estimated at $330 billion.

The economic crisis produced a seismic political change, as the long-ruling Liberal Democratic Party (LDP) was swept from power in November 2009. The LDP had maintained voters' support via clientelistic government spending on infrastructure for rural areas, agricultural subsidies, and expanding social welfare programs. This produced growing deficits well before the Great Recession, and the sudden drop in the economy dealt a devastating blow to the LDP's ability to continue to spend. The new government came to office promising to reduce corruption and the bureaucracy's tight control over economic policy (see chapter 5), though its initial reform efforts were once again met by fierce opposition from entrenched interests. Internal divisions in the new ruling party and the crisis of the tsunami led the Japanese to see the new government as weak and ineffective. They returned the LDP to power in a landslide election in December 2012. The new prime minister, Shinzō Abe, campaigned on a platform of classic Keynesian stimulus in both fiscal and monetary policy to restart economic growth. Shortly after taking office he initiated a large stimulus plan focused on building infrastructure that was equal to 2.6 percent of the country's GDP, bigger in relative terms than President Obama's stimulus plan in 2009. He also replaced the head of the central bank, which has since lowered interest rates to below zero and engaged in "quantitative easing" to pump money into the economy. These policies have improved the economy, but not dramatically so. A second recession actually occurred in 2014 when the government raised sales taxes, with very slow growth of only 0.6 percent returning in 2015. Inflation finally became positive in 2014 but did not reach the government's target of 2 percent, and the central bank could do little else since interest rates were already below zero.

Abe also promised more structural reforms, but few have been implemented. An exception is a new rule on corporate governance that requires Japanese firms to operate much more like firms in LMEs do, with shareholders of stocks having a prominent role. Abe also participated in and signed the controversial Trans-Pacific Partnership trade agreement over the objections of many Japanese businesses; in the long run, it could significantly open up Japanese *keiretsu* to greater international competition, for better or worse. Japan will continue to struggle in the face of globalization and the seeming end of its developmental state model.

CASE Questions

1. Like Germany, Japan had a very successful economic model that fell on hard times in the 1990s. What changed to make the model less successful? How does this compare with the decline of Germany's social market economy model? What do both teach us about the future of CMEs in the face of globalization?

2. What lessons does Japan's long struggle with stagnation have for other countries facing economic problems in the last few years, since the Great Recession?

CONCLUSION

With the extension of the market economy to nearly every corner of the globe, a universal set of issues exists involving the relationship between the market and the state. The state must perform certain tasks so that the market can function efficiently and in turn produce revenue for the state. The market is likely to generate greater wealth if the state is able to go beyond these essential functions by establishing policies to encourage investment and growth. Political pressure can lead to yet other policies, as organized groups in society demand particular state intervention in the market in their favor. Clear and consistent economic theories of how and why the state should intervene serve as intellectual guides for state actions. However, no government's policies follow these blueprints perfectly, as our case studies have shown.

The case studies in this chapter demonstrate the great variation even among the wealthiest in the relationship between the state and the market economy. The United States and United Kingdom are the paradigmatic LMEs, the models of a free-market economy with limited state intervention, though as we have seen, even here the state has intervened and expanded over the past century to try to improve economic outcomes and limit negative market effects. Germany's CME represents the common European alternative, while Japan's variant on the CME model, the developmental state, provides yet another alternative, one toward which a number of poorer countries have gravitated, which we discuss in chapter 11. Like most countries after the first wave of industrialization, Germany and Japan also used state intervention to guide investment into particular sectors.

Globalization has challenged all past economic models. Whether these models were successful or not in earlier decades, they now face rapidly moving capital that seems to limit their options and pushes them all in the direction of greater openness to the market. As our case studies suggest, however, states have not all responded to globalization in the same way. Economic sovereignty, while clearly reduced, still exists. Among the wealthy countries, LMEs have intensified their openness to the market to varying degrees, whereas CMEs have moved in that direction much more slowly, preserving some aspects of their distinct model. Despite challenges, wealthy countries have benefitted more from globalization than they have been hurt by it.

Explaining the variation in state intervention in the market has long been a preoccupation of comparativists. Marxist analysts, whose theories of the dominance of the bourgeoisie are challenged by the existence of extensive welfare states such as Germany's, argue that the elite in capitalist societies sometimes sacrifice the short-term interests of particular businesses in order to preserve the system as a whole. A more widely accepted explanation of variation in state intervention is a pluralist one: countries with stronger workers' movements and unions have created the policies these groups favor.

Weak unions are just one example of weak institutions, which institutionalists argue are the key to explaining the economic paths of different countries. Institutionalists, including the varieties of capitalism approach, see key institutions developing in particular historical junctures and evolving slowly from there, only fundamentally disrupted at times of profound change. The ability of stronger institutions in Germany to discipline their members produced a less confrontational environment that allowed stronger coordination of economic policies. As globalization has weakened those institutions, German economic and social policy has shifted, largely toward a more market-oriented model. Strong bureaucratic institutions similarly help explain the rise of the developmental state in Japan. Globalization also made those institutions weaker over time, helping to undermine what was a widely admired model of economic growth.

KEY CONCEPTS

capitalism (p. 524)

command economy (p. 524)

comparative institutional advantage (p. 546)

convergence (p. 546)

coordinated market economies (CMEs) (p. 536)

deficit spending (p. 532)

developmental state (p. 572)

externality (p. 527)

fiscal policy (p. 532)

globalization (p. 538)

Keynesian theory (p. 532)

liberal market economies (LMEs) (p. 536)

market economy (p. 524)

market failure (p. 527)

monetary policy (p. 532)

monopoly (p. 528)

natural monopoly (p. 529)

neoliberalism (p. 533)

public goods (p. 526)

social market economy (p. 566)

varieties of capitalism (VOC) (p. 536)

 Sharpen your skills with SAGE edge at **edge.sagepub.com/orvis4e.** **SAGE edge for students** provides a personalized approach to help you accomplish your coursework goals in an easy-to-use learning environment.

WORKS CITED

Altman, Roger C. 2009. "Globalization in Retreat." *Foreign Affairs* 88 (4).

Ashbee, Edward. 2014. "The United States: Institutional Continuities, Reform, and 'Critical Junctures.'" In *Moments of Truth: The Politics of Financial Crises in Comparative Perspective,* edited by Francisco Panizza and George Philip, 82–100. New York: Routledge.

Bermeo, Nancy, and Jonas Pontusson. 2012. "Coping with Crisis: An Introduction." In *Coping with Crisis: Government Reactions to the Great Recession,* edited by Nancy Bermeo and Jonas Pontusson, 1–32. New York: Russell Sage Foundation.

Cafruny, Alan W., and Leila Simona Talani. 2013. "The Crisis of the Eurozone." In *Exploring the Global Financial Crisis,* edited by Alan W. Cafruny and Herman M. Schwartz, 13–34. Boulder, CO: Lynne Rienner.

Calmes, Jackie, and Jonathan Weisman. 2013. "Economists See Deficit Emphasis as Impeding Recovery." *New York Times.* May 8 (http://www.nytimes.com/

2013/05/09/us/deficit-reduction-is-seen-by-economists-as-impeding-recovery.html?emc=eta1&_r=0).

Cox, Robert Henry. 2002. "Reforming the German Welfare State: Why Germany Is Slower Than Its Neighbors." *German Policy Studies* 2 (1): 174–196.

Crew, David F. 1998. *Germans on Welfare: From Weimar to Hitler.* New York: Oxford University Press.

Dadush, Uri, and Kemal Dervis. 2013. "The Inequality Challenge." *Current History* 112 (750): 13–19. January (http://www.brookings.edu/research/articles/2013/01/inequality-challenge-dervis).

Edwards, Haley Sweetland. 2013. "He Who Makes the Rules." *Washington Monthly.* March/April (http://www.washingtonmonthly.com/magazine/march_april_2013/features/he_who_makes_the_rules043315.php?page= all).

Faucher-King, Florence, and Patrick Le Galès. 2010. *The New Labour Experiment: Change and Reform under Blair and Brown.* Stanford, CA: Stanford University Press.

Garrett, Geoffrey. 1998. *Partisan Politics in the Global Economy.* Cambridge, UK: Cambridge University Press.

Ginsburg, Norman. 2001. "Globalization and the Liberal Welfare States." In *Globalization and European Welfare States: Challenges and Change*, edited by Robert Sykes, Bruno Palier, and Pauline M. Prior (with Jo Campling), 173–192. New York: Palgrave.

Hall, Peter Andrew, and Daniel Gingerich. 2009. "Varieties of Capitalism and Institutional Complementarities in the Political Economy: An Empirical Analysis." *British Journal of Political Science* 39 (3): 449–482. doi:10.1017/S0007123409000672

Hall, Peter Andrew, and David W. Soskice, eds. 2001. *Varieties of Capitalism: The Institutional Foundations of Comparative Advantage.* Oxford, UK: Oxford University Press.

Hardie, Iain, and David Howarth. 2009. "*Die Krise* but Not *La Crise*? The Financial Crisis and the Transformation of German and French Banking Systems." *JCMS: Journal of Common Market Studies* 47 (5): 1017–1039. doi:10.1111/j.1468-5965.2009.02033.x

Huber, Evelyne, and John D. Stephens. 2001. *Development and Crisis of the Welfare State: Parties and Policies in Global Markets.* Chicago: University of Chicago Press.

Ido, Masanobu. 2012. "Party System Change and the Transformation of the Varieties of Capitalism." In *Varieties of Capitalism, Types of Democracy and Globalization,* edited by Masanobu Ido, 55–79. New York: Routledge.

Johnson, Chalmers A. 1982. *MITI and the Japanese Miracle: The Growth of Industrial Policy, 1925–1975.* Stanford, CA: Stanford University Press.

Kingston, John. 2013. *Contemporary Japan: History, Politics, and Social Change since the 1980s.* 2nd ed. Malden, MA: John Wiley & Sons.

Kotz, David M. 2015. *The Rise and Fall of Neoliberal Capitalism.* Cambridge, MA: Harvard University Press.

Lijphart, Arend. 1999. *Patterns of Democracy: Government Forms and Performance in Thirty-six Countries.* New Haven, CT: Yale University Press.

Lincoln, James, and Masahiro Shimotani. 2009. "Whither the *Keiretsu*, Japan's Business Networks? How Were They Structured? What Did They Do? Why Are They Gone?" Working Paper Series, Institute for Research on Labor and Employment, University of California, Berkeley (http://www.escholarship.org/uc/item/00m7d34g).

Lowrey, Annie. 2013. "The Rich Get Richer through the Recovery." Economix. *New York Times,* September 10 (http://economix.blogs.nytimes.com/2013/09/10/the-rich-get-richer-through-the-recovery/?ref=business&_r=0).

Miura, Mari. 2012. *Welfare through Work: Conservative Ideas, Partisan Dynamics, and Social Protection in Japan.* Ithaca, NY: Cornell University Press.

Ohmae, Kenichi. 1995. *The End of the Nation State: The Rise of Regional Economies.* New York: Simon and Schuster.

Panizza, Francisco, and George Philip, eds. 2014. *Moments of Truth: The Politics of Financial Crises in Comparative Perspective.* New York: Routledge.

Pempel, T. J. 2000. *Regime Shift: Comparative Dynamics of the Japanese Political Economy.* Ithaca, NY: Cornell University Press.

Polanyi, Karl. 1944. *The Great Transformation.* New York: Farrar and Rinehart.

Pontusson, Jonas, and Damian Raess (2012). "How (and Why) Is This Time Different? The Politics of Economic Crisis in Western Europe and the United States." *Annual Review of Political Science* 15: 13–33.

Rattner, Steven. 2011. "The Secrets of Germany's Success." *Foreign Affairs* 90 (4).

Streeck, Wolfgang. 2009. *Re-forming Capitalism: Institutional Change in the German Political Economy.* Oxford, UK: Oxford University Press.

Streeck, Wolfgang, and Anke Hassel. 2003. "The Crumbling Pillars of Social Partnership." *West European Politics* 26 (4): 101–124. doi:10.1080/01402380312331280708

Thelen, Kathleen. 2014. *Varieties of Liberalization and the New Politics of Social Solidarity.* Cambridge, UK: Cambridge University Press.

RESOURCES FOR FURTHER STUDY

Bates, Robert H. 2001. *Prosperity and Violence: The Political Economy of Development.* New York: W. W. Norton.

Friedman, Milton. 1962. *Capitalism and Freedom.* Chicago: University of Chicago Press.

Gilpin, Robert. 2000. *The Challenge of Global Capitalism.* Princeton, NJ: Princeton University Press.

Heilbroner, Robert L. 1985. *The Nature and Logic of Capitalism.* New York: W. W. Norton.

Keynes, John Maynard. 1935. *The General Theory of Employment, Interest, and Money.* New York: Harcourt Brace.

The Levin Institute, The State University of New York. "Globalization 101: A Student's Guide to Globalization" (http://www.globalization101.org).

Rothstein, Bo, and Sven Steinmo, eds. 2002. *Restructuring the Welfare State: Political Institutions and Policy Change.* New York: Palgrave Macmillan.

Siebert, Horst. 2005. *The German Economy: Beyond the Social Market.* Princeton, NJ: Princeton University Press.

Sykes, Robert, Bruno Palier, and Pauline M. Prior (with Jo Campling), eds. 2001. *Globalization and European Welfare States: Challenges and Change.* New York: Palgrave.

Woo-Cumings, Meredith, ed. 1999. *The Developmental State.* Ithaca, NY: Cornell University Press.

WEB RESOURCES

International Labour Organization, LABORSTA Internet
(http://laborsta.ilo.org)

International Monetary Fund, World Economic Outlook Database
(https://www.imf.org/external/pubs/ft/weo/2016/01/weodata/index.aspx)

Organisation for Economic Co-operation and Development (OECD), Stat Extracts
(http://stats.oecd.org)

UNDP Human Development Reports, International Human Development Indicators
(http://hdr.undp.org/en/statistics)

The World Bank, Economic Policy and External Debt
(http://data.worldbank.org/topic/economic-policy-and-external-debt)

11 POLITICAL ECONOMY OF DEVELOPMENT

KEY QUESTIONS

- What is development, and why does it matter?
- What should be the role of the state in the development process?
- What explains the ability of states to pursue development in the context of globalization?
- What types of regimes are able to pursue development more effectively, and why?

In 1995 the average Nigerian was slightly wealthier than the average Chinese, while the average Brazilian was four times wealthier than either. By 2015, the Brazilian was still wealthier than the Chinese, but just barely, while the Nigerian lagged far behind. You can see this story in the first column of the Country and Concept table on page 584, which shows GDP per capita at "purchasing power parity," meaning it takes into account the differences in the cost of living in different countries. These are, of course, gross averages. Much of Nigeria's wealth is in oil, and the truly "average" Nigerian sees relatively little of it. The average Chinese citizen, by contrast, may see far more of her country's wealth, which is based more heavily on labor-intensive manufacturing that employs far more people. Nonetheless, the tale is striking: how did one country, China, increase its wealth so dramatically, and why can't others, like Nigeria, do the same?

The word *development* conjures up images of impoverished children in Africa and gleaming new skyscrapers in China. "Underdeveloped" or "developing" countries are typically thought of as those that are, or recently were, poor on a global scale, the countries that during the Cold War were known as the "Third World" but are now more commonly referred to as the "Global South." As the examples of our five case studies show, dramatic variation and change over time exist within the Global

Middle-school students use virtual reality devices in Beijing, China. While economic inequality has increased markedly, China's economic development model has transformed the country, moving more people out of poverty faster than any other country in history.

(Photo by Zhao Yuhong/VCG via Getty Images)

South, which is the subject of this chapter. In chapter 1, we introduced the concept of "political development" as the rise of modern nation-states and evolution of regimes and institutions. The political economy of development examines the interaction of political and economic development. As in chapter 10, to do this we must understand the economic theories behind various models of development. These economic models, though, include prescriptions for states' role in the process, and some argue that particular types of regimes can better achieve "development" than others. Since World War II, an entire industry and several major international organizations—the International Monetary Fund (IMF) and World Bank in particular—have arisen to try to help poor countries "develop." Governments of the Organisation for Economic Co-operation and Development (OECD), the wealthy countries of the world, spent $135 billion on foreign aid toward this effort in 2014, and that doesn't even include the money spent by international organizations.

But what is "development"? What we mean by it and why it is important are the first questions we must address. In the era of globalization, we must also ask what globalization's effects are in the Global South and how states can navigate globalization to

COUNTRY AND CONCEPT
Political Economy of Development

Country	Per capita GDP (PPP)[1]		Human Development Index[2]		Net foreign direct investment (FDI) inflows as percentage of GDP		Exports and imports of goods and services as percentage of GDP		Portfolio investment equity as percentage of GDP	
	1995	2015	1990	2014	1995	2015	1995	2015	1995	2009*
Brazil	6,622.2	15,359.3	0.608	0.755	0.63	4.2	18.5	27.3	0.36	2.36
China	980	14,238.7	0.501	0.727	4.92	2.3	39.9	42.7	0.00	0.56
Germany	19,032.7	47,268.4	0.801	0.916	0.48	1.4	46.5	84.8	0.48	0.35
India	1,146	6,088.6	0.428	0.609	0.60	2.1	24.2	48.8 (2014)	0.45	1.61
Iran	6,575.6	17,365.8	0.567	0.766	0.02	0.495 (2014)	26.1	43.1 (2014)	0.00	–
Japan	19,229.7	37,321.6	0.814	0.891	0.00	0.00	15.8	36.8	0.96	0.25
Mexico	6019.3	17,276.6	0.648	0.756	3.32	2.6	58.4	72.8	0.18	0.48
Nigeria	1,958.7	5,991.7	–	0.514	3.84	0.6	84.2	30.9 (2014)	0.00	0.3
Russia	8,012.8	24,451.4	0.729	0.798	0.52	0.4	51.9	50.7	0.01	0.27
United Kingdom	17,446.3	41,324.6	0.773	0.907	1.88	1.4	56.8	56.8	0.70	3.52
United States	23,954.5	55,836.8	0.859	0.915	0.79	2.3	24.3	28.1	0.22	1.14

* Data are from 2009, the latest year for which data are available.

[1] Data on per capita GDP (PPP), stock of FDI, imports and exports of goods and services as a percentage of GDP, and portfolio investment equity are from World Bank. Per capita GDP (PPP) are available at http://data.worldbank.org/indicator/NY.GDP.PCAP.PP.CD; FDI data are available at http://data.worldbank.org/indicator/BX.KLT.DINV.WD.GD.ZS; exports data are available at http://data.worldbank.org/indicator/NE.EXP.GNFS.ZS; imports data are available at http://data.worldbank.org/indicator/NE.IMP.GNFS.ZS. Per capita GDP for Iran is for 2014.

[2] Human Development Index data are from the UN Human Development Reports (http://hdr.undp.org/en/composite/trends).

pursue development successfully. That will lead us to the economic theories that have informed the "development debate" over the last half century. The various theories in that debate ask how states can best pursue policies that enhance development and how outside help like foreign aid, if used at all, can be effective. Some argue that democratic or authoritarian regimes are better able to "develop" their societies, a question to which we will also turn.

WHAT IS "DEVELOPMENT"?

Before trying to explain how to achieve something, we need to know what the goal is. That is particularly tricky for the idea of "development." The origin of the concept in its modern usage after World War II was connected to modernization theory (see chapter 3). Put simply, social scientists and policymakers at the time saw "development" as being about the poor countries of the world—what they called the "Third World"—looking more like wealthy, Western countries. Politically, this meant becoming independent, democratic states. Economically, it meant becoming wealthier, which meant industrializing and urbanizing. Chapters 3 and 9 discussed the long, difficult, and still incomplete road to democracy, leaving aside the assumption that everyone should or would want to live in a democracy. The economic road has been equally rocky. Some countries have been spectacularly successful: South Korea went from being part of the "Third World" to being a member of OECD, officially a member of the wealthy world. More recently, China's economic growth has helped make it a global superpower, though it remains only a "middle-income" country. Others, such as Zimbabwe, saw per capita incomes hardly budge over decades.

As we discussed in chapter 3, the economic assumption of modernization theory was that poor countries would largely go through the same process to achieve wealth that the West had in an earlier era. Modernization theorists also assumed that those in the West knew how to help poor countries follow that path, thus justifying foreign aid. Critics questioned those assumptions in the 1960s and 1970s, wondering if poor countries in a different era in the global economy could really follow the same path as the West had, and wondering if wealth generation—economic growth—should be the primary goal. We discuss the first of these concerns below when we turn to globalization. The second, that growth alone should not be the goal, led to a focus on poverty by the 1970s. Economic growth that did not reduce poverty, critics argued, should not be seen as development; instead, development should focus on the "poorest of the poor." Figuring out how the state and external aid could reduce poverty became the goal.

Economist and philosopher Amartya Sen (1999) profoundly influenced thinking on the concept of development in the new millennium with his focus on human capabilities. He argued that neither growth nor poverty reduction alone were adequate goals. The real goal of development anywhere in the world (including in the already wealthy countries) should be enhancing the capabilities of individuals to lead fulfilling lives as they define them. Economic growth that provides higher incomes would certainly be part of that, as would reducing poverty. But helping people achieve greater capabilities also meant they needed to be healthy, educated, and free. Many economists had long recognized that health and education were important parts of developing "human capital," the store of productive labor that would enhance economic growth. Sen, though, argued that health and education were important to individuals themselves, not only to

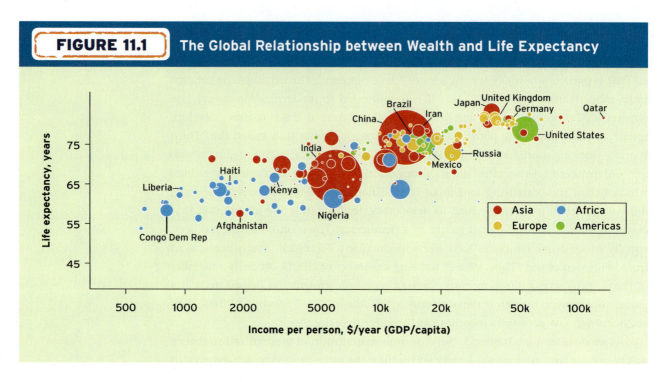

FIGURE 11.1   **The Global Relationship between Wealth and Life Expectancy**

Source: Based on a free chart from www.gapminder.org.

Note: Data are from 2015. The relative size of the circles corresponds to the size of a country's population.

enhance economic growth but also to allow individuals to maximize their own capabilities. Similarly, freedom is essential. Indeed, his book was titled *Development as Freedom*. He argued that people need to be free politically in democracies—only then could they define for themselves what a fulfilling life would be—and they needed to be free from social restrictions such as traditional gender norms that might limit their capabilities.

Sen's concept has become the leading conceptualization of development. It lay behind the creation of what became a widely used index of development, the UN's Human Development Index (HDI) that combines measures of health, education, and income. The Country and Concept table on page 584 shows the difference between this measure and wealth alone: India's per capita GDP is less than half of China's, but the difference in their HDI scores is much closer, while the United States is wealthier than Germany but Germany has a higher HDI score. In practical terms, policymakers still focus on economic growth extensively, as well as poverty, but health and education are also quite important. These tend to go together as well, as Figure 11.1 demonstrates, comparing a basic measure of health (life expectancy at birth) with GDP per capita. The democratization process we discussed in chapter 9 has also been tied to development, at least via foreign aid efforts. Many, though not all, theorists see democratic regimes with strong institutions as most likely to provide the conditions for the greatest development of human capabilities.

While Sen's capabilities theory is certainly the leading understanding of development today, critics of the entire idea of development have also arisen. Using postmodern theories, they argue that the very idea of "development" is an effort by the wealthy countries to control the Global South. They argue that development is still conceived as something the West has and countries of the Global South lack, measured on various scales as deficiencies to be overcome. This, they claim, allows the West to insert itself into domestic economic and political processes in the Global South via foreign aid and other "development" efforts, to impose the West's vision of how these societies ought to be structured. Cast primarily in economic and technical terms, "development" also attempts to depoliticize the process of social and political change in the Global South, removing agency from local actors to chart the course for their societies as they see fit. Rather than an effort to improve people's lives, development as it is conceived and practiced is a continuation of colonialism in a new form (Weber 2014). While this is certainly a minority view, it nonetheless raises profound questions for development practitioners to consider.

DEVELOPMENT AND GLOBALIZATION

In chapter 10, we saw that globalization has clearly affected the ways in which wealthy and powerful states guide their economies. If this is true for those states, it seems likely to apply even more to poorer and less powerful states. Have they in effect lost economic sovereignty to the global market, or can they influence its effects? Poor countries' relationship with globalization is intimately connected with development: How can states in the Global South use economic policies to help them navigate the global economy in ways that are most beneficial to their people? In this section, we examine the effects of globalization before turning to the "development debate" in the next section, which addresses what economic policies states should pursue.

One thing is certain: globalization has helped produce dramatically different levels of economic development around the world. The "Country and Concept" table on page 584 shows key aspects of globalization: **foreign direct investment (FDI),** foreign investment in directly productive activity; **trade,** exports and imports of goods and services; and **international capital flows,** the movement of money across national borders. In most countries, all three areas show marked increases. The greatest increases, though, are in the final column, portfolio investment equity, which partially measures the effects of international capital flows. These have expanded dramatically in almost all countries. The virtual elimination of barriers to moving money across borders and improvement in global communications have resulted in more than $1 trillion crossing international borders daily.

Virtually all governments have followed neoliberal policies to some degree over the last two decades, opening their economies to the global market, but the results have not been consistent. Figure 11.2 compares each region's Economic Globalization Index score—a measure of economies' interactions with the global market—to growth

foreign direct investment (FDI)
Investment from abroad in productive activity in another country

trade
The flow of goods and services across national borders

international capital flows
Movements of capital in the form of money across international borders

rates and poverty rates since 1981. All regions have become more globalized over time, and the gap between the wealthier regions (Europe, East Asia, and Latin America) and the poorer regions (South Asia and Africa) has increased slightly. Economic growth and poverty reduction vary dramatically by region, though. Greater globalization has not systematically produced greater growth, though it appears to be loosely associated with poverty reduction. The rate of poverty reduction, though, varies dramatically as well by region, even though change in the level of globalization does not. The question is, What explains this variation, and what can be done to improve the effects of globalization in the countries that are falling behind?

THE DEVELOPMENT DEBATE

The development debate over the last century has tried to answer these questions. While it long predates the idea of globalization as such, from the start it has addressed these questions implicitly: What explains the success of different development policies, and what should be the role of the state in development in a particular global context? The neoliberal-Keynesian debate that we discussed in chapter 10 also had an influential role in development policy in the Global South. John Maynard Keynes was instrumental in the creation after World War II of the IMF and the World Bank. One basic assumption of the postwar global economic order was that free trade should be as widespread as possible. The economic argument in favor of this is known as **comparative advantage.** It holds that well-being will be maximized if each country uses its resources to produce whatever it can produce relatively efficiently compared with other countries (i.e., it should produce the items that it can produce most efficiently compared with how well other countries produce them, even if it is not the most efficient at anything). It then trades with other countries for goods it does not produce, and all countries gain because they are using their resources as efficiently as possible. What this meant in practical terms was that the poor and agrarian countries of Asia, Africa, and Latin America would, for the foreseeable future, produce primarily agricultural products and raw materials. Their industries, where they existed, were quite new and therefore were not likely to compete successfully against the well-established industrial conglomerates of the wealthy countries.

comparative advantage
Theory of trade that argues that economic efficiency and well-being will be maximized if each country uses its resources to produce whatever it produces relatively well compared with other countries and then trades its own products with other countries for goods it does not produce

The ISI Era Leaders in the Global South and the economists who supported them, however, were not willing to have their countries relegated to producing only agricultural products and raw materials. The new field of "development economics," then, came to be about how a state could intervene in the economy to stimulate rapid industrialization and growth. This meshed with early ideas of development being about economic growth and industrialization, as well as the general Keynesian theory that the state could manage capitalism to enhance growth. In "developing countries," this management would simply take somewhat different forms than in industrialized countries.

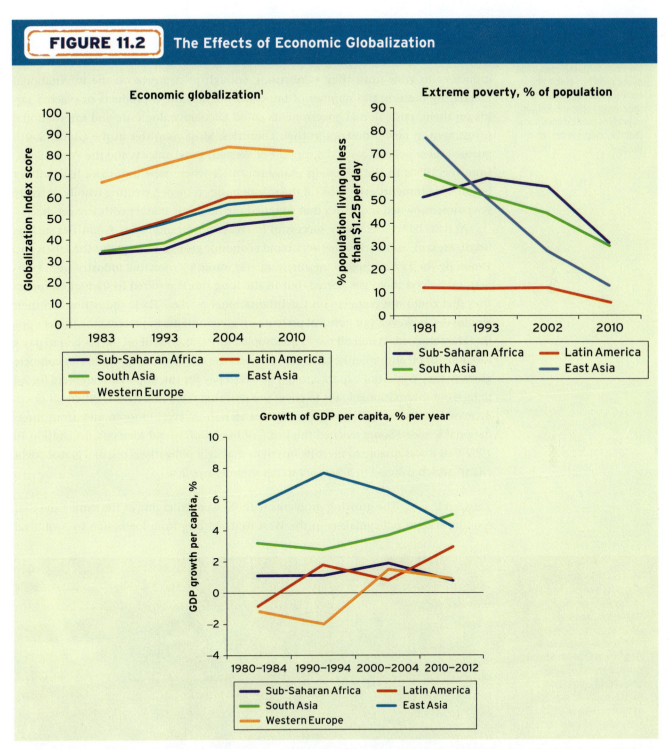

FIGURE 11.2   The Effects of Economic Globalization

Sources: Data for the Economic Globalization Index are from the KOF Index of Globalization, "Economic Globalization" data (http://globalization.kof.ethz .ch/query). Data on GDP growth and extreme poverty are from World Bank (http://data.worldbank.org).

[1]Composite of data on openness to and flows of trade, foreign direct investment, and portfolio investment.

The central policy that developed out of these ideas was **import-substitution industrialization (ISI)**, which stated that a developing nation should protect its new industries by placing restrictions on international trade, thus allowing its new industries to grow until they were strong enough to compete on the international market. By limiting the number of imported manufactured products or placing tariffs on them, postcolonial governments could encourage domestic and international investment in new industries in their countries. Most countries in the Global South pursued these policies, with the support of Western governments and the World Bank, from the 1950s to the 1970s. In many countries where new industries had not yet begun, governments even took on the role of business owner, creating wholly or partly government-owned industries that supplied the domestic market with key goods.

At first, ISI was relatively successful in creating new industries. Countries such as Brazil, Mexico, and Turkey saw very rapid economic growth throughout the 1950s and 1960s. By the 1970s, though, momentum was waning. Protecting industry from competition helped them get started, but in the long run it resulted in inefficient industries that could not compete on the international market. These industries and their employees, however, put political pressure on governments to preserve the protections that they enjoyed. When oil prices quadrupled in 1973, non-oil producers had to pay a lot more for oil and other key imports, but because their industries could not compete globally they could not export enough goods to pay for the imports. They were forced to take out international loans to cover the resulting trade imbalance. When oil prices increased again in 1979, governments had to borrow even more money from international lenders. Some reached the brink of bankruptcy, and Mexico's declaration in 1982 that it was unable to meet its international debt obligations began a global "debt crisis," which ushered in a new era in development policy.

The SAP Era The growing problems with ISI were emerging at the same time that economists and policymakers in the West were shifting from Keynesian to neoliberal

By the 1980s, ISI was becoming discredited, and neoliberals were advocating that developing countries should instead emulate the "East Asian miracle" by promoting export-led growth. In China, workers like these produce millions of pieces of clothing for export annually, helping spur the country's economic transformation over the last generation.

STR/AFP/Getty Images

ideas and becoming increasingly skeptical of the ability of governments to manage the market. The World Bank abruptly shifted its development agenda and prescriptions in 1980, embracing a neoliberal development model. This was partly induced by the great economic success of a handful of East Asian countries that collectively came to be known as the "East Asian miracle." In contrast to most of the postcolonial world, these rapidly growing countries, most notably South Korea, Taiwan, Singapore, and the city of Hong Kong, either had never adopted ISI or had abandoned it early on in favor of focusing on exporting in sectors in which they were competitive. Their success, especially in light of the problems ISI policies had begun to face, suggested to many policymakers that a new approach to development was needed.

The neoliberal model that emerged by 1980 shared neoliberals' skepticism of state interventions in the market. Neoliberal economists argued that developing countries were no different from wealthy ones and, as such, should follow the same basic neoliberal policies. These economists compiled a package of policies that came to be known as **structural adjustment programs (SAPs).** These included directives to end government protection of industries and other restrictions on free trade, privatize (sell off) government-owned industries, and reduce fiscal deficits. SAPs required a drastically reduced government that would participate far less in the economy; this would allow comparative advantage and the market to signal how resources should be invested, which would maximize efficiency and therefore economic growth.

structural adjustment programs (SAPs)
Development programs created in the 1980s; based on neoliberal principles of reduced government protection of industries, fiscal austerity, and privatization

The debt crisis that began in 1982 meant that many governments had to ask the IMF for emergency financial assistance. Working in tandem, the IMF and World Bank demanded that the governments receiving assistance in the 1980s and 1990s implement SAPs, effectively imposing this model on the Global South. This was a slow process in many countries; the necessary steps were politically unpopular because they initially resulted in high inflation, increased unemployment, and drastic cuts in government services, including education and health care. The promise was that if a country could endure these short-term pains, the new policies would maximize efficiency and encourage new investment, producing economic growth in the long term.

Many analysts agree that SAPs were successful in certain cases, such as in Chile and several countries in Southeast Asia, but on the whole their effects were mixed. On the most common measure of development, gross domestic product (GDP) per capita, developing countries grew more quickly than wealthy countries from 1965 to 1980, indicating that development policies prior to SAPs were helping them "catch up" to earlier developers. In the 1980s and 1990s, however, they grew more slowly than wealthy countries, suggesting SAPs might have made things worse, or at least did not help them overcome other factors slowing their growth (Ocampo and Vos 2008, 10). Regional differences, however, were stark, as demonstrated in Figure 11.3. On the one hand, East Asia grew many times faster than the world average. On the other hand, Africa suffered economic contraction through most of the period, and Latin America contracted in the 1980s and saw very low growth of only 1.3 percent per year during the 1990s. Changes in poverty mirrored the changes in growth. The percentage of the world's population living in extreme poverty (earning less than a dollar per day) was cut in half over the two decades, from just over 40 percent to about 22 percent. Virtually that entire decline, however, took place in East and South Asia. Given population growth, the total number of people living in extreme poverty actually increased in Africa and Latin America, and very slightly declined in South Asia, while it was cut by nearly three-quarters in East Asia. East Asia, of course, includes the rapidly growing China, Taiwan, and South Korea. While the latter two served as one of the initial models for SAPs, we will see below that they in fact did not follow the neoliberal model very closely. Many analysts argue that the model was implemented most closely in Latin America, where growth declined and poverty changed little under SAPs.

A large theoretical and policy debate arose over what caused this mixed success among those who (1) viewed the failure of SAPs in some countries as a failure of implementation, (2) believed that the model was applicable only in certain political or economic circumstances, and (3) saw fundamental flaws in the model itself. To secure essential debt relief, poor countries had to accept the policy requirements that the IMF and World Bank imposed. States agreed to make certain policy changes over a period of about three years, and the IMF/World Bank subsequently monitored how the countries followed through on their promises. Often, political leaders only partially fulfilled their obligations, so everything went back to the drawing board. This resulted in very slow and partial implementation of neoliberal policies as countries went through several rounds of negotiation and implementation with the IMF/World Bank. One body of critics, including the IMF/World Bank, concluded that the model's limited success was due to failure of political will. Success happened when top political leaders took "ownership" of the ideas, understood their importance, and committed themselves to accomplishing them. In the absence of this, no amount of external arm-twisting would do the job, and partial implementation often made little economic sense. Chile's government in the 1980s actively embraced the neoliberal model without having it imposed and had the fastest growing economy in Latin America. In contrast, Kenya's leaders were forced to accept Africa's first ever SAP in 1983 and negotiated and renegotiated numerous packages with the IMF over the years, but only very slowly and reluctantly liberalized their economy, resulting in economic stagnation for most of the period.

Other critics contended that the model should have taken political circumstances into account. Lack of implementation, they argued, came not just from lack of understanding and commitment but also from the rational actions of self-interested political leaders. Where leaders' political survival depended on their ability to provide supporters with patronage, they were reluctant to implement SAPs that reduced the size and scope of government and therefore their sources of patronage. Kenya was a prime example. Nimah Mazaheri (2014) used a quantitative analysis to argue that oil producers were less likely to implement neoliberal policies because the volatility of the oil market would be exacerbated by greater openness to global financial and investment markets. Institutionalists contended that markets only work well when embedded in strong institutions, such as clear property rights and contracts. The ultimate goal of the neoliberal model is to improve efficiency to encourage investment and thereby future

---

FIGURE 11.3   Growth and Poverty Reduction in the SAP Era

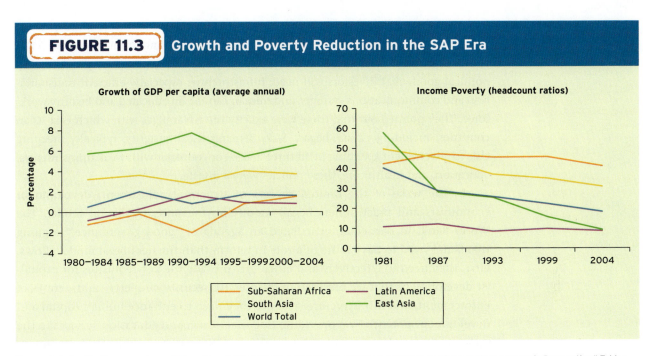

Source: Data for the figures are from Jeffrey Round, "Globalization, Growth, Inequality, and Poverty in Africa: A Macroeconomic Perspective," Tables 11.1 and 11.3, in *The Poor under Globalization in Asia, Latin America, and Africa,* edited by M. Nissanke and E. Thorbecke (Oxford, UK: Oxford University Press, 2010), 330, 334.

growth. Weak states that have weak institutions, however, will never gain greater investment because investors cannot be certain their investments and future profits will be secure. The initial neoliberal model ignored this essential area entirely and so was successful only where key institutions were already relatively strong, such as in Chile.

Another group argued that SAPs worked only in certain economic circumstances. A leading theory for East Asian economic success is the "flying geese" theory (Ozawa 2010). It argues that, like flocks of geese, when one economy in a region is successful, others can follow in its wake by producing goods that the newly wealthy country needs. In East Asia, the original "lead goose" was Japan, followed by South Korea and Taiwan, and later by China. Without a regional leader like Japan, the policies produced few benefits in Africa. Related to this, some analysts argued that the neoliberal model suffered from a *fallacy of composition*: just because something is true in one case does not mean it will be true when applied to all cases. In relation to SAPs, it suggests that market-friendly policies designed to attract investment will succeed in some cases, probably the earliest ones and those with other attractions to investors. When the same policies are extended to all countries, however, there will not be enough investment capital available to respond. Furthermore, the earliest success cases will be likely to attract even more investment, leaving the latecomers empty-handed. Even if later or less attractive states pursue the "right" policies, they still may not see the investment necessary to spark economic growth.

A final school of critics argued that the neoliberal model undermines the real fundamentals of long-term development: infrastructure and human capital. They contended that states succeed at instigating economic development by providing key political goods that investors will need: infrastructure, especially efficient transportation and communications systems; and human capital, an educated and healthy workforce. They pointed out that these were exactly the advantages with which East Asian countries, including China, began. SAPs demand fiscal austerity, typically meaning cuts to government spending in all three areas. For countries with weak infrastructure, education, and health care, these policies were a disaster.

In the wake of the limited success of structural adjustment, development economists and practitioners began modifying the pure, neoliberal model. The World Bank, in particular, articulated an agenda of "good governance," arguing that states need to have more of a role in reform than the neoliberal model allows. First, they need to effectively and efficiently provide the key requisites for capitalist development that we outlined in chapter 10: security, property rights, contract enforcement, and infrastructure. Second, they need to enhance human capital and development potential via providing essential health and education services to the poor, which is also supported by Sen's capabilities conception of development. Virtually all major Western development agencies continue to support the basic principle that states should not distort markets (as they did under ISI), but many now believe that the state does have a role to play in simultaneously attracting capital and alleviating poverty.

Several more significant alternatives, though, have also gained popularity. One is derived originally from the Japanese developmental state model. It has been most prominent in a number of successful Asian developing economies. In Latin America,

CRITICAL inquiry

Structural Adjustment Programs

SAPs were intended to correct economic imbalances in developing countries in order to encourage investment, renew economic growth, and thereby reduce poverty via a shift from the protectionism of ISI to more open economy and export-oriented growth. The IMF along with the World Bank were the major organizations that imposed SAPs on often reluctant governments

around the world. Table 11.1 presents the number of IMF agreements between 1980 and 2000 (the era in which structural adjustment was pursued most actively) for a selection of countries. While this alone does not tell us everything we might want to know about how much individual countries pursued SAPs, it is an indication of the influence of the IMF's policies. The question is, Do these SAPs lead to better economic outcomes? The table also provides data on GDP per capita, trade, poverty, and infant mortality (the best measure of overall health). Based on this table, what trends do you see? Can you use the data to come to conclusions about who is correct in the debate over SAPs? Did they enhance economic growth and improve well-being in developing countries? Did they create even greater poverty, as their critics asserted? What other information would you like to have to answer these questions even better?

TABLE 11.1	Effect of SAPs on Development: Changes in Key Indicators, 1980-2000								
Country	# IMF agreements, 1980-2000	GDP per capita (constant dollars PPP), 1980	GDP per capita (constant dollars PPP), 2000	Trade surplus or deficit (current account balance, % of GDP) 1980*	Trade surplus or deficit (current account balance, % of GDP) 2000*	Absolute poverty level (poverty gap at $1.25 a day PPP, %) 1980	Absolute poverty level (poverty gap at $1.25 a day PPP, %) 2000	Infant mortality rate (per 1,000 live births) 1980	Infant mortality rate (per 1,000 live births) 2000
Argentina	7	10,075	10,282	-1.23	-3.15	0.0 (1986)	2.8	173	95
Ghana	9	993	1,067	-0.21	-6.56	18.0 (1988)	14.4 (1998)	95	64
Indonesia	2	1,323	2,623	3.36	4.84	21.4 (1984)	12.5 (1999)	76	38
Kenya	9	1,375	1,283	-10.72	-2.31	15.4 (1992)	16.9 (2005)	69	70
Mexico	5	10,238	11,853	-4.61	-2.78	3.0 (1984)	1.5	55	24
Nigeria	3	1,645	1,469	8.85	12.47	21.9 (1986)	28.7 (2004)	129	113
Pakistan	8	1,224	1,845	-3.19	-0.29	23.9 (1987)	6.3	111	76
Peru	4	6,083	5,543	-5.06	-2.90	3.0 (1986)	4.6	79	30
Philippines	6	2,827	2,697	-6.91	-2.75	10.3 (1985)	5.5	53	29
Tanzania	4	823 (1998)	868	-7.69	-4.30	29.7 (1992)	41.6	105	78
Zambia	5	1,532	1,028	-15.08	-18.34	40.0 (1991)	26.9 (1998)	98	91

Sources: Data are from International Monetary Fund (number of SAPs, changes to trade surplus and deficit) and World Bank (GDP per capita PPP, absolute poverty rate, infant mortality rate).

*Positive numbers show exports are greater than imports and negative numbers show imports are greater than exports.

a leftist alternative to parts of the neoliberal model arose in the new millennium in several countries, including our case study of Brazil. Finally, in response to the failure to reduce poverty in the poorest countries—what Paul Collier (2007) called "the bottom billion"—policy alternatives involving large investments via aid have gained currency. All of these alternatives accept many of the core neoliberal recommendations for macroeconomic policies and believe that global market forces cannot be ignored, but also that even the poorest states can and must play a significant role in harnessing those forces for the benefit of their citizens.

The Developmental State We outlined the key elements of the developmental state in our examination of Japan in chapter 10. A number of other Asian countries adopted and modified the model, starting with South Korea, as did others elsewhere

export-oriented growth (EOG)
Development policy based on encouraging economic growth via exports of goods and services, usually starting with light manufacturing such as textiles

in the world, although usually less successfully. Developmental states consciously intervene in the market via an aggressive industrial policy: a policy aimed at strengthening particular industries. In contrast to the earlier ISI model, though, developmental states encouraged **export-oriented growth (EOG)**, growth via exports of goods and services, usually starting with light manufactures such as textiles. They tried to "pick winners," subsidizing and protecting new industries but demanding high performance from them and opening them up to global competition as soon as possible. The key aim was not to provide manufactured goods for the domestic market, as under ISI, but manufactured exports for wealthier countries. Light manufacturing is typically labor-intensive, so the new investments employed large numbers of people; Asian developmental states, in particular, used EOG to take advantage of their comparative advantage in large amounts of cheap labor.

While developmental states intervened in the economy, subsidizing and guiding investments into particular areas rather than letting the market fully determine investment patterns, they usually followed neoliberal fiscal and monetary policy, keeping inflation low and their currencies stable and realistically valued vis-à-vis others, thus encouraging investment and exports. Their successes were also based on the fact that their high-quality education systems had produced a highly literate and therefore productive workforce. Another key component of their success was a strong state, one in which economic bureaucracies were insulated from short-term political pressures so that they could pursue consistent, long-term policies. Several major analysts determined that this was a key factor for other states that wanted to pursue similar policies; weaker states that succumbed to short-term domestic pressures were far less successful (Haggard and Kaufman 1995).

The Asian economic miracle that was produced primarily by developmental states has been the biggest development success story of the last generation. A famous comparison is between South Korea and Ghana in West Africa. Upon Ghana's independence in 1957, it and South Korea had nearly identical per capita incomes and economies. Both were poor and mostly agricultural. By 2015, South Korea had a per capita GDP (PPP) of $34,500, compared with Ghana's $4,200. Such rapid growth almost always produces greater inequality, as some people get much richer and others are left behind. Growth in the early developmental states such as South Korea and Taiwan, however, was combined with reduced inequality. This was largely due to earlier policies that supported rural areas; reforms gave peasant farmers more equal access to land, universal education, and good infrastructure, facilitating their participation in economic growth. Labor-intensive manufacturing also helped limit inequality, as it employed large numbers of people at relatively equal wages.

The 1997–1998 East Asian financial crisis shook the foundations of the developmental state model. The crisis started when the government of Thailand was forced to "float" its currency, the baht. The Thai economy had been booming: international capital poured in, factories opened, and the real estate market soared. Much of this activity, however, went through unregulated banks in a relatively weak state, which may be why international investors began to doubt the stability and long-term prospects of the Thai economy. The famous venture capitalist George Soros was one of the first to sell his Thai currency, and as more investors sold their currencies rapidly, getting out of the currency market the way people get out of a stock market when they think it's about to crash, real estate prices and company profits collapsed. Economies that had been booming went into steep decline, and unemployment soared. The economic contagion spread rapidly from Thailand to Indonesia, Malaysia, the Philippines, and South Korea, and later to other developing economies like Brazil and Russia.

The massive loss of wealth in Asia ultimately brought down the government of longtime Indonesian dictator Suharto and threatened the political stability of other countries as well. The crisis produced recession and instability for many middle-income countries, though most recovered and were growing substantially a decade later. In spite of this recovery, the crisis revealed that many developmental states' regulation of the financial sector in particular was very weak. Banks took on unsecured international loans and lent money for dubious investments, often to companies with which they had close, even familial, ties. When the crisis hit, the banks rapidly sank into bankruptcy since their creditors could not repay them and, in turn, they could not repay their own international loans. Neoliberals argued that in spite of East Asia's rapid success, the state's role was not as beneficial as had been assumed. Many began to argue that economic growth would have been even more rapid without state credit and subsidies to key industries. Critics of neoliberalism made the opposite argument: lack of controls of the flow of money across borders allowed the speculative boom and subsequent bust.

Thai farmers step on sheets of rubber to stretch them. The Asian financial crisis that harmed the developmental state model in 1997-1998 began in Thailand when international currency investors decided the country would not be able to pay its debts. The crisis was the largest loss of wealth in the world between the Great Depression and the Great Recession of 2008-2009.

MADAREE TOHLALA/AFP/Getty Images

Even taking the crisis into account, the developmental state has been the most successful developmental model of the last generation, but it seems difficult to imitate in contexts other than where it began. Even in Asia, countries like Thailand and the Philippines, while achieving significant success and becoming middle-income countries, have not duplicated the success of South Korea or Taiwan. Moreover, our case study of China, the greatest success of all, only partly duplicates the developmental state. Nonetheless, the model has helped East and Southeast Asia benefit more from globalization than any other region of the Global South.

The "Pink Tide" in Latin America   The neoliberal model and the IMF probably influenced Latin America more than any other region. The debt crisis that began in Mexico in August 1982 quickly spread to Brazil and Argentina, and the 1980s became known as the "lost decade" in Latin America because of the severe economic downturn that followed the debt crisis. By the mid-1990s, most Latin American countries had engaged in extensive privatization of state-owned activities, reduction of trade barriers, and fiscal restraint. Neoliberal reform, though, did not produce notable improvement in growth or reduction in poverty. Not surprisingly, this produced a political backlash. Citizens in Argentina, Bolivia, Brazil, Chile, Ecuador, and Venezuela elected leftist critics of neoliberal reforms in the new millennium, creating what many called Latin America's "pink tide" (Wylde 2012). These new governing parties and coalitions implemented policies that, while not rejecting all of neoliberalism, significantly modified it.

The "pink tide" governments varied widely. Some, such as Argentina and Brazil, preserved the major macroeconomic foundations of neoliberalism but implemented greater social programs aimed at the poor. Others, most famously that of Hugo Chávez in Venezuela, intervened in the economy in ways that more seriously challenged the market model, including heavily subsidizing certain sectors, such as food and fuel, and nationalizing key industries, especially minerals. Neoliberals feared that the pink tide would undermine what they saw as the gains of neoliberalism, including fiscal austerity and control of inflation. Most of the "pink tide" governments, though, preserved many neoliberal macroeconomic policies, maintaining more or less balanced budgets and keeping the economy open to trade and investment. Through 2007, they achieved slightly higher growth rates and greater fiscal surpluses than other Latin American governments, with only slightly higher inflation (Moreno-Brid and Paunovic 2010). Coupling this with expanded social services resulted in the biggest reduction in poverty in generations in some countries, including our case study of Brazil.

The pink tide in Brazil began with the inauguration of "Lula" as president in 2003 (see chapter 6). He was a union leader who helped lead the democratization movement in the 1980s and helped found the Workers' Party (PT) that ruled the country from 2003 to 2016. During the 2002 presidential campaign, domestic and international business leaders feared a PT government, so the party wrote a manifesto stating that "social development," focused on reducing poverty and inequality, was crucial but that it would be coupled with neoliberal policies to keep inflation low and the government budget in surplus. Lula tried to do these two things sequentially by first securing economic stability and business confidence and then focusing on social programs. While progress was slow, by 2010 unemployment had dropped from 9 percent to under 6 percent, and poverty was cut roughly in half. Lula's government had achieved these gains for the working class and poor via increased and regionally widespread growth and new social programs (see chapter 12).

Growth in Latin America as a whole, and most pink tide countries, peaked in 2010 as the effects of the Great Recession spread. Growth dropped from 5.7 percent in 2010 to only 1 percent in 2014, and the region entered recession, with a 0.9 percent loss of GDP in 2015. Most analysts pointed to falling prices for key exports, especially minerals, as the main reason why. Brazil's economy collapsed in 2015, dropping 3.8 percent, while Venezuela's entered full-scale crisis, dropping nearly 4 percent in 2014 and 5.7 percent in 2015, and producing massive protests against the government of Hugo Chávez's successor. At least in some of the pink tide countries, exceptional growth had relied heavily on selling raw materials, especially to China. As Chinese growth slowed and global mineral prices fell, so did the pink tide experiment, a victim of the effects of globalization. By 2016, the result was leftists being removed from power in Brazil and Argentina, and others being forced to scale back their social programs as government revenue plummeted.

The "Bottom Billion" Economist Paul Collier (2007) coined the term *the bottom billion* to refer to the population of the poorest countries on Earth, most of them in Africa, which seemed to be left behind by globalization. Being poor and heavily indebted, many of these poorest countries were forced to implement structural adjustment in the 1980s and 1990s. The results, however, were even more disappointing than in most Latin American countries. Of 186 countries on the Human Development Index in 2015, some 23 of the bottom 25 were African (the two exceptions were Haiti and Afghanistan). By the new millennium, the continent had become the poster child of economic failure and the subject of growing attention from global development agencies, charitable foundations, and even rock stars. The failure of globalization and neoliberal policies to create growth and reduce poverty in the poorest countries produced a new development debate about both the causes of this failure and what to do about it.

As noted earlier, the World Bank and others began advocating for developing stronger state institutions and human capital. Following an institutionalist approach, they argued that the absence of strong, market-friendly institutions is the problem in the poorest states, in which neopatrimonial forms of authority harm investment and markets by exacting implicit taxes, distributing the revenue gained via patron-client networks, and weakening the rule of law. The World Bank prescribes the creation of effective and efficient governing institutions that help provide strong rule of law, political stability, and key public goods such as infrastructure, education, and health care. At least implicitly, this theory argues that these goals can best be achieved via a democratic regime.

Other analysts, such as Jeffrey Sachs, argued that specific conditions limit growth in the poorest countries, and external aid can help overcome these constraints. Sachs (2005) pointed to geography, disease, and climate as key issues in Africa in particular. Low population densities, few good ports, long distances to major consumer markets, many landlocked countries, and the ravages of tropical diseases all reduce Africa's growth potential in the absence of major foreign assistance. Sachs called for a massive inflow of aid, arguing that a large enough volume targeted the right way could end African poverty in our lifetime. This approach led to the creation of the United Nations' **Millennium Development Goals (MDGs),** a set of targets to reduce poverty and hunger, improve education and health, improve the status of women, and achieve environmental sustainability, all fueled by a call for a large increase in aid. Collier (2007) argued for a more nuanced approach, suggesting that different countries were poor from differing reasons. Some faced a problem of bad governance, as argued above, while others faced a resource curse or debilitating political conflict; each problem, he argued, requires focus on that issue, with aid playing a part, but targeted specifically to that problem.

Neoliberal critics of this approach, such as William Easterly (2006) and Dambisa Moyo (2009), pointed to the fact that Africa has a long history as the world's largest aid recipient and yet has failed to achieve substantial development. Easterly argued that the result of misguided efforts such as Sachs's will be that "the rich have markets" while "the poor have bureaucrats." The former, he suggested, is the only way to achieve growth; the latter will waste and distort resources and leave Africans more impoverished and dependent on Western support. Moyo argued that microfinance and the global bond markets would be better means to achieve development than continued dependence on aid. If poor countries had to use global bond markets to finance investment the way wealthier countries do, they would be forced to implement better policies, and these would foster growth. Stephen Kaplan (2013) found evidence in Latin America to support the disciplining effect of the global bond market: countries that relied more heavily on bonds to finance development maintained stronger fiscal austerity than countries that relied more heavily on loans; he did not examine, however, if this had any effect on economic growth and well-being. The punishing discipline of the international bond market (the same discipline that Greece has faced in the eurozone crisis) would create the incentives governments in poor countries require to develop both stronger institutions and better policies. Foreign aid will never achieve this discipline and therefore, Moyo suggests, will keep poor countries dependent and poor.

Millennium Development Goals (MDGs)
Targets established by the United Nations to reduce poverty and hunger, improve education and health, improve the status of women, and achieve environmental sustainability

As this debate was unfolding, some analysts, including a number of African leaders, began to talk of an "African Renaissance." Overall economic growth improved significantly, averaging nearly 5 percent from 2000 to 2007 and 4.2 percent from 2007 to 2015, in spite of the Great Recession and subsequent decline in commodity prices. The population living in absolute poverty across the continent dropped from 51 percent in 2005 to 39 percent in 2012 (African Development Bank Group 2013). Much of this was fuelled, however, by rising prices for Africa's raw materials, especially oil. Whether improvement can be sustained over the long term in the face of declining commodity prices will determine whether Africa can finally begin to see the benefits of globalization, or whether the "bottom billion" will remain so.

After a half century of debate, no single development theory has proven itself as the key answer to the problem. Most analysts agree with a number of the fundamentals of neoliberalism, at least regarding the need to keep fiscal deficits and debt limited and inflation low to encourage investment. Most also now recognize the importance of the state creating (1) strong institutions providing the core functions we outlined in chapter 10: security, property, and contract rights; and (2) key public goods such as infrastructure, education, and health care. All of these are now seen as essential to achieve both economic growth and enhanced human capabilities. It remains unclear, however, how states with varying levels of wealth and state strength can achieve these goals, especially in the face of globalization and dramatically shifting prices for the goods they export that help finance development. It is also far from clear how much the wealthy countries can and should help. What is clear is that a handful of countries, almost all in Asia, seemed to have figured out a way to pursue successful development, and they account for the vast majority of the success so far.

Regime Type and Development Success

Whichever developmental model seems most effective at navigating globalization to achieve growth and reduce poverty, a subsequent question is, What type of government is most likely to pursue beneficial policies? The classic question in this area has been, Do democracies or dictatorships produce better economic development? Most theorists initially asserted that democracy provides incentives for politicians to pursue policies that will gain them support so they can win elections, and citizens will demand good economic policy. On the other hand, some of the primary development success stories such as South Korea, Taiwan, and China achieved much of their success under authoritarian regimes. Pundits and policymakers used this as evidence to argue that pushing democracy on a poor country too soon will produce neither healthy democracy nor economic development. Many argue that strong states need to be created, as well as healthy economies, before democracy is viable. Sen (1999), of course, argued that democracy is not just a means to development; rather, the freedom democracy provides is part of the definition of development.

Those arguing that democracy enhances growth and reduces poverty focus mostly on accountability, stability, and the rule of law. They hold that democracies provide greater popular accountability, so citizens will demand that their governments pursue beneficial economic policies. Amartya Sen famously noted that no democracy has ever had a famine; the need for popular support ensures that democratic governments will not let their people starve *en masse*. Once consolidated, democracy also enhances political stability; while changes of governmental leaders still occur, elections regularize the process so change does not threaten the ability of investors to predict future returns, and the investment that is the basis of growth will continue to flow. Finally, democracies better protect the rule of law, including the property rights and contracts that are essential elements of capitalist growth. In contrast, dictatorships are less accountable, are more prone to unpredictable instability like coups d'état or revolutions, and do not protect the rule of law from the whims of the ruling elite.

Opponents of this view hypothesize that democracy impedes growth because democratic governments must follow political demands that favor consumption over investment. Long-term economic growth depends on investment, which can only happen if some of society's resources are not consumed. Democracies, this school of thought argues, have to bow to the will of the citizens, and citizens typically want more consumption now and are unwilling to invest and wait for future benefits. This is especially true in poorer societies, where more impoverished people understandably demand consumption now. Furthermore, in democracies with weak institutions and weak political parties, these demands are based on patronage, giving political leaders an incentive to control as many resources as possible. This has the effect of expanding the role of the state, harming the business climate, and again, discouraging investment. Dictatorships, the argument goes, can resist pressure for greater consumption by repressing citizens' demands and can follow more consistent policies over time, as the East Asian success stories demonstrate.

Despite this extensive debate, empirical findings, many using quite sophisticated statistical techniques, have been rather ambiguous. Przeworski et al. (2000) and Yi Feng (2003) analyzed the relationship between regime type and economic growth, taking into account numerous economic factors that influence growth in an effort to isolate the independent effect of regime type. Przeworski et al. demonstrated overall that democracies and dictatorships achieve the same levels of growth, and this is true for both wealthier and poorer countries. Feng also found that democracy has little effect on growth but that this is due to two contradictory results: the direct effect of the level of democracy on growth is slightly negative (i.e., democracy harms growth), but democracy enhances growth indirectly by creating greater political stability. Still, the net result is near zero.

Democracy alone, however, may not be the determining variable in achieving growth and reducing poverty. The type of democracy and other aspects of the state may matter as well. Lijphart (1999) has long argued that consensual democracies produce greater well-being because the compromise they require forces leaders to distribute resources more equitably, which provides greater stability, encouraging investment and growth. Huber and Stephens (2012) found that democracy encouraged the creation of the left-leaning parties in Latin America's "pink tide"; those parties produced more egalitarian social policy, which in turn improved human capital and therefore is likely to improve development in the long run. Flores-Macias (2012) presented a similar but more nuanced argument that the "pink tide" governments that have pursued stable macroeconomic policies that have aided growth, like our case study of Brazil, were characterized by relatively institutionalized party systems. Stronger party systems deter outsiders from entering the system and give leaders and parties incentives to maintain stability. "Pink tide" governments with weaker party systems, such as Venezuela, pursued more erratic and less beneficial policies. Anne Pitcher (2012) similarly argued that in Africa strong parties and quality of democracy lead to better policies and processes of privatization, a key element of neoliberal reform.

Finally, others claimed that the coalition of forces in power is the crucial determinant. Mosley et al. (2012) found that if the elite splits in a democracy, often due to a particular crisis, and one segment of it is astute enough to try to co-opt the poor to help them prevail politically, they will pursue more pro-poor policies. This is not automatic in a democracy, though. The elite in a democracy in a very unequal society may well be able to maintain power, as elite theorists argue, with minimal attention to the bulk of the voters. Similarly, in ethnically divided democracies in which most people vote for "their" ethnic leaders, elites will face little pressure to pursue pro-poor policies because doing so will not affect their ability to garner votes—only ethnicity matters. Carl LeVan (2015) used Nigeria to demonstrate that what matters to sound economic policy is not whether the country has a democratic or authoritarian regime but rather the number of veto players within either type of regime. Among Nigeria's many regimes, those with more veto players produced worse macroeconomic policies such as controlling inflation and providing education; on the other hand, they also kept wasteful spending on patronage limited, creating a dilemma for policymakers between the goals of effective national policy and accountability.

Pippa Norris (2012) argued that the state's bureaucratic capacity, not the characteristics of the particular democracy, is the missing explanatory factor. Like previous studies, she found no clear relationship between democracy and economic growth or other developmental goals. When she added the state's bureaucratic capacity to her statistical model, however, both it and democracy were important in explaining success. She concluded that we need to distinguish between what she called "bureaucratic democracies" with high capacity to implement policies and "patronage democracies" lacking such capacity. Similarly, "bureaucratic autocracies" are more successful than "patronage autocracies," though not as successful as "bureaucratic democracies." Figure 11.4 provides the growth rates of each regime type. Even when controlling for many other factors that affect growth, democracy and state capacity, when considered together, make a difference. These distinctions within both democracies and autocracies, she argued, explain the ambiguous results of prior studies that focused on regime type alone.

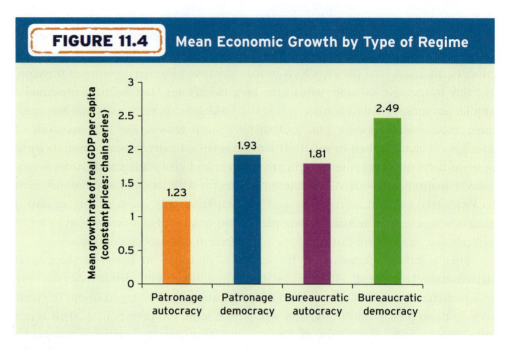

The greatest consensus in this debate is probably that a relatively strong state helps; it can implement policies more effectively, monitor cross-border activities more efficiently, and therefore is more likely to be able to provide the greatest benefits for its citizens. As we discussed in chapters 2 and 8, however, a strong state does not require or even necessarily benefit from an authoritarian regime. While there are examples of authoritarian regimes creating spectacular growth and poverty reduction, their record overall is quite erratic. Authoritarian regimes include some of the most successful, like our case study of China, and some of the worst, like Robert Mugabe's Zimbabwe. Democracy alone, however, does not seem to be a panacea, either. Combined with a strong state, though, it seems likely to help; at least, that is the conclusion of much of the best evidence we currently have available.

CASE STUDIES IN DEVELOPMENT

The Global South includes countries of widely varying levels of wealth and types of economies. Figures 11.5–11.10 provide a comparative glance at key data for our case studies. In spite of their great importance on the world stage, China and India remain poorer on average than the middle-income countries of Iran and Mexico. Indeed, India's per capita GDP is closer to Nigeria's than it is to the average middle-income country. India has seen strong growth over many years now, but it still contains the largest number of poor people in the world. The Human Development Index, reflecting Sen's capabilities definition of development, includes wealth, health, and education. On this, India and China are much closer to wealthier Iran and Mexico; in spite of their relative poverty, they have provided very high levels of education and reasonably good health to their citizens, at least comparatively speaking. Figures 11.7 and 11.8 show that inequality and poverty are not the same thing. Inequality is higher in middle-income countries like Mexico even though absolute poverty is quite low there. Nigeria's oil economy, sadly, has produced both high inequality and poverty. Growth has been far higher in China and India than the other cases and is much more volatile in the oil-producing economies of Nigeria and Iran, which are dependent on global oil prices. Inflation was a serious problem in Mexico and the rest of Latin America in the 1980s but dramatically lower since; this is one area in which neoliberal policies were clearly successful. Our case studies below explore why we see these variations in development outcomes.

MEXICO: FROM PROTECTIONISM TO NEOLIBERALISM

CASE SYNOPSIS

Mexico represents a classic case of the shift from ISI to neoliberal policies, with all of the benefits and costs that entails. ISI combined with oil revenue to create substantial growth until the 1970s, when growing debt and global economic problems undermined it. Mexico started the 1980s debt crisis and was forced to accept neoliberal policies in exchange for Western (especially U.S.) support. The neoliberal shift culminated with the signing of the North American Free Trade Agreement (NAFTA), greatly expanding Mexico's manufactured exports to the United States. This has renewed growth via foreign investment but has also expanded inequality and increased dependence on Mexico's primary export market, the United States, leaving it especially vulnerable to global economic shocks like the Great Recession. The government under President Enrique Peña Nieto instituted significant reforms in 2013, pushing the country further in a neoliberal direction.

- **TYPE OF ECONOMY** ISI initially; shift to neoliberalism in 1980s–1990s

- **DEVELOPMENT OUTCOMES** Middle-income country; heavy reliance on exports

- **RESPONSE TO GREAT RECESSION** Mirrors U.S. economy

- **RECENT REFORM EFFORTS** Liberalization of energy sector

- **CONTINUING PROBLEMS** High inequality; dependence on U.S. market; growing debt

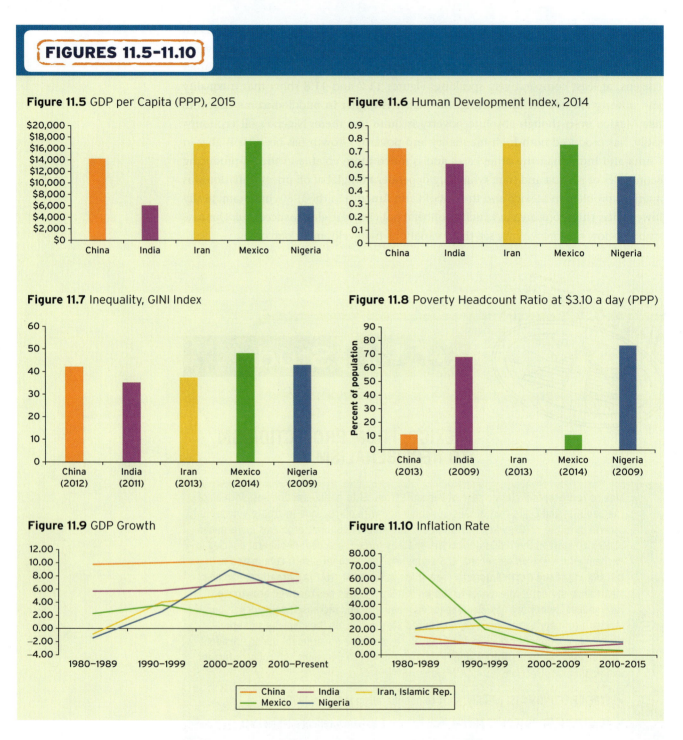

FIGURES 11.5–11.10

Figure 11.5 GDP per Capita (PPP), 2015

Figure 11.6 Human Development Index, 2014

Figure 11.7 Inequality, GINI Index

Figure 11.8 Poverty Headcount Ratio at $3.10 a day (PPP)

Figure 11.9 GDP Growth

Figure 11.10 Inflation Rate

Sources: Data for Figure 11.5 and Figures 11.7–11.10 are from World Bank. Data for Figure 11.6 are from UN Human Development Index (http://hdr.undp.org/en/composite/trends). Data for Figure 11.5 are available at http://data.worldbank.org/indicator/NY.GDP.PCAP.PP.CD; data for Figure 11.7 are available at http://data.worldbank.org/indicator/SI.POV.GINI; data for Figure 11.8 are available at http://data.worldbank.org/indicator/SI.POV.GAP2; data for Figure 11.9 are available at http://data.worldbank.org/indicator/NY.GDP.MKTP.KD.ZG; data for Figure 11.10 are available at http://data.worldbank.org/indicator/FP.CPI.TOTL.ZG.

The prerevolutionary era of dictator Porfirio Díaz gave Mexico its first glimpse of large-scale economic growth, which averaged about 8 percent between 1884 and 1900. The Díaz regime embraced modernizing authoritarianism, which created vast wealth for the upper crust but left many behind. Existing social class distinctions only became more pronounced with the influx of foreign direct investment. The rich simply got richer, while the poor remained poor.

Díaz fell from power in 1911 as a result of the Mexican Revolution. Emerging from the ashes of the revolution was the PRI-led regime that followed a model of corporatism and supported the broad, working-class and peasant constituency that had inspired Díaz's overthrow. Powerful political figures such as presidents Lázaro Cárdenas (1934–1940) and Luís Echeverría (1970–1976) became associated with a staunch, anti-elite populism. Under these leaders, oil nationalization, land redistribution, and ISI became the touted successes of the regime. During the ISI period (1940–1982), economic growth averaged a relatively strong 3.1 percent.

This success was in large part funded through Petróleos Mexicanos (PEMEX), the company that oversaw all of Mexico's oil production. Though it was the world's sixth-largest oil producer at its peak, Mexico has seen its reserves decline while haphazard infrastructure development has limited PEMEX's ability to reap the full benefits of its oil fields. Some of the constraints on the oil sector came from the state's appetite for revenue to fund its public programs, as part of a clientelist effort to maintain the PRI's popularity and legitimacy. In 1976 massive new oil reserves were discovered in the Gulf of Mexico, but the state's disproportionate increase in spending largely cancelled out many of the expected gains.

The first move away from ISI-oriented policies took place when the government was forced to allow the value of the peso to be determined by the currency market, rather than set by the government, in 1976; the peso quickly lost 50 percent of its value. Mexico fell into crisis, and the international community intervened with loans, the first of several such interventions.

Mexico's 1982 debt crisis began with falling oil prices, a recession in the United States, and massive, dollar-denominated debt. Declining oil revenue and the American recession caused the Mexican peso to fall sharply in relation to the dollar, making it much more expensive for Mexico to pay back its debt. As this happened, capital began to flee the country in the billions of dollars. President José López Portillo responded by nationalizing Mexico's banks, which remained state controlled until the 1990s. The crisis ushered in what became the global debt crisis, and it put the IMF and U.S. government in a position to demand fundamental changes in economic policy, creating what Mexicans (and other Latin Americans) refer to as the "lost decade" of economic decline—clearly visible in the negative growth in Figure 11.9.

The country's steady move toward a neoliberal economic model began in earnest during the presidency of Miguel de la Madrid (1982–1988). Foreign-educated experts, disconnected from the politics of the revolution and the PRI's populist heyday, controlled economic policy. By the time Carlos Salinas de Gortari (1988–1994)—a Harvard-educated technocrat himself—left office, Mexico's commitment to neoliberalism was well established and strongly supported by the IMF and U.S. government. The country had joined the General Agreement on Tariffs and Trade (GATT, the predecessor of the WTO) in 1986 and signed NAFTA in 1992. In the late ISI period (1970–1985), GDP growth averaged 4.5 percent per year in the best-performing Mexican states; this figure dropped to only 2.5 percent during the early free-market period (1985–1992). Studies show, however, that without NAFTA, growth would have been 4 to 5 percent lower by the year 2002. While NAFTA increased productivity, it has had only marginal impact on employment. Unemployment has changed little in the past twenty years, and Mexico remains one of the most unequal societies in the world. Indeed, inequality increased as the wealthy benefitted from the new business opportunities neoliberal policies provided while the average wage dropped 40 percent over the 1980s and 1990s and the minimum wage dropped 70 percent. The neoliberal policies did reduce inflation dramatically and improved growth notably in the 1990s, though the economy slowed down in the new millennium.

Mexican oil workers change a drill pipe at a PEMEX facility. One of President Peña Nieto's most controversial economic reforms was ending an eight-decade monopoly that PEMEX, the nationally owned oil company, had on Mexico's oil sector.

Photographer: Susana Gonzalez/Bloomberg via Getty Images

The two most noticeable effects of the shift to neoliberalism and NAFTA were seen in lower inflation (see Figure 11.10) and higher exports, which rose from 15 percent of GDP in 1985 to 35 percent in 2015, with 80 percent destined for the United States. NAFTA not only gives Mexican manufacturers access to the vast U.S. market but invites companies from all over the world to set up manufacturing plants, or *maquiladoras,* just south of the U.S.–Mexico border to take advantage of inexpensive labor and then export their goods to the United States tariff-free, providing Mexico with needed foreign direct investment. Many Chinese and Korean firms, for instance, have opened plants in northern Mexico. After the 1990s boom in *maquila* manufacturing, the sector slowed down in the new millennium in the face of competition from even cheaper labor in China. As wage rates in China began to rise in recent years, however, manufacturing grew again along the U.S.–Mexican border.

As the economy became more dependent on trade, regional disparities became more pronounced, with northern states most able to exploit their proximity to U.S. markets. The less-developed southern states have lagged behind. In the free-trade economy, cheap, state-subsidized corn from the United States displaced traditional and less-developed agriculture meant for local consumption. This resulted in billions of dollars in losses to local growers, negatively affecting already impoverished rural communities and driving many residents to seek better opportunities by migrating to the United States. In 1997 the government began what is widely seen as a relatively successful "conditional cash transfer" (see chapter 12) antipoverty program. Absolute poverty dropped from about 11 percent when the program started to under 3 percent in 2012, though the program cannot be given full credit for that drop, as many factors affect poverty, most importantly economic growth. In spite of this, though, inequality remains exceptionally high (see Figure 11.6).

The transition to a democratic government in 2000 changed economic policy remarkably little. The new ruling party had always been in favor of free-market policies, so it did not change the neoliberal direction of the country. The dependence on exports to the United States meant that the 2008–2009 global recession hit Mexico very hard. Its GDP dropped by 6.5 percent in 2009, though as the United States began to recover, so did Mexico. Growth returned to 5.6 percent in 2010, but it slowed again to about 4 percent through 2012. After 2013, growth dropped further, to 1.5–2.5 percent, largely due to declining world oil prices. The recession also meant higher levels of poverty and reduced migration to the United States as the U.S. job market for immigrants (legal and illegal) dried up.

In the wake of the recession and continued concern about rampant drug-related violence, the PRI regained power in 2012, this time as a democratically elected party. The new president, Enrique Peña Nieto, promised major reforms to revive the economy. Just before he entered office, the Congress passed legislation substantially reducing labor market restrictions. Then Peña Nieto was able to negotiate the "Pact for Mexico," with support of all three major political parties. This promised neoliberal reforms in a wide variety of areas, most importantly in telecommunications, education, and energy. Faced with falling oil revenue, the government also increased taxes on the wealthy in order to keep the fiscal deficit limited. Congress approved the most important element of the Pact for Mexico, liberalization of the oil industry, in December 2013. PEMEX's nationalization and monopoly over the crucial oil industry had been a pillar of the PRI "revolutionary" government since the 1930s. Changing it required a constitutional amendment. The leftist party in the pact withdrew in response to what it saw as unacceptable liberalization. The reforms left PEMEX with control over significant oil fields but for the first time opened up exploration and production to international investment in 2014.

By 2016, Mexico had positive but moderate growth of about 2.5 percent. Neoliberal policies had kept both inflation and unemployment relatively low. Since the Great Recession, though, declining revenue has required cutting government spending to maintain a low fiscal deficit, and the country's external debt has grown substantially. Over the long term, however, the effects of Mexico's shift to neoliberalism remain unclear; growth was negative over the "lost decade" of the 1980s and didn't become consistently positive until 1996. Over the last two decades, per capita growth has been more consistent but modest, averaging around 1.5 percent per year, well below the level of the ISI era.

CASE Questions

1. Mexico is a classic case of the shift from ISI to neoliberal economic policies in developing countries. What have been the benefits and costs of neoliberal policy in Mexico? Weighing these costs and benefits, has the neoliberal model benefitted the country overall?

2. Nineteenth-century dictator Porfirio Díaz famously said, "Poor Mexico, so far from God and so close to the United States!" What have been the major effects of Mexico's modern economic relationship with the United States? Overall, has that relationship strengthened or weakened Mexico's economic development, and why?

CASE Study

CHINA: AN EMERGING POWERHOUSE

CASE SYNOPSIS

China's economic development has been unparalleled since the country's initial entrance into the world market. It has taken more people out of poverty faster than any other country in history. Since economic reforms began shifting the country away from the communist-planned economy in 1978, the population in absolute poverty has dropped from over 90 percent to 11 percent, and GDP per capita has increased sixfold (see Figures 11.5 and 11.8). Success did not result, however, from a rapid conversion to the neoliberal economic model. China's approach was much closer to the developmental state model, consciously choosing sectors in which to invest over time, using state financing to guide investment, and focusing increasingly on export growth. Compared to other developmental states, though, China has maintained a larger role for state-owned enterprises (SOE) and FDI. Foreign companies were encouraged to invest by an increasingly institutionalized state that provided investors assurance that they would be able to keep their profits. The state also invested in expanding public infrastructure and continued the Communist Party's policy of educating the populace. By mid-2016, though, growth had slowed somewhat, and economic analysts began fearing that the world's biggest "growth engine" was finally starting to stall.

- **TYPE OF ECONOMY** Developmental state, with modifications

- **DEVELOPMENT OUTCOMES** World's greatest economic growth and poverty reduction; slowing since 2013

- **RESPONSE TO GREAT RECESSION** Stimulus plan focusing on infrastructure; continued but slower growth

- **RECENT REFORM EFFORTS** Expanding private sector and liberalizing financial sector, but continued role for state-owned industries

- **CONTINUING PROBLEMS** Growing inequality, labor unrest, aging population, environmental concerns

When Mao Zedong died in 1976, China was one of the poorest and most chaotic societies on Earth. A three-year power struggle ensued upon his death, pitting those who wished to continue his legacy against those who saw the need to change directions. By 1979, Deng Xiaoping had emerged as the supreme ruler and immediately set out to move the country away from Mao's ideologically puritanical path to something more pragmatic. As Deng famously said, "It doesn't matter if a cat is black or white, so long as it catches mice."

China's reforms under Deng began gradually and remain incomplete nearly four decades later. The first reforms were focused inward and on agriculture. The "household responsibility system" converted many of China's collective farms into family-leased and operated enterprises in which families could dispose of their surplus production on the open market, giving them an incentive to be more productive. In six years (1978–1984), virtually all farming households had converted to this system, agricultural production was growing at an unprecedented rate of 7 percent per year, and per capita rural incomes increased by more than 50 percent. In rural areas, township and village enterprises (TVEs), mostly owned by local governments, were given even greater freedom to produce what they could for a profit. Their production rose fivefold between 1983 and 1988 (Qian 2006, 235–237).

At the same time, the government gradually began to open to the market, domestically and internationally. It created a "dual-track" market system in 1984 under which state-owned enterprises (SOEs) continued to sell their products at official state prices up to their official state production quota but were free to sell their surplus at whatever market price they could get. Prior to reform, the government had set all retail prices. Over time, a larger and larger share of products were sold at market prices, reaching 95 percent by 1999. Throughout the 1990s, the government gradually but systematically lowered tariffs on imports and loosened restrictions on companies' rights both to import and export, a process that culminated in China's joining the World Trade Organization (WTO) in 2001. The result has been an explosion of international trade for the country: its exports and imports increased nearly tenfold between 2000 and 2014.

Chinese coal miners leave work in Shanxi Province. Overcapacity in state-owned enterprises in sectors like coal was a growing problem as the economy started to slow down after the Great Recession. Adjusting to this may require widespread layoffs of workers, potentially causing political unrest.

VCG/VCG via Getty Images

In 1995 the government announced the start of privatization, selling off the vast majority of SOEs to private investors. The process resulted in the laying off of at least twenty million workers from 1995 to 1997, but the growing economy was able to employ many of them and the government created a pension system for the unemployed, so layoffs did not cause widespread unrest (Frazier 2010; Qian 2006, 243). A decade later, the private sector constituted 70 percent of the economy and the state-owned sector only 30 percent. SOEs still control virtually entire sectors that are natural monopolies or considered "strategic" such as energy and military industry, continue to exist but are much smaller and compete with private firms in sectors such as pharmaceuticals and chemicals, and have been eliminated in highly competitive sectors such as light manufacturing (Pearson 2015). They have also gone from losing money in the mid-1990s to being highly profitable by the mid-2000s, once this transformation was complete (Tsai and Naughton 2015). Indeed, after the Great Recession, SOEs' share of the economy actually increased slightly because the government channeled most of its large stimulus package into infrastructure built mainly by SOEs. China's state sector remains the largest in the world and is a crucial element in the state's effort to guide investment into certain areas.

The government also controls much of the banking system, and uses it, as other developmental states have, to guide investment where it wants. Early in the reform process, the government created a central bank and separated it from four other government-owned banks that the government used to direct large-scale investment in key areas such as energy, steel, and natural resources. By 1998, these banks faced significant losses due to bad loans, instigating a reform process that has reduced the number of bad loans over time, though the government still uses these banks to make loans it thinks are of political or economic importance, regardless of immediate profitability. The growing private sector finances most of its investment via its own burgeoning profits and some via the increasing number of international banks in the country (Knight and Ding 2013).

The role of the state in creating institutionalized incentives for greater efficiency and production has been crucial to China's economic success. A World Bank study (Winters and Yusuf 2007) argued that the institutionalization of Chinese Communist Party (CCP) rule that we delineated in chapter 8 was essential. Local officials and would-be entrepreneurs needed to trust that the central government would follow through on its commitments to allow profits to stay within local enterprises and continue support for the growing market. Given the history of Mao's capricious rule, it was not obvious at the dawn of Deng Xiaoping's era that the government would stick to its new commitments. The CCP gained credibility by institutionalizing its rule, assuring local party leaders and government officials that they would be promoted based on clear criteria tied in part to the success of their local enterprises and economies. As the system worked successfully over the first decade, it gained greater credibility. When China invited increasing foreign investment in the 1990s, greater institutionalization led investors to believe that continued political stability was likely. At the same time, the government began large-scale spending on infrastructure expansion and improvements, facilitating and showing its financial commitment to both domestic and foreign private investment.

China's economic success, measured in terms of economic growth, per capita income, and poverty reduction, is spectacular. This does not mean, however, that no problems exist. China long faced global pressure, especially from the United States, to revalue its currency, the renminbi. It long kept its value low to make its exports cheaper, tying it to the value of the U.S. dollar. This and a large amount of foreign currency from exports and foreign investment allowed China to weather the Asian financial crisis in 1997–1998 and the Great Recession a decade later relatively easily. As growth and exports slowed in 2015 and 2016, however, most analysts began to see the renminbi as overvalued rather than undervalued. Trying to encourage domestic consumption and wanting to become a more important global power, China was keeping its currency at a higher exchange rate than a free market would set. In 2016 the IMF officially included it as a "reserve" currency, recognizing China as a global economic power and the renminbi as a "hard" currency that can be used throughout the world, along with the dollar, euro, and Japanese yen.

Domestically, China has experienced what most countries in the early stages of rapid industrialization do: growing inequality. This is in marked contrast to South Korea and Taiwan, which simultaneously grew and became more equal. China's overall inequality as measured by the Gini Index was 0.42 in 2012, near that of the United States, which is a sharp increase from the Communist era. Since the early 1990s, the urban-rural gap has grown considerably, as foreign investment and manufacturing in coastal cities have exploded. Even though most households have gained from the expanding economy, the wealthiest 20 percent gained far more than their poorer neighbors until about 2010; since then, the pattern began to reverse and the bottom 40 percent's per capita income began to grow more quickly than that of the top 20 percent (Kroeber 2016, 202). The booming coastal regions also have become much wealthier than the distant interior provinces, which remain largely rural and poor. One result has been the massive migration to the coastal cities of workers in search of jobs, and while the state has long tried to regulate this movement, it has been only partially successful. Privatization and migration from the countryside have produced considerable urban unemployment in recent years.

Under Jiang Zemin (2002–2012), the government recognized these problems and officially shifted focus from maximizing growth to providing greater social services, mainly in the form of pensions for unemployed and retired workers. These covered nearly half the workforce by 2005. Pensions provided a way to try to keep social and political peace by providing income to workers who were dislocated by the massive economic changes. SOEs had been the main source of social support such as pensions in the Maoist era. As they were privatized, a new social welfare system had to be created. In 2010 the government passed a comprehensive Social Insurance Law that is designed to guarantee all citizens a right to a pension, medical insurance, employment injury insurance, unemployment insurance, and maternity insurance— a policy that will take years fully to implement.

A key problem in providing social services is the *hukou* system, which requires every citizen to carry identification stating where they are legally allowed to live, the state's effort to control population movements. Changing one's *hukou* is difficult, so many migrant workers are not legally resident in the cities where they work. A 2014 survey found that over 80 percent of legal residents in cities had medical insurance, as opposed to as few as 20 percent of illegal residents, and urban residents generally have far better insurance than rural residents (Dickson 2016, 195). To expand urbanization but ensure the government still maintains control, it announced a plan in 2013 to move 250 million people from rural areas to newly built cities by 2025. In addition to resolving some of the problems with the *hukou* system, more people in urban areas will demand more purchased goods, which should stimulate growth (Johnson 2013). If achieved, the effort will be by far the biggest planned urbanization in human history.

The government also revised the national labor law in 2008 to respond to growing worker unrest. As we discussed in chapter 8, protests have been increasing in China for years, including among workers. Migrant workers not recognized as legal in the *hukou* system are particularly subject to low wages and poor working conditions, not even able to avail themselves of the limited worker protections Chinese law allows. The 2008 law gave full-time workers rights to longer and more secure contracts and streamlined the arbitration process through which workers could demand better wages and working conditions. It stopped short, though, of allowing workers to form their own unions, preserving the monopoly of the official union in the country's state corporatist system. These changes backfired in many ways. Passage of the new law gave workers greater awareness of their rights, and cases flooded the courts. By 2010, the fastest-growing cities were facing a growing shortage of cheap labor. Wages in the manufacturing sector tripled from 2000 to 2008 (Kroeber 2016, 178). Worker protests and strikes expanded, most notably with a strike at a major Honda automobile plant, where workers demanded the right to form their own union. While the government successfully resisted that unionization effort, the tight labor market continues; by 2015, the number of strikes was at least four times what it was in 2011 (Bradsher 2015). The increasing repression under President Xi Jinping fell on labor leaders as well, a number of whom were arrested in December 2015 (Chan 2016).

The Great Recession seemed mainly to augment China's role in the world. Like other "emerging markets," China recovered from the crisis much more quickly than the United States and Europe. It surpassed Japan in 2010 to become the second-largest economy in the world. Part of this success is credited to the government's very large stimulus program in 2009, which invested heavily in infrastructure, including renewable energy and improved road and rail networks. It also used credit from key government-aligned banks to stimulate growth in selected high-technology sectors, consciously following a developmental state model (Naughton 2015, 124). After 2012, growth dropped below 8 percent and in 2015 dipped below 7 percent, still high by world standards but the lowest in China in over a decade. Manufacturing and exports, the heart of the economy, seemed to be slowing particularly quickly, and a boom in urban real estate markets had turned into a collapsing market in many cities.

By 2015, economic analysts became increasingly concerned about whether China could maintain its exceptional economic development model. The global slowdown hurt its exports, the heart of its growth model. In mid-2015, the Shanghai stock market lost about 40 percent of its value, briefly panicking the Chinese government and global investors, though it then stabilized. With exports slowing, the country's debt was increasing. The government under President Xi had already introduced some reforms, relaxing government control of interest rates and the currency's exchange rate. Promised reforms to the state-owned sector were much slower, though. Many analysts believed that with exports slowing, major SOEs such as coal and steel had excess capacity, much of it a result of the stimulus plan after the Great Recession, and were being subsidized by the government. Maintaining growth would require reducing these inefficiencies, portending massive layoffs the government seemed unwilling to pursue (Buckley and Bradsher 2016).

Rising wages in the manufacturing sector simultaneously threatens China's status as the world's chief producer of low-wage goods. As wages rise and workers demand more rights, the country is likely to need to transition to higher-value production like the other East Asian developmental states have done. Developmental states, including China, initially spur growth by "picking winners" in which to invest heavily for export markets. At some point, though, growth has to be spurred via domestic demand as well, and making that transition can be difficult. That appears to be the point China reached after the Great Recession. Its success at navigating that change will profoundly affect not only its citizens but the global economy as well.

CASE Questions

1. In what ways is the Chinese case a good exemplar of the developmental state model? How is it similar to the basic model, and how does it differ?
2. What are the lessons of China's success for other poor countries as they try to develop and navigate globalization? Which elements of its model seem to be replicable and which elements seem not to be, and why?

CASE Study

INDIA: DEVELOPMENT AND DEMOCRACY

CASE SYNOPSIS

India's opening to the global market in 1991 reversed decades of ISI policies and heavy government intervention in the economy. By favoring domestic business in ways that loosely emulate the East Asian development model and then opening further to global markets, the Indian government produced an expanding economy that increased income per capita (PPP) from $1,146 in 1990 to $6,089 in 2015 while reducing overall poverty substantially (see Figures 11.5 and 11.8). New economic activity has been regionally uneven, however, so high levels of poverty remain in poorer areas and overall inequality is increasing. The Great Recession, higher global oil prices, and limits on further reform have raised questions about the rate at which the world's largest democracy can grow, or should. A new government swept into power in 2014 promising to expand neoliberal policies further, but had done so only partially by 2016, as it faced significant opposition to some of its policy changes.

- TYPE OF ECONOMY Elements of developmental state, but partial; shift toward neoliberal more recently

- DEVELOPMENT OUTCOMES Rapid growth in new millennium; limited poverty reduction

- RESPONSE TO GREAT RECESSION Initial stimulus and growth, then collapse and high inflation

- RECENT REFORM EFFORTS Enhanced neoliberal policies and new social programs aimed at the poor

- CONTINUING PROBLEMS Largest population in poverty and the most malnutrition in the world

In a reversal of the typical pattern of globalization, India's giant software company, Infosys, invested $250 million in 2007 to purchase a Polish call center, whose staff can speak and work with clients in half a dozen European languages. Infosys also owns call centers in Mexico and China to serve regional clients in their languages. Bangalore, site of Infosys's headquarters, has become a major global hub for information technology, especially software development and call centers. Infosys is the high-visibility element of India's broader success in dealing with globalization. In 2006–2007, Indian companies spent nearly $13 billion buying companies elsewhere in the world. Yet the country is also home to the largest number of poor people in the world, with nearly one-quarter of its population suffering from undernourishment.

During its first three decades of independence, India pursued a classic ISI policy. While the economy was based on the market, it was highly regulated, both internally and externally. A number of major industrial sectors were reserved exclusively for government investment and control. Doing business required so many governmental forms and licenses that the system came to be known as the "permit, license, quota Raj." The extensive regulations reflected standard development theory in the ISI period, but they also provided numerous sources of patronage for the dominant Congress Party and its supporters. The program produced substantial, albeit inefficient, industrial investment.

Many observers trace India's current high level of growth to the 1991 liberalization of the economy, but comparativist Atul Kohli (2004; 2007) argued that the country's economic success is based on earlier changes that were only partially liberal. Around 1980, elites within the ruling party and bureaucracy, influenced in part by the shift in global development thinking at the time, came to the conclusion that development policies needed to be much more pro-business to achieve economic growth. The government sharply curtailed limits on the size of private business and the sectors in which it could invest, reduced business taxes, liberalized the stock market, passed laws to limit the ability of unions to strike, and made new public investments in infrastructure. The result was a doubling of growth rates in the 1980s to about 5.5 percent. Kohli argued that while these policies only partially followed the neoliberal development model, they were very pro–domestic business. In a modest and gradual way, they paralleled those of the developmental states of East Asia, especially targeting policies designed to encourage growth in the computer sector (Evans 1995).

More dramatic liberalization began in 1991 in response to economic crisis. The growth of the 1980s had been partly fueled by debt. India had to go hat in hand to the IMF in 1991 to secure emergency funding and accept an SAP. The government implemented new policies to lower restrictions on imports, foreign exchange, and foreign

An Indian woman looks at an iris scanner in order to get her new identification. Digital identification and payments may transform the country's antipoverty program from one in which multiple subsidies provide opportunities for widespread corruption to a far less corrupt cash transfer program.

DIBYANGSHU SARKAR/AFP/Getty Images

investment. It also promised to reduce the size of the public sector and the fiscal deficit, privatize state-owned companies, and reform labor laws to further favor business. While these measures helped secure IMF support and were initially received favorably by the population, once the immediate crisis was over, opposition emerged. Farmers feared a reduction in their government subsidies, government bureaucrats resisted the reduction in their power that a more open market would entail, and advocates for the poor feared that the needy would fare even worse in a more open market. Business groups divided over the reforms. Older businesses in what was called the "Bombay Club" opposed opening to the global market, fearing that they wouldn't be able to compete, whereas new businesses in the export-oriented engineering and computing sectors formed a new association that favored liberalization (Sinha 2010). The result of these political forces in India's democracy has been significant but partial reform that continues to unfold.

After the economy recovered from the 1991 crisis, growth resumed at about the same 6 percent rate of the 1980s. The composition of growth, though, changed substantially (Kohli 2007). To reduce the fiscal deficit, the government curtailed public investment, while the reforms encouraged greater private investment, both domestic and international. The greatest growth has come not in manufacturing but in services, including computing services. In 2007 India had two-thirds of the global market in offshore information technology services. Foreign direct investment increased from under $10 billion annually in the 1990s to about $90 billion in 2008, and trade went from 15 percent of the economy in 1990 to 40 percent by 2008. Compared with the most open economies of the world, India remains only partially globalized. Tariffs on imports were still at 22 percent in 2006, and only about one-quarter of the economy was involved in trade at the beginning of the new millennium (Kohli 2007, 105).

India's growth increased in the new millennium, averaging 8 to 9 percent for the five years prior to the Great Recession. The country certainly felt the recession, though growth remained above 5 percent and rebounded to over 7 percent by 2010. The government responded, as did most governments, with a Keynesian-style stimulus plan in early 2009 that lowered interest rates, invested heavily in infrastructure (long seen as a weak spot by domestic and international analysts), and significantly increased deficit spending. Growth averaged 6.6 percent from 2011 to 2015. Renewed growth by 2010 and increasing oil prices (which India must import) produced increased inflation and growing concern about the burgeoning government deficit, leading the central bank to raise interest rates to fight inflation until 2015. While growth remains strong by global standards, the burst of rapid growth in the new millennium may have come to an end, at least until further reforms and/or renewed global growth occur.

Despite India's impressive growth record since 1980, poverty remains a serious problem, and inequality has grown. Absolute poverty dropped from 83 percent in 1983 to 58 percent in 2011. Since the onset of the 1991 liberalization, sixty million people have moved out of poverty, although India still has the largest number of poor people in the world. Economists Jagdish Bhagwati and Arvind Panagariya (2013) noted that the poverty reduction achieved by each percentage increase in GDP has been significantly lower in India than in the East Asian developmental states, including China. They argued that the concentration of growth and investment on relatively high-skill sectors like telecommunications and computing has not provided nearly as many jobs for the poor as the focus on lighter manufacturing like textiles has elsewhere. Indeed, in spite of the great growth over the past decade, the percentage of people employed in agriculture has not dropped noticeably. Small firms dominate the light-manufacturing sector in India, achieving lower productivity and generating less employment than in China, where large firms predominate.

Funding social policies to reduce poverty, though often proclaimed to be important by the government, has also been quite limited (Harriss 2011). Historically, India aided the poor by subsidizing various basic goods like grain and cooking oil, but these subsidies benefited everyone and created black markets and corruption that wasted resources. A more recent work program provides 180 days of paid work to one member of each rural household per year. Corruption is estimated to reduce the benefits that the poor receive from these programs by as much as 70 percent (Yardley 2013). A recent effort to use social expenditures more effectively has been the introduction of a program that provides direct cash subsidies to the poor electronically, who through the program are encouraged to open bank accounts and secure biometric identification from the government. Over 100 million had done so by 2016, a promising start to a program that could greatly reduce the corruption that has long plagued India's social welfare efforts.

Narendra Modi and his party, the BJP, won a sweeping electoral victory in 2014, becoming the first party to win a majority of parliamentary seats in over twenty years (see chapter 6). His campaign promised bold pro-business, neoliberal reforms to restart economic growth. After two years in office, only some of his promised reforms were in place. He had opened up some sectors to greater foreign investment, passed an important new bankruptcy law, and in August 2016 got a long-delayed tax reform through parliament that will replace myriad state sales taxes with a uniform national one. While growth had increased, and inflation and the federal deficit had dropped, supporters of neoliberal policies were disappointed he hadn't achieved more. Whether his policies will put India back on a path of exceptionally high growth, and whether the new social policies can make a more substantial dent in poverty, will be crucial to future assessments of India's increasingly neoliberal development model.

CASE Questions

1. In what ways do India's development policies replicate the developmental state, and in what ways do they not? What have been the implications of these differences between India's history and the developmental state model? What lessons can be learned from this analysis for other countries?
2. What are the implications of the Indian case for the debate over the relationship between democracy and economic development that we outlined earlier in the chapter?

IRAN: STRUGGLING WITH THE BLESSINGS OF OIL

CASE SYNOPSIS

Despite its massive oil revenue, Iran's theocracy has faced many of the same challenges that other middle-income countries in a global economy have navigated. Its attempt at state control of major assets resulted in inefficiency, inflation, and unemployment, though the regime has successfully lowered poverty levels. The Islamist regime uses oil revenue, channeled through *bonyads* (Islamist charities) and its own paramilitary groups, to provide a wide array of subsidies to the population. Thus, the government continues to control a major swath of the economy. Market-oriented reforms have been only partially successful, both in terms of changing policy and improving the economy. The global financial crisis resulted in lower oil prices, sending the Iranian government's budget into a tailspin that finally forced the government to begin to remove some subsidies. Political supporters of the regime in the *bonyads* and Revolutionary Guards, however, continue to control a large share of the economy, and reducing their role further will be politically difficult. International sanctions increased their bite in recent years, at least until the nuclear agreement with the United States lowered the level of sanctions. Throughout the upheavals of revolution, expanding state control, partial liberalization, and sanctions, Iran has remained heavily dependent on oil, though that dependence lessened while it was under the severest sanctions.

- TYPE OF ECONOMY Oil dependent

- DEVELOPMENT OUTCOMES Good growth until 2011; some poverty reduction

- RESPONSE TO GREAT RECESSION Dependence on oil revenue; increased debt

- RECENT REFORM EFFORTS Subsidy cuts; greater foreign investment after nuclear deal with United States

- CONTINUING PROBLEMS High inflation and unemployment; sanctions; political pressure for subsidies; conservative resistance to foreign investment

ran's theocratic regime has not shielded it from the impact of globalization and the problems it brings to middle-income countries, but the revolution and oil have heavily influenced Iran's specific trajectory. The revolutionary government nationalized many economic assets in 1980, including large private companies and banks. They became SOEs, and property confiscated from the shah's family and close associates funded the new Islamic foundations (*bonyads*), which became a key part of revolutionary rule. The eight-year Iran-Iraq War in the 1980s pummeled the economy, which shrank nearly 1.3 percent per capita per year over the decade. The 1990s saw some improvement, but this was accompanied by annual inflation of more than 20 percent and growing unemployment, which reached 16 percent by 2000. Throughout both decades, the country remained critically dependent on oil, which accounted for more than 80 percent of exports and anywhere from one-third to two-thirds of government revenue, depending on world oil prices.

The heavily state-controlled economy resembled the ISI policies of decades earlier in other middle-income countries. The Iranian government, though, intervened more extensively than did governments in many other countries. Government-controlled banks set interest rates uniformly, trade barriers were high, and the government set foreign exchange rates. The government budget provided large subsidies to the *bonyads* and to the SOEs as well, and lack of fiscal discipline played a major role in the high rates of inflation. Government subsidies and protection gave SOEs little incentive to operate efficiently: their losses from 1994 to 1999 equaled nearly 3 percent of the country's GDP (Alizadeh 2003, 273). The subsidies channeled through the *bonyads* and the Revolutionary Guard constituted 27 percent of the economy in 2008–2009; they channel oil revenue to regime supporters to maintain their loyalty.

Facing growing economic problems, in the late 1990s the government under reformist president Mohammad Khatami attempted the first significant liberalization of the economy, a belated response to global trends and pressures. Iran's theocratic government even took advice from the bastion of Western economic imperialism, the IMF, in setting new policies. The most dramatic reforms included the implementation of a floating exchange rate, the sale of some government-controlled banks to the private sector (the government gave up controlling interest rates in the mid-1990s), reduction of import and export barriers, and privatization of SOEs. The last of these was slow and partial. Elites within the regime were divided over privatization, and the Supreme Leader ultimately ensured that much of the equity in and control of the former SOEs would end up in the hands of the *bonyads* and similar groups

Vendors talk to potential customers at an oil, gas, and petrochemical exhibition in Tehran in 2016. Oil has long been the overwhelmingly dominant basis of Iran's wealth. Western sanctions reduced the country's oil income substantially. The partial lifting of sanctions after the 2015 nuclear weapons deal should mean significant economic improvements for the country.

Kaveh Kazemi/Getty Images

with close ties to the regime (Mohseni 2016). Overall, the reforms increased growth in the new millennium to around 5 percent per year and reduced inflation to less than 15 percent, but unemployment and poverty levels remained largely unchanged. Economic growth, fueled by rising oil prices, reached nearly 8 percent before the global financial crisis.

While the direct effects of the Great Recession were relatively slight in economically isolated Iran, the country was nonetheless heavily affected by declining world oil prices. Oil export revenue fell 24 percent in 2009, and overall growth dropped to only 1.5 percent. In response to the crisis, President Mahmoud Ahmadinejad, in spite of his long support for continuing them, began to cut subsidies; his hand was forced by the rapidly growing budget deficit. Past efforts to reduce subsidies had led to widespread protests and reversals of the cuts, but in late 2010 the government allowed gasoline prices to quadruple. This move was met with little visible protest, perhaps because of the severe crackdown on protests after the 2009 election (see chapter 8). Ahmadinejad actively encouraged imports from countries such as India, Pakistan, and China that did not follow the West's sanction regime fully, greatly expanding consumer imports. In the absence of extensive oil exports, though, these had to be paid for by growing debt, producing high inflation. Increased international sanctions starting in 2011 and stagnant oil prices affected the economy heavily. Growth dropped to zero by 2012, and as President Ahmadinejad handed power over to newly elected president Hassan Rouhani, inflation was estimated at over 40 percent and unemployment at around 25 percent.

Rouhani's biggest economic success was the completion of the nuclear deal with the United States and other Western countries that resulted in the removal of some sanctions. Within a year of the accord, Iran's oil exports had doubled and the country had struck numerous deals with European businesses for investment. Growth for 2016 was expected to reach about 4 percent, up from virtually zero a year earlier. Not all political forces in Iran, however, supported the initial changes coming out of the nuclear deal. Supreme Leader Ayatollah Ali Khamenei announced his support for a "resistance economy" two months after the accord was signed, saying he preferred domestic to foreign investment and arguing that the latter would undermine the ideals of the revolution. The sanctions had actually reduced the government's dependence on oil for its revenue, but the ramp-up of oil exports suggested that Iran's long dependence on oil to drive its economy was unlikely to change.

CASE Questions

1. How different does oil make the Iranian case from other middle-income countries?
2. Iran's Islamist regime has long proclaimed a goal of not being influenced by the West and pursuing "Islamist" policies regardless of international opinions. To what extent has it been able to do this? Does regime type make a difference to how much a regime can influence the effects of globalization?

CASE Study

NIGERIA: A WEAK STATE, OIL, AND CORRUPTION

CASE SYNOPSIS

Until the new millennium, Nigeria was a case study of development gone wrong. The largest country in Africa and blessed (or cursed) with abundant oil reserves, it remains one of the world's poorest countries. Despite (or because of) great oil wealth, its growth has been erratic, and poverty and inequality remain high (see Figures 11.5–11.10). The development models pursued—both ISI and SAPs—were justified in terms of reigning theories of economic development in their respective eras, but neither led to significant development. Dependence on vacillating oil markets left the government in crisis when oil prices dropped. Weak institutions, political demands, and massive oil wealth when prices were high produced monumental levels of corruption that undermined virtually all development efforts and expanded debt. Neoliberal policies are designed to encourage investment, but they achieved little in Nigeria outside the oil sector. In the absence of strong and coherent state institutions and a favorable global economic context, economic blueprints do not produce the expected results. The new millennium has been kinder to Nigeria, however. The new democratic government presided over significant economic growth fueled by rising oil prices, reduced corruption somewhat, convinced foreign creditors to forgive the nation's debt, and achieved the first real growth outside the oil sector in decades. Sadly, all that was put at risk when world oil prices collapsed starting in 2014.

- TYPE OF ECONOMY Oil dependence

- DEVELOPMENT OUTCOMES Focused on oil revenue only; little other development; growth in new millennium until 2014

- RESPONSE TO GREAT RECESSION Continued growth until oil prices fell

- RECENT REFORM EFFORTS Reduced subsidies, fiscal stability, and anticorruption policies under democratic regime

- CONTINUING PROBLEMS Falling oil prices; corruption

Like almost all African countries, Nigeria was a poor, agricultural country with little industry of any kind when it gained independence in 1960. As much as 98 percent of the population worked in agriculture, producing 65 percent of the country's GDP and 70 percent of its exports. Like other African states, its new government initially attempted to industrialize via ISI. By the mid-1970s, however, oil production and revenue had overwhelmed all other aspects of the economy and made the government dangerously dependent on the global oil market for political and economic survival. The huge influx of oil revenue and the active involvement of the government in the economy helped make Nigeria one of the most corrupt societies in the world.

As was true throughout sub-Saharan Africa, colonial rulers in Nigeria allowed only particular economic opportunities to Africans. Peasant farmers were encouraged to produce food and export crops, but Nigerians were not allowed any significant opportunity in industry; foreign businesses controlled what little industry there was. Africans' sole route to economic advancement was education and employment in the colonial government. At independence, the educated elite were primarily employed in government and had virtually no involvement or expertise in private industry. They thus saw an expansion of the government's role in the economy as central both to national development and their own interests, which dovetailed well with the reigning development theory at the time, modernization theory and ISI.

The earliest state intervention in the interests of development was in the agricultural sector. Starting during colonial rule, the government had monopoly control over marketing of key export crops, which it bought from farmers at low prices and then sold internationally at much higher prices. Despite farmers' opposition to this unofficial tax, modernization theorists argued that as long as the government used the revenue gained from agricultural exports to make productive investments in industry, its actions were justified. However, in Nigeria's federal system, the bulk of the revenue went to the regional governments, and each one used it to build infrastructure and encourage industrialization, causing wasteful duplication. Export crop revenues also became an early source of corruption, further undermining efficient investment. Given the lack of Nigerian-owned industry, the government, supported by aid donors and advisers, saw joint government investment with foreign companies as crucial to industrialization, a common form of ISI in Africa. By the 1970s, the government had rapidly expanded its investment in large-scale industry. Most of the private Nigerian investors were themselves government officials or political leaders, so participation in the government and politics remained the key means of acquiring wealth.

Children paddle past an oil pipeline near their home in southeastern Nigeria. Nigeria suffers from a classic "resource curse," as dependence on oil has created corruption and massive environmental problems but done little to reduce the poverty that most Nigerians face. The 60 percent drop in global oil prices beginning in 2014 made the problem that much worse.

PIUS UTOMI EKPEI/AFP/Getty Images

In 1961 money from oil exports constituted less than 8 percent of government revenue; by 1974, it was 80 percent, following the quadrupling of world oil prices. Since then, Nigerian governments have invested virtually nothing in agriculture, which has declined from being the most important sector of the economy to one that continues to employ many people but produces very little. The governments of the 1970s used oil wealth to invest in large-scale infrastructure projects, borrowing money against future oil revenues to do so. When the oil market collapsed in the mid-1980s, the government was unable to pay back its loans and faced bankruptcy. Nigeria once again became a fairly typical African state, going to the IMF after 1983 to negotiate an SAP. The politically painful reductions in the government's size and activity that the IMF required were more than even the military governments could bear, and the process of instituting neoliberal policies was long and remains incomplete. Certainly, the government has reduced its involvement in industry (other than oil) and cut its size, but it has still only partially liberalized.

The central role of the state in the economy combined with huge oil revenues to create a situation ripe for corruption. By 2000, Transparency International ranked Nigeria as the world's most corrupt country. As in other parts of the postcolonial world, state intervention in the economy gave government officials many opportunities to grease palms and stuff their own pockets. Every law that required government approval for some economic activity created a point at which an official could ask for a bribe. The legacy of colonial rule exacerbated this problem. Africans saw the colonial government as a source of wealth and resources; it had no other legitimacy in the eyes of the people. The illegitimacy of the colonial government and the newness of democracy after independence meant that governmental institutions were weak, so people did not value them and were not interested in fighting to preserve them. Corruption, then, was easy to engage in. The more it grew, the less legitimacy state institutions had, and a vicious cycle ensued. Clientelism became nearly the sole means of maintaining political support. Nigerian leaders took bribes and stole from government coffers both to feather their own nests and to provide resources to their supporters.

The democratic government that replaced military rule in 1999 initiated a series of anticorruption measures. An initial target was the return of the billions of dollars that Gen. Sani Abacha, the last and most corrupt military leader, had stolen. In subsequent years, several major politicians in the new government also became targets of court cases. For the first time in Nigeria's history, political leaders faced criminal prosecution for stealing the country's wealth. In the run-up to the election in 2007, however, then-president Olusegun Obasanjo used the anticorruption agency to target and eliminate potential opponents. Still, the overall results of the anticorruption campaign have been positive: Nigeria improved in Transparency International's rankings from a score of 1.2 (dead last) in 2000 to 2.6 (136th out of 168 countries) in 2015.

The new democratic government used its international support to gain financial aid and debt relief from Western donors, but in turn was required to make substantial progress in moving its economic policies in a neoliberal direction. By 2006, the country's overall debt had dropped to less than one-tenth of what it had been two years earlier (Gillies 2007, 575). The government also brought inflation under control via tight monetary policy, stabilized government spending and the country's currency, and reduced various tariff barriers. Donors responded not only with debt relief but also with a massive increase in aid, from less than $200 million in 2000 to more than $6 billion in 2005. All this combined with rapidly increasing world oil prices to substantially improve economic growth, which averaged around 5 percent in the new millennium, with non–oil sector growth an impressive 9 percent from 2003 to 2009. In sharp contrast to the 1970s, much of the expanded oil revenue was invested or saved, rather than being consumed or used as the basis to take on additional international debt (Ajakaiye, Collier, and Ekpo 2011). The government's ability to make wise use of oil revenue seemed to have improved considerably under the new democracy, though LeVan (2015) argued that was because of the limited and institutionalized nature of the veto players in the regime.

Nigeria's oil wealth allowed it to weather the immediate effects of the Great Recession without an economic downturn. High oil prices kept its growth rate at a robust 7 percent in 2009 before falling to 6.7 percent in 2011—still a high growth rate by global standards. Oil continues to cause multiple problems, however. Most significant, after years of improved growth, the economy was devastated by the drop in oil prices that began in 2014. With global oil prices falling by 50

Nigeria as an Oil Exporter

The Country and Concept table allows you to compare Nigeria with two other oil exporters, Iran and Russia, but it is also instructive to compare Nigeria with its partners in the Organization of the Petroleum Exporting Countries (OPEC). Nigeria has the largest population and one of the lowest GDPs in OPEC, making it among the poorest countries in the organization. An IMF report found that Nigeria and other sub-Saharan African oil exporters face much greater developmental challenges than exporters from other regions, including running out of oil sooner, lower oil reserves per capita, high oil dependence, and greater infrastructural and human development gaps. All the data below are for 2012.

	Nigeria	OPEC average
Population	163.3 million	34.6 million
Barrels of oil produced per day	1,974,800	2,510,133
Oil export revenue per capita (real $, billions)	$527	$2,331
GDP per capita	$1,443	$23,838
Proven crude oil reserves	37.2 billion barrels	99.9 billion barrels

Source: Organization of the Petroleum Exporting Countries, *Annual Statistical Bulletin 2012* (http://www.opec.org/opec_web/static_files_project/media/downloads/publications/ASB2012.pdf); World Bank.

percent, the country entered a recession in 2016 for the first time in over twenty years and the government, facing a revenue crisis, was considering selling off some of its ownership of the oil sector. It also had to end the tie between its currency and the U.S. dollar, causing a depreciation of 60 percent in 2016. The crisis, though, may finally provide the impetus to reduce corruption in the oil sector. President Goodluck Jonathan in 2012 commissioned a study of the oil sector that found a combination of domestic and international (by international oil companies) malfeasance had cost the government over $100 billion in the last decade, a figure that shocked the nation. The government continues to promise to pass a sweeping reform of the oil sector that has been discussed since 2007. The new president, Muhammadu Buhari, who led the first electoral victory by an opposition party since 1999 (see chapter 9), changed the leadership of the national oil company shortly after taking office, and in 2016 put plans in place to split the company into six separate entities to ease management and reduce corruption.

The steady economic growth from 2000 to 2014 more than doubled Nigeria's per capita GDP, although poverty decreased only slightly and inequality actually increased. Since most of the gains in wealth remain in the oil sector, they have not been distributed widely among the population. In 2009 some 39 percent of Nigerians still survived on less than 3 dollars a day. As long as world oil prices remain low and corruption remains high, it is unlikely this situation will change.

CASE Questions

1. Given the problems oil wealth has caused in Nigeria to date, how might the government go about creating policies that would start to use oil wealth more effectively for the benefit of the country?
2. What does Nigeria suggest for the debate over whether authoritarian or democratic regimes are likely to produce better development?

CONCLUSION

"Development" has been an important political and economic concept since World War II. For most people, it still means creating greater wealth—a process of poor countries becoming more like rich countries over time. Numerous scholars, though, have questioned whether that should be the goal, as well as how it should be achieved. Theories of economic development, in particular, have closely followed the broader debate over economic policy we discussed in chapter 10, including dramatic changes in prescriptions for how the state should be involved in the process.

Poorer countries have virtually all moved in the general direction of economic liberalization, but whether this has been a blessing is not always clear. Various analysts have argued that geography, resource endowment, distance from markets, government policies, and regime type all have a role in explaining why some countries, particularly "the bottom billion," continue to struggle in the face of globalization, while others thrive. The closest thing to consensus is around recommendations for macroeconomic stability, strong institutions, and investment in human capital.

Even with this consensus, though, it isn't always clear why some states have been more successful in the era of globalization than others. Neoliberal policies have often not reduced poverty and have sometimes led to repeated financial crises. In this context, several alternative models have arisen. While pursuit of export-oriented growth in East Asia has generated strong growth and reduced poverty, the developmental state model is based on a strong state that not all countries have. Latin America's "pink tide" governments have some similarities with the East Asian developmental states, but the former prioritized social spending and poverty reduction more than the latter. In "the bottom billion," the debate is over whether the mostly weaker states are able to pursue beneficial developmental goals at all, or instead should either pursue an even purer form of neoliberalism, absent foreign aid, or should be provided a massive influx of aid to overcome their inherent problems.

The Great Recession was only the latest in a series of economic crises in the era of globalization. Each has shaken the foundation of one or another economic development model and has raised questions about who weathers a crisis best and why. The latest crisis has shown perhaps more clearly than ever the force of the global market in limiting states' responses. While most middle-income and poor countries were not as dramatically affected initially, eight years after the crisis the continuing stagnation in the global economy raised questions even in China about how long high growth and poverty reduction could continue. Growing numbers of countries faced stagnation, accompanied by demonstrators in the streets demanding change. The fortunes of the "pink tide," in particular, seemed to raise questions about how much economic sovereignty even relatively large middle-income countries like Brazil could achieve in the face of globalization. A key question in both wealthy and poor countries is how effectively a state can intervene in the market to pursue goals such as greater equality, health, and environmental protection—subjects to which we now turn in chapter 12.

KEY CONCEPTS

comparative advantage (p. 588)
export-oriented growth (EOG) (p. 596)
foreign direct investment (FDI) (p. 587)
import-substitution
　　industrialization (ISI) (p. 590)
international capital flows (p. 587)

Millennium Development
　　Goals (MDGs) (p. 600)
structural adjustment
　　programs (SAPs) (p. 591)
trade (p. 587)

Sharpen your skills with SAGE edge at **edge.sagepub.com/orvis4e.** **SAGE edge for students** provides a personalized approach to help you accomplish your coursework goals in an easy-to-use learning environment.

WORKS CITED

African Development Bank Group. 2013. *Annual Development Effectiveness Review 2013: Toward Sustainable Growth for Africa.* Tunis, Tunisia. July.

Ajakaiye, Olu, Paul Collier, and Akpan H. Ekpo. 2011. "Management of Resource Revenue: Nigeria." In *Plundered Nations? Successes and Failures in Natural Resource*

Extraction, edited by Paul Collier and Anthony J. Venables, 231–261. Basingstoke, UK: Palgrave Macmillan.

Alizadeh, Parvin. 2003. "Iran's Quandary: Economic Reforms and the 'Structural Trap.'" *Brown Journal of World Affairs* 9 (2): 267–281.

Bhagwati, Jagdish, and Arvind Panagariya. 2013. "Introduction." In *Reforms and Economic Transformation in India*, edited by Jagdish Bhagwati and Arvind Panagariya, 1–12. Oxford, UK: Oxford University Press.

Bradsher, Keith. 2015. "China Turned to Risky Devaluation as Export Machine Stalled." *New York Times*. August 17 (http://www.nytimes.com/2015/08/18/business/international/chinas-devaluation-of-its-currency-was-a-call-to-action.html?smid=nytcore-ipad-share&smprod=nytcore-ipad).

Buckley, Chris, and Keith Bradsher. 2016. "In New Economic Plan, China Bets That Hard Choices Can Be Avoided." *New York Times*. March 5 (http://www.nytimes.com/2016/03/06/world/asia/in-new-economic-plan-china-bets-that-hard-choices-can-be-avoided.html?smprod=nytcore-ipad&smid=nytcore-ipad-share).

Chan, Anita. 2016. "Migrant Workers' Fight for Rights in China." *Current History*, 209–213. September.

Collier, Paul. 2007. *The Bottom Billion: Why the Poorest Countries Are Failing and What Can Be Done about It.* Oxford, UK: Oxford University Press.

Dickson, Bruce J. 2016. *The Dictator's Dilemma: The Chinese Communist Party's Strategy for Survival.* Oxford, UK: Oxford University Press.

Easterly, William. 2006. *The White Man's Burden: Why the West's Efforts to Aid the Rest Have Done So Much Ill and So Little Good.* New York: Penguin Press.

Evans, Peter B. 1995. *Embedded Autonomy: States and Industrial Transformation.* Princeton, NJ: Princeton University Press.

Feng, Yi. 2003. *Democracy, Governance, and Economic Performance: Theory and Evidence.* Cambridge, MA: MIT Press.

Flores-Macias, Gustavo A. 2012. *After Neoliberalism: The Left and Economic Reforms in Latin America.* Oxford, UK: Oxford University Press.

Frazier, Mark W. 2010. *Socialist Insecurity: Pensions and the Politics of Uneven Development in China.* Ithaca, NY: Cornell University Press.

Gillies, Alexandra. 2007. "Obasanjo, the Donor Community and Reform Implementation in Nigeria." *The Round Table* 96 (392): 569–586. doi:10.1080/00358530701625992

Haggard, Stephan, and Robert R. Kaufman. 1995. *The Political Economy of Democratic Transitions.* Princeton, NJ: Princeton University Press.

Harriss, John. 2011. "How Far Have India's Economic Reforms Been Guided by Compassion and Justice? Social Policy in the Neoliberal Era." In *Understanding India's New Political Economy: The Great Transformation?*, edited by Sanjay Ruparella, Sanjay Reddy, John Harriss, and Stuart Corbridge, 127–140. New York: Routledge.

Huber, Evelyne, and John D. Stephens. 2012. *Democracy and the Left: Social Policy and Inequality in Latin America.* Chicago: University of Chicago Press.

Johnson, Ian. 2013. "China's Great Uprooting: Moving 250 Million into Cities." *New York Times*, June 15 (http://www.nytimes.com/2013/06/16/world/asia/chinas-great-uprooting-moving-250-million-into-cities.html?emc=eta1).

Kaplan, Stephen B. 2013. *Globalization and Austerity Politics in Latin America.* Cambridge, UK: Cambridge University Press.

Knight, John, and Sai Ding. 2013. *China's Remarkable Economic Growth.* Oxford, UK: Oxford University Press.

Kohli, Atul. 2004. State-Directed Development: Political Power and Industrialization in the Global Periphery. Cambridge, UK: Cambridge University Press.

———. 2007. "State, Business, and Economic Growth in India." *Studies in Comparative International Development* 42 (1–2): 87–114. doi:10.1007/s12116-007-9001-9

Kroeber, Arthur R. 2016. *China's Economy: What Everyone Needs to Know.* Oxford, UK: Oxford University Press.

LeVan, A. Carl. 2015. *Dictators and Democracy in African Development: The Political Economy of Good Governance in Nigeria.* Cambridge, UK: Cambridge University Press.

Lijphart, Arend. 1999. *Patterns of Democracy: Government Forms and Performance in Thirty-six Countries.* New Haven, CT: Yale University Press.

Mazaheri, Nimah. 2014. "Oil Wealth, Colonial Legacies, and the Challenges of Economic Liberalization." *Political Research Quarterly* 67 (4): 769–782. doi:10.1177/1065912914540535

Mohseni, Payam. 2016. "Factionalism, Privatization, and the Political Economy of Regime Transformation." In *Power and Change in Iran: Politics of Contentions and Conciliation,* edited by Daniel Brumberg and Farideh Farhi, 37–69. Bloomington: Indiana University Press.

Moreno-Brid, Juan Carlos, and Igor Paunovic. 2010. "Macroeconomic Policies of the New Left: Rhetoric and Reality." In *Latin America's Left Turns: Politics, Policies, and Trajectories of Change,* edited by Maxwell A. Cameron and Eric Hershberg, 193–232. Boulder, CO: Lynne Rienner.

Mosley, Paul, with Blessing Chiripanhura, Jena Grugel, and Ben Thirkell-White. 2012. *The Politics of Poverty Reduction.* Oxford, UK: Oxford University Press.

Moyo, Dambisa. 2009. *Dead Aid: Why Aid Is Not Working and How There Is a Better Way for Africa.* New York: Farrar, Straus and Giroux.

Naughton, Barry. 2015. "China and the Two Crises: From 1997 to 2009." In *Two Crises, Different Outcomes: East Asia and Global Finance,* edited by T. J. Pempel and Keiichi Tsunekawa, 110–136. Ithaca, NY: Cornell University Press.

Norris, Pippa. 2012. *Making Democratic Governance Work: How Regimes Shape Prosperity, Welfare, and Peace.* Cambridge, UK: Cambridge University Press.

Ocampo, José Antonio, and Rob Vos. 2010. *Uneven Economic Development.* New York: Zed Books.

Ozawa, Terutomo. 2010. "Asia's Labour-Driven Growth, Flying Geese Style: Types of Trade, FDI, and Institutions Matter for the Poor." In *The Poor under Globalization in Asia, Latin America, and Africa,* edited by Machiko Nissanke and Erik Thorbecke, 87–115. Oxford, UK: Oxford University Press.

Pearson, Margaret M. 2015. "State-Owned Business and Party-State Regulations in China's Modern Political Economy." In *State Capitalism, Institutional Adaptation, and the Chinese Miracle,* edited by Barry Naughton and Kellee S. Tsai, 27–45. Cambridge, UK: Cambridge University Press.

Pitcher, M. Anne. 2012. *Party Politics and Economic Reform in Africa's Democracies.* Cambridge, UK: Cambridge University Press.

Przeworski, Adam, Michael Alvarez, José Cheibub, and Fernando Limongi. 2000. *Democracy and Development.* Cambridge, UK: Cambridge University Press.

Qian, Yingyi. 2006. "The Process of China's Market Transition, 1978–1998: The Evolutionary, Historical, and Comparative Perspectives." In *China's Deep Reform: Domestic Politics in Transition*, edited by Lowell Dittmer and Guoili Liu, 229–250. Lanham, MD: Rowman and Littlefield.

Round, Jeffrey. 2010. "Globalization, Growth, Inequality, and Poverty in Africa: A Macroeconomic Perspective." In *The Poor under Globalization in Asia, Latin America, and Africa*, edited by M. Nissanke and E. Thorbecke, 327–367. Oxford, UK: Oxford University Press.

Sachs, Jeffrey D. 2005. *The End of Poverty: Economic Possibilities for Our Time*. New York: Penguin Books.

Sen, Amartya K. 1999. *Development as Freedom*. New York: Anchor Books.

Sinha, Aseema. 2010. "Business and Politics in Changing India: Continuities, Transformations, and Patterns." In *The Oxford Companion to Politics in India*, edited by Niraja Gopal Jayal and Pratap Bhanu Mehta, 459–476. Oxford, UK: Oxford University Press.

Tsai, Kellee S., and Barry Naughton. 2015. "Introduction: State Capitalism and the Chinese Economic Miracle." In *State Capitalism, Institutional Adaptation, and the Chinese Miracle*, edited by Barry Naughton and Kellee S. Tsai, 1–26.

Cambridge, UK: Cambridge University Press.

Weber, Heloise, ed. 2014. *The Politics of Development: A Survey*. New York: Routledge.

Winters, L. Alan, and Shahid Yusuf, eds. 2007. *Dancing with Giants: China, India, and the Global Economy*. Washington, DC: World Bank.

Wylde, Christopher. 2012. *Latin America after Neoliberalism: Developmental Regimes in Post-Crisis States*. New York: Palgrave Macmillan.

Yardley, Jim. 2013. "Ahead of Elections, India's Cabinet Approves Food Security Program." *New York Times*, July 4 (http://india.blogs.nytimes.com/2013/07/04/indias-cabinet-passes-food-security-law).

RESOURCES FOR FURTHER STUDY

Cameron, Maxwell A., and Eric Hershberg, eds. 2010. *Latin America's Left Turns: Politics, Policies, and Trajectories of Change*. Boulder, CO: Lynne Rienner.

Ferreira, Francisco H. G., and Michael Walton. 2005. *Equity and Development*. Washington, DC: World Bank.

Jha, Prem Shankar. 2002. *The Perilous Road to the Market: The Political Economy of Reform in Russia, India, and China*. London: Pluto Press.

Jones, R. J. Barry. 2000. *The World Turned Upside Down? Globalization and the Future of the State*. Manchester, UK: Manchester University Press.

Kohli, Atul, Chung-in Moon, and Georg Sørensen, eds. 2003. *States, Markets, and Just Growth: Development in the*

Twenty-first Century. New York: United Nations University Press.

MacIntyre, Andrew, T. J. Pempel, and John Ravenhill, eds. 2008. *Crisis as Catalyst: Asia's Dynamic Political Economy*. Ithaca, NY: Cornell University Press.

Nissanke, Machiko, and Erik Thorbecke, eds. 2010. *The Poor under Globalization in Asia, Latin America, and Africa*. Oxford, UK: Oxford University Press.

Van de Walle, Nicolas. 2001. *African Economies and the Politics of Permanent Crisis, 1979–1999*. Cambridge, UK: Cambridge University Press.

World Bank. 1993. *The East Asian Miracle: Economic Growth and Public Policy*. New York: Oxford University Press.

WEB RESOURCES

CountryWatch
(http://www.countrywatch.com)

KOF Index of Globalization
(http://globalization.kof.ethz.ch). Based on data from Axel Dreher, "Does Globalization Affect Growth? Evidence from a New Index of Globalization," *Applied Economics* 38, no. 10 (2006): 1091–1110; updated in Axel Dreher, Noel Gaston, and Pim Martens, *Measuring Globalisation: Gauging Its Consequences* (New York: Springer, 2008).

UN Millennium Project, Millennium Villages: A New Approach to Fighting Poverty
(http://www.unmillenniumproject.org/mv/mv_closer.htm)

United Nations University, World Institute for Development Economics Research, World Income Inequality Database
(http://www.wider.unu.edu/research/Database)

World Bank, Economic Policy and External Debt
(http://data.worldbank.org/topic/economic-policy-and-external-debt)

12 PUBLIC POLICIES WHEN MARKETS FAIL
WELFARE, HEALTH, AND THE ENVIRONMENT

KEY QUESTIONS

- What do policy outcomes tell us about who has effective representation and power in a political system?
- Why do states intervene in the market via social, health, and environmental policies?
- Why have many governments pursued significant reforms to welfare states in the era of globalization?
- Why have states found it so difficult to reform health policy and control costs?
- Where and why did more effective welfare and health systems emerge, and can the most effective ones be replicated in other countries?

As globalization spreads the market economy, the issues raised in chapters 10 and 11 about the relationship between the state and the market loom ever larger. The long-standing debate over how much governments ought to intervene in the market in an effort to maximize citizens' well-being continues unabated. This chapter addresses three key areas that have long been subjects of debate in virtually every country: welfare, health care, and the environment. The common thread among them is the call for government to intervene in response to market failure.

We defined market failure in economic terms in chapter 10: markets fail when they do not maximize efficiency, most commonly because of externalities, monopolies, or imperfect information. Environmental damage is a classic example of a market failure to allocate resources efficiently. Markets can also fail, however, in the sense that they don't achieve the results a society collectively desires. In this chapter, then, we broaden the definition of market failure to a more general understanding that markets fail when they do not perform according to widely held social values. For instance, markets do not necessarily reduce inequality or end poverty, even though the alleviation of both is often a widely held social value. Governments develop what Americans call "welfare" policies to respond to market failures to distribute wealth in socially acceptable ways.

Government interventions of this type raise a host of interesting questions because they pit various groups of citizens against one another. The policy outcomes often tell us much about the classic "Who rules?" question: Who is better represented, and thus has power? They also raise major questions focused on why government intervenes in the first place. In recent years, governments in all wealthy countries have reformed welfare policies substantially and tried, with limited suc-

cess, to reform health care policies as well. Why have these trends been so widespread over the past twenty to thirty years, and why have some states been more successful than others at achieving reforms? The Country and Concept table on page 636 shows the great variation in these policy areas across our case study countries. Welfare systems vary from quite extensive to nonexistent, with dramatically different effects on the level of poverty. Key health care indicators like life expectancy and infant mortality vary dramatically as well. The wealthy countries achieve roughly similar health outcomes but at very different costs, while poor countries' health fares far worse. Looking at the most important environmental concern, carbon dioxide emissions that cause global warming, our case studies include the two biggest polluters in the world—the

COUNTRY AND CONCEPT
Welfare, Health, and the Environment

Country	Welfare system	Life expectancy at birth (2015)	Infant mortality rate (deaths per 1,000 births)	Health care system	Public expenditure on health (% of total expenditure on health) (2014)	Per capita total expenditures on health (U.S. dollars, PPP)(2014)	Annual CO_2 emissions (million metric tons of CO_2) (2012)	Per capita CO_2 emissions (tons) (2011)
Brazil	Liberal	75	18	NHS, plus much private financing and some private insurance	46	947	500	2.2
China	Liberal welfare state emerging: social insurance for pensions and unemployment; means-tested programs for others in urban areas	76.1	12.2	NHI emerging, plus much private financing and some private insurance	55.8	420	8,106	6.7
Germany	Christian democratic	81	3.4	NHI	77.0	5,411	788	8.9
India	Minimal: small means-tested programs, such as food subsidies and rural employment	68.3	40.5	NHS, plus much private insurance, direct financing, and NGO provision of health services	30.0	75	1831	1.7
Iran	Mixed: social insurance for retirees; state-funded means-tested programs; Islamic charity via *bonyads* (Islamic foundations)	75.5	37.1	NHI	41.2	351	604	7.8

Japan	Employment-based, with additional means-tested government programs	83.7	2.0	NHI	83.6	3,703	1259	9.3
Mexico	Liberal welfare state	76.7	11.90	NHS, plus much private insurance and direct financing	51.8	677	454	3.9
Nigeria	Minimal: social insurance for small share of workforce only	54.5	71.20	NHS, plus much private financing and NGO provision of health services	25.1	118	86	0.5
Russia	Social insurance for pensions; other benefits targeted to particular groups (in kind until 2007, cash since)	70.5	6.9	NHI	52.2	893	1,782	12.6
United Kingdom	Liberal	81.2	4.3	NHS	83.1	3,935	499	7.1
United States	Liberal	79.3	5.8	Market-based insurance	48.3	9,403	5,270	17.1

Sources: Life expectancy data are from World Health Organization (http://apps.who.int/gho/data/node.main.688?lang=en). Infant mortality data are from *CIA World Factbook* (https://www.cia.gov/library/publications/the-world-factbook/rankorder/2091rank.html). Health care spending data are from World Bank for the most recent year available (http://data.worldbank.org/indicator/SH.XPD.PUBL). Per capita total expenditures on health care data are from World Bank (http://data.worldbank.org/indicator/SH.XPD.PCAP/countries). CO_2 annual emissions data are from International Energy Agency (http://www.eia.gov/cfapps/ipdbproject/iedindex3.cfm?tid=90&pid=44&aid=8). Per capita emissions data are from World Bank (http://data.worldbank.org/indicator/EN.ATM.CO2E.PC).

United States and China—and others that, while likely to suffer the effects of global warming, are only a miniscule part of the problem. The case studies will allow us to examine these policy options and outcomes in widely varying circumstances.

"WELFARE": SOCIAL POLICY IN COMPARATIVE PERSPECTIVE

Most Americans think of welfare as a government handout to poor people. Being "on welfare" is something virtually all Americans want to avoid, as a certain moral

social policy
Policy focused on reducing
poverty and income inequality
and stabilizing individual or
family income

opprobrium seems to go with it. Partly because of this, and partly because different countries relieve poverty in different ways, scholars of public policy prefer the term **social policy** to welfare. Social policy's primary goals are to reduce poverty and income inequality and to stabilize individual or family income. Most people view a market that leaves people in abject poverty, unable to meet their most basic needs, as violating important values. Similarly, when markets produce inequality that goes beyond some particular point (the acceptable level varies widely), many people argue that it should be reversed. Markets also inherently produce instability: in the absence of government intervention, capitalism tends to be associated with boom and bust cycles that result in economic insecurity, especially due to unemployment. Reducing this insecurity has been one of the main impetuses behind modern welfare states.

Various philosophical and practical reasons justify social policies. On purely humanitarian grounds, citizens and governments might wish to alleviate the suffering of the poor. States might also be concerned about social and political stability: high endemic poverty rates and economic instability often are seen as threats to the status quo, including a state's legitimacy, and poverty is associated with higher levels of crime almost everywhere. Keynesians argue as well that policies to reduce poverty and stabilize incomes are economically beneficial for society as a whole because they help increase purchasing power, which stimulates market demand.

Opponents of social policy disagree, criticizing it primarily for producing perverse incentives. Markets maximize efficiency in part by inducing people to be productive by working for wages, salaries, or profits. Neoliberal opponents of social policy argue that providing income or other resources for people whether they are working or not gives them a disincentive to work, which reduces efficiency, productivity, and overall wealth. Critics also argue that financing social policy via taxes discourages work and productivity because higher taxes reduce incentives to work and make a profit.

In liberal democracies, the debate over social policy also raises a fundamental question over the trade-off between citizens' equality and autonomy. According to liberalism, citizens are supposed to be equal and autonomous individuals, yet in a market economy, it's difficult to achieve both. Citizens are never truly socioeconomically equal. As we saw in chapter 3, T. H. Marshall (1963) argued that social rights are the third pillar of citizenship because without some degree of socioeconomic equality, citizens cannot be political equals. Following this line of thought, when the market fails to create an adequate degree of equality, governments should intervene to preserve equal citizenship. On the other hand, in market economies, market participation is a primary means of achieving autonomy. The founders of liberalism believed only male property owners could be citizens because they were the only ones who were truly autonomous; women and nonproperty owners were too economically dependent on others to act effectively as autonomous citizens. All liberal democracies have modified this position, but the fundamental concern remains. Many citizens view only those who participate in the market—whether by owning capital or working for a wage—as fully autonomous. Welfare policies that provide income from nonmarket sources can then be seen as problematic. Traditional liberals argue that social policy undermines equal and autonomous citizenship by creating two classes of citizens: those who earn their income in the market and those who depend on the government (funded by the rest of the citizens). This argument typically makes an exception for family membership: an adult who depends on other family members who participate in the market is implicitly granted full autonomy and citizenship. Social democrats argue, to the contrary, that citizens should be granted full autonomy regardless of their source of income and that social policies that keep income inequality and poverty below certain levels are essential to preserving truly equal citizenship. Different kinds of welfare states are in part based on different values in this debate.

Types of Social Policy

Whatever their justification, social policies can be categorized into four distinct types: universal entitlements, social insurance, means-tested public assistance, and tax expenditures. **Universal entitlements** are benefits that governments provide to all citizens more or less equally, usually funded through general taxation. The only major example in the United States is public education. All communities in the United States must provide access to public education for all school-age residents without exception, making it a universal benefit. Many European countries provide child or family allowances as universal entitlements: all families with children receive a cash benefit to help raise the children. Universal entitlements by nature do not raise questions about equal and autonomous citizenship, even when individual citizens may choose not to take advantage of them. No one questions the equal citizenship of public versus private school graduates in the United States, or those who do not have children and therefore don't get child allowances in the Netherlands. Critics, on the other hand, argue that universal entitlements are wasteful because much of the money goes to relatively wealthy people who do not need the benefits.

Social insurance provides benefits to categories of people who have contributed to a (usually mandatory) public insurance fund. The prime examples in the United States are Social Security, disability benefits, and unemployment insurance. In most cases, both workers and their employers must contribute to the funds. Workers can then benefit from the fund when they need it: after retirement, when temporarily unemployed, or when disabled. Because only those who contribute can gain benefits, fewer questions arise about the beneficiaries deserving their benefits, even though there is usually only a very general relationship between the size of a person's contribution and the amount of his benefit. The average American retiree, for instance, earns substantially more in Social Security benefits than the total of his lifetime contributions with interest, but that gap has never raised questions of equal citizenship. In addition, by covering entire large groups of people—all workers or the spouses of all workers—social insurance is not seen as undermining equal citizenship, because it covers things nearly everyone expects (retirement) or hopes to avoid (unemployment).

universal entitlements
Benefits that governments provide to all citizens more or less equally, usually funded through general taxation; in the United States, public education is an example

social insurance
Provides benefits to categories of people who have contributed to a (usually mandatory) public insurance fund; typically used to provide retirement pensions

means-tested public assistance
Social programs that provide benefits to individuals who fall below a specific income level; TANF is an example in the United States

Means-tested public assistance is what most Americans think of as "welfare." The Supplemental Nutrition Assistance Program (SNAP; also commonly known as "food stamps"), subsidized public housing, and Temporary Assistance to Needy Families (TANF) are examples in the United States. These are programs that individuals qualify for when they fall below a specific income level. Some countries impose additional requirements for public assistance, such as work requirements or time limits, but income level is the defining characteristic. Means-tested programs target assistance at the poor in contrast to the broader distribution of universal entitlements or social insurance, so they may be the most efficient means of poverty relief. Their disadvantage, though, is their impact on recipients' status as equal and autonomous citizens. Because only those below a certain income level can benefit, and benefits are typically financed from general taxation, recipients may be seen as somehow less deserving or not fully equal with other citizens who are paying taxes and not receiving benefits.

tax expenditures
Targeted tax breaks for specific groups of citizens or activities designed to achieve social policy goals

Tax expenditures, targeted tax breaks for specific groups of citizens or activities, have only been included as part of social policy fairly recently. To most people, tax breaks—not collecting taxes from someone—seem different from government spending. The net effect of the two, however, is quite similar. When the government selectively lowers the tax someone would otherwise pay, it is increasing that person's disposable income. A tax break for a particular activity, such as purchasing a home or investing in a retirement pension, subsidizes particular activities that the government presumably believes to be socially beneficial. By giving tax breaks for employees' and employers' contributions to health insurance and retirement pensions, for instance, the U.S. government is subsidizing those activities. A tax break for people with lower incomes has the same effect as the same amount of social spending targeted at that group.

Tax expenditures are an important part of social policy, especially in the United States. They can be restricted to people with low incomes or provided much more widely, with different effects on reducing poverty and inequality. In the United States, for instance, the Earned Income Tax Credit (EITC) aimed at lower-income families has become one of the largest poverty-reduction programs in the country, larger in fact than TANF, the program most Americans think of as "welfare." The tax deduction for interest paid on home mortgages, on the other hand, subsidizes all but the most expensive home purchases; it is a social policy designed to encourage home ownership (presumably improving standards of living and economic security) that provides greater benefits to the middle and upper classes than to the poor.

Different types of social programs are often associated with particular kinds of benefits or groups of recipients. Workers are often covered by social insurance, for instance, while public housing is typically means tested. What is true for tax expenditures, however, is true for all types of social programs; any of them could be used for any type of benefit. For instance, unemployment insurance is fairly restricted in the United States, benefiting only long-term employees and usually for only six to nine months after a worker becomes unemployed; elsewhere, similar programs are more extensive and less distinct from what Americans call "welfare." Preschool is a universal entitlement in France but is means tested via the Head Start program in the United States. Retirement benefits also could be means tested so that when older people no longer earn a market-based income, only those below a certain income level would qualify for benefits. Indeed, this has been one policy suggested in the United States as a way to reduce the long-term cost of the Social Security program. This would target retirement benefits more efficiently at reducing poverty but might raise questions of equal citizenship common to means-tested programs, questions that retirees currently don't face.

Types of Welfare States

Governments combine social programs in different ways and with different levels of generosity, creating distinctive **welfare states.** The Country and Concept table (pages 636–637) gives some idea of the wide variety of combinations states use. Evelyne Huber and John Stephens (2001), modifying the pioneering work of Gøsta Esping-Andersen (1990), classified wealthy countries into three main types of welfare states: social democratic, Christian democratic, and liberal. **Social democratic welfare states** strongly emphasize universal entitlements to achieve greater social equality and promote equal citizenship. Governments typically provide universal entitlements in a wide array of areas, including paid maternity leave, preschool, child allowances, basic retirement pensions, and job training. They use high rates of general taxation to fund their generous social benefits and typically redistribute more income (taxing the wealthy more and giving equal universal entitlements to all) than do other welfare states. Social insurance programs, such as employment-based retirement pensions, also exist, but these usually just supplement the universal entitlements. The primary examples of social democratic welfare states are the Scandinavian countries.

Christian democratic welfare states primarily emphasize income stabilization to mitigate the effects of market-induced income insecurity. Their most common type of social program, therefore, is social insurance, which is designed to replace a relatively high percentage of a family's market-based income when it is disrupted through unemployment, disability, or something similar. Benefits are usually tied to contributions, and financing is mainly through employer and employee payroll taxes rather than general taxation. This means that redistribution is not as broad as under social democratic welfare states. Most Christian democratic welfare states also feature corporatist models of economic governance; that is, social insurance programs tend to be administered by and through sectoral-based organizations such as unions, though under the state's guidance. We explore a prime example, Germany, in detail below.

Liberal welfare states focus on ensuring that all who can work and gain their income in the market do so; they are more concerned about preserving individual autonomy via market participation than reducing poverty or inequality. They

welfare states
Distinct systems of social policies that arose after World War II in wealthy market economies, including social democratic welfare states, Christian democratic welfare states, and liberal welfare states

social democratic welfare states
States whose social policies strongly emphasize universal entitlements to achieve greater social equality and promote equal citizenship; Sweden is a key example

Christian democratic welfare states
States whose social policies are based on the nuclear family with a male breadwinner, designed primarily to achieve income stabilization to mitigate the effects of market-induced income insecurity; Germany is a key example

liberal welfare states
States whose social policies focus on ensuring that all who can do so gain their income in the market; more concerned about preserving individual autonomy than reducing poverty or inequality; the United States is a key example

emphasize means-tested public assistance, targeting very specific groups of recipients for benefits. A great deal of government effort often goes into assessing who is truly deserving of support, which usually boils down to determining who is truly unable to work for a wage. The emphasis on ensuring that only the truly deserving receive benefits often means that some poor people don't get assistance, and the desire to provide incentives for people to work can mean that benefits do not raise people out of poverty. But not all programs are means tested in these countries; retirement benefits are typically provided via social insurance. The United States, to which we turn below, is a prime example of this type of welfare state.

Explaining the Development and Evolution of Welfare States

Comparativists have used rational choice, cultural, institutional, and structural arguments to explain the origins and evolution of welfare states. Though their programs and generosity vary, welfare states exist in all wealthy democracies, begging the question of why. Some early theorists saw welfare states as a product of the structural changes of modernization and industrialization. As capitalism emerged, it created greater wealth, but also winners and losers. The latter demanded help, forcing democratic regimes to respond, and states could use some of the wealth capitalism generated to provide that help. Marxist scholars argued that the welfare state allowed capitalism to postpone social revolution; reducing the misery capitalism created for the poor kept them from pursuing a socialist revolution, allowing the system to survive. More recently, rational choice theorist Philipp Rehm (2016) focused on risk, arguing that all people are risk-averse. Welfare states spread so widely because everyone wants lower risk via insurance. Where risk is more equally distributed, more generous welfare policies emerged, and where risk is less equally distributed, more people will perceive their risks as relatively low, so less generous welfare policies will arise.

Cultural theorists also have tried to explain the variation in welfare states, looking at differences in long-standing values. Anglo-American countries, they argue, have stronger liberal traditions emphasizing the importance of the individual and individual autonomy. Numerous surveys have shown, for instance, that despite upward social

Demonstrators in Sweden protest cuts in public health care in September 2016. Sweden's exceptionally generous social democratic welfare state, while requiring some reforms to control costs over the last two decades, remains very popular.

Tommy Lindholm/Pacific Press/ LightRocket via Getty Images

Sweden's Welfare State

Sweden is a prime example of a social democratic welfare state. The Swedish Social Democratic Party was in power continuously from 1932 to 2006, except for two brief periods. The party instituted the first elements of a welfare state in the 1920s. From the start, it established basic services such as unemployment benefits and retirement pensions as universal social rights of citizenship. In the late 1950s, the party added extra benefits above and beyond the flat-rate universal ones. These were tied to earnings and replaced as much as 90 percent of workers' wages when they were unemployed, disabled, or retired. In the 1970s, the government expanded services designed to induce women into the workforce and support them once they were employed, including the world's most generous maternity and sick-leave policies.

The state combined these benefits with very high tax rates on income (60 percent of the economy at their peak in the 1970s), but it used low corporate tax rates to encourage investment in export industries and had one of the most open trade policies in the world. At its height in the 1970s, Sweden was the world's second-wealthiest country, with robust growth, strong export levels by brand-name companies such as Volvo, virtually no unemployment, and the world's most generous social services. Even after reforms in the 1990s, Sweden's social services and taxes remain among the world's highest. Unemployment benefits still cover about 80 percent of wages and have virtually no time limit. Parental leave provides sixteen months of paid leave at any time during the first eight years of a child's life at 80 percent of full salary. Parents get ten paid "contact days" per year to spend time in their children's schools as volunteers, up to sixty days of benefits per year to care for sick children, and access to a daycare system that enrolls 75 percent of preschoolers, with more than 80 percent

of the cost funded by the state (Olsen 2007, 147–151). To pay for this, government revenue remains more than half of the entire economy (compared with a little more than a third for the United States). In addition, more than 30 percent of all employees work in the public sector.

Sweden's model faced a crisis in the early 1990s. Declining industry and growing outsourcing of business combined with the bursting of a housing bubble (not unlike conditions in the United States in 2008) and demographic changes to increase unemployment, inflation, and the government's debt. When the Social Democrats lost the 1991 election, the newly elected Moderate Party passed what was seen at the time as the most sweeping tax reform in the Western world, with the top income tax rate dropping from 80 to 50 percent and the marginal rate on corporate taxes from 57 to 30 percent (Huber and Stephens 2001, 242). Returning to power in 1994, the Social Democrats expanded the reforms, tying retirement pensions to levels of unemployment and economic growth, dividing the cost of pensions equally between employer and employee (previously, employers paid for virtually all of the benefits), basing retirement benefits on contributions to the system rather than a guaranteed percentage of wages, and reducing unemployment benefits from 90 to 80 percent of income. Unions successfully resisted an attempt to impose a three-year limit on such benefits (nine months is typical in the United States).

While some reforms have been necessary, Sweden's voters have consistently supported their extensive welfare state, indicating a widely held set of values that supports extensive government intervention to reduce poverty, inequality, and economic insecurity. The country's reliance on universal entitlements means extensive social policies do not seem to raise significant questions about equal citizenship.

---

mobility being about the same in the United States and Europe, Americans are much more likely than Europeans to believe that people can work their way out of poverty if they really want to (Alesina and Glaeser 2004, 11–12).

Religious beliefs may also influence welfare states: countries more influenced by Protestantism, especially Calvinism, see wealth as morally superior and have less sympathy for the poor, whereas countries with more Catholics are more generous due to their beliefs in preserving social and family stability. Martin Schroder (2013) noted the high correlation between varieties of capitalism (see chapter 10) and types of welfare states: LMEs have liberal welfare states and CMEs have either social democratic (mainly in Scandinavia) or Christian democratic (elsewhere in Europe) welfare states. He argued that the particular varieties of capitalism and welfare states reinforce one another and both have their origins primarily in cultural differences among the countries, tied to religion and their beliefs about the importance of markets.

A final cultural explanation argues that racial or ethnic heterogeneity matter. Alberto Alesina and Edward Glaeser (2004) claimed that this partly explains the striking difference in the generosity of social spending in the United States and Europe. Surveys show that people (not only Americans) are less sympathetic to those of different races, and in the United States many whites incorrectly perceive the poor as being mostly black or Hispanic. As a result, Americans are relatively unwilling to support policies to assist them. As immigration has diversified many European countries, similar phenomena may be arising there as well. Numerous scholars have noted that the exceptional homogeneity of Scandinavian countries helps account for the generosity of their welfare states and the political threat recent immigration might pose to those policies. Prerna Singh (2015) similarly found that Indian states that have a stronger sense of state-level identity (including a nationalist desire to govern themselves) provide better social welfare than do states without such an identity.

Huber and Stephens (2001) used the influential "power resources theory" to explain variation in welfare states. It combined a structural argument based on class and an institutionalist argument. Welfare states, they argued, primarily reflect the strength and political orientation of the working and lower-middle classes. In countries where these classes were able to organize into strong labor unions and powerful social democratic parties, social democratic welfare states emerged that emphasize wealth redistribution and gender equality. Countries with more Catholics and stronger Christian democratic parties that appealed successfully to working and lower-middle classes saw the emergence of Christian democratic welfare states that emphasize social and family stability, rather than resource redistribution and women's participation in the workplace. Where the working classes were not strong enough to organize to gain political power, liberal welfare states emerged that provide minimal support only for those who are truly unable to work. They combine this with an institutionalist argument: regimes with fewer veto players developed more extensive welfare states. Federal systems and presidential systems, for instance, tend to produce less extensive social policies. Feminist scholars have made similar arguments about the political origins of distinct welfare states but have focused on women's movements: where they were stronger earlier, universal benefits that need not go through a male breadwinner and policies that support women entering the workforce, such as child allowances and universal childcare, developed the most (Sainsbury 2013).

Using a "most similar systems" (see chapter 1) comparison of Spain and Portugal, Sara Watson (2015) questioned Huber and Stephens's explanation for the variation in welfare states. She argued that when the left is divided by the presence of a strong "far-left" party that questions capitalism as a whole, center-left parties create coalitions with more conservative parties to keep the far left out of power; the result is a less generous welfare state, demanded by the conservative parties with whom the center left must cooperate. More generous welfare states emerge, instead, where the left is united behind only a "center-left" party and no strong far-left party exists.

The pressures of globalization initially led scholars to argue that the distinctions among types of welfare states would tend to disappear; global economic forces would pressure all welfare states toward the liberal model of reduced benefits. Pressure on social expenditures also comes from demographic changes: as populations age, fewer workers must somehow pay the benefits for larger dependent populations, particularly the elderly. As we suggested in chapter 10, though, few countries have fundamentally altered their social policies. Indeed, social expenditures in wealthy countries as a whole increased from about 18 percent to 25 percent of GDP from 1980 to 2013 (Obinger and Starke 2015, 471). Institutionalist theorists (Pierson 1996) argued that the welfare state created institutions and their beneficiaries, which then constituted powerful coalitions blocking reform. While governments with different ideological orientations responded differently to the pressures of globalization, as power resources theory would suggest, their differences were diminished compared to earlier eras (Huber and Stephens 2015).

The rise of the service sector and global demands for more flexible labor have led in particular to shifts in unemployment benefits that create greater incentives to get the unemployed back to work. While only a few countries have fundamentally changed policies (as the United Kingdom did under Prime Minister Margaret Thatcher in the 1980s), most have reduced benefits to lower the costs of the traditional programs. Most governments have raised the minimum age at which people can retire, reduced the length of unemployment benefits and the percentage of salary that is replaced, raised employee contributions to social insurance programs, and removed guarantees of benefits so that they can reduce them in the future if necessary (Bonoli, George, and Taylor-Gooby 2000).

Simultaneously, many welfare states have placed greater emphasis on "social investment policies," which provide individual benefits while simultaneously altering the labor market, usually in ways that encourage greater flexibility and employment (Gingrich and Ansell 2015). While traditional retirement pensions may be lowered, governments may spend more on childcare and family leave to encourage women to enter the workforce and job training for the unemployed. These policies, proponents argue, benefit the growing number of part-time and female workers who typically benefit less from traditional social policies. In this way, politicians have been able to put together new coalitions of support for welfare reforms with parties of the left and right emphasizing differing kinds of social investment in line with their ideologies. Globalization has, in a sense, forced change, but change has been filtered through shifting political institutions and coalitions. David Rueda (2015), however, demonstrated that the combination of cuts to traditional programs and social investment policies has lowered welfare states' effects on inequality overall.

Comparing Welfare States

The different types of welfare states initially created significantly different societies in terms of how much of the national income passes through government coffers and how much is redistributed from the rich to the poor. Tables 12.1 and 12.2 provide data comparing the three types of welfare states. Social democratic welfare states used to take the biggest share of the national economy as government revenue to provide extensive social services, reflected in their high social expenditures. In recent years, however, the Christian democratic systems have spent just as much as the costs of their extensive income-maintenance programs for the unemployed and elderly have risen rapidly, while the liberal welfare states spend significantly less.

Table 12.2 shows that when we compare gross (meaning just government expenditures) and net (taking into account taxes recipients of social expenditures pay back to the government) we see a somewhat different picture in terms of overall generosity. While the liberal welfare states still spend the least, the differences between them and the other two models are significantly reduced. A group of scholars (Alber and Gilbert 2010; Garfinkel, Rainwater, and Smeeding 2010) have argued that the three models of the welfare state are not as distinct as has been suggested. While Sweden spends generously on universal programs, for instance, it also has high taxes on consumption (e.g., sales tax), so some of the spending on the poor comes back to the government in taxes. The United States, on the other hand, has very low social spending but much higher tax expenditures targeted at people with low incomes. This helps explain the clear convergence among all wealthy countries in the size of their welfare states over the past three decades (Obinger and Starke 2015).

The extensive social policies of the social democratic and Christian democratic welfare states did not lower economic growth significantly at their height in the 1980s, though liberal welfare states seem to have grown faster recently. Similarly, more generous welfare states actually achieved lower levels of unemployment. Figure 12.1 shows that all three types of welfare states distribute enough income to lower poverty substantially, but the reductions were greatest in social democratic states, followed by Christian democratic states, until recently, when liberal welfare states have improved, though still tolerate more poverty and inequality among their citizens. Note, however, that differences in poverty have narrowed and inequality has increased in all three types of welfare states, reflecting the effects of globalization and demographic pressures in all wealthy countries. Table 12.1 demonstrates differences as well in terms of gender inequality, at least as measured by participation in the paid labor force. Social democratic welfare states facilitated greater female participation via such policies as universal child allowances, paid maternity leave, and subsidized preschool. Liberal and Christian democratic states lagged behind, though they have nearly caught up recently.

Social Policy in the Global South

A welfare state requires a state capable of implementing fairly complex policies. In the weakest states, therefore, social policy is minimal, often involving little more

TABLE 12.1　Comparison of Welfare State Outcomes

	Social expenditure as % of GDP			GDP growth %				Unemployment as percentage of civilian labor force				Women's labor force participation (% of female population ages 15 + in labor force)			
	1980	1995	2010	2014	1981-1990	1991-2000	2001-2010	2011-2015	1991-2000	2001-2010	2011-2014	1990	2000	2010	2014
Social democratic welfare states	21.2	28.3	27.2	27.8	2.51	2.72	1.55	1.1	8.38	5.95	6.64	59.48	58.72	59.1	58.88
Christian democratic welfare states	20.6	24.1	26.7	27.1	2.29	2.16	1.26	0.82	7.49	6.49	7.01	43.31	47.99	51.73	52.34
Liberal welfare states	14.6	17.6	20.8	19.7	3.16	4.03	2.06	2.43	8.58	6.26	8.92	50.6	54.75	57	56.65

Sources: Data for social expenditures are from Organisation for Economic Co-operation and Development (http://stats.oecd.org/Index.aspx?QueryId=4549#); data for GDP growth, unemployment, and women's labor participation are from World Bank (http://data.worldbank.org/indicator/NY.GDP.MKTP.KD.ZG/countries?display=default), (http://data.worldbank.org/indicator/SL.UEM.TOTL.ZS/countries?display=default), and (http://data.worldbank.org/indicator/SL.TLF.CACT.FE.ZS).

TABLE 12.2	Social Expenditure, in Percentage of GDP	
	Gross public social expenditures **2014**	**Net public social expenditures** **2011***
Social democratic welfare states	27.8	21.6
Christian democratic welfare states	27.1	24.1
Liberal welfare states	19.7	19.8

Source: Organisation for Economic Co-operation and Development (http://stats.oecd.org/Index. aspx?datasetcode=SOCX_AGG#).

* Data missing for Switzerland.

than retirement pensions for the relatively small share of the population employed in the government and large companies, as the Country and Concept table (see page 636) shows for our case studies of India and Nigeria. Many governments in the Global South provided benefits for the poor by regulating or subsidizing prices of basic goods they required, particularly food. Neoliberal development strategies have long focused on achieving high economic growth as the best means of reducing poverty. Their implementation, especially in the 1980s and 1990s (see chapter 11), almost always involved cuts to both social services and government subsidies, reducing the minimal programs many states had in place. Ian Gough (2014) terms social provision in most of these societies as "informal security regimes" in which people's social needs are provided mainly by a combination of private markets, formal and informal community organizations, and family networks. Patron-client relationships often are crucial to people's well-being in these societies and therefore also politically influential. Nongovernmental organizations (NGOs) typically provide a large share of whatever formal social services exist, as the state is too weak and poor to do so.

Neoliberalism's limited success, however, led to the emergence of social policy as an important issue in developing countries in the 1990s, especially in middle-income countries. The East Asian developmental states of Taiwan and Korea, for instance, had minimal social welfare states through the 1980s. Their development model, of course, produced far less inequality than most have, and their rapid growth reduced poverty substantially. In the 1980s and 1990s, though, as they democratized, popular demands rose for more social services and expenditures; both countries put many elements of Western-style social welfare states in place by the new millennium (Huber and Niedzwiecki 2015).

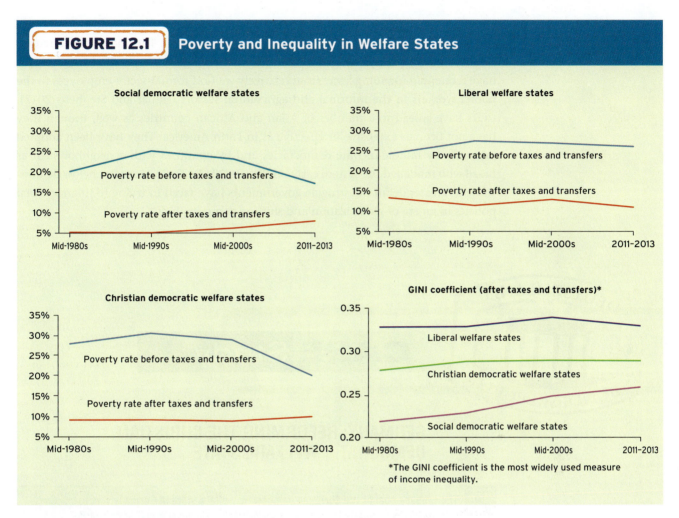

FIGURE 12.1 Poverty and Inequality in Welfare States

Sources: All data are from OECD.Stat. Data for most current date range (shown as 2011–2013 averages) are Poverty Rate before and after taxes and transfers, all working-age household types, and working age-population eighteen to sixty-five. Data for Gini coefficient are Gini (market income, before taxes and transfers). Calculated using the classifications of the three welfare states (liberal welfare state, Christian democratic welfare state, and social democratic welfare state) as defined in Evelyne Huber and John D. Stephens, *Development and Crisis of the Welfare State* (Chicago: University of Chicago Press, 2001).

Democratization also played an important role in improving social policies in Latin America. Older social programs in Latin America were almost all social insurance systems benefitting only workers in the formal sector of the economy, disproportionately in the public sector. These workers are in fact a relatively well-off group in Latin America; the truly poor are in the informal sector (e.g., workers in small enterprises not recognized by the government, street vendors, and day laborers) and agriculture. To reach these truly poor, a number of governments adopted **conditional cash transfer (CCT)** programs, which provide cash grants to the poor in exchange for recipients sending their children to school and to health clinics. These programs, pioneered in our case study of Brazil, are means tested and target the poorest households to gain the maximum impact. CCT programs in Latin America have reduced poverty by

conditional cash transfer (CCT)
Programs that provide cash grants to the poor and in exchange require particular beneficial behavior from the poor, such as children's attendance at school and visits to health clinics

4 to 8 percent, depending on the country, and have increased both school enrollment and use of health care services (Ferreira and Robalino 2011). They have helped reduce poverty and inequality without substantially increasing social spending because they have reoriented spending away from relatively well-off formal-sector employees to the poorer workers in the informal and agricultural sectors (Huber and Stephens 2012). CCTs have spread to a number of Asian and African countries as well, though they have not been as extensive or effective as in Latin America. They have been adopted primarily by middle-income democracies and by countries with a neighbor such as Brazil who modelled the system early on (Brooks 2015). The case studies below demonstrate in greater detail the struggle governments have faced in trying to finance social policies in an era of globalization and shifting demographics.

GERMANY: REFORMING THE CHRISTIAN DEMOCRATIC WELFARE STATE

CASE SYNOPSIS

The primary goal of the Christian democratic welfare state in Germany was to ensure income stability throughout a person's life. Once securely in the workforce, or dependent on someone who was, citizens could count on relative stability, at a minimum of half of their prior salary. This system was far more generous than liberal welfare states but redistributed less income than did social democratic ones. Mounting male unemployment, an aging population, and reunification put great pressure on the system. In response, the government reduced retirement and unemployment benefits, and the unemployment system now guarantees income stability for only one year; permanent support is only at a level just above the poverty line. But the government also included more women, part-time workers, and the self-employed in the benefits. The reforms make Germany's welfare state notably more like a liberal welfare state, but the In Context box shows clearly that differences remain between Christian democratic Germany, the liberal United States, and social democratic Sweden.

- TYPE OF WELFARE STATE Christian democratic

- RECENT PROBLEMS Growing pressure from aging population and need for more flexible labor market

- REFORMS Hartz IV in 2003; major change to unemployment benefit; shift toward liberal welfare state?

Otto von Bismarck created the world's first social insurance program in Germany in 1883. Most of the country's modern Christian democratic welfare state was not put into place until 1949, but it still relies primarily on social insurance. Programs are paid for mainly by roughly equal employer and employee contributions. Following Germany's corporatist model, the system is run by NGOs overseen by employer and employee associations, with the state providing the legal framework and regulations. In the golden era during which the economy was growing rapidly, the system provided relatively generous benefits and was self-financing.

Prior to reforms in 2003, the core social insurance system provided nearly complete income replacement in case of illness, at least 60 percent of an unemployed worker's salary for up to thirty-two months, and a retirement pension that averaged 70 percent of wages. These benefits continue to constitute the great majority of German social spending. Those unemployed for periods longer than three years received unemployment assistance at about 53 percent of their most recent salary, with no time limit. Others who had never worked a full year still received social assistance, a means-tested system that indefinitely provided enough support to keep them above the poverty line. Originally, the system assumed a male breadwinner could support his wife and children. As women entered the workforce, they supported reforms to make the system less focused on male breadwinners. In 1986 child benefits were added, including direct payments to and tax breaks for parents and government-paid contributions into social insurance to provide benefits for parents to take time off from work to care for young children. In the 1970s, maternity benefits of fourteen weeks that covered the full income of many women were added.

German reunification in 1990 dramatically increased the costs of the system: unemployment rates skyrocketed in the former East Germany, and massive transfers of funds from the former West Germany were essential to pay social insurance benefits to these workers. The Christian Democrat (CDU) government made modest reductions

An elderly man eats lunch at a soup kitchen in Berlin in December 2015. Reforms to the German Christian democratic welfare state have meant that the long-term unemployed must live on a means-tested benefit that is barely at the poverty level.

Sean Gallup/Getty Images

The German Welfare State

Germany devotes an unusually large share of its economy to social spending, though not as much as Sweden. Both countries spend more and reduce poverty more than does the United States.

	Germany	Sweden	United States
Gross public social expenditures in 2014 (% of GDP)	25.8	28.1	19.2
Net (after taxes) publicly mandated social expenditures in 2011 (% of GDP)	23.7	22.5	20.1
Poverty rate (pre-tax and transfer) in 2013 (% of population)	32.8	26.7	27.6
Poverty rate (post-tax and transfer) in 2013 (% of population)	9.1	8.8	17.2

Source: Organisation for Economic Co-operation and Development (http://stats.oecd.org/Index.aspx?QueryId=4549#; http://stats.oecd.org/).

to retirement pensions, but it could only do so by abandoning the traditional German neocorporatist process of consulting with business and labor associations before writing legislation. Even these modest reforms were unpopular enough that they were a major issue in the 1998 election, in which German voters ended sixteen years of CDU rule.

While the Social Democratic Party (SDP) criticized the CDU for making the system less generous, once in power the Social Democrats produced even more substantial reforms. In 2003 the SDP/Green government passed what became known as the Hartz reforms. The most controversial part fundamentally changed a key element of Germany's welfare state. Rather than allowing workers to collect full unemployment insurance (set as a percentage of a worker's wage) indefinitely, the government limited it to twelve months, after which an unemployed worker would be placed on "Unemployment Benefit II," which was set at a fixed level (not connected to past earnings). Benefits for the long-term unemployed switched from social insurance to a means-tested benefit more typical of a liberal welfare state. Also, unemployed workers were required to accept jobs at only 80 percent of their prior wage levels, rather than being allowed to wait for positions equivalent to their previous ones (Vail 2004), and retirement pensions were reduced, from 70 percent of retirees' wages in the 1980s to what will eventually be about 45 percent. The Hartz IV reforms sparked massive protests, but the government refused to back down. Leading "leftists" in the SDP responded by forming a new party before the 2005 election, which was a key reason why the SDP lost the election (see chapter 6). In 2010 Germany's Constitutional Court ruled the Unemployment Benefit II was beneath what was necessary for the dignity of the unemployed and their full participation in society (in essence, calling for Marshall's "social rights"). In response, the government increased the benefit, but only slightly, by eight euros (about eleven U.S. dollars) per month.

In the long run, the hope is that these changes will reduce overall social spending, which in 2003 was at 27 percent of gross domestic product (GDP), and by 2014 had dropped to 25.8 percent. The reform is credited with helping to lower the unemployment rate, though critics note that this is because it forced people to take jobs at lower wages. By 2014, the government was providing some benefits to people who were working because their wages still left them below the income level to qualify for Hartz IV. The country implemented its first minimum wage in 2015 in part to deal with this problem. As is often the case with means-tested programs, some stigma that could be undermining a sense of equal citizenship seems to be attached to the reforms: the new verb *hartzen* means "to be unwilling to perform any work" (Grässler 2014). Rehm (2016) argued that the reforms occurred because German reunification reduced support for generous and uniform unemployment benefits; the much higher level of unemployment in the former East Germany led West Germans to conclude that they were paying more and receiving less from the system, undermining support for it, and perhaps also undermining West Germans' sense that East Germans were truly equal citizens.

CASE Questions

1. What does the history of reforms to the German welfare state teach us about the debate over the effects of globalization on social policy? Does globalization force conformity, or do important national distinctions still matter?
2. What values underlie Germany's Christian democratic welfare state, and do these seem to have changed fundamentally in the last decade?

CASE Study

THE UNITED STATES: REFORMING THE LIBERAL WELFARE STATE

CASE SYNOPSIS

The American liberal welfare state recognizes an entitlement to permanent benefits only for the elderly and the disabled. All other spending programs are means tested, and the best known, TANF, is strictly limited in terms of how long people can use it and what they must do to get it. Indeed, tax expenditures have come to constitute a much bigger share of overall social policy than the traditional "welfare" programs. The In Context box on page 652 shows that based on income earned in the market alone, the United States has a comparable percentage of people living in poverty as Germany and Sweden, but taxes and government social programs lower the poverty rate by only about 10 percentage points in the United States compared with

20 or more in the European cases. The shift from means-tested cash assistance to tax expenditures, though, may have the benefit of giving the poor a greater sense of equal citizenship.

- **TYPE OF WELFARE STATE** Liberal
- **RECENT PROBLEMS** Growing poverty, unemployment, and inequality
- **REFORMS** 1996 reform ended entitlement to benefits and required work; tax credit and "food stamps" expanded and are now larger than cash benefit program

Most social policy in the United States began in the Great Depression as part of President Franklin D. Roosevelt's New Deal. The Social Security Act of 1935 established the system and remains the country's primary social program. This social insurance retirement program is similar to Germany's: pensions are tied to individuals' previous earnings and are financed by mandatory employer and employee contributions. Social Security is the country's most successful antipoverty program, and while not as generous as most European pension systems, it nonetheless dramatically reduced poverty among the elderly. Combined with Medicare, the health care plan for the elderly (see the Health Care and Health Policy section below), it reduced American inequality by nearly 10 percent in 2000. (In contrast, "public assistance"—what most Americans think of as "welfare"—reduced American inequality by only 0.4 percent.) Prior to Social Security, the elderly had one of the highest rates of poverty, but now they have one of the lowest.

President Lyndon Johnson's War on Poverty in the 1960s produced the second major expansion of American social policy. It created Aid to Families with Dependent Children (AFDC), which became the main means-tested entitlement benefit for the poor, with each state legally obligated to indefinitely provide a minimum level of support, primarily to poor, single mothers with resident children. Medicaid was created to fund health services for AFDC recipients, food stamps provided vouchers for food purchases by poor families, and subsidized housing was created for some. By 1975, the poverty rate hit a low of about 12 percent of the population, half of what it had been in 1960.

In spite of notable success in reducing poverty, these programs were not widely accepted. Whereas Social Security was regarded as an earned benefit, AFDC was controversial from the outset. Critics argued that its structure of indefinite, per-child payments to families headed by women created perverse incentives for the poor to divorce or have children out of wedlock, and have more children. Benefit levels also varied widely from state to state, with some states providing as much as five times what others did. In spite of the concerns of permanent "welfare dependence" and incentives to have more children, in reality, half of AFDC recipients received benefits for fewer than four years, and the average household size of recipients dropped from 4.0 in 1969 to 2.9 in 1992, meaning an average of only 1.9 children per mother, below the national average of 2.1 (Cammisa 1998, 10–17). Nonetheless, the perception of a perverse incentive structure persisted.

Pressure for reform began as early as the late 1960s, but grew significantly in the 1980s. President Bill Clinton got elected in 1992 on a platform that included a promise to "end welfare as we know it." Two years later, Congress, with Republican support and mostly Democratic opposition, passed and President Clinton signed the most important reform of social policy since the 1960s. The legislation ended AFDC as an entitlement to poor, single mothers and replaced it with a new program, Temporary Assistance for Needy Families (TANF). TANF eliminated the bias against households with fathers, limited recipients to two years of continuous benefits and five years over a lifetime, required virtually all able-bodied recipients to work to keep their benefits, and allowed them to keep a significant share of those benefits after they began working.

Supporters of the reform believed it would reduce welfare dependence, encourage individuals to work, and lower poverty. Critics claimed it meted out harsh punishment to the poor, who would be cut off without the possibility of finding work that would lead them out of poverty. What is clear is that the number of people receiving benefits fell sharply: in 2014, the number of people receiving TANF was one-quarter of the number who received AFDC in 1995 (Edin and Shaefer 2016). In 1995 some 76 percent of poor families with children received AFDC; in 2014 only 23 percent received TANF (Greenstein 2016). The overall number of people in poverty, though, did not change markedly. Some families were able to get out of poverty via work and the tax expenditure programs we discuss below, while others fell deeper into poverty: the number of children living in "deep poverty" (in households with incomes less than half the official poverty level) rose from 2.1 to 3.0 percent between 1995 and 2005, or from 1.5 to 2.2 million children (Greenstein 2016). Kathryn Edin and H. Luke Shaefer (2016) argued that about 3 million American children live in households that for at least three

A man loads free groceries into his car at a food pantry in Jefferson City, Missouri, in 2016. Increased use of food pantries is one way those in the United States in "deep poverty" survive. The American liberal welfare state encourages work and rewards it for people with low incomes with a tax expenditure for the working poor, but many others survive on as little as 2 dollars per day.

AP Photo/David A. Lieb

months a year survive on less than 2 dollars per day, approximately the global standard for "extreme poverty":

> How did they survive? Nearly all had sold plasma from time to time, some regularly. In 2014, so-called "donations" hit an all-time high at 32.5 million, triple the rate recorded a decade prior. They collected tin cans for an average yield of about $1 an hour. They traded away their food stamps, usually at the going rate of 50 or 60 cents on the dollar. Some traded sex for cash or—more commonly—the payment of their cell phone bill, a room to stay in, a meal, or some other kind of help. (2016)

TANF declined so dramatically not only because of the limits the program placed on recipients but because of the way it was administered under American federalism. AFDC had been a national entitlement: states had to provide cash to those eligible at a certain minimum level, and many states supplemented that level. TANF funds from the federal government are a "block grant" given to each state to use on the program with few restrictions. If states do not spend all of the money on TANF, they can use it elsewhere, providing a clear incentive to try not to spend it; just over half of all TANF funding goes to recipients (Schott et al. 2015).

At the same time as "welfare" in the sense of cash benefits declined, other income-support policies expanded. Most important is the Earned Income Tax Credit (EITC), a major tax expenditure that aims to benefit the "working poor" and has been the fastest-growing social program in the country since 1990. Households making less than about $20,000 per year receive a tax credit each spring worth several thousand dollars, usually substantially more than they paid in taxes, which has become a key source of income for many. By 2009, the U.S. government was spending four times more on EITC than TANF. Similarly, the funding and number of recipients of "food stamps," officially the Supplemental Nutrition Assistance Program (SNAP), fell during the 1990s but increased substantially in the first decade of the new millennium. In 2012 EITC and SNAP each lifted approximately 10 million people out of poverty, while TANF lifted only 1.3 million out of poverty (Sherman and Trisi 2015). Sarah Halpern-Meekin and colleagues (2015) argued that because EITC is a tax refund for the working poor that they receive simply by going through the same tax-filing process that other Americans do, it preserves their sense of citizenship much better than programs like TANF that hand them money distinct from what others receive. The division between the working poor who receive EITC and the nonworking poor left to depend on TANF and related programs, who often live on less than 2 dollars per day, is the new reality of poverty in America.

These contradictory trends in American welfare policy mirror debates over how generous the country's social policy really is. As the In Context box on page 652 shows, U.S. "net" social expenditures, which include taxation and therefore programs like EITC, are much closer to European levels than are total U.S. social expenditures (not taking taxation into account). As the In Context box demonstrates, however,

America's liberal welfare state still does not reduce poverty as much as most European welfare states do. The United States channels a lot of money toward education and tax expenditures, which benefit far more people than just the poor.

CASE Questions

1. What does the U.S. reform effort suggest about which type of social policy is most efficient at reducing poverty?
2. Comparing the United States and Germany, how much of a difference is there now between the Christian democratic and liberal welfare state models?

CASE Study

BRAZIL: STARTING A WELFARE STATE IN A DEVELOPING ECONOMY

CASE SYNOPSIS

Bolsa Família, Brazil's CCT program and the largest antipoverty program in Latin America, is a major innovation in the development of the welfare state in developing countries; thirteen Latin American countries had CCT programs in place by 2009. Bolsa Família has substantially reduced poverty and inequality, though in a context of strong economic growth. The country is moving in the direction of creating a liberal welfare state focused primarily on means-tested programs in practice, in spite of lofty language in the constitution about universal social rights. How well Bolsa Família can battle poverty and how much political support it will have in the face of the recent economic downturn remain to be seen.

- TYPE OF WELFARE STATE Liberal (emerging)
- RECENT PROBLEMS Pension spending favors middle class; slowing economic growth
- REFORMS Expansion of pensions to eliminate poverty among the elderly; pioneer CCT program

A t his first presidential inauguration in 2002, former metalworker Luiz "Lula" Inácio da Silva famously declared, "If, by the end of my term of office, every Brazilian has food to eat three times a day, I shall have fulfilled my mission in life" (Hall 2006, 690). When he handed power to his handpicked successor in 2010, there were still hungry Brazilians, but the nation's poverty rate had dropped from nearly 49 percent to under 29 percent, and inequality had declined by 17 percent, one of the most impressive drops in history. Rapid economic growth and raising the minimum wage were important elements in these achievements, but so was Lula's "signature" success, Bolsa Família.

For most of the country's history, Brazilian economic policy focused on achieving growth, while it became one of the most unequal societies in the world. As in many countries, the first systematic government social policy focused on the elderly. Until the 1990s, the pension system covered a small percentage of the population: civil servants, whose pensions were paid for by the government, and formal-sector private employees, whose pensions came from mandatory contributions. This left out the large share of the population that works in the informal sector: most agricultural workers and those in quasi-legal businesses who are not officially recognized and don't pay taxes. Lula's first and largest reform was to the pension system for civil servants. He argued that the generous benefits went to mostly middle-class civil servants (a small proportion of the population). He increased the retirement age, required middle-income civil servants to contribute to their pension system, and reduced its generosity. In the long run, these changes are predicted to save the government a great deal of money, though pensions remain by far the largest social policy in the country.

The 1988 constitution of the new democracy established a right to a minimum income for all elderly people. One new program covers anyone over a certain age who can prove past employment in the agricultural sector. Another offers means-tested benefits to any elderly person in a household with a monthly income less than one-half the minimum wage. While slightly less than half the population contributes to

Members of the Das Neves family hang laundry in their courtyard in a *favela*, an informal settlement, in Rio de Janeiro. The family credits Brazil's innovative CCT program, Bolsa Família, with helping it build a new home after its old one was condemned.

Mario Tama/Getty Images

the pension system, 90 percent of the elderly now receive benefits from the combined programs, financed from general taxation. The result has been a near elimination of poverty among the elderly (Lavinas 2006, 110).

Lula's pledge to end hunger led to the creation of Bolsa Família (Family Grant) early in his first term. The program provides food and cash grants, targeting poor and "very poor" households, and requires recipient parents to send their children to school and utilize children's health services. Local social service councils oversee implementation of the program, an attempt to reduce corrupt and political selection of recipient households. By 2015, it was providing grants to nearly fourteen million families, meaning fifty-five million people, about a quarter of the entire population. The best estimates are that Bolsa Família is responsible for one-sixth of the 12 percent drop in poverty in the new millennium and a third of the drop in extreme poverty (Barrientos et al. 2016). It is also credited with playing a major role in the 50 percent drop in infant mortality and child malnutrition over the same period. Because the cash grants are so small, the program costs only 0.5 percent of GDP, making it one of the most efficient poverty-reduction programs in the world. Since the 2010 presidential election to choose Lula's successor, the program has been so popular that all major presidential candidates have supported it.

Despite the program's success, criticisms and concerns have certainly arisen. Some fear that it will create a "culture of dependency" because it has no time limits on benefits. On the other hand, some critics argue that far more expansive policies are needed, including transferring assets (especially land) to the poor and providing guaranteed and universal benefits. Means-tested programs like Bolsa Família often lead to stigmatization of recipients, which affects the idea of equal citizenship, but a survey of 1,400 recipients "found that rather than feeling stigmatized by their dependence on the government program, three-quarters of respondents said that . . . Bolsa Família has helped them 'lead more autonomous and dignified lives'" (Tepperman 2015, 6–7).

As Brazil's economy went into recession in 2014 and then President Dilma Rousseff, Lula's successor, was impeached, the lingering question became, Would Bolsa Família survive? The recession almost certainly produced an upsurge in poverty, and Bolsa Família never became popular with Brazil's middle and upper classes, but as of late 2016, no major politician had opposed the program, given its popularity with the poor majority of voters.

CASE Questions

1. In what ways does Brazil seem to be moving toward a liberal welfare state? Do you see elements of other types of welfare states in Brazil's system?
2. Look back at the debate in chapter 11 about how to help develop "the bottom billion." What does the striking success of CCT programs suggest about that debate? Can their success in middle-income countries like Brazil be extended to "the bottom billion"? Why or why not?

HEALTH CARE AND HEALTH POLICY

While social policy generates philosophical debate over the proper role of government in most societies, much of the world has adopted the idea that health care is a social right of all citizens. Carsten Jensen (2014) pointed out that health policy is less partisan in most countries than social policy because of the different kinds of risk involved: social policies such as unemployment insurance and social assistance address labor market risks, which many people believe they are unlikely to face, while health policy addresses a life-cycle risk—everyone will get sick. Wealthy countries have the resources to attempt to realize a social right to health via interventions in the health care market, but most others lack the resources to make it a reality. A few countries, notably the United States, do not embrace health care as a social right but nonetheless claim the provision of the best health care possible to the largest number of people as a legitimate political and social goal.

Health Care and Market Failure

Social values are not the only reason for policy intervention in health care markets, however. Market failure takes distinct forms in health care that are based on specific characteristics of the health care market. The key problems are very high risk and poor consumer information, both of which produce inefficiency and misallocation of resources. People will do almost anything—pay any price or undergo any procedure—to restore their health when it is seriously threatened. On the other hand, healthy people need very little medical care. Those who lack the resources to pay for care when sick may face severe harm or even death. Insurance is the typical solution to such high-risk markets. It spreads risks across many people. Paying smaller, regular premiums more or less fixes the cost for each individual in the insurance pool, so catastrophic illness does not mean catastrophic bills. This principle also underlies homeowner's or auto insurance. Governments or private companies can provide insurance as long as a relatively large group of people with diverse risks pool their resources to cover emergencies as necessary.

Although insurance is a potential market-based solution to high risk, it creates its own potential market failure: **moral hazard.** Moral hazard occurs when parties to a transaction behave differently than they otherwise would because they believe they won't have to pay the full costs of their actions. In health insurance, this results from the gap between paying a fixed premium for health care and the costs of the care itself. If insurance covers the full cost of the care, patients have no incentive to economize because their costs (the insurance premium) will not change regardless of how much health care they use. Moreover, many insurance systems pay medical providers for each procedure, giving providers an incentive to oversupply procedures just as the patient has an incentive to overuse them. The obvious results are excessive medical procedures and rising costs. Governments intervene in health care in part to attempt to limit the effects of the moral hazard inherent in an insurance system.

moral hazard
Occurs when parties to a transaction behave in a particular way because they believe they will not have to pay the full costs of their actions

Another market failure, poor information, compounds the problem of overuse. Patients generally rely on medical professionals to know what procedures or drugs are needed to get well. Even highly educated patients usually agree to their doctor's recommended treatment, especially if they are insured and face little direct cost. In the extreme case, a completely unregulated market with poor information can produce the iconic image of nineteenth-century American medical quackery, the "snake-oil salesman," a charlatan selling false remedies to desperate people. To avoid this, virtually all governments regulate both pharmaceuticals and medical practitioners.

Health Care Systems

Wealthy countries have developed three distinct types of health care systems to address these problems. These have served as models for poorer countries as well, though poor countries are severely limited by lack of resources. The earliest and still most common system in wealthy countries is **national health insurance (NHI).** In an NHI system, the government mandates that virtually all citizens have insurance. NHI countries typically allow and encourage multiple, private insurance providers, while the government provides access to insurance to the self-employed or unemployed who do not have access via family members. Since the government mandates the insurance, it also regulates the system, setting or at least limiting premiums and payments to medical providers. In many NHI systems, access to health care is not specific to a particular employer, so workers can keep their insurance when they switch jobs. Germany pioneered this system in the late nineteenth century and continues to use it today, as do many other European countries and Japan. Few poor countries attempt to implement NHI because many of their citizens simply cannot afford insurance, although some do use a limited form of it for wealthier segments of the population, such as civil servants or employees of large corporations.

A **national health system (NHS)** is the second most common type of health care system in wealthy countries and the most common type worldwide. Frequently called a **single-payer system,** NHS is a government-financed and managed system. The government creates a system into which all citizens pay, either through a separate insurance payment (like Medicare in the United States) or via general taxation. The classic example of this type of system is in the United Kingdom, which established its NHS after World War II. In most NHS countries, the majority of medical professionals gain their income directly from the government, which implicitly controls the cost of medical care via payments for procedures, equipment, and drugs. Most poor countries have an NHS through which the government provides most medical care via hospitals and local clinics and in which doctors are direct government employees. With limited resources in poor countries, however, clinics and doctors are few, and many people lack access to or must wait long periods for what is often low-quality care.

national health insurance (NHI)
A health care system in which the government mandates that virtually all citizens must have insurance

national health system (NHS)/single-payer system
A government-financed and managed health care system into which all citizens pay, either through a separate insurance payment or via general taxation, and through which they gain medical care

The third system, a **market-based private insurance system**, is the least common. Although NHI and NHS countries typically permit some private insurance as a supplement for those who can afford it, the United States, Turkey, and Mexico are the only OECD countries that rely on private insurance for the bulk of their health care. In the United States, citizens typically gain insurance through their employment, and medical care is provided mostly by for-profit entities such as private clinics and hospitals. Government programs often exist in market-based systems to cover specific groups without private insurance, such as the poor, the unemployed, and the self-employed. Market-based systems, though, do not guarantee access to health care to all citizens, and even in the wealthiest of these countries, a sizeable minority lacks any insurance.

Common Problems

Almost all countries face a common set of problems regardless of the system they use. The most evident are rising costs (especially in wealthy countries), lack of access to care, and growing public health concerns. Because of the need to contain costs, all countries and systems make decisions about how to ration care: who will get it, when, and how much.

Controlling Costs Wealthier countries are most concerned about cost, because as wealth increases, health care costs rise faster than incomes. This is because wealthier people demand more and better care, and improved but often expensive technology emerges to help provide that care. Wealthier countries also have relatively low birth rates and high life expectancies, so the proportion of the population that is elderly increases over time and needs more health care. From 2000 to 2009, expenditures grew at an annual average of 4 percent, well above overall economic growth, though they slowed considerably after the Great Recession. People in almost all wealthy countries use more and more of their income for health care, regardless of the system in place.

Wealthy countries use several means to try to control costs. A key factor is the size of insurance pools. Larger and more diverse pools of people lower costs because a larger number of healthy people (especially young adults) cover the costs of those (often the elderly) who use health care more heavily, thereby lowering premiums for everyone. NHS and NHI systems that group many or all of a country's citizens into one insurance pool gain a cost-saving advantage. In market-based systems, on the other hand, the risk pools are much smaller (usually the employees of a particular company), so costs tend to be higher. Governments in these countries spend less tax revenue on health care than do other governments, but citizens may spend more on health care overall via private insurance premiums and direct fees. The United States, which depends heavily on private insurance and has very low government expenditures on health care, has by far the highest overall health costs, both in terms of dollars spent per capita and as a share of GDP (compare the wealthy countries in the Country and Concept table on pages 636–637).

Other cost-saving measures focus on limiting the effects of moral hazard. For example, paying doctors on a capitation, or per patient, basis rather than for each procedure creates an incentive to limit unnecessary procedures. Critics, however, argue that this gives providers an incentive to underprescribe, which endangers patients' well-being. A second strategy, "gatekeepers," can limit patients' demands for expensive treatments. Typically, a general practitioner serves as a gatekeeper who must give approval before patients can consult specialists in order to limit unnecessary trips to expensive specialists and procedures. A third approach is to require patients to make copayments, small fees that cover part of the cost of each service. If kept to moderate amounts, copayments can theoretically discourage unnecessary or frivolous procedures; if set too high, however, they may discourage poorer patients from getting medically necessary care.

Clearly, a trade-off exists between cost containment and achieving a healthy population. Meeting all demands for health care instantly might produce the healthiest possible population, but it would be prohibitively expensive and would aggravate moral hazard. No society ever does this; instead, all choose to ration health care in some way, though many people may not perceive it as rationing. NHS countries can control costs most directly simply by limiting the overall health care budget, the payments to medical providers, purchases of new equipment, and/or drug prices. The result can be relatively low-cost but sometimes limited care. Limits typically take the form of patients waiting for certain procedures rather than getting them on demand. NHI countries can set insurance premiums and medical payments as well; they usually don't do so as universally as NHS countries, though Germany has experimented with greater regulation in recent years. Some countries, including the United States (the only wealthy country in this category), provide insurance only to a segment of the population, who thereby have access to fairly extensive care; those without insurance have very limited or no access to care. This is another way to ration.

The data in the Critical Inquiry box (page 665) suggest that the form of rationing does not make a substantial difference to achieving a healthy population among wealthy countries, though it does have a significant effect on costs. Those with the lowest costs, such as Britain, do not have significantly lower health outcomes overall, measured by key data such as infant mortality or life expectancy. For poorer countries, where the main problem is not cost containment but availability of resources, lower costs do seem related to lower-quality health, as the Country and Concept table (pages 636–637) shows.

Access to Health Care Access is a much greater problem than rising costs for the very poorest countries, where limited resources mean much smaller numbers of doctors, hospitals, and clinics per capita. Even though individuals may be nominally covered by a government health plan, they cannot access health care if facilities and

CRITICAL
inquiry

Comparing Health Care Systems

Wealthy countries present us with three distinct models of how to provide health care: NHS, NHI, and market-based. The table below provides some key data on access and cost of health care along with basic health outcomes for all three health care systems. Comparing the three, which do you think is the best overall model of health care? What are the principles or goals on which you base your assessment? Looking at the data, why do you come to the conclusions you do?

	NHS	NHI	Market-based
Costs			
Health care expenditures per capita	$3,829.81	$4,690.86	$5,269.95
Health care expenditures as share of GDP	9.72	11.02	12.46
Outcomes			
Life expectancy at birth	81.8	82.3	80.2
Infant mortality (2015)	3.9	2.9	6.3
Life expectancy at age 65	21.8	22.3	20.2
Access			
Medical doctors (per 1,000 population) (2009)	2.93	3.03	1.7
MRIs (per one million population) (2009)	8.43	19.67	25.9*

Source: All data are from World Bank (2016).

Note: All data are for 2014, unless otherwise noted. Countries in the sample are, for NHS: New Zealand, Spain, and the United Kingdom; for NHI: France, Germany, and Japan; for market-based systems: Chile and the United States.

*United States only; data not available for Chile.

providers are not available. While many have NHS systems, as the Country and Concept table demonstrates, most health care funding still comes from private financing, often direct payments to providers without even the benefit of insurance. As a result of limited access and costs too high for the poor majority, preventable and easily treatable diseases continue to shorten life spans and cause loss of income and productivity in much of the world. The problem of access in wealthy countries with NHS or NHI systems has been virtually eliminated; those systems provide insurance coverage for nearly everyone, and medical facilities and doctors are plentiful. For the

OECD as a whole, well under 5 percent of people reported not receiving adequate care for financial reasons in 2013 (OECD 2015). The only access problem typically is waiting times for some procedures. In market-based systems in wealthy countries, on the other hand, access is not universal: those without health insurance have only very limited access to care because they can't afford to pay for it.

Public Health The third major common problem is public health concerns. These are common to all countries but vary greatly. In the poorest countries, access to enough food and clean water remains a public health issue. Without access to clean water, populations continue to be plagued by a variety of contagious diseases. Furthermore, malnourishment exacerbates the effects of waterborne contagions, as immune systems are weak and resistance low. The health effects in terms of core indicators such as infant mortality and life expectancy are clear in the Country and Concept table (pages 636–637); compare the data for wealthy countries such as the United States, the United Kingdom, or Japan with poorer countries such as India or Nigeria.

The wealthiest countries face a different kind of malnutrition: obesity. The highest rates of obesity in the OECD are in the United States and Mexico, and now include more than 30 percent of the population. Obesity rates are rising in almost all wealthy countries: food is inexpensive compared with incomes, so people overconsume it.

Other public health issues resulting from affluence—alcohol and tobacco consumption—have seen positive change recently. Rates of alcohol use in the OECD declined by 9 percent from 1980 to 2009, while rates of tobacco use declined by about 18 percent from 1999 to 2009. Active public health education programs, along with legal limits and higher taxes on alcohol and tobacco consumption, reaped impressive results in many wealthy countries. Unfortunately, alcohol and tobacco consumption rates are increasing in many poorer countries, as their populations become wealthier and as alcohol and tobacco producers actively market in developing countries to compensate for shrinking consumption in their traditional markets.

Finally, globalization has produced a new set of public health concerns that cross borders as physical interaction among populations increases. These include the expansion of sexually transmitted diseases (especially HIV/AIDS) and insect-borne diseases such as Lyme disease, West Nile virus, malaria, and Zika virus. Increased importation and exportation of products and international travel have also led to the global spread of such conditions as salmonella; hand, foot, and mouth disease; and SARS. The spread of diseases to new populations lowers overall well-being and raises health care costs. Contagious disease is best dealt with via preventative measures such as education campaigns, infrastructure projects, free condoms, and control of insect populations, all of which are public goods and therefore inherently government responsibilities. With increasing globalization, what happens in one country increasingly affects others, meaning that health care policymakers in one country might be well advised to assist the citizens of other countries as well as their own.

CASE Study

GERMANY: PIONEER OF MODERN HEALTH POLICY

CASE SYNOPSIS

Germany has long been a model of the NHI system, but it continues to struggle with rising costs. Reform efforts remained within the corporatist tradition of the German Christian democratic welfare state until the most recent reforms, which have fundamentally altered financing by creating a uniform national premium schedule and shifting costs onto workers. Germany, like all wealthy countries, will continue to struggle with a health care sector that consumes an ever larger share of national income, though Germans have a system that achieves unusually high levels of care coupled with widespread patient choice and universal coverage.

- SYSTEM NHI

- MAJOR BENEFITS Universal access and wide choice

- MAJOR PROBLEMS Growing costs

- REFORMS Aimed at lowering costs via incentives and maintaining equity of access

Germany's NHI system, which dates back to 1883, is corporatist in both organization and management, relying heavily on professional and patient associations to implement it under the overall regulation of the state. It provides very generous benefits, including dental, hospital, preventative care, and even rehabilitative health spa treatments, primarily through a network of sickness funds financed by payroll taxes shared by employers and employees. Cost control has been a major issue (though less so than in the United States) and has prompted a series of reforms to limit costs, increase competition, and shift costs to users.

"Sickness funds," nonprofit organizations run by boards of employers and employees, are the key organizations in the system. They are connected to employer, profession, or locale and are autonomous from the government in setting most of their policies and prices, though the services they must offer are uniform across the country. They negotiate services and payments with regional physician associations; doctors who wish to participate in the system (about 95 percent of them do) must be members of their regional association and abide by the negotiated agreements. All but the wealthiest Germans must belong to a sickness fund; in this way, Germany has long achieved universal coverage. The unemployed must belong to a fund as well, the costs of which are covered by federal and local governments. The wealthiest individuals may opt out of the system and purchase private insurance, though more than 90 percent of the population use the sickness fund system. Residents can also purchase supplemental insurance to give them greater choice in where and how they are treated, and about 10 percent of sickness fund members do so (Adolino and Blake 2001, 225; Green and Irvine 2001, 57).

Employment determined which fund most Germans joined until a 1997 reform allowed citizens to choose their sickness fund and change it annually, introducing competition among funds. This reduced the number of sickness funds from 1,200 in 1985 to 124 in 2015, as competition pushed most out of the market. Nonetheless, German patients have exceptional levels of choice among sickness funds and, once they've selected a fund, among doctors. Despite nearly universal coverage, equity has been a continuous concern, especially for the Social Democratic Party. Some sickness funds have unusually high numbers of poor and unhealthy members, meaning their costs are well above the national average. A 1992 reform attempted to resolve this issue by creating a compensation system in which money is transferred from wealthier to poorer sickness funds. As costs have risen in recent years, relatively young, healthy, and wealthy people have increasingly opted out of the system altogether, taking the lowest-cost members out of the sickness funds and thereby raising premiums for everyone else. Reforms in 2007 for the first time mandated that all citizens have insurance, but the wealthy can still purchase private insurance instead of joining a sickness fund.

Cost containment has long been a major issue in the German system. The key relationship is between the sickness funds and the regional associations of physicians who negotiate agreements over payments to physicians. The first major reform of the system in 1977 established a classic corporatist solution: national negotiations among the sickness funds, physicians' associations, and the government to set

A patient provides ten euros (about thirteen dollars) and his national insurance card to pay for a visit to a doctor's office. Modest copays have become a means of cutting down costs in Germany's NHI system.

Sean Gallup/Getty Images

targets for annual expenditure growth. In 1986 a binding cap on expenditures was established, negotiated each year between the sickness funds and physicians' associations. Finally, in 2007, as costs continued to rise, a more fundamental change in health care financing created a single nationwide premium schedule tied to workers' incomes. The new national fund distributes the premiums plus general tax revenue to sickness funds on a per capita basis, adjusting for the wealth and health of the membership of each fund. Individual sickness funds can give rebates to their members if they can provide services at a cost lower than what they receive from the national fund, or they can charge members additional premiums if necessary. This policy is designed to encourage efficiency as the funds compete for members. Over the years, the government has also increased copayments to give patients incentives to economize on care.

Despite these reforms, cost remains a major concern. An aging population and expensive technological innovations continue to increase the cost of health care. Germany's extraordinarily high number of doctors and hospital beds per capita (see the In Context box, page 669) give patients tremendous choice, but they also cost a great deal. In the face of the global recession, Angela Merkel's Christian Democrat–Free Democrat coalition government implemented a controversial reform in 2011 that raised the insurance premiums from 14.9 to 15.5 percent of wages, with most of the increase paid by employees. More controversially, it allowed future increases that would be paid fully by employees and can be flat fees, rather than a percentage of income. This was modified in 2015, lowering premiums back to 14.6 percent of wages (divided equally between employers and employees), and allowing sickness funds to charge an additional premium of up to 1.3 percent, with wealthier members having to pay more than poorer ones. To try to control rising drug costs, the 2011 reform also required pharmaceutical companies to negotiate prices with insurance funds for new drugs; failure to do so will result in the government setting prices. Overall, the long series of reforms has meant that patients' share of total costs has more than doubled since 1991, providers have new incentives to economize on the number and type of procedures they prescribe, and growing reports suggest some patients are not receiving services in order to keep costs down (Gerlinger 2010).

CASE Questions

1. What does the German NHI system teach us about the costs and benefits of the NHI model?
2. What further reforms might help Germany control costs?

Health Care in Wealthy Countries

Different health care systems in our case study countries have significant differences. Costs, in particular, vary dramatically, while outcomes are similar. Access to doctors, hospitals, and technology depends on how each country chooses to spend its health budget.

	Germany	United Kingdom	United States	OECD average
Costs				
Health care expenditures per capita ($), 2015	$5,267.1	$4,015.2	$9,451.3	$3,739.85
Health care expenditures as percentage of GDP, 2015	11.1	9.8	16.9	9.0
Public share of total health expenditures, 2014	77	83.1	48.3	72.4
Physicians' remuneration (ratio to average wage), 2009	3.3	4.2	3.7	NA
Outcomes				
Life expectancy at birth (years), 2014	80.8	81.1	78.9	80.1
Infant mortality rates (per 1,000 population), 2015	3.1	3.5	5.6	5.9
Childhood measles vaccination rate, 2014	97	93	91	94
Access				
Practicing physicians (per 1,000 population), 2015	4.05	2.77	2.56	NA
Acute care hospital beds (per 1,000 population), 2014	5.34	2.28	2.48	NA
Access to doctor or nurse (% waiting longer than 6 days), 2009	16	8	19	NA
Wait times for elective surgery (% waiting longer than 4 months), 2008	0	21	7	NA

Sources: Organisation for Economic Co-operation and Development (https://data.oecd.org/), (http://www.oecd-library.org/docserver/download/8115071ec025.pdf?expires=1475518210&id=id&accname=guest&checksum=C466A7111E38C2FF49DFD719EC25CA46), (http://data.worldbank.org/indicator/SH.IMM.MEAS); World Bank (http://data.worldbank.org/indicator/SH.XPD.PUBL); access to specialists: Commonwealth Fund (2008).

CASE Study

UNITED KINGDOM: REFORMING THE NHS

CASE SYNOPSIS

In contrast to corporatist and federal Germany, Britain's NHS is a unitary and centralized system of health care. It has always been one of the country's most popular government programs, and it has allowed the government to keep costs relatively low, but at the expense of quality and timeliness of service, or so its critics claim. Britain's majoritarian system has allowed recent governments of both parties to enact significant reforms more easily than in either Germany or the United States. These reforms have focused on reorganization to improve efficiency and quality of service. The Labour government coupled this with sharply increased spending to provide Britons with health care quality closer to that of other European countries. In contrast, the Conservative/LDP government passed reforms to increase competition and the role of the private sector and to drive down costs. Even with this reform, however, British health care will continue to be funded by general taxation and be free or nearly so at the point of service.

- SYSTEM NHS

- MAJOR BENEFITS Universal access and low cost

- MAJOR PROBLEMS Quality of service, waiting times for elective procedures, and growing costs

- REFORMS Instill market mechanisms to increase competition and efficiency

n March 2012, the British Parliament passed what many called the biggest change to British health care since the creation of the NHS after World War II. Pushed by Conservative prime minister David Cameron, the reforms were designed to instill more market-like competition in the system to increase efficiency. They passed after a year of exceptionally acrimonious public debate. Like Germany, the United Kingdom was a pioneer of health care, creating the earliest and most universal NHS based on four key principles: universal services, comprehensive services, free to the patient, and financed by general tax revenue. With minor exceptions, the NHS has worked that way ever since, though both Conservative and Labour governments have made significant reforms in the last twenty years. Britain achieves health outcomes that are about average for wealthy countries at relatively low costs. As the In Context box (page 669) shows, it accomplishes this in part by having fewer doctors and hospital beds than

Germany, and, most important, by rationing nonessential care via long waits (though wait times for simply seeing a primary care doctor or nurse are quite low).

The NHS traditionally functioned like one giant managed care system: it signed contracts with general practitioners (GPs) in each region of the country to deliver primary services to patients. Each region served as one large insurance pool, with an average of about half a million patients. GPs are paid on a combination of fee-for-service and capitation basis, and British patients can sign up with the GP of their choice, usually in their neighborhood, who provides basic care and functions as a gatekeeper, referring them to a specialist or hospital as needed. The NHS regional and district health authorities received national government revenue to provide hospital and specialist services, and most services (except for some pharmaceuticals) are free to the patient at the point of service, having been paid for by general taxes. Waiting times for seeing GPs are very low, but waiting times for specialists and nonemergency hospital stays are among the world's highest.

No one can opt out of the NHS, since it's funded by general taxes, but patients can purchase private supplemental insurance that allows them to see private doctors and get hospital services without the long waits of the public system. As Britons have grown wealthier and have demanded more health care, a growing number supplement NHS coverage with private insurance; in 2012 about 11 percent of the population had private insurance. Patients can use the NHS for routine illnesses and private insurance for procedures that have long waiting lines in the NHS.

The NHS allows the national government to control costs directly: it simply sets the annual overall budget, thereby limiting the system to a certain expenditure level. In 2015 Britain spent less than half of what the United States did as a share of its GDP. Despite the United Kingdom's ability to control costs, health care reform has been a major political issue since the 1980s. The NHS has always been and remains very popular with British citizens, but there are those unhappy with the long wait

Protestors outside the British Parliament opposed Prime Minister David Cameron's proposed changes to Britain's popular NHS. The firestorm of opposition was so great that Cameron took the unusual step of delaying parliamentary approval of the plan for a year while modifications were made.

Photo by In Pictures Ltd./Corbis via Getty Images

times for certain procedures and allegedly lower-quality care, both by-products of cost-control structures.

The NHS as originally structured had no internal incentives for efficiency. The Conservative government under Margaret Thatcher initiated a reform in 1990 that introduced elements of competition to increase efficiency. The idea was never popular, but Thatcher used her majority in Britain's parliamentary system to pass the reform anyway. It created large purchasers and sellers of health care. GPs with large practices (five thousand patients or more) were given their own budget by the NHS, which they used to purchase specialist and hospital services for their patients. Those who negotiated better deals would be likely to get more patients and earn more money.

The results of this bold experiment were mixed. Wait times dropped and there were signs of improved efficiency, but the benefits mainly went to patients of the GPs with the largest practices in the wealthiest areas. The Conservative government also kept overall funding low, so improvements in wait times and quality of care were not dramatic. Indeed, unhappiness with the state of the NHS was one reason why the Labour Party under Tony Blair swept into office in 1997. In a series of reforms, the Labour government modified rather than eliminated the new system. The main reform was to strengthen regional associations, which would purchase services for patients. This kept an element of competition but eliminated the different deals GPs in the same area provided their patients. The Blair government also increased funding to hire more doctors and reduce wait times in hospitals, raising costs substantially.

Cameron's 2012 reforms reversed course again. The new system replaced the regional authorities with groups of GPs, who handle 80 percent of the NHS budget and purchase services for their patients. Most controversially, they are free to use that tax money to purchase services from NHS hospitals or private hospitals and specialists. NHS hospitals and specialists became independent units, required to break even via selling their services to the GP consortia. Reaction to the initial proposals was so negative that the government took the unusual step of "pausing" movement of the bill through Parliament in order to consult more with citizens and medical professionals through several commissions. Many feared that the reform would ultimately allow a full privatization of the system and create greater inequities. The Cameron government and its supporters claimed that the reforms would reduce administrative costs by one-third and instill greater efficiency throughout the system.

By 2016, the results of the reform and continuing financial problems in the system were unclear. A key problem with the new system was practitioners' knowledge and ability to negotiate the wide range of services their patients needed. Competition only works if knowledgeable people operate in the market, and it was not clear that groups of physicians were up to the task. Indeed, fears of privatization appeared to be unfounded; with little real competition in the system, the vast majority of services continued to come from within the NHS (Ham and Murray 2015). In response to the continuing aftershocks of the Great Recession, the Conservative government had also kept NHS funding low, resulting in a funding gap that the NHS estimated will reach 30 billion pounds (about $38 billion) by 2020. The government pledged an additional 8 billion pounds in funding in 2015, leaving a gap of 22 billion pounds to be met by increased efficiency. Britain's 2016 vote to leave the EU also concerned the NHS. In addition to a possible economic downturn further harming funding for the system, a significant number of medical practitioners in the system are citizens of other EU countries whose continued status in the UK would be uncertain.

CASE Questions

1. Comparing the German and British health care systems, what are the primary benefits and costs of each? Which, overall, seems superior, and why?
2. Why has Britain passed more significant reforms to its system over the years than Germany? Is it because the British system needs more changes, or for other reasons?

CASE Study

U.S. HEALTH POLICY: TRIALS AND TRIBULATIONS OF THE MARKET MODEL

CASE SYNOPSIS

The United States spends more on health care—both as a dollar amount and as a share of its total economy—than any other country in the world. In 2011 health spending hit an all-time high of 17.7 percent of the entire economy, falling to 16.9 percent by 2015. The data in the In Context box (page 652) suggest these large expenditures produce health outcomes comparable to, albeit slightly below, those in other wealthy countries. The United States possesses considerably more medical technology than most countries, but this has not produced better health. Prior to the Affordable Care Act (ACA, popularly known as "Obamacare"), a little over half of the U.S. population was covered by employment-based private insurance, with another quarter covered by government programs, and the remaining 15 percent or so had no health insurance. They had to rely on their own resources or free care from mobile clinics, community outreach programs, or hospital emergency rooms, which are required by law to provide aid to anyone who

CASE SYNOPSIS

walks in, though many do not. By 2015, the ACA had reduced the number of uninsured people by twenty million, with the poor and racial minorities being the primary beneficiaries. While overall costs dropped modestly, by 2016 cost remained the major question in the new system, as it had been before implementation of the ACA.

- **SYSTEM** Market-based, supplemented by government programs for the elderly, the poorest, and since 2014 most others without insurance
- **MAJOR BENEFITS** Good access for those insured; high level of services
- **MAJOR PROBLEMS** Highest costs in the world; limited access, particularly for those not insured
- **REFORMS** 2014 reform to expand coverage and perhaps bring down costs

On March 23, 2010, President Barack Obama signed the Affordable Care Act (ACA, commonly known as "Obamacare"), the largest reform of the market-based health care system in the United States at least since the creation of Medicare and Medicaid in 1965. Its chief goals were to expand insurance coverage to 95 percent of the population and reduce overall costs, though it preserved the existing market-based insurance model for all those already served by it. The national debate over the reform was long and exceptionally divisive. Opponents on the right argued that it represented an unprecedented expansion of government into the lives of citizens, while opponents on the left argued that failure to create a true NHS would mean the country would achieve neither universal coverage nor significant cost control.

The American private insurance system became widespread during World War II. After the war, the government encouraged it via tax breaks for health benefits. The system gives advantages to large employers and their employees because each employer negotiates its own insurance rates; larger companies have bigger risk pools and therefore can get lower premiums and better coverage. The authors of this textbook, for

President Barack Obama signs the health care reform bill on March 23, 2010. The reform, the biggest since the creation of Medicare and Medicaid in 1965, provided health insurance to twenty million additional Americans by 2016, though it was less clear that it would reduce the extraordinarily high costs built into the American private-insurance-based health care system.

AP Photo/Charles Dharapak

instance, had the best health coverage of their lives when they were very low-paid teaching assistants in graduate school. Their salaries were near the poverty level, but because they taught at a state university, they were state employees and received the generous benefits a very large employer (the entire state government) provided. Now, they have much higher salaries working at small liberal arts colleges, but not nearly as generous health benefits from employers of only a few hundred employees.

Extensive U.S. government health programs only began in 1965 with the creation of Medicare (for the elderly and disabled) and Medicaid (for the very poorest, mostly TANF recipients). In 1997 the State Children's Health Insurance Program (SCHIP) was created to provide insurance for poor or low-income children. The combination of SCHIP and an expansion of Medicaid coverage reduced the percentage of low-income children who were uninsured from 22.3 percent in 1997 to 14.9 percent in 2005 (CBO 2007, 8). Overall, even before implementation of the ACA, government spending on health was more than 40 percent of total health spending (though that was the second-lowest level in the OECD). Most of this spending went to the expensive Medicare program for the elderly.

Health cost increases reached an alarming rate of nearly 20 percent per year in the late 1980s, leading even large corporations to start demanding some type of intervention to bring costs under control. The issue thus became a major part of the 1992 presidential campaign. After his election, President Bill Clinton proposed a plan that would have set up funds similar to Germany's sickness funds across the country and encouraged them to compete for clients among employers. Coverage would be mandatory and could travel with the employee from one job to the next, and those not employed would be covered by various federal programs and still be part of the funds. Facing fierce opposition from the insurance industry, the reform never passed Congress.

In the absence of national policy reform, employers (the primary purchasers of insurance packages) began reforming the existing system in the 1990s to lower costs via a rapid switch from fee-for-service insurance to HMOs, which try to hold costs down by capitation and gatekeeper rules. As a result, annual cost increases dropped from 18 percent in 1990 to less than 4 percent by 1996, removing health care costs as a significant political concern (Graig 1999, 22–35). By 2006, though, cost increases were rising again, hitting 17.2 percent and putting health care back on the national political agenda.

Obama entered office with a promise, strongly supported by his party—which controlled both houses of Congress—to achieve universal health insurance coverage. Labor unions had long championed creating an NHS. This radical reform, however, did not have majority support even within the Democratic Party, and the private insurance industry and Republicans vigorously opposed it. Many Democrats wanted instead to create what came to be called a "public option"—one health insurance choice among many—that could be achieved by opening up the federal government's insurance plan for its own employees, Medicare, or Medicaid to the broader public. Obama's initial proposal included a public option that would be open only to those not insured through their employers, preserving all existing private insurance as is. Ultimately, even this limited public option proved to be one of the most controversial elements of the plan and was eliminated.

The ACA reduced the number of uninsured people by twenty million in its first two years, from about 15 to 9 percent of the population (CDC 2016). It expanded insurance coverage by mandating that virtually all people must obtain insurance (those who do not must pay a tax penalty) and providing subsidies to premiums for people with low incomes. It created insurance "exchanges" in each state that are available to all those who don't have insurance through their employers. Private insurance companies offer plans in these exchanges that must meet certain minimum standards of service coverage. The exchanges created large pools of previously uninsured people, in theory allowing them to obtain much cheaper coverage than they each could individually. Medium and large employers must offer minimal health insurance to their employees; those who don't pay a fine that helps pay for the subsidies for the uninsured. The reform also prevented insurance companies from denying insurance to people with preexisting medical conditions and allowed young adults to remain on their parents' insurance until age twenty-six to keep them in insurance pools (thereby increasing the diversity and health of the pools).

Implementation of the plan was steeped in controversy. Opponents believed the federal mandate to purchase insurance represented an unconstitutional intrusion into citizens' lives. While the government has long been able to "regulate commerce," opponents argued it could not mandate that citizens purchase a particular item, including health care. In a 5–4 vote, the Supreme Court ultimately held up this central provision of the plan as constitutional, but ruled that state governments did not have to agree to the expansion of the Medicaid program that would pay part of the subsidies for insuring people with lower incomes. By 2016, twenty-one states, almost all of them controlled by Republicans, refused to expand Medicaid even though for the first several years the federal government would pay for it. By 2015, the drop in the number of uninsured citizens was estimated to be twice as great in states with Medicaid expansion as in states without (Courtemanche et al. 2016).

A study comparing the health of the poor and nearly poor in Arkansas and Kentucky, which expanded Medicaid, and Texas, which did not, found that similar residents in the states that expanded coverage had a 12 percent greater increase in access to primary care and similar decrease in missed medication, a 30 percent reduction in out-of-pocket expenses, a 6 percent reduction in emergency room visits, and a 5 percent increase in reporting being in "excellent health" (Sommers et al. 2016). The poor and racial minorities benefitted most from the first two years of the ACA; their access to insurance increased significantly more than whites' and wealthier people's did. Indeed, rates of enrollment in the new exchanges were higher for poorer people, who received larger subsidies, than for those modestly above the poverty line, who received lower subsidies (Tavernise and Gebeloff 2016). The latter often said the premiums were too high for them to afford. While the ACA had not reached its goal of insuring 95 percent of the population by 2016 (when the rate stood at 91 percent), it had nonetheless increased access to health care significantly.

It was less clear that the ACA would reduce the very high overall (private and public) U.S. health costs. The plan was designed to have minimal effect on the already insured, and did. Rates of employer-based insurance and the nature or costs of those plans did not change substantially through 2015 (Abelson 2016). The new exchanges, however, faced growing financial pressure. Although the risk pool expanded and costs dropped 0.1 percent from 2014 to 2015 (Emanuel and Spiro 2016), in late 2016 many insurance companies asked state regulators for very large premium increases, arguing they were losing money because younger and healthier people were not signing up for insurance via the exchanges, leaving a risk pool that was disproportionately older and sicker. Several insurers ultimately decided not to continue participating in the exchanges at all; an estimated 17 percent of the population was projected to have only one insurer in their exchange for 2017 (Abelson and Sanger-Katz 2016). This led some Democrats in Congress to propose the addition of a "public option" that would be available only in areas that had only one private option, in an effort to increase competition and keep costs down. Republicans and private insurers opposed this proposal, with the former arguing the ACA should be replaced with individual health saving accounts. After his 2016 electoral victory, President-elect Trump and Republican leaders, who controlled both houses of Congress, promised to repeal the ACA entirely, though remained uncertain regarding exactly what they would replace it with. Some elements of the ACA were extremely popular so members of Congress hoped to keep them, but without the less popular mandate that everyone gain coverage, it was unclear how the popular elements could be financed.

Judith Feder and Donald Moran (2007) argued a decade ago that until political leaders accept the fact that universal coverage combined with cost containment will require greater limits on what health care the insured can obtain at a given price, no fundamental cost savings will be possible. The implementation of the ACA over the next decade will determine whether or not they were right.

CASE Questions

1. Health care reform has been controversial in all three of our case studies. How can you explain the ability of each government to pass reform into law? Is it easier to do in one of the three countries, and if so, why? Are there particular contexts in which reform is more or less likely to occur?
2. Comparing all three of our cases, which has the superior health care system, and why?

ENVIRONMENTAL PROBLEMS AND POLICY

Climate change is only the latest and largest environmental problem confronting governments around the world. Environmental problems became a significant policy issue later than either health care or welfare, perhaps in part because the environment, in contrast to the other two, is a classic postmaterialist concern, becoming more widespread as wealth rises. Early industrializers in Europe and the United States weren't very concerned about environmental degradation until the 1960s (with the exception of preservation of public land, which began much earlier), when people began to look at the effects of long-term pollution from the new context of economic security. Today, increasing wealth and security in some more recently industrialized countries also seem to be stimulating interest in clean air, water, and other environmental concerns.

The Environment and Market Failure

Environmental damage is an exceptionally clear case of market failure in the form of externalities. No form of pollution is without cost. When a factory pollutes a river with sewage, people downstream get sick and need costly health care while fish and other aquatic life die, raising the cost of fishing and reducing ecosystem diversity. Vehicle exhaust produces cancer-causing smog that results in millions of dollars of health care costs annually. Polluters rarely pay the cost of their own pollution in an unfettered market: many commodities cost less than they would if their true environmental costs were internalized in the production process. The market therefore devotes more resources to those undervalued products than it ought to, creating inefficiency. Meanwhile, other people bear the costs of the pollution produced, a classic externality.

tragedy of the commons
No individual has the incentive or ability to preserve a common, shared good that is free, so without collective effort, it is likely to be overused and perhaps ultimately destroyed

Many environmental goods are inherently public and often free. Unregulated use of free goods like air, water, or public land can lead to the **tragedy of the commons.** This is an old idea. If free public grazing land exists in a farming area, all farmers will use it to graze their herds, and none will have an incentive to preserve it for future use; collectively, they will likely overgraze the land and destroy it so that they all lose out in the end. In wealthy industrial countries, a more current example is clean air, a completely "common" good we all breathe and pollute. Without a collective effort to limit use and abuse, no individual has the incentive or ability to preserve it, so it's likely to be overused. The free market grossly undervalues (at zero cost) a valuable public good.

National governments have been grappling with market interventions to compensate for environmental externalities, trying to avoid the tragedy of the commons, for most of the last hundred years. Recently, globalization has raised new, international challenges in this process. Globalization has spread not only industrialization but also environmental damage. Industrialization always increases the pollution of previously agrarian societies. In addition, many observers fear that the dynamics of global competition will produce a "race to the bottom," as countries use lax environmental rules to attract foreign capital. Many argue that wealthy countries are not only outsourcing factories and jobs but pollution as well. For example, the quality of the air and water around Pittsburgh has dramatically improved as the city's steel industry has declined, while China, now the world's largest steel producer, faces a massive pollution problem. The southeastern region of Nigeria is dotted with nearly 1,500 oil wells, which for many years provided an estimated 40 percent of U.S. oil imports. Estimates suggest as much oil is spilled annually in Nigeria as was spilled by the disastrous Exxon *Valdez* oil spill in Alaska in 1989. Citizens of one of the poorest regions of a poor country thus pay a large share of the environmental costs of U.S. oil consumption.

Opponents of the race-to-the-bottom thesis argue that postmaterialist values will be key: as globalization produces more wealth, it will help lower pollution because wealth and environmental concerns seem to increase in tandem. Analyzing the World Values Survey, however, Dunlap and York (2012) found little correlation between wealth and environmental concerns; citizens of poor nations expressed somewhat different but just as strong (and sometimes stronger) concern for the environment as citizens of wealthier countries. Using a large, quantitative analysis, Gabriele Spilker (2013) found that while higher GDP, trade, and foreign direct investment are associated with more pollution in developing countries, this effect was mitigated by: (1) membership in key international organizations that could help the government respond to environmental problems, and (2) well-established democracy, in which people could demand and politicians would be forced to supply some regulation of environmental damages. Once again, national governments can at least partly mitigate the worst effects of globalization. Whichever argument proves more accurate in the long term, rapidly industrializing countries now face dramatically expanding environmental problems. This is clearest in Asia, as our case study of China shows.

Also tied to globalization are what many term "third-generation" environmental problems: these problems are global and therefore require global responses. Air and water pollution have always crossed borders, but this new concern is distinct. The source of the pollution matters little because the effects are truly global. Scientists have demonstrated measurable effects of China's air pollution on the west coast of the United States. The major third-generation problem, though, is climate change. Burning fossil fuels—full of previously trapped carbon—has pumped excess carbon into the atmosphere. Virtually all scientists now agree that this has increased the entire planet's ambient temperature by an estimated 0.7°C (1.3°F) since the dawn of the industrial age, and the pace is accelerating. A series of reports by the Intergovernmental Panel on Climate Change (IPCC) put together by a large group of the world's top climate scientists has recommended that the world keep the temperature increase to no more than 2°C. Current projections, if no changes are made, go as high as a 5°C rise (UNDP 2007, 3, 7). A new report in 2013 argued that to keep the increase to 2°C or less, total carbon emissions must be restricted to no more than a trillion tons, a level currently projected to be reached around the year 2040 (IPCC 2013). Temperature increases of a few degrees may not sound like much, but the effects would be catastrophic: rising sea levels would flood coastal areas around the world, and severe drought would afflict many areas—especially in the tropics, which are already relatively poor.

Developing countries have long struggled to achieve sustainable development: economic development that can continue over the long term. Development always involves increased use of resources, but if nonrenewable resources are being used quickly, development won't be sustainable. As demand for food and land increases, for instance, farmers and ranchers clear forested areas throughout the tropics. This gives them nutrient-rich soil on which to grow crops and graze cattle, as well as valuable wood to sell on the global market, but tropical rainforest soils are thin and are quickly depleted when put to agricultural use. After a few years, new land must be cleared as the old is exhausted. The result is rapidly disappearing forests and development that is unsustainable in the long run. Deforestation also increases global warming because trees absorb and retain carbon. Farmers' and ranchers' rational response to growing global demand for agricultural products, then, has created unsustainable development and more global warming. Globalization-induced pollution of air and water and rapid use of nonrenewable resources make the goal of sustainable development ever more challenging for many poor countries.

Risk and Uncertainty

While most analysts agree that environmental damage is an externality that must be addressed, a vociferous debate thrives about the uncertainty nearly always present in environmental issues. Scientists can rarely tell us exactly what a particular form or amount of pollution will do. The top climate scientists in the world won the Nobel Peace Prize for their 2007 IPCC Report, but even their most certain predictions were termed "very likely" (90 percent certainty) or "likely" (66 percent certainty) outcomes of climate change. Similarly, we know that air pollution causes lung cancer, but we can't predict with absolute certainty how many cases it will cause, let alone which individuals will be affected. Environmental policy everywhere has to be based on **risk assessment** and **risk management.** Risk assessment tells us what the risks of damaging outcomes are, and risk management is policy used to keep those risks to acceptable levels. The costs of reducing risks must be weighed against the potential (but always uncertain) benefits.

Much of the debate, of course, is over what level of risk is "acceptable." In recent years, the European Union (EU) and its member states have employed the **precautionary principle,** which emphasizes risk avoidance even when the science predicting the risk is uncertain. This principle lies behind the EU ban on genetically modified organisms (GMOs) in food. With limited scientific evidence on whether GMOs are harmful or benign, the EU errs on the side of caution, banning them until the science is clarified. The United States typically errs more toward reducing the costs of environmental fixes. For example, the United States currently allows extensive use of GMOs in the absence of greater scientific evidence of harm.

Policy Options

How do governments respond when they decide that environmental damage is an unacceptable risk? Several approaches exist. The oldest is known as **command and control policies,** which involve direct government regulation. These were the first

risk assessment
Analysis of what the risks of damaging outcomes are in a particular situation

risk management
Policy used to keep risks to acceptable levels

precautionary principle
A policy that emphasizes risk avoidance even when the science predicting a risk is uncertain

command and control policies
Pollution control system in which a government directly regulates the specific amount of pollution each polluting entity is allowed

type of policies most wealthy countries enacted in the 1970s. Based on assessments of health and other risks, a government simply sets a level of pollution no one is allowed to surpass, or requires companies to pay a penalty if they do. Businesses must reduce production or find ways to produce the same goods with less pollution. Command and control policies require governments to set very specific limits on many pollutants from many sources and to inspect possible polluters to ensure they are following the regulations. Both of these tasks are expensive, leading many analysts to argue for what they see as more efficient means of pollution control in the form of incentive systems.

The best-known incentive system is the **cap and trade system,** in which a government sets an overall limit on how much of a pollutant is acceptable from an entire industry or country and issues vouchers to each company that give it the right to a certain number of units of pollution. The individual companies are then free to trade these vouchers. Companies that face high costs to reduce their pollution levels will be interested in buying additional pollution rights, while those that can more cheaply invest in new and cleaner technology will sell their rights. In theory, pollution is reduced in the most efficient way possible and at the least cost.

Critics point out that cap and trade can result in high levels of pollution at particular sources. If you live downriver from the factory that purchased a large number of pollution rights, your water will be particularly polluted, while the water in other locations gets cleaner. Simply taxing pollution directly is another way to provide an incentive to reduce it without dictating specific levels from specific sources. Both cap and trade and taxation systems require the government to set an overall cap or tax at a level that will reduce pollution by the desired amount. While perhaps less complicated than specifying pollution levels from each source, this is still a complex and uncertain task.

Tax or cap and trade systems attempt to set a direct cost on pollution, forcing polluters to internalize an externality. A similar goal is embedded in policies to control use of what otherwise could be free goods, such as public land and the minerals under it, to avoid the tragedy of the commons. User fees on public land exist to limit use so that the overuse inherent in free public goods does not occur. Similarly, governments can charge for access to minerals, including oil. Given that minerals and fossil fuels are nonrenewable, their depletion contains an intergenerational externality: future generations will pay the price of finding alternatives to the finite resources current generations use. Many economists argue that this justifies government intervention to tax mineral extraction, raising the internal cost of mineral production. In practice, many governments, including the United States, pursue exactly the opposite strategy, subsidizing mineral exploration and development in order to maximize production and lower consumer costs in the present. Cheaper minerals and fuels spur economic growth, which all legitimate states strive to achieve. Subsidizing mineral exploration, however, encourages rather than discourages the tragedy of the commons in nonrenewable resources.

cap and trade system
Market-based pollution control system in which the government sets an overall limit on how much of a pollutant is acceptable and issues vouchers to pollute to each company, which companies are then free to trade

Climate Change

The complexity of environmental regulation is magnified at the international level, but the policy options are similar. Risk looms particularly large in the climate change debate because climate change models are all based on probabilities. While no credible scientist disputes that the Earth is warming and greenhouse gases (GHG) are the primary reason why, uncertainty about the extent of the long-term consequences remains. This makes it difficult to judge, both empirically and normatively, how much current generations should give up in terms of economic well-being to reduce the long-term effects of climate change on behalf of future generations. Many economists apply their standard methodology of "discounting" future benefits to present values, assuming any benefit is more valuable today than tomorrow. Others, however, argue that the precautionary principle ought to apply to ensure we avoid the most catastrophic outcomes for future generations, no matter what the cost now. The scientific consensus suggests that significant effects of climate change—including possibly rapid increases in sea levels and severe water shortages in some parts of the world—will start being felt in twenty to thirty years, with much more severe effects taking place by the year 2100.

Two areas of policy response to climate change are possible, and most experts argue both are necessary. *Mitigation* involves reducing the cause of the problem: GHG production. This has been the central focus of efforts at creating international climate change accords over the past twenty years. *Adaptation* involves policies to adapt to the effects of climate change, such as building seawalls to keep rising sea levels from destroying property, farmers switching crops as local climates change, and island nations in the Pacific proposing to move en masse to other countries because their countries are projected to be completely underwater by the end of the century.

Growing scientific consensus and extensive negotiations led to the signing of the Kyoto protocol in 1997, the first major international effort to address climate change. It included mandated targets for developed countries: they would reduce their carbon emissions by an average of 5 percent below their 1990 levels by 2012. It provided no mandates on developing countries, however, which led the United States, the world's largest carbon producer at the time, to reject it. It ultimately only covered 15 percent of global carbon emissions because of the refusal of the United States to participate and the absence of binding agreements on large, developing countries like China and India. A major successor to the Kyoto protocol was to be approved in Copenhagen in 2009, but negotiations failed. In its place, a nonbinding accord was produced in which countries pledged to adopt voluntary measures that would keep twenty-first-century warming to no more than the targeted 2°C. Most observers saw this nonbinding agreement as making very little progress toward addressing the problem.

The Paris agreement completed in December 2015 was the first climate change agreement that was signed by virtually every country in the world. Its approach, however, followed in the spirit of the Copenhagen accords. Rather than legally binding agreements, every nation pledged to implement its own national policy to help the world keep temperature rise to less than 2°C in the twenty-first century, and ideally below 1.5 °C. The countries will meet regularly to share and assess progress, but the agreement will ultimately be a "name and shame" one: no enforcement mechanisms exist to ensure countries create and meet adequate targets. The IPCC estimated that carbon production must drop by 40–70 percent by mid-century and effectively become zero by 2100 to keep the global temperature rise below 2°C. By late 2016, the initial round of national plans was estimated to leave world carbon emissions well above what would be needed to achieve that goal.

In October 2016, an additional climate accord was reached in Kigali, Rwanda, to reduce hydrofluorocarbons (HFCs), powerful GHG used in refrigeration. Unlike the Paris agreement on carbon emissions, the Kigali accord is legally binding and includes enforcement mechanisms, meaning it may have more effect on climate change than the Paris agreement. The accord was reached via a compromise between wealthy and poorer countries under which the wealthier countries will reduce HFC production

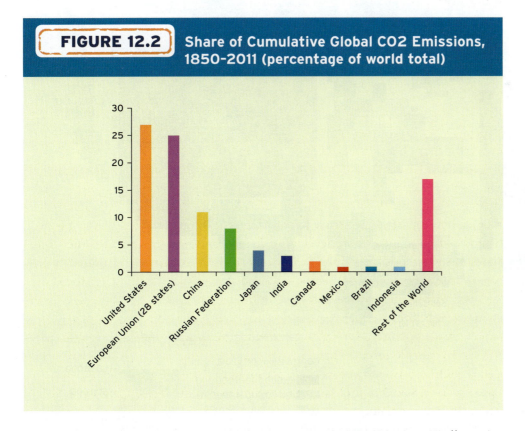

FIGURE 12.2   **Share of Cumulative Global CO2 Emissions, 1850-2011 (percentage of world total)**

Source: Data are from World Resources Institute, "6 Graphs Explain the World's Top 10 Emitters" (http://www.wri.org/blog/2014/11/6-graphs-explain-world%E2%80%99s-top-10-emitters).

sooner than the poorer countries, which will have more time to make the switch to alternative refrigerants. It is binding in part because it is actually an amendment to the binding Montreal protocol of 1987 that lowered production of gases that created the ozone hole.

The battle between wealthy and poorer countries is at the heart of global climate change debates. Figure 12.2 and Maps 12.1 to 12.3 illustrate what this debate is about. Figure 12.2 shows that since the dawn of the industrial era, the wealthy, Western countries have produced the great bulk of carbon emissions. Because these gases do not dissipate, wealthy countries have produced the vast majority of the total GHG to date. The United States alone is estimated to account for nearly 30 percent of the total since 1850. Map 12.1, however, shows that while wealthy countries remain major carbon producers, a few rapidly industrializing countries account for a significant share of CO_2

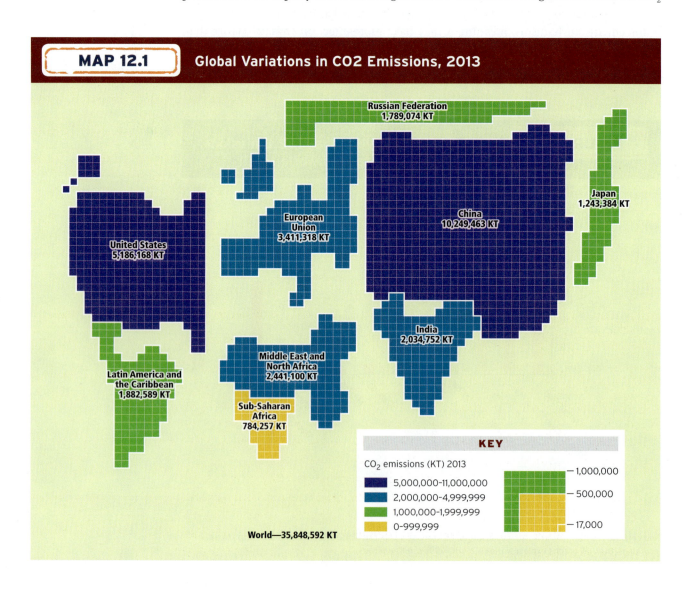

MAP 12.1   **Global Variations in CO2 Emissions, 2013**

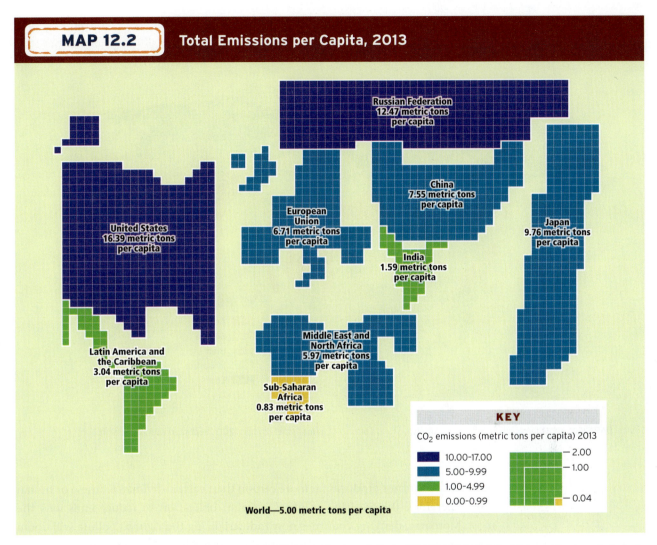

MAP 12.2   **Total Emissions per Capita, 2013**

Russian Federation
12.47 metric tons
per capita

China
7.55 metric tons
per capita

European
Union
6.71 metric tons
per capita

Japan
9.76 metric tons
per capita

India
1.59 metric tons
per capita

United States
16.39 metric tons
per capita

Middle East and
North Africa
5.97 metric tons
per capita

Latin America and
the Caribbean
3.04 metric tons
per capita

Sub-Saharan
Africa
0.83 metric tons
per capita

KEY

CO_2 emissions (metric tons per capita) 2013

10.00–17.00

5.00–9.99

1.00–4.99

0.00–0.99

— 2.00

— 1.00

— 0.04

World—5.00 metric tons per capita

Sources: Data for Maps 12.1 and 12.2 are from World Bank (http://data.worldbank.org/indicator/EN.ATM.CO2E.PC), (http://data.worldbank.org/indicator/EN.ATM.CO2E.KT).

emissions as well, especially China, the world's biggest producer currently. Map 12.2 demonstrates, on the other hand, that in per capita terms, the wealthy countries still produce far more even than China, let alone other developing countries. Each American citizen produces far more carbon annually than does each Chinese citizen. Finally, comparing Maps 12.1 and 12.3 also shows that the countries that produce the least carbon are the most vulnerable to the effects of climate change.

These data make the battle lines of the debate clear. The wealthy countries, led by the United States, argue that they cannot reduce global warming without all of the biggest polluters, including China and India, agreeing to curb their emissions significantly. The developing countries, led by China, counter that the wealthier countries are the main source of the total excess carbon in the atmosphere and that each individual

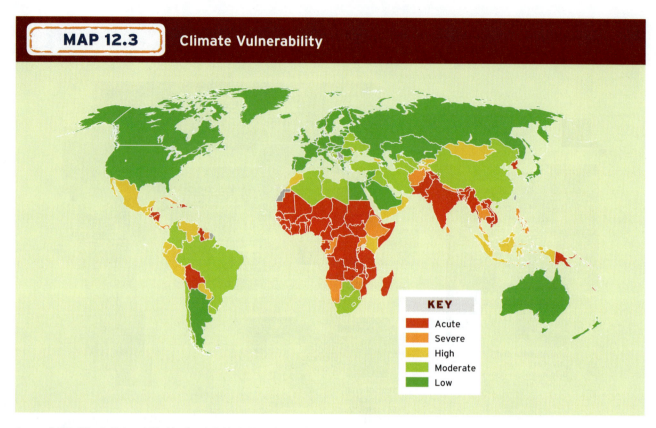

MAP 12.3 **Climate Vulnerability**

KEY

- Acute
- Severe
- High
- Moderate
- Low

Source: DARA, *Climate Vulnerability Monitor: A Guide to the Cold Calculus of a Hot Planet*, 2nd ed., 2012. Reprinted with permission.

in wealthy countries produces far more carbon than each individual Chinese or Indian does. Therefore, the wealthy countries have an obligation to reduce emissions the most. Moreover, denying countries now industrializing the right to pollute will doom them to inferior status forever. The wealthy countries benefitted from unlimited carbon pollution while they were industrializing, for which the entire world will pay the price, and it is unethical to ask countries now industrializing to curb their development prematurely. Furthermore, the poorest countries argue that they have not caused the problem but will suffer the greatest effects, making a moral claim on the major polluters to reduce pollution and pay for adaptation for climate change's worst effects.

Given this structure of interests, numerous formulas for how to share the cost of reducing carbon emissions have been developed. Wealthy countries argue for *grandfathering*, the basis for the Kyoto protocol, under which all countries reduce their emissions relative to a baseline year, so their past emissions are "grandfathered" in. The most common proposal from poorer countries is a *per capita contraction and convergence* principle: every person on the planet would be given the same rights to emissions, which would be reduced over time to lower overall emissions. Countries that exceed their rights would have to reduce their total and/or purchase excess rights from other countries; those with surplus rights could sell them. While not making up for the full historical legacy, this would place much greater burden on wealthier countries (Parks and Roberts 2009). Paul Baer et al. (2009) argued for what they term Greenhouse Development Rights based on countries' capacity to pay (defined as the percentage of their population with incomes above $7,500 per year, chosen as a level that satisfies basic human needs) and responsibility for emissions (based on per capita emissions since 1990). The result in 2009 places about two-thirds of the burden on the wealthy countries, of which the United States would pay 27 percent, while China would be responsible for about 15 percent (Global Development Rights 2013).

Whoever pays the cost, no international consensus exists on exactly which policy mechanisms should be used to reduce greenhouse gases. The most common solutions are a cap and trade system for carbon or a carbon tax. The EU already instituted its own cap and trade system to help it comply with the Kyoto protocol. It initially set a cap that was too generous, leading to a surplus of emissions rights (that no one needed) and a drop in the price to virtually zero. In 2008 the cap was significantly lowered, the trading prices quadrupled, and carbon emissions were reduced the following year. It was estimated to have reduced emissions at participating facilities (utilities, factories, etc.) by 2 to 5 percent (Ellerman et al. 2010).

The Kyoto protocol also included the Clean Development Mechanism (CDM), a system that allows companies and countries to gain emission credits by investing in projects that reduce emissions elsewhere in the world. Because many factories in the developing world use older technology, it's cheaper to reduce emissions there than in wealthy countries. Given that global climate change is just that—global—it doesn't matter where emissions are reduced. A rapidly growing market has emerged that now includes several thousand emissions reduction projects globally, with over half of them located in China. The organization in charge of monitoring it estimated that the CDM had reduced carbon emissions by a billion tons by 2011 (Benney 2015, 42). A truly global cap and trade system would make the CDM unnecessary, as rights to produce carbon would be issued worldwide and could be traded, meaning in theory that reductions in carbon emissions would happen wherever they can be achieved most efficiently. A carbon tax would in theory produce similar results, though knowing the level at which to set the tax remains difficult. Given the lack of global taxation system to date, carbon taxes are a likely national response and might be part of individual countries' responses to the Paris agreement.

Of the three policy areas we discuss in this chapter, the environment is the easiest area in which to justify government intervention in markets. Environmental damage is clearly an externality that should be internalized for efficient allocation of resources and long-term sustainability. This has become particularly clear and urgent in the face of climate change, which threatens to wreak havoc on the lives of millions in the relatively near future. A number of clear policy choices exist as well. Their implementation, however, has been limited and slow. Different policies internalize costs in different ways, resulting in different people paying those costs. Both within individual countries and on a global scale, individual polluters and national governments strive to minimize the costs they will have to pay. Our case studies of perhaps the two countries that are most crucial to the debate—the United States and China—illustrate the conflicts well.

THE UNITED STATES: PIONEER THAT LOST ITS WAY?

CASE SYNOPSIS

The American political system includes numerous veto players. Rational choice scholars have noted that environmental legislation often provides diffuse benefits to many people and high costs for a few (typically businesses), so the latter are often able and highly motivated to block such legislation. Environmental legislation succeeds only at times of generally high concern among the broader public, which leads legislators to override the veto efforts of a few key players. As a result, U.S. policy has a stop-and-go character, with occasional great advances followed by periods of reversal or stagnation. After great advances in the 1970s, progress slowed dramatically, reviving in some areas in the new millennium. While Congress has never approved significant climate change legislation, the Obama administration has used administrative regulations to make significant reductions in GHG at least possible.

- LONG-STANDING ISSUES Protection of land and animals, air, water, endangered species, and ozone
- TYPES OF INTERVENTION Initially, command and control; recently, cap and trade
- RECENT TRENDS Initial opposition to binding treaty on climate change; Obama uses administrative rules to start to address issue
- OVERALL SUCCESS Reduced air and water pollution, but less success preserving endangered species, reducing energy consumption, and mitigating climate change

April 22, 1970, the first Earth Day, marked the coming of age of the environmental movement in the United States. The now annual event emerged out of the fervor of the 1960s and represented a strikingly broad consensus in the country: environmental problems were important, and the government should do something about them. In May 1969, only 1 percent of people mentioned pollution as one of the "most important" problems facing the country, but by May 1971 that number had risen to 25 percent (Layzer 2006, 33). A decade of rapid expansion of the government's role in protecting the environment made the United States a pioneer in the field.

The major U.S. environmental policy that predates 1970 was the protection of public lands for recreational and ecological purposes, from the creation of the national park system in the early 1900s to the preservation of pristine wilderness areas starting in 1964. Landmark legislation of the early 1970s included the creation of the Environmental Protection Agency (EPA), the Clean Air Act (1970), the Clean Water Act (1972), and the Endangered Species Act (1973). In one area, this progress continued in the 1980s, as President Ronald Reagan, generally an opponent of environmental policy, helped champion the Montreal protocol of 1987, which eliminated the use of ozone-depleting chemicals. It is projected to restore the ozone layer to its pre-1980 level by the middle of the twenty-first century. These were all command and control policies, setting specific regulations for allowable levels of pollution from individual sources and protecting specific species and plots of land. Coming from a broad bipartisan consensus, they established the United States as a pioneer in environmental protection, generally seen as being well ahead of most European countries.

Reagan's election in 1980 began a reversal of this environmental trend. His neoliberal economic ideology led him to reduce funding for the EPA and other environmental agencies and appoint opponents of government intervention to key environmental posts. These officials rewrote regulations to reduce their impact on business. By mid-decade, Congress began resisting some of these policies. The most significant congressional reversal was the Superfund Act (1986), which required that thousands of toxic waste sites be cleaned up. A later milestone was a major amendment to the Clean Air Act in 1990, which for the first time included a cap and trade system focused on one

Evacuees settle in at a shelter in Baton Rouge, Louisiana, in August 2016 after unprecedented flooding forced thousands from their homes. Climate science research has shown that rising temperatures are already increasing the frequency and severity of weather-based disasters, the costs of which societies will have to pay as they adapt to climate change.

Joe Raedle/Getty Images

environmental justice movement
A movement focused on exposing and fighting against racial and class inequalities in exposure to pollution, started in the United States in 1982

particular pollutant: sulfur dioxide, a key ingredient in acid rain. The system has significantly reduced this pollutant nationwide, at an estimated cost of only half what a similar reduction under the older command and control model would have incurred (Freeman 2006, 206).

The 1980s also saw the emergence of a new element in U.S. environmental activism in the form of the **environmental justice movement.** It began in 1982, in Warren County, the poorest county in North Carolina, in which 65 percent of residents were African American (three times the state average). When a waste disposal company proposed locating a toxic waste facility in the county, the residents organized demonstrations, and the environmental justice movement began. Focused on environmental damage in particular locales, members argued that poor and, especially, black or Hispanic neighborhoods are much more likely to be sites for polluting industries and toxic waste depositories. The movement has grown significantly since then, and it laid out a clear set of principles at a major conference in 1991. While research results depend on how the researchers define "neighborhood" or "community," it seems that across the United States, black and Hispanic citizens are more likely to live in areas where air and water pollution exceed legal limits and where toxic chemicals are produced or stored (Ringquist 2006). Activists pointed to the state government's slow response to high lead levels in the water supply in Flint, Michigan, a poor and mostly African American city, in 2014 as an example of this continuing injustice.

Bill Clinton's election in 1992 with noted environmentalist Al Gore as his vice president gave environmental advocates hope that the policies of the Reagan/Bush years would be reversed. By the end of the decade, however, environmentalists had mixed assessments of the Clinton administration. A key issue was global warming. Both Republican and Democratic presidents had agreed to voluntary reductions in GHG emissions, but they continued to resist mandatory targets, including the Kyoto protocol. President George W. Bush repudiated the treaty entirely and pursued an energy policy that provided greater incentives for fossil fuel exploration and development. The United States was estimated to spend about $100 billion per year—half the world's total—on fossil fuel subsidies, encouraging rapid use and therefore depletion of these nonrenewable resources and promoting climate change (Hempel 2006, 305).

The most recent element of this is new technology that makes mining shale oil and hydrofracking for natural gas and oil economically feasible, both of which are expanding rapidly in the United States and Canada. By 2016, fracking produced half of all U.S. oil production; increased American production was a major reason why global oil prices began to fall dramatically in 2014, to less than half their previous level, and U.S. oil imports fell from about half to only one-quarter of total consumption. Critics contend that this increased mining will lower fossil fuels' costs and increase their consumption, thereby putting more carbon in the atmosphere. Also, fracking produces 17 percent more carbon per barrel of oil than conventional oil wells do. Supporters of the new technology argue that compared to the alternatives, particularly coal, the new techniques will reduce carbon emissions overall. A major environmental issue arose in

2012 when the government proposed building the Keystone Pipeline from Canada to the Gulf of Mexico to transport shale oil from Canada. While it would have very little projected effect on GHG emissions, the pipeline became a symbolic battle between environmentalists and the fossil fuel industry. Ultimately, the Obama administration rejected the pipeline in November 2015, arguing it would bring few benefits to the United States and potentially increase GHG. Declining oil prices by that point made shale oil production far less competitive, in any case.

Barack Obama came to office having pledged to enact fundamentally new energy and climate change policies. He committed his administration to full involvement in negotiating a replacement for the failed Kyoto protocol and personally helped negotiate the rather weak resolution that emerged from the Copenhagen conference in 2009, as well as the 2015 Paris agreement. Domestically, the administration proposed in 2009 and the House of Representatives passed legislation to create a cap and trade system to reduce GHG by 17 percent by 2020 and over 80 percent by mid-century, but Republican (and some Democratic) opposition in the Senate blocked the measure. This led the administration to pursue EPA regulation of GHG, which the agency ruled substantially harmed health and therefore could be regulated under the Clean Air Act. That act, however, requires reduced emissions only on new and renovated utilities, so the EPA's long-term impact is uncertain. Industry tried to challenge the EPA's right to regulate GHG, but the Supreme Court ruled in 2007, and reaffirmed in a 2011 case, that the EPA does have the right to regulate those gases under the Clean Air Act.

In 2013 Obama announced a new Climate Action Plan that the administration claimed would reduce GHG emissions by about one-quarter by 2025. The EPA finalized rules for carbon reductions and proposed rules for methane reductions in August 2015. The Supreme Court, however, temporarily blocked implementation of a part of the plan that would regulate coal-burning power plants, pending a lower court decision on the issue. The Obama plan also provided various incentives to move the economy toward greater use of carbon-free energy production and improved fuel efficiency for vehicles. While environmentalists applauded the effort, many argued it would not achieve enough, while opponents claimed the regulations would hurt the economy for little benefit. Polls in 2015–2016 found that only about a third of Americans (three-quarters of whom were Democrats) said they "care a great deal" about the issue, as opposed to an average of 54 percent of citizens in a group of forty other countries (Schlossberg 2016). In 2016 President-elect Trump vowed to eliminate the Climate Action Plan entirely.

Despite what environmentalists see as setbacks, U.S. policy has produced a much cleaner environment, though some areas continue to lag behind. The greatest success has been with air pollution. Since the first Earth Day in 1970, production of the six key ingredients of air pollution has dropped by 60 percent in spite of significant population growth and even greater economic growth. The only exceptions were an increase of about 6 percent in emissions of GHG from 1990 to 2014, with peak emissions occurring in 2007. Acid rain, regulated by a cap and trade system, has dropped substantially as well. Surveys of water quality at the turn of the century indicated that 61 percent of rivers and 55 percent of lakes met acceptable standards for clean water, though destruction of wetlands by development continues at about fifty-eight thousand acres per year (Kraft and Vig 2006, 21–24; Yarett 2010). On the other hand, the number of species on the endangered list has quadrupled, energy use per person has not changed and is much higher than in most other wealthy countries, and the average amount of garbage per person has increased 38 percent despite a quintupling of recycling.

CASE Questions

1. Why has the United States shifted from a pioneer of environmentalism to a much more haphazard record in the last two decades?
2. Do domestic or international factors better explain the United States' reluctance to support binding agreements on reducing carbon emissions?

CHINA: SEARCHING FOR SUSTAINABLE DEVELOPMENT

CASE SYNOPSIS

China's rapid industrialization and massive size have made it one of the largest polluters in the world, though on a per capita basis it remains a modest producer of GHG. After decades of nearly complete neglect of environmental protection, the leadership in the new millennium has significantly increased emphasis on the issue. Its efforts are supported by a rapidly growing network of local and national environmental groups. While progress has clearly been made, the fundamental tension between rapid economic growth and environmental protection remains. Under President Xi Jinping, the government has committed itself both to major reductions in urban air pollution and GHG over the coming decades. As the largest producer of GHG and with a rapidly growing economy, China's environmental policies have become crucial not only to its own well-being but to that of the planet as a whole.

- LONG-STANDING ISSUES Rapid economic growth produces massive environmental problems; government prioritized growth over environmental protection

- TYPES OF INTERVENTION Command and control; recently, experimental market-based programs

- **RECENT TRENDS** Increased emphasis on environmental policy since 2002; promise of cap and trade for GHG in 2017
- **OVERALL SUCCESS** Still massive pollution problems—air, water, and greenhouse gases—though modest reductions recently

A s the 2008 Summer Olympics approached, commentators around the world began to question whether Beijing could really host the games adequately, not because of a lack of infrastructure or resources but because of the quality of the air the athletes would be breathing. Even after the government instituted a policy to remove half of Beijing's 3.3 million vehicles from its highways; banned 300,000 aging vehicles found to be especially heavy polluters; encouraged commuters to return to using the bicycles once so ubiquitous across the country; opened three new subway lines; and set up numerous new bus lines, some athletes still bowed out of the competition.

China's environmental degradation and problems are breathtaking, no pun intended. Besides urban air pollution, 30 percent of the nation's water is unfit for human or agricultural use, almost 90 percent of the country's grasslands and forests are suffering degradation, and the Yellow River now dries up before it reaches the ocean, becoming an open sewer (Ho and Vermeer 2006; Morton 2006, 64–65). Severe soil erosion and desertification have doubled since the 1970s and are degrading an area the size of New Jersey each year (Economy 2010, 66). The result of all of this is skyrocketing health problems: air pollution in northern China is estimated to have caused 1.2 million premature deaths in 2010, lowering life expectancy by five years vis-à-vis the less polluted southern China, and cancer rates increased by 30 percent over the past thirty years. In Beijing, where the most polluted days reach forty times the internationally recommended maximum level of air particulates, residents regularly wear facemasks

A long-distance race participant wears a mask to protect himself from the smog as he runs past the National Stadium built for the 2008 Summer Olympics in Beijing. China's rapid industrialization has produced dramatic environmental problems, including many of the most polluted cities in the world. Chinese authorities took numerous measures, such as banning some vehicles and shutting down factories, to clean the air for the Olympics.

Guang Niu/Getty Images

to protect them from air pollution. Those who can afford to choose apartments and schools based partly on the quality of the air filtration system they use. Facing mounting public pressure, the government announced a major new command and control initiative in September 2013 that set upper limits on air particulate levels in major cities, banned the most heavily polluting vehicles, and slightly reduced the nation's dependence on coal. By 2015, air pollution had dropped slightly in most cities, mainly due to reductions in the use of coal, but Beijing still faced its first "red alert," a day so polluted that the government shut down schools and offices and advised citizens to remain indoors. Still, activists saw this alert as positive: the government recognized the problem and was trying to deal with it.

The 2013 law is the latest in a series of moves since 2002 by the Chinese leadership, as it has made a significant commitment to environmental protection. In 2008 it elevated the main environmental protection agency to a full cabinet ministry and doubled its funding. The Ministry of Environmental Protection (MEP) is the key agency governing environmental protection in China. While it has had energetic leaders and been a bureaucratic advocate for the environment, it has had limited ability to enforce China's environmental laws. It is dependent on Environmental Protection Bureaus (EPBs) controlled by local governments for most of its funding and staff. Local government leaders are rewarded in China's system primarily for their ability to further rapid economic growth, so they have had virtually no incentive to slow growth in favor of protecting the environment. Consequently, the effectiveness of environmental policies varies greatly. In some major cities, such as Shanghai and Guangzhou, leaders have become more committed to environmental concerns because of the presence of strong environmental NGOs and the resources to fund better policies. Shanghai, for instance, has committed 3 percent of its GDP to environmental protection, about double the national average (Chan, Lee, and Chan 2008, 297; Economy 2010, 123). Even the doubling of China's national environmental budget falls well below the 2 percent of GDP that most scholars see as essential for it to reverse its most severe environmental problems (Wu 2009).

Most early environmental policies were command and control, though in the last decade the MEP has begun to experiment with market-based policies as well. The two major command and control policies have long been fining excessive polluting from individual sources, such as factories, and requiring environmental impact assessments (EIAs) for new industrial projects. The fines, however, are quite small, so even when the laws are enforced, many firms find it cost-effective to pay the fines and keep polluting. The local EPBs often collude in this because they gain their revenue from the fines, so if they really succeeded at reducing pollution, their revenue would decline. In this context, the EIAs had little effect for many years, though recent trends suggest that may be changing. In 2005 the government began a highly publicized process of rejecting greater numbers of projects on environmental grounds. In what came to be known as "environmental storms," it suspended 30 projects in early 2005, and by August 2008 it had rejected over 400 more. The Great Recession, though, seemed partially to reverse this. To expedite construction projects that were part of the government's successful economic stimulus plan, the MEP created a "green passage" policy that gave quick approval to 150 major projects; provincial authorities radically reduced the time they took to approve EIAs as well (Economy 2010, 78; Johnson 2008, 97–99; Wu 2009, 280). The MEP also started a pilot cap and trade system for air pollution, recognizing that this will be a more efficient way to reduce pollution in the long run.

Another market-based experiment was the 2006 introduction of the concept of a "green GDP" in several major cities, in which an estimate for the cost of environmental damage is subtracted from the cities' annual GDP increase. The intent was to introduce a measure by which local government officials could be held accountable: the central government could use this measure, instead of simple GDP growth, as the chief means of evaluating local officials' performance. The data showed that environmental damage cost 3 percent of the cities' total GDP, though many believed the real figure should be much higher. The central government initially announced that it would expand this green GDP to the entire country the following year, but local governments successfully resisted the plan and the experiment faded away, though the MEP announced in 2015 that it would once again study implementing the idea nationwide (Johnson 2008, 95–97; Ryan 2015).

Concern about the environment among Chinese citizens has grown over the years, with three-quarters saying air and water pollution and climate change were "very big" or "moderately big" problems in 2015 (Gao 2015). In March 2015, a video about air pollution in China went "viral" on the Internet, attracting 150 million viewers before the government shut it down. Reflecting these concerns, environmental NGOs had grown substantially, from the first one legally registered in 1994 to more than 3,500 by 2008. The government often tolerates environmental NGOs and local-level protests, because top officials see them as pushing recalcitrant local officials to enforce environmental policies better while doing little harm on the national level. Indeed, the government has started its own environmental government-organized nongovernmental organizations (GONGOs) as well. In 2012, three days of massive demonstrations ultimately stopped the construction of a petrochemical plant in a coastal city that the local government strongly supported. In Beijing that same year, an online movement convinced the government to begin announcing when air pollution levels exceed acceptable limits, so that citizens can stay indoors to protect themselves.

Internationally, China is best known for its successful opposition to any mandatory limits on production of GHG for developing countries. Although it was one of the main obstacles to a binding agreement at the Copenhagen negotiations in 2009, the Chinese government shifted course under President Xi, announcing agreements with the United States in 2014 and 2015 to cut its carbon emissions substantially and do so via a cap and trade program that will begin in 2017. These agreements between the two largest carbon emitters were one of the main impetuses behind the successful Paris agreement. China has cut its carbon intensity (the amount of carbon produced per dollar of GDP) by more than half since 1990, and committed itself to a further reduction of 60–65 percent below 2005 levels by 2030. Many analysts believe it will actually achieve that goal by 2025 as it reduces its coal production substantially amid slower economic growth.

CASE Questions

1. China, perhaps more than any other country, illustrates the issues involved in the relationship between globalization and the environment. What lessons does our case study provide on this topic?
2. How might greater democracy affect environmental protection in China? What impact, positive or negative, does the authoritarian nature of the regime have on environmental policy?

CONCLUSION

The outcomes of policy battles can tell us much about "Who rules." Policy outcomes reflect the relative strength of various groups in a given political system. More extensive welfare states, especially prior to the 1990s in Europe, likely reflected the greater power of workers and unions in those countries, in contrast to the United States. European countries for the most part have reduced welfare benefits in recent decades, though, suggesting that workers' power is declining relative to other forces, domestic and international. In poorer countries, the poor who would benefit most from social welfare and health care interventions seem to lack significant power, as those countries pursue few such policies, either because the governments are not interested or because they lack the resources. Innovative social policies in Brazil and elsewhere in Latin America, though, suggest that in a democratic setting, it is possible for the poor to overcome these problems at least partially and gain greater benefits.

Environmental policies, which usually assign clear costs and benefits to particular groups, perhaps demonstrate relative power most directly. Self-interested actors are likely to resist paying the costs of environmental improvement, at least until a broader consensus emerges that change is essential for all to survive. For most environmental issues, including climate change, the least powerful player in the game is future generations, who lack any political clout now. They may well end up paying the greatest costs for internalizing externalities in the long run.

State intervention in each of the three policy areas has its own rationale, but in all three, market failure of some sort offers a reason for the state to modify pure market outcomes. States don't intervene solely because they recognize market failures, however. Normative and political motivations also need to be present. Markets can create powerful veto players, which can only be overcome via collective action and/or consensus on the part of broader and usually more diffuse actors who believe they will benefit from intervention. For instance, the Great Depression and World War II helped bring the value of reducing poverty to the fore and led to the growth of modern welfare states. Similarly, wealthy industrial countries have led the way in environmental intervention, reflecting a classic postmaterialist value. Middle-income and rapidly industrializing countries may be attempting to join the bandwagon, but in the very poorest countries, it is difficult to argue convincingly that resources are something to be conserved rather than depleted to meet immediate human needs.

Globalization, too, has had an impact on policies in all countries. On social policy, our cases show a persistence of diverse models but a trend toward at least limited reform in the direction of a more liberal welfare state. Across all three types of welfare states, for instance, workers and the poor have seen social policy benefits reduced, work requirements and limits on social assistance increased, and their contributions to social insurance systems increased.

Globalization, increasing wealth, and an aging population make reform of health policy particularly urgent and difficult. While significant changes occurred after about 2005 in our case study countries, they do not represent wholesale shifts from the long-standing systems in each country. Health care systems create their own institutionalized interests that resist change, from medical practitioners' support of the NHS in the United Kingdom to American insurance companies' opposition to a single-payer model. Health care, perhaps because it affects everyone, including relatively wealthy and powerful players, seems particularly difficult to reform.

In general, wealth seems to raise the prospect that countries can and will act effectively on value consensus in these three policy areas, but we need to explain significant variation among wealthy countries as well. The most widespread explanation for why some governments intervene more extensively than others is implicitly pluralist: in some countries, politically weaker groups have organized better and have more power, and policy reflects this. Institutions can matter as well, though. They create veto players that can be particularly powerful at blocking policy change, toward either more or less intervention. Germany's federal system and less centralized parliament, for instance, seem to make policy change there more incremental than in the more majoritarian United Kingdom.

Judging which set of policies is most "successful" in each of the three issue areas must in part be based on normative values, especially in social policy. If reducing poverty is the key goal, social democratic welfare states seem to be best; if ensuring people are employed is most important, though, a liberal welfare state may seem to be better. In health policy, what is "best" may be a little clearer. If the key criterion is gaining the most health at the least cost, it seems clear that market-based systems fare poorly, and well-established economic arguments explain why. Judging environmental policy success also depends on values: How much do we value clean air and water? How much do we value the well-being of future generations versus our own, right now? In terms of economic theory, environmental policy seems the easiest area in which to justify government intervention, but how much and how it should be done depend very much on larger value questions, including about who should pay how much of the costs, and when.

KEY CONCEPTS

cap and trade system (p. 681)

Christian democratic welfare states (p. 641)

command and control policies (p. 680)

conditional cash transfer (CCT) (p. 649)

environmental justice movement (p. 690)

liberal welfare states (p. 641)

market-based private insurance
system (p. 663)

means-tested public assistance (p. 640)

moral hazard (p. 661)

national health insurance
(NHI) (p. 662)

national health system (NHS)/single-
payer system (p. 662)

precautionary principle (p. 680)

risk assessment (p. 680)

risk management (p. 680)

social democratic welfare states (p. 641)

social insurance (p. 639)

social policy (p. 638)

tax expenditures (p. 640)

tragedy of the commons (p. 678)

universal entitlements (p. 639)

welfare states (p. 641)

Sharpen your skills with SAGE edge at **edge.sagepub.com/orvis4e.**
SAGE edge for students provides a personalized approach to help
you accomplish your coursework goals in an easy-to-use learning
environment.

WORKS CITED

Abelson, Reed. 2016. "Despite Fears, Affordable Care Act Has Not Uprooted Employer
Coverage." *New York Times.* April 4
(http://www.nytimes.com/2016/04/05/
business/employers-keep-health-insur
ance-despite-affordable-care-act.html?
smprod=nytcore-ipad&smid=nytcore-
ipad-share).

Abelson, Reed, and Margot Sanger-Katz. 2016.
"Obamacare Options? In Many Parts of
Country, Only One Insurer Will Remain."
New York Times. August 19 (http://www
.nytimes.com/2016/08/20/upshot/obam
acare-options-in-many-parts-of-coun
try-only-one-insurer-will-remain.html?
smprod=nytcore-ipad&smid=nytcore-
ipad-share).

Adolino, Jessica R., and Charles H. Blake.
2001. *Comparing Public Policies: Issues
and Choices in Six Industrialized Countries.*
Washington, DC: CQ Press.

Alber, Jens, and Neil Gilbert, eds. 2010.
*United in Diversity? Comparing Social
Models in Europe and America.* Oxford,
UK: Oxford University Press.

Alesina, Alberto, and Edward L. Glaeser.
2004. *Fighting Poverty in the U.S. and
Europe: A World of Difference.* Oxford,
UK: Oxford University Press.

Associated Press. 2008a. "Beijing to Take
Half of All Government Cars off the
Road." *USA Today.* June 23 (http://www
.usatoday.com/news/world/environ
ment/2008-06-23-china-cars_N.htm).

Associated Press. 2008b. "Beijing Traffic Cut
to Help Clear Air for Olympics." CNN/
IBNLive.com. July 21 (http://ibnlive
.in.com/news/beijing-traffic-cut-to-help-
clear-air-for-olympics/69238-2.html).

Baer, Paul, Glenn Fieldman, Tom Athana-
siou, and Sivan Kartha. 2009. "Greenhouse Development Rights: Towards an

Equitable Framework for Global Climate Policy." In *The Politics of Climate Change: Environmental Dynamics in International Affairs,* edited by Paul Harris, 192–212. New York: Routledge.

Barrientos, Armando, Darío Debowicz, and Ingrid Woolard. 2016. "Heterogeneity in Bolsa Família Outcomes." *The Quarterly Review of Economics and Finance.* August (http://www.sciencedirect.com/science/article/pii/S1062976916300552).

Benney, Tabitha M. 2015. *Making Environmental Markets Work: The Varieties of Capitalism in the Emerging Economies.* New York: Routledge.

Bonoli, Giuliano, Vic George, and Peter Taylor-Gooby. 2000. *European Welfare Futures: Towards a Theory of Retrenchment.* Cambridge, UK, and Malden, MA: Polity Press and Blackwell.

Brooks, Sarah M. 2015. "Social Protection for the Poorest: The Adoption of Antipoverty Cash Transfer Programs in the Global South." *Politics & Society.* December (43): 551–582. doi:10.1177/0032329215602894

Cammisa, Anne Marie. 1998. *From Rhetoric to Reform? Welfare Policy in American Politics.* Boulder, CO: Westview Press.

CBO (Congressional Budget Office). 2007. *The State Children's Health Insurance Program.* Washington, DC: Government Printing Office.

CDC (Centers for Disease Control). 2016. *Early Release of Selected Estimates Based on Data from the 2015 National Health Interview Survey.* May 24 (http://www.cdc.gov/nchs/nhis/releases/released201605.htm#1).

Chan, Gerald, Pak K. Lee, and Lai-Ha Chan. 2008. "China's Environmental Governance: The Domestic-International Nexus." *Third World Quarterly* 29 (2): 291–314. doi:10.1080/01436590701806863

Commonwealth Fund. 2008. *Commonwealth Fund International Health Policy Survey of Sicker Adults* (http://www.commonwealthfund.org/Content/Surveys/2008/2008-Commonwealth-Fund-International-Health-Policy-Survey-of-Sicker-Adults.aspx).

Courtemanche, Charles, James Marton, Benjamin Ukert, Aaron Yelowitz, and Daniela Zapata. 2016. *Impacts of the Affordable Care Act on Health Insurance Coverage in Medicaid Expansion and Non-Expansion States.* National Bureau of Economic Research Working Paper 22182 (http://www.nber.org/papers/w22182).

Dunlap, Riley E., and Richard York. 2012. "The Globalization of Environmental Concern." In *Comparative Environmental Politics: Theory, Practice, and Prospects,* edited by Paul F. Steinberg and Stacy D. VanDeveer, 89–112. Cambridge, MA: MIT Press.

The Economist. 2010. "Dr. Rösler's Difficult Prescription: The Hard Case of Reforming German Health Care." April 29 (http://www.economist.com/node/16015443? story_id=16015443).

Economy, Elizabeth C. 2010. *The River Runs Black: The Environmental Challenge to China's Future.* 2nd ed. Ithaca, NY: Cornell University Press.

Edin, Kathryn, and H. Luke Shaefer. 2016. "20 Years Since Welfare 'Reform.'" *The Atlantic.* August 22 (http://www.theatlantic.com/business/archive/2016/08/20-years-welfare-reform/496730/).

Ellerman, A. Denny, Frank J. Convery, and Christian de Perthius. 2010. *Pricing Carbon: The European Union Emissions Trading Scheme.* Cambridge, UK: Cambridge University Press.

Emanuel, Ezekiel, and Topher Spiro. 2016. "The Affordable Care Act Is Not in Crisis—But It Could Be Better." *Washington Post.* August 22 (https://www.washingtonpost.com/news/in-theory/wp/2016/08/22/the-affordable-care-act-is-not-in-crisis-but-it-could-be-better/?utm_term=.d2f8f958fcbc).

Esping-Andersen, Gøsta. 1990. *The Three Worlds of Welfare Capitalism.* Princeton, NJ: Princeton University Press.

Feder, Judith, and Donald W. Moran. 2007. "Cost Containment and the Politics of Health Care Reform." In *Restoring Fiscal Sanity 2007: The Health Spending Challenge,* edited by Alice M. Rivlin and Joseph R. Antos. Washington, DC: Brookings Institution Press.

Ferreira, Francisco H. G., and David A. Robalino. 2011. "Social Protection in Latin America: Achievements and Limitations." In *The Oxford Handbook of Latin American Economics,* edited by José Antonio Ocampo and Jaime Ros, 836–862. Oxford, UK: Oxford University Press.

Freeman, A. Myrick, III. 2006. "Economics, Incentives, and Environmental Policy." In *Environmental Policy: New Directions for the Twenty-first Century,* 6th ed., edited by Norman J. Vig and Michael E. Kraft, 193–214. Washington, DC: CQ Press.

Gao, George. 2015. *As Smog Hangs over Beijing, Chinese Cite Air Pollution as Major Concern.* Pew Research Center. December 10 (http://www.pewresearch.org/fact-tank/2015/12/10/as-smog-hangs-over-beijing-chinese-cite-air-pollution-as-major-concern/).

Garfinkel, Irwin, Lee Rainwater, and Timothy Smeeding. 2010. *Wealth and Welfare States: Is America a Laggard or Leader?* Oxford, UK: Oxford University Press.

Gerlinger, Thomas. 2010. "Health Care Reform in Germany." *German Policy Studies/Politikfeldanalyse* 6 (1): 107–142.

Gingrich, Jane, and Ben W. Ansell. 2015. "The Dynamics of Social Investment: Human Capital, Activation, and Care." In *The Politics of Advanced Capitalism,* edited by Pablo Beramendi, Silva Häusermann, Herbert Kitschelt, and Hanspeter Kriesi, 282–304. Cambridge, UK: Cambridge University Press.

Global Development Rights. 2013 (www.gdrights.org/calculator).

Gough, Ian. 2014. "Mapping Social Welfare Regimes beyond the OECD." In *The Politics of Non-state Social Welfare,* edited by Melani Cammett and Lauren M. MacLean, 17–30. Ithaca, NY: Cornell University Press.

Graig, Laurene A. 1999. *Health of Nations: An International Perspective on U.S. Health Care Reform.* 3rd ed. Washington, DC: CQ Press.

Grässler, Bernd. 2014. "The Labor Reforms That Set off a Boom." DW.Com. December 31 (http://www.dw.com/en/the-labor-reforms-that-set-off-a-boom/a-18164351).

Green, David G., and Benedict Irvine. 2001. *Health Care in France and Germany: Lessons for the UK.* London: Institute for the Study of Civil Society.

Greenstein, Robert. 2016. *Welfare Reform and the Safety Net: Evidence Contradicts Likely Assumptions behind Forthcoming GOP Poverty Plan.* Washington, DC: Center on Budget and Policy Priorities. June 6 (http://www.cbpp.org/research/family-income-support/welfare-reform-and-the-safety-net).

Hall, Anthony. 2006. "From Fome Zero to Bolsa Família: Social Policies and Poverty Alleviation under Lula." *Journal of Latin American Studies* 38 (4): 689–709.

Halpern-Meekin, Sarah, Kathryn Edin, Laura Tach, and Jennifer Sykes. 2015. *It's Not Like I'm Poor: How Working Families Make Ends Meet in a Post-Welfare World.* Oakland: University of California Press.

Ham, Chris, and Richard Murray. 2015. "Implementing the NHS Five Year Forward View: Aligning Policies with the Plan." *The King's Fund.* February (https://www.kingsfund.org.uk/sites/files/kf/field/field_publication_file/implementing-the-nhs-five-year-forward-view-kingsfund-feb15.pdf).

Hempel, Lamont C. 2006. "Climate Policy on the Installment Plan." In *Environmental Policy: New Directions for the Twenty-first*

Century, 6th ed., edited by Norman J. Vig and Michael E. Kraft, 288–331. Washington, DC: CQ Press.

Ho, Peter, and Eduard B. Vermeer. 2006. "China's Limits to Growth? The Difference between Absolute, Relative, and Precautionary Limits." *Development and Change* 37 (1): 255–271. doi:10.1111/j.0012-155X.2006.00477.x

Huber, Evelyne, and Sara Niedzwiecki. 2015. "Emerging Welfare States in Latin America and East Asia." In *The Oxford Handbook of Transformations of the State,* edited by Stephan Leibfried, Evelyne Huber, Matthew Lange, Jonah D. Levy, Frank Nullmeier, and John D. Stephens, 796–812. Oxford, UK: Oxford University Press.

Huber, Evelyne, and John D. Stephens. 2001. *Development and Crisis of the Welfare State: Parties and Policies in Global Markets*. Chicago: University of Chicago Press.

_____. 2012. *Democracy and the Left: Social Policy and Inequality in Latin America*. Chicago: University of Chicago Press.

_____. 2015. "Postindustrial Social Policy." In *The Politics of Advanced Capitalism,* edited by Pablo Beramendi, Silva Häusermann, Herbert Kitschelt, and Hanspeter Kriesi, 259–281. Cambridge, UK: Cambridge University Press.

IPCC (Intergovernmental Panel on Climate Change). 2013. *Climate Change 2013: The Physical Science Basis* (http://www.ipcc.ch).

Jensen, Carsten. 2014. *The Right and the Welfare State*. Oxford, UK: Oxford University Press.

Johnson, Thomas R. 2008. "New Opportunities, Same Constraints: Environmental Protection and China's New Development Path." *Politics* 28 (2): 93–102. doi:10.1111/j.1467-9256.2008.00316.x

Kraft, Michael E., and Norman J. Vig. 2006. "Environmental Policy from the 1970s to the Twenty-first Century." In *Environmental Policy: New Directions for the Twenty-first Century*, 6th ed., edited by Norman J. Vig and Michael E. Kraft, 1–33. Washington, DC: CQ Press.

Lavinas, Lena. 2006. "From Means-Test Schemes to Basic Income in Brazil: Exceptionality and Paradox." *International Social Security Review* 59 (3): 103–125. doi:10.1111/j.1468-246X.2006.00249.x

Layzer, Judith A. 2006. *The Environmental Case: Translating Values into Policy*. 2nd ed. Washington, DC: CQ Press.

Marshall, T. H. 1963. *Class, Citizenship, and Social Development: Essays*. Chicago: University of Chicago Press.

McGuire, James W. 2010. *Wealth, Health, and Democracy in East Asia and Latin America*. Cambridge, UK: Cambridge University Press.

Morton, Katherine. 2006. "Surviving an Environmental Crisis: Can China Adapt?" *Brown Journal of World Affairs* 13 (1): 63–75.

Obinger, Herbert, and Peter Starke. 2015. "Welfare State Transformation: Convergence and the Rise of the Supply-Side Model." In *The Oxford Handbook of Transformations of the State,* edited by Stephan Leibfried, Evelyne Huber, Matthew Lange, Jonah D. Levy, Frank Nullmeier, and John D. Stephens, 465–481. Oxford, UK: Oxford University Press.

OECD (Organisation for Economic Cooperation and Development). 2008. *OECD Factbook 2008: Economic, Environmental, and Social Statistics*. Rev. ed. Paris: OECD.

———. 2011a. "Health at a Glance 2011" (http://www.oecd.org/health/health-systems/49105858.pdf).

———. 2011b. "Social Expenditure Database" (http://www.oecd.org/document/9/0,3746,en_2649_33933_38141385_1_1_1_1,00.html).

———. 2015. "Health Care at a Glance" (http://www.health.gov.il/publications-files/healthataglance2015.pdf).

Olsen, Gregg M. 2007. "Toward Global Welfare State Convergence? Family Policy and Health Care in Sweden, Canada, and the United States." *Journal of Sociology and Social Welfare* 34 (2): 143–164.

Parks, Bradley C., and J. Timmons Roberts. 2009. "Inequality and the Global Climate Regime: Breaking the North–South Impasse." In *The Politics of Climate Change: Environmental Dynamics in International Affairs,* edited by Paul Harris, 164–191. New York: Routledge.

Pierson, Paul. 1996. "The New Politics of the Welfare State." *World Politics* 48 (2): 143–179. doi:10.1353/wp.1996.0004

Rehm, Philipp. 2016. *Risk Inequality and Welfare States: Social Policy Preferences, Development, and Dynamics.* Cambridge, UK: Cambridge University Press.

Ringquist, Evan J. 2006. "Environmental Justice: Normative Concerns, Empirical Evidence, and Government Action." In *Environmental Policy: New Directions for the Twenty-first Century*, 6th ed., edited by Norman J. Vig and Michael E. Kraft, 239–263. Washington, DC: CQ Press.

Rueda, David. 2015. "The State of the Welfare State: Unemployment, Labor Market Policy, and Inequality in the Age of Workfare." *Comparative Politics* 47 (3): 296–314. April.

Ryan, Fergus. 2015. "China's 'Green GDP' Dream Could Become a Reality." *The Australian Business Review.* April 20 (http://www.theaustralian.com.au/business/business-spectator/chinas-green-gdp-dream-could-become-a-reality/news-story/cc0d5a387f762a6132cc2e4dc50be554).

Sainsbury, Diane. 2013. "Gender, Care, and Welfare." In *The Oxford Handbook of Gender and Politics,* edited by Georgina Waylen, Karen Celis, Johanna Kantola, and S. Laurel Weldon, 313–336. Oxford, UK: Oxford University Press.

Schlossberg, Tatiana. 2016. "Poll Finds Deep Split on Climate Change. Party Allegiance Is a Big Factor." *New York Times.* October 4 (http://www.nytimes.com/2016/10/05/science/climate-change-poll-pew.html?smprod=nytcore-ipad&smid=nytcore-ipad-share).

Schott, Liz, Ladonna Pavetti, and Ife Floyd. 2015. *How States Use Federal and State Funds under the TANF Block Grant.* Washington, DC: Center on Budget and Policy Priorities. October 15 (http://www.cbpp.org/research/family-income-support/how-states-use-federal-and-state-funds-under-the-tanf-block-grant).

Schroder, Martin. 2013. *Integrating Varieties of Capitalism and Welfare State Research: A Unified Typology of Capitalisms.* New York: Palgrave Macmillan.

Sen, Amartya. 1999. *Development as Freedom.* New York: Knopf.

Sherman, Arloc, and Danilo Trisi. 2015. *Safety Net More Effective against Poverty Than Previously Thought: Correcting for Underreporting of Benefits Reveals Stronger Reductions in Poverty and Deep Poverty in All States.* Washington, DC: Center on Budget and Policy Priorities. May 6 (http://www.cbpp.org/sites/default/files/atoms/files/5-6-15pov.pdf).

Singh, Prerna. 2015. *How Solidarity Works for Welfare: Subnationalism and Social Development in India.* Cambridge, UK: Cambridge University Press.

Smeeding, Timothy. 2005. "Government Programs and Social Outcomes: The United States in Comparative Perspective." Luxembourg Income Study Working Paper Series, Working Paper No. 426 (http://www.lisproject.org/publications/liswps/426.pdf).

Sommers, Benjamin, Robert J. Blendon, and E. John Orav. 2016. "Changes in Utilization and Health among Low-Income Adults after Medicaid Expansion or Expanded Private Insurance." *JAMA Internal Medicine* 176 (10): 1501–1509. doi:10.1001/jamainternmed.2016.4419

Spilker, Gabriele. 2013. *Globalization, Political Institutions and the Environment in Developing Countries.* New York: Routledge.

Tavernise, Sabrina, and Robert Gebeloff. 2016. "Immigrants, the Poor and Minorities Gain Sharply under Affordable Care Act." *New York Times.* April 17 (http://www.nytimes.com/2016/04/18/health/

immigrants-the-poor-and-minorities-gain-sharply-under-health-act.html?smprod=nytcore-ipad&smid=nytcore-ipad-share).

Tepperman, Jonathan. 2015. "Brazil's Anti-poverty Breakthrough: The Surprising Success of Bolsa Família." *Foreign Affairs*. December 14 (https://www.foreignaffairs.com/articles/brazil/2015-12-14/brazils-antipoverty-breakthrough).

UNDP (United Nations Development Programme). 2007. *Human Development Report 2007/2008: Fighting Climate Change; Human Solidarity in a Divided World*. New York: Palgrave Macmillan (http://hdr.undp.org/en/reports/global/hdr2007-8).

Vail, Mark I. 2004. "The Myth of the Frozen Welfare State and the Dynamics of Contemporary French and German Social-Protection Reform." *French Politics* 2 (2): 151–183.

Watson, Sara E. 2015. *The Left Divided: The Development and Transformation of Advanced Welfare States*. Oxford, UK: Oxford University Press.

World Bank. 2010. "Lifting Families out of Poverty in Brazil—Bolsa Família Program" (http://web.worldbank.org/WBSITE/EXTERNAL/NEWS/0,,contentMDK:20754490~menuPK:141310~pagePK:34370~piPK:34424~theSitePK:4607,00.html).

Wu, Joshua Su-Ya. 2009. "The State of China's Environmental Governance after the 17th Party Congress." *East Asia* 26 (4): 265–284. doi:10.1007/s12140-009-9089-9

Yarett, Ian. 2010. "Has Anything Gotten Better since That First Earth Day?" *Newsweek*, April 26, 56.

RESOURCES FOR FURTHER STUDY

Brady, David. 2009. *Rich Democracies, Poor People: How Politics Explain Poverty*. Oxford, UK: Oxford University Press.

Donaldson, Cam, and Karen Gerard. 2005. *Economics of Health Care Financing: The Visible Hand*. New York: Palgrave Macmillan.

Goodin, Robert E., Bruce Headey, Ruud Muffels, and Henk-Jan Dirven. 1999. *The Real Worlds of Welfare Capitalism*. Cambridge, UK: Cambridge University Press.

Huber, Evelyne, and John D. Stephens. 2012. *Democracy and the Left: Social Policy and Inequality in Latin America*. Chicago: University of Chicago Press.

Jacobs, Lawrence R., and Theda Skocpol. 2010. *Health Care Reform and American Politics: What Everyone Needs to Know*. Oxford, UK: Oxford University Press.

———. 2011. "Society at a Glance 2011—OECD Social Indicators" (http://www.oecd.org/document/40/0,3746,en_2649_37419_47507368_1_1_1_37419,00.html).

Schreuder, Yda. 2009. *The Corporate Greenhouse: Climate Change Policy in a Globalizing World*. New York: Zed Books.

WEB RESOURCES

Council on Environmental Quality, U.S. Department of Energy
(http://energy.gov/nepa/council-environmental-quality)

Measure of America of the Social Science Research Council
(http://www.measureofamerica.org/tools/)

Organisation for Economic Co-operation and Development (OECD)
(http://www.oecd.org)

United Nations Statistics Division, Environment
  (http://unstats.un.org/unsd/environment/default.htm)
U.S. Census Bureau, International Database
  (https://www.census.gov/population/international/data/idb/informationGateway.php)
World Health Organization, Global Health Observatory
  (http://www.who.int/gho/en)

Glossary

absolutism Rule by a single monarch who claims complete, exclusive power and sovereignty over a territory and its people (Ch 2)

assimilation A belief that immigrants or other members of minority cultural communities ought to adopt the culture of the majority population (Ch 4)

asymmetrical federal system A federal system in which different subnational governments (states or provinces) have distinct relationships with and rights in relation to the national government (Ch 5)

authoritarian regime A regime lacking democratic characteristics, ruled by a single leader or small group of leaders (Ch 1)

autonomy The ability and right of a group to partially govern itself within a larger state (Ch 4)

bicameral legislature A legislature that has two houses (Ch 5)

bourgeoisie The class that owns capital; according to Marxism, the ruling elite in all capitalist societies (Ch 1)

bureaucracy A large set of appointed officials whose function is to implement the laws of the state, as directed by the executive (Ch 2)

cap and trade system Market-based pollution control system in which the government sets an overall limit on how much of a pollutant is acceptable and issues vouchers to pollute to each company, which companies are then free to trade (Ch 12)

capitalism The combination of a market economy with private property rights (Ch 10)

centripetal approach A means used by democracies to resolve ethnic conflict by giving political leaders and parties incentives to moderate their demands (Ch 4)

charismatic legitimacy The right to rule based on personal virtue, heroism, sanctity, or other extraordinary characteristics (Ch 2)

Christian democratic welfare states States whose social policies are based on the nuclear family with a male breadwinner, designed primarily to achieve income stabilization to mitigate the effects of market-induced income insecurity; Germany is a key example (Ch 12)

citizen A member of a political community or state with certain rights and duties (Ch 3)

civic culture A political culture in which citizens hold values and beliefs that support democracy, including active participation in politics but also enough deference to the leadership to let it govern effectively (Ch 1)

civic nationalism A sense of national unity and purpose based on a set of commonly held political beliefs (Ch 4)

civil rights Those rights that guarantee individual freedom as well as equal, just, and fair treatment by the state (Ch 3)

civil society The sphere of organized, nongovernmental, nonviolent activity by groups larger than individual families or firms (Ch 1)

civil war Two or more armed groups, at least one of which is tied to the most recent regime in power, fight for control of the state (Ch 7)

clientelism The exchange of material resources for political support (Ch 2)

closed-list proportional representation Electoral system in which each party presents a ranked list of candidates, voters vote for the party rather than for individual candidates, and each party awards the seats it wins to the candidates on its list in rank order (Ch 6)

coalition government Government in a parliamentary system in which at least two parties negotiate an agreement to rule together (Ch 5)

code law Legal system originating in ancient Roman law and modified by Napoleon Bonaparte in France, in which judges may only follow the law as written and must ignore past decisions; in contrast to common law (Ch 5)

cohabitation Sharing of power between a president and prime minister from different parties in a semipresidential system (Ch 5)

collective action problem Individuals being unwilling to engage in a particular activity because of their rational belief that their individual actions will have little or no effect, yet collectively suffering adverse consequences when all fail to act (Ch 6)

command economy An economic system in which most prices, property, and production are directly controlled by the state (Ch 10)

common law Legal system originating in Britain in which judges base decisions not only on their understanding of the written law but also on their understanding of past court cases; in contrast to code law (Ch 5)

comparative advantage Theory of trade that argues that economic efficiency and well-being will be maximized if each country uses its resources to produce whatever it produces relatively well compared with other countries and then trades its own products with other countries for goods it does not produce (Ch 11)

comparative institutional advantage Idea in the varieties of capitalism school of thought that different kinds of capitalist systems have different institutional advantages that they usually will try to maintain, resulting in different responses to external economic pressures (Ch 10)

comparative method The means by which scholars try to mimic laboratory conditions by careful selection of cases (Ch 1)

comparative politics One of the major subfields of political science, in which the primary focus is on comparing power and decision making across countries (Ch 1)

conditional cash transfer (CCT) Programs that provide cash grants to the poor and in exchange require particular beneficial behavior from the poor, such as children's attendance at school and visits to health clinics (Ch 12)

consensus democracy A democratic system with multiparty executives in a coalition government, executive-legislative balance, bicameral legislatures, and rigid constitutions that are not easily amended (Ch 5)

consociationalism A democratic system designed to ease ethnic tensions via recognizing the existence of specific groups and granting some share of power in the central government to each, usually codified in specific legal or constitutional guarantees to each group (Ch 4)

constructivism A theory of identity group formation that argues that identities are created through a complex process usually referred to as social construction (Ch 4)

contentious politics Political activity that is at least in part beyond institutional bounds, involving extra-institutional activity such as petitions, protests, riots, violence, civil war, and revolution (Ch 7)

convergence Argument that globalization will force similar neoliberal policies across all countries (Ch 10)

coordinated market economies (CMEs) In the varieties of capitalism approach,

capitalist economies in which firms, financiers, unions, and government consciously coordinate their actions via interlocking ownership and participation; Germany and Japan are key examples (Ch 10)

corporatism System of representation in which one organization represents each important sector of society; two subtypes are societal and state corporatism (Ch 3)

coup d'état When the military forcibly removes an existing regime and establishes a new one (Ch 9)

cultural nationalism National unity based on a common cultural characteristic wherein only those people who share that characteristic can be included in the nation (Ch 4)

deficit spending Government spending more than is collected in revenue (Ch 10)

democracy A regime in which citizens have basic rights of open association and expression and the ability to change the government through some sort of electoral process (Ch 1)

democratic consolidation The widespread acceptance of democracy as the permanent form of political activity; all significant political elites and their followers accept democratic rules and are confident everyone else does as well (Ch 9)

developmental state A state that seeks to create national strength by taking an active and conscious role in the development of specific sectors of the economy (Ch 10)

devolution Partial decentralization of power from central government to subunits such as states or provinces, with subunits' power being dependent on central government and reversible (Ch 5)

dictator's dilemma An authoritarian ruler's repression creates fear, which then breeds uncertainty about how much support the ruler has; in response, the ruler spends more resources than is rational to co-opt the opposition (Ch 8)

dictatorship of the proletariat In the first stage of communism in Marxist thought, characterized by absolute rule by workers as a class over all other classes (Ch 3)

dominant-party system Party system in which multiple parties exist but the same one wins every election and governs continuously (Ch 6)

Duverger's Law Institutionalist argument by French political scientist Maurice Duverger that SMD electoral systems will produce two major parties, eliminating smaller parties (Ch 6)

electoral authoritarian regime Type of hybrid regime in which formal opposition and some open political debate exist and elections are held; these processes are so flawed, however, that the regime cannot be considered truly democratic (Ch 3)

electoral systems Formal, legal mechanisms that translate votes into control over political offices and shares of political power (Ch 6)

elite theories Theories that all argue societies are ruled by a small group that has effective control over virtually all power; contrast to pluralist theory (Ch 1)

empirical theory An argument explaining what actually occurs; empirical theorists first notice and describe a pattern and then attempt to explain what causes it (Ch 1)

environmental justice movement A movement focused on exposing and fighting against racial and class inequalities in exposure to pollution, started in the United States in 1982 (Ch 12)

ethnic group A group of people who see themselves as united by one or more cultural attributes or a sense of common history but do not see themselves as a nation seeking its own state (Ch 4)

executive The branch of government that must exist in all modern states; the chief political power in a state and implements all laws (Ch 5)

export-oriented growth (EOG) Development policy based on encouraging economic growth via exports of goods and services, usually starting with light manufacturing such as textiles (Ch 11)

external sovereignty Sovereignty relative to outside powers that is legally recognized in international law (Ch 2)

externality   A cost or benefit of the production process that is not fully included in the price of the final market transaction when the product is sold (Ch 10)

failed state   A state that is so weak that it loses effective sovereignty over part or all of its territory (Ch 2)

federal systems   Political systems in which a state's power is legally and constitutionally divided among more than one level of government; in contrast to a unitary system (Ch 5)

feudal states   Premodern states in Europe in which power in a territory was divided among multiple and overlapping lords claiming sovereignty (Ch 2)

first dimension of power   The ability of one person or group to get another person or group to do something it otherwise would not do (Ch 1)

"first-past-the-post" (FPTP)   An SMD system in which the candidate with a plurality of votes wins (Ch 6)

fiscal policy   Government budgetary policy (Ch 10)

foreign direct investment (FDI)   Investment from abroad in productive activity in another country (Ch 11)

founding election   The first democratic election in many years (or ever), marking the completion of a transition to democracy (Ch 9)

globalization   A rapid increase in the flow of economic activity, technology, and communications around the globe, and the increased sharing of cultural symbols, political ideas, and movements across countries (Ch 10)

head of government   The key executive power in a state; usually a president or prime minister (Ch 5)

head of state   The official, symbolic representative of a country, authorized to speak on its behalf and represent it, particularly in world affairs; usually a president or monarch (Ch 5)

Hindu nationalism   In India, a movement to define the country as primarily Hindu; the founding ideology of the BJP (Ch 6)

historical institutionalists   Theorists who believe that institutions explain political behavior and shape individuals' political preferences and their perceptions of their self-interests, and that institutions evolve historically in particular countries and change relatively slowly (Ch 1)

historical materialism   The assumption that material forces are the prime movers of history and politics; a key philosophical tenet of Marxism (Ch 3)

horizontal accountability   The ability of state institutions to hold one another accountable (Ch 5)

ideal type   A model of what the purest version of something might be (Ch 2)

ideological hegemony   The ruling class's ability to spread a set of ideas justifying and perpetuating its political dominance (Ch 1)

import-substitution industrialization (ISI)   Development policy popular in the 1950s–1970s that uses trade policy, monetary policy, and currency rates to encourage the creation of new industries to produce goods domestically that the country imported in the past (Ch 11)

institutionalism   An approach to explaining politics that argues that political institutions are crucial to understanding political behavior (Ch 1)

institutionalization   The degree to which government processes and procedures are established, predictable, and routinized (Ch 5)

interest-group pluralism   Interest-group system in which many groups exist to represent particular interests and the government remains officially neutral among them; the United States is a key example (Ch 6)

internal sovereignty   The sole authority within a territory capable of making and enforcing laws and policies (Ch 2)

international capital flows   Movements of capital in the form of money across international borders (Ch 11)

iron triangle   Three-sided cooperative interaction among bureaucrats, legislators, and business leaders in a particular sector that serves the interests of all involved but keeps others out of the policy-making process (Ch 5)

Islamism   The belief that Islamic law, as revealed by God to the Prophet Mohammed, can and should provide the basis for government in Muslim communities, with little equivocation or compromise (Ch 3)

jihad   Derived from an Arabic word for "struggle" and an important concept in Islam; the Quran identifies three kinds of *jihad* (Ch 3)

judicial independence   The belief and ability of judges to decide cases as they think appropriate, regardless of what other people, and especially politically powerful officials or institutions, desire (Ch 5)

judicial review   The authority of the judiciary to decide whether a specific law contradicts a country's constitution (Ch 5)

judiciary   Branch of government that interprets the law and applies it to individual cases (Ch 5)

jus sanguinis   Citizenship based on "blood" ties; for example, in Germany (Ch 4)

jus soli   Citizenship dependent on "soil," or residence within the national territory; for example, in France (Ch 4)

Keynesian theory   Named for British economist John Maynard Keynes, who argued that governments can manage the business cycles of capitalism via active fiscal policy and monetary policy, including deficit spending when necessary (Ch 10)

laïcité   A model of secularism advocating that religion should play no part in the public realm (Ch 4)

legislative oversight   Occurs when members of the legislature, usually in committees, oversee the bureaucracy (Ch 5)

legislature   Branch of government that makes the law in a democracy (Ch 5)

legitimacy   The recognized right to rule (Ch 2)

liberal democracy A system of government that provides eight key guarantees, including freedoms to enable citizen participation in the political process and institutions that make government policies depend on votes and other forms of citizen preferences (Ch 3)

liberal market economies (LMEs) In the varieties of capitalism approach, countries that rely heavily on market relationships to govern economic activity; the United States and United Kingdom are key examples (Ch 10)

liberal welfare states States whose social policies focus on ensuring that all who can do so gain their income in the market; more concerned about preserving individual autonomy than reducing poverty or inequality; the United States is a key example (Ch 12)

liberationist Member of the LGBT movement who seeks to transform sexual and gender norms so that all may gain social acceptance and respect regardless of their conformity to preexisting norms or institutions (Ch 4)

majoritarian democracy A type of democratic system that concentrates power more tightly in a single-party executive with executive dominance over the legislature, a single legislative branch, and constitutions that can be easily amended (Ch 5)

market economy An economic system in which individuals and firms exchange goods and services in a largely unfettered manner (Ch 10)

market failure Phenomenon that occurs when markets fail to perform efficiently or fail to perform according to other widely held social values (Ch 10)

market-based private insurance system Health care system that relies on private insurance for the bulk of the population (Ch 12)

Marxism Structuralist argument that says that economic structures largely determine political behavior; the philosophical underpinning of communism (Ch 1)

means-tested public assistance Social programs that provide benefits to

individuals who fall below a specific income level; TANF is an example in the United States (Ch 12)

member of parliament (MP) An elected member of the legislature in a parliamentary system (Ch 5)

military regime System of government in which military officers control power (Ch 3)

Millennium Development Goals (MDGs) Targets established by the United Nations to reduce poverty and hunger, improve education and health, improve the status of women, and achieve environmental sustainability (Ch 11)

mixed, or semiproportional An electoral system that combines single-member district representation with overall proportionality in allocation of legislative seats to parties; Germany is a key example (Ch 6)

mode of production In Marxist theory, the economic system in any given historical era; feudalism and capitalism in the last millennium in Europe (Ch 3)

modernists Theorists of political culture who believe that clear sets of attitudes, values, and beliefs can be identified in each country that change very rarely and explain much about politics there (Ch 1)

modernization The transformation of poor agrarian societies into wealthy industrial societies, usually seen as the process by which postcolonial societies become more like societies in the West (Ch 1)

modernization theory Theory of development that argues that postcolonial societies need to go through the same process that the West underwent in order to develop (Ch 3)

modernizing authoritarianism A claim to legitimacy based the need to "develop" the country via the rule of a modernizing elite (Ch 3)

monetary policy The amount of money a government prints and puts into circulation and the basic interest rates the government sets (Ch 10)

monopoly The control of the entire supply of a valued good or service by one economic actor (Ch 10)

moral hazard Occurs when parties to a transaction behave in a particular way because they believe they will not have to pay the full costs of their actions (Ch 12)

multicultural integration Accepts that ethnocultural identities matter to citizens, will endure over time, and must be recognized and accommodated within political institutions; in contrast to assimilation (Ch 4)

multiparty systems Party systems in which more than two parties could potentially win a national election and govern (Ch 6)

nation A group that proclaims itself a nation and has or seeks control of a state (Ch 4)

national health insurance (NHI) A health care system in which the government mandates that virtually all citizens must have insurance (Ch 12)

national health system (NHS)/single-payer system A government-financed and managed health care system into which all citizens pay, either through a separate insurance payment or via general taxation, and through which they gain medical care (Ch 12)

nationalism The desire to be a nation and thus to control a national state (Ch 4)

natural monopoly The control of the entire supply of valued goods or services by one economic actor in a sector of the economy in which competition would raise costs and reduce efficiency (Ch 10)

neocolonialism A relationship between postcolonial societies and their former colonizers in which leaders benefit politically and economically by helping outside businesses and states maintain access to the former colonies' wealth and come to serve the interests of the former colonizers and corporations more than they serve their own people (Ch 1)

neocorporatism Also called societal corporatism; corporatism that evolves historically and voluntarily rather than being mandated by the state; Germany is a key example (Ch 6)

neofascist Description given to parties or political movements that espouse a virulent nationalism, often defined on a cultural, racial, or religious basis and opposed to immigrants as threats to national identity (Ch 3)

neoliberalism An economic theory that argues government should balance its budget and minimize its role in the economy to allow the market to allocate resources to maximize efficiency and thereby economic growth (Ch 10)

neopatrimonial authority Power based on a combination of the trappings of modern, bureaucratic states with underlying informal institutions of clientelism that work behind the scenes; most common in Africa (Ch 3)

neutral state model A model of secularism wherein the state is neutral about, but not opposed to, religion (Ch 4)

New Public Management (NPM) Theory of reform of bureaucracies that argues for the privatizing of many government services, creating competition among agencies to simulate a market, focusing on customer satisfaction, and flattening administrative hierarchies (Ch 5)

normative theory An argument explaining what ought to occur rather than what does occur; contrast with empirical theory (Ch 1)

one-party regime A system of government in which a single party gains power, usually after independence in postcolonial states, and systematically eliminates all opposition (Ch 3)

open-list proportional representation Electoral system in which multiple candidates run in each district, voters vote for the individual candidate of their choice, and the candidates with the most votes in the party get the seats the party wins (Ch 6)

pact In a transition to democracy, a conscious agreement among the most important political actors in the authoritarian regime and those in civil society to establish a new form of government (Ch 9)

parliamentarism A term denoting a parliamentary system of democracy in which the executive and legislative branches are fused via parliament's election of the chief executive (Ch 5)

parliamentary sovereignty Parliament is supreme in all matters; key example is the United Kingdom (Ch 3)

participatory democracy A form of democracy that encourages citizens to participate actively, in many ways beyond voting; usually focused at the local level (Ch 3)

party system The number of parties and their relative institutional strength (Ch 6)

patriarchy Rule by men (Ch 1)

peak associations Organizations that bring together all interest groups in a particular sector to influence and negotiate agreements with the state; in the United States, an example is the AFL-CIO (Ch 6)

personalist regime System of government in which a central leader comes to dominate a state, typically not only eliminating all opposition but also weakening the state's institutions to centralize power in his own hands (Ch 3)

personality cult Phenomenon that occurs in the most extreme cases of personalist rule in which followers constantly glorify the ruler and attempt to turn his every utterance into not only government fiat but also divine wisdom (Ch 8)

pluralist theories Explanations of who has power that argue that society is divided into various political groups and that power is dispersed among these groups so that no group has complete or permanent power; contrast to elite theory (Ch 1)

plurality The receipt of the most votes, but not necessarily a majority (Ch 6)

politburo The chief decision-making organ in a communist party; China's politburo is a key example (Ch 3)

political accountability The ability of the citizenry, directly or indirectly, to control political leaders and institutions (Ch 5)

political actor Any person or group engaged in political behavior (Ch 1)

political appointees Officials who serve at the pleasure of the president or prime minister and are assigned the task of overseeing their respective segments of the bureaucracy (Ch 5)

political culture A set of widely held attitudes, values, beliefs, and symbols about politics (Ch 1)

political development The processes through which modern nations and states arise and how political institutions and regimes evolve (Ch 1)

political discourse The ways in which people speak and write about politics; postmodern theorists argue that political discourse influences political attitudes, identity, and actions (Ch 1)

political economy The study of the interaction between political and economic phenomena (Ch 1)

political ideology A systematic set of beliefs about how a political system ought to be structured (Ch 1)

political institution A set of rules, norms, or standard operating procedures that is widely recognized and accepted by the society, structures and constrains political actions, and often serves as the basis for key political organizations (Ch 1)

political opportunity structure The extent to which a regime is open to influence from social movements and other extra-institutional groups (Ch 7)

Political revolution The fundamental transformation of an existing regime, instigated and primarily carried out by a social movement or armed group (Ch 7)

political rights Those rights associated with active political participation—for example, to free association, voting, and running for office (Ch 3)

political saliency The degree to which something is of political importance (Ch 4)

political science The systematic study of politics and power (Ch 1)

political socialization The process through which people, especially young people, learn about politics and are taught a society's common political values and beliefs (Ch 1)

political violence The use of physical force by nonstate actors for political ends (Ch 7)

politics The process by which human communities make collective decisions (Ch 1)

populism A political "style" or ideology emphasizing a united "people" pitted against corrupt elites, denying divisions among the "people," and often led by a charismatic leader (Ch 6)

positive accommodation A model of secularism wherein the state is neutral among but willing to support religions that it recognizes as important elements in civil society (Ch 4)

postmaterialist A set of values in a society in which most citizens are economically secure enough to move beyond immediate economic (materialist) concerns to "quality of life" issues like human rights, civil rights, women's rights, environmentalism, and moral values (Ch 1)

postmodernist An approach that sees cultures not as sets of fixed and clearly defined values but rather as sets of symbols subject to interpretation (Ch 1)

precautionary principle A policy that emphasizes risk avoidance even when the science predicting a risk is uncertain (Ch 12)

presidentialism A term denoting a presidential system of democracy in which the executive and legislature are elected independently and have separate and independent powers (Ch 5)

prime minister (PM) The head of government in parliamentary and semipresidential systems (Ch 5)

primordialism A theory of identity that sees identity groups as being in some sense "natural" or God given, as having existed since "time immemorial," and as defined unambiguously by such clear criteria as kinship, language, culture, or phenotype (Ch 4)

principal-agent problem A problem in which a principal hires an agent to perform a task but the agent's self-interest does not necessarily align with the principal's, so the agent may not carry out the task as assigned (Ch 5)

proletariat A term in Marxist theory for the class of free-wage laborers who own no capital and must sell their labor to survive;

communist parties claim to work on the proletariat's behalf (Ch 1)

proportional representation (PR) Electoral system in which seats in a legislature are apportioned on a purely proportional basis, giving each party the share of seats that matches its share of the total vote (Ch 6)

psychological theories Explanations for political behavior based on psychological analysis of political actors' motives (Ch 1)

public goods Goods or services that cannot or will not be provided via the market because their costs are too high or their benefits are too diffuse (Ch 10)

quantitative statistical techniques Research method used for large-scale studies that reduces evidence to sets of numbers so that statistical analysis can systematically compare a huge number of cases (Ch 1)

quasi-states States that have legal sovereignty and international recognition but lack almost all the domestic attributes of a functioning state (Ch 2)

race A group of people socially defined primarily on the basis of one or more perceived common physical characteristics (Ch 4)

rational choice institutionalists Institutionalist theorists who follow the assumptions of rational choice theory and argue that institutions are the products of the interaction and bargaining of rational actors (Ch 1)

rational choice theory An explanation for political behavior that assumes that individuals are rational beings who bring to the political arena a set of self-defined preferences and adequate knowledge and ability to pursue those preferences (Ch 1)

rational-legal legitimacy The right of leaders to rule based on their selection according to an accepted set of laws, standards, or procedures (Ch 2)

regime A set of formal and informal political institutions that defines a type of government (Ch 3)

regime change The process through which one regime is transformed into another (Ch 9)

relative deprivation A group's or individual's belief that they are not getting their share of something of value relative to others (Ch 7)

rent seeking Gaining an advantage in a market without engaging in equally productive activity; usually involves using government regulations for one's own benefit (Ch 5)

research methods Systematic processes used to ensure that the study of some phenomena is as objective and unbiased as possible (Ch 1)

resource curse Occurs when a state relies on a key resource for almost all of its revenue, allowing it to ignore its citizens and resulting in a weak state (Ch 2)

risk assessment Analysis of what the risks of damaging outcomes are in a particular situation

risk management Policy used to keep risks to acceptable levels

ruling class An elite who possess adequate resources to control a regime; in Marxist theory, the class that controls key sources of wealth in a given epoch (Ch 1)

second dimension of power The ability not only to make people do something but to keep them from doing something (Ch 1)

security dilemma A situation in which two or more groups do not trust and may even fear one another, and do not believe that institutional constraints will protect them, increasing the likelihood that violence will break out between them (Ch 7)

semipresidentialism A term denoting a semipresidential system of democracy in which executive power is divided between a directly elected president and a prime minister elected by a parliament (Ch 5)

separation of powers Constitutionally explicit division of power among the major branches of government (Ch 5)

sharia Muslim law (Ch 3)

single case study Research method that examines a particular political phenomenon in just one country or community and can generate ideas for theories or test theories developed from different cases (Ch 1)

single-member district (SMD) Electoral system in which each geographic district elects a single representative to a legislature (Ch 6)

social capital Social networks and norms of reciprocity that are important for a strong civil society (Ch 6)

social construction Part of constructivist approach to identity, the process through which societies collectively "construct" identities as a wide array of actors continually discuss the question of who "we" are (Ch 4)

social contract theory Philosophical approach underlying liberalism that begins from the premise that legitimate governments are formed when free and independent individuals join in a contract to permit representatives to govern over them in their common interests (Ch 3)

social democracy Combines liberal democracy with much greater provision of social rights of citizenship and typically greater public control of the economy (Ch 3)

social democratic welfare states States whose social policies strongly emphasize universal entitlements to achieve greater social equality and promote equal citizenship; Sweden is a key example (Ch 12)

social insurance Provides benefits to categories of people who have contributed to a (usually mandatory) public insurance fund; typically used to provide retirement pensions (Ch 12)

social market economy In Germany, a postwar economic system that combines a highly productive market economy with an extensive and generous welfare state, as well as unusually active involvement of both business and labor in economic policy (Ch 10)

social movements Part of civil society; they have a loosely defined organizational structure and represent people who perceive themselves to be outside formal institutions, seek major socioeconomic or political changes, or employ noninstitutional forms of collective action (Ch 7)

social policy Policy focused on reducing poverty and income inequality and stabilizing individual or family income (Ch 12)

social insurance Provides benefits to categories of people who have contributed to a (usually mandatory) public insurance fund; typically used to provide retirement pensions (Ch 12)

social revolution In Marxist theory, the transition from one mode of production to another; Marxist understanding of revolution (Ch 7)

social rights Those rights related to basic well-being and socioeconomic equality (Ch 3)

sovereignty Quality of a state in which it is legally recognized by the family of states as the sole legitimate governing authority within its territory and as the legal equal of other states (Ch 2)

state An ongoing administrative apparatus that develops and administers laws and generates and implements public policies in a specific territory (Ch 2)

state corporatism Corporatism mandated by the state; common in fascist regimes (Ch 6)

strong state A state that is generally capable of providing political goods to its citizens (Ch 2)

structural adjustment programs (SAPs) Development programs created in the 1980s; based on neoliberal principles of reduced government protection of industries, fiscal austerity, and privatization (Ch 11)

structuralism Approach to explaining politics that argues that political behavior is at least influenced and limited, and perhaps even determined, by broader structures in a society such as class divisions or enduring institutions (Ch 1)

subcultures Groups that hold partially different beliefs and values from the main political culture of a country (Ch 1)

supreme leader Individual who wields executive power with few formal limits in an authoritarian regime; in the Islamic Republic of Iran, the formal title of the top ruling cleric (Ch 8)

symmetrical federal system A federal system in which all subnational governments (states or provinces) have the same relationship with and rights in relation to the national government (Ch 5)

tax expenditures Targeted tax breaks for specific groups of citizens or activities designed to achieve social policy goals

technocratic legitimacy A claim to rule based on knowledge or expertise (Ch 3)

territory An area with clearly defined borders to which a state lays claim (Ch 2)

terrorism Political violence or the threat of violence by groups or individuals who deliberately target civilians or noncombatants in order to influence the behavior and actions of targeted publics and governments (Ch 7)

theocracy Rule by religious authorities (Ch 3)

theory An abstract argument that provides a systematic explanation of some phenomenon (Ch 1)

third dimension of power The ability to shape or determine individual or group political demands by causing people to think about political issues in ways that are contrary to their own interests (Ch 1)

totalitarian state A state that controls virtually all aspects of society and eliminates all vestiges of civil society; Germany under Hitler and the Soviet Union under Stalin are key examples (Ch 3)

trade The flow of goods and services across national borders (Ch 11)

traditional legitimacy The right to rule based on a society's long-standing patterns and practices (Ch 2)

tragedy of the commons No individual has the incentive or ability to preserve a common, shared good that is free, so without collective effort, it is likely to be overused and perhaps ultimately destroyed (Ch 12)

transition to democracy A regime change typically involving a negotiated process that removes an authoritarian regime and concludes with a founding election of a new, democratic regime (Ch 9)

two-party system Party system in which only two parties are able to garner enough votes to win an election, though more may compete; the United Kingdom and United States are key examples (Ch 6)

universal entitlements Benefits that governments provide to all citizens more or less equally, usually funded through general taxation; in the United States, public education is an example (Ch 12)

unitary systems Political systems in which the central government has sole constitutional sovereignty and power; in contrast to a federal system (Ch 5)

vanguard party Vladimir Lenin's concept of a small party that claims legitimacy to rule based on its understanding of Marxist theory and its ability to represent the interests of the proletariat before they are a majority of the populace (Ch 3)

varieties of capitalism (VOC) School of thought analyzing wealthy market economies that focuses primarily on business firms and how they are governed; divides such economies into liberal market economies and coordinated market economies (Ch 10)

vertical accountability The ability of individuals and groups in a society to hold state institutions accountable (Ch 5)

veto player An individual or collective actor whose agreement is essential for any policy change (Ch 5)

virtual representation When voters' views are represented indirectly in the legislature by their chosen party's candidates who have been elected in districts other than their own (Ch 6)

vote of no confidence In parliamentary systems, a vote by parliament to remove a government (the prime minister and cabinet) from power (Ch 5)

weak state A state that only partially provides political goods to its citizens (Ch 2)

welfare states Distinct systems of social policies that arose after World War II in wealthy market economies, including social democratic welfare states, Christian democratic welfare states, and liberal welfare states (Ch 12)

Index

NOTE: Page numbers with *b, f, m,* or *t* indicate boxes, figures, maps, and tables, respectively. Page numbers in *italics* refer to photographs.